EXPLORING CHÁN

HISTORY, PRACTICE, PERSPECTIVES

SECOND EDITION

CHUAN ZHI

SONGLARK

2025

Exploring Chan, 2nd ed. © 2025 by Chuan Zhi Shakya is licensed under Creative Commons Attribution-NonCommercial-ShareAlike 4.0 International. To view a copy of this license, visit https://creativecommons.org/licenses/by-nc-sa/4.0/

Publisher's Cataloging-In-Publication Data

Names: Zhi, Chuan, author.
Title: Exploring Chán: History, Practice, Perspectives Buddhism (2nd ed.) / Chuan Zhi.
Description: 2nd ed. |Boulder CO: Songlark, 2025. | Includes bibliographical references and index.
Identifiers: ISBN 9781733314350 (hardcover) | ISBN 9781733314343 (softcover) | 9781733314367 (ebook)
Subjects: LCSH: Zen Buddhism--China--History. | Zen Buddhism--China--Influence. | Zen Buddhism--Social aspects. | Spiritual life--Zen Buddhism. | Zen Buddhism--Study and teaching.
Classification: LCC BQ9262.9.C5 H67 2019 | DDC 294.3/927/0951--dc23

Library of Congress Control Number: 2025901049

http://www.songlarkpublishing.com/
editor@songlarkpublishing.com

About the cover illustrations:

The circle, or *yuanxiang* (Jap. *enso*), symbolizes unity, wholeness, and enlightenment. Encircling the yuanxiang are eight petals, commonly representing the Buddha's Eightfold Path—a foundational teaching and guiding framework in Buddhism. At the center of the circle is a wild Asian water buffalo and herder boy, symbols rooted in ancient Chinese mythology, which were repurposed in Chan/Zen to describe the spiritual journey through a series of pictures and poems, commonly referred to as the ox-herding series.

Two illustrations from this series, figures four and six, were produced in 1278 and are featured on the front and rear covers of this book. These represent some of the earliest known Japanese illustrated versions and, according to the Metropolitan Museum of Art, are the only extant examples rendered in color. The poem accompanying the front cover art, translated by Gen Sakamoto, reads:

> With all my energy, I seize the ox. His will is strong, and his power endless, and he cannot be tamed easily. Sometimes he charges to the high plateau. And there he stays, deep in the mist.

The poem accompanying the back cover art, from the same translator, reads:

> Riding the bull, I leisurely wander toward home. Exotic flute melodies echo through sunset clouds. Each beat and each tune is indescribably profound. No words are needed for those who understand music.

There is a secret self that has its own life unpenetrated and unguessed.

— Robert Bulwer-Lytton

Praise for Exploring Chán
(From the first edition)

"[W]ith extraordinary rigor and erudition, debut author Zhi reconstructs both the emergence of Buddhism in general, and of Chinese (or Chan) Buddhism in particular ... [H]is knowledge of the subject matter is astonishing; he not only demonstrates an academic mastery of Buddhism as a historical phenomenon, but also a philosophically profound understanding of its spiritual core ... [A] remarkable study that's intellectually stimulating, historically edifying, and spiritually instructive."

— *Kirkus Review*

"American-born Chán Buddhist monk Zhi combines rich cultural history and practical advice in this in-depth analysis of the religious and mystical traditions of Chinese Chán Buddhism. He charts the complicated evolution and delineation of Chán as a path toward self-knowledge, following Buddhism's spread from India throughout Asia and the West. ... Zhi pairs his discussion of Buddhism's religious institutions with a deep knowledge of individual spiritual practice. His practical advice and well-researched, well-cited cultural histories are equally accessible to readers.

"Readers will be inspired by his encouraging reminders about the objectives of Chán and straightforward guidance on practicing meditation. His succinct explanations for Buddhism-related terms and concepts, extensive footnotes, helpful illustrations, index, and bibliography make this an invaluable resource, highly impressive in both its scope and its complexity. This comprehensive, illuminating guide will benefit both spiritual practitioners and students of world history and religions."

— *Booklife Reviews* (Editor's Pick)

"Chuan Zhi writes with grace, eloquence, and profundity. This work is definitely one of those 'dog-eared' treasures that one returns to again and again as an invaluable resource ... A much-needed piece of research to the long history of Chan."

— *Stacy C. Douglas, Ph.D.*

"Chuan Zhi is deeply conversant with Chan practice, Buddhist history and philosophy, and current scholarship concerning the Chan tradition, as well as with Western psychology, philosophy, literature and music. ... The book's many virtues made it a pleasure to read..."

— *The Existential Buddhist*

"In this illuminating introduction to Chan Buddhism, Zhi offers a sprawling overview of its history and practice. [...] Zhi's overarching concern is to look behind the teachings of Chan (as an authoritative tradition or as a state-sponsored religion) and to position it as "a mystical discipline" concentrated on self-knowledge. [...] [T]hose with an avid interest in the faith would do well to pick this up."

— *Publisher's Weekly*

Contents

EDITOR'S PREFACE TO THE SECOND EDITION XIII
FOREWORD I
INTRODUCTION III

PART ONE
CHAN'S HISTORICAL BACKDROP 1

1. EARLY FOUNDATIONS: INDIA 6
   Jainism & India's religious environment before Buddhism 10
   Buddhism as an independent spiritual journey 22
   Early development of Buddhism in India 24
   The Buddha's Four Noble Truths 28
   The nature of reality and the rise of the Mahāyāna 35
   The Bodhisattva Ideal and the Buddhist trinities 37
   The Triratna, Trishula, and Triple Refuge 39
   Skill-in-means (upāya-kaushalya) 40
   Madhyamaka and Vijñānavāda views 41
   Devotionalism (bhakti) 45
   The sūtras: visionary experience writes the code 46
   The end of Buddhism in India? 61

2. SRI LANKA 63

3. TIBET 66

4. CHINA 72
   Ancestral cults in the Neolithic and Bronze Ages 74
   The Zhou Dynasty 76
   Confucius & The Analects [551 - 479 BCE] 77
   Lao Tzu & The Tao Te Ching 79
   Chuang Chou & the Chuang Tzu 82
   Buddhism's first 500 years in China 86
   Early Nikāya schools in China 91

  Early Mahāyāna schools in China [c. 500 - 600] 92
  The fall & rise of Chinese Buddhism 100
  The legend of Bodhidharma: the first Chan patriarch 108
  The legend of Huineng: "North vs. South" 116
  Esoteric Buddhism and the rise of the Chan master 126
  Encounter Dialogue: the gong-an & hua-tou 127
  Chan lineage & Dharma transmission 131
  The five petals of Chan 136
  Buddhism during and after the Tang Dynasty 137

5. KOREA 142
  The Three Kingdoms period 143
  The Silla period 144
  Korean Sŏn 145

6. VIETNAM 147

7. JAPAN 149
  Early background 151
  The "Nara" schools of Buddhism 153
  The Heian Period: Tendai and Shingon Buddhism 154
  Zen enters the scene 156
  The Ashikaga Period: rise of the Shōgunate 158
  The Tokugawa period: isolationism and art 160
  The Meiji Restoration: return of the emperor 161
  Imperialist expansion and Zen 165
  Imperial Zen on the battlefield 174
  Japanese Zen today 175

8. CHAN'S MIGRATION WEST 179
  Buddhism: a tapestry of disparate beliefs? 181
  The big business of "meditation" 182
  Zen profiteering 184
  The future of Chan in the West? 185

Part Two
Chan Training 187

9. Prerequisites..........190
Revisiting the Buddha's Four Noble Truths 193
Stages of spiritual development 205
Preparing for meditation 213

10. Stage One: Mindfulness 223

11. Stage Two: Concentration 228
Prāṇāyāma ("breath control") 230
Thought retracing 235
Other seeds for concentration 236

12. Stage Three: Contemplation 241
The gong-an 243
The hua-tou 245
Negation practice 250
Countercontemplation 253
Archetypal imagery 253

13. Stage Four: Meditation 256

Part Three
Experiences on the Journey 263

14. Chan's Ox-herding Series............266

15. The Value of a Model............274
"I" vs. "Self"............281
The ubiquitous catuṣkoṭi............287

16. The Theory of Psychological Archetypes 290
Psychological forces 293
Complexes 294
The (enemy) shadow archetype 296
The (friendly) shadow archetype 297
The persona archetype 297

  The anima & animus archetypes..298
  The hero archetype 302
  The child & mother archetypes 303
  The father archetype 303
  The warrior archetype 304
  The Self archetype 304

 17. Dreams and Visions 306
  The science of dreams and visual imagery 309
  Archetypal visions 310
  An example: the snake motif..314

 18. Discovering the "Self" 323
  Jiànxìng (kensho) 325
  Wù (enlightenment or satori) 327

 19. Physical Experiences 338

Part Four
Trials & Tribulations 343

Hindrances 345
 Expectations 346
 Belief..347
 Relinquishing autonomy..348
 Guilt, Painful Memories & Moral Injury....................................359
 Causes and conditions 360
 Judgment..361
 Teachers 362
 Social learning 365
 Clinging..367
 Control 368
 Wrong practice..369
 Fear...371
 Untoward emotions 372
 Existential annihilation..373
 Social media...373
 Effort...374

  Delusion 375
  Sexual desire 377
  Picking and choosing 378
  Secular life 379

21. DANGERS 381
  Skipping steps 381
  Dissociative disorders 383
  Snapping 384
  Overzealousness 388
  Pride 389
  Moral turpitude 390
  Dark emotions 393
  Visionary experience 393
  Institutional allegiance 395

FINAL THOUGHTS 403
  Chinese Chan "vs." Japanese Zen 406
  Returning to the Source 409

NOTES 418
ILLUSTRATION CREDITS 434
WORDS OF THANKS 435
BIBLIOGRAPHY 437
INDEX 452

LIST OF FIGURES

Figure 1. Vesak Day Celebration. 33
Figure 2. Pashupati seal No. 420. 40
Figure 3. The Nèijīng tú. 83
Figure 4. Bodhidharma. 109
Figure 5. Dharma lineage poem. 135
Figure 6. Empty Cloud. 137
Figure 7. Hotei pointing at the moon. 192
Figure 8. The Quadrant Exercise. 240
Figure 9. Picture 8 of Chan's ox-herding series. 269
Figure 10. A Mapping of Conscious States. 284
Figure 11. Nüwa. 315
Figure 12. Fuxi and Nüwa as king and queen. 315
Figure 13. Androgyne with goats' heads. 317
Figure 14. Quetzalcóatl and the Buddha. 318
Figure 15. Neidan Meditation. 325

EXERCISES

Exercise 1: Developing proper sitting form 215
Exercise 2: Becoming aware of the mind 218
Exercise 3: Establishing a routine 219
Exercise 4: Observing the breath 230
Exercise 5: Developing awareness of the breath 231
Exercise 6: Developing breath control 233
Exercise 7: Concentration on natural breathing 234
Exercise 8: Concentration on music 237
Exercise 9: Concentration on ambient sounds 237
Exercise 10: Concentration on the pulse 238
Exercise 11: Concentration on burning incense 238
Exercise 12: Concentration on a concept 238
Exercise 13: Concentration on mental formations 239
Exercise 14: Hua-tou practice 247
Exercise 15: Negation practice 252
Exercise 16: Contemplating archetypal imagery 254

Editor's Preface to the Second Edition

Welcome to the second edition of *Exploring Chan*. Since the first edition was published in 2019, we have received thoughtful feedback from readers, which has guided us in making meaningful updates. This edition features revised content for improved accuracy and clarity, along with new illustrations designed to illuminate key concepts. We've also expanded certain sections to provide deeper insights where they are most needed.

This book will likely resonate with a diverse audience: students of religion, Buddhists seeking to deepen their understanding of their faith's history and practice, practitioners of Chan or Zen eager to enrich their spiritual journey, and Buddhist scholars open to exploring alternative perspectives on the intricate subject of Chan Buddhism.

We hope that the enhancements in this second edition make your exploration of this material both enriching and enjoyable.

February 2025

Foreword

On May 3, 1998, I landed in Hong Kong after a sixteen-hour flight from New York's JFK airport. At thirty-eight years old, I was to meet up with Jy Din Shakya 釋智定, the Abbot, and founder of Hawaii's Hsu Yun Temple. Jy Din, also known as Wei Miao 釋惟淼, was one of China's most senior Chan masters at the time. He would accompany me to the inaugural ordination ceremony at China's new Hong Fa Temple in Shenzhen—a ceremony officially closed to foreigners, with an exception made for me thanks to Jy Din's determined efforts. As a native English speaker from the United States, I spoke no Chinese, had little exposure to Chinese culture or customs, and had minimal experience with religion in general. Yet, for reasons I didn't understand at the time, I felt a profound eagerness to embrace whatever awaited me.

After clearing customs, I changed into monastic vestments: a long gray robe that draped to my feet layered over light-yellow garments that resembled loose-fitting pajamas. This journey was the culmination of a path that began a year earlier when, during a private ceremony at Hsu Yun Temple in Hawaii, Jy Din had bestowed upon me the lineage name *Chuan Zhi Shakya* 釋傳智.

Hong Fa Temple was China's newest monastery in Shenzhen, just north of Hong Kong, and was still in construction under the guidance and direction of the monk Ben Huan. It marked a resurgence of Buddhism in China after many decades of decline that began during the Manchurian Qing dynasty.

Over the thirty-five days that followed, I became immersed in the rich tapestry of Chinese culture and religion. I learned the traditional chants, mastered the art of bowing and offering incense, and navigated the intricate procedures for donning and doffing monastic vestments. I was taught temple etiquette for everything from eating and walking to performing kowtows.

Oddly, I had never thought of myself as a religious person. Yet there I was, immersed in the experience of being initiated into one of the world's oldest religions. What had compelled me to take this journey? This book is not just a narrative about Chinese Chan—it's also a deeply personal account, shared through the lens of nearly three decades of study, practice, and reflection.

Writing about Chan, the mystical practice, is a peculiar endeavor. Reading about it is akin to watching a documentary on mountain climbing: while we may grasp the concepts or appreciate the beauty, true understanding comes only through direct experience. To truly comprehend Chan, we must immerse ourselves in it with the tenacity of a hungry lion and the perseverance of a pronghorn antelope. In Exploring Chán, I aim to sketch a portrait of Chan, but I caution readers not to mistake the map for the territory. Each person's view of Chan is shaped by their unique experiences, interpretations, and emotions, which can lead to vastly different expressions of the subject.

Over the past several decades, I've worked with hundreds of men and women of all ages who have sought Chan for various reasons. Some were drawn to its religious and institutional elements, others to its philosophical and ontological dimensions, and still others to its mystical tradition and practice. Although no book—this one included—can convey the essence of the Chan experience, my hope is that readers will come away with a clearer sense of its nature, its origins, and its enduring relevance for addressing life's many challenges.

— Chuan Zhi

Introduction

SOMETHING STRANGE HAPPENED WHEN I was very young. Our old farmhouse perched atop a small hill that overlooked a tranquil pond nestled within a forty-acre farm in the rural heartland of southern Illinois. A barbed wire fence separated a small grassy yard from a sprawling horse pasture that stretched over acres of green fields.

One hot, humid summer afternoon, I watched a thunderstorm slowly roll across the farm, its lightning and thunder providing a dramatic spectacle. The storm's passing broke a long heat wave, leaving the air fresh and cool. Energized by the change, I eagerly ran down to the old barn to play with my toy cars in the mud left behind by the rain.

At some point, I stopped my play and looked up at a solitary cloud drifting overhead—brilliant white against the deep blue sky. In that instant, a cascade of unsettling questions flooded my mind: What is this? Who am I? Why am I me and not someone else?

Now, over fifty years later, this memory stands out as the oddest from my childhood. It was the first time I can recall reflecting upon the nature of existence and identity. It's also my earliest memory that includes vivid recollections of the day itself, from the sound and smell of the rainstorm to the excitement, fear, and oddity of being alive.

Such moments may be common among us, but the question of existence—*who is it who is experiencing this life?*—continued to gnaw at me throughout my adolescent years and beyond. As a young adult in college, I might have been characterized as nerdy: when I wasn't studying physics or mathematics, I was reading the works of Fyodor Dostoyevsky, Douglas Hofstadter, and Paul Feyerabend, absorbing myself in the orchestrations of Mahler and Shostakovich, or developing my juggling skills. Inwardly, however, I suffered tremendous anxiety and at times severe depression. On the edge of consciousness, existential questions continued to gnaw at me.

As a physics student, one day I encountered the work of Blaise Pascal, a prominent physicist, mathematician, and theologian of the seventeenth century. I was especially moved by a comment he left in his notes:

> For after all what is man in nature? A nothing in relation to infinity, all in relation to nothing, a central point between nothing and all and infinitely far from understanding either. The ends of things and their beginnings are impregnably concealed from him in an impenetrable secret. He is equally incapable of seeing the nothingness out of which he was drawn and the infinite in which he is engulfed.[1]

Pascal's thoughts unsettled me. They reinforced my feeling that the questions to which I was seeking answers were likely unanswerable. Later, during my senior year, I discovered the *Blue Cliff Record*, a collection of Chan (*chán* 禪) writings (*kung-ans*) intended to be used as seeds for contemplation; a Chinese method for becoming aware of something called "Buddha-nature." The book opened new and peculiar pathways for me to explore and gave me a comforting sense that I wasn't alone on my quest to understand reality and my place in it. It also gave me hope that there might be real answers to my existential questions. Maybe Pascal was wrong and the infinite in which we are engulfed *can* be realized. I didn't know, but I had a strong desire to find out.

Years later, I would turn to the ascetic practice of Chinese Chan to which the *Blue Cliff Record* had first introduced me. I would discover, however, that the aspect of Chan I was interested in—that which focused on contemplation and meditation—did not exist independently of its religious framework. This befuddled me. I was interested in the ascetic and mystical disciplines of Chan to help answer burning ontological questions, not the mindless passivity and unquestioned adherence to dogma I associated with religious practices.

Yet I came to learn that embracing Chan meant embracing Buddhism, because Chan was described, explained, and taught through Buddhist language and practice. As I delved into Chan's religious side, I found many aspects paradoxical, confusing, and at odds with the spiritual practice it purported to represent. Looking to others for clarity was futile, for people seemed to view Chan in one of two distinct and mutually exclusive ways: either it was a religion characterized by a specific set of practices, beliefs, and ideologies, or it was a form of mysticism characterized by contemplation, meditation, and detachment from worldly affairs. I found nobody during those early years who could bridge the divide for me, who could connect the two together. So I set out to do it on my own.

Being alive is extraordinary. Perhaps it's our ability to ponder existence in the first place that differentiates us from other forms of life. We often call it self-awareness, but what is self-awareness? When we look closely, we see that what we think of as our "self" is an artifact of the senses which allow us to feel, see, hear, smell, taste, and think. Put them all together, add a bit of experience, and a self is born. Over time, we come to identify ourselves through our experiences, both their sensory aspect and our mental interpretations of them. At some point along the way, we conclude: *this is me.*[*] Soon we learn to judge and evaluate and begin forming opinions and perspectives based on our interpretations of those experiences; we decide what to enjoy and what to dislike, who to hate and who to love. As our sense of identity grows through this

---

[*] Studies have identified the brain's lower-level frontal operculum/ventral premotor cortex and somatosensory cortex to be responsible for manifesting our base sense of self-identity (Barsalou 1999), and the higher-level ventromedial prefrontal cortex has been identified as giving rise to the full perception of self (Lombardo 2010). The cognitive development of a perceived self-identity begins early in the second year of life (Meltzoff 2007) and is fully in place by the age of four or five (Rochat 2003).

process, we become increasingly trapped within it. Our lives may then come to feel fractured, leaving us angry, moody, anxious, depressed, and disillusioned. To alleviate the pain, we may seek distractions with drugs, video games, gossip, social media, sex, talk, careers, social life, TV, radio, books—the list of options is endless. But if we turn our gaze inward, toward the source from which consciousness arises, we can exit the cacophony of this mental anguish and heal the fractures.

To explain what mystical-Chan is about, consider that we each live in a kind of "reality bubble" created by our experiences. Mysticism offers a means to break out of this bubble, to get beyond the limitations imposed by an illusory ego that constructs its own limited and narrow view of reality. From it, we experience salvation because we are freed, or saved, from ourselves—our ego-selves.*

The idea that the ego—that which gives rise to a sense of identity—is a mere illusion has become a recent topic of interest in Western culture and many books have been written about it.† From the Chan perspective, however, we're interested in understanding it only as it pertains to helping us transcend it. The challenge is that this understanding requires we enter a kind of recursive, self-referential loop, because that which is discovered is that which does the discovering. In Part Two, we'll explore Chan's methods for entering this loop.

The landscape of Buddhism is much different today from that of a thousand years ago. Consumerism, social media, science, and technology have all helped create a distinct shape of reality for us that could not have been imagined by our ancient ancestors. While some aspects of modern society obviously distract from living a contemplative life, advances in our understanding of the world through the physical, bio-

---

* In the Buddhist sense, salvation means release from *saṃsāra*, the tumultuous realm of ego-desire that creates suffering. Some people prefer the psychological term *liberation*, or the sociological term *emancipation*, to the soteriological term *salvation*. But, while the three terms have related meanings, their context differentiates them.

† A small selection of recent books on this topic includes: *The Ego Trick, What Does It Mean to be You,* by Julian Baggini, *The Man Who Wasn't There: Investigations into the Strange New Science of the Self,* by Alil Ananthaswamy, *Take Me to the Truth: Undoing the Ego,* by Nouk Sanchez and Tomas Vieira, and *The Self Illusion, How the Social Brain Creates Identity,* by Bruce Hood.

logical, and social sciences have provided unbiased and irrefutable evidence of the value of turning our gaze inward. This simple activity is known to lead to better sleep, fewer medical and psychological problems, improved relationships, and greater overall contentment. Science can't do the work, the "spiritual labor," for us, but, for those of us who embrace the scientific method as a means for better understanding the world we live in, we can use the outcomes of scientific investigations to inspire and motivate us to lead more contemplative lives.

A great deal has been learned over the last century about the meaning, process, and experience of spirituality, as well as the religious institutions that have been created around it. The biological sciences have revealed underlying principles that account for feelings and emotions described as *numinous*, or otherworldly, by those who have experienced them, and functional magnetic resonance imaging (fMRI) and electroencephalography (EEG) have provided many insights into the physiology of mental states experienced during meditation.* Studies have also suggested profound effects at the genetic level which lessen the risk of disease and increase longevity.

Scientific insights aside, Chan as a mystical practice is purely experiential. It eludes attempts to define or explain it. Just as we can't know what it's like to hike the Pacific Crest Trail unless we get on it and start walking, neither can we know Chan's mystical path unless we embark on it. Both require psychological preparedness and physical fitness, as well as courage and discipline. And both require faith that the journey will be worth taking in the first place.

The expression and interpretation of mystical experience, as well as details of the experiences themselves, are necessarily mediated by culture, language, and the religious paradigm, but the *essence* of the experience, I argue, is *not* dependent upon these things (Chapters 10-13,

---

* Although fMRI and EEG studies have yielded some interesting results, because of an often ambiguous understanding of what is meant by *meditation*, it's unclear in many cases whether the groups studied were truly meditating, or were practicing mindfulness, concentration, or contemplation; practices which yield mental states quite different from one another (see Part Two of this book).

18).* If we consider the religious artwork and poetry created by people across the globe for centuries, it's obvious that mystical experience shares uncanny similarities across cultures, religions, and even time itself (Chapter 17).†

Although I began Chan as a mystical practice, a great many people enter through its religious portal, aligning themselves with its institutional form before engaging with it as a spiritual discipline. There are also many who enter through the religious gateway, get stuck there, and go no further. In fact, some Chan scholars, as well as some self-proclaimed Chan/Zen Buddhists I have spoken with, deny that Chan offers a mystical approach to Buddhism in any way. One scholar I know, for example, views Chan entirely as a socioreligious construct mediated by politics, social dynamics, ceremony, and various expressive forms of religious idealization. Similarly, Peter L. Berger, sociologist and theologian, considers Chan's mystical aspect a social construction which induces alienation, veiling reality from anyone who gets caught up in it. While these aspects *can* play into the complex religious structure and identity of Chan, unless we look within—the mystic's "practice"—we will, indeed, as Berger argues, become prisoners of the religious paradigm; our identity will become mediated by the institution, our personal "reality bubble" replaced by that of the religious collective.

---

* By *essence*, I mean the numinous quality of mystical experiences and the archetypal themes which provoke them (Part Three), not the specific experiences themselves. Just as all people experience breathing in much the same way regardless of ethnicity, language, and culture, so is mysticism experienced. This is an admittedly uncommon perspective among scholars (such as Steven T. Katz), but is one which I nonetheless explore throughout this book.

† Some scholars argue that mystical experience is entirely moderated by a social and/or conceptual framework. Stephen Bernhardt cautions against this view as I do: "The recent fashion has been to call into question the old standards in the study of mysticism—Evelyn Underhill, Rudolf Otto, W. T. Stace, R. C. Zaehner, and William James—with their espousals of universal characteristics or typologies for mysticism, which assume that mysticism in its essentials is basically the same everywhere. But as the pendulum swings, I believe there is a tendency to commit the converse error, namely, to conclude that mystical experiences are everywhere different. The pure consciousness event [...] is the most likely available candidate for the title of 'universal mystical experience'" (1990, 225). Descriptions of the mystical experience are indeed necessarily dependent on the social construct of language; however, we cannot say that the description of something is equivalent to the thing being described, nor that flaws or inadequacies of those descriptions subvert the reality of the mystical experience itself.

Chan is most commonly viewed in its institutional context, and Alan Cole, author of *Patriarchs on Paper: A Critical History of Medieval Chan Literature*, offers a plausible explanation for why. Although the term "Chan" means meditation, he suggests that during the mid-Tang dynasty the "perfect master" came to replace the meditation master: "What came to be known as the 'Chan tradition' (*chanzong*) only emerges when *chan* stopped meaning meditation and took on this sense of 'perfect.'"[2] To his point, anyone visiting a traditional Chan temple in China or a Zen temple in Japan will observe veneration for, and often total allegiance to, the principal ecclesiastical authority who may even be regarded as a Buddha. This phenomenon has, to a large extent, carried over to Zen and Chan training centers in the West.

Yet, although devotional ancestor and master worship became a central feature of institutional Chan, there are still tens of thousands of Chan monks and lay practitioners who sit for hours daily in meditation, some of whom participate in devotional Buddhism when off the cushion. Taigen Dan Leighton reasonably suggests, however, that in many cases this type of sitting following formal protocols may be entirely "a ceremonial, ritual expression whose transformative quality is not based on stages of attainment or meditative prowess."[3] Which begs a question: what *is* going on in the minds of those who are, in fact, sitting on a cushion? Are they meditating or not? If so, are they doing it in the context of religious ritual or not? If they are truly meditating, does it matter? Having visited both monastic and home-spun sitting groups in which the only instructions given were "just sit," "watch your breath," "just breathe," or even "watch what other people are doing and copy it," it's likely that some people who practice Zen or Chan don't engage with it as a mystical discipline. Without the right kind of guidance and motivation, practitioners may never experience true meditation. In such cases, the formal act of sitting may indeed be purely ceremonial and unrelated to the spiritual journey. Yet, for those who engage with Chan as a path of salvation—as a vehicle for transcending suffering, which is the foundational principal of Buddhism—I contend that it's nothing other than a mystical discipline, regardless of the institutional context. This view is rarely presented by scholars.

Robert Sharf, author of *Coming to Terms with Chinese Buddhism*, suggests that the reason this subject is so often skirted by scholars is because of "daunting hermeneutic problems involved in what might be called the comparative phenomenology of meditation."[4] For this reason, bias toward viewing Chan predominantly in its institutional form may have evolved naturally, considering the essentially ineffable quality of mystical experience. Since the spiritual realm of feelings doesn't lend itself to analysis or discourse, authors tend to stay away from it. As Chan master Hsu Yun succinctly expressed it, "Learning adds things that can be researched and discussed. The feel of impressions can't be communicated."[5] We might be able to accurately describe a car to someone who has never seen one before, but how do we describe the color blue to someone who is color blind? Herein lies the fundamental challenge for any author who attempts to enter this treacherous domain: spiritual experiences are subjective and can't be communicated. They can only be experienced.

Since we are considering two semi-distinct aspects of Chan, hereafter I'll follow Robert Sharf's convention of referring to small-c chan as the mystical practice and large-C Chan as its institutional religious counterpart, although he explains them slightly differently: "[t]he former refers to Chinese Buddhist *dhyāna* techniques writ large, and encompasses a wide array of practices that made their way from India to China beginning in the first and second centuries C. E. [...] Large-C Chan refers to a specific lineage or school [...] that was based on the mythology of an unbroken, independent lineage of enlightened masters..."[*6]

In the West, the term *Zen* is most commonly associated with Japanese expressions of Chinese Chan. I sometimes use the terms inter-

---

* My ordination from Master Jy Din in 1997, and subsequently again in China, placed me in the Linji or "Southern school" Chan lineage, which was revitalized in China by the monk Hsu Yun, Jy Din's direct "Dharma father." Dharma lineage will be explored in Chapter 4.

changeably, however, since both originate from the transliteration of the same Sanskrit word, *dhyāna*, meaning "to dwell." Although *Zen* is the term more commonly known in the West today, I'll use it principally when referring specifically to Japanese-oriented approaches and reserve the term *Chan* for Chinese approaches.

In Vietnam, the term for Chan is *Thiền*, and in Korea, *Sŏn* (*Seon*), but these terms are less frequently encountered in the Occident. Although they all originated from Chinese Chan, Zen, Sŏn, and Thiền have each developed distinctive characteristics and practices that departed, to various degrees, from Chan's presentation in China. We'll explore how and why in Part I, keeping in mind that the spiritual disciplines presented by each are affected little by the religious forms that contain them.*

Over the last few decades, scholars have examined the political, social, and economic forces that created and shaped Chan during its formative years, and have offered insights on how those forces may have shaped today's presentation of Chan and Zen. Some of those writers we can thank for these insights—most of whom were or are devoted Zen or Chan practitioners themselves—include the late John R. McRae and his wife Jan Nattier, Tilmann Vetter, T. Griffith Foulk, Alan Cole, Brian Victoria, Christopher Ives, Morton Schlütter, Stuart Lachs, Robert H. Sharf, Albert Welter, David Keightley, and Steven Heine. Their valuable thoughts, along with those of others, are sprinkled throughout this book as I attempt to paint a broad picture of Chan Buddhism, exploring its historical, sociological, religious, and mystical contexts. I also reflect on various ways that Chan is conceived and practiced in Western society today in relation to its origins and development in India and China, and offer some practical guidance to readers who may be interested in practicing chan, joining sitting groups, or sharing practice with others.

---

* Contemplation and meditation are activities of the mind as it turns inward away from the phenomenal world, and therefore do not rely on a religious structure. Such a structure, however, can offer entrance and guidance for those interested in pursuing a mystical practice, as well as a framework and model for interpreting and expressing mystical experience (Chapter 15).

Along the way, I will address a series of related questions: (a) How and why did Chan arise in China as a unique expression of Chinese Buddhism? (b) How and why did the Chan institution invent its characteristic lineage system and what is its significance? (c) How has state sponsorship shaped the presentation of Chan and Zen throughout the Orient? (d) Why is there a seeming disparity between the mystical practice of Chan and its religious expression? (e) How does one "do" Chan as a mystical practice, and why would someone want to? (f) How can the religious presentation of Chan be simultaneously supportive and subversive to ascetic practice? And (g) How might a practitioner of Chan best engage with the Chan institution to ensure healthy spiritual growth?

Before we get started, some terms frequently used throughout the book are best explained early, as their meanings in our context may differ from those the reader is familiar with:

BUDDHISM: Buddhism is, of course, a religion, but it differs from the conventional occidental notion of religion in that there are no universally agreed-upon canonical texts defining it, and there is no universal concept of a personified deity. While chan is a practice that can readily be done by anyone—given adequate preparedness and motivation—discussing chan requires the language of Buddhism, as it was Indian Buddhism, combined with other religious and social movements in China, from which it was born. The two terms closest to the heart of Buddhism are *Dharma* and *Buddha*.

DHARMA: *Dharma* (Pāli, *Dhamma*) is often translated as *Universal Law* or *Ultimate Truth*, and refers to the underlying governing principles of reality, which, though not identifiable through the senses or rational thought, are universal, omnipresent, and without beginning or end. Dharma also refers to the teachings of the Buddha, as well as to the myriad "things" (*dharmas*) that flutter in and out of existence in a constant state of flux (*dharmakāya*). In the Buddhist canon, the term has taken on many other meanings, including righteousness, conscience, nature, duty, phenomena, virtue, and justice.⁷ *Dharma* is thought to have originated in pre-Buddhist Vedic culture, where it meant order and law.⁸

BUDDHA: In Sanskrit, *Buddha* means one who is fully awake and conscious. In Buddhism, the term *Buddha* is commonly used in three main contexts: first, as a reference to Siddhārtha Gautama of the Shakya (Śākya) clan—sometimes referred to affectionately as Shakyamuni ("hermit of the Śākyas"); second, as a reference to the *essential-nature* inherent in all things; and third, as a reference to the ideal ("celestial") form of an enlightened being. Other terms for the celestial Buddha are Amitāyus, Amitābha, and Amida. A related term, "Bodhisattva," in early Buddhist texts, refers to the Buddha before he became the Buddha, but the term is now commonly (and confusingly) used to describe either someone who wishes to live in accordance with self-sacrifice and Dharma, or someone who has become fully spiritually awakened and "returns to the world to help others." The Buddhist canon suggests that after experiencing enlightenment, the Buddha referred to himself, illeistically, as the *Tathāgata*, lit. "one who has arrived at suchness." The teachings of the Buddha were posthumously preserved orally in *sutras* (Skt., *sūtras*; Pāli, *suttas*) before being put into writing several hundred years later. The sutra tradition, however, is riddled with questions of authenticity, a (sometimes heated) topic explored in Part One of this book. The basis for all the Buddha's teachings was to transcend suffering.

"SUFFERING": The Sanskrit term *duhkha* (*duḥkha*), simplistically translated as *suffering* in English, describes all the myriad ways that life tortures us: sadness, anger, grief, fear, disillusionment, anxiety, hate, pain, etc. Transcending duhkha is the central theme of Buddhism. In Sanskrit, the realm of suffering in which we live is called *samsāra*, for which there is no English equivalent. Through specific practices described in the Buddha's *Four Noble Truths*, one can escape samsāra and enter *nirvāṇa*, the realm of egoless awareness, sometimes referred to as "Buddha-nature" or "True Self."

SAMSARA: While the notion of suffering, or duhkha, is central to Buddhist thought and practice, the realm in which we participate with suffering, *samsāra*, is central to understanding how suffering arises. The term is important in Hinduism, Jainism, and all flavors of Buddhism, yet there are sometimes subtle, and other times stark, differences in how it's interpreted. In some traditions, it connotes the notion of reincarnation, or rebirth as another human or other life form after the physical death of the body. For some, it suggests a "hell" realm where we go after we die a physical death. But in Mahayana Buddhism—and Chan—it means quite another thing. Literally translated, *saṃsāra* (संसार) means "wandering about in the world". Metaphorically, the term has come to represent the concept of cyclic birth and death, arising and falling, creation and destruction, the ebb and flow of attachments and desires, which the human condition predisposes us toward, and which subsequently creates the condition of suffering. Once we exit this tumultuous cycle of "birth and death" during our life, we experience *nirvāṇa*, the realm of existence freed from it. In *Reflections*, 1994, Ajahn Chah (Chah Subhaddo), a Thai Buddhist monk of the Theravada tradition, beautifully expresses a mystic's interpretation of samsāra:

> The "One Who Knows" clearly knows that all conditioned phenomena are unsubstantial. So this "One Who Knows" does not become happy or sad, for it does not follow changing conditions. To become glad is to be born; to become dejected is to die. Having died, we are born again; having been born, we die again. This birth and death from one moment to the next is the endless spinning wheel of samsāra.
> The Buddha told his disciple Ananda to see impermanence, to see death with every breath. We must know death; we must die in order to live. What does this mean? To die is to come to the end of all our doubt, all our questions, and just be here with the present reality. You

can never die tomorrow; you must die now. Can you do it? If you can do it, you will know the peace of no more questions.

For mystics, the notion of reincarnation—rebirth of one's self following physical death—does not arise. When the self is seen clearly as an illusion, there is nothing to reincarnate. When we recognize that we have no fixed identity we are freed from the cycle of life and death. Mahayana Buddhists recognize samsāra as the tumultuous and painful existence we endure when attached to the mundane world, and the resulting emotional roller coaster that keeps us in its grip.

"TRUE SELF": The term *True Self* describes awareness when it's stripped of ego-identity, or ego-self.* Common synonyms for True Self include *Buddha-nature* or *Dharma-nature* (*fó xìng* 佛性; Skt., *Tathāgatagarbha*), *essential nature*, *essential being*, *original nature*, and *essential Self*. In the Indian *Vedas* and *Upanishads*, it's referred to as *Brahman* or *Atman*†, and in China as *Xīn* 心. *Xīn* is typically translated to English as *Mind*, but it also includes the concepts of heart, intelligence, center, core, and soul. Chan training employs various methods for gaining awareness of this "Self," which is ever-present yet rarely known because of the ego's overwhelming bias toward sensory modes of perception.

"Host and guest" is a similar concept in mysticism, and often found in chan literature. Imagine you are a traveler and you stop at an inn for the night. The host takes you in and gives you a place to stay. In the morning you leave, while the host remains. The Self is the host who welcomes the foreigner, and is always there, never leaving. The ego-self is the guest, a foreigner to the host. The guest travels from place to place, but takes rest and comfort from the host. *Host and guest* is an

---

* I use the term *ego* throughout this book in the conventional psychological sense to mean that part of the mind that gives rise to a sense of personal identity.

† Brahman is the ultimate underlying reality of everything; Atman is one's True Self, which is identical to Brahman.

allegorical tool that can be used to contemplate the nature of, and relationship between, ego-self and Self.

MEDITATION (*Dhyāna*): *Meditation* is a broad categorical term that, in popular culture, describes both mindfulness and contemplation, as well as meditation.* The term *meditation* is now often identified with various practices and states of mind which are precursors to meditation (in its original intended meaning), such as *mindfulness* practices that lead to withdrawal of the senses (*pratyahara*) and *concentration* practices (*dhāraṇā*) that lead to calmness of mind (*santi*).† Dhāraṇā involves focusing the mind on a specific thing, or "seed," such as an idea or thought, an image held in the mind, a sensation, etc.; while dhyāna implies a mind which has entered an egoless state of awareness. The term *Chán*—though derived from *Chán-na*, the early Chinese transliteration of *dhyāna*—has acquired additional meanings that differentiate it from its Sanskrit namesake, a topic we'll explore throughout this book.

SPIRITUALITY: Spirituality (*jīn gshén xìng* 精神性) derives from the Latin term *spiritus*, meaning breath, soul, courage, and vigor, and refers to connecting with our "inner life" (*nèixiǎn* 內想), which is devoid of judgment, bias, interpretation, opinion, and belief. Spirituality is characterized by Self-absorption and contemplation (*chénsī* 沉思).

The term *spirituality* is often used broadly and indiscriminately in contemporary culture to mean a variety of things, from belief in ghosts to a religious belief in a personified God. In this book, I use *spirituality* to refer to the ascetic's practice of contemplating and detaching

---

* The terms *meditation, contemplation,* and *concentration* are encountered frequently in Buddhism, and they are often, and for good reason, confused with one another. While Sanskrit offers literally dozens of terms to describe various mental states achieved when we turn our gaze inward, English has very few. Translators thus have had few options when converting these Sanskrit concepts to English, resulting in different Sanskrit terms being correlated with the same English word. For the purpose of this work, meditation refers to *dhyāna*, concentration refers to *dhāraṇā*, and contemplation, even though it's often synonymous with meditation, refers to a transitory state between concentration and meditation.

† There are significant qualitative differences between *dhyāna* and *dhāraṇā*, and research has shown that there are quantitative differences as well (Jian Xu 2014); thus, using the same term—*meditation*—to refer to any or all of them is misleading. We will examine this issue more in Part Two.

from worldly affairs. I don't use the term in a religious context, which would associate it more with institutional forms of worship than with Self-absorption.

ENLIGHTENMENT: Enlightenment refers to spiritual awakening, or the recognition of the ineffable Self. In the 1930s, D. T. Suzuki, one of the foremost voices in Japanese Zen during the early 20th century, popularized the term *enlightenment* from his translation of the Japanese term, *satori*; a convention started by Max Müeller (1823-1900). Originally, enlightenment referred to a European social movement during the 18th century described by Immanuel Kant as "freedom to use one's own intelligence."[9] In Chinese, the experience of enlightenment or "new spiritual awareness" is *wù* 悟. In Sanskrit, the term for spiritual awakening is *bodhi* (बोधि), and the term for ultimate liberation or salvation is *nirvāṇa* (निर्वाण). In the early Buddhist canon, enlightenment was closely linked to the release from suffering.[10]

There are various enlightenment experiences, from small glimpses of Self to full-blown ecstatic "revelation" (Chapter 18). The experience of enlightenment—mystical awakening—is not unique to Chan. Other mystical traditions recognize the same thing using different terminology and models to express it. It has, for example, been regarded as akin to the Christian alchemists' *philosopher's stone*, the Sufis' (Islamic mystics') *Marifa* (المعرفة), and the Jewish Kabbalists' *ayin*.*

RELIGION: Religion, in the context of this work, is an institutional social framework governed by rules, beliefs, ethical codes of conduct, procedures, and rituals, all of which ensure conformity of thought and action within its body of followers. Religion is embodied by subliminal (unconscious) archetypal motifs. At its heart is a shared belief system that strengthens and perpetuates the institution but can isolate it and

---

* Joseph Gikatilla wrote, "The depth of primordial being...is called Boundless. It is also called *ayin* because of its concealment from all creatures above and below.... If one asks, 'what is it?,' the answer is, Ayin, that is, no one can understand anything about it.... It is negated of every conception" (as quoted by Matt 1990, 128). In other words, Ayin, like Dharma, is that which cannot be known intellectually, is infinite, is concealed from the intellect, and can only be realized through a process of negation.

its members from the world at large—a phenomenon Peter Berger calls *alienation*—as well as from those outside the institution who do not share its core beliefs.*

ARCHETYPAL MOTIFS: Archetype (*diǎnxíng* 典型) derives from the Greek noun *archetupon* (ἀρχέτυπον), which means first-molded, beginning, origin, pattern, or model. An archetype is thus the distilled essence of something that reveals its fundamental intrinsic form or nature. For example, a triangle drawn on paper may be considered the archetype of a structural principle[11] and a statue of the Buddha an archetypal representation of Self. Psychological archetypal motifs are visual and emotional themes that are believed to have arisen through evolutionary processes,[12] and manifest across all cultures and civilizations. They are especially prominent in religions, being represented in statuary, frescos, paintings, hymns, chants, and canonical texts.†

MYSTICISM: The term mysticism (*sham zhǔyì* 神秘主義) evolved from the Greek word *mustērion* (μυστηριον), meaning that which is secret, hidden, and remains unknown. A mystic is one who delves into that which is unknown—more specifically, *that which cannot be known through the senses*. This concept arises in many religious traditions, including Chan, where the aim is to abandon what is known in favor of what is not known, through disengagement with worldly affairs. As "mysteries" are discovered, the mystic assimilates them and continues further into the unknown. Chan provides a mystical (*shénmì* 神秘) tradition of Chinese Buddhism, just as Judaism offers Kabbalism, Islam

---

* Peter L. Berger, author of *The Sacred Canopy*, describes religion as the result of an endeavor to construct a sacred world distinct from the mundane world: "Religion is the human enterprise by which a sacred cosmos is established" (1990, 25). Berger argues that this leads to alienation of a religious person from himself and from the natural world through the construction of a false consciousness (Ibid., 87). This phenomenon can sometimes become a problem for Chan, and for its adherents. I will explore some of these issues and examine why they may occur throughout this book. In Part Four, I'll suggest ways to avoid the psychological entrapment that religion can sometimes impose on Chan/Zen training.

† Visual archetypal themes are commonly encountered in meditation (Chapter 17) and can impart great significance to those who encounter them. James Hillman wrote that archetypal images are "valued as universal, trans-historical, basically profound, generative, highly intentional, and necessary" (Hillman 2013).

offers Sufism, and Christianity offers spiritual alchemy (insofar as the ancient alchemists identified as Christians).*

"self" vs. "Self": Throughout this book I refer to the concept of self in two ways: small-s "self" (zìwǒ 自我; Skt., *ahaṃkāra*) refers to our usual notion of who we are—our identity—which is created and shaped through sensory experience, while large-S "Self" (Skt., *antarātma*) I use to refer to our *original nature,* our *fundamental essence,* aspects of which can be known once we are able to see beyond ego-moderated awareness. I also use the term *Self* to refer to evolved instinctual patterns beyond our conscious awareness which manifest as emotions to spur us to action. In Chan, *Self* is sometimes represented symbolically with an ox, or more specifically, a wild Asian water buffalo (Chapter 14).

A NOTE ON LANGUAGE

Many of the terms used in Buddhism originate from Sanskrit or Pāli sources, the primary languages through which Buddhism spread as it moved out of India and split into different schools.† Today, we recognize the Pāli canon as associated with *Theravāda* Buddhism, that school which evolved as Buddhism spread south from India into Sri Lanka, Myanmar, Thailand, Cambodia, and Malaysia. *Mahāyāna* Buddhism, which spread dominantly into central Asia and China, adopted the older classical language of Sanskrit.‡

---

* Some writers consider mysticism from the viewpoint of *constructivism,* namely, that mystical experience is shaped and formed entirely by our beliefs and expectations. This is an understandable perspective for one who has not had mystical experience. But there may also be people who consider themselves to have had mystical experience they haven't had, and who base their belief in mystical experience on their expectations of what they imagine it to be—the accusation levied by constructivists. Defining clearly what mystical experience *is* is an epistemological challenge, considering that intellectual knowledge is dependent upon words and thoughts, while spiritual experience is not. This problem will be explored in parts Three and Four.

† Buddhist texts were written in other languages of the Indo-Aryan (MIA) family as well, including Prakrit, Apabhraṃsa, Māgdhī, and Paiśācī.

‡ Because of the rifts that developed between Buddhist schools across cultures, the world's collection of sutras, represented as teachings of the Buddha, are not widely agreed upon between the adherents of Theravāda, Vajrayāna, and Mahāyāna traditions; each has its own favored collection that evolved to reflect distinct religious and cultural environments.

Linguists warn us that our worldview is shaped profoundly by our language and its grammar.[196] In discussing religions endemic to cultures whose languages are significantly different from ours, we must consider that it may be fundamentally impossible to accurately describe and interpret them. To address this problem, I sometimes include original terms in Chinese Hanyu Pinyin and hanzi (pictographic characters), as well as Sanskrit and Pāli transliterations, to allow the reader the opportunity to investigate key concepts elsewhere if desired.

In Summary

This book represents the culmination of my observations, insights, and experiences drawn from decades of engagement with Chan in both its mystical and institutional dimensions. Inevitably, my perspective is woven into the narrative, making it inseparable from the story told here. My hope is that readers will approach these pages with healthy skepticism, using it as a spark for their own critical exploration of what is true or false, imaginary or real. After all, no one else's words on matters of the spirit can ever match the satisfaction of one's own discoveries.

In Part One, we'll delve into the religious and spiritual context from which Chan emerged, tracing its journey from ancient India to the present day. We'll uncover how Chan evolved over nearly a millennium through a dynamic interplay of invention, spiritual insight, political maneuvering, and literary creativity. Along the way, we'll explore the possible roots of Chan's mystical traditions in antiquity and examine the effects of Buddhism's institutionalization, politicization, and militarization. In Part Two, we'll turn our attention to chan training methods, including specific exercises for readers interested in exploring them firsthand. In Part Three, we'll discuss a range of experiences commonly encountered when engaging deeply with our inner lives. Finally, in Part Four, we'll address potential challenges and dangers that may arise on this path and provide guidance on how to navigate them effectively.

My journey with Chan began as a deep fascination with the philosophical and ontological insights embedded in its canonical texts, some of which I share in Part One. It was only much later that I embarked on the practice of chan itself, a journey that forms the heart of the remainder of this book. More recently, I've developed an interest in the institutional dimensions of Chan, and I have woven my reflections on this topic—alongside the perspectives of contemporary scholars—throughout the narrative.

I hope you enjoy this exploration into the mysterious realm of Self and the religious expression that emerged from it in China called Chan.

PART ONE

Chan's Historical Backdrop

...the writer of history works to evoke scenes and events that, though invisible, can be made to appear to the reader as integral parts of reality, albeit in the past. In this overlay of the past onto the present, the way we get back to those past events is via imagination and fantasy. In the writing of history, then, there is a kind of alchemy at work in which words disappear as they magically turn into quasi-visible events, and these events then are given various meanings that can be shaped for the audience's instruction and entertainment. In short, however fictional or factual a history might be, it is born of imagination—the author's and the reader's.

– Alan Cole, *Patriarchs on Paper*[*]

THE ORIGIN OF MEDITATION, and those practices that lead to meditation, are likely lost to history, but there are clues that suggest quite ancient roots. Harappan stone seal artifacts, discovered from the Indus Valley Civilization (2300-1900 BCE or earlier), depict

---

[*] Alan Cole is an independent scholar specializing in medieval Chan literature. He has taught at Lewis & Clark College, Reed College, Harvard University, the University of Illinois, the University of Oregon, and the National University of Singapore.

people sitting in lotus position, a posture still commonly used today in meditation halls and living room floors, and one often associated with Zen and meditation. We can thus posit that meditation, as a means for cultivating spiritual insight, may have endured in some form for over four millennia. Shortly after knowledge of meditation entered China with Buddhism, it became central to a new socioreligious and spiritual movement called *Chan*, the Chinese transliteration of the Sanskrit term *dhyāna*, meaning, *to dwell within, to contemplate*.

As an expression of Chinese Buddhism, Chan developed in two distinct but codependent directions: one religious, characterized by specific beliefs, attitudes, and behaviors, and one spiritual, characterized by contemplation and meditation. They were distinct because the experience of meditation excludes the social environment of its religious counterpart. When we turn our gaze inward, into the domain of Self, the religious framework vanishes as we become consumed by an entirely different kind of reality. When our gaze returns to the outer world we are confronted with the challenge of reconciliation, of understanding our inner experience in the context of the society in which we live and the religious structure in which we might participate. These become the two different windows through which we can view Chan: the religious, or institutional, and the mystical, or spiritual inner realm.

The purpose of chan as a spiritual discipline is Self-knowledge. But not all Chan Buddhists engage in Chan with the intent of gaining spiritual insight; a great many are born into the religion* or may have adopted it for a variety of other reasons.† When we talk about Chan, context will influence whether we are addressing the spiritual, contemplative aspect or its religious counterpart. Historically, however, the two aspects—religious and spiritual—have always been closely interconnected.

---

* This is not to suggest that being born into the religion precludes one from participating with its spiritual/mystical framework, just that when one does not enter the religion by choice, one is likely to relate to it differently from someone who adopts it for purposes of spiritual pursuit.

† For example, some people may be attracted to religion because they fear death, because it belongs to their cultural tradition, because they harbor guilt for which they seek amelioration, because they enjoy its social environment, or because they are seeking someone or something else to solve their problems.

The expression of Chan Buddhism, in both its religious and mystical forms, evolved from a complex dance of cultures, philosophies, social movements, politics, religious expressions, and individual epiphanies. To try to understand how and why Chan may have evolved as it did, we'll begin in ancient India, where the Vedas, whose origins date to 2000 BCE or earlier, helped inspire the birth of Buddhism, from which Chan later arose in China. We'll explore how Chan developed, why it came to be presented differently in neighboring countries, and how these presentations have influenced the practice and perception of Chan throughout the Americas, Europe, and other parts of the world. We'll also note how Tibetan (Himalayan) Buddhism has influenced people's perception of all forms of Buddhism, including Chan.

While the practice of chan is a personal, contemplative journey into *being*, the story of Chan is a story of people, their experiences with meditation, and the religious, cultural, and political environments in which many of them lived their lives. It's also a story that is often indistinct and obscure. Much of Chan's development, as well as its spiritual heritage, has happened through anonymous contributors, memories (or fabrications) of encounters with meditation masters, and—often overlooked but equally relevant—visionary experience.* The expression of Chan was further developed through a synthesis of cultures, ideologies, hagiographies, interpretations, idealizations, and "spin" (Chapter 4).

Simplistically, we can view Chan's invention as an organic response to the religious, social, and political environment of the time. As Buddhist ideas and practices were evolving, Taoist and Confucian sensibilities were incorporated, just as Westerners today are melding Buddhism with Islam, Christianity, and Judaism.†

---

* Meditation produces brain-wave states similar to those which produce dream imagery during sleep. Because a meditator is fully conscious as such imagery is produced, the visual experience can take on extraordinary significance. We will examine this in Chapter 17.

† The interested reader will find a plethora of books available through online book sellers linking Buddhism to Judaism, Christianity, and Islam. Some examples are: *Common Ground between Islam and Buddhism; Spiritual and Ethical Affinities*, by Reza Shah Kazemi; *The Lotus & The Rose: A Conversation Between Tibetan Buddhism & Mystical Christianity*, by Lama Tsomo; and *Torah and Dharma: Jewish Seekers in Eastern Religions*, by Judith Linzer.

State sponsorship further shaped the presentation of Chan in China, Sŏn in Korea, and Zen in Japan. While Chan, Sŏn, and Zen institutions enjoyed the financial benefits of state sponsorship, they also became unduly influenced by political, patriotic, and economic forces—to the extent, even, that warrior monks were trained to wield their spiritual prowess on the battlefield. Arguably, no nation became more adept at Zen warfare than Japan (Chapter 7).

There are a great many excellent works available on the historical interpretation of Chan.[14] My objective in Part One in recounting historical events is not to compete with these works or to add to them, but to select and highlight some relevant circumstances that allowed Chan to emerge and evolve, and to address some contemporary critical perspectives on history. We'll explore through this investigation how Buddhism's mystical path may have developed through a synthesis of religious, ethnic, and spiritual practices that long preceded the written record. We'll also be led to conjecture that the essence of chan as a mystical practice may not be based as much on historical precursors as on humankind's intrinsic desire to know the Self, a desire that does not arise out of religious form, but inspires and creates that form.

If Chan was entirely an inner practice, there would be no historical record of it. History is created through our interaction with the physical world—the opposite of the spiritual "inner" domain where the mystic travels. So as we explore Chan, we'll look at both the outer presentation and the inner experience. Part One, *Chan's Historical Backdrop*, focuses predominantly on the outer expressions of the spiritual experience and the institutional frameworks that have evolved from them.

While individual Buddhist teachers in China may have fought to persuade others of their particular beliefs, the collective Chinese Buddhist mind has historically been open to diverse interpretations of Buddhist thought and practice. The Buddhisms of India, Sri Lanka, Tibet, Korea, Vietnam, and Japan may seem distinct from Chinese Buddhism, but not only did cross-pollination of religious ideas and practices between them play a role in shaping the Chinese form, those expressions have greatly affected our view of Buddhism today. For these reasons, Part One offers a broad overview of the development of Buddhism in these countries and draws attention to differences and similarities among them.

For the spiritually inclined, studying history may not seem relevant, but as Robert Penn Warren has aptly observed, "History can give us a fuller understanding of ourselves, and of our common humanity." Yet, we must be careful about how we interpret historical "facts." As Wendi L. Adamek observes, "a quest for 'facts' often reveals more about its own context than that of the apparent subject, while the fault-lines of fiction may admit echoes from the past that have been expunged from more authoritative works."[15]

Indeed, the stories and lore of Chan, while sometimes embellished or allegorical, can provide rich insights into the social, and political landscapes from which they arose, offering echoes of the environments that shaped them and suggesting truths that rigid historical accounts may easily overlook.

With this perspective, our journey begins in ancient India, a time when religious groups flourished as abundantly as the creative and spiritual minds that shaped them.

I

Early Foundations: India

When religious movements are in their infancy, they often inspire excitement and foster creative expression. Over time, however, this vitality can fade as institutional identity and group solidarity take precedence over the pursuit of spiritual insight. Many religions and sects, if they endure long enough, pass through periods of decline where the creative spirit is eclipsed by rigid adherence to doctrine and tradition. Some fade away entirely, while others experience a revival after centuries of stagnation. Occasionally, a dwindling sect becomes the spark for a new movement, rekindling the energy and vitality of its origins. Such dynamics shaped the religious landscape of India during the 5th and 6th centuries BCE, as visionary leaders challenged the authority of Vedism and addressed the deep social inequalities of the time.[16] Buddhist texts refer to as many as sixty-two religious sects, and Jain texts refer to as many as 636 sects during the 6th century BCE alone.[17]

In this dynamic religious environment, one voice stood out among many, one that would transform religious and spiritual life throughout the Orient and, eventually, the world. It was the voice of Siddhārtha

Gautama, who would become known as the Buddha—the Awakened One.

Although we have no records of Siddhārtha from his lifetime, it's generally agreed, considering the assortment of accounts written nearly five centuries later, that he lived somewhere between 563 and 483 BCE in Bihar, India.*[18] It was many generations after his death that his story and teachings were first recorded, having previously been transmitted only orally.† It's possible that what we know today about Siddhārtha and his teachings is as much myth as fact, considering the natural tendencies of zealous followers to create elaborate hagiographies, and considering the vague and often contradictory records left by successive generations of Buddhists.‡ But fact or fiction, the religions and social movements that arose due to this provocative individual would attract hundreds of millions and alter the course of civilizations.§

The story of the Buddha is perhaps as famous with Buddhists as the story of Jesus is with Christians, or the story of Muhammad is with Muslims. Each of these posthumous religious founders has yielded two types of stories as well: some based on evidence synthesized from written and archeological records, and others mythological, the result of

---

* Tilmann Vetter has noted that "[t]he basis of the calculation of these dates can be found in the Ceylonese tradition which maintains that the Buddha died 218 years before the coronation of Asoka" (1988, XIII).

† Written language during this time in India's history had essentially vanished for unknown reasons. In its place, extremely accurate oral recitation practices were used to retain important information.

‡ Priest and Buddhist scholar Etienne Lamotte wrote that "teeming" contradictions between early Buddhist texts present substantial challenges for historians: "The Brahmanical, Jaina, and Buddhist sources rarely agree and, inside Buddhism, the Sinhalese chronicle often deviates from the written or oral traditions which prevailed on the Indian continent, and adopts a different chronological computation. Completely opposed versions of one and the same fact circulated" (Lamotte, 1998).

§ Buddhism has influenced modern culture in many ways. It has inspired "new-age" groups, advertising campaigns, medical and psychological research; it has also influenced politics, philosophy, and even science. According to the Pew Research Center, as of 2010 there were about 488 million Buddhists worldwide, representing 7% of the world's population (Pew Research Center 2012).

hagiography and religious idealization.* We will focus here on the historical Buddha, Siddhārtha Gautama.

The common narrative is that he was born into a wealthy family of the Shakya (Śākya) clan and lived a luxurious life as a prince, isolated from the world around him. At age sixteen, he married Princess Yasodharā and they had a son, Rāhula. On Siddhārtha's twenty-ninth year he became aware of suffering in the world, a world which he apparently had known little to nothing about. Profoundly affected by observing old age, death, and disease, he was compelled to understand the nature of suffering and, if at all possible, find a solution to it. So, he left his royal life of privilege and set out to find someone who could help with his quest.†

Moving through a succession of teachers over the course of several years, he tried many of the austere practices in vogue at the time and eventually found himself near death from self-imposed starvation. He purportedly gave this account of that time:

> I was unclothed, indecent, licking my hands. ... I took food only once a day, or once in two or seven days. I lived under the discipline of eating rice only at fortnightly intervals. ... I subsisted on the roots and fruits of the forest, eating only those which fell [of their own accord]. I wore coarse hempen cloth ... rags from a rubbish heap ... clothes of grass and of bark. ... I became one who stands [always] refusing to sit. ... I made my bed on thorns. ... The dust and dirt of years accumulated on my body. ... I subsisted on the dung of suckling calves.

---

* The knowledge we have of the Buddha's actual life comes from the Pali canon, from the Mahāyāna canon written in Sanskrit, from Sanskrit sources that were lost but whose translations survived in Chinese, and from writings in Sinhalese from Sri Lanka. The most factual story can be pieced together from the collection of different accounts preserved in writing by comparing what they share in common. Mythologically, the Buddha is said to have been conceived without intercourse and birthed from his mother's right side without piercing her body (Williams, 2009, 21). The *Mahāvastu* of the *Lokottaravāda* school (no longer extant) describes the supramundane qualities of the Buddha explicitly and in great detail (P. M. Harrison 1982, 216-218).

† For reasons described later, it's unlikely that his motivation to undertake an arduous spiritual journey was solely altruistic. He likely experienced grief and suffering himself. In fact, according to the sutras, he preached that recognition of suffering in one's own life was a prerequisite for success in transcending it, a foundational tenet upon which his subsequent teachings were based.

... So long as my own dung and urine held out, I subsisted on that.

... Because I ate so little, my limbs became like the knotted joints of withered creepers, my buttocks like a bullock's hoof, my protruding backbone like a string of beads, my gaunt ribs like the crazy rafters of a tumble-down shed. My eyes were sunken deep in their sockets.

... My scalp was shriveled. ... The hair, rotted at the roots, fell out if I stroked my limbs with my hand.[19]

Near death and unable to make progress on his spiritual quest, he finally decided to give up ascetic extremes. Soon after, on one fateful morning while sitting under an Aśvattha tree,* he looked up and saw the morning star, Vega,† and, in a sudden flash, experienced bodhi, spiritual awakening.

Although his followers would refer to him as the Buddha, lit. *the Awakened One*, the sutras suggest he may not have claimed enlightenment for himself,‡ as he repeatedly makes references to himself as the *Tathāgata*, lit. *the one who has arrived at suchness*, rather than the "enlightened" or "awakened" one.§ Over the next forty-five years, he wandered India helping others discover for themselves what he had found for himself: freedom from the ego, that aspect of the psyche that gives

---

* *Ficus religiosa* is also referred to as a bodhi tree, *pippala tree* (Sanskrit), and peepal tree. Descendants of this tree are still believed to be living at Bodh Gaya in Bihar, India, the spot where Siddhārtha purportedly experienced enlightenment.

† Vega is the fifth brightest star in the sky and holds special significance in many religious traditions, including Taoism and Buddhism. It's a prominent symbol of the *anima* (*divine feminine*) in the Taoist *Neijing tu*, and in Chan's ox-herding pictures (Chapter 14). Vega is also one of three stars that comprise the Summer Triangle. The other two are Deneb and Altair. The trio became important symbols in Taoism and Chan (Chapters 4 and 14).

‡ One who has experienced spiritual awakening sees no "self" that can be enlightened. To "attain enlightenment" is an oxymoron to one who has experienced spiritual awakening. The concept exists only as an *expedient means* by which one can be guided. We will explore this in later chapters. The Buddha does, however, refer to himself as having "awakened," in the sense of being "freed from suffering." Of course, as always, we need to keep in mind that there are a great many versions of the sutras, some of which are written in Sanskrit and some in Pali, and that translations and embellishments over the centuries may easily have altered the messages. We can't know how much of the sutras represent the Buddha's actual words vs. the interpretations and ideologies of their writers, translators, and commentators.

§ Enlightenment—spiritual awakening—is not something one "gets," or "has," but is an experience in which one *sees*. There is nothing gained nor lost from enlightenment: rather, it's a shift in awareness, perspective, and understanding, an entrance into the dharmakāya. This will be explored in more depth in Chapter 18.

rise to desire, grasping, and attachment. In short time, he would consolidate what he had learned into the *Four Noble Truths*, referring to it as a *Middle Way* to contrast it with the harsh asceticism he had endured for years without benefit. The Four Noble Truths and the *Eightfold Path* contained therein, while simple, were also provocative. Their simplicity allowed them to be passed down accurately using oral recitation traditions common to the era, and their inspirational message became the foundation for virtually all schools and sects of Buddhism throughout the world.

It's common for Buddhists to attribute to Siddhārtha Gautama, exclusively, the teachings he propounded during his life. Yet when we look closer, we find that he didn't entirely pull a rabbit out of a hat. The methods he used, along with their philosophical and spiritual framework, had existed in various forms in the pre-Buddhist Vedic culture before he adapted and synthesized them in a new way that reflected his own experience and understanding.*

But Buddhism wasn't the only new religion to take root and enjoy rapid growth during the first millennium BCE. Jainism, with beginnings a few hundred years before Buddhism, may have had a significant influence on the formation of Buddhism, courtesy of a possible contemporary of the Buddha: Vardhamâna Mahâvîra.†

Jainism & India's religious environment before Buddhism

The first (historical) Jain leader, Parshvanatha (Pārśvanāth or Pārśva), c. 800 BCE, preached four fundamental principles: no killing, no steal-

---

* Scholars attest that much of the terminology Siddhārtha used to describe the spiritual landscape was borrowed from earlier Vedic sources, but that he sometimes altered their meanings by putting them in new perspectives. See Jantrasrisalai 2008, p. 28, for examples.

† There is debate over the age of Jainism. Historians generally attribute its birth to the 8th century BCE. Jainist scripture claims that Jainism has always been and will always be, and some Jainist sources tell of Rishabha, the founder of Jainism, as having lived for 8.4 million years (Georg Feuerstein 2008, 140). In addition, there is debate among historians whether Vardhamâna Mahâvîra was indeed a contemporary of Siddhārtha Gautama (Vetter 1988, XII).

ing, no property ownership, and no dishonesty. These tenets formed the core identity of Jainism. Jainism was, however, a small player on the religious scene until Vardhamâna Mahâvîra brought it to prominence in the Indus Valley several centuries later. The narrative goes that, at the age of thirty, after having married and had a daughter (Anojjâ), Vardhamâna left them both and wandered as an ascetic for twelve years.

On the thirteenth year, while engaging in extreme penance and meditation, he reached *kaivalya*—a "sublime state of solitude, detachment, and isolation"—while sitting under a Sala tree on the bank of the Rijupālika river; he then spent the rest of his life preaching his religious ideas.[20] Unlike Buddhism, however, which the Buddha would describe as the "Middle Way," Jainism, and Vardhamâna in particular, advocated extreme self-mortification, including long periods of food- and water-fasting, and unwavering practice of nonviolence.* As Tilmann Vetter, author of *The Ideas and Meditative Practices of Early Buddhism*, describes it,

> What is paramount in Jainism is that one abstains from karma ("work") and expiates karma that has already been done by self-mortification, thereby liberating oneself completely from the burdening and obscuring material particles which penetrate the soul through work. In Jainism the soul is bound to a cycle of rebirth through karma and is robbed by karma of its innate qualities, such as all-knowing and bliss.[21]

Both Siddhārtha and Vardhamâna began their spiritual quests under the umbrella of the existing religious and spiritual framework of the time that was also influencing early Hinduism: the *Upanishads*, *Ājīvakism*,†

---

* Any form of injury to any living being was to be avoided, including accidentally stepping on an ant or inhaling microbes from the air. For the former, Jainists would use a broom to clean the path in front of them as they walked. For the latter, they would wear face-masks to help prevent anything living from entering their mouth as they breathed. These practices are still alive today.

† The only existing information we have about *Ājīvakism* comes from accounts written by rival religious groups, so the accuracy may be tainted by differing sectarian and ideological views. From what the writings have in common, however, we can surmise that the *Ājīvakas:* 1] did not believe in a god as an absolute supreme being that created the universe (they were *atheists*); 2] did not believe in free will (they believed in *absolute determinism*); 3]

and early Jainism,* all of which evolved from Brahmanism and its predecessor, Vedism (the *Rigveda*, a collection of spiritual hymns, evolved between 4000 and 2000 BCE).† It's possible, if not likely, that it was Jainist practitioners, or yogis influenced by Jainism, who introduced Siddhārtha to fasting and other self-mortification practices.

Both spiritual seekers rejected popular Brahman traditions which encouraged and often centered around brutal animal sacrifices, a carryover from older Vedic traditions. While not all sacrifices involved killing animals,[22] those that did could involve extreme brutality. For example, the horse-sacrifice (*aśvamedha*) was one of the bloodiest and longest of them all, with preparations taking a year or more. It began with the bathing of a chosen sacrificial horse while a man, "chosen for his contemptible demeanor," slaughtered a dog with a club.[23] After the horse was sacrificed along with 600 bulls, the chief queen would lie down beside the dead horse and simulate copulation. The ceremony would conclude with a sacrifice of twenty-one sterile cows.[24] While this ceremony is no longer practiced today, animal sacrifices following ancient Vedic tradition are still common in parts of India.‡ Considering the brutality of such ritual slaughter, we may wonder if the precept of

---

believed that everything was composed of tiny "atoms" of matter (they were *atomistic*); and 4] believed that there are no objective moral laws (They followed *antinomian ethics*: grace alone is necessary for salvation). It is thought they lived simple lives without possessions and practiced nonviolence and vegetarianism (Basham 2009).

* While the precise timeline is uncertain, it's well agreed among historians that many of the religious concepts and spiritual practices found in both the Upanishads and Jain texts had existed for centuries before Siddhārtha's birth.

† The *Rigveda* (*r̥gveda*) had been passed down orally since at least 2500 BCE, and possibly as far back as 4500 BCE, based on references to stellar patterns (Gerog Feuerstein 1995, 106). Donald Lopez has observed that many of the religious symbols and spiritual practices extolled in the *Rigveda* strongly influenced Buddhism (Lopez 2015, 83-101). Their ancient hymns also describe remarkable knowledge of metallurgy, cosmology, and mathematics, including the binary number system used today for computing (Osborn 2014).

‡ From the canonical record, Siddhārtha warned in his first sermon, albeit obliquely, against giving reverence to such practices: "Reading the Vedas, making offerings to priests, or sacrifices to the gods, self-mortification by heat or cold, and many such penances performed for the sake of immortality, these do not cleanse the man who is not free from delusions" (Carus 1894, 49). There is a slow trend towards stopping animal sacrifices taking place in India today. One remote part of northern India ruled, on Sept. 1, 2014, to ban animal sacrifices in any place of worship, including lands and buildings. Apparently, having been ignorant of these practices, the court announced: "A startling revelation has been made… thousands of animals are sacrificed every year in the name of worship… Sacrifice causes im-

non-killing, and the resulting convention of not eating meat popular with many Buddhists today, originated at least in part as a response to the inhumanity of such sacrificial practices.*

So, while Jainism got its lift from Vardhamâna, who is said to have reached the pinnacle of spiritual experience because of and during a period of extreme ascetic practice, Buddhism took birth from Siddhārtha, who gave up extreme ascetic practices because they failed to give him the answers he was seeking—and because they nearly killed him. Striking out on his own, he took a path devoid of both extreme self-indulgence and extreme self-mortification, a formula that, for him, led to spiritual awakening. The course that each religion took came to reflect the distinctly different experiences of each of these men: one would advocate extreme asceticism, which Jainism is still known for today; the other would encourage a "Middle Way," a phrase still used today to describe Chan.

The very different approaches these two men took were reflected in other similar opposing sentiments of the time: while Jainists advocated extreme physical asceticism to realize Self-nature, Upanishadic sages advocated the cultivation of grace through breathing and other techniques. But these divergent approaches had much earlier origins.

Nearly a thousand years before, while the followers of the Vedic folk religion were enacting elaborate and torturous animal sacrifices, another group broke away from the Vedic orthodoxy to roam the Indian northeast and practice their own way of spiritual life devoid of such sacrifices. Known as *Vrâtyas*, the Brahmanas characterized them as "ascetics roaming about in an intoxicated state," and as "guardians

---

mense pain and suffering to innocent animals. They cannot be permitted to be sacrificed to appease a god or deity in a barbaric manner" (Shimla 2014).

* Vegetarianism is a convention among many Buddhists, but not all. Chinese monastics have a purely vegetarian diet, but lay Buddhists are often not vegetarians. There is no specific precept against eating meat, although many consider the precept against killing to imply that meat should not be eaten. Theravāda Buddhists believe the Buddha specifically permitted the eating of fish, poultry, and pork if it was known that the animal did not die for them to eat it. I have known as many devout Buddhists who eat meat as I have Buddhists who don't. Stigma associated with eating meat as a Buddhist varies between cultures.

of the truth."*²⁵ Their teachings and religious philosophies are known from parts of the *Atharva-Veda*. In it, we find the first written record of practices that were precursors to yoga as we know it today, practices that would be inherited by Buddhism and, indirectly, by Chan through the *Yogācāra* school to be popularized by Xuan Zang.† Of special significance was a description of pranayama (*prāṇāyāma*) which explained how life-forces circulate in the body as the breath is inhaled, retained, and exhaled.²⁶ This, combined with a novel model that described its spiritual and physical effects from channels of energy circulating within the body, offered a ready technique that anyone could use to attain knowledge of the Absolute.‡ The *Atharva Veda* describes the unifying and timeless nature of this *Absolute Reality*:

> *That which stirs, flies, stands still, breathes, or breathes not, closes [the eyes] but exists, sustains the earth and, being all-formed, is singular only.*
>
> *That which is endless is extended in every direction: the endless and the ending come together. These the Guardian [i.e., the sun] of the firmament (nâka), who knows past and future, continues to hold apart.*²⁷

It may not have been for another few hundred years, until the emergence of the *Upanishads* around 900 BCE, that *internalization* practices began to be refined and developed as general methods for gaining spiritual insight.

The Upanishadic sages followed in the footsteps of the *Vrâtyas* by insisting that, rather than worshiping external gods and goddesses, and sacrificing animals to them, such practices could be internalized through contemplation and meditation. Sacrifice, too, was turned in-

---

* Might we imagine that the "intoxicated state" refers to a state of spiritual joy?

† Although many historians consider the Aryans' Vedic culture to have developed the formative seeds of yoga, Edward Fitzpatrick Crangle, author of *The Origin and Development of Early Indian Contemplative Practices*, presents evidence that suggests yogic techniques originated much earlier with pre-Aryan yogi aboriginals (1994).

‡ Chinese Taoism, which was developing around the same time that Siddhārtha was meditating under a ficus tree, created a similar model which will be briefly described in Chapter 4. We might wonder how much of the Chinese model may have been influenced by Indian sages traveling the Silk Road into China, sharing their knowledge of the Upanishads.

side out: rather than sacrifice animals, they would sacrifice themselves through meditation. This "inner sacrifice" would lead to knowledge of Self: "A person—as long as he or she is a spiritual practitioner—*is* a sacrifice."[28]

One set of stanzas from the early Upanishads, attributed to Yâjnavalkya in the 7th century BCE, uses an analogy of a tree to express the dichotomy between one whose life is disconnected from Ultimate Reality (Self) and one who abides in It:

As a tree of the forest,
just so, surely, is man.
His hairs are leaves,
his skin the outer bark.

From his skin blood,
sap from the bark flows forth.
From him when pierced there comes forth
a stream, as from the tree when struck.

His pieces of flesh are under-layers of wood.
The fiber is muscle-like, strong.
The bones are the wood within.
The marrow is made resembling pith.

A tree, when it is felled, grows up
from the root, more new again;
a mortal, when cut down by death—
From what root does he grow up?

Say not 'from semen,'
for that is produced from the living,
as the tree, forsooth, springing from seed,
clearly arises without having died.

If with its roots they should pull up the tree,
it would not come into being again.
A mortal, when cut down by death—
From what root does he grow up?

When born, indeed, he is not born [again].
Who would again beget him?

The Absolute (Brahman) is knowledge, is bliss,
the final goal of the giver of offerings,
Of him, too, who stands still (stops)
and knows (abides in) It.[29]

A tree, Yâjnavalkya explains, can be reborn from the roots if its trunk topples. We have likely all seen a fallen tree which has sprung new shoots from its roots. If the root is removed, the tree won't come back, but otherwise it may give birth to a new one. Yâjnavalkya says a mortal human is like the tree, and the root is to the tree as the Absolute is to he who "stands still and knows It." The mortal human (who is mortal because he does *not* know It), when he dies, will not be born again, because "who would again beget him?" Not knowing, in other words, is like having no root. Yâjnavalkya argues that one who has merged with the Absolute (Self), being no longer separate from It, is beyond the duality of life and death, self and other, root and tree, and that person has thus discovered immortality in this lifetime.

To go further, we might interpret the above stanzas as "Until one has merged with the Absolute in one's lifetime, one is destined to live with the constant flux of birth and death in this lifetime; that is, with the dualities of creation and destruction, attachment and alienation, good and evil, etc." Birth and death become metaphors for creation and annihilation, which are the conditions of a person separated from Self, and who therefore exists in a constant churning of opposing forces: those opposing forces are themselves the direct cause of suffering (duhkha). It's possible that these stanzas might suggest an early seed for the belief in reincarnation; however, there's no indication to me that Yâjnavalkya had in mind a physical rebirth; that is, a reincarnation into another person or animal. Metaphor, analogy, and simile are ubiquitous within the Upanishads; literal interpretations can blind us to intended alternate meanings.

Yâjnavalkya elaborates further:

He who has found and has awakened to the Soul (Self)
That has entered this conglomerate abode—
He is the maker of everything, for he is the creator of all;
The world is his: indeed, he is the world itself.
Verily, while we are here we may know this.
If you have known it not, great is the destruction.
Those who know this become immortal,
But others go only to sorrow.[30]

Yâjnavalkya also describes negation practice—"*Not thus!, Not thus!*" (*Neti!, Neti!*)—which would become important in Vedânta as well as Chan.* Its purpose is to stop the mind from attempting to describe or qualify ultimate reality (Self-nature) since, he explains, ultimate reality is beyond the limitations of words and thoughts; that is, because it's ultimate and absolute, it cannot be an object of knowledge. Any attempt, therefore, to conceptualize Self-nature will be in error. The only way to get to "It" is to deny or negate everything else, everything that is *not* It.[31]

The following stanzas from the *Kena-Upanishad* describe Brahma, the Absolute—or in the parlance of Buddhism, Dharma or Self-Nature—as that which becomes known once we detach from the sensory stimuli generated by the mind (thought), the breath (breathing), the ear (hearing), and the eye (seeing), and suggests that the means for gaining this awareness is through a process of negation; that is, the Absolute is witnessed when we think not with the mind, breathe not with the breath, hear not with the ears, and see not with the eyes. These thoughts would propagate into later Mahāyāna canonical texts, including many of those central to Chan.

[Question:]
1. By whom impelled soars forth the mind projected?
By whom enjoined goes forth the earliest breathing?
By whom impelled this speech do people utter?

---

* See Zhao Zhou's "*Wú!*", Chapter 12.

The eye, the ear—what god, pray, them enjoined?
The all-conditioning, yet inscrutable agent, Brahma [the Absolute].

[Answer:]
2. That which is the hearing of the ear, the thought of the mind,
The voice of speech, as also the breathing of the breath,
And the sight of the eye! Past these escaping, the wise,
On departing from this world [of the senses], become immortal.

3. There the eye goes not;
Speech goes not, nor the mind.
We know not, we understand not
How one would teach It.
Other, indeed, is It than the known,
And moreover above the unknown.
—Thus have we heard of the ancients (pūrva)
Who to us have explained It.

4. That which is unexpressed with speech (vāc, voice),
That with which speech is expressed—
That indeed know as Brahma [the Absolute],
Not this that people worship as this.

5. That which one thinks not with thought (manas, mind),
[or, That which thinks not with a mind,]
That with which they say thought (manas, mind) is thought—
That indeed know as Brahma,
Not this that people worship as this.

6. That which one sees not with sight (cak us, eye),
[or, That which sees not with an eye,]
That with which one sees sights (cakṣūmsi)
That indeed know as Brahma,
Not this that people worship as this.

7. That which one hears not with hearing (śrolra, ear),
[or, That which hears not with an ear,]
That with which hearing here is heard—
That indeed know as Brahma,
Not this that people worship as this.

8. That which one breathes (prāṇith) not with breathing (pramyate, breath),
[or, That which breathes not with breath,]
That with which breathing (prāṇa) is conducted (pramyate)
That indeed know as Brahma,
Not this that people worship as this.

Next, the *Katha-Upanishad* suggested that it was worldly desires which led to suffering and that by turning away from them and practicing meditation, one could discover the Self, the "absolutely unqualified Soul" or Ātman.*

1. The better (śreyas) is one thing, and the pleasanter (preyas) quite another.
Both these, of different aim, bind a person.
Of these two, well is it for him who takes the better;
He fails of his aim who chooses the pleasanter.

2. Both the better and the pleasanter come to a man.
Going all around the two, the wise man discriminates.
The wise man chooses the better, indeed, rather than the pleasanter.
The stupid man, from getting-and-keeping (yoga-kṣema), chooses the pleasanter.

3. Thou indeed, upon the pleasant and pleasantly appearing desires
Meditating, hast let them go, O Naciketas.†

---

* Ātman (आत्मन्) has a complex meaning in Indian culture. It's variously used to mean *essence, Self, nature, breath,* and *soul*. It appears in the *Atharva Veda*, which is thought to have been composed at least 3000 years ago (Griffith n.d., 1436).

† Nachiketa (Naciketas), son of the sage Vajashravasa, is the literary vehicle used in this Upanishad to create a dialogue between teacher and student, much in the same way that Glaucon, Plato's older brother, was Socrates' muse in much of *The Republic*. Chan's famous

*Thou art not one who has taken that garland of wealth
In which many men sink down.*

*4. Widely opposite and asunder are these two:
Ignorance (avidyā) and what is known as 'knowledge' (vidyā).
I think Naciketas desirous of obtaining knowledge!
Many desires rend thee not.*

*5. Those abiding in the midst of ignorance,
Self-wise, thinking themselves learned,
Running hither and thither, go around deluded,
Like blind men led by one who is himself blind,*

*6. The passing-on is not clear to him who is childish,
Heedless, deluded with the delusion of wealth.
Thinking 'This is the world! There is no other!'—
Again and again he comes under my control.*

*7. He who by many is not obtainable even to hear of,
He whom many, even when hearing, know not—
Wonderful is the declarer, proficient the obtainer of Him!
Wonderful the knower, proficiently taught!*

*8. Not, when proclaimed by an inferior man, is He
To be well understood, [though] being manifoldly considered.
Unless declared by another, there is no going thither;
For He is inconceivably more subtle than what is of subtle measure.*

*9. Not by reasoning (tarka) is this thought [sacred view] (mati) to be attained.
Proclaimed by another, indeed, it is for easy understanding, dearest friend (preṣṭha)!—
This which thou hast attained! Ah, thou art of true steadfastness
May there be for us a questioner (praṣṭā) the like of thee, O Naciketas!*

---

encounter dialogues use the same literary technique. References to Nachiketa (or another similar person) arises in the *Rigveda* as well as the *Taittiriya Brahmana* and *Mahābhārata*.

10. *I know that what is known as treasure is something in-constant.*
For truly, that which is steadfast is not obtained by those who are unsteadfast.
Therefore, the Naciketas-fire has been built up by me,
And with means which are in-constant I have obtained that which is constant.

11. *The obtainment of desire, the foundation of the world (jagat),*
The endlessness of work, the safe shore of fearlessness,
The greatness of pause, the wide extent, the foundation (having seen).
Thou, O Naciketas, a wise one, hast with steadfastness let [these] go.

12. *Him who is hard to see, entered into the hidden,*
Set in the secret place [of the heart], dwelling in the depth, primeval—
By considering him as God, through the Yoga-study of what pertains to Self,
The wise man leaves joy and sorrow behind.

13. *When a mortal has heard this and fully comprehended,*
Has torn off what is concerned with the right (dharmya),
and has taken Him as the subtle,
Then he rejoices, for indeed he has obtained what is to be rejoiced in.
*I regard Naciketas a dwelling open [for Ātman].*³²

Recurring thoughts found in the *Upanishads* include:*

- The reality of the universe is identical to our own Self-nature.†

- The realization of Self liberates us from suffering.

- Our thoughts and actions (*karma*) determine our sense of identity.

---

* The *Upanishads* were not written down, but memorized and transmitted orally from teacher to student, as was the entire early Buddhist canon. It is referred to as mnemonic literature prior to being assembled in the form of written sutras during the early part of the first century CE. It was common practice for monks then, and still is today, to memorize extremely long passages as a concentration practice. According to Georg Feuerstein, some could (and still can) recite the entire *Mahābhārata* (2008, 128).

† In Sanskrit, the word for unconditional reality is *Brahman*, derived from the root *brih* meaning "to grow." Buddhists use the term *Dharma*. Self-nature is referred to as *ātman*; hence, ultimate reality is the same as our own Self-nature, i.e., *ātman* = *Brahman*.

- Until the Self is realized, we will be continually subjected to the forces of karma, enduring continual birth and death in this lifetime.

Some of these thoughts are expressed again in the Buddha's explanations of his Noble Truths.*

Jainism was not closely connected with Upanishadic thought, and followed its own independent trajectory, yet both were offshoots of Brahmanism/Vedism and both advocated seeking knowledge of the Absolute, referred to as Brahman in the Upanishads, and kevala-jnana in the Jain canon.

BUDDHISM AS AN INDEPENDENT SPIRITUAL JOURNEY

We don't know why extreme ascetic methods didn't work for Siddhārtha while they apparently did for Vardhamâna. All we know is that one day he said "Enough!" and went his own way using more moderate methods.† This led Siddhārtha to teach that "awakening" required that we pursue it of our own accord and not follow in the footsteps of others. For this reason, Buddhism has lacked a central authority figure from the beginning; the Buddha, having left no successor, told his followers that they didn't need him or any other person to lead them.‡ They

---

* Crangle, however, argues that the inclusion of yogic concepts and practices in the latter, post-Buddhist Upanishads originated "most probably" from Buddhism. Moreover, "[t]he evidence suggests that early Indian contemplative practices developed neither in a simple linear fashion nor as a result of a single synthesis. It indicates, rather, a zigzag progression wherein Aryan/Brâhmanical contemplative practices both influenced, and were influenced by, indigenous yogic disciplines" (1994, 270, 274).

† Vetter surmises that, "According to Majjhima Nikāya 36, the Buddha, when he no longer saw any sense in self-mortification, remembered experiencing non-sensual happiness in his youth and this led him to a possible path to salvation. He did not abandon the concept that sensual pleasure is not beneficial. But when a convincing path to salvation presented itself, he no longer thought it necessary to avoid non-sensual happiness. In order to follow this path that, as far as he knew, no one had followed before, he had to take a step that was inconceivable to his former companions: he began to eat food again" (1988, XXIX).

‡ Nonetheless, different Buddhist schools/sects began creating their own (and different) lists of Dharma-master succession several centuries after the Buddha's death. The version that made it to China was a list of five *Dharmācāryas* compiled in the second century CE by the Sarvāstivādins and Mūlasarvāstivādins; however, it was not accepted by other sects,

only needed the Dharma, discipline, and themselves.* He left behind his simple teachings, which encouraged people to investigate their True Nature for themselves, by themselves.† In fact, his purported last words before his death were: "All things are impermanent. Work out your own salvation with diligence."³³ The *Sarvāstivāda Mahāpari Nirvāṇa Sūtra* includes the same message, as he tells his attendant, Ānanda:

> From the beginning, Ananda, I have taught you that whatever things are delightful and desirable, joyful and pleasing, these are subject to separation and destruction, to disintegration and dissociation. So Ananda, whether now or after my decease, whoever you are, you must remain as islands to yourselves, as defences to yourselves with the Dharma as your island and the Dharma as your defence, remaining unconcerned with other islands and other defences.³⁴

If we take this passage as representative of Siddhārtha's actual thoughts, it's evident that following a spiritual authority outside one's own Self was antithetical to his teaching. It was a sentiment that would also characterize Chan for some of its most vocal proponents nearly a thousand years later (Chapter 4).‡

Buddhism quickly flourished. Unlike Jainism, whose austere practices made recruitment difficult (and still do), Buddhism was easily approachable. In short time, Buddhism was assimilated by remarkably

---

nor did it become part of Sri Lanka's Buddhist narrative. Historian Étienne Lamotte comments, "The lack of uniformity which characterizes the Buddhist tradition in relation to the succession of Masters shows that the Saṃgha taken as a whole—the community of the Four Regions—was without a universal, unanimously accepted leader, but that the various limited saṃghas scattered throughout India were never deprived of spiritual heads who exercised authority over larger or smaller groups of devotees" (1988, 203).

* This is clearly stated in the *Mahā-parinibbāna Sutta* (Nikāya, 1921, II. P.100). Dharma, in this context, means *Universal Law*.

† Although his teachings were simple, they were nonetheless hard for some people to grasp. After his spiritual awakening, Siddhārtha spent years explaining his thoughts in ways compatible with different people's needs, questions, and aptitudes.

‡ Chan's lineage system, however, would complicate things by introducing *ancestral worship*, which effectively created deified lineage-holders, placing them in a role that inspired supplication and veneration from their students, which effectively weakened independence and autonomy. Nonetheless, numerous influential Chan teachers have taught that we must become our own spiritual authority, including Linji, Hsu Yun, and Jy Din (Chapter 4).

diverse cultures, perhaps, in part, because its core beliefs did not conflict with pre-existing folk religions.* Buddhism would merge with the Bön religion of Tibet to become what we know today as Tibetan, or Himalayan, Buddhism,† and it would combine with Taoism, Confucianism, and China's indigenous folk religion to become Chan Buddhism and Pure Land Buddhism.‡ Along the way, various distinct branches would develop and prosper. The three branches surviving today are *Theravāda*, *Mahāyāna*, and *Vajrayāna* (tantric Buddhism).

Early development of Buddhism in India

After the Buddha died, the sangha 僧伽 (Skt., *saṃgha*; Pali, *saṅgha*)—his group of followers—were left to their own devices to figure out what to do. With a leader no longer available, fierce arguments about how to interpret his teachings split the sangha into different camps. With many people living together, often in caves, conflicts quickly began to erode the health of the sangha, so rules of monastic discipline became essential. Devout members who abstained from sex, intoxicants, and other forms of frivolous behavior became, by default, the new leaders.§

To ensure that the Buddha's teachings would survive, a disciplined sangha was essential. To address the issue, a group of some 500 followers (*arahats*) are thought to have convened a meeting, or *council*, to

---

* In India especially, the growth of Buddhism was rapid, largely due to Buddhism's acceptance of members of lower castes and the lifting of taboos around approaching people of lower societal castes for food (JHA 20011, 76).

† Tibetan Buddhism is popular today in much of the world, including Mongolia, Tuva, Bhutan, Kalmykia, Nepal, and various districts of India. It is now commonly referred to as *Himalayan Buddhism* since it prospers throughout the region.

‡ Pure Land Buddhism is, by far, the dominant school of Buddhism practiced in China today. Foulk has pointed out, however, that there is long precedent in China for practices and beliefs to be mixed together: "[t]he elite ranks of Ch'an masters in the Sung included not only meditation specialists but also Pure Land devotees, tantric ritualists, experts on monastic discipline, exegetes of sutra and philosophical literature, poets, artists, and even monks with leanings to Neo-Confucianism. Thus, apart from a familiarity with the mythology of the Ch'an lineage and an ability to mimic its rhetorical style in certain ritual settings, the only indispensable external marks of a Ch'an master in the Sung were the regalia of Dharma transmission, chief among them his inheritance certificate" (1992, 28).

§ For more on this topic, see *Ancient India In Historic Outline* by D. N. JHA, 2011.

make decisions on how to best move forward. Mahā Kassapa, the most senior monk, is considered to have led this first council meeting in the town of *Rājagaha*: its objective was to establish collective agreement on the Buddha's teachings and to establish a set of rules, or tenets, to end growing conflicts among monks holding differing interpretations.* The outcome of this council is ambiguous because different Buddhist schools reported vastly different things, but they all agreed, in general, on the first rules of conduct (which over time evolved into the *Buddhist precepts*) as well as on the content of the first sutras. The first set of rules was known as the *Prátimokṣa* and covered everything from sexual intercourse to murder to how to build huts for secluded living and meditation.[35] Over time, the group of canonical texts grew and eventually became known, collectively, as the *Vinaya Pitaka* (lit. *leading out, education, discipline*), of which the *Prátimokṣa* was but one part.†

Successive councils were called throughout the first five hundred years of Buddhism in India but, again, historical sources, taken collectively, offer ambiguous conclusions about what really happened in these meetings, as sectarian biases led different schools to report significantly different "facts." In light of this, some scholars question whether these council meetings happened at all. Could they have been entirely fabricated by later generations to substantiate particular aspects (and versions) of the developing Buddhist canon?‡ We may never know.

Regardless of whether these early councils happened or not, Lamotte writes,

---

* Based on the autobiographical writings of Xuan Zang, Dan Lusthaus commented in his article, *Xuanzang and Kuiji on Madhyamaka*: "In India, debate was taken very seriously—it could literally be a death sport, with the loser expected to forfeit his life, freedom, or livelihood as a consequence of failure. [...] Debate was a bloodsport, sometimes eliciting homocidal passions. But its purpose was noble, as was the hoped-for outcome." (2015)

† As Buddhism spread into different parts of the world, the Vinaya Pitaka was modified to adapt to the needs of new cultures. Various versions of the Vinaya monastic rules spread into China, the most popular being the *Dharmaguptaka*. They were substantially rewritten by the monk Changlu Zongze in 1103; known as the Chányuàn qīngguī 禪苑清規, they retained much the same flavor as the original doctrines and are still a dominant presence in Chinese monastic life today (Yifa 2003).

‡ Hermann Oldenberg, for example, argues in his introduction to *The Vinaya* (1879, xxxii) that, from a historical perspective, these councils were "pure invention."

...the records devoted to these councils are riddled with improbabilities, anachronisms and contradictions; in the course of history, they were exploited to very different ends. It remains nonetheless a fact that the work done by the early disciples (*sthavira*) during the two centuries which followed the Nirvāṇa supplied the original community with a law (*Dharma*) and a set of rules (*prátimokṣa*) which were more or less definitive: a sacred trust which constituted the common heritage of the schools which were to develop later.

It was on this basis that the canonical writings were elaborated, but their compilation required many centuries and was still not completed in the fifth century of the Christian era, nearly a millennia after the Buddha's death. Each sect claimed to possess its own code of writings and attempted, without always succeeding, to institute it by exploiting the common doctrinal fund, while enriching it with more or less authentic new compositions. This work was not carried out systematically, but with much classifying and reclassifying of the texts.[36]

Historians generally agree, however, that about one hundred years following the Buddha's death, a group of renegades, rejecting the authority of the Elders—those who were trying to establish an orthodoxy—initiated a schism over disagreements in the monastic code of conduct. They would become known as the *Mahāsaṅghika*, or the "majority group," and later evolve into the Mahāyāna branch of Buddhism, from which Chan would appear.*

But the representation of Buddhism by the Elders was short-lived. Individuals in the sangha contested the Elders' authority to both set doctrine (recall that the Buddha is thought to have intentionally left nobody in charge and told his followers to seek salvation on their own), and to be adequately knowledgeable and enlightened to do so in the first place. Historical evidence suggests that the Elders' Buddhism split into as many as seventeen distinct sects, only one of which has survived

---

* Jan Nattier infers from the early *Parirccha Sutra* that "the Mahāyāna is not a school, a sect, or a movement, but a particular spiritual *vocation*, to be pursued within the existing Buddhist community. To be a 'Mahayanist'—that is, to be a bodhisattva—thus does not mean to adhere to some new kind of 'Buddhism,' but simply to practice Buddhism in its most rigorous and demanding form" (J. Nattier 2003, 195).

today as *Theravāda*. Collectively, this early group of seventeen sects that split from the Elders was derisively referred to by the Mahāsaṅghika group as the "Small, Inferior Vehicle," or *Hīnayāna*. The nonderogatory term now commonly used is *Nikāya*.

Perhaps no person characterizes Buddhism's early and substantial influence on Indian culture and society more than Ashoka (Aśoka), the third ruler of the Indian Mauryan Empire. He not only brought Buddhism to prominence, but substantially influenced its spread throughout Asia. Ashoka came to power during the early third century when the empire was still fractured into many small kingdoms. Seeking unification, he lead bloody and ruthless campaigns that ultimately created the India much as we know it today. What made Ashoka especially unusual as a military ruler, however, is that, after all the bloodshed was over, he apologized for his brutality and issued an edict which he had carved into stone pillars and rocks around the country. The edict was an apology to the people for the suffering he inflicted, and an assurance to them that he had renounced war and embraced the Buddha Dharma.

He would become revered by many as the most benevolent and progressive ruler of India, and his ruling style would become a model for successive generations of rulers. Adopting Buddhism, not as an official national religion but as a model for a moral way for living, he sent missionaries to Sri Lanka (they would establish Theravāda Buddhism there) and re-introduced writing which had been abandoned for over a millennium.* Ashoka sought unification of all the various Buddhist sects that had formed, encouraged tolerance of all religions, set up programs to help the poor and sick, and built numerous public medical facilities. He also established an environment for Buddhism to flourish and expand outside India, encouraging missionaries to "spread the word" by traveling the Silk Road as far as Syria, Egypt, and Greece to the west, China to the east, Tibet to the north, and Sri Lanka to the south. Which

---

* The Indus River Valley writings, indecipherable to this day, stopped around 1500 BC for unknown reasons, while the ancient language of the Vedas was preserved orally. That language, once put into writing, is now referred to as Vedic Sanskrit, the predecessor of modern Sanskrit. Its linguistic history is traceable to Proto-Indo-Iranian and Proto-Indo European languages.

flavors of Buddhism would be spread, however, was apparently left up to the missionaries themselves. To Ashoka, they were all good.

THE BUDDHA'S FOUR NOBLE TRUTHS

The *Four Noble Truths* (*Catvāri āryasatyāni*) are considered by many the foundational teachings of the Buddha.* They would be preserved in all expressions of Buddhism, bridging cultures, societies, and languages. While many of the Buddha's teachings are disputed between, and even within, the various Buddhist schools or sects that evolved, they all take these Four Truths, and the Eightfold Path contained therein, to represent the quintessential principles from which the rest of his teachings arose.† They were put into writing some 500 years later in the *Dharmacakra Pravartana Sūtra* (*Setting in Motion of the Wheel of Dharma*), considered his first sermon. There, he presents a spiritual path he calls the *Middle Way*, which introduces the *Four Noble Truths* in the form of a medical diagnosis and treatment, first identifying the problem (suffering), then identifying the cause (desire), then attesting that there is a cure (eliminate desire), then giving that cure (the Eightfold Path).‡

The term *Catvāri āryasatyāni* is most commonly translated as the *Four Noble Truths*, or the *Noble Four Truths*; however, these translations

---

* Vetter suggests that a second "path" presented in the Buddhist canon is equally relevant to the Buddha's fundamental teaching but observes that its presentation in relation to the Four Noble Truths is ambiguous. This alternative path, he describes, "states that one is freed from desire—and thereby from rebirth and future suffering (samsāra)—when, with discriminating insight, one perceives the five constituents of one's person as being transient, and therefore suffering (i.e., unsatisfactory), and that because of this they can neither be the self nor belong to the self" (1988, XXIII).

† Japanese Buddhism, at least in some of its presentations, may be an exception. During my time attending several Japanese-style Zen groups and monasteries in the 1980s, the Four Noble Truths were neither mentioned nor discussed, including during introductory training *sesshins* for beginners. Reasons for this neglect will be postulated in Chapter 7.

‡ Andrew Skilton, Senior Research Fellow in Buddhist Studies at Kings College London, describes this method as "...an ancient medical formula, in which one first states the nature of an illness, then the conditions which have given rise to its existence, next whether the condition can be cured, and finally the means for bringing about that cessation." He continues, "There are various other instances in which other states or conditions are analysed in this way by the Buddha and his disciples, and it would be wrong to think that it was only suffering, only duhkha, that was accorded this kind of treatment" (2001, 28).

miss some important nuances. It's not the *truths* themselves that are noble, but those who understand them and live according to that understanding who are noble, and it's *for them* that they are, in fact, truths.* For others, they are *not* truths. Hence, possible alternate translations could be the "*four truths of the noble*," or the "*four ennobling truths*".[37] The term "noble" may be misunderstood here as well. In English, the term is often understood to refer to wealthy royalty, the elite, or those with special rank or social status. "Noble" here means "one who is exceptionally wise." Hence, we could also refer to the *Catvāri āryasatyāni* as the "*four truths of the wise*" or the "*four truths of wisdom*." For convention's sake, however, I'll continue to refer to them as the Four Noble Truths.

These Four Truths and the Eightfold Path they contain are at the heart of Buddhist thought and practice and references to them appear throughout the sutra literature. If we return to the original Sanskrit, they are presented simply with four words: *duḥkha*, *samudaya*, *nirodha*, and *mārga*. Because of their significance to Buddhism—and ultimately to the spiritual disciplines of Chan—we'll take a closer look at what the Buddha may have meant by them according to the sutras.

The First Noble Truth: Duhkha (suffering) Abounds

> Now this, bhikkhus, is the noble truth of suffering: birth is suffering, aging is suffering, illness is suffering, death is suffering; union with what is displeasing is suffering; separation from what is pleasing is suffering; not to get what one wants is suffering...†[38]

The Buddha used the term duhkha (*duḥkha*) to describe a certain kind of illness to which we are all susceptible. Duhkha is derived from the terms dur ("bad") and kha ("state"). Aside from the most common (and overly simplistic) translation as "suffering," it also means impermanence, sorrow, imperfection, grief, and transience. Just as the word

---

* The prefix *ārya*, in *Catvāri āryasatyāni*, includes the notion of "pertaining to ourselves," wise, excellent, auspicious, respectable, and honorable (Majumdar 2015).

† From the *Dhammachakkappavattana Sutta*, translated from the Pali by Bhikku Bodhi.

"lavender" conjures a color, a flower, a scent, and a certain feeling—regardless of the contextual meaning intended—the word duhkha, too, carries with it all the connotations of its complex character, reflecting its history of usage. We can't begin to know that full history, but we can infer important aspects: life is imperfect, everything is always changing, everything is empty of intrinsic meaning, there is sorrow, and there is suffering. According to the sutras, it seems the Buddha considered duhkha to be a fundamental fact and insisted that recognizing the reality of duhkha was essential before one could be freed of it. He contended that not realizing the reality of duhkha is a state of ignorance that confines us to its domain, to samsāra: the endless karmic cycle of *dependent origination* (*pratītyasamutpāda*).

Siddhārtha, the story goes, wanted to truly understand why suffering existed and whether there was a way out of it. The yearning for genuine answers, we are told, inspired his quest. The insights he gained from his ensuing journey enabled him to understand suffering, its cause, and how to eliminate it. Simply put, the cause of suffering was desire and the attachment it creates; the way to eliminate desire was by detachment; and a method for doing so was to follow his *Eightfold Path*.

The Second Noble Truth:
The Cause of Suffering Is Samudaya (Mental Formations)

According to the *Śālistamba Sūtra*, duhkha is the consequence of the aggregation of "mental formations" (*samudaya*), often translated into English as *desire*:*

> What, then, is the causal relation in subjective conditioned arising?
> It is as follows: Ignorance conditions (mental) formations. (Mental) formations condition consciousness. Consciousness conditions name and form. Name-and-form conditions the six (sense) entrances. The six (sense) entrances condition contact. Contact conditions sensation.

---

* The term *samudaya* is often translated as *desire*, or *craving*, or *grasping*, but these are all separate aspects which, collectively, form the meaning. The Buddha used the term *samudaya*, meaning the "aggregate of the constituent elements or factors of any being or existence" (Monier-Williams 2011).

Sensation conditions desire. Desire conditions grasping. Grasping conditions becoming. Becoming conditions birth. Birth conditions decay and death, and grief, lamentation, suffering, depression, and anxiety come to be. Thus the arising of this entire great mass of suffering occurs.[39]

So the root cause of suffering—the beginning state from which it arises—is ignorance, *avidyā*.* This is not meant in a derogatory way. Ignorance is simply our starting-off point of "not-knowing" which, of course, is how we all begin life. The mind does its best to try to figure things out as we go along, but because it's locked within itself, it can only see what's created by it and from it—nothing more and nothing less. In ignorance, then, the mind directs and guides according to the sensory input it receives, the experiences it has, and the thoughts it generates as it tries to put it all together. This, in turn, conditions a sense of reality and self-identity. In this way, avidyā thus predisposes us to mistake mental formations for reality. The mind, then, is set up (provides the condition) to experience sensation, which begets grasping and desire, which begets "becoming," i.e., self-identity. What would happen without the originating seed of ignorance? The birth of an ego-self would not arise and none of this would happen:

> Were there no ignorance, (mental) formations would not be known, and so on until: were there no birth, decay and death would not be known. But when there is ignorance, the development of (mental) formations occurs, and so on until when there is birth, the development of decay and death occurs. Herein, it does not occur to ignorance, "I cause the (mental) formations to develop." Nor does it occur to the (mental) formations, "We are developed by ignorance," and so on until: it does not occur to birth, "I develop decay and death." Nor does it occur to decay and death, "I am developed by birth." But still, when there is ignorance, the development, the manifestation of (mental) formations occurs, and so on until, when there is birth, the develop-

---

* The more complete translation of *Avidyā* includes *delusion*: mistaking the illusory for the real.

ment, the manifestation of decay and death, occurs. Thus is the causal relation in subjective conditioned arising to be seen.[40]

We humans can't be anything other than who we are, which means we are manifestly destined to go through the process of psychological entrapment and deal with its consequences. But being aware of what's happening allows us the opportunity—and ability—to break out of it, to release the bonds of conditional arising or, metaphorically, to transcend birth and death (saṃsāra). The Mahāyāna concept of the dharmakāya would help clarify the nature of ceaseless arising and decaying ("birth and death") as an essential principle, not related to the physical birth or death of the body, but to reality's primordial, ever present, flow.*

The Third Noble Truth: Nirodha (Suffering) can be eliminated

The key to eliminating suffering, according to the sutras, is *nirodha*: annihilation of *samudaya*, or cessation of desire. Here we are offered hope, a way out: all we have to do is sever our attachments, to cease clinging to "mental formations." But how do we do that? If the mind naturally clings to things, and if that clinging is unconscious, how is it possible? Would it not be like telling our heart to stop beating or our cells to stop dividing? The Third Noble Truth baits us into asking how, which prepares us for the answer:

The Fourth Noble Truth: Mārga (the path) Eliminates Suffering

The Buddha's remedy for suffering was the *Eightfold Path of the Noble* (*Āryāṣṭāṅgamārga*):

> And what, bhikkhus, is that Middle Way awakened to by the Tathāgata, which gives rise to vision ... which leads to Nibbāna? It is this Noble Eightfold Path; that is, right view, right intention, right

---

* The term *dharmakāya* (*fa-shen* 法身) appears in the *Aṣṭasāhasrikā Prajñāpāramitā*, one of the earliest Mahāyāna texts.

speech, right action, right livelihood, right effort, right mindfulness, right concentration. This, bhikkhus, is that Middle Way awakened to by the Tathagata, which gives rise to vision, which gives rise to knowledge, which leads to peace, to direct knowledge, to enlightenment, to Nibbāna."[41]

FIGURE 1. VESAK DAY CELEBRATION.
A crowd gathers to celebrate Vesak Day in Indonesia, paying reverence to a large Dharma wheel whose eight spokes represent each of the steps on the Eightfold Path. Vesak day commemorates the enlightenment of Buddha Siddhārtha Gautama and falls in the month of May or June, according to the lunar calendar.

The Eightfold Path—which came to be symbolized by an eight-petaled lotus flower or eight-spoked wheel, and referred to as the *wheel of the Dharma* (Figure 1)—instructs us to deconstruct our lives, to act caringly instead of selfishly, to observe the motivations behind what we do, to question not what we think, but *why* we think what we think. In short, the first seven steps of the Eightfold Path require that we look deeply

---

* This excerpt is from the *Dhammachakkappavattana Sutta*, translated from the Pali by Bhikkhu Bodhi. The term *bhikkhus* refers to the followers of the Buddha at the time, and "*Nibbana*" is the Pali spelling for nirvana (Skt., *nirvāṇa*) meaning extinguished, or ultimate liberation.

into things rather than act mindlessly and selfishly. Collectively, they lead to the eighth and final: meditation.

> *Samyag-dṛṣṭi* – Right Understanding
> *Samyak-saṃkalpa* – Right Intention
> *Samyag-vāc* – Right Speech
> *Samyak-karmānta* – Right Action
> *Samyag-ājīva* – Right Livelihood
> *Samyag-vyāyāma* – Right Effort
> *Samyak-smṛti*—Right Mindfulness*
> *Samyak-samādhi* – Right Meditative Absorption

The term samyak (or *samyag*) can be translated into English as *perfectly, fully, completely, correctly,* and *properly*. Most often, the term is translated as "right," but this misses the aspect of perfection. Perfection implies an ideal we can strive for rather than something we can necessarily attain. It conjures the image of a platonic *ideal form*, an idealized abstraction which serves as a vehicle for discovery and insight into that which it represents. *Perfection* implies there is a process through which we can develop ourselves, improve the way we live, act, and think. The term "right," as in "right intention," may falsely suggest an ethical quality which is *not* the intent of the Eightfold Path. Its intent is not to measure if one is right or wrong, good or bad, nor to judge others, but to serve as a guide to help propel us forward out of samsāra, out of the state of duhkha. The Eightfold Path encourages us to work at perfecting our thoughts, our understanding, our actions, and our mental development.† Compatible moral thought and action arise as a natural result of this effort.

Once one has become accomplished with the first seven steps of the Eightfold Path, one enters a new domain, which Vetter, drawing upon the Pali canon, describes as four stages:

---

* *Smṛti* is more accurately translated as *memory*, or *thinking of or upon*, but the term *mindfulness* has been the preferred translation for the last century.

† Vetter has noted that the Aṅguttara Nikāya of the Theravāda branch of Buddhism added an additional two items to the Eightfold Path: ñāṇa (discriminating insight) and vimutti (liberation/salvation) (1988, xxxvii).

This first stage is a state of joy and happiness, which arises from separation (i.e., the previously practiced renunciation of objects of pleasure as well as the solitariness of the place), accompanied by contemplation and reflection. In the course of time contemplation and reflection cease, giving way to inner calm and becoming one of the heart. Joy and happiness remain, though they are no longer explained by separation, but as originating from concentration (samādhi). This is the second stage. Then the joy disappears, but happiness conceived as physical well-being remains. This happiness is joined by equanimity and awareness (*sati*). This is the third stage. Finally, even the feeling of happiness disappears and equanimity and awareness reach a state of perfection. This is the fourth stage.[42]

We will examine the Four Noble Truths as they relate to chan practice in Part Two.

Next, we'll explore Buddhism's spread out of India into neighboring civilizations, and see how that migration created distinct, unique, and, to varying degrees, independent expressions of Buddhism. While most religious sects can claim to be linked by common roots,* people calling themselves Buddhists around the world may embrace views, beliefs, and practices as different from one another as the Islamic views of Muslims are from the Shintō views of the Japanese. In the remaining part of this chapter, we'll investigate how and why Buddhism may have fractured into so many disparate forms, and how this, in turn, would influence Chan.

THE NATURE OF REALITY AND THE RISE OF THE MAHĀYĀNA

I have mentioned several major schools of Buddhism up to this point. To review, the *Nikāya* refers to the collection of various sects of Bud-

---

* For example, Christianity has the Protestants, Catholics, Eastern Orthodox, Oriental Orthodox, Ahe mosnglicans, and others, yet they are all in close agreement with fundamental tenets of Christianity as represented by the Christian Bible. There is no singular written source in Buddhism available to unify Buddhist ideologies, practices, and beliefs.

dhism, each claiming to be "the authentic" Buddhism, as represented by a group of arhats referred to as The Elders; *Theravāda* refers to the lone survivor of these Nikāya sects, and *Mahāyāna* refers to the group of dissenters from the Nikāya orthodoxy, originally referred to as the Mahāsaṅghika.* The divergences of religious thought during the first few hundred years after Siddhārtha's death occurred simultaneously with the beginnings of Hinduism. Hinduism, however, followed a different stream of ideologies taken from the Upanishads and Brahmanism.

As noted earlier, the Mahāsaṅghika did not diverge much from the orthodoxy of The Elders on any significant theological concepts, but they picked out and emphasized certain elements from the Pāli canon and de-emphasized others, which gave some appearance of divergence. In time, though, significant theological distinctions did arise as successive generations expanded on concepts they considered critically important. Among them, two would come to clearly distinguish Mahāyāna from Theravāda. They addressed two quintessential questions: Is reality dualistic or nondualistic? Is Buddha-nature mundane—relating solely to the external, physical realm—or supra-mundane, relating to a spiritual or "celestial" realm? The Mahāyāna sided with the latter in both cases, Theravāda with the former. This would have profound implications in China for the genesis of Chan, which adopted the Mahāyāna view. An additional concept introduced by the Mahāyāna was the *Bodhisattva Ideal*: after one is spiritually awakened, he or she must return to the mundane world to help others. One of the first canonical texts to expound these new views—views which would become hallmarks of the Mahāyāna—was the *Pratyutpannabuddha Saṃmukhāvasthita Samādhi Sūtra*, which translates as *Sūtra on the Samādhi for Encountering Face-to-Face the Buddhas of the Present*. It was one of the first sutras to be

---

* The third important Buddhist school, *Vajrayāna*, would not appear for another several hundred years. While not significant to the development of Chan, it will be discussed briefly later.

translated into Chinese and promptly became revered as the *Banzhou Sanmei Jing* 般舟三昧經.*

THE BODHISATTVA IDEAL AND THE BUDDHIST TRINITIES

Nikāya Buddhism held that the highest achievement for a follower of the Buddha Dharma was nirvāṇa, arguing that only once one has entered nirvāṇa will one become free of the infinite cycle of birth and death (samsāra). The Mahāyāna argued that this is an egoistic goal that serves nobody. Using the Buddha himself as a role model, as one who "stayed behind" to help others, the Mahāyāna argued that just arriving at nirvāṇa is not enough; one must return to the world of *conditional arising* to help others discover nirvāṇa as well. This distinction wasn't accepted by the Nikāya, who equated enlightenment with nirvāṇa. The Bodhisattva Ideal thus arose within the Mahāyāna to emphasize the altruistic imperative to help liberate all sentient beings from suffering.

The term *Bodhisattva*, when dissected (according to Buddhist theology), has three properties: compassion, wisdom, and benevolence. These qualities became represented by three *celestial beings*: *Avalokiteśvara*, *Mañjuśrī*, and *Maitreya*, respectively. Because they are *essential essences*—ideal forms that represent archetypal aspects of being—they are said to be *celestial*.† In Part Two, we'll explore how, through contemplation and meditation, these celestial beings can become directly known.

Unlike Nikāya literature, the Mahāyāna sutras refer to the Buddha sometimes as a man and sometimes as one or more aspects of an ideal (celestial) form, often without making a clear distinction. For example,

---

* Lokakṣema is credited with bringing Mahāyāna Buddhism to China during the 2nd century CE because of his translation of this sutra and other texts.

† The concept of an ideal form dates historically to ancient Greece (Plato), but its exact origins are unknown. The idea is that for everything we interact with in our lives—forms of all kinds, be they dogs, men, women, lamps, trees, toads—the mind unconsciously relates them to their ideal form, i.e., the perfect dog, the perfect man, the perfect woman, the perfect lamp, etc. Plato suggested that actual "things" we encounter in the world we "see" not as they are, but as "shadows" of their ideal forms (Plato 1987, 255-264).

the beginning of the *Śālistamba Sūtra* (Mahāyāna) expresses this supramundane quality of the Buddha by referencing him as Maitreya:

> Thus have I heard: [At one time,] the Lord was staying at Rājagrha on Vulture Peak Mountain with a large company of monks, 1,250 monks, and many Bodhisattvas, [Mahāsattvas]. At that time, the Venerable Śāriputra* approached the place frequented by Maitreya Bodhisattva-mahāsattva. When he approached, they exchanged many kinds of good and joyful words, and sat down together on a flat stone.[43]

Compare this to a typical example from the Nikāya (Theravāda) canon which expresses the solely mundane aspect of the Buddha:

> Thus have I heard. On one occasion the Blessed One was dwelling at Savatthi in Jeta's Grove, Anathapindika's Park. Then, when the night had advanced, a certain devata of stunning beauty, illuminating the entire Jeta's Grove, approached the Blessed One. Having approached, he paid homage to the Blessed One, stood to one side, and said to him...[†44]

It was the Buddha's life itself, rather than his teachings, per se, that inspired Mahāyāna's Bodhisattva Ideal and led to observations of elemental principles (psychological archetypes) that transcended not only the Buddha, but all sentient beings. Mahāyānists depicted the three-fold aspects of the archetypal Self—compassion (*Avalokiteśvara*), wisdom (*Mañjuśrī*), and benevolence (*Maitreya*)—in statuary, frescos, and other forms of religious art.[‡]

Around 300 CE, through systemization of doctrines conducted by the Yogācāra (lit. "Yoga Practice") school of Mahāyāna Buddhism, another trinity arrived, this one expressing not aspects of *being*, but aspects of the *experience* of being: the Dharma-*kāya*, or Truth-body,

---

* Śāriputra is considered one of the most important of the Buddha's disciples in the Theravāda tradition.

† From *The Book with Verses* (*Saglithlivagga*), Chapter I: *Devatlisamyutta*.

‡ This is an act of *reification*, bringing abstract realities into concrete forms so that they can be more readily accessed. For more on this topic, see Chapter 18 and Berger 1990, 85-87.

the *Sambhoga-kāya*, or *Bliss-body*, and the *Nirmana-kāya*, or *Transformation-body*. Both sets of trinities become known through meditation, where archetypal images of celestial beings are commonly encountered in visions, along with rapturous states of bliss (Chapters 4, 12, 15, 17, 18). Similarly, through the continuing development of mental clarity, truth manifests, which is experienced as transformative. Hsu Yun* alludes to this *Trikāya*, or *Three bodies*, in his Ox-herding poems, which are presented and discussed in Chapter 14.

The number of celestial saviors would increase to include *Amitābha*, the *Buddha of infinite light*, and *Amitāyus*, the *Buddha of infinite time*.

THE TRIRATNA, TRISHULA, AND TRIPLE REFUGE

Another foundational triad introduced into the early Buddhist canon was the Three Jewels: the Buddha, the Dharma, and the Sangha. Together, they represent the core pillars of Buddhism. Taking refuge in the Three Jewels became a universal ritual for all devotees upon joining a Buddhist community, marking the adoption of the earliest and most fundamental Buddhist precepts.

बुद्धंशरणंगच्छामि Buddhaṃ śaraṇaṃ gacchāmi   I take refuge in the Buddha
धर्मंशरणंगच्छामि Dharmaṃ śaraṇaṃ gacchāmi   I take refuge in the Dharma
संघंशरणंगच्छामि Saṅghaṃ śaraṇaṃ gacchāmi   I take refuge in the Sangha

In early Buddhism, the Three Jewels were represented symbolically by a *trishula*, a three-pronged spear resting atop a lotus blossom. The trishula is thought to have evolved from a much more ancient sym-

---

* Hsu Yun (Hsü Yün—Empty Cloud) was an influential Chinese Chan master of the late 19th century and early 20th century. He changed his name from his original tonsure name, Yen-Ch'e, to Hsu Yun—Empty Cloud—because, according to Holmes Welch, he desired privacy and wanted to live incognito (1967, 280). Incognito was not to be, however. Hsu Yun became famous in China and throughout the world for his persistent work to revitalize Chan throughout China, to establish harmonious relations with the government, and to help form the Chinese Buddhist Association at Kuang Chi Monastery, which helped smooth relations with the government. For more about Hsu Yun's life and teachings, see *Empty Cloud: The Teachings of Xu (Hsu) Yun*, by Chuan Yuan Shakya, 1996.

bol, the *triratna*, a graceful "W" sitting atop a wheel. The oldest triratna symbol known to date is on a Pashupati seal from Mohenjodaro, Pakistan. circa 2500 - 2400 BCE. The trishula, as a trinity symbol, though now more commonly associated with Hinduism, is commonly seen in early Buddhist statuary, reliefs, and paintings, and archeological evidence suggests its symbolism was later adopted by Hindus.

FIGURE 2. PASHUPATI SEAL NO. 420.
From Mohenjodaro, Pakistan. circa 2500 - 2400 BCE. Note the triratna atop the head of a meditator in the yogic *padmasana* pose.

SKILL-IN-MEANS (UPĀYA-KAUSHALYA)

The Buddha purportedly said, "Whatever is conducive to liberation and not to bondage, that is my teaching." Buddhism, in other words, is an open book with innumerable blank pages, left to be filled in as needs and means arise: as civilizations and cultures evolve, so do the requirements for expressing its teachings. In the Vinaya (*Cullavagga*, X 4) and in the *Aṅguttara-nikāya*, the Buddha purportedly offered some principles to help identify what exactly was "conducive to liberation and not to bondage":

> [Of] whatever teachings (dhamme), O Gotami, you can assure yourself "these teachings lead to dispassion (virāga), not to passion (sarāga), to freedom from bondage (visamyoga), not to bondage (samyoga), to decrease [in possessions], not to increase; to few desires, not to many; to contentment, not to discontent; to solitude, not to socializing; to exertion, not to indolence; to ease in maintaining oneself,

not to difficulty" - indeed you may consider "this is the Dhamma, this is the Vinaya, this is the teaching of the Teacher (sasthusāsana)."[45]

From this point of view, we can understand the Mahāyāna doctrine of *skill-in-means*, or *skillful means*, (*upāya kausalya*) as a vehicle through which the Buddha's teachings—the *Dhamma*—can be actualized and propagated as societies and cultures change over time. *Upāya* refers to a quality of selflessness which allows one to strategically adapt to the changing needs of individuals and societies to convey the Buddha's teachings in ways that can be understood. It further encourages "expedients" or "stratagems" that are cleverly suited to this goal. Rather than adhering to any particular teaching, it requires one to be infinitely flexible, creative, and open to new ideas and ways of expressing the Buddha Dharma. Paul Williams, former President of the UK Association for Buddhist Studies, postulates that, through the concept of upāya, "Buddhism could open itself out to new and perhaps originally non-Buddhist ideas."[46] This may be, at least in part, why Buddhism presents in so many different ways today.*

Madhyamaka and Vijñānavāda Views

Different interpretations of ontological concepts led to two schools within the Mahāyāna: the *Madhyamaka* (the "Dialectical school") and the *Vijñānavāda* (the "Consciousness school"). The Madhyamaka, considered to have been founded by Nagarjuna (Nāgārjuna) in the second century CE, propounded that the fundamental nature of everything is emptiness (*śūnyatā, śūnyam*) and that all phenomenal existence is illusory—without self-existence (*svabhāva*). Nagarjuna popularized the *catuṣkoṭi*, or *tetralemma*, by using it as both a means to explain this perspective and as a tool or mechanism to apprehend it.† It states that, with reference to any logical proposition P, there are four possibilities: P, not

---

* The interested reader may enjoy the *Upāyakauśalya Sūtra*, which is entirely devoted to explaining the principle of upāya.

† Alex Wayman's article "Who understands the four alternatives of the Buddhist Texts?" well supports the claim that Nagarjuna was not interested as much in using the *catuṣkoṭi* as a

P, both P and not P, and neither P nor not P. These four possibilities are independently exclusive of the others and together are exhaustive of all possibilities; that is, there are no other possible options.* Nagarjuna used catuṣkoṭi logic to describe the fundamental nature of Self:

> "Self" is taught, "non-Self" is also taught, "no Self nor non-self at all" is also taught by the Buddhas. Everything is true, or not true, both true and not true, neither true nor not true—this is the instruction of the Buddhas.
>
> If something arises interdependently, it is not *that*, nor, more-over, is it *other*; therefore, it is neither continuity nor interruption. If the Self were the aggregates (*skandhas*†), it would be subject to arising and disappearance; if the Self were other than the aggregates, it would be without the characteristics of the aggregates.
> Consequently, the Self (*ātman*) cannot be either identical or different from the dependency (on the *skandhas*); the self does not exist apart from this dependency, nor is it certain that it does not exist.[47]

Considering Nagarjuna's expansive use of the catuṣkoṭi, Kaisa Puhakka concludes, justifiably, that

> Nāgārjuna's dialectic aims not at a synthesis but at liberating the mind from attachment to any new view or position. Because his approach is to neither affirm nor deny anything, it is called the dialectic of the Middle Way [...] Nāgārjuna shows that every one of the four possibilities is untenable or self-contradictory, and thus one is left with nothing to assert, no ground to stand on.[48]

Nāgārjuna solidified a new Mahāyāna view that ultimate reality is free of the four extremes: *existence, nonexistence, existence* and *nonexistence*,

---

means for arguing ontological perspectives as he was to use it as a means for penetrating the nature of reality directly. (1984, 225-250)

* The catuṣkoṭi will be revisited again in Chapter 15 when we examine several models for describing spiritual experience.

† *Skandhas*, translated usually as "aggregates," refers to the five-fold collection of forms, sensations, perceptions, mental formations, and consciousness.

and *neither existence nor nonexistence*, a perspective that would come to be represented in Chan by an "empty circle."

Madhyamaka split again into two more schools, the *Svātantrika* and the *Prāsaṅgiga*. The *Svātantrika* school explained the existence of physical "things" as illusory, because any thing can be decomposed into various parts and each of those parts can, in turn, be decomposed into smaller parts, *ad infinitum*, until all that's left is emptiness.* It's only through a sequence of causes and conditions that the world appears as it does. The essence of *śūnyatā*, the *Svātantrika* explains, is truth itself—Dharma.

The *Prāsaṅgiga* school took the position that the *Svātantrika* school was completely off-base, because not only was its theory empty, devoid of self-existence, but it was also fundamentally impossible to create any kind of theory of causation from it; that is, one cannot prove that something is caused by itself, caused by something else, both, or neither.

Nagarjuna did not originate catuṣkoṭi logic but used it to argue that the fundamental nature of reality is emptiness. The *Pratyutpanna Samādhi Sūtra* makes frequent reference to catuṣkoṭi logic as in this passage describing the nature of dharmas:†

> All dharmas are originally nonexistent. To think that they exist causes attachment. If they do not exist, to say perversely that they do is also attachment. One neither thinks of these two, nor does one incline to what is between them. It is for this reason alone that they are not on either side, nor in the middle, they neither exist, nor do they not exist. Why? All dharmas are empty; they are like nirvāṇa; they are indestructible, imperishable, and unsteady; they are neither here nor there, they are markless, they are unwavering.[49]

---

*This conceptualization foreshadowed modern elementary particle physics, which still searches for explanations for why some particles transform from one type of particle into another, and why others are completely annihilated. These elementary particles are, collectively, the stuff we are all made of, according to the standard atomistic conceptualization of the physical world.

† "Dharmas," in this context, represents a "physical or mental 'factor,' or fundamental 'constituent element,' or simply 'phenomenon'" (Lopez 2014, 424).

Nikāya literature (such as the *Aggivacchagotta Sutta* from the *Majjhima Nikāya*) also suggests that the Buddha sometimes used catuṣkoṭi logic when responding to questions asked of him:

> The speculative view that the world is not eternal...that the world is finite...that the world is infinite...that the soul and the body are the same...that the soul is one thing and the body another...that after death a Tathagata exists...that after death a Tathagata does not exist...that after death a Tathagata both exists and does not exist...that after death a Tathagata neither exists nor does not exist is a thicket of views, a wilderness of views, a contortion of views, a vacillation of views, a fetter of views. It is beset by suffering, by vexation, by despair, and by fever, and it does not lead to disenchantment, to dispassion, to cessation, to peace, to direct knowledge, to enlightenment, to Nibbana. Seeing this danger, I do not take up any of these speculative views.[50]

The tenets of both the *Prāsaṅgiga* and *Svātantrika* would be incorporated into the general Mahāyāna view because, in effect, they both built on the Nikāya and on each other, a process that would continue to characterize the creative development of the Mahāyāna for centuries to come. The *Svātantrika* emphasized the illusion of self-existence, while the *Prāsaṅgiga* emphasized the rejection of any and all concepts and doctrines. The first major branch of Mahāyāna Buddhism, *Madhyamaka*, to which both schools belonged, propounded the doctrine of emptiness (*śūnyatā*). Chan would embrace all three positions.

Followers of the second major Mahāyāna school, the *Vijñānavāda*, extolled that consciousness, apart from any sense of an objective external world, is the ultimate nature of reality.* Through our sensory perceptions, they argued, we create an imagined reality from mental images and imbue it with the character of an objective reality, i.e., one that's understood to be the same for everyone. The *Vijñānavāda* took it further and argued that it was these mental formations themselves that were real, and they alone. For example, a tree has no objective reality; it

---

* Two brothers, Asaṅga and Vasubandhu, are credited with founding the *Vijñānavāda* school in the 4th century CE.

is only our *experience* of it through our senses that is real. To imagine an external world, consequently, is illusory, just as is imagining an internal world.* Pure consciousness is without objects and subjects, that is, non-dualistic; thus, to see objects and subjects as objective reality is to be deluded by illusion. This way of witnessing reality required meditation, for which the yoga tradition supplied the requisite techniques. The *Vijñānavāda* came to be referred to as the Yogācāra or "yoga-practice" school and established meditation as an essential aspect of Mahāyāna Buddhism. Its principle views were taken from the *Saṃdhinirmocana Sūtra* and the *Laṅkāvatāra Sūtra*, the latter becoming a foundational sutra for Chan (Chapter 4).

Even though these early Mahāyāna concepts came directly from Nikāya literature, the Mahāyāna view, by this time, had become substantially distinct from the Nikāya (Theravāda). The Buddha was no longer just an enlightened person who had taught about the Truth (Dharma), but had become a supra-human "force," a *celestial savior* with various identifying aspects. The nature of Dharma, or *Ultimate Universal Truth*, became, in effect, emptiness. Yet because the Mahāyāna built off the same sources that were identified with the Nikāya, it may not be accurate to consider that early Mahāyāna and Theravāda represented two distinct schools of Buddhism; each, we might conjecture, simply followed different sets of contextual thought that were developed in different directions by different people.

Devotionalism (bhakti)

At the same time that the philosophical and theological foundations of the Mahāyāna were being established, devotionalism, the practice of reverent worship, also became integrated into the daily lives of the sangha. Unlike expressions of piety common to many other religions,

---

* This is not to say that an external world does or does not exist. It says only that what we can perceive of any possible external world with our senses *is not it*. What is *not* illusory, then, is our *experience* of the world through our senses. We can say no more about it than that. To draw inferences from it is to err—like mistaking the reflection of a tree for the tree that reflects.

where worshiping gods or people is common, Buddhist worship was not about gods (of which there were none, at least not in the Western sense), nor people, but about ideal forms or archetypes of psychological principles that one could tap into through devotion to them.* To this end, Buddha statues, representing the celestial essence of an enlightened being, were erected in vast numbers during the last few centuries BCE, beginning with the reign of Ashoka and continuing through the reign of Kanishka. Other statues which served as inspirational themes for devotional activities would soon follow, notably, Mañjuśrī, Avalokiteśvara, and Maitreya, the celestial representations of wisdom, compassion, and benevolence, respectively.

As a side note, secular people tend to react with bewilderment toward religious/spiritual worship. But there is a corollary with devotionalism we express routinely toward belongings, pets, family members, and famous personalities. We attach strong feelings of care, concern, love, and idealization to a wide variety of things and people in our lives. The difference between religious (or spiritual) devotionalism and secular devotionalism is that the former helps sever ourselves from the ego while the latter serves to strengthen it.† Devotional worship of an ideal form, such as Avalokiteśvara, encourages us to connect with a particular obscure essence within us—in this case, compassion.

The sūtras: visionary experience writes the code

Sūtra is derived from the root *siv*, meaning to sew or stitch together, and describes the original format in which information in ancient India was retained and passed orally through generations. While the orally

---

* It could be argued, however, that the Western Jewish/Christian god is also archetypal—an ideal form in the Platonic sense—a topic discussed in Part Three.

† Not all people respond to, or engage in, religious worship this way, however. Unless there is a willingness and desire to transcend the ego, either consciously or subconsciously, religious devotionalism will not lead to spiritual awakening (Chapter 9). Simply following religious protocols won't help us out of the roiling waters of samsāra; we must also be willing to abandon ourselves.

recounted Buddhist sutras would eventually be sewn together on palm leaves, the original meaning was metaphorical: to sew together thoughts to best preserve them, as succinctly as possible, through memorization and recitation (*śruti*). Extraordinary effort went into it, resulting in remarkable accuracy.[51] The Vedas, for example, were memorized and recited in up to eleven different ways, then "proof-read" by comparing them with each other to detect and correct errors, a method that scholars believe preserved their integrity for centuries.[52]

As an example, one form of recitation was the *jatā-pātha*, or "mesh recitation." With this method, two adjacent words were recited in correct order, then recited in reverse order, then again in correct order.[53] Using this method, the six-word phrase, "That which stirs, flies, stands still...," quoted earlier from the *Atharva Veda*, would have been recited as:

> That which which that that which
> Which stirs stirs which which stirs
> Stirs flies flies stirs stirs flies
> Flies stands stands flies flies stands
> Stands still still stands stands still

As complex as this seems, it was among the least complex of the systems according to Sanskrit scholar, Pierre-Sylvain Filliozat. The most complex was the *ghana-pātha*, lit. "dense recitation," which took the form:[54]

> word1word2, word2word1, word1word2word3, word3word2word1, word1word2word3;
>
> word2word3, word3word2, word2word3word4, word4word3word2, word2word3word4;
>
> ...

Using the same six-word phrase from the *Atharva Veda* and applying this recitation approach yields a fifty-two-word stanza:

That which, which that, that which stirs, stirs which that, that which stirs;

Which stirs, stirs which, which stirs flies, flies stirs which, which stirs flies;

Stirs flies, flies stirs, stirs flies stands, stands flies stirs, stirs flies stands;

Flies stands, stands flies, flies stands still, still stands flies, flies stands still;

We can clearly see that, unlike the "Telephone" game played by children—where one person whispers a word or sentence in the ear of another, who passes it on to another, and so forth, until it returns back to the original person as a completely different word or phrase—these mnemonic recitation devices left little to no chance of mistakes happening without them being easily caught and corrected.

Scholars attest to the high precision rendered by these approaches for retaining information throughout countless generations without the use of written language. As well as preserving religious information deemed of utmost importance, the technique preserved mathematics, literary style, and even pronunciation nuances of phonetics (śikṣā) and metrics (chhandas): according to Filliozat, even the Rigveda (ṛgveda) was accurately preserved for over a millennium without any variations using such techniques.[55]

Filliozat describes the early sutras as a unique form of oral literature in that the information in them was intentionally compressed for extreme brevity: "The knowers of the sūtra know it as having few phonemes, being devoid of ambiguity, containing the essence, facing everything, being without pause and unobjectionable."[56] Because of their brevity, interpretation of the sutras required special knowledge and training. In the monastic tradition, this would have been provided by the senior monks for the junior monks.

Since memorization skills were well-honed by many in the sangha, it's likely that much of the earliest sutra literature accurately represents the words of the Buddha. Yet, whether the sutras are verbatim accounts of the Buddha's teachings is not as important to Buddhism as that they are *considered* to be his actual teachings, either directly or indirectly. This was essential for the sangha in defining themselves as Buddhists. The specific collection of sutras they accepted as authentic, e.g., Mahāyāna or Theravāda versions, defined them further as belonging to that specific ideological/theological branch.

Since a sutra (in the oral tradition) sought to compress information as much as possible, it's likely that the first sutras written down were much shorter than they are now, even when additional information needed to explain them accurately was included. We also know that, over the centuries, scribes embellished them, adding and repeating phrases to intentionally lengthen them.* By comparing later versions of sutras with earlier versions of the same sutra, it's possible to see what new content was added and what old content was later embellished.† Additionally, a sutra war seems to have taken place between the followers of the Mahāyāna and Theravāda branches based on derogatory remarks made—sometimes subtle, sometimes overt—toward each by the other.[57]

Aside from the variations in doctrine that grew between Theravāda and Mahāyāna, their approaches to formulating and organizing the teachings were also quite different. Theravāda followers preferred systematic organization of ideas and principles. They liked to make numbered lists, organize concepts into groups of different lengths, and then apply the organizational structure itself to memory with recitation.‡ Mahāyāna followers, on the other hand, preferred to leave organiza-

---

* We can speculate that this would have served the purpose of occupying the sangha with extended chanting sessions, as well as helping to ensure that the message would not be lost, improperly remembered, or misunderstood.

† For example, Lewis Lancaster examined the *Perfection of Wisdom Sutra* (*Aṣṭasāhasrikā*), comparing later versions with the earliest known, to discover that many significant Mahāyāna concepts are not evident in the original (Williams 2009, 29).

‡ For example, the *Sutta Piṭaka* from the *Tripiṭaka* is divided into five groups known as *Nikāyas*: The *Dīgha Nikāya* ("Long Group"), the *Majjhima Nikāya* ("Middle-Length Group"), the *Saṃyutta Nikāya* ("Connected Group"), the *Aṅguttara Nikāya* ("Numerical Group") and the *Khuddaka Nikāya* ("Minor Group").

tion to the sutras themselves, presumably feeling that they did not need organizing any further, which, as previously discussed, was the original intention of the sutra literary format. To this day, whenever we encounter Buddhist doctrines organized with numerical lists or groups, they likely belong to the Theravāda Buddhist canon.

The first Mahāyāna sutra to be written, the *Śālistamba Sūtra*, appears to have been the first subtle departure from the Nikāya/Theravāda doctrines in that, while previous writings claimed to represent the historical record of the Buddha's teachings, this one included slight deviations that would become seeds for developing the Mahāyāna identity in centuries to follow. Most thoughts in the *Śālistamba Sūtra* are similar to early Nikāya/Theravāda texts, leading scholars to conclude that, while it likely was not written until sometime between the first century BCE and the first century CE, the ideas presented may be dated to only a hundred years or less after the Buddha's death, and may even represent the Buddha's own actual thoughts.[58] Regardless, the *Śālistamba Sūtra* is considered by some scholars to represent the oldest extant proto-Mahāyāna text.

An important aspect of the early development of the two schools of Buddhism was the interpretation of *anātman*, or *not-self*.* Those interpretations would further distinguish Buddhism from Hinduism. An early departure from the Hindu view arose in the *Śālistamba Sūtra*, which argued that there was nothing that would remain and/or return after the death of the body. All Buddhist schools acknowledged the same guidance from the Buddha on this subject at the time, namely that there is no *ātman*, no soul in the sense of an eternal "essence of self," or

---

* Anātman has commonly been translated as both *no-self* and *not-self*, each of which have different, subtle but important, connotations. "No-self" suggests a nihilistic interpretation that we do not exist, offering no possibility for discovery of anything beyond the known—which is the mystic's quest. According to Tao Jiang, author of *Contexts and Dialogue: Yogacara Buddhism and Modern Psychology on the Subliminal Mind*, *not-self* is the more accurate interpretation if we consider early Buddhist literature. The *Sutta Nipāta* and the *Saṃyutta Nikāya*, thought to be among the earliest records of the Buddha's teaching, describe it as a denial of identification of thought-objects with the self: "This is not mine, this is not what I am, this is not my self" (as cited in Jiang 2006, 24). In this way, there is no denial of existence, per se, but denial of an illusory existence created by the mind's attachments.

ego-self;* rather, the notion of a self that is real is only an illusion, an effect of causes and conditions (*karma*).† However, from the Theravāda view, this meant that there *is* something other than self, something born of our actions in this life, which is reborn in future lives, either in human or other animal forms. The *Śālistamba Sūtra* asserts that it's only the *consequences* of our actions in this life (karma) which continue after our physical death, nothing more. Translated from the Chinese version:

> Again Śāriputra, (it is) as the moon (in) the beautiful sky 42,000 leagues above the earth. The water flows below and the moon shines above. Although its mysterious image is single, (its) reflection appears in many waters. The moon's body does not descend and the water's substance does not rise. Thus, Śāriputra, creatures do not go from this world to an after-world, or from an after-world again to this world. But there are the fruits of karma (and) the outcomes of causes and conditions which cannot be diminished.
>
> Again, Venerable Śāriputra, (it is) as (when) fire has fuel it burns, and when the fuel is gone it stops. Likewise, karma bondage produces consciousness everywhere (in) all realms. (It) can produce the result name-and-form, (which is) not self, not a master, not a recipient, like empty space, like summer heat (mirages), like an illusion, like a dream, not having substance. Yet its virtuous and evil causes and conditions, fruits and results follow karma undiminished.[59]

This short text developed some allegorical allusions that would be embellished and repeated in many contexts in future Mahāyāna literature, notably Chan: the moon reflecting, water flowing, and fire burning. The text also touched on topics that have led to mainstream discussions today, not only in religious and spiritual circles, but secular ones

---

* Hinduism took a nearly opposite interpretation and sided with the doctrine of atman: there *is* an eternal soul which can either be reborn after death into another body (*transmigration*), or released from rebirth altogether (*moksha*).

† In Mahāyāna Buddhism's canonical literature, karma describes the principle of cause and effect. When I walk in the rain, I get wet. Western culture popularly considers karma a moral principle. If I hurt someone, it will come back to me and I will be hurt. If I help someone, it will come back to me and someone will someday help me. This is an egoistic interpretation of karma because it's all about "me." Remove the ego and there is no longer good and bad, just actions and their consequences: effects and their causes.

as well, including: 1) the notion that our sense of identity is an illusion; 2) that the illusion is created by causes and conditions; 3) that the illusion creates bondage; and 4) that the illusion gives the false impression that there is an eternal *"essence"* of being which will be reborn when the body dies.*

The *Śālistamba Sūtra* also expresses the Mahāyāna viewpoint on reincarnation with the idea that a past or future *being of self* is irrelevant to one who has discovered that the nature of self is, in fact, emptiness, and that it only seems to exist because of *conditional arising*:

> Whoever, Venerable Śāriputra, with perfect wisdom, sees this conditioned arising, perfectly set forth by the Lord, as it actually is: always and ever without soul, devoid of soul, truly undistorted, unborn, not become, not made, not compounded, unobstructed, unobscured, glorious, fearless, ungraspable, inexhaustible and by nature never stilled, (whoever) sees it well and fully as unreal, as vanity, void, unsubstantial, as a sickness, a boil, a dart, as dangerous, impermanent, suffering, as empty and without self; such a one does not reflect upon the past (thinking): "Was I in the past, or was I not? What was I in the past? How was I in the past?" Nor again does he reflect upon the future (thinking): "Will I be in the future, or will I not be? What will I be in the future? How will I be in the future?" Nor again does he reflect upon the present (thinking): "What is this? How is this? Being what, what will we become? Where does this being come from? Where will it go when departed from here?"[60]

The *Pratyutpanna Samādhi Sūtra* further explains that the self can neither perceive itself nor be grasped rationally, and that even to hold the conception of self is delusional:

---

* The bulk of the *Śālistamba Sūtra* explains these postulates as effects of *conditional arising* through the metaphor of a seed which, when conditions are right, will germinate and give birth to a sprout, which will flower giving rise to a fruit, which will give rise to a seed, which will fall to earth at the right place and germinate, and the cycle will repeat. The conditions involve earth, water, heat, wind, space, and seasons.

Because he [a bodhisattva with conceptual thoughts] has the concept of 'self' he lacks understanding. If one searches for the basis of a self it cannot be apprehended, and it does not undergo birth and death or nirvāṇa...[61]

The *Ajitasena Sūtra*, also considered to be one of the earliest Mahāyāna sutras, introduced the formative concept of ideal forms as internal representations of Self which can be visualized through *archetypal meditations* (Chapter 12), and set the stage for what would become the Pure Land school of Buddhism in China, advocating recitation of the Buddha's name as a vehicle for accessing Buddha-nature.[62]

At this early time in the history of Buddhism, however, the distinction between Mahāyāna and Theravāda conceptualizations was still virtually nonexistent. It would take time for the evolution of new sutras before clear division arose and the term "Mahāyāna" would be used.* The *Aṣṭasāhasrikā prajñāpāramitā* would present the earliest definitively Mahāyāna position, incorporating the most divergences from Theravāda.† This sutra taught that once one reaches the stage of a Bodhisattva (fully enlightened being), one must postpone entering the final realm of the Buddha (*ultimate nirvāṇa*) and return to the world to help others, a theme that would later be presented in Chan's ox-herding pictures and poems. It also confronts the problem of how not to get so consumed in samādhi that one wishes not to leave it—a paradoxical egoistic situation (Part Four)—and gives instructions for the three meditations on *emptiness, signlessness,* and *wishlessness.*

The *Aṣṭasāhasrikā prajñāpāramitā* is one of the first writings to use the concept of *śūnyatā*, which translates as *void*, or *emptiness*. This concept would eventually become known as "zero" by the world, and play the important role in mathematics that we've come to know.‡

---

* The term "Mahāyāna" first appears in the *Lotus Sutra*, but its first historical appearance was in the recording of a large land grant to a Mahāyāna monastery (Schopen 2004, 494-95).

† Carbon dating of a birch-bark manuscript of this sutra places it between about 47 and 147 CE. The title of the sutra translates as *"The Perfection of Wisdom in Eight Thousand Lines."*

‡ The idea that emptiness was actually *something* appears to have been a purely Indian invention. While other civilizations had notations for *nothing*, the zero we have today as a

The *Aṣṭasāhasrikā prajñāpāramitā Sūtra* also acknowledges visionary experiences of ideal forms during meditation—specifically the sage archetype (*divine being*)—and describes our tendency to attribute improper value to visionary encounters instead of seeing them as internal manifestations of the psyche.* Misinterpreting them this way can lead one to mistakenly believe that their appearance and disappearance is objectively real:†

> Dharmodgata:... A sleeping man might in his dreams see one Tathāgata, or two, or three, or up to one thousand, or still more. On waking up he would, however, no longer see even one single Tathagata. What do you think, son of good family, have these Tathagatas come from anywhere, or gone to anywhere?
>
> Sadaprarudita: One cannot conceive that in that dream any dharma at all had the status of a full and perfect reality, for the dream was deceptive.
>
> Dharmodgata: Just so the Tathagata has taught that all dharmas are like a dream. All those who do not wisely know all dharmas as they really are, i.e. as like a dream, as the Tathagata has pointed out, they adhere to the Tathagatas through their name-body and their form-body, and in consequence they imagine that the Tathagatas come and go. Those who in their ignorance of the true nature of dharmas imagine a coming or going of the Tathagatas, they are just foolish common people, at all times they belong to birth-and-death with its six places of rebirth, and they are far from the perfection of wisdom, far away from the dharmas of a Buddha. On the contrary, however, those who know as they really are all dharmas as like a dream, in agreement with the teaching of the Tathagata, they do not imagine the coming or going of any dharma, nor its production or stopping. They wisely know

---

digit in a counting system, a placeholder, and a representation of emptiness was purely Indian. It was first unambiguously presented in writing in the 7th century (Bourbaki 1998, 46), although earlier Jain texts such as the *Lokavibhāga*, dated to 458 CE, also convey its meaning this way (Georges 2000).

* I use the term *psyche* in the standard psychological sense to mean the totality of the mind's cognitive (conscious and unconscious) state.

† The often-overlooked significance of this will be examined in Part Three.

the Tathagata in his true nature, and they do not imagine a coming or going of the Tathagatas. And those who wisely know this true nature of a Tathagata, they course near to full enlightenment and they course in the perfection of wisdom.[63]

The *Aṣṭasāhasrikā prajñāpāramitā Sūtra* further suggests that *all* experience has the nature of a dream or illusion:

> Gods: Beings that are like a magical illusion, are they not just an illusion?
>
> Subhuti: Like a magical illusion are those beings, like a dream. For not two different things are magical illusion and beings, are dreams and beings. All objective facts also are like a magical illusion, like a dream. The various classes of saints, from Stream-winner to Buddhahood, also are like a magical illusion, like a dream.
>
> Gods: A fully enlightened Buddha also, you say, is like a magical illusion, is like a dream? Buddhahood also, you say, is like a magical illusion, is like a dream?
>
> Subhuti: Even Nirvāṇa, I say, is like a magical illusion, is like a dream. How much more so anything else!
>
> Gods: Even Nirvāṇa, Holy Subhuti, you say, is like an illusion, is like a dream?
>
> Subhuti: Even if perchance there could be anything more distinguished, of that too I would say that it is like an illusion, like a dream. For not two different things are illusion and Nirvāṇa, are dreams and Nirvāṇa.

While a notable exposition on the nature of reality as a dream, the *Aṣṭasāhasrikā Prajñāpāramitā Sūtra* is not alone in offering this insight. A modern spin on the idea came in 2003 from philosopher Nick Bostrom who suggested that perhaps we live in a computer simulation.[64] Others, such as James Hillman, have offered similar thoughts: "It is not we who imagine, but we who are imagined."[65] And of course there is the famous parable of the butterfly from the early Taoist master, Chuang Tzu (aka, Zhuang Zi and Chuang Chou) c. 300 BCE:

> Once upon a time, I, Chuang Chou, dreamt I was a butterfly, fluttering hither and thither, to all intents and purposes a butterfly. I was conscious only of my happiness as a butterfly, unaware that I was Chou. Soon I awaked, and there I was, veritably myself again. Now I do not know whether I was then a man dreaming I was a butterfly, or whether I am now a butterfly, dreaming I am a man.*[66]

Prajñāpāramitā means "the perfection of transcendent wisdom" and refers to a large collection of sutras within this specific category. A particular sutra from this collection, the *Large Sūtra on Perfect Wisdom*, would become the basis for the famous *Heart Sūtra* (*Prajñāpāramitāhṛdaya*) which, Jan Nattier's research convincingly suggests, was likely been produced in East Asia between the 5th and 7th centuries.†

There are many other important concepts presented in these early Mahāyāna texts that are pertinent to our story; however, the task here is not to extract them all, but to give a sense of the early philosophical and spiritual framework from which Chan would later emerge.

We have noted differences between the Theravāda and Mahāyāna traditions as they diverged during these early years, but divergences originally began only because of early disagreements in minor aspects

---

* These similar insights from the Aṣṭasāhasrikā Prajñāpāramitā Sūtra, Nick Bostrom, James Hillman and Chuang Tzu can be understood if we consider that the conscious and unconscious minds are distinct from each other, and therefore cannot directly know one another (Chapter 15); nonetheless, the conscious mind may have a sense that there is something real on the "other side" to which it is blind, and likewise, the unconscious mind (which is inhabited during meditation and stages of sleep) can feel the same way toward the conscious mind. This curious relationship between conscious and unconscious states will be explored in Chapters 15, 17, and 18, beginning with work carried out by Albert Hoffman.

† By comparing Chinese, Tibetan, and Indian texts, she concludes that "a flow chart of the relationships among the Sanskrit and Chinese versions of the *Large Sūtra* and the *Heart Sūtra* can reasonably be drawn in only one sequence: from the Sanskrit *Large Sūtra* to the Chinese *Large Sūtra* of Kumārajīva to the Chinese *Heart Sūtra* popularized by Hsüan-tsang to the Sanskrit *Heart Sūtra*" (J. Nattier 1992, 198). Interestingly, if true, this implies that the Sanskrit *Heart Sūtra* came about through a convoluted process of translations and adaptations in China before being translated into Sanskrit and presented back as an authentic Indian sutra. To the devotee of Chan/Zen, however, its origins are of little significance—it's the message it conveys that counts.

of the early Buddhist canon, mainly disagreements about monastic rules. According to Buddhist scholar, Nobel Ross Reat, the early departures of the Mahāsaṅghika as recorded in the *Śālistamba Sūtra* were vague and raised no significant concern with the Nikāya.[67] It was only because of the rift that grew between the two groups as they spread across the world, and because Buddhism had no established doctrinal boundaries (and never would), that more significant divergences would develop; specifically, Mahāyāna would meet Confucianism and Taoism in China, and Theravāda would meet Brahmanism, Jainism, and Ājīvakism in Sri Lanka.

Sociological principles offer another way to understand the rift that eventually led to these two divergent expressions of Buddhism. While one group of Buddhists was interested in preserving a fixed set of doctrines according to the teachings of a venerated holy man, the other was more interested in preserving the message than the man who presented it, a man who was, after all, gone. Rather than venerating the Buddha as a person, they venerated the Buddha Dharma. That is, while one group, Nikāya, embraced a more literalist thinking, the other, Mahāsaṅghika, embraced a more fluid, creative approach, one strongly grounded in meditation and visionary experience. Indeed, visionary experiences would significantly shape the Mahāyāna view and the sutras that would come to define it.

Historical evidence supports this. There were effectively two different kinds of Buddhist monks: those who chose monastic life, and those who chose seclusion in the ascetic tradition, building huts in the forest or finding caves where solitude could provide better opportunity for contemplation and meditation. Referred to as forest hermits, this latter group was met with ambivalence, if not scorn and ridicule, by the monastics, who viewed them as neglecting their duties as monks.[68] Those duties included taking money from donors (to give the donor merit) and managing the monastery's money and property.*[69] With much to

---

* "The primary role of their fellow Buddhist monks was not to 'work out their own salvation with diligence' but to diligently generate merit for lay donors by using what they provided or what belonged to them" (Schopen 2004, 245-6).

do to maintain the monastic institution, we can imagine that life within it may not have provided an environment conducive to meditation for those who sought it.* Gregory Schopen, Professor of Buddhist Studies at the University of California, describes early monastic life as one in which

> ...normal monks lived in monasteries and had free access to and use of monastic property and objects of worship; they lived communally and could interact with the laity. The norm here, the ideal, is not of ascetic practice but of sedentary, socially engaged, permanently housed monasticism.[70]

While not all ascetics would have chosen to live a reclusive life in the forests, some apparently did, and Williams and others have speculated that the early development of the Mahāyāna may have originated from this very loosely organized group of monastic "renegades."[71] Renegades they may have been, but the path they chose was not without precedent in the scriptures of the time. The *Ugrapariprcchā Sūtra* goes to great length to explain the advantages of living as a forest hermit as a means to gain isolation from other people in order to focus on meditation. Although this was probably not entirely literal—historians think monastic life could have provided opportunities for isolation also—it may have helped establish a precedent for the importance of isolation.

The speculation that proto-Mahāyāna began with these "forest dwellers" comes in part from the *Sarvadharmāpravrttinirdeśa Sūtra*, in which great accolades are bestowed upon forest dwellers who love meditation, and scorn is derisively bestowed upon all others, criticizing them for merely "pretending" to be followers of the Mahāyāna.†[72]

---

* This is made especially apparent in Buddhaghosa's *Visuddhimagga* (Buddhaghosa 2010).

† Williams speculates that the intent of the forest hermits was to return to what they considered the original objective of the Buddha's teaching, which included a great deal of devotion to meditation and detachment from property, social interactions, etc., something the monastics were accused of neglecting by the Mahāsaṅghika. Schopen speculates that the first Mahāyāna sutras may have originally been writings from these forest hermits in the form of pamphlets espousing their views, and that it was not until later that they were put into the form of sutras (2009, 38).

But in the eyes of the Mahāyānists, what justified the creation of a whole new canon of sutras which would depart (sometimes radically) from the Nikāya canon? The *Pratyutpanna Sūtra* provided an answer by arguing that, through visualization meditations, a devotee could visit the *Buddha Fields* ("Pure Lands"), where they would have direct access to the wisdom (Dharma) of the Buddha. In this way, the meditator can listen to Bodhisattvas preaching the Doctrine and

> ... retain, master, and preserve those dharmas after hearing them expounded. They honor, revere, venerate and worship that Lord ... Amitāyus. And on emerging from that samādhi [meditative absorption] the bodhisattvas also expound at length to others those dharmas, just as they have heard, retained and mastered them.[73]

In other words, sutras could now be written based on *direct revelation* through the practice of meditation.* This further solidified the Mahāyāna as being predominantly focused on meditation; moreover, devotees were encouraged to read the sutras from the viewpoint of *being* in meditation. Sutras such as the *Sukhāvatīvyūha* and *Akṣobhyavyūha* give instructions for attaining such absorptive states through visualization techniques, some of which will be described in Part Two.

I would again like to emphasize at this point the importance that visual imagery played in the early development of the Mahāyāna tradition. Not only was it acknowledged as an important aspect of practice, *but from it grew the Mahāyāna itself.* The *Āryasvapnanirdeśa Sūtra* is devoted entirely to dreams/visions and their interpretations, listing 108 dream signs†, and explicitly states that one can acquire the inspiration

---

* Some sutras written using this justification, however, were not based on visionary experience but instead on the desire to establish an inarguable theological point of view. One view espoused in such a sutra was self-immolation as a vehicle for achieving Buddhahood (Williams 2009, 346, note 36). Later dismissed as a forgery, burning oneself, nonetheless, is still a symbolic Buddhist practice of renunciation in China. Many monks and nuns participate in ceremonies in which small cones of incense are placed on the forehead or forearm. Once lit, they burn themselves out on the skin to leave lasting scars symbolic of their renunciation of worldly affairs.

† The number 108 is considered sacred in Buddhism, Jainism, and Hinduism and occurs in many contexts. This number may have been known to early Indian civilization as the number of sun-diameters between the sun and the Earth, as well as the number of moon-

(*pratibhāna*) to produce sutras through visions. The content of sutras, which was spawned from visionary meditative states, did not necessarily diverge from the teachings of the Buddha as reflected in the Nikāya literature; rather, the new Mahāyāna literature generally elaborated on them based on insights into pre-existing themes. Paul Harrison, author of "Mediums and messages: Reflections on the production of Mahayana sutras," suggests, as well, that the advent of writing further inspired these literary works:

> What I am suggesting here, then, is a convergence of meditation and textual transmission in the forest environment, stimulated into a new burst of creativity as a result of a technological development, the advent of writing. Here the specific circumstances of the real world combine with visions in deep states of meditation or dream to transform received oral tradition into a new kind of Buddhism. The resulting revelations are not completely novel, but deeply conditioned by context and by tradition. Although dismissed as poetic fabrications ... or even demonically inspired nonsense by their opponents ... they are in fact creative recasting of material already accepted as authentic buddhavacana ['words of the Buddha'] by the wider community.[74]

The legitimacy of this approach for sutra-writing, Williams argues, is firmly established not only in the Mahāyāna canon (see the *Śikṣāsamuccaya Sūtra*), but also in the Pāli canon (see the *Uttaravipatti Sutta*), the *Vinaya* (see the *Cullavagga*), and the *Aṅguttara Nikāya*.[75,76] It was the Mahāyānists, though, who fully embraced it because it aligned with the imperative to express the Dharma in different ways in accordance with the principle of upāya. Williams writes:

---

diameters between the Earth and the moon. From this knowledge, India may have been the first civilization to arrive at a value for π, which they could have known to three decimal places (Kak 1993, 135). For math enthusiasts, 108 has other interesting properties as well: it's the *hyperfactorial* of 3, an *abundant number*, a *semiperfect number*, and a *tetranacci number*; it's *refactorable*, and both a *Harshad* number and *self-number* in base 10. It's related to the *golden ratio*, an irrational number that can be computed by $2\sin(108°/2)$; Adolf Zeising describes the golden ratio as representing a universal law, as it is found ubiquitously in nature (Zeising 1854). Physicists have also identified it at the quantum level of matter (Helmholtz Association 2010).

The Mahāyāna took up the Buddha's assertion that the Dharma should guide his followers after his death, and stressed that the Lord had described the Dharma as whatever leads to enlightenment, that is, whatever is spiritually helpful. What is spiritually helpful will vary considerably, depending on person, time and place. As time, place, and person change, so some sort of innovation becomes inevitable.[77]

Such a situation, where the scriptural backbone of a religion is acknowledged to be—*and desired to be*—fluid, is practically unheard of in other religions. The consequences of such a position enabled Buddhism to easily adapt to other cultures and evolve in quite unexpected and diverse ways wherever it went.

China was the only country to continue to develop Mahāyāna Buddhism in the sutra tradition initiated by the Indian Madhyamaka, creating new sutras to reinforce particular aspects of developing Buddhist thought and practice. To the Nikāya purists, however, they were apocryphal, and this furthered the rift between the two schools. The Chinese, however, believed in the fluid nature of reality—the dharmakāya—and this was reflected in the way they adopted Buddhism. For the religion to live, they believed people needed to be able to understand it, relate to it, and use it, and that, in turn, required dynamic invention and creative expression.

THE END OF BUDDHISM IN INDIA?

Hinduism and Buddhism coexisted easily in India during their first few centuries together. This isn't surprising, considering that both evolved from the same spiritual traditions preserved in Vedic culture. But as rulers came and went, Buddhism found itself in or out of favor with the state. It prospered most under Ashoka, but thereafter, Hindus fought against Buddhism, which pushed it into isolation in monasteries and universities. The Hindu caste system, which came to define social and religious structures, furthered adversarial relationships with Buddhism.

Śaṅkara, one of the formative proponents and developers of Classical Hinduism, was also one of the loudest voices condemning Buddhism. Ironically, however, in the eighth century Śaṅkara founded a sect of Hinduism called *Advaita Vedānta* (non-dualist *Vedānta*) which shared much in common with Nāgārjuna's *Vijñānavāda*. In fact, some scholars discern so little difference between Advaita Vedānta and Vijñānavāda that they suggest Buddhism lives on in India in the form of Advaita Vedānta Hinduism. Reat comments:

> The only important philosophical difference between Śaṅkara and Nagarjuna is that for Śaṅkara ultimate reality (*Brahman* or *ātman*) is the source of the self and the universe, whereas for Nāgārjuna ultimate reality is the emptiness (*Śūnyatā*) of all things and the self. Given that both thinkers reject the validity of verbal and conceptual formulations of the nature of ultimate reality, it is difficult if not impossible to distinguish meaningfully between Śaṅkara's ultimate "something" and Nāgārjuna's ultimate "nothing," especially since both thinkers would reject the labels "something" or "nothing" as being far too crude to characterize accurately the ultimate real.[78]

By the end of the first millennium CE, after Muslim invaders had further decimated Buddhist influences, Buddhism was relegated to little more than a footnote in Indian history.* Nonetheless, Buddhism had long-lasting influence, shaping the direction of Hinduism and Indian life in general. While the religion was declining in India, other countries began developing their own styles of Buddhism. It was, however, the small country of Kashmir, bordering northern India and Pakistan, that would become the incubator and protector of Indian-style Buddhism, allowing it to eventually find its way into Tibet.†

---

* Islam was, by its nature, not prone to spread as other religions were. The Qur'an encouraged Muslims to spread the rule of Islam, but not the faith: "Arab Muslims had strong reasons not to want non-Arabs to join the faith... The problem was that a non-Arab, even after converting to Islam, had no tribal affiliation which could provide him an identity within Arab society..." (The American Forum of Global Education 2000, 279).

† Buddhism lost its influence in Kashmir in the 14th century when the Rinchan Shah took power and converted to Islam. He was eventually killed by the Kashmiris, but not before Buddhism had gone underground. Most vestiges of Buddhism had disappeared from

2

Sri Lanka

Buddha, the blessed wanderer through the world, when he perceived the anger of the Serpent kings, (and saw) that the island was being destroyed, thought, in order to prevent this, many kind thoughts, for the sake of the highest bliss of (men) and gods. (He thus reflected:) "If I do not go (to Lanka), the Serpents will not become happy; the island will be destroyed, and there will be no welfare in future time. Out of compassion for the Nagas, for the sake of happiness (of men) I shall go there; may the happiness of the island prosper.

– Excerpt from the *Dīpavaṃsa**

BUDDHISM WAS ONLY ONE of many religious movements during its early formation in India, and far from the most popular. It wasn't until Ashoka's reign around 200 BCE that Buddhism first came to flourish. During this time, there were many different independent interpretations of Buddhism (as there still are today), so what

---

Kashmir entirely by the end of the 15th century (Reat 1994, 81). It was replaced, in large part, by what would become known as *Kashmir Shaivism*, a Hindu sect of *Tantric Shaiva*.

* The *Dīpavaṃsa* ("Island Chronicle") is a Pali text written by author(s) unknown. The work is the earliest extant text from Sri Lanka and chronicles the history of the island from ancient times to the reign of Mahasena (277-304 CE), including the Buddha's legendary visit there. This excerpt is from H. Oldenberg's book, 1879.

Ashoka's missionaries spread depended upon their personal beliefs and interpretations of doctrines as well as the "school" with which they identified. Ashoka's missionaries may have introduced the *Sthaviravada school* (one of many that no longer exists) to Tibet during this time, and Theravāda to Sri Lanka. It was in Sri Lanka that the first systematized and formalized version of Theravāda Buddhism was written down to become what is popularly known today as the Pāli canon.*

Over the next few hundred years, Sri Lanka would embrace both Theravāda and Mahāyāna (Mahīśāsaka) sects. The Mahāyāna, however, was a minority group and eventually became absorbed into the Theravāda branch.[79]

Owing in large part to the natural isolation accorded an island country, the admixture of Theravāda with Mahāyāna created a distinct expression of Buddhism in Sri Lanka. An abundance of *Mahāyāna Nātha* (*Avalokiteśvara*) statuary and practices common to the Mahāyāna, such as recitation of certain mantras and specific use of prayer beads, created a unique synthesis that was neither entirely Theravāda nor Mahāyāna, but distinctly Sri Lankan.†

When Buddhism was introduced to Sri Lanka, it was thrown into a preexisting melting pot of religious ideologies, including Brahmanism, Jainism, and Ājīvakism, with no particular one dominating. In an environment of acceptance, diverse forms of religious expressions were common, and many became integrated into the mélange. Some people performed sacrificial rites similar to those practiced in the Vedic tradition known to India, while others participated in a variety of flourishing aboriginal cults known for worshiping various types of spirits (including trees). All these practices would, to varying degrees, become absorbed into Sri Lankan Buddhism. Spirit worship remains an integral aspect of popular Buddhism in Sri Lanka today.

---

  * The canon drew largely from previously recorded Sinhalese texts (the native language of Sri Lanka) written by Buddhaghosa around the 5th century CE (Reat 1994, 89).

  † While Sri Lanka is considered an entirely Theravāda Buddhist country by most people today, its religious practice is distinct from Theravāda expressions in surrounding countries.

Two practices unique to Sri Lankan Buddhism with roots in its ancient past are the *Bali* and *Tovil* ceremonies. The Bali ceremony invokes the presiding deities of the planets (*graha*) and placates them to protect people from their evil influences, while the Tovil ("devil-dancing") ceremony, Kariyawasam writes,

> ...is essentially a demonic ritual mainly exorcistic in character, and hence a healing ceremony. In its exorcist form it is meant to curb and drive away any one or several of the innumerable hosts of malevolent spirits, known as yakkhas, who are capable of bringing about pathological states of body and mind. Petas or departed spirits of the malevolent type, referred to as mala-yakku (mala means dead) or mala-peta, are also brought under the exorcist power of tovil.[80]

Over the centuries, Buddhism went cyclically in and out of favor with the government and, at times, underwent extreme repression. Sri-Lankan-style Theravāda Buddhism was ultimately saved by Burma, which received a copy of the *Pāli canon* and not only preserved this unique style of Buddhism, but became a geographical transfer point for it to reach other countries, most notably Cambodia, Laos, and Thailand.*

Buddhism continues to be the dominant religion in Sri Lanka, with approximately 70% of the population identifying as Buddhists according to its 2011 census. Sadly, although Muslims account for under 10% of the population, Buddhist nationalism in the country is on the rise, with Buddhists—principally those following strict Theravāda traditions—launching violent attacks against Muslims to force them to leave the country, fearing that they may otherwise take over and eradicate Buddhism, according to Hannah Beech, Southeast Asia Bureau Chief for the *New York Times*.[81]

---

*In 1989, the military arm of the Burmese government renamed the country Myanmar following a massive military campaign against its population, during which hundreds of monks, students, and school children were killed. A strongly Buddhist country (nearly 90% of the population is Buddhist), the Myanmar military continues aggressive campaigns against its minority populations, especially the Muslim Rohingya.

3

Tibet

When the bright radiances of the Five Wisdoms shine upon me now, Let it come that I, neither awed nor terrified, may recognize them to be of myself;

When the apparitions of the Peaceful and Wrathful forms are dawning upon me here, Let it come that I, obtaining the assurance of fearlessness, may recognize the Bardo.

– from the *Tibetan Book of the Dead (Bardo Thodol)*

By the time Buddhism reached the remote Tibetan plateau during the beginning of the first millennium, it had already become firmly established in China, where it had fused with Taoism and Confucianism. During Buddhism's last stand in India, as Muslim migrants were increasingly hostile to Buddhist communities, monks fled north across the mountains for refuge in Tibet's high, cold, and largely inaccessible terrain. At somewhat over three million, Tibet's population remains small for a country its size due to significant challenges growing crops.

The pre-Buddhist religious environment in Tibet is obscure, in part due to the lack of a written language at that time.* But, as is common when a religion is introduced to a culture, the sensibilities of pre-existing customs and beliefs are not replaced with new ones but added to them. There is no way to know with clarity what these pre-Buddhist religious beliefs were, but by comparing the Buddhism that evolved in Tibet with that of its Indian neighbor, and by observing other religious groups that did not assimilate Buddhism, some aspects can be deduced.

Referred to now as Bön (བོན་), the indigenous folk religion was highly shamanistic, with magic playing a dominant role in ceremonies and beliefs. A variety of capricious and dangerous gods and daemons ruled the spiritual landscape, requiring a good deal of appeasement to win their favor, including by animal sacrifice. It was the shaman's (*gShen*†) job to enter a trance to pacify the spirits of the dead and appease these angry gods. The shaman could likewise invoke spells to cure or harm others if needed. To this day, many characteristics of this ancient shamanistic religion co-mingle with Tibetan Buddhism, Reat notes, and can be readily observed in ceremonies where, for example, human thigh bones are fashioned into horns and human skulls into bowls.

The Bön religious tradition still exists in Tibet, but any distinction from its Buddhist counterpart may seem marginal, at least to an outsider. The *Bön-po*, as its adherents are called, use a set of literature called the *gTer-ma*, or "treasure texts," which exhibit many Buddhist characteristics. An outsider observing a Bön ceremony and then a Buddhist ceremony, Reat observes, would notice little difference between the two, perhaps with the exception that Bön-po walk counterclockwise around temples and shrines while Buddhists walk clockwise. Similarly, the Buddhist swastika is reversed in orientation by the Bön-po, so that

---

* It's traditionally believed that during the second half of the first millennium the linguist Thönmi Sambhoṭa single-handedly created the Tibetan written language as it is today (Reat 1994, 224).

† Tibetan terms and names are presented here as Wylie transliterations. The Wylie system, published in 1959 by Turrell V. Wylie, was designed to accurately represent the characters of the Tibetan alphabet rather than the pronunciation. Because of its accuracy, it's widely used in academia today.

it too may travel counterclockwise. Both incorporate much magic and supernatural divination into their practices and ceremonies.

The first introduction of Buddhism to Tibet, the story goes, occurred in the middle of the seventh century when King Srong bTsan sGam-po took two princesses as wives to help secure sociopolitical alliances with neighboring countries: one came from China, the other from Nepal.* At that time, Chan Buddhism, already firmly established in China and the most popular religious presence in the country, was the preferred religion of the Chinese princess. The Nepalese princess, on the other hand, favored Indian Buddhism. Uncertainty ensued over which teachings to follow: should they adopt Chinese Chan Buddhism, which emphasized meditation and the value of spiritual awakening, or should they go with Indian Buddhism, which was believed to better emphasize morality? The matter was settled near the turn of the eighth century by a debate that was settled in favor of Indian Buddhism.†

The first Buddhist sect in Tibet, referred to as the *Nyingmapa*, borrowed heavily from the established Bön religion. Simultaneously, Bön incorporated much of Buddhism into its doctrines and practices. Tibetan Buddhism would thus become a unique convergence of seemingly disparate religious ideologies. It continues to survive to this day in all the sects that have splintered from the original.

Due to the large contingent of fleeing Buddhist monks from Northern India, a variety of Buddhisms (as well as Hinduism) were introduced to Tibet, and Tibetan Buddhism would draw from these different faiths as well. Not only were Mahāyāna and Theravāda schools represented, the traditional folk religions of northern India, along with remnants of the ancient Vedic religion which had merged with Mahāyāna Buddhism, added additional flavors to the broth. Tibetan Buddhism evolved tantric or secret ("esoteric") rituals and teachings that could

---

* Today, these wives are widely venerated as goddesses in Tibet: the wife from China is known as the White Dolma and the wife from Nepal is known as the Green Dolma. Both are considered to be manifestations of the god Tārā, the consort of Avalokiteśvara.

† This debate, the story goes, was between Śāntarakshita and his Indian disciple Kamalaśīla. While the details are not known, it was this singular event that would decisively establish Indian-style Buddhism in Tibet (Reat 1994, 225-6).

only be conveyed from teacher to disciple. Rituals included chanting magic phrases or words (*mantras*), using magical objects (such as the *vajra*), creating magical diagrams (*mandalas*), and performing ceremonial sexual intercourse. This new form of Buddhism would later be referred to as *Vajrayāna*.*

A consequence of esoteric teachings is the strong student-teacher relationship that develops. The guru, seen as an object of spiritual perfection, becomes a profound devotional idol for his disciple: for all intents and purposes, he is a deity to worship. To encourage this relationship, during Dharma talks and other training sessions and events, the guru sits on an ornately decorated platform, elevated several feet above his audience.

Like Hindus, Tibetan Buddhists believe in reincarnation of the human soul into another form—either human or other animal—after death. But Tibetans expanded on the theme. One of the most famous books of Tibetan Buddhism, the *Bardo Thodol*, commonly known as the *Tibetan Book of the Dead*, describes how to navigate the many realms of existence one encounters after physical death, a journey lasting up to forty-nine days when one is neither alive nor dead. If navigated successfully, the traveler will be able to choose a new body in which to reincarnate, a feat only the most advanced gurus are said to be able to accomplish. This practice began during the twelfth century and proved a valuable way for the *Karmapa* sect to preserve the lineage of abbots in a monastery by replacing one who had died with their found reincarnation, generally a child of only a few years born into a wealthy family with strong Buddhist connections to the temple.[82] Indoctrination during infancy ensured proper training for the abbacy that would later claim him. (The Chinese would address the same "lineage problem,"

---

* Vajrayāna is also sometimes referred to as the *Vehicle of Spells*, or the *Adamantine Vehicle*. It's commonly considered a separate school of Buddhism, alongside Mahāyāna and Theravāda; however, few Buddhist scholars consider Tantric Buddhism relevant to Buddhism because its approaches are so far removed from original Buddhist doctrines and practices. They instead believe it deserves independent consideration as something unique unto itself. Indeed, many historical and theological treatises on Buddhism fail to mention the term *Vajrayāna* at all and may only mention the term *tantra* quickly in passing.

instead, by establishing a patriarchal lineage system, something we'll explore in the next chapter.)

During the middle of the fifteenth century, the abbot of the contentious Gelugpa sect, dGe 'Dun Grub, announced that he too would reincarnate, just as the abbots of the Karmapa sect did. Unbeknownst to him, however, he would (posthumously) become the first *Dalai Lama*, and would undergo transmigrations that have continued to this day.

The honorary title *Ta-le* (now written as *Dalai*), meaning "ocean," was bequeathed to the third reincarnation of dGe 'Dun Grub by the Mongol Kublai Khan, effectively making him ruler, or *God-king*, of Tibet. This is how and why the Dalai Lama, to this day, is considered the spiritual-head of Tibet.[83] Only recently, on May 29, 2011, did the Tibetan Parliament ratify an amendment to replace the office of the Dalai Lama as head of state with a democratically elected Kalon Tripa, or prime minister. The Dalai Lama was clear, however, that he would continue to play a role in the government and continue to serve as a representative of the Tibetan people.

The story of the succession of Dalai Lamas is fascinating but beyond the scope of this book. It's worth mentioning, though, that the individuals bearing this title have ranged from a flamboyant miscreant playboy who enjoyed wine and women (the sixth Dalai Lama*), to a Nobel Peace Prize recipient (the present, fourteenth, Dalai Lama).

Tibetan Buddhism has intrigued and inspired countless people. Tibetan monks, characteristically wearing red and yellow robes, commonly use meditation to raise or lower their body temperature, speed up or slow down their pulse, and eliminate the need for sleep. While any advanced meditator can attain these abilities regardless of religious affiliation, it's possible that the isolation provided by a secretive teaching method offers an environment well-suited to learning such advanced states of meditative absorption—although the potential for abuse because of that secrecy is also quite high (Chapter 20).

---

* Since Dalai Lamas are deified, they are considered above and beyond the domain of worldly ethical and moral behavior: any behavior is considered acceptable since their actions are believed to not be within the realm of human understanding.

Tibetan Buddhism would spread into Nepal in the southern Himalayas* as well as into Bhutan and a region of Northern India now known as Sikkim. In Nepal, Buddhism merged with Hinduism to form another unique religious blend, while in Bhutan it remained nearly entirely Buddhist. Because of Tibetan Buddhism's wide dispersion throughout the region, it's now commonly referred to as Himalayan Buddhism.

Although Himalayan Buddhists today represent less than five percent of Buddhists worldwide,[84] its influence has been great, in large part due to the many books written by the exiled Dalai Lama condemning China's aggression in the region. Widespread publicity of Tibetan Buddhism has led many in the West to believe that Buddhism writ large shares the same beliefs as Tibetan Buddhism: reincarnation, guru worship, and various magical practices. Surprisingly, there are also a great many people who falsely believe that the Dalai Lama represents all Buddhists worldwide. Nothing could be farther from the truth. The diversity of religious beliefs among Buddhists around the world is enormous: no one person could ever hope to adequately speak for such a broad, amorphous, socioreligious population, despite some who desperately try.

And in China, a great many did try. The quest to identify the "true identity" of Buddhism was fierce and would lead to an entirely new perspective on Buddhist thought and practice.

It would be called Chan.

---

* Nepal is important to Buddhists around the world because it contains the birthplace of the Buddha. Before the eighteenth century, Nepal was only 200 square miles of land in the Kathmandu Valley; it wasn't until its expansion during recent times that it gained this fame.

4

China

Here, O Sâriputra, all things have the character of emptiness, they have no beginning, no end, they are faultless and not faultless, they are not imperfect and not perfect. Therefore, O Sâriputra, in this emptiness there is no form, no perception, no name, no concepts, no knowledge. No eye, ear, nose, tongue, body, mind. No form, sound, smell, taste, touch, objects.

— Excerpt from the *Heart Sūtra**

THE FIRST CONTACT BETWEEN India and China may have occurred from Buddhist missionaries or traders finding their way around the rugged Himalayas during the second and first centuries BCE. Following a circuitous and dangerous route westward through what today is Pakistan, they may have climbed over the Khyber Pass and into the area now known as Afghanistan, then back across the Pamir Mountains and eventually to the Silk Road at Kashgar, which, today, is on the far western edge of China.[85] The scarcity of records from this time, however, permit only speculation. But when Buddhism

---

* This sutra is recited daily in Chan and Zen monasteries around the world. Note the use of the catuṣkoṭi described in Chapter 1.

finally arrived in China, it was confronted with more formidable obstacles than geography: namely, Confucianism, Taoism, and xenophobia.*

During the Later Han dynasty (25-250 CE), China slowly began taking notice of Buddhism.† Over a few centuries, Buddhist concepts were interpreted using Taoist and Confucian terminology, just as the occidental world would interpret them borrowing terminology from Christianity, psychology, and sociology thousands of years later. Paul Williams has noted that *prajñā* ("wisdom") was translated as *tao* ("the Way"), *śūnyatā* ("emptiness") was translated as *wú* ("non-being"), and *nirvāṇa* was translated as *wu-wei* ("non-action").[86] Harrison observed that, in Lokakṣema's Chinese translation of the *Pratyutpanna Samādhi Sūtra*, he translated *bodhi* ("spiritual awakening") as *Dao* ("the Way"), and *tathatā* ("suchness") as *benwu* ("original nonbeing").[87]

The influence of Taoism, Confucianism, and indigenous folk religion on early Buddhism was not trivial. Together, their worldviews sculpted Buddhism in ways that made its Chinese presentation nearly unrecognizable from Mahāyāna Buddhism in other countries. In fact, if we inspect Taoism and Confucianism along with Chinese folk religion today, we observe so much overlap in terminology, ceremony, and beliefs that it's apparent they aren't truly distinct from one another. Although each claims its own set of distinguishing features, they each share many with the others. What I will attempt in this chapter is to give the reader a sense of the enduring influences the preexisting Chinese mind had on the development of Buddhism, and ultimately on Chan.

But before we get started, some clarifications may be helpful. Historical data on Buddhism in China during the first millennium is sparse. There are many beliefs popularly held by the Chinese people today that do not necessarily correspond with the few facts that have been

---

* Paul Williams notes that "[t]he Chinese tended to be intensely xenophobic, and a foreign religion, and barbarians in strange garb, could at most be curious. In addition, the Confucian Chinese found certain aspects of Buddhism, such as celibate monasticism, morally and socially repellent. Monks who renounced the world might fail to pay proper respect to their ancestors, either through appropriate rituals or through begetting sons to continue the family lineage" (2009, 130).

† The earliest extant Buddhist writing in Chinese dates to 65 CE (Jong 1979).

unearthed or deduced by archeologists, historians, and scholars, and available information is frequently contradictory. Furthermore, historical dates of events are often not available, and sources containing them are often challenged by other sources which list different dates for the same event, sometimes differing by a century or more. The historicity of who did what and who said what is also often ambiguous, if not impossible to determine. It's common for those who adulate a revered teacher to posthumously speak for him, ascribing dialogues and sayings to him that likely never happened. We encounter this often in writings attributed to Confucius and Lao Tzu, as well as the famous (real or invented) Chan masters. I don't consider this to have had a negative impact on Buddhism, for if we look beyond the words to the message, the process can be viewed as a creative means for keeping the spirit of the teachings alive, and as a natural response to the sociopolitical environment in which Buddhism was developing. We'll see that there were likely many ulterior motives involved in the creation of the early Chinese Buddhist canon. Considering all these things, parts of this chapter will not be presented using a traditional historical timeline; however, when dates are known and help tell the story, I'll offer them.

ANCESTRAL CULTS IN THE NEOLITHIC AND BRONZE AGES

David N. Keightley has been a valuable contributor to our understanding of the early Chinese mind, producing a plethora of articles and several books on the early formation of Chinese civilization in the Neolithic (c. 10,000 – 8,000 BCE) and early Bronze (c. 3300 – 1200 BCE) Ages. Particularly relevant to Chan, he has explored the origins of ancestral worship, drawing extensively from archeological and inscriptional evidence. Much of the Chinese way of thinking about the world today, Keightley asserts, can be firmly traced to the Shang dynasty, c. 1600 – 1045 BC, or earlier.[88]

During the Shang dynasty, ancestral cults were central to Chinese life, and divination practices using tortoise shells and ox scapulae became a common means for communicating with the deceased. Archeological remains of oracle bones suggest this custom likely originated in the much earlier Neolithic period. Divination would inspire the *I-Ching* or *Classic of Changes*, palm reading, tea-leaf reading, and dozens of other divination practices still common in Chinese culture today.

To help us grapple with the differences between Eastern and Western views, broadly, Keightley offers comparisons between the culture of China, which developed ancestral cults, and ancient Mesopotamia and Greece, which instead developed dramatic anecdotal mythologies. Ancestral cults, he proposes, seek to establish harmonious order and design and therefore have no need to attribute personalities to the deceased. By comparison, anecdotal mythologies of the gods in classic Greek epics commonly attribute elaborate stories to personalities that describe their lives, a mechanism that addresses the perceived chaos of existence. Since ancestral cults create an ordered universe, there is no need to address chaos, so such mythologies are not needed:

> [A]n inverse relationship exists between an emphasis on hierarchical roles of authority, whether for the living or the dead, and the vagueness with which the afterlife is conceived. The cultures that depict the afterworld, or even this one, with some attention to specific detail may not need, or may do so precisely because they do not have, a well-defined social hierarchy or ancestral cult. When the authority of the elders and ancestors functions well in this world, there is less need to depict the environs of the next. This suggestion [...] would also help explain the well-known fact that, although there are many mythic personages alluded to in ancient China, there is little evidence of a sustained, anecdotal mythology.[89]

We might imagine that ancestral worship, and the relationship between man and spirit in general, touched all aspects of life in early China. Evidence suggests that not only was man intimately connected to ancestral spirits as their progeny, but rulers were legitimized by their special relations with them.[90] Keightley argues that procuring one's place in a genealogical succession was extremely important: "the supreme obligation to one's ancestors was to become an ancestor oneself."[91] This theme was revisited recently by Alan Cole to examine the formation of early Chan. In his provocative book, *Fathering your Father, The Zen of Fabrication in Tang Buddhism*, Cole deftly explores the genesis of Chan's lineage system through the lens of ancestral cults and the Chinese mind which inhabits them, challenging many long-held assumptions.

THE ZHOU DYNASTY

Ancestral cults were integral to Chinese culture by the time the Zhou dynasty (c. 1050 – 256 BCE) arrived. The Zhou was the longest-lived dynasty in the history of China and the third dynasty in its recorded history, following the Xià (2070 – 1600 BCE), and the Shang (1600-1050 BCE).* The Zhou saw the birth of the Bronze Age, the discovery of magnetism, and the advent of astronomy, geometry, trigonometry, and acupuncture. It saw the building of the Great Wall, the invention of book-binding, and the creation of silk textiles. It famously contributed several of the oldest written works now known to humankind: the *Book of Odes* (*Shijing* 詩), the *I Ching* (*Zhōu yì* 易經) or *Classic of Changes*, the *Classic of History* (*Shujing* 書經), and the *Record of Rites* (*Liji* 禮記). As they had for millennia, the people of the Zhou practiced ancestral worship, believing that spirits of the deceased would protect them as long as they were venerated in accordance with the principle of *tian* (*tiān* 天: heaven). Their folk religion, now referred to as *Shendao* 神道 ("Way of the Gods"),† focused on a form of shamanism called *Wuism* (*Wū Jiào* 巫教). Wu masters are still revered in Chinese culture today.

---

* *Zhou* was not the clan name in this instance—which was *Jy*. Zhou may have been the name of their homeland.

† Traditional Chinese folk religion goes by a variety of names, including *Shenism* (*Shénjiào* 神教) and *Shenxianis* (*Shénxiānjiào* 神仙教: "religion of gods and immortals").

Although the Zhou dynasty endured, it did not always prosper. Its initial peaceful era was followed by feudalism (c. 770-250 BCE), a period during which China split into independent states or kingdoms, each vying for dominion. The era subsequently became known as the Warring States period. During this time, two men would appear and forever change the social, religious, and spiritual landscape of East Asia: Confucius and Lao Tzu.

Confucius & The Analects [551 - 479 BCE]

Around the time that the Buddha was reaching enlightenment in northern India, in China, Kǒng Qiū 孔丘 was developing a social framework that would transform Chinese culture. Eventually known as Confucius (also K'ung Fu-tzu, Master Kong, Kongzi, and Kǒng Qiū), he is now considered by many scholars to be a purely legendary figure in light of the numerous contradictory facts and fictions regarding him.[92]

Whether he was a real historical figure or not, writings attributed to Confucius suggest the author had extensive literary knowledge of the time, which included texts from the Zhou dynasty, and that these works shaped many of his ideas. He became a popular voice in society not only because his thoughts were in harmony with the social and political atmosphere of the time, but because they spoke of a means to help society get out of the endemic turmoil of the Warring States period. He presented a way to live life that was logical, thoughtfully conceived, and comprehensive, while also supportive of peace, social stability, and economic growth. He also preserved the quintessential values of ancestral veneration, inherited from the earlier Shang. Following his death, his thoughts would become codified by multiple generations of his disciples into the *Analects*.

I use the term "disciples" loosely, however. Although he purportedly had followers, Confucius was not a religious icon. His teachings centered principally on how to live an ethical life without religious ideologies or dogma, in order to create and preserve social harmony and order. This is not to say that Confucius did not embrace the religious notions of the time—at least according to the *Analects* themselves, in which, for example, the belief in ancestral spirits and the importance of venerating those spirits was often implied if not directly stated. Confucius' ideology was grounded principally in the physical world of here and now. He was not concerned with an afterlife or spiritual transformation, but with social order and harmony.

Confucius and his followers are credited with resurrecting several literary works from the Zhou dynasty: the *I Ching* (*Book of Changes*), the *Classic of Poetry* (*Book of Songs*), the *Book of Documents* (*Book of History*), the *Book of Rites*, and the *Spring and Summer Annals*. Although Chinese tradition considers these works to have been composed by Confucius, historical evidence suggests that he, if not his followers centuries later, likely took what writings were already extant from the earlier Zhou dynasty, expanded on them, and put them into a language that was more accessible for people of the time.[93] In any event, these works came to be identified with Confucius and revered as Confucian classics. By the time Buddhism entered the country, the ideologies of Confucius had been well absorbed into Chinese culture, and the writings attributed to him through the *Analects* were common popular knowledge.[94]

Jeffrey Riegel writes for the *Stanford Encyclopedia of Philosophy* that "Confucius' goal was to create gentlemen who carry themselves with grace, speak correctly, and demonstrate integrity in all things."[95] Confucius advanced the principles that one should:

- cultivate compassion for others *(ren)*,
- show devotion to parents and older siblings,
- practice self-restraint and discipline to cultivate altruism,
- seek to gain respect and admiration through study and the mastery of *li*—ritual formalities defined by specific social rules of conduct,
- offer sacrifices to the spirits as if they were present,

- strive to live in accordance with the natural law of heaven and the universe, Tian (Tiān), and

- recognize that a ruler who lives according to Tian has the "Mandate of Heaven," which gives him irrefutable authority to rule over all of China and to pass his reign to progeny who will inherit the Mandate, thus ensuring an enduring empire.[96]

The practice of ancestral worship and engaged filial piety (xiào 孝) would become quintessential attributes of Chinese Buddhism in all its sects, including Chan. Buddhist monasteries in China to this day include an *ancestor's hall* (cítáng 宗祠)—a separate building devoted to the veneration of ancestors. In it, "soul-tablets" of former abbots and monks are worshiped ceremonially twice a month.[97]

LAO TZU & THE TAO TE CHING

As with Confucius, little to nothing is known about Lao Tzu (Lǎozǐ 老子; lit. *the Old One;* also, Lao Tze) as a historical figure. What is available about him comes from stories, many of which were created decades or centuries after his death. According to stories recounted in the *Zhuangzi*, a text from the Warring States period (476–221 BC), it's possible that Lao Tzu and Confucius were contemporaries and knew each other. The stories about who Lao Tzu really was, however, are so vastly different from one another that there's no way to know anything at all about him with any confidence, nor about what he actually wrote. For example, Jeaneane Fowler, author of *An Introduction to the Philosophy and Religion of Taoism*, notes that one ancient account has him a contemporary of Confucius with the surname Li and personal name Er or Dan, and as an official working in the Imperial Archives who wrote a book in two parts; another has him as a different contemporary of Confucius with the name Lao Laizi who wrote a book in fifteen parts; and yet another has him as a court astrologer, Lao Dan, who lived in the 4th century BCE.[98]

Regardless, the work he is most famously credited for is the *Tao Te Ching* (*Dàodé Jīng* 道德經).* While Confucius provided a solid ethical guide with the *Analects*, the *Tao Te Ching* provided a rich spiritual and philosophical framework that would evolve through an interplay with Buddhism to become Taoism, and subsequently influence Buddhism in many ways. Whether it was composed (or compiled) by Lao Tzu is only of academic interest. If the value of a written work is measured by its ability to improve lives and societies, the *Tao Te Ching* did not fall short of the highest achievements.

The title of Lao Tzu's work—the *Tao* (the Way), *Te* (Virtue), *Ching* (Great Book)—is ambiguous. As we read, we learn that this "Way" is the natural primordial flow of the universe and all it encompasses: something that eludes the senses and the mind but can be touched directly by emptying ourselves and living according to its principles. The "Great Book" examines the nature of this "Way" and gives instructions on how to live in accordance with it to achieve wholeness.† The text of the *Tao Te Ching* is extraordinarily terse, which has led to a variety of translations over the centuries.

In poetic form, the *Tao Te Ching* addresses the nature of a mind that has succeeded in stepping outside of the personal ego-self and has merged with the Absolute. A few selections from John Stubbs' translation offer the flavor of the work:

The wise avoid judgement
And teach without words.
They accept all things as they are,
Is it not paradox?
Only by letting selfishness go
May the self be found.

---

* An archeological find in 1993 near the town of Guodian in Wingmen, Hubei uncovered the oldest extant version of the *Tao Te Ching* known to date. It was dated to 300 BCE (Chan 2013).

† It may be worth noting that the literary technique invoked here, in which a work self-references itself as "great," would appear again centuries later in the developing Mahāyāna canon; notably, in the Indian *Pratyutpanna Samādhi Sūtra* and the Chinese *Heart Sūtra*.

...
Bring things forth and help them grow.
Produce but do not possess.
Act without anxiety for results.
Lead but do not manipulate.
Such is the subtle nature of the Way.
...
Passionate pursuits lead to madness.
Desire for rare goods is a distraction.
The wise, therefore,
Focus on their inner state and not externals.
They cleave to the one and let the other go.[99]

The inspirational *Tao Te Ching* led to a socioreligious movement in 142 CE, when Zhang Daoling (Zhāng Dàolíng 張陵) wrapped religious garb around the text to create the *Way of the Celestial Masters* (*Tiān Shī Dào* 天師道). Also known as the *Way of the Five Pecks* (grains) *of Rice*—because that's what people had to pay to join—it became the first expression of religious Taoism. The theme of Zhang Daoling's teaching, however, was longevity and immortality and how to get it.*

Taoist mystics, on the other hand, interpreted immortality differently, describing it as an awakening into egoless existence. Death of the body was irrelevant. The origins of mystical Taoism, or *Neidan* (*nèidān shù* 內丹術), date to the second century, with the publication of the *Cantong qi* by Wei Boyang. Neidan, also known as the *Way of the Golden Elixir* (*jindan zhi dao*), was firmly established as a mystical Taoist tradition during the Tang dynasty.

Mystical Taoism imagines the human body as a vessel through which transformation occurs when proper meditation techniques are applied. the *Neijing tu* (*Nèijīng tú* 內經圖), shown in Figure 3, and the

---

* Reat describes the Chinese appetite for immortality at the time: "By the time of the introduction of Buddhism to China, the Daoist ideal of immortality had degenerated into the practice of a sort of dietary alchemy designed to stave off physical death. This practice is very likely responsible for the remarkable variety of Chinese cuisine, which in its traditional form offers such delicacies as monkey brains, turtle eggs, and shark fin soup" (1994, 136-7).

Xiuzhen Tu (*Xiūzhēn tú* 修真圖), also known as the *Chart for the Cultivation of Reality*, depicted several important mystical experiences, including *divine union* (*taijitu* 太極圖)—the integration of male and female elements of the psyche. The close affinity between Chan and Taoism is clearly identified in the Neijing tu with the depiction (and accompanying annotations) of Lao Tze and Bodhidharma in the head, above and below the eyes, respectively.

As Taoism mixed with Buddhism, new sects developed and prospered throughout China, bringing with them new art, poetry, and alchemical practices.* Along the way, a story expressing the inextricable closeness between Taoism and Buddhism emerged: one day Lao Tzu mounted an ox and rode out of China to India, where he eventually became known as the Buddha.

CHUANG CHOU & THE CHUANG TZU

Other seminal writings on Taoist thought come from a collection of texts known as the *Chuang Tzu* (or the *Zhuang Zi*). Again, authorship is ambiguous due to conflicting accounts and hagiographies surrounding the work and its creator, but it's popularly considered to be authored by a man named Chuang Chou (Zhuang Zhou/Chuangtse), c. 200 BCE. The version extant today comes to us via Kuo Hsiang of the third century CE,[100] who compiled and edited it and added his own commentary.[101]

A central theme throughout the *Chuang Tzu* is "going along with the way things are":

> Words are like wind and waves; actions are a matter of gain and loss. Wind and waves are easily moved; questions of gain and loss easily lead to danger. Hence anger arises from no other cause than clever

---

* I use the term *alchemy* here as it pertains to the esoteric spiritual/mystical domain from which the term originates. In ancient India, it provided a means for the creation of a divine body (*divya-deham*) and immortality in one's life (*jīvan-mukti*). In China, alchemy provided a means for giving birth to an *immortal fetus*. For more on Chinese alchemy, see *The Secret of the Golden Flower* by Richard Wilhelm, 1962, Harcourt Brace & Company.

FIGURE 3. THE NÈIJĪNG TÚ.

"Chart of the Inner Passageways."

The Nèijīng tú depicts the spiritual journey from the conjoined Taoist/Buddhist perspective. We can see Lao Tse as an old man seated toward the top of the head, with Bodhidharma seated under him, arms raised to the heavens. The ox-herder and spinning maiden appear prominently in the lower half.

Of note also, toward the middle of the drawing we see the spinning maiden directly beneath the ox-herder who is grasping the Little Dipper (described in the text as the ox-herder constellation), containing the star Polaris, about which the universe revolves; a clear reference to the Nüwa/Fuxi myth depicting *divine union*, to be discussed in Chapter 17.

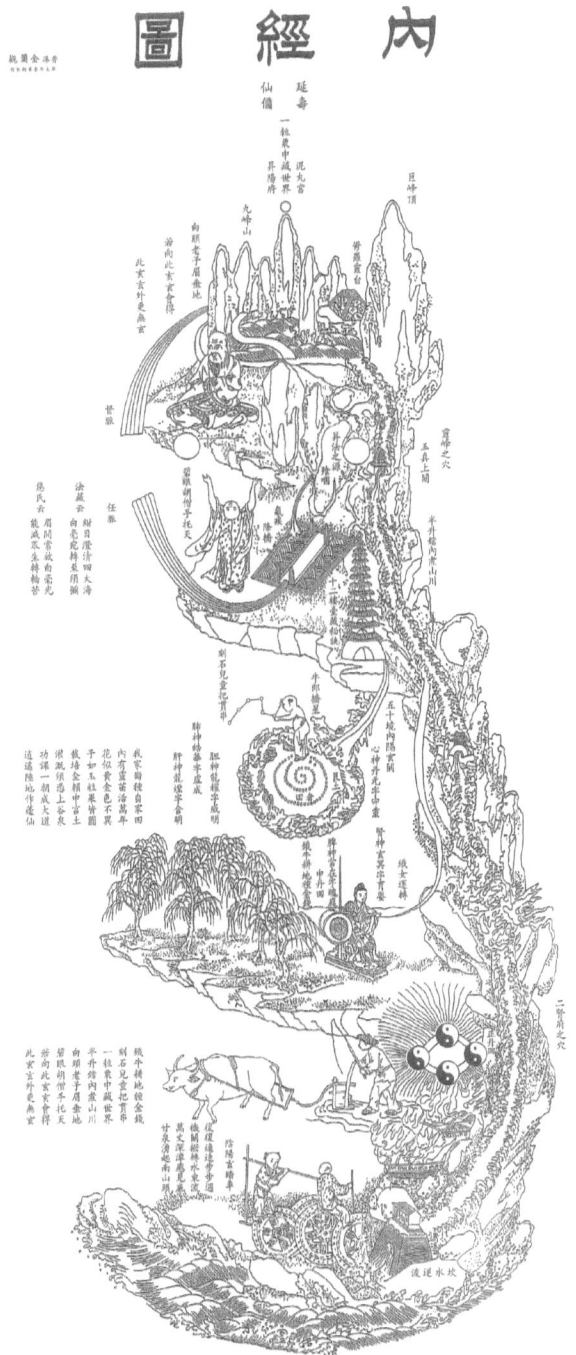

words and one-sided speeches. ... Just go along with things and let your mind move freely. Resign yourself to what cannot be avoided and nourish what is within you—this is best. What more do you have to do to fulfill your mission?[102]

Do not be an embodier of fame; do not be a storehouse of schemes; do not be an undertaker of projects; do not be a proprietor of wisdom. Embody to the fullest what has no end and wander where there is no trail. Hold on to all that you have received from Heaven but do not think you have gotten anything. Be empty, that is all. The Perfect Man uses his mind like a mirror—going after nothing, welcoming nothing, responding but not storing. Therefore, he can win out over things and not hurt himself.[103]

The concept of *wu-wei* (*wú-wéi* 無爲)—of "non-acting"—would arise many times in Chan literature. Wu-wei directs us to not act according to how we desire things to be, but rather to act according to the way things are.

Much of the *Chuang Tzu* uses short parables contextually relevant to the Eastern Zhou period in which they were written. The author's choice of subjects, which can be not only sages like Confucius or Lao Tzu but also fictitious people and even insects, often give a lighthearted touch to serious subjects. Amusing non sequiturs also help break the reader out of conditioned ways of seeing things, a technique that foreshadowed Chan's *gong-an* (*gōng'àn*; Jap., *Kōan*) tradition that would arrive nearly a millennium later. Hui Tzu, who appears often in the *Chuang Tzu*, plays the sometimes amusing role of someone who tries desperately, yet futilely, to understand spiritual concepts. The following excerpt expresses the lightheartedness of the work as well as the seriousness of the subject:

Hui Tzu said to Chuang Tzu, "Can a man really be without feelings?"

Chuang Tzu: "Yes."

Hui Tzu: "But a man who has no feelings—how can you call him a man?"

Chuang Tzu: "The Way gave him a face; Heaven gave him a form—why can't you call him a man?"

Hui Tzu: "But if you've already called him a man, how can he be without feelings?"

Chuang Tzu: "That's not what I mean by feelings. When I talk about having no feelings, I mean that a man doesn't allow likes or dislikes to get in and do him harm. He just lets things be the way they are and doesn't try to help life along."

Hui Tzu: "If he doesn't try to help life along, then how can he keep himself alive?"

Chuang Tzu: "The Way gave him a face; Heaven gave him form. He doesn't let likes and dislikes get in and do him harm. You wear out your energy, leaning on a tree and moaning, slumping at your desk and dozing—Heaven picked out a body for you and you use it to gibber about 'hard' and 'white'!"[104]

Macabre humor in the following excerpt may have reflected the mood of the times, considering the context of the Warring States period:

> The emperor of the South Sea was called Shu [Brief], the emperor of the North Sea was called Hu [Sudden], and the emperor of the central region was called Hun-tun [Chaos]. Shu and Hu from time to time came together for a meeting in the territory of Hun-tun, and Hun-tun treated them very generously. Shu and Hu discussed how they could repay his kindness. "All men," they said, "have seven openings so they can see, hear, eat and breathe. But Hun-tun alone doesn't have any. Let's try boring him some!"
>
> Every day they bored another hole, and on the seventh day Hun-tun died.[105]

From their literary styles, Lin Yutang compares the personalities of Laotse and Chuangtse to Walt Whitman and Henry David Thoreau:

> The fundamental basis of thinking and the character of ideas of the two philosophers were the same. But while Laotse spoke in apho-

rism, Chuangtse wrote long, discursive philosophical essays. While Laotse was all intuition, Chuangtse was all intellect. Laotse smiled; Chuangtse laughed. Laotse taught: Chuangtse scoffed. Laotse spoke to the heart; Chuangtse spoke to the mind. Laotse was like Whitman, with the large and generous humanity of Whitman, Chuangtse was like Thoreau, with the ruggedness and hardness and impatience of an individualist.[106]

Laotse and Chuangtse reveal elements of Chinese thinking that would eventually characterize Buddhism: the openness to diverse modes of personal expression, the extensive use of metaphor, and the literary form of dialogue between a knower and a seeker to convey spiritual and mystical concepts.

Buddhism's first 500 years in China

Buddhism may have arrived in China as early as the second century BCE, around the time that Ashoka is thought to have sent Buddhist missionaries to surrounding countries, and around the time that trade routes were being established between India and other parts of the world. By the middle of the first century CE, Buddhism was well-known in China and receiving accolades from the second Han Emperor, Ming.[107]

With the fall of the Han dynasty in 220 CE, came the rise of the Three Kingdoms period and sixty years of social upheaval and warfare, a period that would mark a critical turning point for Chinese Buddhism.* After sixty years of widespread war and significant population reduction, China was weak and susceptible to foreign invasion from the north. That invasion came in the form of a large and powerful tribal group of Eurasian nomads, known as the Xiong Nu (Hsiung Nu). They took control of China's northern regions after capturing and executing its two reigning emperors. Intelligentsia and gentry in the north

---

* The country during this time was separated into three states: the Wei 魏 in the north, Shu 蜀 in the southwest, and Wu 吳 in the southeast.

fled south in exile where the Xiong Nu had little power, initiating what would become an effective bifurcation of China.*

The ensuing sociopolitical separation between northern and southern China would have long-lasting repercussions for Buddhism, especially Chan. Devotional Buddhism would become widely popular in the north and controlled by the state, while in the south, where northern rulers had little influence, Buddhism would enjoy relative autonomy and freedom in an environment conducive to creative expression—a hallmark of the Mahayana from its earliest origins. Under the rule of weak ethnic dynasties, Buddhism in the south developed predominantly under the influence of the exiled intelligentsia who favored meditation disciplines and ontological discussions to devotional worship.[108] Eventually, ideological differences between Buddhist representatives in the north and and those in the south would lead to conflicts that split Chan into "northern" and "southern" versions, each with its own character, beliefs, and practices.

The northern school, which identified the emperor with the Buddha, would be primarily responsible for spreading Buddhism to Korea and Japan, while its more isolated southern counterpart would effectively become a state within a state, its adherents occupying their time with contemplation and meditation, and working to integrate Taoist principles into Buddhist training and practice.[109] Reat comments on the significance of this on the development of Buddhism in the south:

> In either circle, Daoist philosophy, resigned to the inevitable succession of yin and yang in the Way of nature, was better suited to the needs of a people in humiliating exile than was the dynamic, optimistic political philosophy of Confucianism. Increasingly, the aristocrats and contemplatives in southern China turned to the Daoist ideal of wu-wei, non-action, and from it extrapolated the theory that

---

* Chinese Intelligentsia refers generally to the intellectual class which Shu-Ching Lee describes as comprised of three different groups: "The first was the *shih ta-fu*, who were Confucian scholars and civil administrators before the establishment of the civil examination system. The second were the literati, who elevated themselves through the various examinations. The third group contained those who graduated from modern colleges and universities in China and in foreign lands" (S.-C. Lee 1947).

all reality is grounded in the single metaphysical principle of wu, or non-being. The Buddhist doctrine of Sunyata (emptiness) is of course remarkably similar to this "neo-Daoist" position and is at least partly responsible for its development.[110]

While Buddhist principles were being integrated with Taoist concepts in the south, Buddhism in the north developed in different directions. The complexity of a "barbarian" people ruling over the ethnic Chinese population, many of whom were now Buddhists, presented the rulers with opportunities to gain control of the population. The imperial court devised a grand scheme to legitimize their rule and collect taxes from its newly conquered population by declaring Buddhism the official religion of China. It subsequently erected large, lavish monasteries to entice Buddhists to congregate, emphasized devotional Buddhism, which was more accessible to the average person, and proclaimed the reigning emperor a living incarnation of the Buddha. It was a successful tactic that would be copied by the governments of Korea and Japan, as they both would receive Buddhism from northern China, inheriting its state-sponsored model.

In time, however, the system imploded on itself. While Buddhists in the south were experiencing a renaissance of sorts, enjoying freedom of spiritual exploration, northern Buddhists experienced religious oppression from state politicization. Because Buddhist temples were government property, they effectively became "...large feudal estates, administering large tracts of land and large pools of labor."[111] With land came wealth, and with wealth came power, and the rulers did not want to share; violent suppression of Buddhism was their eventual response.

As the appetite for Buddhism was growing in both the north and the south, albeit in different ways, so too was the appetite for Indian literature. Indian missionaries were welcomed, and as they came, they brought new canonical texts that further expanded the growing tapestry of Buddhist knowledge. As the canon expanded, monks branched off into new areas, advocating those texts they believed best represented the Buddha Dharma. Proselytizers who drew the most enthusiasm from the population became the de facto founders of new sects. Three of the most influential early advocates of Buddhism were Fotudeng, Fa Xian, and Zhi Yi.

Fotudeng and Pranayama (the Ānāpānasmṛti Sūtra)

Buddhacinga arrived in China from Kucha in Central Asia in 310 CE and became renowned for teaching meditation through breathing practices, or *pranayama*. Popularly known as Fotudeng (Fótúdéng 佛圖澄), his teachings would eventually become integrated into Chan training. Fotudeng used the *Ānāpānasmṛti Sūtra* as his principal guide, which teaches meditation through attentiveness to bodily phenomena. According to Bhikkhu Anālayo, the *Ānāpānasmṛti Sūtra* is the most widely utilized sutra across all Buddhist traditions to this day.[112]

The term *Ānāpānasmṛti* is often translated as *mindfulness* in English, but this can be confusing, as "mindfulness" is more popularly understood as referring to the application of nondirected attention (Chapter 10). *Ānāpānasmṛti* may be better interpreted here as meaning *immediacy of the experience of conscious awareness through observation and contemplation*.

The *Ānāpānasmṛti Sūtra* describes directed concentration and contemplation techniques that build upon one another in such a way as to eventually lead to meditation (*samādhi*). It progresses the devotee from the first stage—becoming conscious of the breath—to stages requiring successively more demanding contemplations. The final stage is characterized by complete detachment from all mental states.

Fotudeng also taught the still popular method of breath-counting, among others, as a precursor to the more advanced contemplative practices described in the *Ānāpānasmṛti Sūtra*.

Fa Xian, Zhi Yi, and Devotionalism (the Lotus Sūtra)

Another influential monk, Fa Xian (Fǎxiǎn 法顯), took an arduous journey to India in 399 CE to collect more Buddhist literature. Following his journey, he translated his large collection of new texts, beginning a new tradition of translation that later generations of monks would perform as religious practice. One of the most significant contributors to the growing Chinese Buddhist canon during this time was Kumārajīva (344-413), who built a translating team of hundreds.

By the mid-fifth century, Buddhist institutions in the north had become wealthy and powerful under state sponsorship. Fearful of government overthrow, Emperor Wu began a campaign to demolish Buddhism in the region. He instituted policies of Buddhist suppression, killing monks and destroying temples, sutras, and artworks: a phenomenon that would repeat itself throughout Buddhism's long history in China, Korea, and Japan. Buddhism would not experience significant revival until Emperor Wen (581-604 CE) came to power. Under Wen, China not only became whole again, but Buddhism was nurtured back to health, thanks largely to the efforts of an eminent monk from the south, Zhi Yi (Zhì Yǐ 智顗).

When Zhi Yi appeared on the scene, Buddhism was in a state of confusion. Texts were arriving from India in vast quantities, expounding every imaginable Buddhist view. Not only did each sutra have something unique to say, but also entirely different Buddhist schools were represented: some Nikāya, some Mahāyāna, some devotional, some philosophical, some written recently, and others written much closer to the time of the Buddha. Imported Buddhism had become a mishmash of religious ideologies and spiritual practices, and Zhi Yi decided to devote his life to the formidable challenge of organizing it all.

Zhi Yi, however, was a devotionalist at heart, and his favorite sutra was the *Lotus Sūtra* which, to him, best expressed the essence of devotional Buddhism. This approach to Buddhism was also in harmony with emperor worship, which resulted in a strong, popularist Buddhism, accessible to the masses and controllable by the state. This in turn strengthened the governing power of emperor Wen. Zhi Yi's teachings would be codified into the first highly formulated expression of Buddhism in the country: *Tian Tai* (*Tiāntái zōng* 天台宗), named after the mountains where Zhi Yi lived.

Emperor Wen died in 604 at the hands of his son, Yang Di. Fourteen years later, he, too, was murdered, making way for the Tang dynasty (618-907 CE).

Following Zhi Yi's organization of Buddhist doctrines came a new approach to Buddhism, one based on specific texts—mostly sutras—which appealed to specific monks. Unlike Indian Buddhist schools at this time, which propounded radically different doctrines, the Chinese schools were not differentiated as much by doctrine as by favored texts from the growing canon. The exception, and challenge, was that there were two fundamentally different Indian schools of thought that vied for popular favor: Nikāya and Mahāyāna.

EARLY NIKĀYA SCHOOLS IN CHINA

Nikāya Buddhism expressed itself in the *Lü*, or *Vinaya* school, and the *Ju She* (*Chü She*) school. The Lü school, started by Dao Xuan (Dàoxuān 道宣, 596-667 CE), emphasized strict adherence to the Vinaya Tripitaka rules of monastic propriety. As a separate school, it failed to gain much support and died out quickly. Before it disappeared in China, however, it made its way to Japan via Jianzhen (Jap., *Ganjin*).* The Lü school did, however, strongly influence monasticism in all successive Buddhist schools in China. Strict enforcement of the rules of discipline remains a ubiquitous feature of Chinese monasticism today.

The Ju She school based itself on the *Abhidharmakośakārikā*, translated by Paramārtha (563-67 CE). It, too, was short-lived, but its teachings and perspectives would be preserved in the Mahāyāna *Wei Shi* school.[113]

---

* In Japan it became the *Risshū* school, one of the six early *Nara* schools (Chapter 7).

Early Mahāyāna schools in China [c. 500 - 600]

The San Lun (Mādhyamaka) school

As Buddhism was beginning to enter China, a rift widened between Theravādists and Mahāyānists over doctrinal interpretations. In the early fifth century, Kumārajīva produced a new collection of translations, including Nāgārjuna's *Mādhyamaka*, or *Middle Way*, which rejuvenated interest in the Mahāyāna school in southern China, especially among Taoists, because of the similarity between the Buddhist notion of emptiness (*śūnatā*) and the Taoist notion of nonbeing (*wú-wèi*).* Kumārajīva's translations would also set the stage for neo-Taoism.[114] The principal contribution of the San Lun school to Chinese Buddhism was the notion that all phenomena are empty of intrinsic nature, or essence (*svabhāva*). Instead, phenomena arise out of emptiness (*śūnya*) in codependence with the observer.†

The Wei Shi (Yoga) school

Indian Yoga (Yogācāra, or "yoga practice") strongly influenced the early development of Buddhism in China, especially its emphasis on pranayama (breath control) and its perspective that all existence is of "mind only." One of Yogācāra's principle doctrines is *vijñapti-mātra*, often translated as "consciousness only". Yogācāra would become central to the *Wei Shi* school, also known, variously, as the *Fa Xiang* (*Fa Hsiang*) school, the Yogācāra school, the *Consciousness* school, as well as the *Vijñānavāda* school. The Wei Shi school was already known in China

---

* Wang Bi, an early neo-Taoist philosopher, described *wú* similarly to the *Neti! Neti!* of the *Upanishads* (Chapter 12): there is the essence of what is known and constantly changing and restless, and there is its negation, *wú*, which is unknown, inactive, silent, and ineffable (Smart 2008, 86).

† This view is harmonious with the principles of quantum mechanics and is now being formally modeled and tested by Donald Hoffman, professor of cognitive science at the University of California, Irvine.

by the second or third century, but grew to some dominance during the sixth through the efforts of Xuan Zang (Hsüan-tsang 玄奘).

Xuan Zang was an especially zealous monk with an insatiable desire to learn as much as he could about Buddhism, both from doctrinal and experiential perspectives. Raised in a conservative Confucian home, he was intrigued with Buddhism from an early age. When he was nine, he entered Jingtu monastery 淨土寺 and immediately began studying Mahāyāna Buddhism with fervor. At thirteen, he received Buddhist precepts, and seven years later, full ordination. Much of the first part of his life thereafter was spent traveling throughout China seeking new texts about Buddhism in an effort to reconcile seemingly contradictory doctrines propounded by the many schools that had developed. During these early years, he became especially enamored with a small group of discourses written by two brothers, Asaṅga and Vasubandhu (predominantly the former), in fourth-century India. Their complex epistemological perspectives became known as the Yogācāra school. *Yoga*, here, refers to its original meaning, *mystical union*, and *cāra* to spiritual practice.

Having gleaned as much as he could from China's still relatively sparse collection of Buddhist texts, and still unable to reconcile many of the diverse views presented by them, Xuan Zang embarked on a trip to India to acquire more Buddhist literature in hopes of eventually formulating a cohesive, sensible, and comprehensive set of texts. The political and logistical challenges of such a journey, however, were numerous. As is common in spiritual life when seemingly insurmountable obstacles arise, solutions are often presented in the form of visionary 霊夢 encounters during meditation or sleep.* His recounted vision:

---

* In China, dreams and visions are rarely disregarded. Visions have long been held to represent communications between celestial beings and man. Alex Wu describes visions as referring "to a place where the divine and humans communicate. This particular thought reveals the ancient Chinese people's understanding of multiple realities" (2013). Indeed, it is nearly impossible to read an account of spiritual life from monks or nuns without encountering tales of dreams and visions that inspired and directed them. Xuan Zang documented many visionary experiences during his travels.

>...he sees Mount Sumeru, a sacred mountain at the center of the universe, made of gold, silver, beryl, and crystal surrounded by a Great Sea. Lotus flowers of stone support him as he crosses the waters, but too slippery and steep is the way up this Asian Mount Olympus that each time he tries to climb its sides, he slides to the bottom. [All] of a sudden, a mighty whirlwind raises him to the summit; the world stretches out as far as the eye can see. ... In an ecstasy of joy, he awakes; he has been shown a vision of what he must do.[115]

This vision purportedly gave Xuan Zang the courage to undertake what would become one of the most challenging and historic adventures in the annals of human exploration, a journey that would last nearly seventeen years and earn him posthumous accolades from Chinese Buddhists to the present day.*

Arriving finally in India after numerous trials, including almost dying while crossing the Gobi Desert, Xuan Zang spent over a decade visiting dozens of monasteries and studying under many teachers. When he returned to China, it was with over six hundred Mahāyāna texts, including a large number on his favorite subject, Yogācāra.† Xuan Zang's *Chéng Wéishì Lùn* 成唯識論—*Discourse on the Perfection of Consciousness-only*‡—established the *Weishi* (or *Faxiang*) school of Yogācāra in China.[116]

Yogācāra literature is vast and branches in many esoteric directions, but there are aspects of this Buddhist school that are central to understanding Chan. The earliest and perhaps most influential of the Yogācāra texts is the *Saṃdhinirmocana Sūtra*, attributed to Asaṅga.§ Asaṅga was

---

* The journey was recorded in detail in the Chinese classic *Great Tang Record on the Western Regions*. Nine hundred years later, it led to a romanticized version of the story, *Journey to the West*, by Wú Chéng'ēn 吳承恩.

† Xuan Zang's enormous contribution to Chinese Buddhism was further realized when it was discovered that many of the writings he returned with became the only extant copies in the world, as Muslim invaders would destroy the majority of Buddhist literature in India during the latter part of the first millennium. His biography states that he returned with, "over six hundred Mahāyāna and Hīnayāna texts, seven statues of the Buddha and more than a hundred sarira relics" (Strong 2004, 188).

‡ *Chéng Wéishì Lùn* is also known as the *Vijñaptimātratāsiddhi*.

§ The *Saṃdhinirmocana Sūtra* extolled its own significance by claiming itself the third and last "turning of the wheel of the Dharma." The first turning was considered to be the

especially known for his many years of intensive meditation, and for his accounts of encounters with "celestial beings"—particular archetypal motifs accessed during meditation (Chapter 12). The sutra presents the perspective that all perceived experience—even that of celestial beings (i.e., "Buddha Realms") encountered during meditation—is entirely of the mind, and the mind alone, and that it is folly to consider otherwise. This idea is expressed in terms of *Three Natures: conceptualized nature (parikalpitasvabhāva), dependent nature (paratantrasvabhāva),* and *perfected nature (parinispannasvabhāva).* In Xuan Zang's translation of the *Saṃdhinirmocana Sūtra,* they are described as the *threefold marks of all things*:

> In sum, the marks of all things are threefold. The first is the characteristic pattern of clinging to what is entirely imagined. The second is the characteristic pattern of other-dependency. The third is the characteristic pattern of full perfection.
>
> The pattern of clinging to what is entirely imagined refers to the establishing of names and symbols for all things and the distinguishing of their essences, whereby they come to be expressed in language.
>
> The pattern of other-dependency refers to the pattern whereby all things arise co-dependently: for if this exists, then that exists, and if this arises, then that arises. This refers to [the twelvefold conditions, starting with] 'conditioned by ignorance are karmic formations,' [and ending with] 'conditioned by origination is this grand mass of suffering,' [the last of the twelve conditions].
>
> The pattern of full perfection refers to the universally equal suchness of all things. Bodhisattvas penetrate to this suchness because of their resolute zeal, intelligent focusing, and true reflection. By gradually cultivating this penetration, they reach unsurpassed true awakening and actually realize perfection.

Buddha's teaching of the *Four Noble Truths* and *Eightfold Path,* and the second turning was the teaching of emptiness and compassion as presented in the *Prajñāpāramitā* canon, referred to as *bodhicitta.* The *Saṃdhinirmocana Sūtra* may have been the last of the contributions to the Mahāyāna canon in India before Buddhism's final extinction at the hands of Muslims.

Good son, the pattern of clinging to what is entirely imagined is like the defective vision of one who has cataracts in his eyes. The pattern of other-dependency is like those deceptive images in the confused vision of the one with the cataracts, for they appear to be distinct images, such as hairs, flies, small particles, or patches of different colors. The pattern of full perfection is like the unconfused objects seen by the pure vision of one with sound eyes and no cataracts.[117]

So first, in our base state of ignorance, we are aware of the first mark of existence: we hypostatize, believing that what we see exists independently of our perception. We give things names, describe them by their attributes, and form a bond, or attachment to them. When we name things, they take on the semblance, through this mentation, of an independent existence;* thus, subject-object duality arises, which produces a false understanding of reality and consequently gives rise to samsāra's realm of suffering (duhkha).†

In the second mark of all things, the *pattern of other-dependency* is realized as we recognize that our minds create the observed world of things; i.e., things are recognized as not possessing an independent existence apart from us, the observer: they are, in fact, fully dependent upon us. In reality, Xuan Zang offered, there is merely an ever-changing flow of perceptions (*vijñaptimātra*), and if we project this flow of perceptions upon that which is created as a mental image (*cittamātra*), we will exist in the base state of samsāra, described above as the *first mark of all things*.

---

* From the *Treatise on the Two Entrances and Four Practices*, attributed to Bodhidharma: "[People] arbitrarily posit names where there are no names, and these names lead to the generation of [distinctions between] 'this' and 'not-this.' [They also] arbitrarily formulate principles [explaining this reality] where there are no principles, and these principles lead to the occurrence of disputation. The phantasmagorical transformations [of phenomenal reality] are not real, so who can say 'this' and 'not-this'? [All is] false and without reality, so what are 'being' and 'non-being'?" (McRae 1986, 106)

† Subject-object duality describes the codependent relationship between our perception of something (the object) and we who perceive it (the subject), and our tendency to mistakenly believe that the object exists independently of us, the observer. This codependent relationship between object and observer was hypothesized by physicist Erwin Schrödinger and later demonstrated experimentally with matter by Clinton Davisson and Lester Germer in 1927. It remains the fundamental basis for the field of quantum mechanics, which has brought us televisions, radios, cell phones, and computers.

The third mark of all things is realized once the mind penetrates the realm of *suchness* or *thusness* (*tathātā*), an awareness that can be attained through meditation (samādhi). Here we experience reality as the dharmakāya, the flux of perceptions of things as they come and go in a cycle of perpetual creation and destruction, birth and death. That which is real is only this ever-flowing perception itself, and even it lacks a fixed existence. Reality is perceived as devoid of duality, lacking nothing, empty of attributes, while all-consuming and all-expansive.

A commentary to the *Mahāyānasamgraha* of the Yogācāra school offers an analogy to these three marks: imagine seeing a mirage of water. Its perception as water by someone hallucinating is its conceptualized nature (first mark); its perception as a mirage is its dependent nature (second mark); and the recognition of the absence of water in the image of the water is its perfected nature (third mark).[118]

The Yogācāra school professed eight types of consciousness, all of which would become important players in the development of Chan. The first of them correspond to each of the six sensory organs: eye (sight), ear (sound), body (touch), nose (smell), tongue (taste), and brain (mind, or *manovijñāna*): for each of these sensations, there is a corresponding consciousness which permits its experience.[*] Together, these six sense-realities had already been described in the *Tipitaka* of the Pāli Canon. Yogācāra added two additional types of consciousnesses: the substratum (*ālayavijñāna*[†]) and the tainted-mind (*kliṣṭamanas*).

Substratum consciousness refers to the realm of *thusness* or *suchness* (*tathātā*), where all is perceived as a flow of conditioned arisings and departures, always changing from moment to moment in an eternal flux. Substratum consciousness explains the nature of karma, cause and effect: one action (seed) begets another action in response, which progresses in an endless flow of causes and effects or actions and reactions.

---

[*] Recall the predecessor to this idea from the Kena-Upanishad (Chapter 1).

[†] More commonly translated as *storehouse consciousness*, *ālayavijñāna* is an analog to the modern notion of the unconscious as envisioned in analytical psychology. Tao Jiang describes it as "...a key concept in the Yogacara system. It is a subliminal reservoir of memories, habits, tendencies, and future possibilities" (Jiang 2006).

Substratum consciousness can explain our propensity to live within an illusory "bubble world" of forms and experiences, with aspects seemed to be shared with others.*

Substratum consciousness is described variously in Yogācāra literature. Although some have equated it with the contemporary concept of "universal consciousness," we might better understand it in terms of Pierre Janet's (1850-1947) concept of the subconscious, in which he described a powerful awareness underneath our layers of critical thought. As with the subconscious, substratum consciousness is uniquely determined for each person (so there are many of them), and allows for the processes of thinking and action, as well as the experience of existence itself.

In another way, the "seed" of personal karmic action need not be the only kind of seed from which action, experience, and awareness can arise. Another kind of seed can be "inherited."[119] This corresponds (albeit loosely) to Carl Jung's concept of the collective unconscious (Chapters 16 and 17), and accounts for the many remarkably similar archetypal encounters meditators experience regardless of ethnicity, culture, or religious persuasion (Chapter 17).†

Substratum consciousness cannot be isolated or directly apprehended. Like many terms and ideas used to describe spiritual insight and experience, it is a teleological concept, one created to explain a phenomenon (Chapter 16). The term refers, essentially, to flux, like a flowing stream, and is best viewed as a condition or basis through which life is experienced. If we falsely identify with it as something separate

---

* The *ālayavijñāna*, Schmithausen writes, explains why we collectively agree on the existence of an outer world: "...the whole world, especially the outer world, is only a subjective mental production of each living being. Our conviction to live in one and the same world is therefore merely an imagination based on the fact that there are certain common features in our *karman* which cause our *ālayavijñānas* to produce *similar* mental images of the outer world" (as quoted in Williams 2009, 309, f.n. 37).

† Of course, during this time nobody had yet conceived of a medium of inheritance, such as DNA, nor the principles of evolution, so it was natural to assume that similar traits appearing in successive generations were due to some kind of rebirth of an *essence* which continued after one's physical death. For Yogacara, this was explained as types of *seeds* which could transmigrate after death of the body. There are striking similarities to our present understanding of the functioning of genes.

from ourselves, we again enter saṃsāra's realm of dualities; however, if rightly experienced, we witness the eternal realm of the dharmakāya.*

Much Yogācāra literature is concerned with describing the essential aspects of reality as interpreted, or experienced, through consciousness (*cittamātra*). Readers interested in the philosophical and ontological insights offered by the meditation masters of the Yogācāra school may be interested in reading the *Yogācārabhūmi-śāstra*, the *Saṃdhinirmocana Sūtra*, the *Pratyutpanna Sūtra*, the *Daśabhūmika Sūtra* and, of special relevance to Chan, the *Laṅkāvatāra Sūtra*. Also significant are *The Five Treatises of Maitreya*, attributed to Asaṅga, and claimed to have been expounded to him during meditation by the celestial Buddha, Maitreya.

Although Yogācāra was known in China well before Xuan Zang returned from India, it was through his efforts that it was given new life and became a major influence on Chan.

The Zhen Yan (Tantric) school

The *Zhen Yan* (*Chen Yen*) school, known for impressing people with feats of magic and fortune-telling, made its dominant imprint during the Tang dynasty in northern China under the influence of three of its proponents: Śubhākarasiṃha, Vajrabodhi, and Amoghavajra. The school was short-lived in China, but became popular and enduring in Japan. During its short life in China, many Japanese monks flocked to study Tantrism at the Qing Long Temple, headquarters to the Zhen Yan school.[120] The school came to be known as *Shingon Buddhism* in Japan and remains a dominant Buddhist presence there today.

---

* In this sense, upon death of the body, it's only the *tainted* or misunderstood aspects of the substratum consciousness which perish. The flow remains. Paramārtha, founder of the Shelun school of Yogacara in China, differentiated this eternal flow as a ninth consciousness which he termed the *immaculate consciousness* (*amalavijñāna*)—the permanent, ultimate, true reality (Williams 2009, 99).

The Fall & Rise of Chinese Buddhism

Chinese Buddhism developed most of its distinctive schools during the Tang dynasty and, while many died out, some continue today. From roughly 600-900 CE, temples became extremely wealthy in northern China from the grains they milled and sold, from the donations they received (on which they were not required to pay taxes), and from advantages they took from tax-avoidance schemes. With their increased power and social influence, the northern Buddhist institutions fell into disfavor with the government and religious persecution ensued. Thousands of monasteries and tens of thousands of shrines were destroyed, hundreds of thousands of monks and nuns were forced back to laity, and lands and valuables were confiscated.[121] It was a devastating blow to Buddhism in northern China.

Those Mahāyāna schools that survived developed distinct flavors: the *San Jie Jiao* (*San Chieh Chiao*) or *Three Ages* school, the *Tian Tai* (*T'ien T'ai*) school, the *Hua Yan* (*Hua Yen*) school, the *Jing Tu* (*Ching T'u*) or *Pure Land* school, and the Chan school.

I would like to pause at this point to remind the reader that these schools were not profoundly different from one another. If compared to the Western public-school system, each Buddhist school was like one high school within a district of many, each of which specializes in something different: maybe one school is most notable for its sports teams, another for its science program, and another for its special-needs classes. Chinese Buddhists were typically not strict adherents to any one school, and many monks would often receive training and education in more than one as part of their spiritual and religious explorations. From this openness to diversity, a melding of thoughts and practices came to characterize Chinese Buddhism in its broadest sense. While some schools died out, many of their teachings were preserved in others that adopted their views in various ways.* This characteristic

---

* As a contemporary example, when I was a resident monk several decades ago at Hong Fa Temple in Shenzhen, China, I observed that the dominant school was Pure Land, but there was also a meditation hall that many monks used regularly in the Chan tradition, and the abbot himself was a noted Chan master (Ben Huan). The Vinaya rules were integrated

of Buddhism is perhaps unique to China; Japan would respond differently, with divisive and often violent quarrels common between rival sects and schools (Chapter 7).

Of five purely Chinese Mahāyāna schools, only two popularly survive today as separate schools: Pure Land (devotional) and Chan (meditational). The other three—San Jie Jiao, Tian Tai, and Hua Yan—were absorbed into these two, to varying degrees (although there are still monks claiming lineages in them, perhaps to symbolize their inclusive embrace of Buddhist diversity).

The San Jie Jiao school

Also known as the *Three Ages* school 三階教, San Jie Jio was founded by the monk Xinxing (also known as Hsin Hsing 信行禪師) during the late 6th century. Followers lived in strict accordance with many austere practices, including begging, which brought substantial wealth. Their central tenet was that they were living in the *Dharma Ending Age*. The idea was that once the Dharma is made known upon the earth, knowledge of it deteriorates in three stages, and they happened to be living in the third and last of them—hence the name, Three Ages school. This meant that there was little hope left, and the best one could do was live in austerity.* Which they did. Unfortunately for them, however, belief in such an abysmal state of affairs undermined their relationship with the government, for they believed that in this degenerate Third Age, no government could possibly govern adequately, much less earn their allegiance or respect.

---

into monastic training, a feature passed down from the early Lü school. The Ancestor's Hall resided prominently and proudly near the main Buddha Hall, honoring deceased monks and abbots from centuries past in the tradition inherited from Confucianism and China's ancient folk religion.

*Some people interpret "Dharma decline" as meaning that the Dharma itself is in decline, rather than knowledge of it. Apparently, this was a common misconception of members of this school itself, for according to the Buddhist principles of Dharma, it's not only everlasting and all-encompassing, it's the foundation of reality. Its decline is thus an impossibility. From the earliest sutra literature, it's apparent that knowledge of the Dharma has always been rare because it's not easily fathomed by the intellect and requires a "spiritual eye" to see.

They should not have been surprised when, in 713, Empress Wu (Wu Ze Tian) declared the sect heretical and confiscated much of its vast wealth. We still hear about the "Dharma Ending Age" and, while begging for money is not an aspect of Chinese Buddhism, the ritual offering of money to monks in small red envelopes by laity continues as a cultural tradition. Although it's common for monks today to accept monetary offerings, they will not directly ask for them.* However, begging for food with an alms bowl continues to be an accepted means of survival for many traveling monks.

Although Xinxing's Three Ages school officially died an unpleasant death, he initiated a radical paradigm shift in Buddhism by proclaiming that all older forms of Buddhism were false and only his was the "True Buddhism." His Buddhism did away with sutra-study and replaced it with meditation, begging, and asceticism. Chan would adopt his perspective that sutra-study, as a means for spiritual awakening, was ineffective by itself, breaking a long-established tradition of Buddhist practice.†122

The Tian Tai school

As mentioned previously, Zhi Yi (532-597) created the devotional Tian Tai school based on his favorite expression of Buddhism, the *Lotus Sūtra*. His teaching approach relied on the Buddhist concept of skillful- or *expedient-means* (upāya). Simply put, this means that the appropriate teaching is chosen according to the aptitude and disposition of the individual receiving it; i.e., there is no single formula that works for everyone: some people are better served by hearing one thing, and others something else; some are ready for advanced teachings and practices,

---

* When I was in residence at Hong Fa Temple in 1998, one of the monks residing there told me that much of the money received by the temple is distributed back into the country to help the poor and impoverished. He said that this has also helped to endear the Chinese government to Buddhism, fostering the resurgence of Buddhist expression that had been quelled for decades.

† Sutra study has not been eliminated from monastic life, however. For many monks and nuns, sutra study continues to be a part of the daily routine. Buddhist temples throughout China offer libraries where monks are free, and encouraged, to study canonical texts.

others only for an introduction. Teachings, therefore, must be flexible and adaptable to circumstance. Zhi Yi considered the teachings of the Buddha to fall within one of five categories: the highest and most difficult to understand was presented in the *Avataṃsaka Sūtra*, the last and easiest to understand is the *Lotus Sutra*. In his view, the *Lotus Sutra* was the most accessible teaching for the greatest number of people.

Zhi Yi would posthumously become an important figure in Chan because of narratives later written about him by Guanding (561-632) under the political influence of emperor Sui Yangdi.[123]

The Hua Yan school

Fa Shun is credited with founding the Hua Yan school, also known as the *Avataṃsaka* (*Flower Garland*) school, after his favorite sutra, for which it's named. Aside from the difference in sutra orientation, the Hua Yan and Tian Tai schools were very similar. Both held the perspective that all which exists resides within the realm of Buddha-nature (ultimate reality). This was also the basic Vijñānavāda metaphysical perspective. The Hua Yan school took the concept further, however, by saying that not only did all things exist within Buddha-nature, but that Buddha-nature exists simultaneously in all things, interchangeably, as might be envisioned with a modern holographic image, or hologram. To create a hologram—a three-dimensional visual reconstruction of an object from a 2-dimensional image—a thick transparent film is exposed by reflecting a highly coherent laser beam off an object onto the film where it interferes with another beam from the same source which did not reflect off the object —the reference beam. The resulting image stored in the film can then be cut in half to again reveal the full three-dimensional image of the object in each half, and each of those halves can be cut in half again to reveal the full image in each of those halves. This can continue ad infinitum, assuming a perfect system, because the whole image exists within every part of the medium.*

---

* Laser coherence, film granularity, and vibration of the system limit the actual recursive properties of this process in the laboratory. But the possibility that the entire universe may be a holographic projection has received recent attention following research published by

This metaphysical perspective was greatly appreciated by the emperor, because the idea that all things were unified under the Buddha, and that the Buddha was unified under all things, equated to everything being unified under the emperor and the emperor unified under all things.[124] Not a bad situation for any emperor!

The Jing Tu school (Pure Land)

The Pure Land school began with Hui Yuan in 402 as the *Pure Land Society*, and based itself principally on the *Sukhāvatīvyūhaḥ Sūtras* and the *Amitāyurdhyāna Sūtra*.* The Pure Land and Chan schools ended up, in some ways, on opposite sides of the religious spectrum in terms of beliefs and practices. Followers of the Pure Land school believed that, considering we are in the age of Dharma-decline (a notion taken from the Three Ages school), the best we can do is pray to be reborn in the Pure Land upon death. If Chinese Buddhism got a reputation for being pessimistic, I imagine it came largely from here: "There is no hope. Let's pray that we are reborn in a better place after we die, the radiant heavenly paradise of Buddha Amitābha." While this was not actually the message presented in the *Sukhāvatīvyūhaḥ Sutra*, it became the popular interpretation. Psychologically, it acknowledged suffering and the sense of futility many people felt in life, it offered hope in the next life as long as the celestial Buddha was venerated in this one, and it didn't require substantial effort, such as learning to meditate or applying the Eightfold Path. These sentiments, for many, made Pure Land easy to identify with, easy to follow, and easy to believe in.

---

physicists Niayesh Afshordi, Claudio Corianò, Luigi Delle Rose, Elizabeth Gould, and Kostas Skenderis (Niayesh Afshordi 2017). As a hologram is a projection of three dimensions onto a two-dimensional plane, we can say that the information of the 3-dimensional realm is preserved in the projection. Likewise, theorists speculate, the universe we experience may actually be a projection of three dimentions onto a 2-dimensional "surface", which gives us our experience of reality as 3-dimensional. Because all the information of the 3-dimensional realm is preserved on the 2-dimensional projection, we are left with the illusion that we live in a 3-dimensional realm.

* The *Sukhāvatīvyūhaḥ* is a pair of sutras, referred to as the *Larger* and *Smaller*. They are also known as the *Sutra of Infinite Light* and the *Sutra of Infinite Compassion*, respectively. The *Amitāyurdhyāna Sūtra* was a later sutra which historians think may not have originated in India, but may have instead been produced in East Asia (Williams 2009, 239).

There were, however, two differing views proffered by the Pure Land school: one expounded by Dao Zhuo, the other by his disciple Shan Dao. Dao Zhuo taught that single-minded devotion to the Buddha Amitābha through chanting was enough to gain rebirth in the Pure Land, while Shan Dao favored the inclusion of chanting sutras and meditating upon Buddha images (archetypal motifs), meditations that required much preparation (Chapter 12). Dao Zhuo's easier approach, in general, won out over Shan Dao's; however, Pure Land as practiced in China today continues to present both teachings.[125]

Sutras representing the Pure Land school predominantly teach the practice of meditation on ideal forms, especially Self (Buddha-nature). The *Larger Sukhāvatīvyūhaḥ Sūtra* is thought to be the older of the pair, originating between 100 BCE and 100 CE by some estimates.[126] It identifies "Buddha Fields" as realms that can be visualized through meditation where one can not only meet and be guided by a Buddha (as a celestial being), but can also be born into that realm, or Land, oneself.* Two Buddha Lands described in the sutra are those of *Amitābha Buddha* and *Amitāyus Buddha*: Amitābha is the *Buddha of infinite compassion and life*, and Amitāyus is the *Buddha of infinite light and wisdom*.† Pure Land Buddhism is reputed to be the most popular and practiced form of Buddhism in all dominantly Mahāyāna Buddhist countries today.

Although Chinese Buddhism was forming a character distinct from its Indian origins, largely due to the production of new sutras and other canonical texts, Buddhism would not be fully embraced by China until it could adequately address the "ancestor problem." When it did, things changed radically.

---

* There are two ways to interpret this. The most common is the literal interpretation: when we die, we will go to heaven, and that heaven is a Buddha Field or Buddha Realm. The mystics' understanding is different: when we encounter "Buddha fields" in meditation, the effect is to be born into them, i.e., to inhabit them, there and then, in the timelessness of samādhi.

† The *Larger Sukhāvatīvyūhaḥ Sūtra* attempts to describe the nature of reality experienced when encountering ideal forms in meditation, a reality that can seem more real than when we are *not* meditating. We will explore this phenomenon in Part Two.

The Chan school

Chan's origins are ambiguous. Over the last few decades, however, new insights have been offered by scholars and historians such as John McRae, Alan Cole, Mark Csikszentmihalyi, Bernard Faure, Wendi Adamek, T. Griffith Foulk, Tillman Vetter, Mario Poceski, and John Jorgensen. In *The Mystique of Transmission*, Adamek, associate professor of Buddhist Studies at the University of Calgary, loosely connects the origins of something called "Chan" to the short-lived *Bao Tang* sect of the Tang dynasty, whose members "saw themselves as members of a school that they broadly defined as 'Chan'..." But what we now think of as Chan, contemporary scholars believe, was the result of a new literary framing of Buddhism during the Song dynasty that glorified and fabricated events during the previous Tang dynasty.* Additionally, Adamek has noted that the term "Chan school" itself is controversial:

> Thanks to careful research into Tang sources in recent decades, it has become clear that the image of the late Tang as the "golden age" of Chan is a retrospective illusion heightened by the sectarian biases of later Japanese scholars.[127]

Nonetheless, central to this new Chinese Buddhism called Chan were the principles of ancestral worship and filial piety (*xiào* 孝), both of which had been integral to Chinese culture since at least the time of Confucius. The glue that bonded Buddhist and Confucian ideologies, was the invention of "Dharma transmission."

Anyone who has delved into medieval Chan literature has quickly encountered an array of fantastic stories: stories of enlightenment, of encounters with Chan masters, and of amazing, harrowing, and mysterious adventures of pious monks as they trekked from temple to temple in search of the Dharma. Many of these stories are now believed to

---

* As a reminder to the reader, throughout this book I differentiate the religious façade of Chan from its spiritual/mystical practice, as I consider them to be largely distinct—though mutually interdependent. The religious framework is, in part, the outer representation of inner experience, and is necessarily framed in a context commensurate with a particular society's values, beliefs, and social customs.

have originated during the Song dynasty to help solidify a Chan patriarchy. Adamek writes:

> The lore of the Chan patriarchy was reworked in numerous iterations over the course of several centuries, such that most traces of the stories' original contexts were erased or submerged. The historicity of the biographies and lineages of renowned Chan masters has been undermined not only by the Dunhuang find, but also by scholarly recognition that Chan classics on the Tang masters are largely products of the Song dynasty (960-1279), when Chan was a prestigious religious and cultural institution that enjoyed the privilege of canonizing a romanticized view of its origins.[128]

Cole further suggests we consider the stories of Chan as we might other works of art, belonging

> ...within a highly developed literary culture, which, even before Buddhism showed up, delighted in just this kind of story—presented in elegant and erudite Chinese—that exalted the value and power of all things beyond language and culture. Now, a hundred years or so into Chan studies, it is clear that reading Chan texts without this literary, historical, and political context in mind is a lot like looking at Chinese nature paintings and thinking that they reflect real mountains and rivers, when in fact they were more often than not painted from other paintings, in comfortable urban studios.[129]

Given what we know today, it's likely that the stories of Chan originated as teaching stories and as mechanisms to define a religious culture, rather than as historical accounts of actual events. Essential for the institution, they became mechanisms to solidify and strengthen viewpoints and define and establish lineages. Philip Yampolsky, former director of the C. V. Starr East Asian Library of Columbia University and specialist in Chinese and Japanese religious traditions, argues that

> [t]he Ch'an biographical works ... aimed to establish Ch'an as a legitimate school of Buddhism traceable to its Indian origins, and at the same time championed a particular form of Ch'an. Historical accuracy was of little concern to the compilers; old legends were repeated, new stories were invented and reiterated until they too became legends.[130]

Considering the strong influence story-telling had on the early development of Chan, we'll look at two of the most important early stories that came to solidify the Chan institution and which continue to be retold today to novice monks, nuns, and laity: those of Bodhidharma and Huineng.

THE LEGEND OF BODHIDHARMA: THE FIRST CHAN PATRIARCH

Chan is popularly considered to have begun with the first proclaimed Chan patriarch, Bodhidharma (Figure 4). Many scholars, however, argue that Bodhidharma was purely legendary, if not a full fabrication; that he was a literary invention created for the purpose of establishing a new sect of Buddhism.[131] It may seem implausible that such a pivotal and important figure could be a fabrication, but the type of historical writing that may have produced him was not at odds with the Chinese approach toward historicity at the time or for centuries prior, according to Cole who contends that historiographies, commonly written since at least the Warring States period, were not intended to produce accurate documentation, but to fictionally "shape the past to improve the present."[132] He also suggests that the Chinese mind was content and felt morally justified in fabricating a historical truth as long as it was believed to help lead to a better present and future. Whether Bodhidharma was a literary invention or not, stories of him, reinforced through their retelling, embellishment, and expansion, set a precedent for a new way of conceptualizing Buddhism and Buddhist practice.

According to Cole, the first mention of Bodhidharma occurs in the *Records of the Buddhist Monasteries of Luoyang*, written by Xuan Zhi in 547. In the account, Bodhidharma is a wandering monk from Persia who notices a beautiful stupa (a memorial edifice for a deceased person) and exclaims, "Truly this is the work of spirit.... I am 150 years old, and I have passed through numerous countries. There is no country that I have not visited and yet nowhere on earth has a monastery this beautiful."[133] The second encounter with Bodhidharma occurs in the preface to *The Treatise on the Two Entrances and Four Practices* (*èrrú sìxíng*), written by an anonymous source in the early seventh century. It gives a vague and fractured biographical sketch of Bodhidharma which closely resembles the biography of Buddhabhadra (Bátuó 跋陀), the founder of Shaolin monastery, in 495 CE.

Later historical analysis suggests that Bodhidharma may not have been a real person, because early historical accounts vary substantially both in the time in which he is purported to have lived (either the 5th or 6th century CE) and the teachings he purportedly espoused. In addition, no records of his existence at the time he was purported to have lived seem to exist.[134] We should note that, for the purpose of chan, the question of

FIGURE 4. BODHIDHARMA.

Bodhidharma (Jap. Daruma) depicted with wide lidless eyes, a beard and an angry or otherwise unhappy expression. By Kawanabe Kyōsai.

his existence is irrelevant, and for the purpose of the Chan institution, it's not his historicity that's important, but the symbolism encompassed by his legend; for he came to be considered not only the 28th patriarch of Indian Buddhism, but the *first* patriarch of Chan.

Chinese historiography presents Bodhidharma as a Buddhist Indian Brahman prince of the early 6th century who was disillusioned by the futility he saw in reciting sutras and building temples. He traveled to China and eventually crossed the Yangtze River "on a reed."* Traveling north, he eventually came to a monastery, where he stayed for the next nine years seated in meditation facing a wall.† To avoid falling asleep, he cut off his eyelids, and because he sat for so long, his legs severely atrophied. Bodhidharma is thus often depicted in sketches, statues, and dolls with no legs, wide lidless eyes, a beard, and sometimes an angry or fierce expression. He is referred to as the "Blue-Eyed Daemon," or the "Blue-Eyed Barbarian", in some Chinese texts, suggesting possible Aryan descent.

A dialogue purported to have happened between Bodhidharma and Emperor Wu of the Liang dynasty helped establish the character and reality of the Bodhidharma legend, as well as provide the context of Chan as a mystical approach to Buddhism:

> The emperor asked, "Since ascending to the throne, I have had temples built, sutras transcribed, and monks ordained. What merit have I gained?"
>
> The master (Bodhidharma) answered: "No merit at all."
>
> The emperor replied: "Why no merit at all?"
>
> The master replied: "All these are but impure motives for merit; they mature the paltry fruit of rebirth as a human being or a deva (a god).

---

* Reed boats were commonly used for river activities, so this was likely a reference to such a boat. Oddly, translators and commentators have offered a wide range of alternate interpretations, including a reed-flute. For a contemporary view of the Bodhidharma legend, see John McRae's *Seeing Through Zen*, 2003, pp. 22-33.

† For a discussion of the origin and meaning of wall-meditation, see McRae's *The Northern School and the Formation of Early Chan Buddhism*, 1986, pp. 112-115.

They are like shadows that follow the form, having no reality of their own."

The emperor said: "Then of what kind is true merit?"

He answered: "It is pure knowing, wonderful and perfect. Its essence is emptiness. One cannot gain such merit by worldly means."

Thereupon the emperor asked: "What is the sacred truth's first principle?"

The master replied: "Vast emptiness."

The emperor said: "Who is this who faces me?"

The master replied: "I don't know."[135]

Bodhidharma has also been credited with bringing martial arts to China, specifically to the Shaolin temple, which is still renowned for its rigorous martial arts training today. Chinese historians (such as Tang Hao, Xu Zhen, and Lin Boyuan) discount this, however, since the only reference to Bodhidharma teaching martial arts comes from the *Yin Jin Jing* (*Muscle Change Classic*), a qigong text* written in 1624 by a Taoist priest who attributed it, apocryphally, to Bodhidharma.[136]

Because Bodhidharma's favorite sutra was said to be the *Laṅkāvatāra Sūtra*—popular with the Yogācāra school, which described the mind as the creator of the phenomenal world—early Chan literature refers to the Chan school as the *Laṅkāvatāra* school or *Mind-only* school (*Léngqié zōng* 楞伽宗). Florin Giripescu Sutton, author of *Existence and Enlightenment in the Laṅkāvatāra Sūtra*, describes the purpose of the *Laṅkāvatāra Sūtra* as helping people realize their Self-nature:

> [T]he entire epistemological reasoning of the *Laṅkāvatāra sūtra* is geared toward [...] the achievment of Self-realization, or Self-actualization, refered to by various terms (Siddhānta, Āryajñāna, Prayātmagocara, Tathata, etc). All theoretical constructs elaborated

---

* Qigong, meaning "life energy cultivation," is a Chinese holistic approach to spiritual development that includes physical exercises, visualization practices, diet, breathing practices, and meditation.

in the *Sūtra* are treated as nothing more than mere stepping stones toward, or rungs on the ladder of Self-realization.¹³⁷

There are several texts attributed to Bodhidharma, but according to John McRae, author of *Seeing Through Zen: Encounter, Transformation, and Genealogy in Chinese Chan Buddhism*, there is only one that might possibly be from him should he be a real historical figure: *The Treatise on the Two Entrances and Four Practices*.* The first of the *Two Entrances* gives two prerequisites for Chan:

- One must have faith in the teaching and recognize that we all have the same fundamental "True Nature," a nature which becomes obscured from view when we misidentify sensory experience for reality.

- One must live according to four practices: being unaffected by suffering; accepting one's circumstances, whatever they may be (recall the *Chuang Tzu*); discarding desires; and acting in accordance with the nature of emptiness, i.e., recognizing the non-substantiality of all things.

But how might Bodhidharma have become the first patriarch of Chan? And what, exactly, does that mean?

Perhaps the most distinguishing aspect of (institutional) Chinese Chan is the lineage system that came to characterize it. In its popular understanding, it works like this: an ineffable essence called Dharma is transmitted wordlessly from teacher to disciple, a process that began with the Buddha and has continued to the present day. Only those people who have received Dharma transmission from a previously-transmitted monk are considered by the Chan institution to be legitimate "carriers of the flame"; with this transmission, they are also considered to be living Buddhas.† In this way, Dharma transmission was conceived

---

* Cole posits that this text, written in the fashionable literary style of the time, was more likely posthumously attributed to Bodhidharma in order to present him as a perfect representation of Buddhism. Cole also observes that the "enhanced, but still very vague, account of Bodhidharma drew on details found in the biography of the Indian master Buddhabhadra (*fotuo*), who appears to have been a real historical figure and who, once in China, founded Shaolin monastery in 495" (2016, 30).

† For some, the act of ordination is viewed as a ceremonial acknowledgment of transmission, or as a process through which transmission occurs. Others interpret transmission,

as a gift which one could own and, for some, was equated with enlightenment itself, according to Cole, author of *Conspiracy's Truth: The Zen of Narrative Cunning in the Platform Sutra*. He also suggests broadly that the term *ownership*

> ...best reflects Chan's claim that enlightenment is a kind of private property (sometimes referred to as a "dharmajewel 法寶") that is passed down in lineages that are modeled, to some extent, on Confucian and imperial styles of patriarchal succession. That is, the whole logic of Chan rests on the conceit that enlightenment, as the final and fullest form of tradition, can be privately held as a Thing-like entity by members of a Chan lineage; of course, too, as a kind of heirloom, enlightenment supposedly can also be given from one man to another in sudden and inexplicable moments of transmission.[138]

To our benefit, a great many historians and religious scholars have investigated the origins of Chan lineage and Dharma transmission, and while their conclusions are still debated, a general picture has begun to emerge which sheds light on the early development of Chan.

We can begin the Chan lineage story with Guanding, who wrote a biography of Zhi Yi entitled *Great Calming and Contemplation* (*Móhē zhǐguān* 摩訶止観). In his preface, he includes Zhi Yi in a genealogical list of twenty-four Indian masters who are spiritual descendents of the Buddha. Although the list of Indian sages had appeared earlier in another text produced in China (*History of the Transmission of the Dharma-Treasury*), Guanding took the list and manipulated it to create a Dharma-lineage to Zhi Yi based on the principle of transmission.[139] After some lengthening and slight modification, this list would become the one we know today that connects transmitted Chan monks to the Buddha.

---

in whatever form it's given, as the imparting of enlightenment upon the receiver. Transmission has thus come to be viewed as something bestowed upon someone as a kind of prize, a formal indoctrination into the Buddha's family and Buddhahood. Of course, receiving such acknowledgment of worth and value can make some people feel and act grandiose; inflated egos are, ironically perhaps, not uncommon in religious groups and present a common obstacle for many chan practitioners (Chapter 21).

The "perfect master" attribute of Chan, Cole suggests in his engaging sardonic style, was influenced by another monk of the same time, Xinxing:

> ...Xinxing is a good example of creating an "absolute master" who supposedly held the totality of Buddhist tradition in his own person. In short, for his followers, Xinxing *the man* was more important than all other Chinese monks and, equally stunning, more important than all the imported Buddhist literature. And, finally, even though Xinxing insisted on an unbridgeable gulf between himself and his followers, he also preached a seductive ideology in which his followers were consoled in their permanent secondary status by an emphasis on their inherent Buddhahood.[140]

Pivotal to the development of Chan's lineage tradition was a biography of the monk Faru in the form of a funerary stele carved into stone at Shaolin Temple in 690. The anonymous author continued the Dharma lineage concept, presumably initiated by Guanding, by adding five Chinese monks to the collection of Indian ancestors, attesting that each had inherited the Buddha Dharma wordlessly, in succession, from Bodhidharma to Huike to Sengcan to Daoxin to Hongren and then to Faru. It's hard to imagine a purpose for this other than to install Faru as a perfect and incontestable representative of the Buddha Dharma, and of Buddhism itself.[141]

Du Fei was next to develop the lineage tree. His work, *Record of the Transmission of the Dharma-Jewel,* c. 780, picked up Faru's lineage story from the Shaolin stele and modified it to proclaim the monk, Shenxiu, the rightful Dharma heir to Faru. Further, Du Fei created biographies of each Dharma ancestor beginning with Huike and added embellishing details to the life of Bodhidharma. Cole writes,

> ...Du Fei's text is basically organized like a freight train, with each master's biography set up as a car filled with various materials and linked to the cars before and after it. In broader terms, by organizing a text that treated each master in the Bodhidharma family at length,

> Du Fei deserves credit for solidifying a whole new genre of literature—the free-standing genealogy of the masters. In time, this kind of text would become known as a "flame history" (denglu or dengshi)—because each master is like a lamp that receives the flame from his predecessor and hands it off to his descendant [...].[142]

One of the more colorful stories from Du Fei is that of the second Chan patriarch, Huike (Huikě 慧可). Huike sought out Bodhidharma as a teacher, and on one cold and snowy day visited him at his cave and asked to be accepted as his student. Bodhidharma refused. Resolute, Huike stood in the snow outside the cave all night. In the morning, Bodhidharma appeared and asked him why he was still there. He replied that he sought a teacher to "open the gate of the elixir of universal compassion to liberate all beings." Bodhidharma responded, "How can you hope for true religion with little virtue, little wisdom, a shallow heart, and an arrogant mind? It would just be a waste of effort."[143] To show his resolve, Huike severed his arm and handed it to Bodhidharma as a token of his sincerity. Only then did Bodhidharma accept him as his student.

According to Heinrich Dumoulin, historical accounts suggest that his arm was most likely cut off by thieves.[144] More recently, Cole, McRae, and others have contested this, asserting that it was more likely an altogether different person, Tanlin (ca. 506-74), who was commonly known as "one-armed Lin" because his arm was cut off by bandits. Tanlin's story, then, could have been transposed onto Huike by Du Fei to help establish a convincing and credible successor to Bodhidharma, as well as to emphasize Bodhidharma as Chan's rightful founder.[145] For Chan Buddhists, however, the medium is the important message, not the historical accuracy of events: the valued teaching of the story is that it takes extreme commitment, humility, and self-sacrifice to undergo chan training. For the Chan institution, it helps establish a strong ecclesiastical hierarchy.

The next quintessential Chan story further developed Chan's self-definition while also effecting divisions within the greater Chan community, divisions that would be referred to as "Northern" and "Southern."

The legend of Huineng: "North vs. South"

Over Chan's long history, we have observed great variations in methods and approaches to its training and teaching. Teachers may support methods used by another teacher, even if they don't use or recommend them themselves, or they may vehemently attack those methods as unproductive or even dangerous. It was in the latter context that a monk from the south, Shenhui (Heze Shenhui 菏泽神會/神会, 684—758), would mount tireless campaigns against a rival monk from the North, Shenxiu (Yùquán Shénxiù 玉泉神秀, 606?—706), initiating a division within Chan that has been preserved to this day.

How Shenhui's divisive rhetoric came to fracture the Chan establishment may be illuminated by some historical context. Buddhist identity was a significant problem during the 8th century, according to Yampolsky:

> Throughout the eighth century a two-fold movement took place: the attempt to establish Ch'an as a sect within the Buddhist teaching in general, and the attempt to gain acceptance for a particular school of Ch'an within the Chinese society in which it existed. ... To achieve the aura of legitimacy so urgently needed, histories were compiled, tracing the Ch'an sect back to the historical Buddha, and at the same time stories of the Patriarchs in China were composed, their teachings outlined, their histories written, and their legends collected. Treatises were manufactured to which the names of the Patriarchs, the heroes of Ch'an, were attached, so as to lend such works the dignity and authority of the Patriarch's name.[146]

Later generations would refer to this early Tang era (ca. 618-907) as the "golden age of Chan" since, through centuries of hagiography, the patriarchs inhabiting it had been portrayed as near-deities. Dialogues and sayings attributed to them became frequent subjects for Dharma sermons, discussions, debates, and even new canonical texts, all of which further enhanced their saintly status and lent a sense of reality to their past existence.*

Fragments of the historical record of this period were unearthed in 1900 when the Taoist monk Wang Yuanlu discovered a trove of ancient texts in a hidden library in the Mogao caves at Dunhuang, a location along the Silk Road linking India with China. Among the documents found was the *Ch'uan fa-pao chi*, a text describing much of the early history of Chan, dating contextually to the first decade of the eighth century. It lists the first five patriarchs, including Bodhidharma, along with the stories about him as described above. In this particular lineage, the sixth patriarch is named Fa-ju, and a seventh patriarch is named Shenxiu. Huineng is nowhere mentioned. Another document from the same collection, the *Leng-chia shih-tzu chi*, is now the oldest extant document to refer to Huineng and attribute to him the *Platform Sutra* (*Liùzǔ Tánjīng* 六祖壇經), also known as the *Sutra of Huineng*.[147]

These writings, and all other Chan texts detailing historical events of the time, agree on the first five patriarchs, but because the fifth patriarch, Hongren (Hóngrěn 弘忍), had numerous disciples (some of whom started their own schools), disagreement arose over who was the rightful sixth. Shenxiu was mentioned as the Sixth Patriarch of Chan according to later followers in his lineage—a lineage that would be referred to derisively as "Northern school teachings" by another of Hongren's disciples, Shenhui. In counterpoint, Shenhui's approach to Chan would become referred to as "Southern school."†

---

* It's not uncommon in the history of Chan for Dharma sermons to be crafted around a certain topic appropriate for the time and place, in order to address issues or problems that have arisen within the sangha. Invoking the principle of *upāya*—*skill-in-means*—an abbot could legitimately, for example, create a dialogue between a historic master and a monk that would illustrate and emphasize a particular point. When that point can be expressed by a past sage, it makes the message seem more believable and important.

† Prior to the identification of northern and southern Chan schools, the "northern" approach which Shenxiu propagated (and which is thought to have originated with Dàoxìn and Hóngrěn) came to be referred to as the "East Mountain Teaching." Of note, however,

Since many Chan and Zen practitioners today identify themselves exclusively with either the Northern ("gradual method") or Southern ("sudden method") school, it may be helpful to consider possible origins of the division and investigate if there were indeed significant differences between them.

Shenxiu was a highly respected monk in northern China, favored by the empire and scholars of the time, and a disciple of Hongren, who would be identified as the fifth Chan Patriarch. A generation later, Shenhui emerged in southen China as a disciple of Huineng, another of Hongren's disciples. In 730, about two decades after Shenxiu's death, Shenhui began efforts to discredit Shenxiu's teachings, a story pieced together by Yampolsky from the Mogao Cave texts.[148] Shenhui derisively called Shenxiu's teachings "Northern school" and launched a tireless campaign to discredit them, which ultimately succeeded.*[149]

Despite Shenhui's attacks on Shenxiu's teachings, the differences between their approaches to teaching were more strongly influenced by the context in which they taught than by fundamental differences in their insight into the Dharma.

This is a good time to pause and remind the reader that the experience of enlightenment, or spiritual awakening, is transformative (Chapter 18). It leads to new understanding, new awareness, and for many, a desire to share it with others so that they too may escape the illusory entrapment of self-identity. Yet the expression of the experience will naturally be different for everyone; it will be influenced by the experiences that led us there, by our language and culture, by our personalities, etc. For this reason, everyone who experiences enlightenment

---

McRae has commented that "the defining characteristics of the 'East Mountain Teaching' can only be approached through texts produced and/or edited during the later 'Northern school' phase" (1986, 118).

* McRae speculates that there was another force at work that led to the Northern school's demise in China: Shenxiu was extremely popular among government officials and the intellectuals of the time, and as the power of the dynasty receded from favor, so did Shenxiu, who was seen as closely connected to it. Before the Northern school fell out of favor in China, however, visiting monks from Korea and Japan transported it to their homelands, where it has enjoyed a lasting life. Northern school Chan would also make its way to Tibet during the eighth century, but as it merged with other religious ideologies, it lost much of its identity, contrary to its future longevity in Korea and Japan.

has something different to say about it, offers different insights into the experience, and propounds different methods for "getting there" commensurate with their own individual experiences. While the qualitative experience of enlightenment is undeniable to those who have encountered it, expressions of the enlightenment experience are highly diverse.

This may be what we see with Shenxiu and Shenhui: two different people, two different ways of describing things and teaching, each based on his own individual experiences, sensibilities, aptitudes, and contextual relationships with his community. When we fail to recognize that there can be different ways of expressing mystical experiences, it's natural that squabbles may arise over who is right and who is wrong. In the case of Shenxiu and Shenhui, each may have considered his own experience and understanding to be the only valid one. At least from Shenhui's records, we know he had grave objections to Shenxiu's expression of Buddhism as a gradual process dependent upon seated meditation.

Shenxiu's writings are less clear, at least what we have of them. He mostly discusses the state of mind referred to as *samādhi*, or *meditation* in the original Indian meaning of the term. This state is sometimes described as expansive-awareness, emptiness, and vastness. Shenxiu encouraged people to go directly into this place:

> To view the mind as pure is called "to purify the mind-ground."
> Do not constrict the body and mind and then unfold the body and mind—view afar in expansive release. View with universal "sameness."
> Exhaust space with your viewing.[150]

To one who has experienced this level of meditation, Shenxiu's description and instruction is appropriate, but for others it likely offers little help, and may even hinder one's ability to "get there" (Chapters 9 and 21). Shenxiu taught in the context of monasticism, in which monks were first trained with concentration practices before being presented with advanced contemplative practices. The context of Shenxiu's training environment is thus extremely relevant for understanding his teaching approach.

Shenhui, on the other hand, was less monastically inclined and more aligned with the role of inspirational orator and evangelist, preaching on an ordination platform to people who had no formal monastic experience. He taught that anyone could awaken in this very moment, and that awakening was not dependent upon any particular method at all. Unlike Shenxiu's teaching, Shenhui taught that anyone could experience spiritual awakening, young and old, poor and rich alike; moreover, awakening was not dependent upon monastic life or monastic rule. Shenhui disapproved of sitting-meditation as the singular means through which one could awaken. When asked by Chongyuan why he preached Chan without sitting, Shenhui replied:

> To teach people to sit [in meditation this way] ... is to obstruct bodhi (i.e., spiritual awakening). When I say 'sit' now, [I mean that] 'sitting' is for thought not to be activated. When I say 'meditation' now, [I mean that] 'meditation' is to see the fundamental nature. Therefore, I do not teach people to have their bodies sit and their minds abide in entrance into concentration. If it were correct to declare such a teaching, then Vimalakīrti would not have scolded Śāripūtra for sitting in meditation.[151]

Shenhui refers to a passage in the *Vimalakīrti Nirdesa Sūtra* in which Śāriputra recounts to the Buddha being admonished by Vimalakīrti for sitting in contemplation:

> I remember one day, when I was sitting at the foot of a tree in the forest, absorbed in contemplation, the Licchavi Vimalakīrti came to the foot of that tree and said to me, 'Reverend Śāriputra, this is not the way to absorb yourself in contemplation. You should absorb yourself in contemplation so that neither body nor mind appear anywhere in the triple world. You should absorb yourself in contemplation in such a way that you can manifest all ordinary behavior without forsaking cessation. You should absorb yourself in contemplation in such a way

that you can manifest the nature of an ordinary person without abandoning your cultivated spiritual nature. You should absorb yourself in contemplation so that the mind neither settles within nor moves without toward external forms. You should absorb yourself in contemplation in such a way that the thirty-seven aids to enlightenment are manifest without deviation toward any convictions. You should absorb yourself in contemplation in such a way that you are released in liberation without abandoning the passions that are the province of the world.[152]

In other words, it's not the act of sitting that's important, but where we direct the mind: what's happening with our physical body is of secondary importance.

So, we might differentiate the two monks this way: Shenxiu taught Buddhism in the accepted monastic tradition, using seated forms of practice in accordance with the example established by the Bodhidharma legend, while Shenhui taught people not to limit themselves that way, and that confining practice to the seated position is a hindrance, "obstructing bodhi." Shenhui did not suggest that seated forms of meditation should be avoided, but that Buddha-mind must be cultivated at all times in all circumstances and not be impeded by dependencies of any kind. Alternately, Shenxiu taught a formal method in the context of a rigid ecclesiastical system, which relied on seated forms of meditation, unlike Shenhui's approach which was essentially independent of method. Shenhui derisively referred to Shenxiu's methodical approach as "gradual" (spiritual growth happens gradually as you practice seated meditation); in contrast, his devotees would refer to his approach as "sudden"* (spiritual awakening happens spontaneously and independently of any particular method).

As we find throughout the history of Chan, teachers go about teaching the same thing in many different ways—an approach encouraged as an application of upāya, or skill-in-means. While we may consider

---

* Sudden awakening was expressed in the Vinaya canon as well, in what is referred to as the Buddha's *Second Sermon at Benares*. The sermon declares, for example, that salvation can be found immediately from merely hearing the sermon (Vetter, 1988, XXXXIV).

it unfortunate that Shenhui created a rift in Buddhism, one that has fractured Zen Buddhists into two different camps to this day, we might also consider that without his devotion to destroying the status quo of formal Chan training methods, Chan may have lost its vitality in the centuries to follow and may never have invented the *encounter dialogues* which came to characterize the classical, or middle, period (c. 750-1000 CE) as an even more distinctive and creative expression of Buddhism in China.

But what does all this have to do with Huineng, the subject of this section? Why is Huineng the pivotal figure of this period instead of Shenhui, who was recorded as preaching essentially the same thing as Huineng, according to documents such as the *Li-tai fa-pao chi*? The *Platform Sutra* makes no mention of Shenhui as an important monk, yet some of the texts of the period state that Shenhui is the seventh patriarch and Huineng the sixth.[153] All we have to go on are fragments of preserved texts to help identify a particular Chan school along with the mystique that surrounds Huineng. We are left only to speculate about what may have happened by examining the literary intent and methods employed by the authors who are, more often than not, anonymous. The conclusions of researchers, such as John McRae and John Jorgensen,[154] seem plausible: the Huineng legend was invented for the purpose of solidifying the Chan school.[155] While Huineng may have existed as a monk who received transmission from Hongren, and he may have indeed been Shenhui's master, there seems to be no historical evidence that he was a significant player in the socioreligious Chan movement during his lifetime."[156] It seems possible that Shenhui, and/or his heirs, may have sought to establish a new lineage that emphasized his values by means of creating a new legend—a legend that, ironically perhaps, would remove Shenhui as an important figure in Chan's quint-

---

*McRae writes that there is "good evidence to show that in the late 730s Shenhui was ignorant of most of the details of Huineng's life" (2003, 67). He continues, "It is striking, even stunning, how little Shenhui knows about the person who is supposed to be his own master. . . . It is probably fair to think of the historical Huineng as a reasonably conventional Chinese monk, whose teachings differed only slightly if at all from those of other members of the Northern school" (2003, 68).

essential story line.¹⁵⁷ Huineng's putative mummy on prominent display at Nan Hua temple in China is testimony to his great importance to the Chan tradition (monks are normally cremated and rarely mummified).

We can keep in mind that this was a period when Chan was still trying to define itself. Ancestor veneration, when applied to Buddhism, required that knowledge of the Dharma must be securely transmitted to the next generation *or it would be lost*. It was thus essential to establish a solid connection from Hongren to seal the identity of Chan.

The stories of Huineng are valuable from the point of view of defining a quintessential person/legend in Chan's storyline, and for explaining the early character of Chan thought and training. A passage from the *Platform Sutra* commonly used in Chan monasteries to begin Dharma talks, or sermons, is the story of the Wind and the Flag: One gusty evening while Huineng was sheltered under the eaves of Fa-hsing Temple, he heard two monks arguing over the stirring temple flag:

> One said it was the flag that was moving, the other that it was the wind. Back and forth they argued, but they were unable to realize the true principle.
>
> Hui-neng said: "Pardon a common layman for intruding into your lofty discussion, but it is neither the banner nor the wind that is moving; it is only your own mind that moves." Yin-tsung overheard this remark and his flesh crept at the strangeness of it. The next day he invited Hui-neng to his room, and in response to his intense questions about the meaning of [his remark about] the banner and the wind, Hui-neng explained the principle in detail. Yin-tsung involuntarily arose, saying: "You are no ordinary man. Who was your teacher?" Hui-neng, hiding nothing, at once told him of how he obtained the Dharma. Then Yin-tsung assumed the position of a disciple and begged for instruction in the essentials of Ch'an.¹⁵⁸

As with many of the stories contained in the *Platform Sutra*, this one serves multiple purposes: it frames Chan as the "Mind Only" school,* it

---

* The mind, in this context, is not the reasoning, thinking, mind, but the mind of awareness. The "mind only" Chan school was characterized in the early *Pratyutpanna Samādhi*

reinforces the importance of Huineng's Dharma lineage, and it emphasizes the importance of the Master-disciple relationship characteristic of monastic training. The *Platform Sutra* is the only text to have been given the status of a sutra without being attributed to the Buddha directly, an act that assigned Huineng status equal to the Buddha himself.

But the value of the *Platform Sutra* to Chan practitioners, aside from clearly linking Buddhism with Taoism and Confucianism, has less to do with whom it's attributed to than to several strong positions it takes in defining Chan, among them:

- One cannot attain merit through good deeds.

- The fundamental nature of reality is emptiness.

- It's preferable to practice Chan as a layman, outside the walls of a monastery, than to follow the forms of monasticism without applying an inner-practice.

- The essence of practice is to eliminate false thoughts.

- The "sudden" and "gradual" approaches (i.e., "South" and "North") are simply two different ways, each appropriate for different "kinds" of people. From the Platform Sutra:*

    > What is meant by 'gradual' and 'sudden?' The Dharma itself is the same, but in seeing it there is a slow way and a fast way. Seen slowly, it is the gradual; seen fast it is the sudden [teaching]. Dharma is without sudden or gradual, but some people are keen and others dull; hence the names 'sudden' and 'gradual'[159]

- Sitting, focused on "mind-blanking," is a deluded way. From the Platform Sutra:

Sūtra: "The mind creates the Buddha. The mind itself sees him. The mind is the Buddha. The mind is the Tathagata. The mind is the body, the mind sees the Buddha. The mind does not itself know the mind, the mind does not itself see the mind. A mind with conceptions is stupidity, a mind without conceptions is nirvāṇa" (Paul Harrison and John R. McRae 1998, 26).

* In the following except, note the derisive language used to describe people who follow the "gradual" or "Northern school" approach.

> The deluded man clings to the characteristics of things, adheres to the samādhi of oneness, [thinks] that straightforward mind is sitting without moving and casting aside delusions without letting things arise in the mind. [...] If sitting in meditation without moving is good, why did Vimalakīrti scold Śāriputra for sitting in meditation in the forest?[160]

(Note the close similarity of this to the comment ascribed to Shenhui, presented earlier.)

- On the path of salvation, everything needed is within us, and it's up to us alone to do the work. No one can do it for us. From the Platform Sutra:

  > "Good friends, when I say 'I vow to save all sentient beings everywhere,' it is not that I will save you, but that sentient beings, each with their own natures, must save themselves. What is meant by 'saving yourselves with your own natures'? Despite heterodox views, passions, ignorance, and delusions, in your own physical bodies you have in yourselves the attributes of inherent enlightenment, so that with correct views you can be saved. If you are awakened to correct views, the wisdom of prajñā will wipe away ignorance and delusion, and you all will save yourselves. If false views come, with correct views you will be saved; if delusion comes, with awakening you will be saved; if ignorance comes, with wisdom you will be saved; if evil comes, with good you will be saved; if the passions come, with bodhi you will be saved. Being saved in this way is known as true salvation."[161]

- The mind that seeks enlightenment is deluded. From the *Platform Sutra*: "Although enlightenment [bodhi] is originally pure, creating the mind that seeks it is then delusion."[162]

Esoteric Buddhism and the rise of the Chan master

During the early eighth century, while Shenxiu was setting the stage for what would become known as Northern school Chan, Śubhākarasiṃha (and soon after, Vajrabodhi and Amoghavajra) was bringing a new interpretation of Buddhism to China from India: Vajrayāna, or esoteric Buddhism, eventually codified as the *Zhen Yan* (Jap., *Shingon*), or *Mantra* school. Esoteric Buddhism involved the use of visualization techniques and impressive ritual enactments to control weather, disease, and military victories, and, according to McRae, came to pervade the entire East Asian consciousness.[163] It also further alienated Northern school Chan from its southern counterpart because Śubhākarasiṃha frequently criticized Shenxiu's approach, contending that "single-mindedly maintaining nonthought (*wunian*) as the ultimate, the [longer you] search, the more unattainable [is your goal]."[164] In other words, he professed that people who followed the Northern school teachings of Shenxiu would get nowhere spiritually.

Esoteric Buddhism influenced the Chan school in multiple ways, especially its emphasis on master-student relationships, which helped solidify the Dharma-lineage tradition and establish the teacher, or master, as a Buddha. This would produce an environment ripe for hagiographical accounts of past teachers in the yulu-genre: *encounter dialogues*.* "What is ironic," Albert Welter writes, "is that although yulu grew out of a movement that challenged the very nature of authority, especially as codified through existing canonical texts, yulu established a new authority, constituting what might be characterized as a kind of anti-authoritarian authority, a new anti-orthodox orthodoxy."[165]

Encounter dialogues would produce some of the most unusual canonical texts of any religion in world history and characterize Chan

---

* The yulu genre of Chan are records of a specific master that include poetry, anecdotes, sermons, and conversations. It is thought to have developed originally from the platform talks given by Shenhui (*tanyu*).

as an entirely distinct and purely Chinese expression of mystical Buddhism.

Encounter Dialogue: the gong-an & hua-tou

> Ta-chu Hui-hai, an eighth-century Buddhist, once went to visit the great master Ma-tsu (Kiangsi Tao-i). The Master asked him, "Why do you come here?"
>
> Ta-chu replied, "I come seeking enlightenment."
>
> The Master said, "Why should you leave your home to wander about and neglect your own precious treasure? There is nothing I can give you. Why do you seek enlightenment from me?"
>
> The visitor pressed him for the truth: "But what is my treasure?"
>
> The Master answered, "It is he who has just asked the question. It contains everything and lacks nothing. There is no need to seek it outside yourself."
>
> – Record of the Transmission of the Lamp[166]

The *Records of the Transmission of the Lamp* (*Jǐngdé Chuándēnglù* 景德傳燈錄) was the first substantial expression of what is now referred to as *Classical Chan*, following the *Anthology of the Patriarchal Hall* in 952. Producing it was not a minor undertaking. Written in thirty volumes during the Song dynasty by Daoyuan (*Dàoyuán* 釋道原), it sought to clearly define Chan, from its history and genealogy to its philosophy and practices. It paved the way for three successive works which would further refine and popularize the format of encounter-dialogues: the *Blue Cliff Record* (*Bìyán Lù* 碧巖錄), which was produced during the early 12th century,* the *Book of Equanimity* (*Cóngróng lù* 從容錄), and

---

* The *Blue Cliff Record* was the product of a collection of teachings from Chan masters accumulated by Dahui Zonggao.

The Gateless Barrier (*Wúménguān* 無門關), produced by Wansong Xingxiu and Wumen Huikai, respectively, during the early 13th century.

Encounter dialogues, however, were known much earlier in China. The reader may recall that numerous anecdotal stories of Chuang Tzu were written in this format many centuries earlier, suggesting it was already a familiar and respected literary form when it reappeared during the formative years of Chan. As an expression of Chan, encounter dialogues became more than just storytelling devices; they would define Chan as a path that:

- relies on insight, Self-awareness and meditation,
- engages both inner (contemplation) and outer (action) aspects,
- has a precisely known lineage traceable to the Buddha,
- exists because of that lineage,
- emphasizes the importance of venerating Dharma ancestors,
- seeks to transcend the rational mind by whatever means possible,
- encourages independent investigation and admonishes seeking solutions from others, and
- does not rely on scriptures.

These positions, in general, came to comprise Chan's self-definition and, as such, became implicit axioms. We may note historical discrepancies when it comes to lineage; we may question how the lineage was created or established; we may even question the actual existence of some of Chan's purported lineage-holders. But from the point of view of Chan, such questions are outside its realm of interest.* Although we may justifiably endorse Cole's conclusion that, "In effect, the Song authors created the perfect masters of the Tang in order to be their

---

* We may consider, for example, that when a Chan monk is acknowledged by the collective Chan community as a lineage-holder, that makes him de facto so, regardless of factual circumstances surrounding Dharma transmission, historical context, etc.

descendants—a grand case of fathering your father..."; [167] it's also worth considering the development of the Chan storyline in light of the literary medium of encounter dialogue itself. It provided a framework from which Chan could establish an identity and grow. But neither that framework nor the expression that came from it were as important, independently, as the fact that one begot the other; that is, through the medium of this form of expression, Chan emerged.

Encounter dialogues, which evolved into the literary format of gong-ans, use a variety of literary techniques to achieve their goals: vernacular speech makes them resemble precise renderings of actual encounters, lending plausibility; they typically pair a clueless student with an enlightened master to juxtapose "nonenlightened" discursive thought (the student) with "enlightened" nondiscursive thought (the master);* they install the Chan master above and beyond the understanding of the unenlightened, enabling him free recourse to use any and all teaching methods that might help the student break out of the conditioned mind; they provide a clear approach to teaching that could be used in the monastic setting; and they offer useful topics for extemporaneous talks and sermons, allowing for embellishment as needed to fit the circumstances.

How, exactly, encounter dialogues evolved, however, remains unknown. Albert Welter, author of *The Linji Lu and the Creation of Chan Orthodoxy*, writes that

> ...[i]t will never be clear whether the encounter dialogues in Chan yulu are the product of storytelling or of literary embellishment. Did practitioners recounting the tales around the fire, or in some other venue, produce them, or were they the product of the literary imagination of those who wrote them down? It is likely that both played a role, and it is perhaps best to consider these as two aspects of a continuum that coproduced the encounter dialogues as they appear to us today. Whoever was responsible, all involved were keen to cre-

---

* This mirrored the literary techniques we observe centuries earlier in the *Chuang Tzu* dialogues, c. 4th century BCE. Discursive and nondiscursive modes of thought reflect dualistic and nondualistic perspectives, respectively. See Chapter 18 for further discussion.

ate a new, uniquely Chan interpretation of Buddhism. The past (i.e., Buddhist scriptures and doctrines) was no longer an encumbrance that dictated the terms with which present reality was understood. The imagination intervened to create a new sense of the past, and this creation was transcribed through yulu as the accepted version. Living memory, as it were, trumped received wisdom. In this process, fictionalization was not seen as the falsification of events but as the verification of truth.[168]

Well after gong-ans became an accepted method of Chan training, the Linji master Dahui Zonggao 大慧宗杲 (1089-1163) began teaching the importance of pondering their *critical phrase* (*kan huatou*), an approach that later came to be known as *kanhua* 看話 Chan. It would lead to the *hua-tou* 話頭 as a Chan training method that could be used independently of gong-ans and would be popularized centuries later by monks such as Han Shan, Hsu Yun, and his disciples Jy Din, and Ben Huan. The hua-tou will be described in detail in Chapter 12.

While "Southern school" approaches to Chan training were gaining momentum, "Northern school" approaches, as presented by the Caodong sect, were losing steam. During the 12th century, Dahui was among the most vocal adversaries of Caodong's silent illumination approach, and was largely responsible for its reduced popularity in China.* Nonetheless, "Northern school" teachings eventually returned to being considered equally legitimate to the Linji "sudden illumination" approach, unlike in Japan, where the two schools continue their conflict.†[169]

---

* For a thorough examination of Dahui Zonggao's profound influence on Chan, and the effect of local governing officials and literati on the Chan institution during the Song dynasty, see Morten Schlütter's *How Zen Became Zen, The Dispute Over Enlightenment and the Formation of Chan Buddhism in Song-Dynasty China*, 2008, University of Hawaii Press.

† In general, it's understood in China that different methods serve different people's needs, so a great diversity of methods and approaches are encouraged. There are enough dissimilarities between Caodong and Linji approaches, however, that chan teachers generally present one, but not both, according to their own experiences and preferences.

Chan lineage & Dharma transmission

The forces which created and shaped the Chan lineage system, we have seen, can be traced to the Chinese practice of ancestor veneration, a characteristic of traditional folk religion with origins dating to the Neolithic period.*[170] Although Buddhism is not concerned with traditional familial lineages, such as those represented by Chinese *kinship churches* (*zōngzú tang* 宗族堂), Buddhists could not easily abandon the cultural imperative to revere the deceased.† Their solution was to venerate their Dharma ancestors instead. For this substitution to work, however, a mechanism was needed to connect one Dharma generation with the next. That mechanism would become known as *Dharma transmission*; it relied on an ineffable *something* called Dharma that could be conveyed from monk to monk (master to disciple). Dharma transmission allowed ancestors to be venerated while preserving the perfect teaching and understanding of Buddhism. The event of transmission itself could happen either publicly and ceremonially, or privately and without fanfare. It could even happen in dreams.[171]

In practice, Dharma transmission has served purposes other than just establishing lineage and enabling ancestral worship. Just as we have identified two types of Chan, one institutional and one spiritual (or mystical), we can also identify two corresponding types of transmission: one serving the institution (ecclesiastical), and one reflecting or acknowledging spiritual awakening or enlightenment (*wù* 悟).

Ecclesiastical transmission has historically been used for practical purposes, such as installing a monk as an abbot of a monastery.‡ This

---

* The importance of Lineage to the Buddha was established in India before Buddhism entered China. The *Pratyutpanna Sūtra*—one of the first sutras to begin establishing a distinctive Mahāyāna voice—emphasized its importance.

† To be a follower of the *Buddha Dharma* means severing attachments to family and friends and devoting oneself entirely to Buddhist principles and practices; thus, for a Buddhist, it is unacceptable to venerate one's parents or genealogical ancestors.

‡ Welsh has noted that Dharma transmission has been a fluid concept for the Chinese. It could be freely applied for different purposes as situations warranted: "...sometimes receiving the dharma was the prerequisite for becoming abbot; sometimes becoming abbot was the prelude to receiving the dharma. In still other cases, the dharma had nothing to do with abbotship. The practice differed from monastery to monastery, and any one of them could

form of transmission acknowledges a monk as a teacher or administrator, making him eligible to perform ceremonies—some of which are essential for the temple's financial (and political) health, as well as the social stability of the institution.[172] In such cases, transmission could be given ceremonially to a monk who had been selected to be abbot by council appointment—assuming he had not already received transmission[173]—and proof of transmission could be provided by the issuance of a Dharma scroll or certificate. Spiritual transmission, on the other hand, has never been dependent upon a master or teacher to give it, but relies solely on one's own spiritual awakening. Hsu Yun, for example, taught that "enlightenment is the only medium of transmission."*[174]

Dharma lineage offered a means for tracking a succession of monks back to a common Dharma-ancestor: the Buddha. Each branch of the resulting "Dharma family tree" could be identified by the teachings of a specific monk who had been acknowledged as having received transmission. The branches are all considered to represent the Dharma equally; for this reason, it's been common for a monk of one sect to serve as abbot of another, and for some monks to "receive the Dharma" in all of them, a practice still common in the present era. To illustrate, Welsh offers the following account of the fluidity of Chan lineage-affiliations:

> "... one of my informants [when researching for this book] was Lin-chi by tonsure and began his career practicing meditation at a Lin-chi monastery. After a year and a half, he found that this was too 'lofty' (*kao-shang*) and hard to understand, so he tried T'ien-t'ai meditation (*chih-kuan*). After eight years of unsatisfactory progress in the latter, he finally shifted to the Pure Land practice of reciting Buddha's name.

---

change its practice as circumstances required" (1963, 96). Alternatively, in Japan, abbacy is traditionally (though not always) proffered through father-to-son inheritance.

* This contradicts Cole's assertion of the opposite, that transmission is the medium of enlightenment; however, transmission can be viewed both as a mechanism that supports and sustains the religion (Cole's point), as well as a means for expressing and acknowledging spiritual insight (Hsu Yun's point). The context in which the term is invoked—either mystical or religious—distinguishes its meaning. From Hsu Yun's perspective, transmission can not happen without spiritual awakening, and from Cole's perspective, enlightenment is bestowed upon someone who "receives transmission" in a formal, ecclesial, sense, and carries no particular spiritual or mystical significance.

But he still considered himself either Lin-chi on the basis of tonsure or T'ien-t'ai on the basis of the T'ien-t'ai dharma that he had received. The Venerable Tao-chieh, who acted as a witness at the ordination of T'ai-hsü in 1904, is described as following the T'ien't'ai sect and concurrently (*chien*) the Avatamsaka and Dharmalaksana sects. This was in respect to doctrine. In respect to tonsure, he was Lin-chi, and in 1924 he served as abbot of one of the leading monasteries of the Vinaya sect, the Fa-yüan Ssu in Peking. Another eminent monk, Hsü-Yün, made it a point to receive the dharma not only of Lin-chi and Ts'ao tung, but of Yün-men, Fa-yen, and Kui-yang—sects whose lineage had terminated centuries before."[175]

Welsh further notes that, in China, receiving a Dharma scroll as a symbol of Dharma transmission "was not exclusive. One could become a dharma disciple in more than one lineage and more than one sect."[176] Contrary to Japanese Zen sects, which were often at war with one another over their differing interpretations of Buddhism (Chapter 7),† many Chinese monasteries readily combined the views and practices of multiple sects:

> [t]he former abbot of the T'ien-ning Ssu told me that, although its bell and board were Lin-chi, the monastery 'did not belong to a single sect'. It advocated and practiced Ch'an, Pure Land, recitation of the Diamond Sutra (in a special hall for the purpose), and the study in its seminary of T'ien-t'ai, Wei-shih (Idealist) and Hsien-shou (Hua-yen) doctrines.[177]

---

*During my stay at Hong Fa Temple in Shenzhen, I met several monks who had previously been ordained in other lineages, including one monk from Tibet who practiced in the uniquely Tibetan tradition. Considering the fluidity of lineage in Chinese Buddhism, it's not surprising that precise lineage trees are rarely encountered, and when they are, they are invariably incomplete if not substantially wrong, historically.

† In Japan, rigid doctrinal distinctions between sects created isolation and discord. The lack of rigid distinctions between sects in China, Welch has commented, has led many Japanese Buddhists to discount Chinese Buddhism, as they have believed it to represent "... evidence of decay and this may be one of the reasons why they have avoided the study of modern Chinese Buddhism" (1967, 397).

As we have observed repeatedly throughout the history of Buddhism, differences in interpretations of Buddhist philosophy and practice, along with broad variation in spiritual experiences themselves, have led to a colorful variety of schools, sects, and sub-sects. And throughout Chan's history, teachers have expressed the Dharma according to their own sensibilities and experiences. Along the way, teachers who gained a significant following became pivotal figures for separate sects, or "houses"; of them, five received notoriety: *Gui Yang*, *Linji*, *Caodong*, *Fayan*, and *Yunmen*.* Rather than referring to them as separate sects or schools, however, they came to be referred to, poetically, as *petals*. Together, they are said to represent the flower that is Chan.†

To track a monk's lineage in a particular house, a convention was adopted during the late Ming period to use generation characters (*beizi* 輩字). By the mid-Qing dynasty, they had been formalized into poems:[178] a monk giving transmission would assign the next character of the poem from his own and choose a second character to accompany it. Together, the two characters would form the complete tonsure name (*tidu ming* 剃度名) of the newly ordained monk or nun. A second name—referred to as a courtesy name or style name (*zì* 字)—would be given when entering adulthood, or later if one had not been previously assigned. Figure 6 shows a stanza from the Linji tonsure poem in hanzi, pinyin, and English.

This poetic approach to Dharma transmission might seem like a clever and functional way to track lineage, but situations arise that make backward tracking of lineage extremely challenging. For example, Hsuan-Li Wang has observed that,

> in the case when the master and the heir belonged to different Chan tonsure lineages, when the heir received a new name in the dharma

---

* There may have been other popular sects which failed to make a mark on the literary record for geographical or sociopolitical reasons.

† The "five petals" allegory may have originated with the *Platform Sutra*, which ascribes a petal to each of the five patriarchs preceding Huineng. The petals were said to have been opened by Bodhidharma (as he was the common Dharma ancestor of them all) to reveal a flower.

transmission, for the heir, it was the name of the dharma transmission, not the name of the tonsure, but for the master, the new name was named following the transmission poem of his own Chan tonsure lineage. It is at this point that the transmission poems of the Chan tonsure lineages and the transmission poems of the dharma transmission lineages got entangled and resulted in complexities which perplex scholars who attempt to check.[179]

For the monk or nun, however, backward tracking of lineage is of little importance. It's enough to know that one is recognized as a legitimate lineage-holder in a tradition that is ipso facto continuous: even if there might be breaks in the person-to-person transmission somewhere in the tree (recall that transmission could happen even in a dream), the transmission of Dharma as a means of expressing and/or acknowledging spiritual awakening, is absolute and inalienable.

Traditional Chinese (hànzì)	Pinyin	English
心源廣續	Xin Yuan Guang Xu	The heart/mind is the source, all-embracing and ever-continuing.
本覺昌隆	Ben Jue Chang Long	The source is conscious, good, and abundant.
能仁聖果	Neng Ren Sheng Guo	Being benevolent brings the sacred fruit.
常漢寬宏	Chang Yan Kuan Hong	Always exercise expansiveness and spaciousness.
惟傳法印	Wei Chuan Fa Yin	Only transmit the Dharma seal.
證悟會融	Zheng Wu Hui Rong	Witness realization to gather harmony.
堅持戒定	Jian Chi Jie Ding	Resolutely sustain sila with determination.
永繼祖宗	Yong Ji Zu Zong	Forever continue the ancestral lineage.

FIGURE 6. DHARMA LINEAGE POEM.

A stanza from a tonsure poem used to select ordination names for monks and nuns and identify them with a specific Dharma lineage.

THE FIVE PETALS OF CHAN

The first of Chan's petals was *Gui Yang* (*Kui Yang*), named after two monks during the 9th century: Guishan Lingyou and Yangshan Huiji. Also known as the *Weiyang* school, it did not last long and in short time was absorbed into *Linji*.

The Linji petal was named after the teachings of the monk Línjì Yìxuán, who was renowned for using dramatic and sudden acts, such as shouting and hitting with sticks.

The *Caodong* petal, founded by Dongshan Liangjie and later developed by his heirs, emphasized sitting meditation. Japan would become the predominant heir to Caodong. Through the work of Dōgen, it would adapt to Shintō, the term ascribed to Japan's indigenous folk religion, and become known as Sōtō Zen (Chapter 7).

The *Fayan* petal received its name from the monk Fayan Wenyi (885-958).

Finally, the *Yunmen* petal was named after the monk Yunmen Wenyan, who was known as an exceptional orator and the originator of "one-word barriers." For example, he would shout "*Guan!*", referring to a barrier which a student must penetrate. His often-ambiguous teachings would become popular topics for gong-ans, chan training devices we'll explore in Part Two. Yunmen's thoughts on Chan survive in the *Yunmen Quinzhee Chánshī Guǎnglù*. In addition, eighteen gong-ans in the *Blue Cliff Record* reference him.

Again, it's important to point out that each of these sects or schools shaped Chan into what it is today: for the Chinese, it is a flower with many petals, each contributing to the whole, each offering different perspectives on the same thing. In China, Chan has historically preferred inclusion to exclusion; monks are encouraged to read and study canonical texts and other writings regardless of their affiliated sects. Understanding comes from synthesizing information, from piecing seemingly unconnected pieces together to create a whole. It was in this spirit of unification that the famous Chan monk of the 20th century, Hsu Yun

(Figure 5), is said to have become a transmitted lineage holder in all five petals.*

Buddhism during and after the Tang Dynasty

The Tang dynasty (618-907) was generally one of growth and prosperity for Buddhism, and Chan in particular, until national economic troubles developed. In the mid-ninth century, and again in the tenth, Buddhism was severely persecuted. As mentioned earlier, temples were destroyed, and many monks and nuns were forced back into lay life.[180] Buddhist schools that relied on religious texts, such as the Tian Tai and Hua Yan, suffered the most, as many of their texts were destroyed (they would later recover copies of some of them from Korea and Japan). Schools that did not rely on scriptures, namely Chan and Pure Land, survived the period more easily.

FIGURE 5. EMPTY CLOUD.

Chan Master Hsu Yun—Empty Cloud—attested to lineage in all five Chan schools and was credited for establishing the Chinese Buddhist Association at Kuang Chi Monastery, which continues to help smooth relations with the Chinese government today. He was also responsible for re-popularizing the hua-tou practice. Visibly deformed fingers were a result of beatings by the red guards during China's Cultural Revolution.

---

* This was confirmed during discussions I had with monks at Hsu Yun Temple in Honolulu, Hawaii, in 1997, a temple founded by Hsu Yun's "Dharma descendent," Jy Din. Hsu Yun's means of receiving Dharma transmission in all lineages, however, remains unknown to me. Does this reference spiritual transmission (which can happen even in dreams) or ecclesial transmission, which must be proffered by an ordained monk who has "received transmission" in the school's respective lineage? If going by Hsu Yun's thoughts on the subject, it implies the former. Regardless, from the institution's perspective, it implies that all of Hsu Yun's heirs (Dharma descendents) likewise share lineages with all five sects.

If there was much disharmony between Buddhism, neo-Taoism, and neo-Confucianism before the end of the Tang dynasty, it gradually vanished during the Sung dynasty (960-1279), as efforts were made to unite the three. To this day, many Chinese offer devotions to all three "founders"—the Buddha, Confucius, and Lao Tzu—at monasteries and temples throughout China, and the distinctions between them have, for many, blurred into insignificance.*[181] Chan monks also worked to harmonize Pure Land practices with Chan, combining recitation practices of the Pure Land school in the Buddha hall with Chan concentration and contemplation practices in the meditation hall.†[182]

The Ming dynasty (1368–1644) is noted especially for the work of the monk Zhu Hung, who helped meld the three socioreligious "isms" into one and emphasized the value of lay practice. For the average Chinese of the time, religious life was a (various) mix of Buddhism, Taoism, Confucianism, and folk religion.

During the Manchurian Qing dynasty (1644-1912), Buddhism decayed, along with Chinese culture,[183] giving rise to secret Buddhist societies. Social, political, and religious tensions finally led to the Tai Ping Rebellion in 1850. During its fourteen years, up to thirty million people died, many due to plague and famine. By the end of the Qing dynasty, Buddhism was effectively on its knees. Severe poverty prevailed around the nation, and Buddhist monasteries were abandoned or converted for other uses. The Chan monk Jy Din Shakya recalled his experience as a boy visiting Nan Hua Temple in Shao Guan (where Huineng is purported to have lived and taught) during the early part of the 20th century:

---

* There is still controversy on this topic, Adamek suggests: "The study of Buddhist-Daoist interactions involves such hotly contested issues as whether it is misleading to speak of Buddhism, Daoism, and Confucianism as 'religions,' whether one can speak of 'syncretism' among these traditions, whether it is possible to draw distinctions between 'elite' and 'popular' religion, how the relationship between belief and practice should be conceived, and the ways in which the history of interaction between Asia and the West has influenced the construction of such categories" (Adamek 2007, 237).

† To this day, Chan monasteries are little different in appearance from Pure Land monasteries—they are, for all intents and purposes, the same thing. Dharma talks (sermons) frequently comingle Pure Land concepts with Chan concepts, Taoist ideologies, and Confucian principles.

... no one seemed to be in charge of it. About a hundred monks and a few dozen nuns lived there, but mostly they busied themselves with bickering. Nuns argued with nuns. Monks argued with monks. Nuns argued with monks. And the buildings of this great religious center were merely the places in which all these arguments took place. It didn't seem to matter that the wood was rotting and the stonework was crumbling and the ironwork of the old red and white pagoda was rusting. The decay had merely kept pace with the decline in monastic discipline.[184]

During the following Republican period (1912-1949), Buddhist associations again began forming, this time to help build bridges between Buddhist monastics and laity, and between the Buddhist institution and the government:

> These modern Buddhist associations, the first of which was founded in 1900, had precedents in the Buddhist societies that had existed since the fourteenth century and had helped overthrow the Mongol and Manchurian dynasties. The Buddhist associations of the twentieth century, however, attempted to adapt Buddhism to modern realities and to negotiate with rather than overthrow governments. These associations worked to improve monastic education, enhance Buddhism's social relevance by establishing schools and orphanages, and make monasteries economically viable through fund-raising activities.[185]

In 1928, Chiang Kai-shek (Jiang Jieshi or Jiang Zhongzheng) entered China's political arena to try to reestablish national stability under a communist authoritarian government. Other communist insurgents had different aspirations, however, and soon a conflict arose which ultimately led to civil war. In 1949, following Mao's victory over Chiang Kai-shek, the People's Republic of China was established and Chiang fled mainland China for Taiwan. The government he established there (The Republic of China) still considers itself the rightful and legitimate government of China.

Buddhism flourished in Taiwan and, to a lesser degree, in mainland China. But that changed when Mao Zedong began a brutal campaign to eradicate Buddhism from the country soon after he became chairman of the Communist Party in 1949. Jy Din describes the harsh treatment his master, Hsu Yun, received during this time:

> Not long after I arrived in Hong Kong in 1949, the Chinese Civil War ended, and the Communists took control of the government. Cadres of Communist thugs, supposing that Churches and Temples were repositories of hidden gold and other valuables, marched on the defenseless religious buildings and demanded that the clergymen turn over these nonexistent treasures to them.
>
> In 1951, while I was in Hong Kong, a cadre of these thugs came to Yun Men Monastery and demanded that Xu [Hsu] Yun give them the temple's gold and valuables. Xu Yun tried to explain that there were no such valuables at Yun Men Monastery. But they refused to believe him and one by one, they beat the monks in an effort to force a disclosure of the treasure's location. One monk was actually beaten to death; several monks disappeared and their bodies were never found. Many suffered serious injuries such as broken arms and ribs. During the three months the thugs occupied the monastery, they would regularly interrogate and beat Xu Yun and then throw him into a small dark room for days, depriving him of food and water. Several times he was beaten into senselessness and left for dead.*[186]

Mao's objective was to wipe out all traces of what he saw as superstitious nonsense. His policies would lead to one of China's bloodiest campaigns against its own people, and one of the most destructive wars the world has seen, the Great Proletarian Cultural Revolution (1966-69). His vision was to bring modernization and industry to China through "grassroots socialism," and ancient religious traditions could play no

---

* Hsu Yun would become instrumental in effecting a peace accord with the government in 1953 through the Chinese Buddhist Association at Kuang Chi Monastery, which he helped establish. The Association won its appeal for the government to halt its attack against Buddhists and their property, to return previously confiscated property, and to provide Buddhist temples with enough arable land to allow them to be self-supporting.

part. Buddhist monks were tortured and killed, and temples, statues, and texts were destroyed. After Mao's death in 1976, Buddhism began a slow and cautious return.

In 2017, China began what it calls "sinicization" of religion: a "far-reaching strategy to control, govern, and manipulate all aspects of faith into a socialist mold infused with 'Chinese characteristics.'"[187] While foreign religions such as Christianity and Islam are now under extreme persecution, Buddhist associations have helped establish harmonious relations with the government and have also helped rebuild the infrastructure of Buddhism within the country. Nonetheless, Buddhism remains under strict government control and supervision. Hong Fa Temple 弘法寺, just north of Hong Kong in the city of Shenzhen, symbolizes a new era of Buddhism in China as the government begins to rekindle a flame with Buddhism. Built from scratch starting in 1985 under the supervision and direction of the Chan monk Ben Huan, the expansive and elegant monastery is now one of China's most eminent temples, drawing Buddhists and tourists alike from around the world.

5

Korea

For millennia, Korea has endured conflicts with China to the East and Japan to the West. The Economist notes that "Chinese dynasties have seen Korea as a tributary to be protected, a prize to be coveted, or as a dangerous land bridge which might convey 'outer barbarians' into China."[188] Yet despite China's long interest in Korea—exhibited by its numerous invasions—and despite Japan's long interest in expanding its empire into Korea (and its many attempts to do so), Korea has maintained its sovereignty, albeit now in divided form. Its culture is as distinct from its neighbors as its expression of Buddhism.

Before Buddhism appeared in Korea during China's Three Kingdoms period, Koreans practiced a form of Shamanism called *Muism* 무교, also known as *Sinism* 신교. Considering Korea's proximity to China and Japan, it's not surprising that Muism bears striking similarities to both Chinese *Wuism* and Japanese *Shintō*. All share animistic beliefs in which spirits inhabit the natural world. Just as Chinese folk religion strongly influenced the expression of Buddhism in China, so too did Muism influence the expression of Chinese Buddhism in Korea.

Central to Muism are shaman-priests, or mu 巫, known as *mudang* if female and *baksu* if male. Mudang are intermediaries between spirits, gods, and human beings, who perform rituals to solve problems within the human sphere of existence. The mu are considered descendants of deities, and their authority as mu is passed genealogically through female lineage. Myths tell of the origins of the mu residing with a mother goddess.

The source of all being is *Haneullium*, which represents God or *supreme Mind*, and is fundamental to all religions in Korea.[189] Ritual (*gut*) is central to Muism, and involves ancestral worship and sacrifices to the gods. Gut ceremonies are colorful, with abundant song and dance performed to appease the gods.

Over recent centuries, Muism has been attacked as antiquated and obsolete by foreigners and Christian missionaries; consequently, the number of people practicing Muism today is small. Nonetheless, Muism has had a strong influence on Korea's expression of Buddhism.

The Three Kingdoms period

Between the first and fifth centuries CE, the Korean peninsula was occupied by three independent kings claiming their own territories: Koguryŏ, Paekche, and Silla. Three centuries of conflict among the kingdoms ensued as each vied for dominion over the others. China and Japan, meanwhile, both took sides with one kingdom or another, each with an eye toward getting a foothold in the region. Popular local history suggests that, in 372 CE, China attempted to settle disputes by sending Buddhist scriptures to King Sŏngmun of Koguryŏ through a monk named Sundo. It's thought that King Sŏngmun built the first Buddhist structure—Hŭnguk Monastery—for Sundo, who is considered the first Buddhist monk of Korea. Reat has observed, however, that Buddhism was known in Korea before, and that it was already well established by the fourth century.[190]

The specific form of Buddhism introduced by China during the Three Kingdoms period is unknown, but it may have been mostly shamanistic, a form with which Koreans were already comfortable. From early in its history, Buddhism followed a state-sponsored model like northern China's.

Tian Tai was the first Buddhist school to establish a following in Korea's Silla territory. From 589-599, the Korean monk Wŏn'gwang studied in China, specializing in scriptures that would identify the doctrinal principles of Tian Tai, then still under development by Zhi Yi in China. After returning to Silla, Wŏn'gwang, having gained some notoriety, opened doors for Korean monks to travel to and from both China and India. Successive monks continued to develop Buddhism in Silla, and it eventually dominated the entire peninsula.

Three monks came to prominence for their contributions to Buddhism during the seventh-century: Chajang, Ŭisang, and Wŏnhyo. Chajang became famous for developing the Vinaya school. He instituted rigorous scriptural study, bi-annual examinations of clergy, fine-tuned ordination procedures, and established a government agency to maintain and oversee Buddhist temples and properties. Following his studies in China under Zhi Yan and Fa Zang, Ŭisang became known for temple-building, and for developing the Hua Yan school. The colorful monk Wŏnhyo was renowned for composing and performing songs on lute or drums, and enjoying the pleasures of wine and women at the local brothels when he wasn't busy writing treatises and commentaries on sutras.[191] Wŏnhyo's charismatic style, along with his voluminous written output, made him especially popular. He would dramatically influence the character of Korean Buddhism.[192]

THE SILLA PERIOD

Silla came to occupy what is now mostly South Korea, and it was during this era that Korean Buddhism became distinct from its Chinese heritage and separated into schools: Tian Tai, Hua Yan, Haedong, Yŏlban

(Nirvāṇa), and Zhen Yan (tantric; Jap., Shingon), among others. While Chinese Buddhism in the south remained mostly autonomous during this time, Korean Buddhism, in all its flavors, continued as a branch of the state. A government-run ordination center, established and managed by Chajang, was the only access point for those seeking monastic life. All Buddhist schools emphasized, to various degrees, Korean nationalism and shamanic ritual. *Sŏn* (Chan) would not begin to grow significantly until the decline of Silla.

Korean Sŏn

Chan is said to have entered Korea via the monk Pŏmnang after he returned from northern China in the mid-seventh century, having purportedly studied under Dàoxìn 道信 (580 - 651), Chan's fourth patriarch, who's teachings emphasized seated meditation. Known as Sŏn, it eventually evolved into the "Nine Mountains" school, named after the mountain range in which the main monastery was built.

Widespread disharmony arose between the Sŏn school, which de-emphasized reliance on scripture study, and other schools, which depended upon it. Nonetheless, all Buddhist schools enjoyed the benefits of being under the umbrella of the government, which encouraged Buddhism in all its forms. Monastic life assured people of exemption from military service, taxes, and compulsory labor. Corruption, however, was a natural consequence. Those monks at the top of the hierarchy amassed great wealth, while those at the bottom served as warriors to guard temples, and as workers to erect new buildings to house the steady influx of monks. With the arrival of Chinul in the 12th century, however, all that would change.

Chinul was a self-made monk who started with Sŏn when he was seven years old. He spent roughly two decades studying and meditating in solitude without a regular teacher before taking and passing the entrance examination to become a monk.[193] Soon, though, his frustrations with monastic life discouraged him and he left the priesthood. He was not done with Sŏn, however. He went on to found the first Buddhist Society in Korea in the spirit of China's Buddhist associations of the time, which emphasized meditation and study. Then, in the late 12th century, Chinul established the "Chan Cultivation" (Susŏn) Monastery. It opened with great fanfare. Now called the Piney Expanse Monastery (Songgwangsa), it remains a center for Korean Sŏn Buddhism today, offering frequent meditation retreats and hosting ceremonies and festivals throughout the year.

During the Chosŏn period (1392-1910), Confucianism replaced Buddhism as the state religion, as Buddhism was believed not to offer adequate supernatural protection following the Mongol domination of previous centuries.[194] Buddhism thereafter diminished in relevance and split into two distinct forms: one emphasizing doctrinal study (Kyo), and the other emphasizing meditation (Sŏn).

During the 16th and 17th centuries, Christian missionaries sought to convert Buddhists to their cause, which led to the Great Persecution in the nineteenth century. Catholic priests and their followers were killed by the thousands. By the end of the 19th century, as modernization became a state objective, Confucian ideologies, too, became suppressed, just as Buddhism had centuries before.

Today, Buddhism is sparsely represented in Korea. According to the 2015 national census, approximately 56% of the population consider themselves nonreligious, 27% consider themselves Christian, and only 15% consider themselves Buddhist. Other religious sects account for only 0.8% of the population.

In 1983, the Korean monk Seung Sahn (1927-2004) brought knowledge of Korean Sŏn to the West by establishing the international Kwan Um school of Zen at Providence Zen Center, Rhode Island. Unfortunately, the Center was victim to numerous sex scandals surrounding Seung Sahn throughout his tenure there.[195] Nonetheless, the Zen center continues today, maintaining traditions of Korean Sŏn.

6

Vietnam

VIETNAM BORDERS CHINA TO the north and Laos and Cambodia to the west and contains over three thousand miles of coastline along the Gulf of Thailand, the Gulf of Tonkin, and the Pacific Sea. It was thus well situated to receive Mahāyāna Buddhism from southern China, becoming a conduit for Chinese Buddhism to spread south into Malaysia. Vietnam's indigenous folk religion shared customs, ceremonies, and beliefs similar to those of ancient China. Taoism and Confucianism had also been introduced to Vietnam long before Buddhism arrived. Considering Vietnam's proximity to China, and the fact that China had annexed Vietnam twice over the last two millennia, it's not surprising that, of all the other countries that adopted Chan from China, Vietnam's version remains the closest to the original Chinese form.

Although Buddhism had been popular in Vietnam, and was even established as the state religion during the Đinh dynasty (968-980), Chan (*Thiền*) was never a dominant sect. It reached its greatest popularity during the Lý dynasty (1009–1225), but thereafter, as Confucianism gained favor with the government, Buddhism's popularity waned until it finally fell out of favor with state officials during the Later Lê dynasty (1428–1789). Christianity played a role in the further decline of Buddhism over the next several centuries.

When Buddhism ('đạo Phật or Phật giáo') was first introduced to the area, the southern half of Vietnam (as it is today) was not distinctly Vietnamese, as it was occupied by the kingdom of Champa. It wasn't until the 19th century that the region would be annexed by Vietnam to the north. With its long border with Cambodia, this region was greatly influenced by eclectic Cambodian religions: Animism, Hinduism (Shaivism), Buddhism (both Theravāda and Mahāyāna), Islam, and later, Christianity. Religious culture became a largely undifferentiated melting pot of beliefs and practices taken from all of them.

Chan made its debut, according to local history, via the Indian monk Vinītaruci, who purportedly studied Chan under Jianzhi Sengcan, the third Chan patriarch. Later, Wu Yantong (Vô Ngôn Thông) and Thao Duong (Thảo Đường) sects were established by Chinese monks in the tradition of Mazu Daoyi's Hongzhou school and the Pure Land school, respectively. The Trúc Lâm school, which combined Taoist and Confucian ideologies, also emerged. Additional schools developed during the 17th century.

According to the Pew-Templeton Global Religious Futures Project, as of 2010, only 16.4 percent of the population of Vietnam was Buddhist. There is only a small Thiền presence in Vietnam today. As in China, those who follow Mahāyāna Buddhism generally prefer ritualized devotional practices over meditation. Most of the remaining Buddhists practice in Theravāda traditions. Some resurgent interest in Thiền has been sparked by two contemporary monks, Thích Nhất Hạnh and Thích Thanh Từ, but only the latter resides in Vietnam. In 1970, Thích Thiên-Ân, a philosophy teacher at the University of California, founded the International Buddhist Meditation Center in Los Angeles, California. The center has continued to provide instruction in Thiền since his death in 1980, and his 1975 book, *Buddhism and Zen in Vietnam*, continues to be circulated.

7

Japan

The Emperor is identical to the Great [Sun] Goddess Amaterasu. He is the supreme and only God of the universe, the supreme sovereign of the universe. All of the many components [of country] including such things as its laws and constitution, its religion, ethics, learning, and art, are expedient means by which to promote unity with the emperor.*

– Sugimoto Gorō, as quoted by B. D. Victoria[197]

THE HISTORY OF ZEN in Japan has been the subject of much analysis and debate in recent decades as historians, Buddhists, and others have struggled to understand how and why Zen became such a powerful tool for advancing the Japanese war machine of World War II, and imperialist expansion in general. Brian Victoria's *Zen at War*, Christopher Ives' *Imperial-Way Zen*, and Xue Yu's *Buddhism, War, and Nationalism*, all published within the last two decades, have been

---

* Sugimoto Gorō was a Japanese general and an ardent Sōtō Zen practitioner. This excerpt was posthumously published in a collection of his writings called *Great Duty* (*Taigi*) which became popular among soldiers during World War II, selling over a million copies between 1938 and 1945. His writings reflected the general spirit of Japanese Imperial Buddhism during the early part of the 20th century.

instrumental in opening a discussion on these important, and often confounding, topics.

Acknowledging that there are various approaches we can take to understand Japanese Zen, my approach here will be in keeping with my earlier implicit thesis: when an alien religion assimilates into a new culture, some aspects of that religion will be embraced while others will either be discarded or replaced with viable substitutes; through this process, the foreign religion loses its original identity and acquires a new one.

The degree to which a culture's worldview differs from another's suggests the degree to which a religion imported from one to the other may also be subject to change. The practice of Chinese Chan as a contemplative activity is no different from that of Japanese Zen, but the institutional expression of Zen became distinct from its Chinese heritage, just as the institutional expression of Buddhism in China developed distinctive characteristics from its Indian counterpart. In China, Indian Buddhism merged with Confucianism and Taoism, and in Japan, Chinese Buddhism merged with what would become known as *Shintō*.

As we have seen, state sponsorship of religion has had a significant impact on religious ideologies and practices throughout history. During Ashoka's reign in India, Buddhism saw some of its most inspired growth in a time of peace. In other countries, including China, Buddhism at times became militarized.* Considering the many conflicts in which Buddhist monks have fought throughout East Asia,[198] it's not surprising that Japan, too, would employ Buddhist monks for purposes of war. What may be unique to Japan is the degree to which Buddhists, and specifically Zen Buddhists, learned to excel at violence and employ it on the battlefield. Indeed, the sword, the arrow, and many lethal

---

* The marriage of Chan with martial arts had its origins at Shaolin Monastery, which played a likely role in the Bodhidharma legend, and in the establishment of Chan's patriarchal lineage system, as examined in Chapter 4. Meir Shahar speculates that training in martial arts there may have been prompted by the need for monks to protect themselves and their large estate (Shahar 2008, 2). Inscriptions at Shaolin Monastery during the Tang dynasty (618-907) attest to monks fighting in battles, and during the Ming dynasty (1368-1644), Shaolin monks and monks from other monasteries around the country were drafted to fight in numerous military campaigns (Ibid., 3-4).

martial arts came to be regarded as hallmarks of Japanese Zen, and many Zen masters would include training in such disciplines as part of their rigorous teachings.[199] It would be a tremendous challenge to try to understand Japanese Zen without investigating the roles that state sponsorship, tribalism, and preexisting folk religion played in shaping the Buddhist institution.

Early background

Buddhism is considered to have officially entered Japan in its Chinese form by way of Korea, its closest neighbor, around 550 CE, via a peace offering from a Korean king.[200] Japan's indigenous belief system made for some early but short-lived conflicts, as Buddhism was seen by some as a threat to Japan's culture and identity. But Buddhism was soon embraced and, under the appointment of the devout Buddhist prince, Shōtoku, Buddhism was proclaimed the official religion of Japan c. 593.

As an island nation, Japan's isolation set it back technologically from its contemporaries in neighboring China, which had already entered the Bronze Age a thousand years earlier. During the first century CE, Japan was still in the Stone Age; Chinese writings tell of a meeting with a Japanese delegation in 57 CE, describing them as "heavily tattooed" and "carrying bone-tipped arrows."[201] At that time, Japan was inhabited by clans, or *uji*, each of which was associated with a primary deity, or *kami*, unique to its clan. The chieftain of each clan was also its high priest and was closely identified with its kami.*

As clans became extinct, being either killed off or conquered by rival clans, so did their kamis. By the fifth century, the political and social hierarchy was represented by the dominant clan, the *Yamato*, and its defining deity, Amaterasu, a sun goddess who "created Japan by paint-

---

* Kami is a broad term that embraces the idea of a spirit-essence which can be found in things, people, and phenomena. Aspects of the natural world too, such as powerful forces of nature, may also be considered kami, as may animals, spirits of the deceased, certain tools and weapons, and strong charismatic leaders (such as the emperors who came to replace the uji chieftains).

ing the landscape with her siblings."[202] The chieftains of the Yamato were considered Amaterasu's direct earthly descendants.

The term *Shintō*, meaning *Way of the Gods*, was not applied to indigenous Japanese socioreligious beliefs until the need to differentiate it from Buddhism arose during the sixth century.[203] Reat describes Shintō as "a deification of Japan and the Japanese way of life, reflected in observance of Japanese traditions, patriotic allegiance to Japan, and a nature-based polytheism expressing appreciation of the natural beauty of Japan."[204]

The transition from chieftain to emperor was a natural one, and the bloodline is popularly believed to be intact to this day. The first (purely legendary) emperor of the archipelago was Jimmu (Kan'yamato Iwarebiko). He is said to have reigned from 660 to 585 BCE and to have descended from Amaterasu.[205] All successive emperors are likewise considered in Japanese culture to be descendants of this goddess, from the first to the present, Naruhito. Until a constitutional monarchy was established in 1947 following Japan's surrender at the end of World War II, Japanese society had been governed by these deified emperors who, in principle if not always in fact, took center stage in all aspects of society, from religion, to government operations, to war.* As we will see, the emperor tradition had tremendous consequences for Buddhism and significant repercussions for Zen as it made its way to the West during the 20th century.†

---

* The emperor tradition continues today, although the position holds no power in the government according to the latest constitution. Akihito, the eldest son of the Emperor Shōwa (Hirohito) who led Japan into WWII, was the 125th emperor until he abdicated to his son, Naruhito, on April 30, 2019. Naruhito now serves as the head of the Imperial House of Japan and the ceremonial head of state. He is widely claimed to represent the spirit of the Japanese people. In the past, emperors have had varying degrees of influence and control over the government and military, from complete authority to none at all. When Japan went to war during WWII, it was under the Meiji constitution, which stipulated in Article 6 that "The emperor gives sanction to laws and orders them to be promulgated and executed" and in Article 11, "The Emperor has the supreme command of the Army and the Navy."

† The last reigning emperor, Hirohito, embraced himself as a descendent of the gods, though he was forced to publicly reject such claims after his defeat in WWII. Hirohito commented, "It is permissible to say that the idea that the Japanese are descendants of the gods is a false conception; but it is absolutely impermissible to call chimerical the idea that the Emperor is a descendant of the gods" (Wetzler 1998, 3).

The "Nara" schools of Buddhism

By the early 8th century, Buddhism had grown into six dominant schools, all imported from China, and all patronized by the state. In 710, Japan's capital, along with the Emperor and his entourage, moved to Nara, taking with them the locus of all existing Buddhist schools at the time. These came to be known as the *Six Schools of Nara*.* The Buddhist establishment at this time was entirely subservient to the whims of the state, to the extent, even, that the sangha was listed as a government department.[206] Buddhist monasteries soon became wealthy and corrupt, mirroring the process that occurred in Korea and Northern China, where Buddhism had also been nationalized.

Of the six early Nara schools, three sealed the bonds between Shintō and Buddhism. One was the *Hossō* school (the Chinese Wei Shi school), which created the "Double Aspect" (*Ryōbu*) Shintō movement that identified Buddhist and Shintō deities as the same. Another was the *Kegon* school (the Chinese *Hua Yan* school) which identified Vairocana—the celestial Buddha from whom the *Avataṃsaka Sūtra* is said to have originated—with Amaterasu. Since Vairocana was associated with the sun in Buddhism and Amaterasu with the sun goddess in Shintō, the Emperor became identified equally with the Celestial Buddha of Buddhism and the sun goddess (Mahāvairocana) of Shintō.[207] Finally, the Ritsu school completed the merging of Shintō with Buddhism when it erected a bronze statue of Vairocana in 752 to represent the imperial throne: Vairocana appeared atop a large six-petal lotus, each petal representing a province of Japan. Buddhism and Shintō were now joined at the hip. Today it's still common for Buddhist monks to preside over Shintō ceremonies, and Shintō shrines commonly appear within Buddhist temple complexes.[208]

Although the marriage between Shintō and Buddhism was complete, they would often struggle to coexist in harmony.

---

* The six schools were *Hossō-shū* (法相宗), *Jōjitsu-shū* (成実宗), *Kegon-shū* (華厳宗 or 花嚴宗), *Kusha-shū* (倶舎宗), *Ritsu-shū* or *Risshū* (律宗), and *Sanron-shū* (三論宗).

The Heian Period: Tendai and Shingon Buddhism

In 794, the seat of government moved from Nara to Kyoto and stayed there until 1185, a period known as the Heian. During this time, Tendai and Shingon schools appeared. Unlike the early Nara schools, which sought to remain close to their Chinese roots, these two developed distinct doctrines and practices that would provide a foundation from which successive Japanese Buddhist schools would evolve.[209]

The Tendai and Shingon sects, however, were not happy partners. By the middle of the Heian period, both had become wealthy and powerful from government patronage, which led to fierce, and at times violent, rivalries between the two.[210] In the 12th and 13th centuries, fighting between sects became common, especially between Honen and Shinran of the Pure Land tradition, and Dōgen of the Zen sect. Winston L. King, author of *Death Was His Koan, The Samurai-Zen of Suzuki Shōsan*, described the period as one of competition for patronage from the imperial court and Shōgun. Patronage meant they could construct large temples and monasteries, increase their land holding, and gain wealth.[211] Religious establishments furthered the shōguns' political purposes by providing monk-soldiers. Rivalries were common between the Nara sects and the Tendai and Shingon sects of the 9th century, between Tendai and Shingon sects and the Pure Land and Zen sects of the 13th century, and between Nichiren and all other sects.[212]

Following Tendai and Shingon sects, the *Jōdo* (Pure Land) sect (now usually referred to as *Jōdoshū*) became firmly established by Hōnen, c. 1175 CE. Hōnen was banished from the Sangha in 1207, however, due to divergent views he had adopted from the Tendai school in which he was trained. He gave up his robe, married, and had children. Honen's disciple, Shinran, continued the Jodo school after Honen's departure, but in accordance with his own interpretation of it. He believed that rebirth in the Pure Land was not something that could happen from any action on our part, but purely from Amitābha's compassion; therefore, all that was needed was to have faith in that compassion. He called his school *Jōdo-shin-shū*, or the "True Pure Land school." Today, it's commonly referred to as *Shin Buddhism*.

Shinran rejected the priestly lifestyle, along with the Vinaya rules of conduct which accompanied it. He favored living a regular life as laity and rejected celibacy and vegetarianism. His disciples followed his lead accordingly. Today, many Japanese Buddhists are not vegetarians in the strict sense of the term,* and a great many monks and nuns marry (celibacy is generally not considered necessary). For the most part, Buddhist temples became institutions whose abbacy was (and still is) inherited, passed down through generations from father to son.†

Buddhism, stripped of ethical constraints imposed by the Vinaya, emboldened the *Jōdo Shinshū* sect to become excellent and ferocious warriors. Although they were not a monastic bunch, during the warring times of the later Ashikaga Period (1336-1600) they built fortresses—provincial fortified temples—from which they could plan and stage attacks against other sects as well as against feudal warlords. With full allegiance to the Shōgun—the de facto seat of military power during this period—they would fight in dozens of large-scale military battles.[213] It was during this time that weaponsmithing techniques became refined and extremely hard, flexible, and sharp blades like the katana would be invented.‡

---

* From a survey by the Animal Rights Center of Japan in 2014, only about 4.7% of Japanese are vegetarians. Although the number of vegetarians is greater in strongly Buddhist communities, many dishes which may appear to be free of animal products are cooked and served with beef, fish stock, or pork. (Japan Experience, 2015)

† Richard Jaffe writes in *Neither Monk nor Layman: Clerical Marriage in Modern Japanese Buddhism*, "The overwhelming majority of Sōtō temples are inhabited by a cleric and his family. The same ratio between training monasteries and local temples is true for most other Buddhist denominations today as well. Buddhist clerical marriage has become so entrenched in Japanese life that the majority of the laity prefer having a married cleric serve as abbot of their temple. As a 1993 Sōtō denomination survey demonstrated, only 5 percent of the Sōtō laity explicitly preferred an unmarried cleric. An overwhelming 73 percent expressed a preference for a married cleric, with the rest of the survey group not expressing a preference" (Jaffe 2002, 1).

‡ Forging a blade was complex and time-consuming, taking days or weeks. The process itself was considered sacred and involved many Shintō religious rituals (Irvine 2000).

Shin Buddhism is the largest Buddhist sect in Japan today. Accurate statistics are scarce, but in 1998 Esben Andreasen estimated that Jōdoshū and Shin Buddhism, combined, had roughly 20 million followers in Japan.[214]

The *Nichiren* sect, named after its founder, followed shortly after the introduction of Zen by Eisai and Dōgen, c. 1243 CE. Nichiren (Zeshō-bō Renchō) was a radical extremist and met with hostility because of his extreme behavior and divergent views from the orthodoxy. He was exiled twice by government authorities. In 1253, he initiated a vehement attack against Pure Land Buddhism and all other forms of Buddhism in Japan, except the Jōdo Shinshū sect (which would be attacked by his followers a few centuries later). He denounced the country's Buddhist authorities, both secular and religious, as traitors, liars, and hypocrites, identified himself with the Bodhisattva Viśiṣṭacārita, prominent in the *Lotus Sūtra,* and referred to himself as "the pillar of Japan, the eye of the Nation."[215] In 1274, when Japan discovered that the Mongols were preparing to attack, Nichiren "insisted that the only way to save the nation was to obliterate all other forms of religion, punish their leaders, and adopt his own faith as the national creed of Japan."[216] Although that obviously didn't happen, Nichiren's Buddhism quickly became popular. Over twenty sects of Nichiren Buddhism have evolved to this day, along with over a dozen Nichiren social movements and lay organizations.*

Zen enters the scene

Zen had a rough start in Japan. Although Zen-style meditation halls were established during the Nara period, the practice was not particularly popular. Unlike the other schools, it de-emphasized sutra study

---

* The Nichiren sect did go through a dark period from the 16th century to the end of World War II. In 1532, heavily armed, the sect destroyed the headquarters of the Jōdo Shinshu sect, which had been established in 1480. This caused other Buddhist sects to team up and fight against the Nichiren sect: "...monks and their followers fought a pitched battle in the city streets. By all accounts, both sides fought bravely with the disregard for death that faith in a heavenly reward instills. The Nichiren sect suffered a crushing defeat, resulting in the deaths of over fifty thousand of its followers and the destruction of all the twenty-one Nichiren temples in the capital" (Reat, 1994, 212).

and doctrine, and instead emphasized rigorous meditation. It wasn't until the Kamakura period (1185–1333) that Zen started to become popular, but not so much with the aristocracy or even the general population; Zen was taken up by the military, especially the samurai soldiers.[217]

Zen began (more or less) in 1168, when Myōan Eisai, a Tendai monk frustrated with Buddhism in Japan, wanted to understand Buddhism in greater depth, so set off for China. He made two separate trips there and arrived home after the second trip a full-fledged Chan master in the Linji lineage. But he wasn't interested in establishing a Zen sect; he wanted to popularize meditation practice among *all* Buddhist sects in the country, including his own Tendai sect. His strongly nationalistic essay *The Propagation of Zen for the Protection of the Nation*, along with his close affiliations with the shōgun and samurai, brought him favor from the Empire, and in 1202 he was named *Dai Sōjō*—the highest possible rank in Japanese Buddhism. He was then handed the abbacy of his own temple. Eisai is considered the founder of the Japanese *Rinzai* Zen school, the term "Rinzai" evolving from the Japanese transliteration of the Chinese Linji Chan school.

A second Zen sect, Sōtō, was established during the 13th century by a monk with imperial blood named Dōgen. Although some of the acclaimed events of his life have been questioned by scholars,[218] it's said that his Chinese teacher Tiāntóng Rújìng 天童如淨 (Jap., Tendō Nyōjo) of China's Cáodòng school named him his Dharma successor and the next patriarch of the Cáodòng lineage.* Dōgen's expansive collection of essays, published as the *Shōbōgenzō*, firmly established him and his lineage in Japanese Buddhism, and Sōtō continues to be the dominant Zen sect in Japan today, as well as in other parts of the world.†

---

* Chinese Buddhism today generally considers Chan patriarchy—which bases itself broadly on "Southern school" lineage—to have ended in the 7th century with Huineng, the proclaimed sixth Chan patriarch. Some followers of Japanese Zen independently continued the patriarchy system in an alternate direction, a common point of contention between Chinese Chan Buddhists and Japanese Zen Buddhists.

† Tracing the lineage of Dōgen back to its Chinese roots, we find the origins of the Sōtō school with a monk named Hong Zhi (Hóngzhì Zhēngjué 宏智正覺; 1090-1157), who opposed a goal-oriented, dualistic approach, which he believed Huineng and Shenhui advo-

Dōgen's Zen was extreme and austere, demanding long hours of strict sitting meditation (zazen) to the exclusion of nearly all else. He often characterized this practice as "just sitting," or *shikan-taza*. From a Dharma-sermon given in 1240, Dōgen preached:

> ... It is only due to the cognition of sounds and sights and ceaseless mental calculation that one is not yet able to gain liberation. How pitiable! What such a person gets as a result is only suffering as they come and go in the defiled world of sights and sounds. But now you have come to a time when you have an opportunity [to practice]. Dispense with (*hōkyaku*) burning incense (*shōkō*), prostrations (*raihai*), buddha-mindfulness (*nenbutsu*), repentances (*shusan*), and sutra reading (*kankin*), and just (*shikan*) sit (*taza*).[219]

THE ASHIKAGA PERIOD: RISE OF THE SHŌGUNATE

Buddhism became dominant in Japan not only through imperial decree, but also through military favor. Those who practiced Buddhism could be strong warriors, for Buddhist disciplines built resilience, fearlessness, concentration, and stamina. Moreover, in the popular Japanese interpretation of the Pure Land tradition, Buddhism instilled a belief in the afterlife; a devoted follower of the Buddha Way, if killed, would be born into the *Western Paradise*, the *Pure Land*.* The training of samurai warriors was often Zen training in part, so it's not surprising that, as the

---

cated. Hong Zhi adopted the term "Silent Illumination" for his teaching, which is now commonly referred to as the "gradual approach" by the opposing "sudden approach" group, who argue that spiritual awakening happens in a brief instant and not gradually as one practices seated meditation.

* Pure Land Buddhism historically focuses on the "pure land of bliss" inhabited by Buddhas, most specifically Amitābha, the archetypal *Buddha realm* of one's True Self. The Mahāyāna sutras most venerated by Pure Land Buddhists are the *Amitābha Sūtra*, the *Sukhāvatīvyūhaḥ Sūtra*, and the *Amitāyurdhyāna Sūtra*. These sutras all describe the Pure Land not as a life-after-death "heaven of bliss," but as a state of bliss encountered from meditation on the ideal form, Amitābha—contrary to the popular view of Pure Land in most parts of the world. More will be said about archetypal meditations in Chapter 12.

samurai adapted to Zen, Zen adapted to the needs of the samurai.* Zen training would become nearly universally militaristic and nationalistic.

Feudalism during Japan's most violent Ashikaga Period† was extreme. The Emperor, devoid of practical power during this period (although he was still considered the official ruler) was replaced by the Shōgunate as the military head of state. The shōguns were, however, careful not to let the general population know that the Emperor had no real authority over them: for all they knew, the will of the Shōgun was the will of the Emperor.[220] As warlords fought among themselves to rule the land, so did Buddhist sects, and soon, warlords forged alliances with them. One group of influential rebels during the 15th and 16th centuries followed after the Jōdo Shinshū sect and created the *Ikkō-ikki* ("*Single Minded*") movement. Its fighters became Japan's "holy warriors" par excellence, according to Stephen Turnbull, author of *Warriors of Medieval Japan*.[221]

Feudalism ensued throughout the era as hundreds of thousands perished at the hands of highly skilled, highly trained monk-soldiers and ninja mercenaries. In this tumultuous and violent environment, the educated faction of society sought refuge and protection. Rinzai monks came to their rescue and established provincial schools around the country where they could find safety and continue their academic studies. The symbiotic relationship between monks and scholars that followed brought Zen to the forefront of the Ashikaga period and established it as the leading representative of Japanese moral, aesthetic, and cultural values.[222]

Toward the end of this feudal era in the late sixteenth century, three warlords formed an alliance in order that they might dominate all of Japan. Buddhist temples and monasteries were destroyed and Buddhist monks and nuns were killed by the thousands. Eventually, only one of

---

* *Bushido*, or *Way of the Warrior*, was a code of ethics that samurai adopted between the 16th and 20th centuries. Although it was influenced by both Shintō and Zen values, a variety of different versions have been used throughout the centuries. A version offered by Nitobe Inazo emphasized righteousness, heroic courage, benevolence, compassion, respect, integrity, honor, duty, loyalty, self-control, filial piety, wisdom, and fraternity. (Nitobe 2002)

† The Ashikaga Period, also known as the *Muromachi* period, was named after the first Shōgun, Ashikaga Takauji. Muromachi is the name of the district of Kyoto where Ashikaga established his administrative headquarters.

the warlords survived: Tokugawa Ieyasu. He would rebuild Japan and bring a long-awaited peace, initiating what would become known as the Tokugawa period [1603 - 1867].

The Tokugawa period: isolationism and art

The last of the powerful warlords to survive, Tokugawa Ieyasu, was determined to bring peace to the country. To do so, he looked toward the Jōdo (Pure Land) school, which was the only Buddhist school that had not been militarized. Favoring it had the intended effect. The mood of the country calmed and Jōdo, for the first time, became a popular Buddhist sect in Japan. Over subsequent years, Ieyasu also brought peace and growth to the other Buddhist schools in Japan, including those which had been nearly destroyed during the Ashikaga Period.

But, as fond as Ieyasu was of Buddhism, he was equally disdainful of Christianity, which had been escalating its presence in Japan since the middle of the 16th century. Considering Christianity a form of foreign invasion, Ieyasu initiated widespread persecutions of all Christians, torturing and killing them until nearly all traces of Christianity were wiped away from the Japanese Empire.[223] To prevent a resurgence of Christian "invaders," he required all people to register as members of a Buddhist temple and attend its ceremonies according to its customs. Christianity was now effectively gone, or at least dormant, and Buddhism would struggle under rigid state control.

The third shōgun and grandson of Tokugawa Ieyasu, Tokugawa Iemitsu, ruled from 1623 to 1651. He continued the offensive against foreigners and Christians, and went to even further extremes. He instituted a *Sakoku*, or "closed country," policy to prevent people from either entering or leaving Japan. While the policy didn't do exactly that—trade continued quite well—laws enforced severe restrictions on whomever the state wanted to keep out; specifically, anyone who might be perceived as a threat to the shōgunate. Tokugawa Iemitsu would eventually expel virtually all Christians from Japan by force.

As a likely result of isolationist policies, Japan saw a blooming of art: gardening, architecture, the tea ceremony, the popularization of Haiku by the poet Bashō, and the refinement and further development of origami and calligraphy. These became cultural hallmarks of the era and would influence the presentation of Zen and Japanese culture in centuries to follow.

But while the Japanese population may have enjoyed the relatively peaceful era, they no longer favored Buddhism. Being forced to participate in government-run Buddhist establishments—having to attend ceremonies and regular services—brought acrimonious distrust of the religion. Buddhism became viewed more as a tax-collection agency and a means of monitoring the population than as a place for spiritual or religious refuge.[224]

In 1866, Tokugawa Yoshinobu was selected to take over as the 15th shōgun following the death of Tokugawa Iemoch. Yoshinobu immediately began building up Japan's military capabilities with assistance from the French, English, and Americans.

But despite the robust show of international support, the Shōgunate was losing its hold on power and would soon collapse.

The Meiji Restoration: return of the emperor

With the decline of Buddhism over the previous two and a half centuries came a resurgence of Shintō, giving new hope for the Emperor to regain state control. The vast majority of the population by this time was unhappy with the shōgunate system, a system they saw as unjust and unfair. Two samurai decided to do something about it and devised a plan to bring about its end. The plan succeeded on November 9, 1867, when the last shōgun resigned, leaving an Emperor truly in charge of Japan for the first time in centuries.

In 1868, the Meiji "Enlightened Government" was established, and Emperor Meiji quickly made Shintō the state religion. It was an easy decision, considering the population was ready to be rid of the stifling, state-run Buddhist institutions, and the nationalistic ethics of Shintō helped strengthen his power.

He issued the *Charter Oath*, or *Oath in Five Parts*. The fourth part read, "All absurd usages of the old regime shall be abolished and all measures conducted in conformity with the righteous way of heaven and earth." This meant celebration for Shintō and grave warnings for Buddhism. The *Charter Oath* was quickly followed by the *Separation Edicts* (*Shinbutsu bunri*) and the ensuing *haibutsu kishaku* movement, which sought to expunge Buddhism from Japan. The Meiji regime expelled Buddhist priests from the priesthood, divorced Shintō from Buddhism, closed down tens of thousands of Buddhist temples, and destroyed thousands of Buddhist artifacts.[225] These actions were all in response to Emperor Meiji's quest for Japan to regain national pride by re-establishing its Shintō identity. Industrialization was taking place, the world was changing fast, and Meiji believed it had moved ahead without them during Japan's long period of isolation: he would do away with the old and bring in the new.

With Westernization as his goal, Japan imported advisers from around the world to help bring the country up to speed in banking, education, military affairs, and transportation, as well as in the sciences and engineering. Japan also adopted the West's Gregorian calendar, along with its fashions in clothes and hairstyles.* In short time, Japan became a world power, a position that would be interrupted only briefly following the end of World War II, after which it arose again quickly as an economic world power.

While Japan was trying to be more like the West, the Buddhist establishment—or what was left of it—was regrouping and trying to figure out a way to resurrect itself. Japan was becoming a formidable nation once again, with an emperor at the helm and Shintō manning the sails.

---

* The Japanese interest in modeling Western culture continues today. One of the more unusual examples is the popular double eyelid surgery (blepharoplasty) used to make the Asian epicanthic fold look more caucasian. It's one of the most popular forms of cosmetic surgery in Japan, according to Yumi Nakata (2014).

The only way to stay on board was to join the crew, and that meant reaffirming allegiance to the emperor. Buddhists banded together to help the Emperor "refute evil and exalt righteousness" (*haja kenshō*) and rallied behind him to help expel Christian influences from the country. Meanwhile, the general population, largely Buddhist, was still upset at the government's widespread condemnation of Buddhism. Protests were public, large, and at times violent. Eventually, the emperor conceded and denounced persecution of Buddhism in all its forms.

But in exchange for state support, Buddhists had to give up their autonomy. In 1872, the Meiji government decreed the *Great Teaching* (*Daikyō*), which put forth three tenets:

- The principles of reverence for the national deities and of patriotism shall be observed;

- The heavenly reason and the way of humanity shall be promulgated; and

- The throne shall be revered and the authorities obeyed.[226]

Buddhism was back, although it was again to be Shintō-controlled. Buddhist priests were forced to receive training under the leadership of a government-appointed *Doctrinal Instructor*. Without government training and certification, priests were not allowed to perform ceremonies, lecture, or even live in a Buddhist temple.[227]

While Buddhism was resurrected largely to appease the population, it was in symbol only that Buddhism was allowed. Buddhist ceremonies could still only be conducted in accordance with Shintō practices and beliefs that were enforced by government authority. To further weaken Buddhism, the government issued Order Number 133, allowing Buddhists to eat meat, grow long hair, get married, and wear regular clothing—reversals of long-held customs that served to undermine traditional Buddhist ethics and weaken the Buddhist institution.*

---

* Ironically, the idea came from the prominent Sōtō Zen priest, Ōtori Sessō (Victoria 2006, 9).

What followed was a great deal of turmoil among Buddhists. Some took sides with the government, and some vehemently disapproved of it. As Western culture continued to grow its influence, the government had the idea to split Shintō into two groups: one cultic, focused on the emperor and State, and well-funded, and the other religiously oriented and mostly ignored. So in 1882, *State Shintō* was officially established. It would dominate its religious alter ego, Sect-Shintō (*Kyōha Shintō*), which, as planned, received no government funding or support. Under State Shintō, religious freedom was granted—to some degree. In 1889, the Meiji constitution included the words "Japanese subjects shall, within limits, not prejudicial to peace and order, and not antagonistic to their duties as subjects, enjoy freedom of religious belief."[228] The emphasis of the statement was clearly not religious freedom, but national ethics, patriotism, and imperial servitude.

Buddhism was back and would come to serve as a weapon Japan could wield to justify expansionist war. The rhetoric of Buddhism and Zen, combined with patriotic zeal, led Japan to identify itself not only as a world power, but as a Buddhist superpower. As such, it was up to Japan to spread its wisdom throughout the rest of the world. Anesaki Masaharu, an eminent Buddhist scholar, expressed the common sentiment of the time: "Our nation [Japan] is the only true Buddhist nation of all the nations in the world. It is thus upon the shoulders of this nation that the responsibility for the unification of Eastern and Western thought and the continued advancement of the East falls."[229]

Buddhism became viewed as representing the interests of the empire, and it was thought that, as Buddhism grew, so would the empire grow with it. Growth meant the conquest of new territory, for which Japan needed to look no further than China and Korea. Buddhism would be used as an excuse by Buddhists, including some prominent Zen Masters, to not only support foreign invasion, but to call for it.

Buddhist imperialism, once again fueled by government patronage, prospered. Those Buddhists who denounced it wielded little to no power. In 1889, a group of Buddhists created a new organization that would further enhance Japanese expansionist sentiment, the *United Movement for Revering the Emperor and Worshiping the Buddha* (*Sonnō Hōbutsu Daidōdan*). Its objective was to preserve the imperial family and increase Buddhist influence to enhance Japan.[230]

The movement was vocal, violent, and a prelude to war.

Imperialist expansion and Zen

Complete and total domination of Korea was Japan's goal, but to get Korea, Japan had to first deal with China. Japan's interpretation of Buddhist ethics provided the needed arguments. One of the most effective arguments calling for the conquest of Korea, and therefore a war with China, was Japan's perceived superiority as a Buddhist nation. It had a *responsibility* to share that superior wisdom with those less fortunate countries, especially those countries they wished to conquer. Brian Victoria explains:

> While there was almost no peace movement among Buddhists, there was no lack of Buddhist leaders who justified the war. One line of reasoning they adopted was based on Japanese Buddhism's supposed preeminent position within all of Asian Buddhism. An editorial entitled "Buddhists During Wartime" appeared in the August 8, 1894 issue of the newspaper *Nōnin Shimpō*. It asserted that Japanese Buddhists had a duty to "awaken" Chinese and Korean Buddhists from their indifference to the war, an indifference which allegedly stemmed from the pessimistic nature of the Buddhism in those two countries.[231]

With support from prominent Buddhist authorities, Japan launched military campaigns against China on August 1, 1894, which ended favorably for Japan the following year with the signing of the treaty of Shimonoseki. Japan received over 16 million pounds of silver from China along with the island of Taiwan. In addition, Korea became independent from China by a proclamation stipulated in Article 1 of the Treaty of Shimonoseki. All this made Korea's conquest seem ever more possible. Japan would finally annex Korea, but not until August 29, 1910, at the ratification of the Japan-Korea Annexation Treaty, signed by Korean officials under duress, threat of force, and bribes.*

Japan, however, was not entirely happy with the outcome of the war. It wanted a piece of the mainland to demonstrate its ultimate victory. Although Japan had taken the Liaotung Peninsula, Russia, France, and Germany had teamed up against it and forced it to give the land back.

Humiliated over having to give back the peninsula, but emboldened by its victory in China, Japan was determined to continue its military campaigns abroad. Its new connections with the West through growing trade allowed it to acquire and build new weapons, which it did at ferocious speed. By the middle of the first decade of the twentieth century, Japan had four battleships, sixteen cruisers, and twenty-three destroyers among its arsenal.[232] Japan fought successfully against Russia in 1904, and in 1914, entered the First World War as an ally of Britain.

Around the turn of the twentieth century, another movement took shape called the *Association of New Buddhists* (*Shin Bukkyōto Dōshikai*). It would be referred to by the name of a monthly journal it published called *New Buddhism* (*Shin Bukkyō*).† New Buddhism has been described as

> ... a religious world view that emphasized the duties of citizenship, such as patriotism, loyalty, and hard work, and coupled these goals with Buddhist ideals of compassion, service, and faith or practice. This combination was then translated into socially conscious, politically astute, and communally minded organizations that were as devoted to issues of public health and education as they were to doctrinal exegesis and spiritual training.[233]

---

* This "treaty" continued to be a thorn in Korea's foot for decades thereafter. As recently as 2010, its legality was still being debated. It was mutually agreed by both Korea and Japan at that time that "it was never valid in the first place" (Chung-weon 2010).

† This was a renaming of the *Buddhist Puritan Association of New Buddhists* (*Bukkyo Seito Soshi Kai*).

Shin Bukkyō sought to publish reform-minded articles, which trended toward radical reform of society, abandonment of superstitions and traditional Buddhist ceremonies, and political protection.[234] It was banned by the government twice and finally shut down in 1915.[235]

A notable contributor to *Shin Bukkyō* (yet one who may have helped lead it to its final demise) was Inoue Shūten, who was, according to Tomoe, influenced by the "absolute pacifism of Chinese Southern school Buddhism."[236] Inoue wrote articles critical of war and imperial allegiance and expressed contempt for the Japanese people's lack of spirituality.[237] His critical anti-establishment stance ultimately led to persistent surveillance by state and military police for the remainder of his life.[238] In 1911, he daringly wrote:

> War is the greatest sin, whatever the name be given it… In sum, war is an uncharitable act to make a profit out of it and commit murder… which is indeed far from humanity… The true advocates of peace should stand between the warring nations to promote peace for the people as well as to remember "the tremendous evil-doing of war."[239]

D. T. Suzuki also wrote numerous articles for Shin Bukkyō; however, his position was more conservative and variable than Inoue's. For the most part, Suzuki fiercely advocated for a strong relationship between Buddhism and Imperial Japan: "…religion and the state must necessarily support each other if they are to achieve wholeness…" and, "religion should, first of all, seek to preserve the existence of the state, abiding by its history and the feelings of its people."*[240] This was not a sentiment unique to Japan, as Buddhism in many other countries also enjoyed the benefits of state sponsorship. But it was a sentiment that, at the time, helped frame Buddhism as supporting imperial expansion through military force.

---

* Suzuki did not always take a pro-state position, which suggests he may have struggled with conflicting views. In 1911, he wrote to Paul Carus, "The Japanese are very narrow-minded. The government seems to be trying to suppress every new doctrine that may conflict with the old notions of loyalty or patriotism. Since the war reactionaries are in full power, and militarism runs wild" (as quoted by Tomoe 2005, 291).

Suzuki continued to be outspoken on the subject of Buddhism and imperial filial piety.* Victoria summarizes the overall gist of his positions at the time:

> Suzuki laid out ... fundamental positions that Buddhist leaders would collectively adhere to until Japan's defeat in 1945: (1) Japan has the right to pursue its commercial and trade ambitions as it sees fit; (2) should "unruly heathens" (*jama gedō*) of any country interfere with that right, they deserve to be punished for interfering with the progress of all humanity; (3) such punishment will be carried out with the full and unconditional support of Japan's religions, for it is undertaken with no other goal in mind than to ensure that justice prevails; (4) soldiers must, without the slightest hesitation or regret, offer up their lives to the state in carrying out such religion-sanctioned punishment; and (5) discharging one's duty to the state on the battlefield is a religious act.[241]

These sentiments were shared by other contemporary Buddhist voices, including Suzuki's teacher, Shaku Sōen, who was perhaps even more vocal and extreme in his views than Suzuki. An acknowledged fully-enlightened Zen master in the Rinzai tradition, Sōen wrote to Leo Tolstoy in response to Tolstoy's request to join him in condemning the war:

> Even though the Buddha forbade the taking of life, he also taught that until all sentient beings are united together through the exercise of infinite compassion, there will never be peace. Therefore, as a means of bringing into harmony those things which are incompatible, killing and war are necessary.[242]

As prominent Buddhist voices were giving just cause for war, scholars and proclaimed enlightened Zen masters were preaching not only

---

* Suzuki's view of Buddhism was multi-faceted and changed over the course of his life. Tomoe describes his general worldview of religion as being composed of three aspects, or phases: "rationalism, social criticism, and non-political, individualistic spirituality (2005, 292).

the *need* for war, but the *imperative* for war for preserving the Buddha Dharma.

Zealous fervor for battle encouraged wanton violence on the battlefield. The prominent Sōtō Zen master Sawaki Kōdō, for example, would later brag of his morbid accomplishments during the Russo-Japanese War (1904-5).[*] For Kōdō, Buddhism offered supreme justification for killing, and he argued that it was the precept *forbidding* killing that in fact allowed it.[†]

Zen training in Japan continued to be conveyed from teacher to disciple in the age-old lineage tradition established in China. But what was being transmitted? Was it Dharma, or the imperative for uncompromising allegiance to nationalistic Shintō values? Were they perceived as different or one-and-the-same?

Exploring these questions, Victoria offers the example of Nogi Maresuke, who would become a general and commander of the Third Army in the Russo-Japanese War, and eventually a famous war hero.

Nogi was trained under the Rinzai Zen master Nakahara Nantembō, a devout nationalist with fervent military inclinations. Nantembō was neither humble nor dispassionate. Among his more notable remarks, he declared, "I am the only one in today's Japan who possesses the true transmission of the Buddhas and Patriarchs. Zen that only looks like Zen must be smashed!" and "...no bodhisattva practice [is] superior to the compassionate taking of life."[243] Under Nantembō's tutelage, Nogi was seen as such an exemplary general and commander that Sōtō

---

[*] Kōdō proudly recounted: "My comrades and I gorged ourselves on killing people. Especially at the battle of Baolisi temple, I chased our enemies into a hole where I was able to pick them off very efficiently. Because of this, my company commander requested that I be given a letter of commendation, but it wasn't issued" (Kōdō 1984, 6, as quoted by Victoria, 2006, 35).

[†] Kōdō stated, "The Lotus Sūtra states that 'the Three Worlds [of desire, form, and formlessness] are my existence and all sentient beings therein are my children.' From this point of view, everything, including friend and foe, are my children. Superior officers are my existence as are their subordinates. The same can be said of both Japan and the world. Given this, it is just to punish those who disturb the public order. Whether one kills or does not kill, the precept forbidding killing [is preserved]. It is the precept forbidding killing that wields the sword. It is this precept that throws the bomb. It is for this reason that you must seek to study and practice this precept" (Kōdō, Zen-kai Hongi o kataru 1942, 107, as quoted by Victoria, 2006, 35-36).

Zen master Iida Tōin bestowed upon him the achievement of "Great Enlightenment" (*daigo*), and Nantembō appointed him one of his own Dharma heirs.[244]

While not all Buddhists participated with or believed in Imperialist Buddhism, many did, and those who didn't struggled to be heard. The relationship between Buddhism and imperialism was officially established in the 1930s with the formation of *Imperial-Way Buddhism* (*kōdō Bukkyō*), a formalization of the relationship that was already extant. Imperial-Way Buddhism "represented the total and unequivocal subjugation of the Law of the Buddha [Dharma] to the Law of the Sovereign. In political terms, it meant subjugation of institutional Buddhism to the state and its policies."[245] Moreover, the Emperor was to be venerated as supreme to the extent that "The emperor's edicts, being holy and divine, are inviolable…and they must always be revered."[246]

Such sentiments were popularized through a wide variety of arguments linking Buddhist theology to the veneration of the Emperor, by writers such as Fukuda Gyōei, a Tendai priest; distinguished Sōtō Zen master Harada Sōgaku; Sōtō Zen master Yasutani Haku'un; and Dr. Shiio Benkyō, a Jōdo priest and future president of Taishō University.

The war machine required ongoing justification for its mission from the Buddhist community, and Yasutani was among many to offer it. He wrote:

> Of course one should kill, killing as many as possible. One should, fighting hard, kill everyone in the enemy army. The reason for this is that in order to carry [Buddhist] compassion and filial obedience through to perfection it is necessary to assist good and punish evil…. Failing to kill an evil man who ought to be killed, or destroying an enemy army that ought to be destroyed, would be to betray compassion and filial obedience, to break the precept forbidding the taking of life. This is a special characteristic of the Mahāyāna precepts.[247]

In 1937, Japan engaged in numerous battles against the Chinese, including the now infamous "Nanjing Massacre," also known as the "Rape of Nanjing," in which an estimated 200,000 to 300,000, mostly civilians, were killed, raped and tortured.* Shortly after the Japanese offensive against China began, Professor Hayashiya Tomojirō, with the help of Shimakage Chikai, published the book *The Buddhist View of War* (*Bukkyō no Sensō Kan*), defending Japan's aggression against the Chinese. Among its notable passages justifying war in the name of Buddhism was this:

> We believe it is time to effect a major change in the course of human history, which has been centered on Caucasians and inequality among humanity. To realize the true happiness of a peaceful humanity and construct a new civilization, it is necessary to redirect the path of world history's advance from this false path to the true path. Rooted in this sublime view of history, the mission and responsibility of Mahāyāna Buddhists is to bring into being true friendship between Japan and China.
>
> ...In general, it can be said that Chinese Buddhists believe that war should absolutely be avoided no matter what the reason. Japanese Buddhists, on the other hand, believe that war conducted for a [good] reason is in accord with the great benevolence and compassion of Buddhism.[248]

To attempt to comprehend this interpretation of Buddhist ethics, we can start by remembering that Japanese Buddhism is a combination of Chinese Buddhism and Shintō, so, in the context presented here, the supreme ruler is necessarily not the Buddha Dharma, but the emperor; the supreme cause is not Buddhism, but Japan. The ramifications of this are stark. When a State is supreme in all ways, including its expression of Buddhism; when its imperialistic worldview inclines it to dominate other countries; when Buddhist institutions can be manipulated by the state to serve its nationalistic agenda; and when monks and nuns serve the state above all else, then the state can readily exert the power and

---

*For details, see the 1997 book by Iris Chang, *The Rape of Nanking, the Forgotten Holocaust of World War II*, and the 2018 book by Angie Timmons, *The Nanjing Massacre: Bearing Witness: Genocide and Ethnic Cleansing*.

influence needed to contort Buddhist ethics to serve its interests as it pleases. In this case, Tomojirō and Chikai tied the core values of Buddhism and Shintō together by suggesting that compassion (a Buddhist ideal) justified wars that served imperialist objectives (a Shintō imperative). Even if their ideas may have contradicted previously established Buddhist values, their status within the Buddhist institution, and society at large, lent them credibility.

Japan's expansionist ideology was described succinctly by Shimizu Ryūzan, then president of the Nichiren-affiliated Risshō University, in response to Japan's systematic evangelization efforts in Manchuria. Believing that Japan's Buddhism was superior to China's, he explained that it was in the spirit of Japan to "enlighten the world with truth," to "lead all nations of the world into righteousness," and to create a world "where all men shall be Buddhist saints."[249]

This widely held sentiment, combined with the popular nationalistic views of D. T. Suzuki and others, would help lead to the most violent, brutal, and highly-trained army the world has ever known, an army ready and eager to fight fearlessly to the death in whatever battle came its way.*

Suzuki believed that Zen was not only superior to other Buddhist sects, but that it was the most valuable form of Buddhism for supporting the war effort:

> We have the saying in Japan: "The Tendai is for the royal family, the Shingon for the nobility, the Zen for the warrior classes, and the Jodo for the masses." This saying fitly characterizes each sect of Buddhism in Japan. The Tendai and the Shingon are rich in ritualism and their ceremonies are conducted in a most elaborate and pompous style ap-

---

* In the end, even an atomic bomb dropped on Hiroshima would not immediately dissuade Japan from continuing its conquest of the world. The United States believed a second was needed to convince it to stop, so dropped another bomb on Nagasaki, a major ship-building center. Did this reflect the enormous strength of Japan's conviction in the righteousness of their cause, their heavenly duty to spread Imperial Buddhism around the globe? Whether the US was truly justified in dropping atomic bombs on Japan is a topic of continued debate, but it undeniably brought one of the most destructive wars in human history to a conclusive end.

propriate to the taste of the refined classes. The Jodo appeals naturally more to plebeian requirements because of the simpleness of its faith and teaching. Besides its direct method of reaching final faith, Zen is a religion of will-power, and will-power is what is urgently needed by the warriors..."[250]

In the case of Japan's expansionist goals, the enemy was anyone who resisted the perceived heavenly right to expand the empire. Neither Suzuki nor his contemporaries appear to have addressed the morality of such a stance: we can speculate that since this view was sanctified by the Emperor, a descendent of Amaterasu, it was beyond reproach, its morality unquestionable.*

In 1940, Japan joined forces with Hitler and Mussolini. Lieutenant Colonel Sugimoto Gorō, a major in the army during WWII with many years of Zen training, wrote:

> The emperor is identical to the Great [Sun] Goddess Amaterasu. He is the supreme and only God of the universe, the supreme sovereign of the universe. All of the many components [of a country] including such things as its laws and constitution, its religion, ethics, learning, and art, are expedient means by which to promote unity with the emperor. That is to say, the greatest mission of these components is to promote an awareness of the nonexistence of the self and the absolute nature of the emperor. Because of the nonexistence of the self, everything in the universe is a manifestation of the emperor...including even the insect chirping in the hedge, or the gentle spring breeze. Stop such foolishness as respecting Confucius, revering Christ, or believing in Shakyamuni! Believe in the emperor, the embodiment of Supreme Truth, the one God of the universe![251]

Although it's been common throughout history for religions to be cited as justification for war, and Buddhism has not been exempt, Gorō's commentary suggests that the just cause for war, at least from his perspective, was inspired more by Shintō ethics than Buddhism. But con-

---

* A possible explanation for this attitude will be offered in Chapter 20.

sidering that Shintō framed Zen, Zen became equally culpable in the battlefield atrocities that would follow.

IMPERIAL ZEN ON THE BATTLEFIELD

While Zen masters extolled the holiness of "compassionate killing" in their sermons, compassion was in short supply on the battlefield. Not all fighting troops were Zen Buddhists, but the disciplines and attitudes of Imperial Zen Buddhism had, by now, penetrated the Japanese psyche, as well as its military machine.

War is black and white, good vs. evil. When people see each other as evil, they become dehumanized, and when soldiers are trained in the extreme forms of mental discipline provided by Zen and believe that they are fundamentally superior to people of other nationalities by divine law, horrors can ensue.[252] Japanese war crimes in WWII included: cannibalism of dead and live victims as a way for soldiers to "get a feeling for victory, and to give the soldiers nerves of steel;"[253] beating and starving tens of thousands of prisoners of war as they marched from the peninsula of Bataan;* killing competitions between officers as sport;[254] and the Nanjing Massacre, during which an estimated 300,000 disarmed combatants and civilians were brutally killed and women raped.†

Zen, detached from its ethical foundations, can become a lethal tool for those who wield it. When the ego has been diminished through

---

* "They were beaten, and they were starved as they marched. Those who fell were bayoneted. Some of those who fell were beheaded by Japanese officers who were practicing with their samurai swords from horseback. The Japanese culture at that time reflected the view that any warrior who surrendered had no honor; thus was not to be treated like a human being. Thus, they were not committing crimes against human beings. [...] The Japanese soldiers at that time [...] felt they were dealing with subhumans and animals" (Rohrabacher, U.S. Congressional Representative 2001).

† Victoria quotes the words of military correspondent Omata Yuko in *Zen War Stories*: "Those in the first row were beheaded, those in the second row were forced to dump the severed bodies into the river before they themselves were beheaded. The killing went on non-stop, from morning until night, but they were only able to kill 20,000 persons in this way. The next day, tired of killing in this fashion, they set up machine guns. Two of them raked a cross-fire at the lined-up prisoners. Rat-a-tat. Triggers were pulled. The prisoners fled into the water, but no one was able to make it to the other shore" (2003, 12).

Zen practice, we can lose our sense of agency. If we then entrust that agency to others, it can lead us to commit atrocities, a phenomenon we'll examine in Chapter 20 when we review the research of Stanley Milgram. While we can't claim that needless battlefield violence was a direct product of Zen training, given the evidence, it's reasonable to assert that Zen training at least established conditions that facilitated it.

Japanese Zen Today

Although militarization and politicization of Buddhism, especially Zen, were profoundly influential in shaping and defining Buddhist religious institutions in Japan, as a spiritual practice, we should be careful when attempting to draw distinctions between Japanese Zen and Chinese Chan. The differences lie in their institutional presentations, not the ascetic, mystical, practice. As I emphasize throughout this book, there are two interrelated dimensions to Chan/Zen: the religious—the institution, which is shaped by culture—and the spiritual, our personal contemplative practice. These two aspects don't always support one another, as each has its own objectives which may be at odds with those of the other. The religious institution seeks to grow and survive, and if conjoined with the interests of the state, it seeks the political objectives of bureaucrats as well. The individual seeks salvation. The objectives of each can clearly be incompatible. The resulting tensions between the two can help explain numerous conflicts that have been waged throughout history, in the name of religions of all kinds.

When the religious and the spiritual work together in harmony, things go well, but maintaining the balance can be a challenge. In Japan's recent history, balance, it seems, was neither sought nor desired, as the pursuit of individual liberation and spiritual awakening conflicted, fundamentally, with Shintō's core values, which have historically been sacrosanct and at the forefront of Japanese Culture. When greed, power, and nationalism become involved with religion, the spiritual needs of the individual inevitably become sidelined, redirected, or simply ignored.

Christopher Ives, professor of Religious Studies at Stonehill College, explains the closeness between Zen and the Japanese state as one of lifelong mutual interdependence:

> From the time of its introduction to Japan in the sixth century, Buddhism has usually functioned interdependently with those in political power, whether aristocrats, the imperial family, warrior governments, shōguns, oligarchs in the late nineteenth century, or military leaders during WWII. With few exceptions, Buddhists and rulers have cultivated a mutually beneficial and mutually legitimating relationship. This symbiosis has taken the form of patronage offered by those in power and, in a quid pro quo arrangement, Buddhist support for the "state." Buddhists offered their support ritually by performing ceremonies and chanting sutras deemed to protect the ruler and his realm; institutionally with temples playing administrative roles for the state; and doctrinally through political readings of key Buddhist doctrines. One can safely construe the "nationalism" if not militarism of modern Buddhist institutions as a continuation of this traditional symbiotic relationship between Buddhism and the government.[255]

Shintō exerted tremendous influence on Buddhism because Buddhism was absorbed into Japanese culture as an add-on to—not a replacement for—Shintō ethics and values. This cultural absorption of Buddhism followed a similar process to that which occurred in China, where it was integrated with Taoism, Confucianism, and folk religion, but with stark contrasts. As D.T. Suzuki explained, "We Buddhists bow in front of the emperor's picture, but for us this isn't a religious act. The emperor is no god because god can be something very low for us. We see the emperor in an area high above all religions."[256]

Japan's long history of war, from early clans fighting for territory to the imperialism of the early 20th century, created a militaristic Buddhism that many of its adherents believed to be superior to all other expressions of Buddhism around the world.* The "selflessness" of Indian Buddhism† was reframed to create soldiers who could kill without remorse and die with honor, knowing they would be reborn in the Western Pure Land.‡ Considering Japan's aggressions against Korea and China in the 19th and 20th centuries, it's understandable that the populations of China and Korea hold the highest anti-Japanese sentiments of any countries in the world—a 90% and 79% negative view of Japan, respectively, according to a 2014 BBC World Service poll.[257] Many Japanese today don't understand why so many Koreans and Chinese don't like them, because Japan's history of violent wanton aggression toward these two countries has been largely expunged from Japan's educational system.[258]

The Zen of Japan and the Chan of China evolved in two distinct directions in response to different cultural, political, and socioreligious environments. Although Japanese Zen became a tool that could be utilized by the state to assist with its nationalistic agenda, Zen nevertheless offered a valuable spiritual haven for a great many of those who undertook it as an ascetic practice. The elegant simplicity that came to characterize Japanese Zen through architecture, poetry, ceramics, clothing, music, and ceremony has become a hallmark of its spirit.

Zen Buddhism today has an enormous following around the world, and thanks to the World War II era being over, and thanks to government policies established in 1954 that limit military use to defense only, the ensuing peace has reached into its expression of Buddhism. The still-popular practice of martial arts has moved away from developing soldiers, and toward helping people build stamina, discipline, and concentration—all essential ingredients for success with mystical-Zen.

---

* This is not without precedent in other Buddhist countries. Ives notes that in the 1970s, the Thai Buddhist monk Kittivuddho condoned killing communists "because whoever destroys the nation, the religion, the monarchy, such bestial types are not complete persons. Thus, we must intend not to kill people but to kill the Devil (Mara); this is the duty of all Thai" (Kittivuddho, as quoted by Ives, 1996). Myanmar has also endured much aggression led by Buddhist monks, and as we explored in Chapter 4, China has also not been exempt from Buddhists fighting for the state.

† As discussed in Chapter 1, the concept of anatman, or not-self, expressed the state of egoless awareness encountered in meditation. When we exit the meditative state, we are again in the presence of ego-self, although we may be simultaneously aware of its illusory nature. This phenomenon will be explored in more depth in Part Three.

‡ Possible reasons for this will be offered in Chapter 20.

A developing trend in the West is the creation of Japanese-style Zen centers with accompanying Japanese-style approaches to practice, led entirely by Westerners who, for cultural reasons, have no direct connection with Shintō ideologies.* This mirrors the phenomena we have seen for centuries as Buddhism, and Zen in particular, has spread from country to country, adapting to new, and often diverse cultures.

---

* Nonetheless, I have encountered Westerners who promote Japanese-style Zen and echo some Japanese teachers' rhetoric claiming superiority over Chinese Chan. I have also heard Western Japanese-style Zen practitioners repeat the occasional Japanese claim that Chan in China no longer exists, despite overwhelming evidence to the contrary (and my own first-hand experience).

8

Chan's Migration West

THE OCCIDENT HAS BEEN a welcoming beneficiary of the philosophies, foods, literature, and religions of the Orient for centuries. A visit to any major city of the West will reveal a tremendous variety of ethnic, religious, and cultural expressions of the East, which have arisen as migrants established new homes far from their native lands. As Buddhism has worked its way west, it has done so predominantly to serve a sociocultural need—religion offers comfort and provides a connection with one's home, family, and heritage; it offers a place to socialize and connect with others of the same culture who speak the same native tongue; it offers a place for meetings and gatherings, and a place to school young children in a cultural and religious heritage.

Because the vast majority of Buddhist temples were established to serve these needs, visitors who do not share the same ethnic background as the congregation may understandably be met with some confusion, and possibly discomfort. A monk at such a temple may wonder why someone who isn't a part of their culture would knock on their door, someone who doesn't know their language or their religious and social customs. Western spiritual seekers may not understand this. While temple doors may be open to everybody, the prerequisites for true entrance are often not based on spiritual aspiration so much as cultural identification.

Some Buddhist temples and monasteries, however, have been established to serve a different purpose: to teach meditation and introduce Westerners to an Eastern religious paradigm. For example, in 1980, Sheng-yen founded the Chán Meditation Society in Queens, New York, in the Chinese Chan tradition; in 1982, Thích Nhất Hạnh and Chân Không founded Plum Village in France in the Vietnamese Thiền tradition; and in 1972, Seung Sahn founded Providence Zen Center in Rhode Island in the Korean Sŏn tradition.

Of all the cultural spin-offs of Chinese Chan, none are as prominent around the world as Japanese Zen. This can, at least partially, be attributed to Shintō values, which, during the early- and middle-part of the 20th century, inspired the Japanese people to spread their nationalistic Buddhist identity throughout the world. But it has also been due to the work of translators and commentators such as D. T. Suzuki during the same period. Zen monks from Japan have since established Zen training centers in North and South America, Europe, Australia, and New Zealand. These prominent training facilities, however, are not the only players on the scene: perhaps the greater number of people practicing Zen in the West are affiliated not with temples or monasteries, but with small groups that meet in a living room or a rented space in an office building. Some of these groups have teachers who have been trained by seasoned Zen monks, while others may have teachers who are entirely self-taught. Among them, some may have had robust spiritual experiences, and others not. Some teachers have also integrated Zen with other religions, such as Catholicism, Judaism, and Islam. There is tremendous diversity in the way Zen is expressed in the West.

Chinese Chan was poorly represented when Japanese Zen was being introduced to Westerners, first by Soen Shaku in 1893 at the World's Parliament of Religions in Chicago, and later by D. T. Suzuki. This was likely not only because Buddhism was being suppressed by Chinese Nationalists during that time, but also due to strict U.S. immigration policies toward Asians, especially Chinese.* It may be that Chinese Chan will fail to make headway in the West; time will tell, but more likely, as history has repeatedly demonstrated, Chinese Chan will assimilate into westernized Japanese Zen, and Western culture in general, to create something, yet again, new.

Buddhism: a tapestry of disparate beliefs?

As we have seen, Chan arose within the context of Buddhism, Taoism, and Confucianism. To try to separate Chan from these composite influences would be like trying to separate nucleotides from DNA; it would destroy the very thing that gives it life. Chan cannot exist outside of Buddhism. Buddhism gives it the language, the ethical foundations, and the spiritual and social contexts that sustain and nurture it. But when we ask ourselves, "What, then, is Buddhism?" we are left with more questions than answers. The beliefs among people around the world who profess to be Buddhists vary so widely that we might consider identifying a singular "Buddhism" impossible. As we have seen, Buddhism adopted different beliefs and practices in different cultures because of pre-existing shamanistic folk religions and social and political ideologies. Moreover, as Buddhism spread, it cross-pollinated with itself: Himalayan and Mahāyāna Buddhism influenced one another, as did Theravāda and Mahāyāna Buddhism. This resulted in popular Buddhisms with vast assortments of beliefs, including beliefs in ghosts and spirits, realms of existence after death, reincarnation,† and divina-

---

* The Chinese Exclusion Act of 1882 was intended to prevent Chinese immigrants from entering the U.S. for ten years, but it was repeatedly renewed and lasted sixty years. Due to widespread racism and bigotry toward Chinese, Chinese immigrants endured extreme discrimination and persecution during this time. In fact, the largest mass-lynching in U.S. history was of 18 Chinese in Los Angeles in 1871.

† Many people find comfort in believing that a personal identity will continue after death. For the mystic, however, any sense of identity is illusory and the notion of wanting to hang onto an illusion does not arise: it would be like wanting to preserve the shadow of Yâjnavalkya's allegorical tree after the sun sets (Chapter 1).

tion. Buddhists were free to select whichever beliefs they desired, and if their chosen beliefs were not de facto aspects of their desired style of practice, they could attribute them to it anyway, for if one wants to believe something, attaching that belief to one's religion further reinforces and justifies it.

Although I have tried to convey how Buddhism arose in the principal countries that adopted it, and to show how it has been influenced by state sponsorship and pre-existing sociocultural religious beliefs, I have also tried to give the reader a sense of some quintessential aspects of Buddhist thought and practice as it evolved from the ancient Indus Valley civilization to become a dominant world religion in its own right.

The Four Noble Truths can be considered a fundamental basis for all forms of Buddhism, as they define its purpose—to escape from duhkha, or suffering—and give the methods for doing so in an Eightfold Path. Through the message of these Noble Truths, spiritual practices assert themselves. Chan (the mystical aspect) takes us on a journey inspired by our desire to understand who we are, to uncover deeper truths, and to penetrate the nature of existence itself. It seeks denial of all that is illusory in favor of all that is not. It seeks elimination of ignorance and false views by attacking beliefs with great doubt.

When we begin chan's spiritual journey, the robust assortment of beliefs, rituals, artistic expressions, and ethnic customs surrounding its religious façade can make the path seem complex, difficult, and confusing. But as we apply ourselves to the process of looking within—a process that's both simple and straight-forward—the journey becomes progressively clearer. We start to recognize what is important and what is not, what is conditioned by false views, and what is unconditioned reality.

The big business of "meditation"

Mindfulness meditation has become a multibillion-dollar industry according to Emma Barnett, an editor for The Telegraph and producer of a documentary on the subject. She has identified a problem inherent in separating a spiritual practice from its purpose: detached from its Buddhist roots, she argues, the "snack-sized" portions in which mindfulness meditations are offered can give no lasting effect unless the root causes of people's unhappiness are first confronted. As she puts it,

> It is our lives and how we lead them that really needs to change if we are to improve our mental well-being. Ironically, this is what the Buddhist version of mindfulness teaches—a moral and ethical world view—as opposed to this new corporatized McMindfulness—which in the long term will do as much as a McDonald's Happy Meal to sate a person's gnawing hunger for a richer life.[259]

Unfortunately, commercialization of meditation and "mindfulness," largely inspired by Buddhism, has come to dominate much of society's understanding of what Chan/Zen is about. Just as Japan modified Chinese Chan to adapt it to Shintō, so too is capitalism in the West modifying it in other ways, sometimes to the extent that it becomes nearly unrecognizable from its roots in India centuries ago. Imagine the art of shipbuilding reduced to merely nailing boards together so that water doesn't seep through the cracks. Should Chan/Zen likewise be reduced to such a simplistic level, its value as a path for salvation will be lost: just as a poorly crafted boat will fail to deliver its passengers to their destination, so will chan fail to deliver its advocates out of the roiling waters of samsāra.

Yet our capitalist society is doing just that by selling mindfulness. Advertisers and marketers have led us to become infatuated with mindfulness. As an example, in 2010 Andy Puddicombe started Headspace, an online service with cute animations where people can "learn how to meditate." With 3 million users in over 150 countries, Sean Brecker, CEO, explained during an interview that people use the app when they are "stressed out" or suffering relationship problems or preparing to play golf, while others use it "as people do with going to the gym."[260] At the time of this writing, Headspace, valued at $250 million by Forbes in 2017, offered four subscription plans ranging from $12.99 monthly to $399.99 for a lifetime subscription. Ironically, Andy Puddicombe, its founder, spent a decade as a celibate monk in Burma before returning to the United Kingdom to turn his life around as an entrepreneur. In a 2014 interview with Benjamin Russel, he explained that when he returned from his travels, he met a "burned-out executive," Rich Pierson, and together they created the business idea of the Headspace app, as in "Get some 'Headspace' offering thinkers a daily dose of Zen."[261] He wasn't concerned about being affected by his new wealth, though: "If I can have my surfboard and my juggling balls, I'm pretty happy."[262]

Other tremendously popular (and highly profitable) online businesses touting "mindfulness meditation" are *calm.com, buddhify, Insight Timer, Smiling Mind, MINDBODY, Meditation Timer Pro, Sattva, Breathe, Simply Being, Omvana,* and *10% Happier.*

ZEN PROFITEERING

In a market economy, what people want will be provided at whatever price the market can sustain, and when the market is large enough, the quality of services rendered will reflect a normal distribution comparable to that of any business sector. The savvy entrepreneur will take quick advantage of the opportunity to profit when the demand for a service is high and there is a deficit of providers to meet its demand. The Western free market economy has created an environment ripe for attracting leaders to Chan/Zen training centers who exploit people to satisfy their thirst for power, prestige, and greed (Chapter 20). It's one thing to ask for an optional donation, and another to charge a fee for services. When there is true value in a teacher's teachings, people freely offer donations and seek their counsel. When value is defined by the amount of money it costs, it will lure people who equate money with value, but what they get may be empty of heart. Extolling the virtues of Zen in exchange for profit is antithetical to the spirit of Zen, a practice which leads to the transcendence of ego. Without ego-desire, there is no motivation to profit at the expense of another; we don't take in order to give. We give in order to give.

THE FUTURE OF CHAN IN THE WEST?

Just as the Chinese reshaped Indian Buddhism to align it with Confucianism and Taoism, and the Japanese adapted Chinese Chan to integrate it with Shintōism, the West is now reinterpreting Zen/Chan to fit its own values and sensibilities. While I do not advocate for blind religiosity, I firmly believe in appreciating the religious and cultural context of Chinese Chan—or any mystical tradition, for that matter. Stripped of its foundational context, Chan loses its depth and meaning; it becomes akin to attending an opera only to find the performers silent.

If we sever Chan from its rich Buddhist heritage—a heritage that breathes life into it through art, music, literature, and the promise of solutions to life's profound challenges—then we risk reducing it to mere triviality. Such a diluted version of Chan becomes vulnerable to exploitation by "mindfulness" businesses, superficial parodies, and inevitable scandals.

For Chan to thrive in the West, its advocates and representatives must embrace not only its spiritual and religious heritage, but also understand the broader social contexts from which it arose—contexts that addressed both individual and collective needs. With this foundation can we begin the thoughtful process of adapting Chan to Western culture, striving to preserve the essence that gives it life and meaning and serves as a profound vehicle for personal transformation.

PART TWO

Chan Training

Don't be content to study the Dharma, to memorize its surface. Plunge into it. Go as deeply as you can.

– Han Shan[*]

IN PART ONE, WE followed the evolution of Buddhism from its origins in India through its migrations into Tibet, China, Myanmar, Thailand, Cambodia, Korea, Vietnam, and Japan to the east, Sri Lanka to the south, and Malaysia to the southeast. We observed how Buddhism adapted to pre-existing religious beliefs and social customs in these countries, and how that adaptation led to distinct expressions of Buddhism. We also explored how institutionalization and state sponsorship often had dramatic influences on the religion.

We further observed that Chan arose in China as a unique expression of Buddhism which combined its Indian roots with Confucianism and Taoism. We then followed Chan's development as it evolved to

---

[*] Han Shan is one of China's revered poets of the sixteenth century, who Guo-gu Shi describes as "one of the four most eminent Buddhist monks in the late Ming dynasty [1338-1644]" (Te-ching n.d.).

focus more on spiritual experience through contemplation and meditation than on philosophical or doctrinal study. We observed that different teachers throughout Chan's long history have offered distinct approaches to training according to their own experiences and sensibilities, and speculated that this enabled Chan, as both an expression of mysticism and religious idealism, to evolve dynamically across cultures.

We also identified the important role visionary experience played, both in early Indian Buddhism and later in China, to help create a new genre of sutras that came to represent the Mahāyāna, and how these sutras provided a foundation upon which Chan could emerge. What we haven't yet explored is how chan practice—the mystical aspect of Chan—is accomplished. So, in the remainder of this book, I switch gears to describe this practice from a personal, contemporary, and Western perspective, drawing largely on my own experiences. I present this material in an instructional format, offering general guidance and an assortment of exercises, which I hope will be helpful for any aspiring chan practitioner.

Although chan's spiritual journey begins once we learn to "dwell," practically, most of us need preparation before we're ready and able to enter the meditative state. As the journey progresses, we typically move through a sequence of stages, beginning with mindfulness, which focuses on *ānāpānasmṛti*—developing awareness of the breath. During the second stage we develop the ability of concentration, *dhāraṇā*, by focusing the mind on an object, or "seed." In the third stage we develop skills of contemplation, *dhyāna*, and in the fourth and ultimate stage, we arrive at meditation, *samādhi*.*

---

* I separate the progression of chan training into these four stages in part based on my own experience and in part from my observations of successful practitioners. These stages follow, generally, the last of the eight stages of Yoga as described by Patanjali: *Pratyahara* (withdrawal of the senses), *dhāraṇā* (concentration), *dhyāna* (contemplation), and *samādhi* (meditative absorption). See *Light on the Yoga Sūtras of Patañjali*, 3rd ed., by B.K.S. Iyengar, 2002, for a more thorough presentation of Patañjali's spiritual stages. I use the idea of stages only to facilitate discussion and understanding of the journey; they are not fundamentally real, as there are no discrete separations between them. The journey is best viewed as a continuum comprised of both gradual cultivation and sudden shifts of cognition.

Before we delve into the details of these four stages, reviewing some important prerequisites will help insure success with practice for readers inclined to give chan a try.

9

Prerequisites

TRADITIONALLY, CHAN HAS BEEN available principally only to those entering the gates of a monastery to become monks and nuns. Not all people who entered, however, would necessarily be given instruction in chan: it would be made available only to those who were ready in mind, spirit, and body, and only to those who desired it.* Those who were eager for it but weren't ready would prepare themselves by laboring in the vegetable gardens and performing long sessions of chanting, kneeling, and bowing. These activities would help build physical strength, discipline, and endurance, all necessary for success with chan. Ultimately, chan training would be carried out by a senior monk who had demonstrated adequate depth of understanding of chan through his own practice. Today, chan/zen has been made available to everyone. In theory, we can buy a book on the subject or go to a web page and get started instantly. We can also sign up for a meditation session at a temple or zendo or participate in a one- or two-week

---

* Variations in approach would naturally arise according to geographical region and the disposition and experience of the temple Abbot. Pure Land, or devotional Buddhism, has been the more popular form of Buddhism in China, as discussed in Chapter 4, and even in dedicated Chan monasteries, many monks will practice this form of devotional Buddhism instead of, or alongside, Chan.

intensive meditation retreat. However, without oversight provided by the monastic environment, we may find ourselves unprepared for the rigors of chan training.

Consider, for example, the characteristics of someone who decides to leave home, job, family, friends, and personal belongings to take spiritual refuge in a monastery where his head is shaved, he receives little more than four hours of sleep each night, eats only simple food, and sleeps side-by-side on the floor next to dozens, or hundreds, of other monks. Such an individual, unless he or she has entered monastic life for worldly reasons, has already met several important prerequisites: spiritual readiness or a sincere desire to become spiritually ready, an unwavering desire to escape suffering (duhkha), firm commitment, and, perhaps most importantly, faith in the program. This faith McRae aptly describes as "...not an emotional commitment or outpouring of devotion, but rather an unswerving conviction, a total absence of even the slightest doubt about the nature of reality as described by the Buddhist teachings." It connotes "...complete acceptance of the existence of the Buddha-nature within the veil of illusions, or even the decision to rely on the existence of that Buddha-nature as the guiding principle of all one's actions."*[263]

When we start with chan it behooves us to ask ourselves, honestly and sincerely, some important questions: Are we adequately committed? Do we have faith in the program? Are we psychologically and physically prepared? Is our motivation to practice chan harmonious with its purpose as a mystical discipline? It may be that we're more interested in participating in its religious form for worldly reasons without a clear understanding of what motivates them. For example, we may be lonely and looking for a community to give us a sense of belonging, we may be seeking structure to overcome a sense of personal chaos, or, as Westerners, we may be Sinophiles or Japanophiles, attracted to a

---

* In my case, I simply wanted to get out of my state of misery. My faith was based on a conviction that zen/chan could make that happen: I was not convinced that a thing called "Buddha nature" was a reality, but I was willing to entertain it as a possibility. I was, however, convinced of the efficacy of chan to get me out of the dark place I was in, which gave me the needed motivation to stick with it.

culture because of its differences from our own. Chan, as an ascetic or spiritual practice, can only serve its intended purpose if we are malcontent with our life and seeking to make it better in ways harmonious with Buddhist principles.

Many Westerners today are introduced to Chan or Zen through the internet, where sutras and commentaries on Chan are readily available. It's easy to become enamored with the philosophical and spiritual insights that have been produced by enlightened minds over the centuries and represented in Chan's canonical texts; yet we may fail to truly understand these insights and mistake their intellectual expression for their experiential discovery, a discovery that affects us more viscerally than intellectually. As with Chan's allusion of the moon and the finger pointing to it (Figure 7), we may not recognize that it's not about the finger or the moon, but about something else entirely.

FIGURE 7. HOTEI POINTING AT THE MOON.
Is it about the finger, or the moon?

To avoid misinterpretation of chan—a spiritual discipline which is, at its essence, experiential and *not* intellectual—I'll begin by addressing prerequisites for chan training, starting with those that are generally taken for granted in the Chinese monastic tradition. Many of these are often overlooked or ignored by lay practitioners.

Revisiting the Buddha's Four Noble Truths

> When we are well we wonder what we would do if we were ill, but when we are ill we take medicine cheerfully; the illness persuades us to do so. We have no longer the passions and desires for amusements and promenades which health gave to us, but which are incompatible with the necessities of illness. Nature gives us, then, passions and desires suitable to our present state. We are only troubled by the fears which we, and not nature, give ourselves...
>
> – Blaise Pascal, from *Pascal's Pensées*[264]

Many chan teachers offer their own version of prerequisites, but the Buddha's First Noble Truth is perhaps the simplest and most profound: we must have an acute understanding, awareness, and experience of duhkha—suffering—and a strong desire to get out of it. Unlike Western culture, which treats mental states such as depression as illnesses, Buddhism valorizes them as gateways to spiritual awakening. Chan is a difficult path to follow, requiring fierce determination, unrelenting perseverance, and ceaseless courage. If we simply go through the motions we're unlikely to make headway, but once we can scream *"Get me out of here!"* we find the fierce resolve needed to accomplish the task. As Chan master Ben Huan described it, "The sense of serious urgency required for Ch'an training is similar to mourning for ones parents, looking into an abyss, or walking on thin ice." When we approach chan with this mental state, we will succeed. Chan master Dahui Zonggao (1089-1163) described it this way:

> Constantly take the two concerns—not knowing where we come from at birth and not knowing where we go at death—and stick them on the point of your nose. Whether eating or drinking, whether in quiet or noisy places, you should make scrupulous efforts from moment to moment, always as if you owed someone millions with no way out, your heart sorely troubled, with no opening to escape. Searching for birth, it cannot be found; searching for death, it cannot be found—at

such a moment, the roads of good and evil are immediately cut off. When your awareness has gotten like this, this is precisely the time to apply effort: contemplate the story right here.[265]

Ultimately, whether duhkha is a truth for us or not is up to us to determine. If we feel it's not a truth, then perhaps it's not: we can go about our lives and not concern ourselves with it any further—chan will serve no purpose for us. But to understand the full implications of duhkha requires fearless honesty and considerable contemplation. A flippant response may prevent us from finding a deeper truth. We may, in fact, be blind to our suffering. The Greeks use the term *agnōsía* (ἀγνωσία) to describe such blindness; it means to be unaware of something, ignorant, unable to recognize something that's there. In English, the term is used in medicine to describe cognitive defects due to brain injuries or various diseases such as Alzheimer's. For example, the clinical term, *anosognosia*, is used to describe the fact that people who have Alzheimer's disease (and some other mental illnesses) are unaware that they have it; *prosopagnosia* is used to describe people who can't recognize faces of familiar people.

Agnōsía can present in many ways. Anil Ananthaswamy, author of *The Man Who Wasn't There*, recounts the story of a man who felt that he shouldn't have one of his legs because he didn't recognize it as "being of himself."[266] He tried killing it off with a tourniquet, but that didn't work, so he decided to submerge it in dry ice. He gave up on that idea when he couldn't obtain strong enough painkillers to allow him to endure the pain of the procedure. Finally, he had the leg amputated by a willing surgeon. After the leg was gone, he said it was the first time in his life he felt whole.[267] This phenomenon occurs frequently enough that it's been termed *body integrity dysphoria* (BID).

Another manifestation of agnōsía was revealed from research in the late 20th century conducted by David Dunning and Justin Kruger from the psychology department of Cornell University. Their research suggested that we all have difficulty assessing our own skill level and competency, a phenomenon now commonly referred to as the Dunning-

Kruger effect. Dunning and Kruger looked at both low-ability people and high-ability people to see how they rated their level of competence. They found that low-ability people tend to overrate their ability and exhibit high levels of confidence contrary to their ability-level, while high-ability people tend to underrate their ability and overrate the ability of others. "The miscalibration of the incompetent stems from an error about the self, whereas the miscalibration of the highly competent stems from an error about others."[268] Dunning explains this in terms of anosognosia: "If you're incompetent, you can't know you're incompetent [because the] skills you need to produce a right answer are exactly the skills you need to recognize what a right answer is."[269] The chan approach to dealing with this is, of course, to recognize that we can't know what we don't know—which is obviously an enormous amount—so we approach everything with an attitude of *not* knowing. If we always assume we know less than we *think* we do, and if we apply doubt to the things we think we know, we are likely to be more realistic and better able to make good decisions. It will also encourage us to enhance our knowledge and understanding, a task we may otherwise neglect.

Some years ago, I sat for dinner with two psychiatrist friends. During the meal, I offered the hypothesis that should everyone in the world be screened for mental illness, at least twenty percent would qualify for it in some form, a number I thought was pretty high. They looked at each other and laughed. "More like seventy," they said together, in near unison, obviously amused by my naiveté. While they may have been exaggerating, their point was clearly made: mental illness is extremely common.* We will never know just how common it is in the

---

* Not all cultures perceive mental illness in the same way. In some, the mental states we label as illnesses may not be seen as illnesses at all but rather as variations of normal mental states. Ethan Watters, in his book *Crazy Like Us: The Globalization of the American Psyche*, wrote "Because the troubled mind has been perceived in terms of diverse religious, scientific, and social beliefs of discrete cultures, the forms of madness from one place and time in history often look remarkably different from the forms of madness in another." (2020) In some cultures, like Asia's, much of what we would describe as mental illness is relatively uncommon. For example, June De Vaus and others determined that depression and anxiety in the West are 4 to 10 times greater than rates in Asia. (De Vaus 2017) Additionally, '"mental illness" can be a by-product of harmful societal norms, which can vary from culture to culture.

world because only a small fraction of people who suffer from it are evaluated by a professional. In developing countries, that number may drop to nearly zero. The National Alliance on Mental Illness assembled a fact sheet in 2013 that put the breadth and scope of mental illness in perspective.[270] About 18.1 percent of American adults—about 42 million people—live with diagnosed anxiety disorders, such as panic disorder, obsessive-compulsive disorder (OCD), post-traumatic stress disorder (PTSD), generalized anxiety disorder, and phobias. Mood disorders such as depression were the third most common cause of hospitalization in the U.S. for both youth and adults ages 18 to 44. Suicide was the tenth leading cause of death in the U.S. (more common than homicide) and was the third leading cause of death for ages 15 to 24. More than 90 percent of those who died by suicide had one or more mental disorders. Troy Brown, of *Medscape Medical News*, reports that for the month of March 2015, the antipsychotic medication *aripiprazole* (*Abilify*)—used to treat mood disorders such as bipolar disorder, schizophrenia, Tourette's syndrome, irritability associated with autism, and depression—was the second largest seller and the 12th most prescribed medication of all medications sold that month, bringing in $8.3 billion dollars for the pharmaceutical companies from nearly one billion pills sold.[271]

Considering the large number of people suffering from poor mental health, it seems realistic to posit that each of us exists somewhere on the "duhkha spectrum."

The Second Noble Truth explains that the cause of duhkha is desire and the attachment that manifests from it. The *participation mystique*, first coined and described by French philosopher Lucien Levy-Bruhl, offers a model to help understand the nature of attachment. It refers to our tendency to create an emotional relationship—an attachment—with an object, idea, person, or group. Carl Jung explained it as "...a peculiar kind of psychological connection with objects and consists in the fact that the subject cannot clearly distinguish himself from the object but is bound to it by a direct relationship which amounts to partial identity."[272]

As an example of the participation mystique, consider how, as children, we may have been given a new toy and came to adore it, carrying it around with us everywhere, maybe even sleeping with it. Our sense of identity became enmeshed with the object. We do this as adults too. We buy a new car and "fall in love" with it. Or it may be a house, a bicycle, a pair of shoes, or a cell phone. Stronger sentiments may arise for a girlfriend, boyfriend, wife, husband, or child. Identification with objects (or people) creates psychological bonds with them.

The participation mystique expresses itself in other ways as well. We might meet a famous actor, musician, or political figure and, in reverence, ask for their autograph so that we might take a part of them home with us. We can also become attached to beliefs, attitudes toward people, and political and religious ideologies and figureheads. Regardless, all attachments, when we trace them to their source, originate with desire. We may, for example, want to be accepted by a particular social, religious, or political group, or to be loved by our parents. In general, desire arises in response to some unmet emotional need.

Our unique collection of attachments leads us to identify ourselves with an equally unique personal reality that's composed of and defined by them. Within this illusory reality, we can become slaves to those attachments and isolated in a particular kind of "reality field" created by them. And that isolation can bring enormous grief.

There is a way out of this predicament, though, according to the Third Noble Truth: we just need to stop craving and kill our desires. While it may sound simple, this is extremely difficult and requires extraordinary effort. But if we're truly experiencing misery and are aware of that fact, and if we want to get out of it, then the motivation is there. The next step is to do it. Han Shan offered this advice:

> What is the best way to sever our attachment to material things? First, we need a good sharp sword, a sword of discrimination, one that cuts through appearance to expose the real. We begin by making a point of noticing how quickly we become dissatisfied with material things and how soon our sensory pleasures also fade into discontent. With

persistent awareness we sharpen and hone this sword. Before long, we find that we seldom have to use it. We've cut down all old desires and new ones don't dare to bother us.[273]

The Fourth Noble Truth gives a structured approach to severing attachments. Siddhārtha used the metaphor of a path that leads, eventually, to blissful meditation. Since the steps of his *Eightfold Path* were presented in a specific order in his first sermon, and later in others, he may have intended them to be followed in sequential steps. Indeed, when analyzed, each step supports the next; however, considering many practitioners successfully work with all of them together, Vetter's conclusion is reasonable that "the eightfold path is no path which one has to traverse from one stage to the next, but only a list of important means."[274] The liturgical basis of the Eightfold Path was presented in Chapter One, so here we'll look at it in a more practical context as it pertains to preparing us for chan.

1. Samyag-drsti: Right View — Perfection of Understanding

Right View begins with recognizing that life in *samsāra* means suffering.* There is no way to understand this intellectually; we have to realize it directly. Why is this so important to the path? Because illumination, *bodhi*, requires us to throw away our old self, to abandon everything we've identified ourselves with, including our self-image, our profession, our friends, and our family. They all must go. It doesn't mean we literally leave them or throw them away—that would not necessarily sever our attachment to them—it means we *psychologically* sever attachment to them; we detach our sense of self-identity from them; that is, we stop engaging the participation mystique. The willpower for doing this arises from our determination to exit samsāra—the tumultuous cyclic realm of suffering, where desires are continuously arising and falling.

---

* The *Saccavibhanga-sutta* provides this explanation of Right View: "And what, your reverences, is right view? Whatever ... is knowledge of anguish, knowledge of the arising of anguish, knowledge of the stopping of anguish, knowledge of the course leading to the stopping of anguish—this, your reverences, is called right view" (as quoted by Crangle, 1994, 157-8).

Right View also means paying attention to the *way* we look at things. Many of us don't consider our perspectives, we just have them. They create our opinions, judgments, attitudes, and beliefs, all of which convey a sense of identity and define a narrative for our lives. Right View challenges us to find the source of these perspectives and observe their effects. Do our views allow us to observe reality *as it is*, or might they distort our interpretation of it through prejudicial wishes and desires for how we want reality to be?

Right View means we work to understand things from different perspectives and avoid judgment on a topic until we have contemplated it from as many perspectives as possible. This open-minded process of inquiry, nurtured by harboring great doubt, is highly engaging and leads us to realize that there are so many ways to look at things that we can't possibly know them all. Any opinion we may form might easily be wrong, because we may have overlooked something. With this attitude, the mind becomes more open, receptive, unbiased, and clear.

2. Samyak-samkalpa: Right Intention – Perfection of Thought

Right Intention engages us to seek actions motivated by what's helpful and valuable. It also encourages us to look at the reasons for our actions and determine whether they are based on motivations that are beneficial to us and others.

How often do we do something mindlessly, without thinking about it, and how often does this get us into trouble? Perhaps we have an accident while driving because we're distracted by our phone, or we inadvertently insult someone, or intentionally cause someone harm because we harbor enmity toward them. Right Intention requires that we avoid actions that are motivated by selfish intentions, and that we work on aligning action with intention to help improve the outcomes of our actions—not just for ourselves, but for others as well.

This doesn't mean, however, that an act motivated by good intention will always result in a positive outcome. Positive outcomes are not the point of Right Intention.

A story may help illustrate this. A woman is driving her car and notices a turtle plodding across the busy road. She stops in front of it, blocking traffic, then gets out of her car and carries it to the side of the road and places it in the foliage. She returns to her car and drives away (I had been driving the car immediately behind her). Can we assume that her action resulted in the turtle's ultimate safety? No. What if it wanted to be on the opposite side of the road from where she placed it, so it crossed the road again and was subsequently hit by a passing car when otherwise it might not have been? Or what if she placed it in an area that was recently sprayed with pesticide and it died of poisoning? There's no way to know if the turtle was better off because of her intervention. So how might we assess if her behavior was in harmony with Right Intention? The answer would depend on whether it was based on a desire to make her feel good about herself, or if instead it was a selfless act of kindness. It would also depend on whether she considered Right View, contemplating many possible outcomes her actions might bring. Did she consider the danger to herself and others from stopping in the middle of a busy road? Only she could know if her action was in harmony with Right Intention, irrespective of the ultimate outcome for the turtle, herself, and other drivers.

There is no objective right or wrong when it comes to doing the "right thing"—there is rarely, if ever, a perfect option. The second step simply encourages us to assess our intention to determine if our motivation for an action is based on selfish interest or true concern for a greater good.

3. Samyag-vāc: Right Speech – Perfection of Speech

The Buddha purportedly said, "Words have the power to both destroy and heal. When words are both true and kind, they can change our world." This is apparent and obvious, yet speech has a power often overlooked. Words can injure or heal; they can send a call to war, or they can invoke peace; they can show empathy, indifference, or disdain. Of all the steps on the Eightfold Path, many people find Right Speech the most difficult. How much of what we say is said on impulse? How much of what we speak is thoughtlessly thrown out to land wherever it may, without regard to who is hearing it, or what impact it may have on others? How many of us mindlessly speak aloud whatever thoughts are cascading through our mind at the moment, indifferent to whether they need to be heard? How many of us know people who talk incessantly as long as there is someone to listen? How many of us fit this description ourselves?

Right Speech challenges us to pay attention to the words we speak and consider their impact on whomever may hear them. It suggests that we consider their value and whether they will help or harm. More than the words we speak, our motivation determines whether we are properly regarding Right Speech. Are we trying to impress people with our knowledge of a subject? To coerce them into believing what we believe? Maybe we want to insult them? Are we trying to sell ourselves to them so they will like us? Are we trying to position ourselves in a dominant, authoritative role to gain a position of power or prestige? Are we trying to fill a void of loneliness? Might we just be habituated to speaking our thoughts aloud, heedless of the unnecessary attention it demands from others?

If we are preoccupied with self-serving motives, an often-unconscious pretense for speech, we will not be engaging Right Speech. Our words will instead be motivated by wanting our ego satiated in some way. As we gain the ability to see things from another's point of view, to step out of our isolated ego-world, we can then begin to watch and correct our speech more easily. By inquiring into the motivations for what we say, we can observe whether our thoughts and words are self-serving and, if so, make adjustments so that we may speak more thoughtfully and caringly.

4. Samyak-karmānta: Right Action – Perfection of Conduct

In the wake of Donald Trump's quest for the White House, violence against minorities in the United States rose sharply according to many sources, especially crimes against Muslims, Hispanics, Blacks, and Jews. On December 5, 2016, CBS New York posted an article about a woman wearing a turban who was pushed down stairs in a New York City subway.[275] The article described a scene in which most people witnessing the event did nothing; only one person stopped to help the victim.

Every day we are faced with situations that require a decisive course of action. We may be waiting for a red light to turn green so we can drive through the intersection, or perhaps waiting for a cashier to tell us how much we owe so we can pay. But these are trivial actions that take little attention—there's no question about what we need to do.

But when something new and unexpected happens, determining the best course of action can sometimes be difficult. When there are established rules to follow, it's easy: all we have to do is follow those rules, and our decisions will at least be accepted by society. But when there are no fixed rules, no firm guidelines to follow, what then?

In the Muslim hate crime described above, many pedestrians made the decision to not get involved; perhaps some took solace in thinking that by not taking action they would be exonerated from the incident. Maybe some didn't want to jeopardize their own safety or soil their clothes. Maybe their neglect was in response to unconscious (or conscious) racism or bigotry. Regardless, any of them who witnessed and assessed the event, and who could have stopped to help, were not applying Right Action because they were thinking of themselves first.

Right Action means we conduct our behavior in accordance with what's helpful to others when we are in a situation to help. It means we consider other people, other animals and creatures—all part of our extended family of living beings—with respect and dignity. When, by our action or non-action, we deny help to others when we are able to give it, we deny them respect and compassion, and we fail to embrace our mutually shared humanity.

Avoiding wrong actions comes naturally when we're attentive to right actions. As we work toward becoming more aware of our actions and inactions, as well as the resulting effects they have on our lives and the lives of others, we can better act with awareness of the consequences those actions bring. With that awareness, we can then make adjustments as needed to bring them into harmony with Right Action.

5. Samyag-ājīva: Right Livelihood – Perfection of Living

"Your work is to discover your work and then with all your heart to give yourself to it," the Buddha purportedly said. All societies depend on a vast assortment of jobs. Refuse collectors are as important to the health of a society as doctors and firefighters, teachers and artists. Right Livelihood is not about how much money or prestige we gain from a job or career, nor even whether the work we engage in is more or less ethical than another;* Right Livelihood is about how we approach our livelihood, whatever it might be.

Right Livelihood means that, regardless of what type of work we do, we strive to disengage the ego from it; we apply ourselves to do the best job we can, without regard for personal reward. When approached this way, reward comes automatically, and it's invariably more enduring and satisfying than the fleeting rewards gained from appeasing transient ego-desires.

6. Samyag-vyāyāma: Right Effort – Perfection of Diligence

As difficult as it can be to turn our gaze inward while sensory pleasures beckon us to indulge in them, if we don't, our inner lives go unexplored, if not undiscovered.

Often, we pay little or no attention to our inner lives, and as a result we may suffer depression, fear, anxiety, or other unpleasant emotions. Having neglected our spiritual life, we may squander our resources on drugs, clothes, pets, cars, or countless other things. We may even take on good-deed causes to give our lives a sense of meaning and purpose or join or start groups of one kind or another. All such activity dis-

---

* Clearly, being a mafia hitman or illicit drug dealer would not qualify as Right Livelihood, but such a person would not be applying the first four steps on the Path, which serve to align thoughts and actions with compatible moral behavior.

tracts us from the uncomfortable and sometimes painful task of looking inward.

Staying the spiritual course once we're on it is much easier than getting on it in the first place. It's all to easy to look for shortcuts to try to avoid the difficult work. But shortcuts lure us away from applying the effort needed to sever attachments to the sensory world, and the resulting frustration often leads to giving up. Han Shan contended that

> [p]eople who don't appreciate the struggles of climbing lack understanding of where they've been, awareness of who they are, and determination to continue climbing. That's why they never attain the Dharma. The hard way—the way learned by difficult experience and painful realizations—doesn't interest them. They want a short-cut. True Dharma seekers are afraid of short-cuts. They know better. They know that without effort, there's no sense of accomplishment. It's that sense that keeps them going.[276]

Success with the last two steps on the path require that we are not only content to leave behind the world of sensory affections, but eager. If our motive is selfish, directed solely at trying to achieve something for personal gain, our efforts will fail. Christmas Humphries, author of *Concentration and Meditation*, instructed that our motivation must be "an impersonal turning of the will towards the removal of all suffering, without undue attention to one's own, and an effort to uncover within each form of life that 'Essence of Mind,' which, as the *Sūtra of Huineng* points out, 'is intrinsically pure.'"[277]

7. Samyak-smṛti: Right Mindfulness – Perfection of Attention

Right Mindfulness, or *Perfection of Attention*, can be viewed as the culmination of the first six steps on the path. It directs us to be attentive to everything we do and think to the highest possible degree. Through Right Mindfulness, we develop clarity and harmony of thought and action, yielding a mind that is focused, resilient, and contemplative.

Right Mindfulness can be further honed during seated practice by using any of the exercises available for developing mental clarity, some of which I'll discuss in the next three chapters. It can also be practiced during daily activities by utilizing other chan practices, such as the *huatou*, which I'll describe in Chapter 12.

8. Samyak-samādhi: Right Meditation — Perfection of Meditation

We can interpret *Samyak-samādhi*, as "perfection of meditative absorption." Meditation arises naturally and without effort once the mind has been adequately prepared through concentration and contemplation.* That preparation begins by learning to focus the mind intently on a subject or "seed." Any subject of concentration can be effective: it can be a thing, like a shoelace, a candle, a flower, or a stick of burning incense; it can be an idea, a thought, a sound, a mathematical puzzle, or a physical sensation like the pulse or breath; it can also be a quality, such as equanimity, compassion, or tranquility. When the mind is finally ready for meditation, it slips into it naturally and automatically. At that point, the knower and the known merge and the ego-self disappears.

STAGES OF SPIRITUAL DEVELOPMENT

The principles of the Eightfold Path are helpful when we apply them mindfully and when we desperately want to transform our lives. Working and talking with people over the years about chan practice, I have observed that those expressing an interest in practicing chan generally fit into one of several categories: those eager and prepared for a struggle; those eager but unprepared for the discipline and effort required; those unmotivated or unwilling to take charge of their own spiritual

---

* *Samyak-samādhi* is sometimes translated as *perfection of concentration*, which may be equally ambiguous to the English reader. Sanskrit has many terms to describe types or stages of concentration, all of which fit broadly within the categorical term *dhāraṇā*. *Samādhi* is generally used to refer to concentration on mind or Self to the degree that one enters a state of ecstatic absorption, but *samādhi* is also a container term that includes a variety of other states of "intense mental collectedness" (Feuerstein, 2008, p. 162.).

development; those seeking some tangential benefit that religious affiliation brings; and those who, for whatever reason, are uninterested in applying effort. People who fit into the first two groups are a minority but have a high chance of success with chan practice, while those in the latter groups rarely make headway. Because chan is so demanding, many people who start a chan practice soon give up and take alternate paths.

A subset of people eager for chan suffer from psychological disturbances that completely confound the spiritual training process, arresting our ability to acquire the concentration skills required for spiritual growth and keeping us stuck in the muck of duhkha. This was my situation when I tried meditation for the first time in the early 1980s. Anxiety, depression, and nihilistic pessimism erected a seemingly impenetrable psychological barrier. It was a decade from the time I was introduced to chan before I was ready for it.

While such mental states are not uncommon among those who eventually follow chan, it's common for us all to suffer under the ego's uncompromising rule, which we can consider a kind of mental disturbance itself. One person recently exclaimed to me, "My life is a horror but at least I'm holding on to myself!" Such existential conflict can be a launching pad for people attracted to chan: once the "horror" element is strong enough, there's a tipping point when the desire to "hold onto oneself" falls away. This is when we need a different kind of knowledge and guidance to navigate our lives in a new direction.

"The crucial knowledge is the knowledge obtained by which one is transformed," Erwin Rousselle wrote in *Spiritual Guidance in Contemporary Taoism*.[278] Knowledge that does not transform is of little value to one who wants to get out of the roiling waters of duhkha. For the Eightfold Path to impart transformative benefits, we need to be ready and able to be transformed. Fortunately, when this condition befell me, I had already been introduced to chan and the basics of Buddhist mysticism. I knew the path would be there when I was ready for it, and it was.

There have been many attempts to quantify spirituality, or more specifically, spiritual awareness. Some people have offered valuable insights. James Fowler, for example, proposed that all people fit, generally, into one of six stages of spiritual development, and that the mechanisms for moving forward from one to the next are uniquely different for each of us, i.e., that spiritual development is dependent on where we are and whether we use the right means for moving forward.* He also recognized that many people get stuck in one of the earlier stages and remain there their entire lives. In 1981, he published his thoughts in *Stages of Faith: The Psychology of Human Development and the Quest for Meaning*. Although Fowler proposed the stages as universally relevant and independent of one's religious or spiritual identity, it's useful to present a summary of them as they relate, broadly, to chan because they offer useful perspectives on our own lives, and the human condition in general.

STAGE ONE: *Intuitive-Projective Faith* applies to the fantasy world of the very young child. At this stage there is no concept yet of self and other—our entire universe is egocentric, the outside world a shadow of a fantasy:

> Intuitive-Projective faith is the fantasy-filled, imitative phase in which the child can be powerfully and permanently influenced by examples, moods, actions and stories of the visible faith of primally related adults.
>
> ...The imaginative processes underlying fantasy are unrestrained and uninhibited by logical thought... This is the stage of first self-awareness. The 'self-aware' child is egocentric as regards the perspectives of others. ...

---

* James Fowler received his Ph.D. from Harvard University in Religion and Society, focusing on ethics and sociology of religion. He subsequently taught at Harvard Divinity school, Boston College, and Emory's Candler school of Theology, where he was named Charles Howard Candler Professor of Theology and Human Development in 1987. He became internationally recognized as a research pioneer in the theory of faith (Center for Ethics at Emory 2015).

The gift of emergent strength of this stage is the birth of imagination, the ability to unify and grasp the experience-world in powerful images and as presented in stories that register the child's intuitive understandings and feelings toward the ultimate conditions of existence.

The Dangers in this stage arise from the possible 'possession' of the child's imagination by unrestrained images of terror and destructiveness, or from the witting or unwitting exploitation of her or his imagination in the reinforcement of taboos and moral or doctrinal expectations.[279]

STAGE TWO: *Mythic-Literal Faith* is when we personally identify with the belief system given to us by our family and community, even though it's perceived as fractured and discordant. This is when we first begin forming an identity by connecting with external belief structures offered by political parties, religions, families, and other social institutions. While we still exist dominantly within a self-absorbed world, we are beginning to yearn for acceptance from both family and community. Each opportunity employed to gain acceptance strengthens self-identity within the scope of a larger world which is just beginning to be discovered.

For us to make sense of our beliefs, they are

> ... appropriated with literal interpretations, as are moral rules and attitudes. Symbols are taken as one-dimensional and literal in meaning. ... A factor initiating transition to Stage Three is the implicit clash or contradictions in stories that leads to reflection on meanings. The transition to formal operational thought makes such reflection possible and necessary. Previous literalism breaks down, new "cognitive conceit" leads to disillusionment with previous teachers and teachings. Conflicts between authoritative stories must be faced.

The new capacity or strength in this stage is the rise of narrative and the emergence of story, drama and myth as ways of finding and giving coherence to experience.

The limitations of literalness and an excessive reliance upon reciprocity as a principle for constructing an ultimate environment can result either in an overcontrolling, stilted perfectionism or 'works righteousness' or in their opposite, an abasing sense of badness embraced because of mistreatment, neglect or the apparent disfavor of significant others.[280]

STAGE THREE: *Synthetic-Conventional Faith* arises when we begin to yearn for strict belief structures. Once we embrace them, we will identify with them exclusively and repel any notions that don't fit within the confined and limited worldview they present. Often strongly opinionated, we are neither individuated nor free thinkers, but gauge ourselves exclusively within the context of our selected paradigm, whether it's religious or secular. At this stage, we will identify strongly with specific social or religious groups, rejecting others as being inferior or incorrect, regardless of any facts or evidence that may draw into question the validity of our beliefs.

Fowler writes of Stage Three:

> Stage Three typically has its rise and ascendancy in adolescence, but for many adults it becomes a permanent place of equilibrium. It structures the ultimate environment in interpersonal terms. Its images of unifying value and power derive from the extension of qualities experienced in personal relationships. It is a 'conformist' stage in the sense that it is acutely tuned to the expectations and judgments of significant others and does not have a sure enough grasp on its own identity and autonomous judgment to construct and maintain an independent perspective.
>
> The emergent capacity of this stage is the forming of a personal myth – the myth of one's own becoming in identity and faith, incorporating one's past and anticipated future in an image of the ultimate environment unified by characteristics of personality.
>
> The dangers of deficiencies in this stage are twofold. The expectations and evaluations of others can be so compellingly internalized

(and sacralized) that later autonomy of judgment and action can be jeopardized; or interpersonal betrayals can give rise either to nihilistic despair about a personal principle of ultimate being or to a compensatory intimacy with God unrelated to mundane relations.[281]

If we get stuck in Stage Three, we become susceptible to self-identification with cults and cult-like groups that others may look upon as extremist. If we are sports enthusiasts, for example, we may strongly identify with a particular team, acquiring logo-paraphernalia to display proudly in our home and wear on the street. If we are politically oriented, we may develop extremist political views on whichever side of the political spectrum we support. If we have religious affiliations, we may acquire extremist ideologies and project them onto the religion with which we identify. The longer we stay in this stage, the harder it can be to get out of it. Many adults never escape from it.

STAGE FOUR: *Individuative-Reflective Faith* is characterized by a critical reflection on identity and outlook. In this stage, we rely dominantly on thinking and reasoning processes to help define and guide our lives. The mind is "fact-based" over "feeling-based." During this stage, the mind's eye has not yet glimpsed beyond our manufactured self-identity to a more all-inclusive aspect of self. It's characterized by

> ...critical reflection on identity (self) and outlook (ideology). Its dangers inhere in its strengths: an excessive confidence in the conscious mind and in critical thought and a kind of second narcissism in which the now clearly bounded, reflective self overassimilates "reality" and the perspectives of others into its own world view.[282]

At Stage Four we may be attracted to Chan because of a perceived logical or philosophical aspect that appeals to our sense of reason. We may consider the scriptural foundations of Chan to be the limit of what Chan has to offer, blind to any deeper significance. We often find people in Stage Four entering professions in academics, research, medicine, journalism, business, and various other "thinking" fields. Chan and Zen groups may also have leaders and teachers who fit into this stage of development.

STAGE FIVE: *Conjunctive Faith* begins when we become receptive to seeing into the deeper nature of being and correlates with the first step on chan's journey. Entering Stage Five, however, we still experience a rift in the psyche as a result of tension between our spiritual and banal identities. From this tension we acquire the desire for a spiritual grounding-post—a way to resolve the tension, to become progressively more rooted within our Self. Fowler describes this stage as an "opening to the voices of one's 'deeper self.'"

> Alive to paradox and the truth in apparent contradictions, this stage strives to unify opposites in mind and experience. It generates and maintains vulnerability to the strange truths of those who are 'other.' Ready for closeness to that which is different and threatening to self and outlook (including new depths of experience in spirituality and religious revelation), this stage's commitment to justice is freed from the confines of tribe, class, religious community or nation.
>
> The new strength of this stage comes in the rise of the ironic imagination—a capacity to see and be in one's or one's group's most powerful meanings, while simultaneously recognizing that they are relative, partial and inevitable distorting apprehensions of transcendent reality. Its danger lies in the direction of a paralyzing passivity or inaction, giving rise to complacency or cynical withdrawal, due to its paradoxical understanding of truth.
>
> ... But this stage remains divided. It lives and acts between an untransformed world and a transforming vision and loyalties. In some few cases this division yields to the call of the radical actualization that we call Stage 6.[283]

Stage Five is reflected in the first stanza of Chan's famous ox-herding series, which will be presented in its entirety in Chapter 14. Hsu Yun offered this verse:

I. Pushing Aside the Grass to Look for the Ox*

Wanting to break through to Emptiness with my white cudgel
I cried out louder than the bellowing Ox, mooing through my senses.
I followed mountain and stream searching for the Ox, seeking it everywhere.
But I couldn't tell in which direction it had gone...west?... or east?[284]

Alternatively, the Chan monk Kuo An Zhe wrote:

I. Searching for the Ox

Alone in the wilderness, lost in the jungle, the boy is searching, searching!
The swelling waters, the far-away mountains, and the unending path;
Exhausted and in despair, he knows not where to go.
He only hears the evening cicadas singing in the maple-woods.[285]

From the Buddhist perspective, prior to this stage, we are presumed to exist in one of the *six realms of desire*, i.e., we seek to satisfy desires through any and all means and exist at the mercy of the senses which rule over us: we are completely detached from, and unaware of, our fuller nature. The subsequent ox-herding stanzas pertain to Fowler's *Stage Six*, Buddhism's *seventh realm*, which collectively pertain to his final stage of spiritual development.

STAGE SIX: *Universalizing Faith* describes the development of awareness that's inclusive of all being. In this stage, we have transcended personal identity as the nexus of existence and experience life from the perspective of *universal essence*. Existence takes on a boundless and all-encompassing nature for us: we reside in the harmonious unification of all things and follow natural universal laws (Dharma). Having ceased to differentiate between self and other, we perceive all people, in every walk of life, of every nationality, culture, age, and gender, collectively, as One. Every person is seen as an essential interconnected aspect of

---

* The ox of Chan's ox-herding series represents one's *essential nature*, which is initially unknown but becomes known through a quest to discover it.

reality; even rocks, trees, planets, and stars are seen as an aspect of Self as they equally share the realm of existence. Hsu Yun expressed this feeling of wholeness and unity in his tenth ox-herding stanza:

X. Coming Home with Folded Hands

How wide are the horizons of the spinning earth!
The moonlight leads the tides and the sun's light will not be
*   confined within the net of heaven.*
But in the end, all things return to the One.
The deaf and dumb, the crippled and deformed
*   are all restored to the One's Perfection.*[286]

The corresponding verse by Kuo An Zhe reads:

X. Entering the city with Bliss-bestowing Hands

Bare-chested and bare-footed, he comes out into the market-place;
Daubed with mud and ashes, how broadly he smiles!
There is no need for the miraculous power of the gods,
For he touches, and lo! the dead trees are in full bloom.[287]

Some may question whether Fowler's stages truly relate to Buddhism's Four Noble Truths and chan's Journey, and whether it's pertinent to present them here. Their value, to me, is that they illustrate that each of us is at some point along a continuum of experience, understanding, and awareness, and that to move forward, we must move in the direction away from where we are into the unknown. We can never truly know the path in front of us—that which we have not yet experienced—because we can't know what we don't know; but we *can* open our minds to great doubt and let that propel us forward into whatever may lie ahead.

Preparing for meditation

Many people equate chan practice with sitting on a cushion on the floor for long periods of time, but this practice is meant to complement a fuller regimen that engages us at all times, regardless of whether we are sitting, jogging along a mountain path, eating a meal, or talking on the phone.* In fact, in early Chan literature, we find many references to Chan as having no reliance on meditation, but never is meditation ruled out as a valuable tool. "No reliance" means we can do it, but we must not rely upon it as our sole spiritual activity. Moreover, we should form no attachment to it. With this in mind, many Chinese monks and nuns, to this day, incorporate hours of meditation sessions into their daily lives. A sitting regimen (*zuò chán* 坐禪; Jap., *zazen*) provides an opportunity to intensely focus the gaze inward, something that can be difficult when we are cleaning the kitchen, shopping for groceries, or tending the needs of children, yet something which can be very helpful if we can allocate a small amount of time for it each day. But how do we go about it?

In a traditional Chinese monastery, meditation methods are generally tailored to each person's specific psychological constitution, mental framework, and developmental readiness. But regardless of method, they all require an understanding of correct posture, breathing, and mental attitude.

Sitting practice: zuò chán

Correct posture (Skt., *āsana*) is important for several reasons: it helps strengthen the muscles around the spine, it helps keep us alert and awake, and it allows us to sit with great stability, which becomes increasingly valuable later when we enter the timelessness of samādhi. Attention to posture also helps us develop a keen awareness of the body.

Regardless of the many sitting options we might choose, it's important to keep the spine "straight" and upright, the body relaxed. We don't want to slump forward or lean to one side or the other. I put "straight"

---

* This was emphasized by Han Shan: "True Dharma seekers who live in the world use their daily activity as a polishing tool. Outwardly they may appear to be very busy, like flint striking steel, making sparks everywhere. But inwardly they silently grow. For although they may be working very hard, they are working for the sake of the work and not for the profits it will bring them. Unattached to the results of their labor, they transcend the frenetic to reach the Way's essential tranquility. Doesn't a rough and tumbling stream also sparkle like striking flints – while it polishes into smoothness every stone in its path" (2014)?

in quotes because the spine is not naturally straight, but forms an "S" shape. "Straight" just means we use our core muscles in such a way that our bodies become as vertical and balanced as possible.

Beginners often find it most comfortable to use a chair, either with a hard seat or a thin cushion, and sit on the front half to one-third without leaning on the backrest. When using a chair, we position our legs so they don't put a leveraging force on the body, pushing it backward or pulling it forward. Some experimentation may be needed: it may, for example, be necessary to cross the calves slightly if the legs are too long or place a book under the feet if they are too short.

Another popular option employs the Japanese zafu and zabuton. The zafu is a round cushion about eight inches high and fourteen inches in diameter. It's usually placed on top of a zabuton, a cushion of twenty to thirty inches square and about an inch thick. When using these, we sit on the front third to half of the zafu cushion and fold our legs comfortably in front of us without them overlapping. Alternately, we can sit in the "half lotus" (*ardha padmasana*) position with one foot lifted onto the thigh of the opposing leg. For this position, it may be necessary to remove the zafu and sit only on the zabuton. The "full lotus" (*padmasana*) position, in which each foot rests on top of the opposing thigh, while being the most stable and conducive to long meditation periods, is best not attempted until adequate stretching exercises have enabled the legs to easily move into this position. In the full lotus position, no pillow is needed to raise the spine.

EXERCISE 1: DEVELOPING PROPER SITTING FORM

Take your preferred sitting position from one of those described above. Gently rock the body left and right until you feel the most centered position, then do the same by gently rocking front to back. To further help find the right position, imagine a thin string running up along the spine, rising through the top of the head. Imagine it being pulled taut and your body straightening along with it. Feel your spine rooted firmly to the chair and feel a stretch up the torso, all the way through the neck to the top of the head. Imagine the body stretching upwards, the spine rising up along the path of the taut string, aligning the vertebrae, neck, and head. Use the muscles to make it happen. Sitting in front of a mirror is often helpful: sometimes we may think we're sitting perfectly, but when we have visual feedback, we may realize we need to make adjustments.

Next, slowly roll the shoulders forward, upward, then back, then let them drop naturally. If there is tightness in the shoulders, perform this motion several times in each direction.

Now concentrate to hold the posture. At first it may be difficult because we're using muscles in ways we aren't accustomed, and because we're breaking old habits; but with practice, the muscles strengthen and the effort needed to hold this posture decreases. Eventually, the right posture comes automatically. When beginning, go slowly; sit for, say, two ten-minute sessions per day for the first week, then on the second week extend it to two fifteen-minute sessions twice a day. Always keep goals attainable. It's better to take small steps forward than to attempt giant leaps.

For experienced sitters, the half- or full-lotus positions are usually used because they allow the body to have three points of contact, like a tripod, which gives great stability and allows us to stay comfortably seated for a long time without fatigue. It also puts the spine in a natural prone position. When we're first learning to sit, however, we don't want to start with these positions because the process of getting comfortable with them can be quite painful and undermine our objective—to learn to meditate.* To learn these positions, we practice them gradually over the course of several weeks, starting with the half-lotus and alternating

---

* Pain induces a stress response. During any stress response, heart rate increases, breathing quickens, muscles tighten, and blood pressure rises. The body's chemistry responds as well, releasing adrenaline, norepinephrine, and cortisol. Such conditions are not conducive to meditation. Concentration practices can allow us to gain control over these responses and tune them out; however, beginners lack the experience needed for this.

which leg goes on top. In short time, we're able to take the position effortlessly and comfortably.

Once we're in the right position we'll feel balanced and there will be no tendency to lean one way or another. We'll feel immovable, like the trunk of a strong old oak tree rooted to the earth. Solid.

One sitting position to avoid is the *Vajrasana*, or vajra pose, a position sometimes taught by contemporary yoga instructors in which we sit on our heels. Extended periods of time in this position can lead to peroneal neural damage, or what is colloquially known as *yoga foot drop*.

What do we do with the hands? Traditionally, hands are placed in specific positions called *mudras*. Each mudra has its own associated symbolic meaning in terms of how it's conceived to affect the body's "life-energy," or Qi.* The most common hand positions for seated meditation are the *bhairava* and *hairavi* mudras. In each case, the hands are placed one on top of the other on the lap just under the navel, palms up, with adjacent thumbs lightly touching. In the case of the *bhairava mudra*, the right hand is placed in the left; in the case of the *hairavi mudra*, the left hand is placed in the right. The *bhairava mudra* is associated with the *Shiva* aspect—the aspect of *Supreme Self*, or *Essential Law*, and is considered masculine in nature. The *hairavi mudra* is associated with the *Shakti* aspect—the aspect of consciousness and manifestation, power and energy, and is feminine in nature.†

Mental attitude

The right mental attitude is essential for success with chan practice: if we don't have it, we may give up before we've begun, or simply fail to make progress. For chan, we must be prepared to wage a battle with our ego-desires and confront the "daemons" that lurk as repressed

---

* The term Qi 氣 corresponds to similar terms in other languages. In Sanskrit, it's prāṇa (प्राण), *pneuma* (πνεῦμα) in Greek, and *mana* in Hawaiian. In Latin, the term is *spiritus*, from whence the English term *spirit* originates. Qi refers to the vital life energy, or life force, within a person and is most often associated with the breath and breathing.

† Shiva and Shakti are codependent opposites analogous to Taoism's Yang/Yin duo.

emotions in our psyches. We must be prepared and willing to experience feelings of all kinds, from wonderful to terrifying.

Without the right mental attitude, we may also become self-critical, convincing ourselves that we aren't up to the challenge, or we may engage in sabotaging self-talk: *Why am I doing this? This isn't going anywhere! Is this really a legitimate practice? This is too hard! I can't do this!* These are all sentiments I've heard from beginners (myself included). This is a phase we get out of if we don't give up. I have known no successful chan practitioners who haven't past through it. There's nothing the ego wants more than to see us give up; after all, this practice threatens its existence, so why should it *not* want to fight back? The solution is to gather up courage and, rather than fight such thoughts, watch them arise, let them go, and continue. We can imagine ourselves as an arrow traveling through the sky, piercing every obstacle we encounter; observing any mental chatter, acknowledging it as harmless, and refusing to let it coerce or cajole as we fly by.

EXERCISE 2: BECOMING AWARE OF THE MIND

Assume a proper sitting posture (Exercise 1) and take three full slow breaths, then breathe normally. Watch the mind as it travels from one thought to another. Is it a little bit unnerving? Our minds do this all the time; the difference is we're just now becoming aware of it. Simply by watching the mind, the chaotic chatter will slow down. With continued practice, the chaos can be eliminated altogether.

Enabling Time for Solitude

Solitude is essential for any successful spiritual regimen. Without it, we remain mired in endless engagements with people and activities, all of which divert attention from the inward-looking eye of contemplation. Sometimes we may have to go to great lengths to get it.

Many well-known artists and scientists have also lauded the value of solitude for nurturing the creative spirit:

Kafka: "You need not leave your room. Remain sitting at your table and listen. You need not even listen, simply wait, just learn to become quiet, and still, and solitary. The world will freely offer itself to you to be unmasked. It has no choice; it will roll in ecstasy at your feet."

Tesla: "The mind is sharper and keener in seclusion and uninterrupted solitude. Originality thrives in seclusion free of outside influences beating upon us to cripple the creative mind. Be alone—that is the secret of invention: be alone, that is when ideas are born."

Picasso: "Without great solitude no serious work is possible."

If we live hectic lives, it's all the more valuable to our mental and spiritual health to create time for solitude daily.

Establishing a routine

If we rearrange our daily schedule to insert some time for practice we will be more apt to stick with a regimen and make progress, even if it's only for five or ten minutes a day. Many people have found the following routine effective in various modified forms:

Exercise 3: Establishing a routine

Stake out a corner of a room by rearranging furniture and perhaps erecting a barrier such as a shoji screen* to isolate it from the rest of the room. Place a small altar in the area on which you can place a small bowl of salt or sand to hold incense sticks.† Arrange one or two other things you find inspiring on the altar. Place a chair or a zafu and zabutan on the floor a few feet in front of the altar. Before breakfast in the morning, light a stick of incense and place it in the prepared incense bowl, then take a seat on the cushion or chair and begin the practice you are working with. When the incense stick has finished burning, conclude your sitting time, or light another stick and repeat.

---

* A type of lightweight foldable and portable wall traditionally made with wood or bamboo and rice paper.

† Some people prefer to use an oil diffuser which produces no smoke.

Incorporating ritual into the routine

Action performed with a focused and attentive mind, directed entirely on a specific activity to the exclusion of all else, is the essence of ritual. Ritual helps us exit the cacophony of daily life and enter the mental space conducive to spiritual work. Erika Bourguignon, author of *Psychological Anthropology: An Introduction to Human Nature and Cultural Difference*, describes ritual as a

> kind of learning, through which the world is simplified for the individual: the complex world of experience is transformed [through ritual] into an orderly world of symbols. At the same time, there is also a transformation of the individual, who acquires new understandings, or ... "new cognitive structures," and a new transformed identity.[288]

Chan training in the Orient is highly ritualized, and many rituals are ceremonial. A well-known example is the tea ceremony, popular among both Chinese and Japanese Buddhists and non-Buddhists alike. For monks living in a monastery in China, nearly every aspect of life is ritualized, from walking to the dining hall, to lighting incense, to bowing, to washing clothes. Ritual provides the opportunity to practice Right Mindfulness, induces calm, and helps maintain a concentrated, reflective mind.

Religious rituals serve an additional purpose. They work with symbols that tap into the unconscious, facilitating a transformation of awareness from the outer realm of the senses to the inner realm of Self. Common symbolic structures accessed through ritual in Chinese Buddhism are the celestial Buddha (Amitābha, Amida, or Amitāyus), who embodies the essence of Self, and the celestial trinity: Avalokiteśvara (Guan Yin), who embodies compassion, Mañjuśrī, who embodies wisdom, and Maitreya, who embodies kindness. Represented ubiquitously in statuary, frescos, paintings, and liturgical texts, these four transformational symbols are commonly used as seeds for contemplation and meditation to foster awareness of Self and inspire the archetypal aspects they symbolize: compassion, wisdom, and kindness, respectfully.*

Maintaining effort

Chan master Ben Huan offered this advice:

> ...remember never to let your energy level slip when you are training. Although it is not easy, always maintain the right kind of effort or your training will be in vain. At the Gao Ming Temple, a venerable old monk said: 'If you walk this path, make a great effort. If you do not make a great effort, then do not walk this path."[289]

There is perhaps no stronger bond to sever than that of the ego—the illusory self. This is the singular reason the chan path is so difficult. It takes every bit of effort we can muster to detach from this capricious aspect of the psyche.

When we no longer identify ourselves with our professions, our families, our likes and dislikes, our opinions, etc., the ego's command over us dissolves. Collectively, attachments are the raw constituents of ego: sever ourselves from them, and we sever ourselves from the ego — we remove the foundation of, and cause for, its existence. This process, however, is not only difficult, it's often painfully so. Successful navigation out of the ego's domain requires great courage and commitment. We also have to believe that we will win the battle and that the rewards will be worth it—that is, we must have faith in the program.

Imagine being out at sea on a sinking ship. On this ship is a pole—a tall mast—so you grab onto it and climb to the top, hoping for your life that you won't go down with the ship. But as you look down and see the water approaching, you know that you must make a choice: do you continue hanging on to the last solid object in sight, or do you let go and allow whatever might happen to happen? If you keep hanging on to the pole, you know you will sink with the ship and drown. If you let go,

---

* Because Japanese Zen is largely bereft of archetypal meditations, these transformation symbols are less commonly encountered in Japanese Zen traditions.

what then?* The pole represents all the things we cling to, that drag us down and make us miserable: attachments to belongings, people, pets, social media; but, most drastically, our pesky sense of self-identity. Letting go of our attachments requires a giant leap into the frightening unknown because we lose the comforting security these attachments had convinced us we couldn't live without.

Entrance into chan often begins with feeling like we're on a sinking ship that's out of control. We may feel intense dread as we recognize we can't continue living as we have. We know we can't hang on to the pole because it will drown us if we do, yet we don't know what will happen if we let go. It can be terrifying. The pole offers the only sense of security we have left, yet we know that when it sinks into the abyss, that sense of security will be our doom unless we give it up. So, we apply effort, muster the faith and courage to let go and take our chances with the unknown. Once we've taken the leap, we quickly realize we didn't need the pole at all. Without the pole we are free.

---

* This popular Chan story has been told in many ways. It is presented in case 46 of the *Gateless Barrier* (the *Wu-men kuan*): "The priest Shih-shuang said, 'How do you step from the top of a hundred-foot pole?' Another eminent master of former times said: 'You who sit on top of a hundred-foot pole, although you have entered the Way, it is not yet genuine. Take a step from the top of the pole and worlds of the Ten Directions are your total body'" (Aitken 1995, 273).

10

Stage One: Mindfulness

ALTHOUGH THE PREREQUISITES DISCUSSED earlier are essential for chan in the broad sense, they aren't essential for gaining the benefits of preliminary practices. Stages One and Two, as I describe them here, develop mindfulness and concentration, and are readily accessible to anyone with a desire to try them.

The term "mindfulness" originates with Thomas W. Rhys Davids' (1843-1922) translation of the Sanskrit term *smṛti*, lit. *that which is remembered*.[291] Mindfulness is generally used today to mean *attentiveness* or *awareness*. In the context of chan, however, it's more than this. The Chinese character for mindfulness is nian 念, which is composed of the character jin 今, meaning "now" and "this," and xin 心, meaning both "heart" and "mind"; thus, the term also includes the notion of harmonizing heart (feeling) and mind (thinking) in the present moment, of "heartfulness" or compassion, of living in the "now," and of living in "thusness" (Skt., *tathātā*).*

The primary objective of mindfulness is to break out of conditioned ways of interacting with the world around us. The brain is accustomed to spending most of its time processing inputs from the environment

---

* The concept of mindfulness may seem to contradict the Chinese concept of no-mindfulness (*wunian*), i.e., when one is mindful of "not-mind," or "no mind." The problem is reconciled by recognizing that "mindfulness of no-mind" is a later development, arising in the contemplation phase which I describe as Stage Three.

and, as a result, becomes biased towards externalized forms of perception. Looking within then becomes minimized or even eliminated, sometimes to the extent that we come to know only half of ourselves—the externalized half—and totally ignorant of the other half. Mindfulness practices help us balance an otherwise unbalanced mode of perception.

"Mindfulness meditation" is variously referred to in contemporary literature as *nondirective meditation, open-monitoring meditation, Transcendental Meditation* (TM), and by some as *Vipassana*.* In Norway, it has been popularized under the name *Acem meditation*. In this stage, the practitioner is generally directed to passively observe any and all inputs from the senses as they arise, acknowledge them, then watch them as they go. Mental effort is not exerted to try to control the thoughts or to concentrate on any specific thing.

Robert Sharf traces the origins of contemporary mindfulness practice to Theravāda sources that became popular in the twentieth century, such as Buddhaghosa's *Path of Purification* (*Visuddhimagga*), written in Sri Lanka in the 5th century, and from techniques developed by various Burmese teachers, such as Mahāsī Sayādaw.[292] Sayādaw (1904-1982) created a method that was easy to learn and approachable for people who had no Buddhist background. It eliminated concentration practices and emphasized "moment-to-moment lucid awareness of whatever arises in the mind."[293] His student, Nyanaponika Thera (Siegmund Feniger, 1904-1994) named the method "bare attention" and popularized it through his 1954 book, *The Heart of Buddhist Meditation*. Sharf comments that, because Mahāsī's method

---

* *Vipassana* is a Pali term for a popular practice from the *Theravāda* Buddhist tradition. A respected teacher of this tradition, Bhante Henepola Gunaratana, describes it as "looking into something with clarity and precision, seeing each component as distinct and separate, and piercing all the way through so as to perceive the most fundamental reality of that thing" (Gunaratana 2002). In this way, he refers to it as *directive meditation* in which there is a subject or object that must be investigated thoroughly, with full concentration, until its essence is revealed. Crangle supports this view and asserts that the sutras, in fact, place Vipassana as an "exclusive and original discovery" of the Buddha, "as a discrete meditation following on form (through continuing to utilize) concentration (*samatha*)," and that it "distinguishes the Buddha's course of practice from those of other meditative schools, including both early Vedic and Upanisadic practices with their particular world-views" (1994, 272).

...did not require familiarity with Buddhist literature and was designed to be taught in a delimited period of time in a retreat format, it proved easy to export beyond the realm of Burmese Theravāda. The method has been influential not only in Southeast Asian Theravāda but also among modern Tibetan, Chinese, Korean, Japanese, and Vietnamese religious reformers. By the end of the twentieth century, Mahāsī's approach to sati or mindfulness, interpreted as "bare attention" and "full awareness of the here and now," had emerged as one of the foundations of Buddhist modernism—an approach to Buddhism that cut across geographical, cultural, and sectarian boundaries.[294]

From my experience, the Sōtō Zen lineage of Japan, the most prevalent Zen school in the United States and other parts of the Western hemisphere, teaches largely, if not exclusively, nondirective, Stage One practices.* In fact, at the time of this writing, the popular Japanese-based Sōtō Zen website, global.Sotozen-net.or.jp, describes nondirective approaches as the essence of sitting-practice:

> Do not concentrate on any particular object or control your thought. When you maintain a proper posture and your breathing settles down, your mind will naturally become tranquil. When various thoughts arise in your mind, do not become caught up by them or struggle with them; neither pursue nor try to escape from them. Just leave thoughts alone, allowing them to come up and go away freely. The essential thing in doing zazen is to awaken (kakusoku) from distraction and dullness and return to the right posture moment by moment.[295]

This description bears a striking similarity to a passage in the *Zuochan yi* 坐禅仪, presumably written by Changlu Zongze in the 12th century.†

---

* Some former followers of Soto Zen have told me they never received training in mindfulness meditation, nor any other particular type of meditation, but were told to "just sit and empty the mind." People's experience with Soto (or other) training methods will be largely determined by the teacher's experience and depth of understanding of the spiritual development process as well as their philosophical and soteriological perspectives as shaped by their cultural and religious traditions.

† The *Zuochan yi* described standard meditation practices of the Northern Song Chan school, some of which became adopted in Japan by monks such as Dogen (Schlütter 2008, 170).

After describing the proper sitting posture, it states, "Do not think of any good or evil whatsoever. Whenever a thought occurs, be aware of it; as soon as you are aware of it, it will vanish ... this is the essential art of seated meditation."[296] The emphasis on nondirective technique is considered by some to be the dominant difference between the Linji (Jap., Rinzai) and Caodong (Jap., Sōtō) schools of Zen, as discussed in Chapter 4.*

Although there are few, if any, extant records of nondirective methods promoted as an exclusive practice in the Chan tradition,† and they don't appear as topics of the Buddha's teachings conveyed in the sutras, they are nonetheless beneficial and accessible for many people, as the widespread adoption of Mahāsī's methods has attested to. Health benefits are numerous, progress can be made quickly, and they help prepare us for the next stage.

A study of people practicing mindfulness methods was carried out by Jian Xu and others in 2014 to compare "nondirective" methods with "directive" methods (to be discussed in Stage Two). Utilizing Functional Magnetic Resonance Imaging (fMRI), the results showed the brain to be active across more regions when using nondirective methods than when using focused, directed methods which concentrate mental activity. Specifically, it was found that people who practice nondirective techniques experience "higher activity in the right medial temporal lobe (parahippocampal gyrus and amygdala)," which supports a conclusion that it "involves more extensive activation of brain areas associated with episodic memories and emotional processing, than during concentrative practicing or regular rest."[297]

---

* Some people understand Soto Zen as a "mind-blanking" approach, in which we pay attention to nothing. Such a conceptualization of Zen training is not compatible with Chinese chan, as it does not belong to the broad category of mindfulness or any other chan training disciplines.

† It may be of interest to note that the origin of Dogen's "Silent Illumination" teachings originated with Hong Zhi, who coined the term for his teaching. Hong Zhi, however, also strongly advocated directive methods. As editor of the *Book of Serenity*, he not only taught gong-an (koan) methods, but described the "six subtle methods" of directive meditation practice that lead ultimately to "essential purity," formulated by Zhi Yi (T. Cleary 1988, xx). Consequently, it has been suggested by some that Dogen cherry-picked practices according to his own selective biases.

In a different independent study in 2006, B. R. Cahn and J. Polich demonstrated that mindfulness practices stimulated the middle prefrontal brain associated with metacognition and self-observation.[298] Juergen Fell and others observed that first-time meditators quickly learn to moderate alpha-wave activity (8 to 12 Hz, characteristic of pre-sleeping/pre-waking states), slowing its rhythm while increasing its power, and observed that this effect was independent of how much experience a person had with mindfulness methods, as well as the school with which they identified.[299] Some people practicing mindfulness meditation may enter theta brain-wave states, where the conscious and subconscious mind coexist and dream imagery manifests.

To reach "deeper" states, we must be able to command ourselves to stay awake, because the natural response of the body, when in them, is to sleep.* The way we learn to stay awake is to work with concentration practices. If we limit ourselves to Stage One mindfulness practices and fail to move on to this next stage, we can get stuck here and fail to reach full meditation, a state of consciousness in which the brain inhabits the slower theta (4 Hz to 8 Hz) and delta (0.5 Hz to 4 Hz) states.

---

* People sometimes talk about meditation in terms of how "deep" they go. This ambiguous terminology can be misleading. "Depth" of meditation indicates our ability to stay alert and conscious as the brain's neural-synapses come into phase. The "deepest" state of meditation happens when we can stay conscious while the brain produces delta waves, thought to be the slowest wave-state possible, and one normally associated with deep sleep. I'm not fond of talking about meditation in terms of depth because it elicits notions of "going down" and darkness, as well as states such as hypnosis, where awareness becomes diminished rather than heightened. When we remain conscious as the brain's neuroactivity becomes progressively more in-phase, the clarity and tranquility experienced is tremendously illuminating. To corroborate this, psychologists Peter Lush and Zoltan Dienes, researchers at the University of Sussex, have identified meditators as being significantly more aware of self-cognitive functions such as intentional-awareness than nonmeditators, and to an even greater degree compared with people in hypnosis (Dienes 2016). Hillman more appropriately describes depth as it relates to the psychological activity of "vertical" or "downward" interiorizing: "Depth is [...] not literally hidden, deep down, inside. Rather, the fantasy of depth encourages us to look at the world again, to read each event for 'something deeper,' to 'insearch' rather than to research, yet further significance below what seems merely evident and natural" (2013, 37).

11

Stage Two: Concentration

As emphasized throughout this book, chan requires effort and discipline directed by will. Without the will to effect change, the kind of change we are looking for won't happen. Techniques for learning meditation are simple, but the task of implementing them—of learning to sustain mental focus—takes time, practice, and discipline.

Concentration (dhāraṇā) facilitates calmness of mind and breath, enhances mental power and clarity, eliminates stress and anxiety, and develops the ability for sustained attention, observation, and reflection. Edward Crangle, author of *The Origin and Development of Early Indian Contemplative Practices*, writes that the term's use in the sutras "means literally 'collection or concentration of the mind (joined with the retention of the breath).'"[300] Ernest Wood, author of *Concentration – An Approach to Meditation* and *Yoga*, describes concentration and its purpose as[*]

> ...the narrowing of the field of attention in a manner and for a time determined by the will. Our consciousness may at any given time be

---

[*] Ernest Wood (1883-1965) was a theosophist, Sanskrit scholar, and Indologist whose two books, *Concentration – An Approach to Meditation* and *Yoga and The Pinnacle of Indian Thought*, are still widely circulated and available in recent reprints.

diffused over a large area, in which everything is indefinite, or it may be focused on some chosen object. In the latter case, we obtain the clearest mental vision and the most vivid consciousness of which we are capable. The practice of concentration is intended to produce this condition...[301]

Concentration breaks down conditioned mental and emotional patterns when we apply willful effort to the process. Without effort, we'll continue to be slaves to a chaotic mind, and the skill of concentration will elude us. But what, exactly, is willful effort?

Jeffrey Schwartz MD, research professor of psychiatry at the UCLA school of Medicine, suggests in *The Mind and the Brain, Neuroplasticity and the Power of Mental Force* that the question of will does not reside with what we choose to do, but with what we choose *not* to do. That is, it's our ability to throw on the brakes—to arrest preconditioned ways of thinking and reacting—that fosters mindfulness.[302] A study at the Max Planck Institute for Human Cognitive and Brain Sciences supports this hypothesis. Through the use of brain imaging techniques, researchers found that the brain makes decisions for us an incredible seven seconds before we are consciously aware of making them. That is, when we think we are making a conscious decision to *do* something, that decision has already been made automatically through unconscious processes.[303] Schwartz thus suggests that it's only when we choose to arrest an action that conscious will manifests, and that it's therefore more realistic to talk about "free won't" than "free will."[304]

Considering these observations, when we act on unconscious urges there is no free will, but the moment we deny those urges through an act of negation, free will manifests. We can learn to overcome preconditioned ways of thinking, feeling, and acting by disciplining ourselves to concentrate: when distracting thoughts, feelings, or sensations interfere, we can remember the negation practice from the *Upanishads* (Chapter 1) and turn them off by telling ourselves, *Not thus! Not thus!*

Exercises for developing concentration need not necessarily be related to spiritual discipline: they can be activities we use to gain a skill, as a musician practices scales or a bodybuilder lifts weights. Developing concentration prepares the mind for contemplation (Stage Three) and meditation (Stage Four).

Prānāyāma ("breath control")

There are many activities that can help us learn to concentrate, but one of the best is through the breath—*pranayama*. Training in any of the sciences, mathematics, music, sports, martial arts, and many other disciplines also develops concentration powers; however, the breath offers additional advantages as a focus for concentration: it directs our gaze inward instead of outward, forging a connection with our inner life.

One of the most ancient terms for breath comes from the *Rig Veda*: *ātman*, meaning not only breath, but soul, and the principle of life and sensation.* It also encompasses the concept of "absolute Self."†305

Pranayama practices typically begin with *ānāpānasmṛti*,‡ lit. "mindfulness of the breath,"§ which leads to *pratyāhāra*, or *withdrawal of the senses*.¶

Exercise 4: Observing the breath

Close your eyes and watch the breath as you inhale and exhale five times. Don't try to control it. What is it doing? Is it shallow or deep? Is it regular and even, or irregular? Is it fast or slow?

---

* The Sanskrit grammarian Yāska describes *ātman* as "the pervading principle, the organism in which other elements are united and the ultimate sentient principle" (Baumer 2001, 42).

† "He who knows the *ātman* crosses over [the ocean of suffering]" (Chāndogyopaniṣad, VII, 1, 3).

‡ The *Ekottara Āgama* (*Zēngyī-ahánjīng* 增壹阿含經), also known as *The Great Ānāpānasmṛti Sūtra* 大安般守意經, was one of the first sutras to be translated into Chinese during the second century CE. A century later, the breathing practices advocated in this scripture, promoted by the monk Fotudeng 佛圖澄, rapidly spread Buddhism throughout China (Nan 1997).

§ The Chinese use the term xī 息—a compound character composed of the symbols for heart, 心 (xīn), and the character for nose 自—to represent the breath in stillness and rest (C. Luk 1964, 125).

¶ According to Whalen Lai, the practice of "withdrawal of the senses" had long been employed by Taoists before the Buddhist monk, Hui Yuan 慧遠, popularized it as a Buddhist practice during the early part of the first century CE (Lai 2009, 331).

Most of us use a very small part of the lungs when we breathe unless, of course, we are exercising, and our body is working to consume higher levels of oxygen and expel higher levels of carbon dioxide. Vigorous exercise forces us to breathe deeply, fully, and rhythmically, but we can also learn to breathe this way while quietly sitting.

EXERCISE 5: DEVELOPING AWARENESS OF THE BREATH

Assume the correct sitting posture, exhale, then begin a breath from the bottom up: inhale slowly using the diaphragm and feel the abdomen expand outward as air rushes in through the nostrils and down the trachea. Pay attention to every nuance of the breath—the feeling of muscles contracting, the feeling of air as it flows in through the nose, sinuses, and the back of the throat. Keep the mouth closed, the tongue lightly touching the roof of the mouth. Once you've reached maximum air capacity from the bottom, the abdomen fully expanded, begin filling the rest of the lungs by expanding the chest to let more air enter. Check that the shoulders are relaxed. Feel the stretch, the pressure, as air fills the lungs. Once the lungs are fully expanded, take one last inhale using all the diaphragm's power to grasp a last few bits of air—you may be surprised how much air your lungs can actually hold. Now hold the breath for a few moments, then raise a hand, placing the palm approximately three inches in front of your mouth. Very slowly release the breath, blowing on the hand as you would blow out candles on a birthday cake, so the flow is smooth and even against your hand. When you think you've expelled all the air you can, use the abdominal muscles to push out even more air. Repeat this process five times, then take a break before doing it again. Continue until the pressure of air on your hand is even and constant throughout the entire exhale.

Next, sit for a couple minutes breathing normally. Feel balanced and grounded. Now exhale naturally until it's no longer comfortable to do so, then slowly inhale until it becomes uncomfortable to inhale further. Slowly exhale. Unlike the previous exercise, don't try to force extra air in at the top of the breath, or out at the bottom of the breath. Continue taking slow, natural, deep breaths, inhaling to full capacity, then exhaling fully. With some experimentation you'll soon be able to establish a rhythm and will be breathing in and exhaling out more deeply and rhythmically than you normally would. Focus all your attention on breathing. If you get dizzy, lightheaded, or anxious, stop and wait a few minutes, review the instructions, then try it again. Some people find that practicing five minutes at a time works best, while others like going for ten or fifteen. It's better to practice for short periods when we can focus intently than for long periods when we may be prone to losing concentration. I have found many people have the best success with this exercise when they practice for five minutes, take a break, then practice for another five minutes, repeating it three or four times a day. But if you can only do it once a day, that's good too.

Once we have mastered this exercise, we can extend it to times we're doing other things. When we're involved in daily routines, it's difficult to maintain regular deep breathing, but it's valuable to try. Over time, this practice will automatically change the way we breathe all the time. It will also help reduce our stress and anxiety and improve our overall sense of well-being. When we find ourselves stressed, angry, upset, or even struggling with insomnia, simply by pointing the mind at the breath—producing slow, deep, even breaths—we can bring ourselves back to the calm of the moment.

It's important not to move on to the next exercise until this one is mastered. When I first started to learn to meditate over thirty years ago, I was unable to sit for more than a couple minutes without becoming extremely agitated. Being alone with my mind was torture. In fact, after the first attempt, I could not even bring myself to try it again for another five years. Being psychologically, mentally, and physically ready for each successive practice is essential for success; trying to jump ahead before we're ready can sabotage our efforts (Part Four).

As discussed previously, when we focus the mind on something, we refer to that "something" as a *seed*. A seed starts out very small, but as we cultivate it, it sprouts, turning into something entirely different.

Our first seed has been the breath, and the first objective has been to simply become aware of it. Our next task is to make the seed sprout, and for this we can use another pranayama exercise. Pranayama can be translated as *extension of the breath*, or *extension of the life-force*. In the next exercise we are going to take our seed—our life-force—and extend it.

Exercise 6: Developing breath control

This exercise is performed in three parts in a carefully regulated pattern, or ratio: a "1:4:2" sequence. It begins with an inhale (*pūraka*) for one count, then is followed by a hold (*kumbhaka*) for four counts and concludes with an exhale (*rechaka*) for two counts. This means that the breath is held for four times the amount of time taken to perform the inhale, and the exhale is completed in half the time the breath is held. Begin with a ratio sequence of 3:12:6, where each count is approximately one second. As you work with the practice, gradually extend the number of counts for longer durations, maintaining the same ratio and one-second count-interval; for example, 4:16:8, 6:24:12, 8:32:16.

Practice this exercise until the sequence can be repeated continuously for ten minutes or more. Be careful not to close the throat during the breath-hold—air should stay in the lungs using muscle control alone. At the end of the exhale, immediately begin inhaling to start the next cycle. If the 3:12:6 cycle is too challenging, begin with 1:4:2 or 2:8:4 using the same approach, and work your way to longer cycles over the course of several days or weeks.

If you are a smoker, have asthma, or another condition that impairs breathing, long ratio sequences may not be feasible, but don't let that deter you from mastering shorter ones. They can work just as well.

An audible clock or metronome can be used to monitor the time in one-second intervals, or if the heartbeat can be felt, it can be used instead. Another option is to silently repeat the words for each part: as you inhale, repeat the word *pūraka* three times, then hold the breath while repeating *kumbhaka* twelve times, then expel the breath while repeating *rechaka* six times. While doing this practice, uninterrupted concentration is essential. Within days or weeks, you'll begin to notice subtle changes in your mood, physical energy, and awareness.*

As we work with various concentration practices, it's helpful to occasionally pause and return to natural breathing. This allows us the opportunity to observe the effects of practice.

Exercise 7: Concentration on Natural Breathing

After you are able to complete ten minutes or more of the pranayama exercise described above without interruption, follow it with simply observing the breath. That is, instead of trying to control it, let the breath happen naturally and be aware of it in its entirety. Breathing should be regular and comfortable, and you should feel relaxed and at ease as you attentively watch the entire breathing process. Feel the air flow into the nose and into the lungs on the inhale as the lungs expand. On the exhale, feel the air leave along the same path it entered as the diaphragm relaxes. Continue this watchful breathing for five to ten minutes. Take notice when the mind wanders and gently bring attention back to the breath.

It can take anywhere from weeks to months to train the mind to concentrate well. The more we work at it, the faster it happens. Exercises 6 and 7 can also be effective initial transition exercises for more advanced practices, which I'll describe next.

---

* This exercise is sometimes presented to practitioners of hatha-yoga and is referred to as a *Healing Breath* (Wood 1959, 84-85).

Thought retracing

Thought retracing enhances awareness of our mental process and reduces the chaotic cascading of random thoughts that interfere with our attention of the present moment. The first time we sit down and attempt to quiet the mind, we usually notice how noisy it is, how many fragmented thoughts are seemingly tangled up with each other. It can sometimes be so chaotic that we can't tell where one thought ends and another begins. *Thought retracing,* attacks this problem directly. Amidst the mind's chaos, we take a moment to isolate a particular thought fragment—it doesn't matter which. Once identified, we recall which thought immediately preceded it, then which one preceded that. We keep going back along the chain of thoughts until we can identify an effective starting point from which the final thought arose. Christmas Humphreys offers a clear example of this technique:*

> To take a simple example, one may begin to concentrate on an orange. Before one is aware of it, the mind has leapt from orange to fruit in general, from fruit to the need of buying some for lunch, from this to the play which the people coming to lunch are taking one to see, from this to tickets one promised to pick up on the way, and thence the best way of arriving at the theatre and the proper time to leave the house in order to get there in time. With a start you realize how far you have travelled from the orange, but instead of returning direct to the orange and beginning again, force the attention to travel back the way it came. From planning times and routes, return to tickets, and thence to visitors, lunch, fruit and the need for it, and so back to the orange sitting in front of you. This habit of thought recalling is a valuable exercise in itself, and much may be learnt from it.[306]

With continued practice, a peaceful silence arises through which thoughts can be observed with extreme clarity. It can seem like they take on their own reality, distinct and separate from us. We become an

---

* Christmas Humphreys (1901-1983) was a lawyer who later converted to Buddhism and founded the London Buddhist Society, which became influential in bringing Buddhist thought and practice to England.

observer looking in on them rather than a participant in their formation—like watching a movie. This new perspective of awareness leads to the next stage, contemplation. Han Shan offered this guidance:

> If you can [...] engage in contemplation, then whenever a thought arises, you should find its source. Never haphazardly allow it to pass you by [without seeing through it]. Do not be deceived by it! If this is how you work, then you will be doing some genuine practice. Do not try to gather up some abstract and intellectual view on it or try to fabricate some clever understanding about it.[307]

Other seeds for concentration

In the *Śūraṅgama Sūtra*,[*] the Buddha asks twenty-five bodhisattvas—people who have experienced spiritual awakening—to explain the seed of concentration that led to it. Telling their stories, each seed fits into one of four categories: the "six sensory data," the "five sense organs," the "six consciousnesses," and the "seven elements." The *Śūraṅgama Sūtra* suggests that the Buddha was aware that different people are best suited for different seeds, and that each is an equally valid and useful tool for transcending the conditioned mind. Once the ability to concentrate for prolonged periods has been mastered using the breath, we're free to explore any of these seeds.[†]

Sound or music

Many people find sound to be the most direct means to enter meditation. Whether we listen to music, sounds that naturally arise in our

---

* McRae describes the *Śūraṅgama samādhi*, which is explained in this sutra, as being "so conceptually abstruse that it amounts to an encapsulation of the entirety of the Mahāyāna Buddhist path" (Paul Harrison and John R. McRae 1998, 114).

† There is risk in selecting our own seed when we are beginning, as the ego can get involved and we can end up jumping about from one seed to another without ever "germinating" any of them. For this reason, it's best to pick a seed and stick with it, resisting the temptation to change it until it has illuminated us: the specific seed used is of less importance than the effort we put into the process. Once concentration has matured adequately—i.e., we have learned to *cultivate* our seed—we can apply the method to any seed we might choose, because at this point, they will all point us in the same direction.

environment, or chant, we simply let the sound enter and consume us, keeping our attention always on sound while not engaging with it emotionally. If listening to music, choosing music that doesn't have an easily recognizable tune or pattern will make it harder for the ego to become involved. The music of Philip Glass, György Ligeti, John Cage, Richard Wagner, John Coltrane, Tōru Takemitsu, Baba Allaudin Khan, Ravi Shankar, and G. S. Sachdev, or any of the shakuhachi masters, are among many good choices.

Exercise 8: Concentration on music

Play your selected music on speakers or headphones. Take the proper sitting position and focus your attention entirely on the music. Watch how the mind moves as the music moves. Observe and identify any emotions that may arise.

Exercise 9: Concentration on ambient sounds

Take a proper sitting position and focus the mind on ambient sounds in the environment. The mind will initially jump from one sound to another, which is okay. The objective is to keep it focused on sound alone. When the mind begins thinking random thoughts, gently return it back to the sounds. Challenge yourself to hear soft sounds that are largely obscured by louder ones. How long can you maintain focus?

The pulse, incense, concepts, and mental formations

The heart is always with us and beats all the time, so it's a natural object for concentration. We can use the pulse to become aware of another of our body's autonomic processes:

Exercise 10: Concentration on the pulse

After having attained a relaxed and concentrated mind, place your hands in the *aakaash mudra*, the thumb lightly touching the tip of the middle finger, the back of the hands resting on the legs. Focus attention on the contact surfaces between the two fingers of your right hand until you feel a light throb of the pulse. Continue concentrating on the sensation. How long can you maintain awareness of the pulse?

Next, shift attention from the fingers to the hand. Concentrate on the hand until you feel the pulse there. Alternate between the right and left hands and then try it with both simultaneously. Once mastered, try this same seed on any point of the body: simply point your attention to a location and concentrate it there until you feel the pulse. Even if you are unable to sense the pulse, this exercise will quickly develop concentration power.

Exercise 11: Concentration on burning incense

Light a stick of incense and place it in a small bowl containing salt or fine sand. Place the bowl on the floor four to five feet directly in front of where you sit (if you sit on a chair, place it on a short table at approximately the same distance). After assuming the proper sitting position, fix your gaze on the burning incense stick and observe the smoke as it rises and vanishes. Continue until it has completed burning.

Exercise 12: Concentration on a concept

Before sitting for practice, choose a concept of interest. It can be an abstract philosophical question, such as "Can we observe anything objectively?" or "What is a number?"; it can be a social concept like liberty, peace, or freedom; or it can be an emotional concept like joy, love, hate, fear, grief, or solace. Hold the concept or question in your mind and investigate it from every possible vantage.

Exercise 13: Concentration on mental formations

Working directly with mental formations (*saṃskāra*) offers another approach to concentration practice. Take your position for seated meditation and concentrate on your thoughts and their associated feelings. Visualize a Cartesian coordinate system, with horizontal and vertical axes intersecting each other perpendicularly to form four quadrants. When you clearly identify a thought, place it in one of the quadrants according to its emotional tone, which is identified as either internal or projected, and as either positive or negative. See Figure 8 for examples. Note that the top quadrants receive thoughts that correlate with positive feelings and the bottom quadrants receive thoughts that correlate with negative feelings; while the left quadrants receive thoughts with projected feelings, and the right quadrants receive thoughts with internal feelings; that is, thoughts elicit emotions which can be identified as having two qualities: one internal or external and another positive or negative.

As an example, say a thought arises of a conflict you had with a coworker earlier in the day. Examine the emotional tone of the thought. If it elicits anger, place it in the lower left quadrant; if it elicits remorse, place it in the lower right quadrant, if the conflict ended in a positive outcome that makes you happy, put it in the upper right quadrant, or if it elicits compassion toward your coworker, put it in the upper left quadrant. If it's a complex emotion, eliciting both positive and negative, or both interior and exterior feelings, label it by the first one that comes to mind. It's not necessary to define the specific emotional aspect of the thought (e.g., tranquility, hate, guilt, etc.), only to determine which quadrant to assign it to. It doesn't matter if you make a mistake, and it's not necessary to remember the succession of thoughts or feelings: once a thought's emotional tone has been identified and placed in its appropriate quadrant, let it pass and move on to the next one that arises. Avoid being judgmental: be an analyst making an objective decision based on the evidence observed. This exercise works well on or off the cushion and can also be invoked during normal daily activities.

POSITIVE FEELINGS

PROJECTED FEELINGS	INTERNAL FEELINGS
Kindness	Tranquility
Compassion	Peace
Love	Happiness
Sympathy	Joy
...	...
Anger	Craving
Hate	Remorse
Jealousy	Guilt
Resentment	Fear
...	...

NEGATIVE FEELINGS

FIGURE 8. THE QUADRANT EXERCISE.
When a thought arises, identify its tone and place the thought in the quadrant corresponding to whether it expresses itself as a projected feeling or an inward feeling, and whether it has a positive or negative emotional tone.

12

Stage Three: Contemplation

CONTEMPLATION ALLOWS US TO investigate a supra-conscious (*asamprajnāta*) state of mind. We can liken it to developing an independent "third eye"—a passive observer, or witness, of our mental and physical activity. While concentration practices help focus the mind, contemplation practices work on developing a mind that's open, receptive, and free of mental formations: a mind that can reflect upon itself. In this phase of practice, we may experience a variety of "enlightenment experiences" including *jianxing* (*jiànxìng* 見性; Jap., *kensho*) and *wù* 悟 (Skt., *bodhi* बोधि; Jap., *satori*) and become, for the first time, directly aware of the elusive Self.

Moving from concentration to contemplation happens automatically, without our having to force it. As we concentrate, we'll notice a shift in awareness as we become an observer to the process of concentration itself. If we're able to maintain the experience, we'll begin to watch the mind as we might watch a movie, but unlike a movie, we'll be able to interact with its thoughts, changing and directing them fluidly, with a sense of extreme clarity. The sense that we are in charge of the experience, however, is oddly absent—it's more like the experience is in charge of us and we are interactive spectators. In this state, we're able to investigate our seed from a much wider vantage point, integrating its various aspects into a cohesive whole. Rather than zooming in on it to observe details—as we did when learning to concentrate—the mind now zooms out, observing the totality of the seed-object, inclusive of all the details we observed when concentrating on its parts. The seed simultaneously becomes inclusive of us, the observer.

Shenxiu, who came to represent the early teachings of "Northern school" Chan (Chapter 4), advised beginning chan practice with contemplations of external objects:

> If you wish to cultivate contemplation, you must proceed first from the contemplation of the external. Why is this necessary? Because the external sensory realms constitute the causes and conditions of the generated mind, the locus of the activated illusions. [...] One must simply follow each and every [object upon which the] mind is conditioned, investigating it intimately. Know that there is only this mind and no external realms.[308]

Although we can choose anything for our seed, the feelings we experience from contemplation will be affected by the type of seed we use. If our seed is a pencil, for example, we will be less likely to experience ecstatic feelings of joy than if our seed is a concept like beauty, grace, or compassion. Ernest Wood, author of *Seven Schools of Yoga*, describes the numinous feeling that accompanies the experience of contemplating such seeds:

> Contemplation is concentration at the top end of your line of thought. Thus a new platform is produced in the mind. [...] This state is sometimes reached involuntarily by devotees in whom a chosen image or picture, or the sight perhaps of some glorious natural beauty, awakens an ecstatic feeling, and they stand transfixed, drinking in, in complete self-forgetfulness, the beautiful realities. This is worship, the highest human faculty, in which man contacts truth, goodness and beauty

beyond the limited personally relative experiences and conceptions of them which are already familiar to him.[309]

For contemplation practice off the cushion, we might engage in *gong-an*, *hua-tou*, or *negation* practices, as described next. Practices on the cushion may include the three practices on emptiness, signlessness, and wishlessness, as described in the *Aṣṭasāhasrikā prajñāpāramitā Sūtra* (Chapter 1).

The gong-an

The *gong-an* (*gōngàn* 公案; Jap., *kōan*) is one of many techniques employed to break through the rigid mental framework that obscures the Self. Readers may be familiar with the gong-an, "What is the sound of one hand clapping?", now, unfortunately, more often used to present a satirical or whimsical joke.* Gong-ans present problems other than misrepresentation as well. Students may intellectualize them or compete with other students to see who can get the "right answer" first. The effect, then, is to strengthen the ego rather than transcend it.

Gong-ans are now predominantly used in some, though not all, Japanese Rinzai and Korean sects as a means of initiating students with a practice. They are also commonly used as topics for sermons. Translated, gong-an means "public case." An example from *The Book of Serenity* is titled "The World Honored One Ascends The Seat." The dialogue contains an introduction, a case (the heart of the gong-an), a commentary, a verse, another commentary, and some added sayings. In this example, the case is:

> One day the World Honored One [the Buddha] ascended the seat. Manjusri† struck the gavel and said, "Clearly observe the Dharma of

---

* For example, a cartoon by GD & Aalif poses one monk saying to the other, "Brother, I just heard the sound of one hand clapping." The other monk says, "Sorry brother, those were the baked beans I had for lunch."

† Mañjuśrī is a prominent bodhisattva in Mahāyāna Buddhism and represents the ideal form, or archetype, of a fully enlightened sage, or Buddha. Many sutras involve dialogues between Mañjuśrī and the Buddha.

the King of Dharma; the Dharma of the King of Dharma is thus." The World Honored One then got down from the seat.[310]

With some historical background, this short exposition elicits more questions and ideas than may be initially obvious. What is Dharma? How can someone be king of it? How does the Buddha getting off his seat, into which he just climbed, illustrate it? Clearly there is no logical answer. Nonetheless, the questions taunt us. They beckon us to seek answers. The intriguing nature of these literary devices leaves little wonder why collections of gong-ans have been preserved and revered for generations, and why they are still used today.

Many traditional gong-ans, however, require explanation that would have been unnecessary during the era in which they were written. Theological concepts that were common knowledge to students a thousand years ago are no longer part of the common Buddhist lexicon (Chapter 4); consequently, gong-ans may now be of more academic interest than useful tools for gaining spiritual insight.

Consider, for example, this short encounter dialogue from the Classical Chan period: A monk asked Dongshan, "What is 'Buddha'?" Dongshan replied, "Three pounds of hemp." This last line has been interpreted (and translated) in many ways and inspired numerous Dharma talks. Dōgen's response was:

> Dongshan's Buddha is three pounds of sesame. When debt of gratitude is deep, enmity also deepens. Wishing to see the ocean dried all the way down to the bottom, one finally knows that a dead person has no mind remaining.[311]

John Daido Loori presented a lengthy sermon on this "flax problem" in 2001. He commented:

> From the outset, we should understand that "three pounds of flax" is not just a reply to the question about buddhas. What is Dongshan responding to, answering this way? What is he addressing? He's answering all of those questions that people keep bringing up about

practice: "Where am I going? What is the goal? What do I get?" Isn't that how we approach our undertakings? How much does it cost? How much do I get? Can you imagine doing this practice simply because of being called to it, without intent? And to be able to practice that calling with great excitement and great energy?[312]

While both Loori and Dōgen may have offered insightful—albeit unrelated—commentaries, it appears that neither knew that three pounds of hemp (or flax) was the quantity required to make a monk's robe during the Tang dynasty, according to John McRae.[313] How sesame got involved we may never know. But with this information in hand, information which would have clearly been known to the generations for whom the encounter was memorialized, there is no mystery. The allusion to a monk's robe points an arrow from the Buddha to the monk. From the Self to the Self. From Mind to Mind. We can also now imagine a wry smile from Dongshan when he quipped, "Three pounds of hemp." The intended meanings of many gong-ans can easily be lost to contemporary cultures, and any lightheartedness that may have originally been present can be lost through generations of translations, annotations, and commentaries.* For us, a monk's robe can be ordered online from Amazon, flax is something we take for constipation, hemp is something we use to make rope, and sesame seeds are tasty garnishes on salads.

The hua-tou

> Search back into your own vision—think back to the mind that thinks. Who is it?
>
> – Foyan

The hua-tou (huà-tóu 話頭) was the next step in the evolution of this practice, courtesy of the Linji master, Dahui Zonggao, who advocated contemplating the critical phrase of a gong-an (Chapter 4). It is used

---

* This is not to suggest, however, that new interpretations of ancient gong-ans that relate them to contemporary subjects can not be of value; just that those interpretations may be unrelated to the original intended message.

extensively throughout China today. Chan master Hsu Yun wrote, "The four Chinese characters *zhao gu hua-tou* are prominently exhibited in all Chan halls. '*Zhao*' is to turn inward the light, and *gu* is to care for. These two characters together mean '*to turn inward the light on the Self-nature.*'"[314] In Japan, the hua-tou is not used, to my knowledge, however, gong-an (koan) study is still a common practice among some sects. Like the gong-an, the hua-tou engages us to look directly into Mind, or in Hsu Yun's description, Self-nature. Literally translated as "word head," or "critical phrase," it originally referred to the main idea of a literary passage. Once adapted by Chan, it came to signify the origin of a thought, word, or phrase that arises in the mind, or in Hsu Yun's more poetic words, to "the mind before it is stirred."*[315] Some examples of hua-tous suggest a common theme:

> Who is dragging this corpse about?
> What is this?
> All things are returnable to One, to what is the One returnable?
> What was my original face before I was born?†

Hua-tou practice engages us to look deeply into the nature of being by contemplating an open-ended question which points back upon itself. After locking it in our minds, we return to it again and again until it reveals its secrets. The objective is not to answer it intellectually, but to play with it, letting it taunt, tease, and torment. Eventually, we enter a recursive loop in which the observer and observed, the question and the mind that ponders it, merge into one, an experience that will be examined in Chapter 18.

---

* Fa Hsing Shakya has observed that a similar method to the Chinese hua-tou was promulgated by 3rd century Christian ascetics and recorded in *Sayings of the Desert Fathers* as the key phrase "give me a word." Christine Valters Paintner explains that "[t]his tradition of asking for a word was a way of seeking something on which to ponder for many days, weeks, months, sometimes even a whole lifetime. The word was often a short phrase to nourish and challenge the receiver. The word was meant to be wrestled with and slowly grown into" (2012, 3). A similar approach was apparently used in the ancient Indus Valley civilization: the *Aitareya Aranyaka* offered the question to ponder, "Who is the Atman (self) whom we worship (*upâsmahe*)?" (as quoted by Crangle 1994, p. 61)

† This may have originated from case 23 of the *Wúménguān* (Jap., *Mumonkan*), a popular collection of gong-ans.

Exercise 14: Hua-tou Practice

Select a hua-tou, then stick with it and don't switch to another. If you are concerned that you may have chosen the wrong one, that's the ego trying to interfere. Don't let it manipulate you. Once you get going with the practice, you'll see that they all share the same purpose and you can use any of them and even come up with your own, as they will all point you in the same direction. But when starting out, it's essential to work with only one.

"Lock in" your hua-tou. During your regular sitting schedule, use this hua-tou for the entire period. Focus your entire being on it. Don't give in and give yourself some artificial answer to the question, like: *I am just sitting here trying to figure out this hua-tou.* Open the mind and engage great doubt.[*] Perform this "lock in" session daily for three weeks. After that time, the hua-tou will be firmly implanted in your mind.

Let the hua-tou consume you day and night but push it back when you have to do other things that take concentration. Just because it's not the central focus of attention doesn't mean it won't be working for you.[†] Work with the hua-tou whenever you are doing something that doesn't require lots of attention, like washing dishes, walking down the street, or getting dressed. Apply it to whatever you are doing. Who is washing this cup? Who is crossing this street? Who is putting on this sock?

Be merciless! If you feel the hua-tou practice is not working for you, ask yourself, *Who is it who thinks the hua-tou practice is not working?* The (ego-) mind can be our worst enemy and can sabo-

---

[*] Doubt, in this context, does not suggest questioning the truthfulness or validity of something, but maintaining a mind that is wide open, receptive, questioning, and non-judgmental.

[†] I liken this to the common experience of losing a key and searching for it without success. In frustration, we finally give up and do something else, then suddenly have a "eureka moment" and know where it is. Because of the strong desire to find the key, the question of where it might be had lingered in the back of our minds even though it wasn't part of our conscious attention. Finally, the answer is revealed. The hua-tou works this way too.

tage even the best of intentions. When it interferes, turn the hua-tou back onto itself.

If you find yourself forgetting to attend to the hua-tou, noncritically bring the mind back to it. The amount of effort will lessen as you continue the practice. In short time, the practice will happen automatically.

Observe the results of practice. Take the practice seriously, but lightly. It should not be a chore or a burden, but something to enjoy doing for the reward of uncovering hidden mysteries.

Avoid preconceptions. Everyone who has done this practice has his or her own experiences to tell. Don't develop expectations of what will happen for you based on accounts from others.

Clearly, strong concentration skills are needed for hua-tou practice, which is why the practice is not often given to beginners. Without the ability to concentrate deeply on the hua-tou, progress will be difficult: we may get discouraged and give up or spend our wheels endlessly without moving forward.

The hua-tou offers a simpler practice than the gong-an, but one no less challenging. Instead of dialogues and commentaries and verses, we have a single question to ponder: "Before I was born, what was my original face?" or "Who is reciting the mantras?" or "Who is dragging this corpse around?" or even, simply, "Who?" With the hua-tou, there is no place for discussion or intellectualization, just a simple unanswered question to contemplate that directs attention toward the Self. Success with hua-tou practice requires fierce, unrelenting, and unmitigated effort. Chan master Hsu Yun compared a mind focused on a hua-tou to a mouse determined to chew its way out of a coffin; its success is a matter of life and death: it doesn't give up until it has chewed through to freedom.[316]

In a talk at a Chan training retreat, Hsu Yun commented further:

All hua-tous have only one meaning which is very ordinary and has nothing peculiar about it. If you look into 'Who is walking on the road?' or 'Who is sleeping?' The reply to 'Who?' will invariably be the same: 'It is Mind.' Word arises from Mind and Mind is head of Thought. Myriad things come from Mind and Mind is head of myriad things. In reality, a hua-tou is the head of a thought. The head of thought is nothing but Mind. To make it plain, before a thought arises, it is a hua-tou. From the above, we know that to look into the hua-tou is to look into the Mind. The fundamental face before one's birth is Mind. Self-nature is Mind. To 'turn inwards the hearing to hear the Self-nature' is to 'turn inward one's contemplation to contemplate the self-mind.'

Usually, beginners give rise to a doubt which is very coarse: they are apt to stop abruptly, then continue again. Practice may seem suddenly familiar, then suddenly unfamiliar. This is not doubt, it is thinking. When the wandering mind has gradually been brought under control, one will be able to apply the brake on the thinking process, and only then can this be called 'looking into'. Little by little, as one gains experience from training, there will be no need to give rise to doubt; it will rise of itself, automatically. In reality, at the beginning, there is no effective training at all; there is only the effort to end false thinking. When real doubt rises of itself, this can be called true training. This is the moment when one reaches a *strategic gateway*.[318]

Han Shan offered the following advice when obstacles are encountered while working with the hua-tou:

Sometimes desire and lust well up; sometimes restlessness comes in. Numerous hindrances can arise inside of you, making you feel mentally and physically exhausted. You will not know what to do. Hindrances will all come out. At that critical point, you must be able to discern and see through them then pass beyond them. Never be controlled and manipulated by them and, most of all, never take them to be real. At that point, you must refresh your spirit and arouse your courage and diligence, then bring forth this existential concern with your investigation of the hua-tou. Fix your attention at the point from which thoughts arise, and continuously push forward, on and on, and ask, "Originally there is nothing inside of me, so where does the obstacle come from? What is it?" You must be determined to find out the bottom of this matter. Pressing on just like this, killing every delusion in sight without leaving a single trace, until even the demons and spirits burst out in tears. If you can practice like this, naturally good news will come to you.[319]

It's important to work with hua-tous independently: we don't want to compare notes with others—the practice belongs to us, and us alone. I have been asked how one can know if they've succeeded in penetrating a hua-tou (or gong-an) without the validation of a master. When we approach the practice with honesty, devotion, and intensity, it will be obvious whether it's still opaque or whether it's opened itself to illuminate us. Once we "get it," the need for validation will seem as silly as needing someone to confirm that the sun shines. If we question our success—as we will if we feel the need for validation—we return to the practice and keep working with it. As always, the goal isn't the destination, it's the journey.

NEGATION PRACTICE

> The prerequisite of [Chan] training is the eradication of false thinking. As to how to wipe it out, we have already many sayings of Shakyamuni Buddha and nothing is simpler than the word 'Halt' in His saying: 'If it halts, it is enlightenment (bodhi).'
>
> – Hsu Yun, from the *Hsu Yun Ho Shang Fa Hui*

Tathātā (*zhēn rú* 真如), often translated as "suchness" or "thusness," describes seeing things exactly as they are and, as such, existing in a state of perfection.* Absent this view, we experience reality dualistically. We name things, compare and contrast them, make judgements and form opinions. This subject/object relationship separates the observer (us)

---

* Recall that the Buddha referred to himself as the Tathāgata, which literally means "one who has arrived at suchness;" that is, a person who has come to see things clearly as they are.

from the observed (everything experienced as "not us"), diminishing our ability to recognize the perfection and wholeness of reality, which, without our mental intervention, becomes clearly visible. Gong-an and hua-tou practices are both designed to help break out of this dualistic way of viewing reality. Negation practice is another, and appears in the first gong-an of the *Gateless Barrier*:*

> A monk asked Zhao zhou, "Does a dog have Buddha-nature or not?"
>
> Zhao zhou replied, "*wú!*"†

Wú 無 is most often used along with another word to negate it, as in 爲無爲 (wei wú-wei, action without action), and 無爲 (wú-wei, non-action‡). In common usage, it may appear with most any noun, such as 無情 (without heart, heartless), 無理 (without reason, unreasonable), and 無邊 (without limit, limitless). But what does it signify when used alone, as a statement or exclamation? It calls to mind the ancient Vedic negation practice, *Neti! Neti!*—"Not thus! Not thus!"—as described in Chapter 1. By negating our normal perceptual relationships with things, the mind has the opportunity to see deeper into their nature, a nature that is, in essence, empty, without distinction, without separation, whole, and unified (*śūnyatā*). Zhao zhou was not saying that a dog does not have Buddha nature, he was negating the entire question, leaving it empty of intrinsic meaning. He was seeking to open the monk's eyes to a new way of seeing.

Whenever we interact with something, from a tree to a toad, attachment arises between us and that thing and perceptual biases arise. The practice of negation permits experience without such attachments;

---

* In Chinese, this is called the *Wúménguān* 無門關. It is the first collection of gong-ans assembled together during the 13th Century by Wumen Huikai 無門慧開. In Japanese, it is known as the *Mumonkan*, and its author as Mumon Ekai.

† Wumen Huikai would tell his disciples "…concentrate yourself into this 'Wú'… making your whole body one great inquiry. Day and night work intently at it. Do not attempt nihilistic or dualistic interpretations" (Shibayama 1974).

‡ Wú-wei is an ancient concept in China that dates to the era of Confucius (Kong Zi). It "…represents a perfect harmony between one's inner dispositions and external movements, and thus is perceived by the subject to be 'effortless' and free of strain" (Slingerland 2009, 112).

that is, by denying what we *think* is real, we get closer to what actually *is* real. For example, if we invoke this mechanism when we see a tree, it will lose its properties of "treeness"; that is, its individuality, created by a mental definition, will be absent. We will still see the tree as a tree, but we will bypass the "identification-as-object" circuitry of the brain—which is mediated by ego—and this gets us closer to seeing it as it is.

Following the *Heart Sutra*, the *Platform Sūtra* continued to establish negation as a central aspect of chan training:

> Good friends, in this teaching of mine, from ancient times up to the present, all have set up no-thought as the main doctrine, non-form as the substance, and non-abiding as the basis. Non-form is to be separated from form even when associated with form. No-thought is not to think even when involved in thought. Non-abiding is the original nature of man.[320]

Exercise 15: Negation practice

> Wherever the mind moves, observe its motion and, whatever it becomes fixated upon, observe this too and think to yourself, *Not thus!* If you look across the room and see a lamp, observe the mind's connection with it and deny that connection: *Not thus!* If you have a thought about something you did yesterday that makes you feel a certain way, recognize the mind taking you to this thought and feeling and negate it: *Not thus!* As you are walking to your car, observe the motion of your feet, your breath, and your arms moving and negate it all with: *not thus!* If you prefer Chinese: *wú!*

Eventually, this practice becomes habituated and we don't have to remind ourselves to negate the mind's targets of attention; it happens automatically.

Countercontemplation

Shenxiu (Chapter 4) advocated *countercontemplation,* which he described as follows:

> When you can maintain the mind [on this subject] for some time, then you must "countercontemplate" (chieh-kuan, i.e., turn around and contemplate) this false mind [itself]. Whether it is existent or nonexistent, [whether it is generated or] extinguished, [the discriminatory mind] is ultimately not apprehendable, [no matter how one may attempt] various methods of searching for it. The mind of the present is not maintained [beyond the immediate moment]. Also, because [every] two [states of] mind are dissimilar, when one realizes the generation of [one state of] mind, one does not realize the extinction [of another state of] mind.[321]

Explaining what he means by "countercontemplation," Shenxiu wrote:

> ...countercontemplation is only to be constantly mindful of the contemplating mind's countercontemplation of itself—there is no subject and object. [Just as] a knife cannot cut itself and a finger cannot point at itself, the mind cannot contemplate itself [dualistically]. When there is no contemplation (i.e., when you are just trying to imagine what this practice might be like), subject and object of contemplation exist, but in actual countercontemplation there are no subjects and objects of contemplation. This [practice] transcends words and characteristics, the path of words being eradicated, and the locus of mental activity extinguished.[322]

Archetypal imagery

The psyche always seems to need a grounding point, a reference from which to establish itself. Before we acquire knowledge of the spiritual realm, that reference is the ego. Being grounded to the ego allows us to connect and identify with the physical world, but as we pursue the spiritual realm, ego-identification becomes replaced with something else. In Mahāyāna Buddhism, that grounding reference point shifts, ideally, to a "celestial savior" (Chapters 1 and 16)—a representation of an archetypal form such as the celestial Buddha—Amitābha, Amida, or Amitāyus—or one of the aspects of the celestial Buddha—Guan Yin/Avalokiteśvara, Mañjuśrī, or Maitreya (Chapter 9).*

Archetypal imagery helps shift us away from our ego-oriented perspective and toward the Self, in one or more of its essential aspects. The *Amitāyurdhyāna Sūtra*, for example, describes this method applied to the archetype of the perfect (i.e., celestial) enlightened being, *Amitāyus/Amitābha*.†

EXERCISE 16: CONTEMPLATING ARCHETYPAL IMAGERY

Take the proper sitting position and focus the mind on the mental image of the celestial Buddha. Contemplate the ideal form of a perfect being.

Alternatively, contemplate Avalokiteśvara, the celestial embodiment of compassion. Statuary or other visuals can assist in developing the apropriate mental imagry.

Archetypal contemplation is also an excellent way to work with images that arise in dreams and visions during sleep or meditation. For example, if we receive a visual image of riding on a powerful horse, we can uncover its meaning through this form of contemplation.‡ The

---

* I say "ideally" because it's not uncommon for people to instead shift that reference point to a senior monk or other perceived spiritual authority. In Japan, that reference point became the Emperor (Chapter 7). When this happens, it can lead to a wide assortment of problems (Part Four).

† As celestial beings, *Amitābha* represents the Buddha of infinite light and *Amitāyus* the Buddha of infinite life. A composite term derived from them, *Amida*, which translates literally as "without measure," added the concepts of infinite time and infinite space.

‡ It's often not helpful to try to interpret dreams or visions rationally or analytically. For the mystic, their value lies in their feeling—*numinosity*—and that feeling, along with its accompanying image, becomes a seed for contemplation, whereby its meaning is revealed. We can work to process visual imagery in various ways. James Hillman writes: "Although an archetypal image presents itself as impacted with meaning, this is not given simply as revela-

reader is encouraged to consult the *Amitāyurdhyāna Sūtra* and the *Sukhāvatīvyūhaḥ* for examples of many more archetypal meditations.

Because the mind is the source of archetypal imagery, we can consider mind contemplation quintessential to all archetypal meditations. Daoxin described formless archetypes as nothing other than mind:

> The very mind that is reflecting on buddha is called "reflecting without an object." Apart from mind there is no buddha. Apart from buddha there is no mind. Reflecting on buddha is identical to reflecting on mind. To seek the mind is to seek the buddha. Why is this so? Consciousness is without form. Buddha too is without form and without manifest attributes. To understand this principle is to pacify the mind.[323]

Any seed we might choose for meditation, from a spoon to the celestial Buddha, is still inherently separate and distinct until we penetrate its nature. Once we experience the seed and eye that sees it to be one and the same, we will have been led directly into meditation.

---

tion. It must be made through 'image work' and 'dream work.' The modes of this work may be concrete and physical as in art, movement, play, and occupational therapies, but more importantly (because less fixedly symbolic), this work is done by 'sticking to the image' as a psychological penetration of what is actually presented including the stance of consciousness that is attempting the hermeneutic" (Hillman 2013, 23-4).

13

Stage Four: Meditation

EXPERIENCES ENCOUNTERED DURING MEDITATION (samādhi) include *divine union* (integration of male-female aspects of the psyche), a variety of archetypal encounters (discussed later in Part Three), and the *"Void."* Once the mind achieves meditation, progressive changes occur in our perception of the world when we're not in meditation. Notably, dualities become deconstructed: right and wrong, good and bad, light and dark are all seen as two aspects of the same thing, each dependent upon the other for existence, each devoid of independent, intrinsic, nature. Likewise, an object no longer appears as it does through its named construction. Viewing things this way removes the need for naming—mental framing—which relies on outer appearances, comparisons, and conceptual biases: we continue to reference things by name, but both those names and their references are understood as empty of intrinsic form. If this makes no sense, it's because seeing this way requires a different mode of perception than we are accustomed, one which can be achieved with meditation.

As I mentioned in the introduction to this book, the term *meditation* is now commonly used to represent many forms of mental activity, ranging from mindfulness practices (Chapter 10), to contemplation practices (Chapter 12), as well as to actual meditation, which I will attempt to describe here. When terms originally meant to describe something specific devolve into describing something much broader and more ambiguous, confusion can arise. This is especially true of the term *meditation*, considering that the qualitative experiences of these various mental states—dhāraṇā, dhyāna, and samādhi—are significantly different.* Referring to them all as meditation is like using the term *car* to refer to all forms of vehicles; people will know we're speaking about something that transports, but not whether we're talking about a tricycle, a truck, an airplane, or a wagon. I thus reserve the term *meditation* here to refer specifically to *samādhi*, that mental state wherein the ego is completely subsumed by consciousness: a state of *ecstatic absorption*.[324]

In samādhi, there is no longer a personal will to give direction and no longer methods of cultivation to be applied. The first stage of samādhi, *samprajnata samādhi* (also called *savikalpa samādhi* and *sabija samādhi*) happens when we're engaged in deep contemplation on a seed and the mind becomes so absorbed in that seed that all else vanishes from awareness. The seed, which previously had an independent existence, has now merged with the observer: any sense that the object is separate from the observer has vanished, along with the sense that the observer is in any way apart from the object. In meditation, we enter a timeless, spaceless realm and are in effortless union with the object of contemplation.

During the second stage of samādhi, the object of meditation also vanishes. This is called *asamprajnata samādhi* (also *nirvikalpa samādhi* and *nirbija samādhi*) and corresponds to the Buddha's eighth step on his Eightfold Path: *Samyak-samādhi*, perfection of meditation. There is now no longer an action to engage in, no longer an object of concentration or seed as there is in dhāraṇā and dhyāna because the self—the ego-self—is fully transcended: it has gone completely off the grid. The

---

* The *Yoga Sūtras of Patanjali* use the Sanskrit term *samyama* to collectively describe all three.

meditator, along with that which is meditated upon, merges consciously into an infinite wholeness; a brain state that may correlate with delta-rhythms, the slowest brain-wave state we can enter, normally associated with the deepest sleep (Chapter 17).

The *Yoga Sūtras of Patanjali* describe a variety of qualities of samādhi, but I believe it's best at this stage to leave their discovery to the explorer. When we try to explain or describe a spiritual experience, we invariably fall short. Even to say that we "merge into an infinite wholeness" is ambiguous, if not meaningless, to one who has not experienced it. Such descriptions easily lead to misunderstanding and may prompt practitioners to want to seek the description of the experience rather than the experience itself. In addition, few languages have adequately robust vocabularies to describe the inner-world of Self. Translating spiritual terms into a different language that doesn't have direct correlates can easily lead to oversimplifications, misinterpretations, and misrepresentations.

With that said, we can still talk about the effects of meditation on our lives when we return to the sensory realm where language provides agency.

Over the last several decades, studies of the brains of meditators using fMRIs, EEGs, positron emission tomography (PET), and single-photon emission computed tomography (SPECT) scans have revealed permanent enhanced brain function in frequent meditators compared to nonmeditating control groups. This research has connected meditation with genuine cognitive shifts in awareness and demonstrates that qualitative effects are accompanied by distinct quantitative physiological changes.

In the *Scientific American* article "Mind of the Meditator," Matthieu Ricard and others summarize research on various neurological changes that happen in the brain of a meditator, including physical changes.[325] Of note was: 1) frequent meditation decreases the size of the amygdala, that part of the brain responsible for our sense of fear; 2) meditators have an increased number of axons, the fibers that connect different parts of the brain; and 3) meditation can reduce the activity of inflammation-related genes, and can influence genes to turn off or on. In addition, there is evidence that meditation increases telomerase activity, the caps at the end of DNA segments responsible for cell reproduction. When the caps get too short, the cell stops dividing, a phenomenon that has been causally implicated in the death of all living things.[326] If meditation causes these caps to grow, could it provide a natural way to extend life?* In addition, research studies by Eileen Luders and others have observed that the brains of long-time meditators tend to have a statistically-significant reduced loss of gray matter (the cell bodies, dendrites, and axon terminals) as a result of the aging process.[327]

The transition from a normal resting state, as achieved from non-directed practices, to a meditating state, as achieved with directed "on-seed" practices, has been caught on fMRI and electroencephalogram (EEG). The analysis shows a sudden change in brain states—a transition taking anywhere from five to fifteen seconds depending on the experience of the meditator—that happens in a sudden burst of high-amplitude gamma wave activity and cross-hemisphere synchronicity.[328] This suggests that the brain becomes coordinated, or *in phase*, across the hemispheres during meditation, a quantitative description of this uniquely qualitative experience that distinguishes it from brain states acquired during concentration and contemplation.†

My first encounter with meditation was startling. I had heard a lot about meditation, and in fact thought I had already mastered it. But the first time I slipped into meditation I knew my thoughts about it had been wrong. There had previously been no change to the quality

---

* I don't intend to suggest that seeking to extend one's life is commensurate with the objective of chan, but perhaps such a desire may prompt some people to give chan a try.

† A research team at Kiel University designed a circuit that utilizes a pair of coupled oscillators to mimic brain function. Using adaptive memory devices called memristors, the oscillations in the circuit synchronized, modeling the behavior of neural networks of the brain. Neurologist Thorsten Bartsch, a member of the research group, speculates that consciousness itself may be closely linked to the brain's neural synchronization (PhysOrg 2016). If this is true, might we speculate that the experience of consciousness itself may be lesser or greater for a person depending on the degree of neural synchronicity, a phenomenon that can be enhanced through meditation?

of of consciousness which this new experience provoked. The first thing I noticed was that my breath had become threadlike, slow, rhythmical, and relaxed. As I watched it, it seemed as if I had stopped breathing altogether.* My mind became exceptionally clear and focused. As I watched myself watch my mind move, the "I" that was watching vanished, leaving the mind to itself. The transition out of meditation was gradual. Afterward, as I walked about the room in solitude, everything I looked at seemed to come alive. It felt like I was seeing things for the first time, things that I had seen thousands of times before. All my senses seemed to be in a state of relaxed hyper-alertness: the incense in the room smelled heavenly, the birds sang beautifully through the windowpanes, and my mind was peculiarly absent of mental chatter. Regardless of our own individual response, our first meditation experience is unlike any other, and extremely engaging. The specific practices we engage with prior to entering meditation can have a significant effect on the nature of the experience as well. If we used Pure Land practices, for example, visualizing the ideal forms of a Buddha Land, or visualizing the archetypal Buddha directly, then in meditation those images may come alive and seem startlingly real and the emotions they render, spellbinding.

Once we slip into meditation, we know it, for there's nothing else like it. The first time it happens, we may be so startled that we come out of it quickly. Staying in meditation takes practice, time, and commitment. But the more we do it, the more quickly and easily it happens. After we've experienced it once, we know where to direct the mind to enter it again.

---

* In Taoism, this is referred to as *embryonic breathing* (*tai xi* 胎息).

PART THREE

Experiences on the Journey

A human being is part of the whole called by us universe, a part limited in time and space. We experience ourselves, our thoughts and feelings, as something separate from the rest. A kind of optical delusion of consciousness. This delusion is a kind of prison for us, restricting us to our personal desires and to affection for a few persons nearest to us. Our task must be to free ourselves from the prison by widening our circle of compassion to embrace all living creatures and the whole of nature in its beauty. The true value of a human being is determined primarily by the measure and the sense in which they have obtained liberation from the self.

– Albert Einstein

So far, I've described some of Chan's historical and institutional dimensions, and have explored various stages of chan's journey, but I've said little about the psychological, spiritual, and physical effects of chan practice. While some experiences can suggest we're on the right track, others might warn that we've taken a detour or, sometimes, fallen off a cliff. Recognizing the effects of spiritual practice is helpful in navigating the path because it helps us determine if we're doing things right or wrong. If we're doing things right, we can continue as we are; if we're doing things wrong, we can assess where we've erred and make appropriate course corrections to get back on track.

When we encounter something unfamiliar, having a framework or model to interpret and understand it can be immensely helpful. We often use such models unconsciously. Imagine walking through a forest and coming across a strange tree, one you've never seen before. Despite its unfamiliarity, you instinctively categorize it as a "tree." By doing so, you bring it within your sphere of knowledge—recognizing that it likely has roots and bark, harnesses energy through photosynthesis, and shares other characteristics of trees. This mental model provides clarity and helps you make sense of what might otherwise seem perplexing.

But what happens when we encounter something entirely outside our existing models? Imagine, for instance, stumbling upon a three-legged marsupial with green antlers, pink wings, juggling large boulders while whistling Christmas jingles. If we eliminate the possibility of a costume or an elaborate prank, we're left with a puzzle that existing models can't explain. In such cases, we must either expand an existing model or invent a new one to make sense of the unfamiliar. This process is how we continually evolve our understanding of the world.

The stages we traverse on Chan's journey are as ineffable as they are enigmatic. The language of mysticism is rooted in imagery and feelings, not in words.[*] How, then, does one convey this profound and mysterious experience called Chan to someone who has not yet stepped into its realm? How might we provide a model that serves as a guide for the traveler, a framework to navigate this hidden and elusive territory?

---

[*] Although we use words to describe the experience of chan and to guide others to it, the words are not the experience. Some argue that chan is defined by its literature, its institutionalized representation, its stories and lore, etc., but these all represent external expressions of chan and fail to communicate the inner experience. We can study Chan by examining its institutional, externalized, form, but we can only know chan—the mystical practice—through our own participation with it.

The challenge is far from trivial, because it demands the use of language to express something that, by its very nature, defies linguistic expression. It's akin to describing the color green to someone who is colorblind or explaining the flavor of a banana to someone who has never tasted one.

The sutras rarely try to accomplish such a task. Instead, they focus on trying to guide the seeker to the hidden domain of Self directly. Perhaps their authors, or even Siddhārtha himself, recognized that since a description of an experience is not the experience, the mind may easily mistake the description *for* the experience, compounding ignorance instead of reducing it.

Yet this hasn't kept people throughout the centuries from trying to develop models to help travelers understand what they are doing, where they are going, what experiences to expect, and how to get out of situations that hinder or undermine healthy spiritual growth.

Before we look at some contemporary Western models, we'll look at a description of the journey from the Chinese perspective as presented by its ox-herding series, a collection of poems and pictures that draw upon an ancient myth of an ox-herder and spinning maiden.

14

Chan's Ox-herding Series

THE CLASSIC OF POETRY (*Shijing* 詩經), compiled between the 11th and 7th centuries BCE, contains one of the oldest known mythical allegories of Self-symbolism. Elements of the myth also made their way into the Pāli (Theravāda) *Mahā-gopālaka Sutta* (the *Greater Cowherd Discourse*). In China it continues to be celebrated annually with the Qixi festival.

Central to the Chinese myth is the wild Asian water buffalo (*shuǐniú* 水牛), which has commonly been mistranslated to English as "ox" or "cow." There is relevant symbolic significance to this distinction. Asian water buffalo (*Bubalus arnee*) are huge, weighing up to 3000 lbs., while oxen (*Bos taurus*) generally weigh well under 1000 lbs.; oxen are castrated, while water buffalo are not; oxen are easy to domesticate, while water buffalo are not; water buffalo are used for carrying heavy loads, while oxen are used for much lighter labor. For convention's sake, I'll continue to use the terms ox and ox-herder, but the reader should be aware that the animal referred to is neither a cow, an ox, nor a North American buffalo; in contrast, it's a large, powerful, and unruly beast.

The Chinese myth is framed as a love story between a spinning maiden or "weaving girl" (Zhinü or Chih Nü) and an ox-herder (Niulang or Chien Niu), who are represented by the stars Vega and Altair respectively. Because they were not permitted to conjoin in union, they were banished to opposite sides of the sky (the "Silver River" or Milky Way, represented by the star Deneb);* but once a year on the seventh day of the seventh lunar month, they are united by a flock of magpies in divine union. The spinning maiden returns as a symbol of the female element (*anima*) in the *Neijing tu* (Figure 3, Chapter 4) as well as in some versions of the ox-herding poems. The ox-herder symbolizes the male principal (*animus*) in both, and in the Neijing tu, he cultivates the seeds that germinate into a *golden elixir* (Chapter 4).

Alternatively, the parallel Indian story, as presented in the *Mahā-gopālaka Sutta*, adopts the myth to juxtapose the difference between someone who is on the correct spiritual path with one who isn't. It begins with an analogy of a novice monk, or beginning spiritual traveler (ox-herder), who is unable to progress on the journey (to tend the herd) because he is unskilled, ignorant, unknowing of the spiritual path, lacking of respect for those who have more experience and wisdom, at the mercy of emotions, lacking restraint, falling victim to greed, failing to ask the right questions to resolve doubts, ignorant of the Dharma and the joy it brings, and incapable of tending to the Self (the ox) because it remains unknown.

The second part of the *Mahā-gopālaka Sutta* presents a spiritual traveler (ox-herder) who is able to progress on the path because he has skill, knows the path, respects those who have gone before, can tend the herd so that it prospers, sees things clearly for what they are, dispels thoughts of harmfulness if they arise, practices restraint when greed and desire arise, questions the meaning of doctrine to reach a better understanding, comprehends the Dharma and the Eightfold Path, and gains insight by viewing things from various perspectives.

---

* Altair, Vega and Deneb form the Summer Triangle astronomical asterism.

We may never know the source of inspiration for the Chinese ox-herding series, but, as we can see, its mystical symbolism had been widely known when it became adopted by Chan monks to depict stages of the spiritual journey. Unlike the *Mahā-gopālaka Sutta*, however, which uses the motifs to differentiate those who "get it" from those who don't, Chan's ox-herding series use them to describe qualitative aspects of the spiritual journey rather than the journeymen themselves.

After Chan's ox-herding series first emerged—the earliest known to date is thought to have been produced by Ching Chu 清居 (Jap., Seikyo) during the 10th century[329]—it thereafter became a popular format for future monks to use to offer their own interpretations. Today, we have a variety of ox-herding series to study and compare: among the most popular are those by the monks Ching-chu, Tzu-te Hui, and Kuòān Shīyuǎn (Jap., Kaku-an). Another by Hsu Yun is recently becoming widely known. Some ox-herding series are collaborations between poet and artist, while others are thought to have been produced by the same person. Others, such as Hsu Yun's, may not have been produced with accompanying pictures. Ching-chu, who was possibly the first to introduce the stylistic form, presented five pictures with accompanying poems (now lost), while later versions have included various numbers of pictures and stanzas, most often ten. From Hsu Yun we have eleven stanzas. The ox symbolism varies, too, by author: sometimes it represents the Buddha-Self, sometimes the unruly ego, and sometimes both.

Ching-chu's pictures describe the journey of Self-discovery with imagery of a wild Asian water buffalo that turns gradually from black to white and eventually disappears. At first, when the chaotic and difficult-to-control ego-self dominates consciousness, the unruly and powerful ox appears black. As we progress and begin to see glimpses of the Self, the ox transitions from black to white. Eventually, the ego is transcended entirely and is seen as the illusion it is, depicted by an ox which is entirely white. The ox (ego-self), in all its mental manifestations, finally vanishes into the Void and the ox-herder (as his Self), ascends to nirvāṇa. Figure 9 shows picture eight of the ten-picture series produced in China by an unknown artist.*330

FIGURE 9. PICTURE 8 OF CHAN'S OX-HERDING SERIES.
The ox-herder has ascended into nirvana's heavenly bliss, completely freed from ego-self (the ox when it was black) and worldly affairs. Hovering above the ox, he observes it clearly for what it is, and they exist together in harmony. Note the star pattern low on the horizon which, based on the geometry and proximity to the horizon, may be the summer triangle, composed of the stars Deneb, Altair and Vega; a reference to *divine union* from the Fuxi and Nüwa myth (Chapter 17). Vega is also symbolic of spiritual awakening (Chapter 1). The top-right star may be Rasalhague 候 (Alpha Ophiuchi).

---

* This series of pictures is commonly attributed to Pu-ming. According to Suzuki, however, Pu-ming composed the accompanying verses for them, but was not the artist, who is unknown. (1994, 129)

The complete eleven-stanza ox-herding series, written by Hsu Yun in the early 20th century, is presented below and followed by a brief commentary.[*]

1. Pushing Aside the Grass to Look for the Ox

Wanting to break through to Emptiness with my white cudgel[†]
I cried out louder than the bellowing Ox, mooing through my senses.
I followed mountain and stream searching for the Ox, seeking it everywhere.
But I couldn't tell in which direction it had gone... west?... or east?

2. Suddenly Seeing Tracks

On I searched... into the mountains and along the river banks.
But in every direction I went, I went in vain.
Who would have suspected that it was right where I stood;
That I needed only nod my head and my true Self would appear before me.

3. Seeing the Ox

Its wild nature is now calmed in lazy sleep.
By the stream, under the trees, crushing the blades of dew laden grass
The Ox sleeps without a care.
At last I have found it... there with its great head and horns.

4. Piercing the Ox's Nose

I rush forward and pierce the Ox's nose!
It wildly jerks and jumps
But I feed it when it is hungry and give it water when it thirsts.
Then I allow the Oxherding Boy to take care of it.

---

[*] Hsu Yun produced these poems as part of *Eleven Stanzas on the Song in Praise of Tending an Ox, as Requested by the Students of Gushan Buddhist Institute.* This rendering is the result of a translation collaboration sponsored by the Zen Buddhist Order of Hsu Yun in 1997, an organization established by Jy Din Shakya, one of Hsu Yun's Dharma heirs, in the same year.

[†] "White cudgel" has meaningful contextual symbolism here. White is the color of purity, clarity, and perfection, and a cudgel—a stick or club used for protection—is symbolic of the Dharma and spiritual protection. Together, they suggest an *object of transformation*. The shakuhachi, popular in Japan today and introduced to Japan from China during the first millennium, was one such version of a cudgel, being fashioned from the root-end of a bamboo stalk in such a way that it could be both a formidable weapon and a musical instrument. In Japan, playing the shakuhachi became a popular form of meditation among the monks of the now defunct *Fuke-shū* Zen sect.

5. Training the Ox

I have supported you with great care for many years
And you plow - not mud and water, but clouds!
From dawn until dusk, the natural grass sustains you
And you keep your master company by sleeping out of doors.

6. Returning Home Riding the Ox

What place in these cloudy mountains is not my home?
There's greenery everywhere - so lush it's hard to tell
Crops from wild grasses. I don't intrude on planted fields.
I ride the Ox and let him graze along the roadside.

7. Keeping the Person Because of the Ox

I went from the city to the edge of the sea
I returned riding backwards on a white ox cart.
Into this painted hall comes a spinning red wheel.
The New Bride finally arrives, and from my own house!

8. The Bride and the Ox are Forgotten

I remember the old days as I brush out dead ashes from the cold stove.
Silently, without a trace, I pace back and forth for no reason.
But today the ice is broken by a plum blossom!
A tiger roars, a dragon growls, and all the creatures of the universe
  surround me.

9. Returning to the Origin and the Essence

Every thing and every creature under the sun has its own nature.
Hasn't this knowledge been passed down through generations?
When the Ox suddenly roars like a lion
Everything in the universe reveals such infinite variety.

10. Coming Home with Folded Hands

How wide are the horizons of the spinning earth!
The moonlight leads the tides and the sun's light will not be confined
  within the net of heaven.
But in the end all things return to the One.
The deaf and dumb, the crippled and deformed are all restored to the
  One's Perfection.

11. The Concluding Song

In the beginning there was nothing, nor was anything lacking.
The paper was blank. We pick up the paint brush and create the
    scene...
The landscape, the wind whipping water into waves.
Everything depends upon the stroke of our brush.
Our Ox lets the good earth lead it,
Just as our brush allows our hand to move it.
Take any direction, roam the world to its farthest edge.
All comes back to where it started... to blessed Emptiness.[331]

Poetry translations are invariably dependent on the translator's degree of understanding of the emotional tone intended and the subject used to convey it. The challenge of translating poetry to English is further compounded when working with the Chinese sinitic language, which can represent multiple complex ideas with a single character, and which relies strongly on context to determine a character's meaning. All these factors make reliable English translations of Chinese mystical poetry notoriously hard to render, if not impossible. Nonetheless, we can attempt some interpretations of Hsu Yun's verses as they relate to chan's spiritual journey and the stages through which a traveler passes. From Hsu Yun's perspective, those stages unfold sequentially with: [1] recognizing pain and suffering (duhkha) and desiring to get out of it, but being unable to see the way; [2] seeing the first glimpse of *Self* (*jiànxìng* 見性; Jap., *kensho*); [3] recognizing Self in its entirety, i.e., experiencing full spiritual awakening or "enlightenment"; [4] recognizing that the ego-self is still around and that the Self must continue to be cared for and cultivated; [5] engaging in years of cultivation, nurturing the Self until it, alone, remains; [6] allowing the will to acquiesce to the Self while not permitting the ego-self to intrude on others' "planted fields," that is, other people's spiritual lives; [7] experiencing spiritual androgyny; [8] seeing all the universe as an aspect of enlightened nature, in perfect suchness (tathātā): the Self, now fully integrated in male/female unity, is abandoned as the Dharmakāya (*Truth body or reality body*) becomes fully realized; [9] recognizing that dharmas (all independent "things" in their infinite variety—the *Nirmāṇakāya*) manifest to create the world; [10] experiencing the dissolution of dualities, which leads to witnessing the *Saṃbhogakāya* ("*bliss body*"); and ends with: [11] reflecting on life's journey from the beginning, when there was nothing, to the end, when the nature of that nothingness is again realized in "blessed Emptiness," chan's empty circle.

From Hsu Yun's perspective, we begin chan's journey when our Self (ox) is unknown/unfound, but we long to know it. The ox arises from emptiness into the Trikāya,* and finally returns to a state of emptiness in which even *it* disappears: at this stage, Self manifests to awareness, but does not appear as distinct from all else, so cannot be separately identified. Note that, in his depiction of the journey, discovery of Self: 1) happens early, 2) is far from the end of the journey, 3) is not causally dependent on method but 4) is causally dependent on the quest for seeking it, 5) is followed by years of cultivation, and 6) is instantaneous—we have only to "nod our head."†

Although the ox-herding theme succinctly describes experiences of the journey from beginning to end, many of us never make it to the second, or even the first, stage depicted by these poems and pictures. For me, it took nearly a decade after first learning about chan in my late teens before I was ready to "push aside the grass to look for the ox." To prepare us for chan, other models can help.

---

* The *trikāya* is a Mahāyāna concept that expresses a three-fold aspect of the celestial Buddha: *Dharmakāya* is the body of essence, fundamental truth, and natural law; *Saṃbhogakāya* is the body of bliss and ecstasy; and *Nirmāṇakāya* is the body of transformation and creation. Each of these relate to experiences encountered in and from meditation. For an in-depth examination of the trikaya and Dharmakāya, see *Early Buddhist Dhammakāya: Its Philosophical and Soteriological Significance* by Chanida Jantrasrisalai, 2008.

† The popular Japanese interpretation of Zen (Chapter 7) is often presented as nearly the opposite: the quest for enlightenment is the objective of practice, not the discovery of Self (the former is a mental projection, a quest for something externally projected—like a pot of gold at the end of a rainbow—and the latter is a search for something within); enlightenment is the end of the journey, not an early experience on a much longer one; enlightenment is attained by particular methods such as "just sitting" (*zazen*) and is not the result of a search or quest motivated by the desire to be freed of duhkha; and the journey begins with seated meditation practice, not the realization of suffering and the desire to be freed from it.

15

The Value of a Model

Remember that all models are wrong; the practical question is how wrong do they have to be to not be useful.

– George E.P. Box

Monks practicing Chan in Chinese monasteries are immersed in a rich tapestry of archetypal motifs*—manifested in statuary, frescoes, paintings, sutras, and gāthās—that guide the practitioner deep into the inner sanctums of the psyche. For lone lay practitioners, who often lack access to such immersive symbolic expressions, finding alternative ways to engage with the realm of the psyche revealed through spiritual practice becomes essential. In this case, a meaningful model can serve as a helpful guide. If we are able to derive insight from it, a model can deepen our understanding and direct our progress. However, if a particular model doesn't resonate with us, there's no need to force it; instead, we can explore others. When

---

* Carl Jung referred to these as *motifs* because of their repetitive tendencies: "There are types of situations and types of figures that repeat themselves frequently and have a corresponding meaning. I therefore employ the term 'motif' to designate these repetitions" (Jung 1941, par 309).

we find one that speaks to us, we can adopt it, learn from it, and, once we've drawn all the wisdom it offers, let it go and continue on our path.

Some psychological models offer especially useful tools for the Western mind. Although psychology, in general, deals with ego-consciousness—most branches of psychology either ignore or deny the presence of underlying unconscious elements that affect and shape our actions and emotions*—*analytical psychology*, developed by Carl Gustav Jung, offers an especially compelling and useful model for interpreting and understanding the experiences we have when we focus our attention inward. Analytical psychology examines human behavior in relation to psychological archetypes, which sometimes reveal themselves through visual imagery. It's the only model I know of that attempts to map out the terrain of the unconscious with a comprehensive, methodical approach (though others have built off his work). Unlike most other descriptive models of the psyche, analytical psychology fully acknowledges the effects of evolutionary forces which have shaped our behaviors and simultaneously blinded us to them. In *Archetype Revisited: An Updated Natural History of the Self*, Anthony Stevens emphasizes this often overlooked but important point:

> The human being is [...] a psychological system with a built-in 'biological clock': its structure and life-cycle is predetermined by the evolutionary history of its genes. As the biological clock ticks away and the life-cycle unfolds, so the system accepts and incorporates into itself the life-experience of the individual. But what you and I experience as the whole process is only the end result. We are [conscious] only of the ontogenetic (personal developmental) aspects of our own maturation, being largely unconscious of the phylogenetic blueprint on whose basis it proceeds.[332]

---

* In broad strokes, Western psychology addresses how the mind interprets, responds to, and assimilates or suppresses experiences, and how those experiences, in turn, affect our behavior and relationships with ourselves and the world around us. That is, it addresses our *agency of externalization* rather than the inner realm experienced through internalization.

Our cumulative experience of existence, in other words, is causally, and necessarily, dependent upon all that has gone into the evolutionary process of creating us. We are largely blind to it, however, because it's distinct from our development as individuals. We can consider this unconscious realm of hidden "blueprint knowledge" the source from which insights reveal themselves as we delve within, and from which we can come to know our Selves in greater completeness, in both our localized and evolutionary forms.

Until we have come to recognize this unconscious domain as a real aspect of being, however, any model for interpreting it might seem useless or even absurd. Indeed, it may be because some people don't believe the unconscious is real that they question the relevance of Jung's theories or even express revulsion to them.* I have heard some people argue that because Chan has survived for centuries without his theories, they are irrelevant. Others have different reasons for dismissing them. Anti-Jung sentiment seems so common that I feel addressing it is important before we can move on to examine its relevance to the chan experience. Following are my responses to some of the critical arguments I have heard against Carl Jung and his theories as they relate to chan:†

[1] *Chan has existed successfully for hundreds of years, so why bother with Jung?* Chan has not survived so well for those hundreds of years. Buddhism has suffered numerous persecutions by governments throughout the centuries, and in Western countries chan is virtually unknown. For chan to provide a viable spiritual solution for new gen-

---

* Jung accused many of his critics of just this: because they had no knowledge of the unconscious, they were incapable of understanding his ideas.

† This section is based on my private communications with scholars, clinicians, and practitioners of Chinese Chan and Japanese Zen. Among them are Alan Cole, author of *Fathering Your Father, the Zen Fabrication of Tang Buddhism* and *Patriarchs on Paper: A Critical History of Medieval Chan Literature*, and Stuart Lachs, author of *Coming Down from the Zen Clouds: A Critique of the Current State of American Zen and Richard Baker* and *The Myth of the Zen Roshi*. Both are longtime practitioners of Zen. While the important connection between Jung's theories and Zen is now well established, there is resistance to Jung's ideas among many people I have worked with privately, as well as among scholars, psychologists and therapists I have spoken with. The range of arguments refuting Jung's work that I have heard are summarized here.

erations, it needs to speak to the modern mind in terms it can understand and relate to.

[2] *Why bother with other perspectives when Chan offers everything that's needed?* To overlook the insights of others, especially those that may offer new understandings of the human experience, is to put a bag over our heads. We can choose to remain ignorant, or we can choose to examine things from different perspectives. Chan encourages us to investigate life with an open mind, leaving no stone unturned. Regardless of what we know, if we are open to considering the tentative nature of knowledge, we can allow for the possibility that future information may lead to new insights that will further enhance our understanding.

Having a model to help navigate the inner realm is no different from having a model to help investigate the outer realm. The purposes of each are the same: to enhance understanding. When we are led entirely by religious faith—i.e., faith in the religious institution and the dogma it propounds—rather than by reason and insight or spiritual intuition, our minds can become not only inflexible, but dangerous (Part Four).

[3] *Archetypal visions such as those Jung describes are just dreams, so we can ignore them because they aren't real.* One of the greatest dangers when getting deep into a spiritual life is misinterpreting and misunderstanding visionary experiences, which we all eventually have if we stick with the practice.* Yet, many Zen teachers tell their students to simply ignore visionary encounters and move on. Although this does help avoid getting attached to them, it also encourages students to ignore experiences that may be instructional. We can get stuck, psychologically and spiritually, if we don't adequately process the messages of visionary material. Worse, we can develop psychotic symptoms, or become susceptible to suggestions from a religious authority which may not be in our best interest (Part Four). To flippantly assume dreams aren't real not only denies their existence—that is, our experience of them—but blinds us to their impact on our lives from the messages they convey.

---

* As we learn to meditate, brain-wave states slow down, and we enter the domain normally associated with sleep. Unlike sleep, however, during meditation we remain conscious as visual imagery arises.

[4] *Chan and Buddhism have nothing to do with Jung's psychological archetypes.* As we discussed in Part One, it was partially through visionary experiences that Mahāyāna Buddhism arose. Many of the Mahāyāna sutras evolved largely out of insights gained through meditation and, specifically, meditations focused on archetypal motifs (Chapters 1 and 4). Only in the last century have we developed new ways of understanding this from an ontological perspective. Why would we want to ignore or discount that?

In addition, Jung had a keen interest in Chinese and Japanese Buddhism. Ideas he developed through frequent correspondences with Richard Wilhelm and D. T. Suzuki helped Westerners understand the Asian Mind in a way few others of his generation had. His insightful commentaries on works by them, including *The Secret of the Golden Flower*, the *I Ching*, and *An Introduction to Zen Buddhism*, helped forge a harmonious link between East and West.

[5] *Jung was a Nazi sympathizer, so we should have nothing to do with him.* Some people discredit Jung because they accuse him of having had Nazi sympathies. This charge has been thoroughly debunked.*

On a side note, a great many Germans and Austrians who supported the Nazi regime contributed substantially to the arts and sciences: to discount a person's contributions to the greater welfare of humanity because of flawed beliefs they may have held, destructive actions they may have once taken, or party affiliation they were coerced into joining, is foolhardy.†

[6] *Jung changed his views throughout his lifetime, so why should we believe anything he said?* We all change our views throughout our life-

---

* Jung, in fact, offered grave public warnings against the Third Reich as it started coming into power: The "blond beast [is] stirring in its subterranean prison...threatening us with an outbreak that will have devastating consequences" (as cited in Welsh, et al., 1947). Jung's vocal opposition to the Nazi regime landed him on Hitler's "blacklist" (Ibid.). The accusations of antisemitism leveled at Jung in the 1930s are now known to have been instigated by Freud in response to his feuds with Freud (who was Jewish), and whose views he strongly opposed. According to Gallard (and others), it was Freud who emphasized the religious and cultural differences between the two of them as a means to discredit Jung (1994).

† As we will see in Chapter 20, Stanley Milgram's experiments demonstrated that we are likely all susceptible to performing violence against others if we fall under the spell of someone who commands us to carry out such acts.

time, but that doesn't make all the views irrelevant. Moreover, theories don't need to be *believed* to be useful. Even Einstein's famous theory of general relativity is considered by physicists to be only provisionally true. Another theory may come along someday that supersedes or modifies it. Regardless, while Jung's views about analytical psychology developed over his life, his later thoughts primarily expanded on earlier ideas, which he did not refute.

[7] *Jung's theories are the same as Freud's and the field of psychology has moved on from them.* It's interesting that the only people I have heard this view from are professional psychologists. This may be because Jung's theories are rarely presented in the formal educational system. It's well known that he and Freud—who is considered the father of modern psychology—collaborated for many years, but less well known, it seems, that Jung departed from Freud in substantial ways as he developed his own independent ideas and wrote expansively on them.

[8] *People who are into Jung are crazy nuts.* This sentiment follows in the same vein as those who say that Muslims are fanatical, Blacks are lazy, Americans are loud, arrogant and entitled, or any other stereotype derisively applied to a population of people. Surprisingly, I have heard this most often from Buddhist scholars and people who identify themselves proudly as long-time practicing Buddhists and self-proclaimed experts on the subject. Such an arrogant and dehumanizing attitude can arise in response to an emotionally-charged revulsion to a group of people who one sees as different from oneself and hence a threat. When we feel threatened, it's not uncommon to attack—to discredit the perceived source of the threat.

[9] *Jungians are cultists.* One religious scholar, when he learned that I planned to include a chapter on Jungian psychology in this book, exclaimed to me vehemently "the Jung movement is a cult!" The idea that Jung's model of the psyche is a social movement is no different from saying that Freudian psychoanalytic theory is a social movement, or that Erikson's stage theory is a social movement, which is absurd. These

are all just different models we might use to better understand human nature.

The idea that Jung had something to do with cults was suggested in the late twentieth century by Richard Noll, whose 1997 book, *The Jung Cult: Origins of a Charismatic Movement*, popularized the idea among a group of Jung adversaries. An op-ed Noll had written previously for the New York Times, which propounded the same idea, met with a quick response from the prominent historian Olivier Bernier, who wrote:

> Richard Noll makes an unwarranted and wholly uninformed comparison between Luc Jouret, the dead cult leader, and Carl Gustav Jung. Mr. Jouret was a self-immolated madman. Jung was a universally recognized psychoanalyst, the author of many respected books and a man who, far from leading his disciples to an early death, brought his patients back to psychological health. There was, and is, no Jung cult. [...] Like Freudian psychoanalysis, Jungian psychoanalysis is recognized worldwide.
> Other distortions by Mr. Noll are evidently due to his inability to distinguish symbol and reality. Jung never claimed to a be a god; he made a plea for a reintegration into the psychic structure of a recognition of the divine; the two are hardly the same.
> Carl Gustav Jung died in his bed at the age of 86. Today, 30-odd years later, his contribution to psychoanalysis and to the study of myth and symbol is recognized everywhere ..."[333]

Once an idea is put forth, it can take on a life of its own through the complexities of social dynamics, something Richard Dawkins investigated in his acclaimed 1976 book, *The Selfish Gene*. In it, Dawkins coined the term *meme* to "convey the idea of a unit of cultural transmission, or unit of imitation:"

> Just as genes propagate themselves in the gene pool by leaping from body to body via sperms or eggs, so memes propagate themselves in the meme pool by leaping from brain to brain via a process which, in the broad sense, can be called imitation.[334]

As ridiculous as the idea that Jung was a cult figurehead may be—he was not a charismatic individual, and was "wary of anyone who claimed to be his disciple"[335]—or that people who study analytical psychology today are followers of a "Jung cult," the simple act of putting forth such an idea, or meme, was enough for it to gain traction among a group of people who already opposed Jung's ideas and theories for any number of reasons (some of which I discussed above). The meme became an easy and quick way to dismiss and simultaneously discredit the thousands of hours of research, and voluminous writings, which consumed Jung for most of his lifetime, and which have since been valued by countless patients, scholars, researchers, and therapists around the world.

In upcoming chapters, we'll explore some of the salient aspects of analytical psychology as it pertains to chan practice and experience. I don't present Jung's model of the psyche as the sole means through which one might gain insight into the spiritual realm, just one that I've found helpful for myself. Many spiritual travelers have had success without ever learning about analytical psychology.

First, however, we'll look at a 20th-century model of the mystic experience through the eyes of Roland Fischer, an experimental psychiatrist at Ohio State University from 1958 to 1971. His model was developed by studying the effects of LSD and, despite some obvious flaws, as we'll see, it offers valuable insights into the relationship between ego-identity—"I"—and egoless "Self."

"I" vs. "Self"

On November 16, 1938, Albert Hoffman synthesized the first LSD (lysergic acid diethylamide) while looking for an analeptic—a respiratory and circulatory stimulant drug. On April 16, 1943, he touched his hand to his face and inadvertently ingested a small amount. Describing the experiences that followed, he said he was

... affected by a remarkable restlessness, combined with a slight dizziness. At home I lay down and sank into a not unpleasant intoxicated[-]like condition, characterized by an extremely stimulated imagination. In a dreamlike state, with eyes closed (I found the daylight to be unpleasantly glaring), I perceived an uninterrupted stream of fantastic pictures, extraordinary shapes with intense, kaleidoscopic play of colors. After some two hours this condition faded away.[336]

The Central Intelligence Agency (CIA) of the U.S. government soon became interested in LSD for potential uses in interrogations and torture. In the early 1950s, a covert operation named Project MKUltra was created to study the effects of LSD both in the laboratory and on the general population of the United States:

The program consisted of some 149 subprojects which the Agency contracted out to various universities, research foundations, and similar institutions. At least 80 institutions and 185 private researchers participated. Because the Agency funded MKUltra indirectly, many of the participating individuals were unaware that they were dealing with the Agency.[337]

LSD was distributed covertly by front-organizations in the U.S. and Canada to colleges and universities, hospitals, prisons, and pharmaceutical companies. There was a new drug on the street, and virtually none of the tens of thousands of people who took it knew they were participating in a conspiratorial experiment conducted by the CIA. Though the program was shut down in 1973, LSD would not be ruled illegal by the Supreme Court until 1985, three decades after it had begun to be freely distributed. Because of MKUltra, LSD became a popular counterculture drug during the late 1950s through the 1960s, and inspired the birth of the Beat Generation, popularized by such writers as Allen Ginsberg, William S. Burroughs, Jack Kerouac, Lucian Carr, Herbert Huncke, and Gary Snyder.

But the discovery of the effects of LSD also sparked research into the nature of altered states of consciousness. One prominent researcher in this area was Roland Fischer. Fischer used EEGs and biofeedback techniques to study the cognitive effects of LSD as a means to better understand schizophrenia. From his research, he derived a model which he believed accurately represented both drug- and naturally-induced states encountered during meditation and contemplation. His theories received scrutiny and attack within the field for a variety of reasons; among them, drug-induced states are markedly different, both qualitatively and quantitatively, from those naturally induced. Nonetheless, Fischer's work offered some valuable insights.

Fischer proposed that there are two distinct and independent aspects of the experience of consciousness, which are expressed either through "excited" (*ergotropic*) states or "relaxed" (*trophotropic*) states.* These distinguish the (psycho-perceptual) experience of activities that we do in our daily life, such as weeding our garden (ergotropic), from experiences such as relaxing in a bath (trophotropic). He then proposed that different people exhibit different magnitudes of ergotropic and trophotropic experience, and related this to the relative perception of ego-self ("I") and egoless Self. When the Self is fully encountered, he correlated the experience with samādhi on the trophotropic side, and mystical rapture on the ergotropic side (Figure 10):

> Thus, the mutual exclusiveness of the "normal" and the exalted
> states, both ecstasy and samādhi, allows us to postulate that man, the
> self-referential system, exists on two levels: as "Self" in the mental
> dimension of exalted states; and as "I" in the objective world, where
> he is able and willing to change the physical dimension "out there."
> In fact, the "I" and the "Self" can be postulated on purely logical
> grounds. See, for instance, Brown's reasoning that the universe is apparently "...constructed in order (and thus in such a way as to be able)

---

* "Ergotropic arousal denotes behavioral patterns preparatory to positive action and is characterized by increased activity of the sympathetic nervous system and activated psychic state. These states may be induced either naturally or, for example, through hallucinogenic drugs. Trophotropic arousal results from an integration of parasympathetic with somatomotor activities to produce behavioral patterns that conserve and restore energy, a decrease in sensitivity to external stimuli, and sedation" (R. Fischer 1971, f.n. 1, 903). The two terms were first coined by Swiss psychologist, Walter Rudolf Hess.

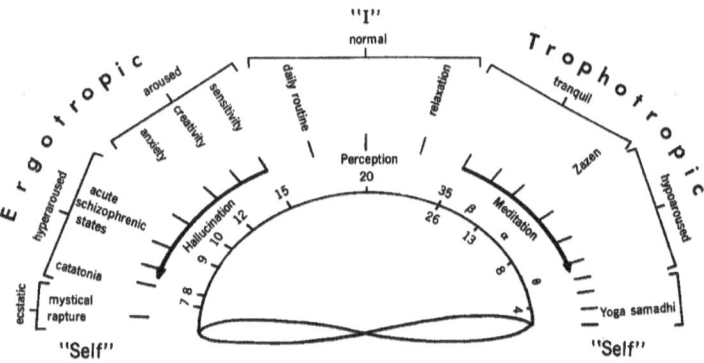

FIGURE 10. A MAPPING OF CONSCIOUS STATES.
Varieties of conscious states mapped on a perception-hallucination continuum of increasing ergotropic arousal (left) and perception-meditation continuum of increasing trophotropic arousal (right). These levels of hyper- and hypoarousal are interpreted by man as normal, creative, psychotic, and ecstatic states (left) and Zazen and samādhi (right). The loop connecting ecstasy and samādhi represents ergotropic excitation. The numbers 35 to 7 on the perception-hallucination continuum are Goldstein's coefficient of variation [see L. Goldstein, H. Murphree, A. Sugarman, C. Pfeiffer, and E. Jenney, Clin. Pharmacol. Ther. 4 (1963), 10], specifying the decrease in variability of the EEG amplitude with increasing ergotropic arousal. The numbers 26-4 on the perception-meditation continuum, on the other hand, refer to those beta, alpha, and theta EEG waves (measured in hertz) that predominate during, but are not specific to, these states. Reprinted with permission from R. Fischer, "A Cartography of Understanding Mysticism," Science, vol. 174, November 26, 1971, pp. 897-904. Copyright 1971 by the AAAS.

to see itself. But in order to do so, evidently it must first cut itself up into at least one state which sees, and at least one other state which is seen. In this severed and mutilated condition, whatever it sees is only partially itself... but, in any attempt to see itself as an object, it must, equally undoubtedly, act so as to make itself distinct from, and therefore, false to, itself. In this condition it will always partially elude itself."[338]

Throughout most of this book, I have focused more on the ergotropic nature of the mystical experience. Much of the rest of the book continues in this vein, with discussions of "awakening" experiences (such as "enlightenment") and other psychological, emotional, and cognitive experiences. The trophotropic side of the spiritual journey is just as important, but there is less to say about it because it happens naturally as our practice evolves, presenting itself through feelings of profound contentment, joy, and harmony. If we fail to maintain a balance between the two states, though, we can get in trouble, a topic I address in Chapter 21.

Expressions of the chan experience usually reflect one state or the other. Trophotropic expression is most often used to convey the *experience* of mystical insight, while ergotropic expression is more often used to help guide people to that trophotropic experience. The monk Ta Hui (1089 – 1163), for example, often expressed the trophotropic state, describing the spiritual experience:

> This affair is like the bright sun in the blue sky, shining clearly, changeless and motionless, without diminishing or increasing. It shines everywhere in the daily activities of everyone, appearing in everything. Though you try to grasp it, you cannot get it; though you try to abandon it, it always remains. It is vast and unobstructed, utterly empty. Like a gourd floating on water, it cannot be reined in or held down. Since ancient times, when good people of the Path have attained this, they've appeared and disappeared in the sea of birth and death, able to use it fully. There is no deficit or surplus: like cutting up sandalwood, each piece is it.[339]

Han Shan, on the other hand, often expressed ergotropic dimensions that lead to the trophotropic spiritual experience:

> ...if we want to melt ice we have to apply heat. The hotter the fire, the quicker the ice melts. So it is with wisdom. The more intense our scrutiny, the quicker we will attain wisdom. When we grow large in wisdom we dwarf our old egotistical self. The contest is then over.[340]

Fischer's model does not imply a continuous path through which one progresses, beginning with awareness of ego-identity and ending with full awareness of Self, but rather a set of static points on a continuum between ego-self and Self where one may reside. Most people live entirely within the "I-knowledge" domain (the top of the graph), unaware of Self. When we enter meditation (samādhi), we exist entirely within the Self and are, likewise, unaware of ego-identity. When we come out of samādhi, however, we return to the domain of the ego-self, and again exist within I-ness. Fischer explains that,

> In our terminology, the "Self" of exalted states is that which sees and knows, while the "I" is the interpretation, that which is seen and known in the physical space-time of the world "out there." The mutually exclusive relation between the "seer" and the "seen," or the elusiveness of the "Self" and the "I," may have its physiological basis in the mutual exclusiveness of the ergotropic and trophotropic systems.[341]

There are, however, regions along the continuum in which we are simultaneously aware of ego-self and Self and their interaction with one another; these correspond, according to Fischer, to coefficients of variation between 10 and 13 on the perception-hallucination continuum and between 9 and 12 hertz EEG range on the perception-meditation continuum, identifiable in Figure 10. For the chan traveler, this interaction between ego-self and Self happens once we have experienced an "awakening event," during which the Self becomes known (Chapter 18).

Fischer approached the problem of mystical experience from the perspective of a researcher studying psychiatric patients and the effects of hallucinogens (LSD) on test subjects. Although he was insightful on many points (the ergotropic/trophotropic system nicely depicts how Self is unknown when we live in our "I" existence), he was weak on the naturally-induced states of mystical experience. What he meant by "zazen" is unclear, especially considering that he distinguishes it from samādhi, which, of course, is where we finally arrive when we become adept at sitting meditation (zazen). Also, meditators—those in samādhi—encounter hallucinations, or what I more often refer to as visions (numinous dreams occurring during conscious states of awareness), so to suggest they cannot be co-occurring—unknown to each other—is faulty. The mistake was likely a natural consequence of studying drug-induced states, not naturally occurring states of altered consciousness, and his own lack of personal experience meditating.

Fischer's work offers a good example for how we should consider any model: as a mechanism from which we might either gain new insights, be misled, or both. It's up to us to apply our own sensibilities to the task of assessment and evaluation. In the process, it helps to remember that models are not representations of reality, but merely expressions of our desire to better understand reality. Whether a model is true or false, good or bad, is not the point; it's whether we can extract something meaningful from it that enhances understanding. We can take away what's useful and discard what's not. It's always helpful to keep a critical, open, and questioning mind as we consider a model of any kind, and recognize that different models and conceptual strategies can help us understand different aspects of the same thing.

One quite different and unique model often encountered in Buddhism is the *catuṣkoṭi*. It has been used for millennia to describe spiritual experience as well as to help guide people to it.

The ubiquitous catuṣkoṭi

> Thirty years ago, before I practiced Chan, I saw that mountains are mountains and rivers are rivers. However, after having achieved intimate knowledge and having gotten a way in, I saw that mountains are not mountains and rivers are not rivers. But now that I have found rest, as before I see mountains are mountains and rivers are rivers.*
>
> – Qingyuan Weixin 青原惟信

---

* This common chan aphorism is attributed to Wudeng Huiyuan (1252) in the *Compendium of the Five Lamps*.

The Catuṣkoṭi, first described in Chapter 1, has provided a mechanism for mystics to express how the experience of reality shifts as we progress on the spiritual journey. As a reminder, if we consider some proposition, then what we can say about it is that it must be either true, false, not true or false, or neither true nor false. There are no other options. Consider, for example, Qingyuan's mountain. By catuṣkoṭi logic, the experience of the mountain will align exclusively with one and only one of the following conditions for us:*

1) the mountain is real
2) the mountain is not real
3) the mountain is both real and not real
4) the mountain is neither real nor not real

At the beginning, before we engage in a spiritual practice such as chan, we live in the outer world created by sensory perceptions—the realm of subject-object duality: we (the subjects) interact with "things" (the objects), which give the impression of a distinct and separate reality for both subject and object. We are in catuṣkoṭi stage 1: the mountain is real.

Both negation and hua-tou practices assist in breaking the bonds between ourselves and the objects we perceive through our senses. This, in turn, helps us see a deeper aspect of being. We come to recognize that, by observing something, we participate in bringing it to awareness, that any sense of an objective reality—one that's independent of us—is a construction of our imagination. Objects thus lose their previous sense of substantive, or objective, reality. We are in catuṣkoṭi stage 2: the mountain is not real.

With persistence and continued effort, we break entirely through our conditioned way of perception to see things unfiltered through the ego's lens. The reality of the mountain returns but is no longer mediated by its abstraction as a "mountain"; i.e., it exists, but not as a mental

---

* For chan, how we interpret a mountain, or feel about it, is significant, not debating the nature of its existence.

formation. We are in catuṣkoṭi stage 3: the mountain is not real as an object apart from ourselves, but its perception as a mountain is real; i.e., the mountain is both real and not real.

When we enter samādhi, personal consciousness becomes subsumed entirely by Self-consciousness, and the distinction between real and not real vanishes because there's no thinker left to think about such things. We enter Chan's empty circle. We are in catuṣkoṭi stage 4: the mountain is neither real nor not real (recall Zhao zhou's *wú!* from Chapter 12).

Catuṣkoṭi logic may be useful to describe some aspects of the spiritual journey for someone who has lived it, but, in my opinion, it does little to illuminate it for those who haven't. There's no way to view life nondualistically unless we have done the work necessary to shed the ego's bonds. Despite Nagarjuna's persistent effort to try to help people understand mystical experience through the catuṣkoṭi (Chapter 1), there's no way to understand the state of consciousness we experience when we enter samādhi until we have been there.

The catuṣkoṭi offers a useful tool to describe spiritual experience, but it's not as helpful for teaching us how to achieve it. It also says nothing about the experiences we have when we start out on a spiritual journey. For that, we need to look to other models that help us understand the psychological forces that shape our interactions with the world and ourselves.

We'll next take a look at analytical psychology, which I found especially helpful during the early years of my own journey.*

---

* The reader who remains averse to considering the possible usefulness of analytical psychology is welcome to skip this next chapter, although some of the ideas presented will be referenced in following chapters as I attempt to describe and explain some of the challenges and dangers that can be encountered on chan's journey.

16

The Theory of Psychological Archetypes

> We must constantly bear in mind that what we mean by "archetype" is in itself irrepresentable, but has effects which make visualizations of it possible, namely, the archetypal images and ideas. We meet with a similar situation in physics: there the smallest particles are themselves irrepresentable but have effects from the nature of which we can build up a model.
>
> – C. G. Jung

IN THIS CHAPTER, I review Jung's principal thoughts relating to psychological archetypes as they evolved throughout his life. As emphasized earlier, the objective is not to present them as fundamental truths, but as a means for looking at and interpreting our own lives in a broader context. We'll begin by explaining some fundamental terminology. In later chapters, we'll explore the relationship of analytical psychology to experiences encountered on chan's journey.

Central to all of Jung's theories is the notion of a *collective unconscious*,* a storehouse of inherited psychological forces, which he calls *archetypes*:

---

*The term *unconscious* originated long before Jung and Freud, with the philosopher Friedrich Schelling; however, Paracelsus is credited with first proposing the existence of

> In addition to our immediate consciousness, which is of a thoroughly personal nature and which we believe to be the only empirical psyche, [...] there exists a second psychic system of a collective, universal, and impersonal nature which is identical in all individuals, This collective unconscious does not develop individually but is inherited. It consists of pre-existing forms, the archetypes, which can only become conscious secondarily and which give definite form to certain psychic contents.[342]

> ...archetypes are, by definition, factors and motifs that arrange the psychic elements into certain images, characterized as archetypal, but in such a way that they can be recognized only from the effects they produce. They exist preconsciously, and presumably they form the structural dominants of the psyche in general.... As *a priori* conditioning factors they represent a special psychological instance of the biological 'pattern of behavior,' which gives all things their specific qualities. Just as the manifestations of this biological ground plan may change in the course of development, so also can those of the archetype. Empirically considered, however, the archetype did not ever come into existence as a phenomenon of organic life, but entered into the picture with life itself.[343]

Jung used the term "archetype," variously, to describe both the characteristic *image* or *pattern* of an instinct as well as the force or energy—numinosity—residing with the instinct.* He also described it as an organizing principle through which an instinct acts.† Instincts are those programs that direct and guide us to survive and procreate:

---

unconscious cognition during the 16th Century.

* In Greek, *archetypon* means a model or pattern; in Latin, *archetyp* means an original. Jung uses the term in the same context in which it had been used for centuries. His contribution was to apply the concept to instinctual mechanisms and forces. "The first element 'arche' signifies 'beginning, origin, cause, primal source and principle,' but it also signifies 'position of a leader, supreme rule and government' (in other words a kind of 'dominant'); the second element 'type' means 'blow and what is produced by a blow, the imprint of a coin ... form, image, copy, prototype, model, order, and norm,' ... in the figurative, modern sense, 'pattern underlying form, primordial form' (the form, for example 'underlying' a number of similar human, animal, or vegetable specimens)" (Schmitt 1945, 98).

† "The unconscious, as the totality of all archetypes, is the deposit of all human experience right back to its remotest beginnings. Not, indeed, a dead deposit, a sort of abandoned

> The instincts are not vague and indefinite by nature, but are specifically formed motive forces which, long before there is any consciousness, and in spite of any degree of consciousness later on, pursue their inherent goals. Consequently, they form very close analogies to the archetypes, so close in fact, that there is good reason for supposing that the archetypes are the unconscious images of the instincts themselves, in other words, they are patterns of instinctual behavior.[344]

Jung describes two aspects of the unconscious: the *personal* unconscious, which relates to our localized psyche, and the *collective* unconscious, which relates to its evolutionary form.

Jung's theories are relevant to chan because they address a domain mediated not by words and thoughts, but by unusual imagery, auditory hallucinations, and peculiar emotions, all commonly experienced when we engage in meditation (dhyāna and samādhi).* Jung's models present a vehicle for interpreting and understanding these experiences by positing that there are elemental psychological forces at work which shape our interaction with the world. Psychologist James Hillman, founder of the field of Archetypal Psychology (which he based largely on analytical psychology), wrote:

> The primary, and irreducible, language of [...] archetypal patterns is the metaphorical discourse of myths. These can therefore be understood as the most fundamental patterns of human existence. To study human nature at its most basic level, one must turn to culture (mythology, religion, art, architecture, epic, drama, ritual) where these patterns are portrayed.[345]

---

rubbish heap, but a living system of reactions and aptitudes that determine the individual's life in invisible ways—all the more effective because invisible. It is not just a gigantic historical prejudice, so to speak, an *a priori* historical condition, but it is also the source of the instincts, for the archetypes are simply the forms which the instincts assume" (Jung 1969, § 339).

* Of note, I have met and corresponded with a number of people who claimed to have meditated for many decades and who attest that they have never had any such experiences. I attribute this phenomena, at least in part, to the Japanese Zen paradigm which tends to keep people in Stage 1, mindfulness, practices (see Part One) and consequently fails to help people enter the "deeper" levels of meditation.

Jung used the term *individuation* to describe the process through which we integrate these archetypal elements into consciousness.

Psychological Forces

According to Jung, a psychological archetype is an "instinct-force" which is "a living organism, endowed with generative force."[346] Since Jung often refers to archetypes as they pertain to instinctual forces, it may be helpful to first examine the idea of a psychological "force." An instinct, as an internal principle or force that commands our actions and emotions, is analogous to external forces which influence the physical world. In both cases, "force" is a teleological concept, something that's conceived to explain a phenomenon by the purpose it serves rather than by some postulated cause.*

Without the natural forces, there would be no physics. In fact, there would be nothing at all, because it's those forces that create things, that give substance to our world and make things happen. If we take a rock to be real, we also acknowledge that the forces that make it behave like a rock—that give it "rockness"—are real. Likewise, if we get angry and consider that anger to be real, we can also consider that there must be a force, or mechanism, that produces that anger, even if its nature is unknown. We can then observe it, describe it, do experiments to learn more about it, and speculate about it. We can name such interior forces anything we want; the name isn't important, but recognizing their existence is valuable, because it brings us closer to understanding ourselves and the world we live in. It also helps us come to understand that we are not our emotions—they are simply an aspect of being human and do not define us. Drawing on an analogy with physics, without interior forces we would have no emotions and no impetus for action.

---

* Much of science is based on teleological constructs. If something happens, we propose a reason—a mechanism—for it and give it a name. If a rock falls, we attribute it to something we decide to call *gravity*. If two magnets repel, we say it's because of something we have decided to call *electromagnetism*. Once a "force" concept is identified, we can investigate it further to understand its function and properties and unlock its secrets.

Like the forces that govern our physical world, archetypal forces can be viewed as governing our interior world.* Until we become conscious of these interior forces, however, they act upon us without oversight, directing us to think and behave as if we are robots following a set of programmed instructions, instructions which have been assembled from our collective inherited experience.

Jung posited that the number of archetypes in the human psyche is vast, and that they exist within a hierarchical structure.† The primary archetypes are those that cannot be reduced and are thus the basis for all other psychological archetypes: the Self, the persona, the shadow (both the enemy shadow and friendly shadow), and the anima/animus. Secondary archetypes include the hero, the child, the mother, and the father. Tertiary and other successive groups continue to build the tree, each progressively containing a larger mix of more elemental archetypes. When we turn our gaze inward, as we do with chan disciplines, we come into conscious contact with them, a process which integrates them into consciousness. Eventually, all archetypes may become known, a spiritual transcendent state alluded to in Chan's classic ox-herding series (Chapter 14), as well as the Neijing tu (Chapter 4).

COMPLEXES

Jung proposed that archetypes manifest in the psyche (in the personal unconscious) through *complexes*. Complexes, as he describes them, are

---

* Psychological archetypes can also be described as processes, or happenings. For example, we could draw the analogy that the enemy-shadow archetype is to anger as gravity is to falling. They are both the same kind of thing—teleological constructs that serve to describe why certain phenomena occur—but while an archetype makes itself known through *internal* observation (e.g., a visionary encounter with it, or an emotional reaction from it), external happenings make themselves known through *external* observation, from, say, watching a rock roll down a hill, or feeling it land on our head.

† "In the world of the archetypes we can accordingly establish a certain hierarchical order. We designate as "primary" those archetypes which are not susceptible of further reduction, which represent, as it were, the 'first parents'; we term the next in line, their 'children,' 'secondary,' their 'grandchildren' tertiary,' etc., until we arrive at those highly diversified archetypes which stand closest to the familiar domain of our consciousness and hence possess the least richness of meaning and numinosity or energy charge" (Jacobi 1974, 56-57).

patterns of emotions, perceptions, desires, and memories that become organized around some theme,* and are naturally present in all people.† Each complex has a positive and a negative aspect; that is, they are bipolar.‡ The further from consciousness, the greater the autonomy of the complex;³⁴⁷ however, through assimilation, a complex can be dissolved, and its energy discharged.³⁴⁸

The *root* of a specific complex resides with a specific archetype—or the specific collection of *connected* archetypes—and forms when experiences combine with archetypal influences and move into the personal unconscious.§ The ego is an example of such a composite complex: ego-consciousness is "the realm organized by the ego, which itself originates from the personal unconscious as a complex."³⁴⁹

We can imagine a complex manifesting negative behavior because of psychological imbalances originating perhaps from trauma or abuse during childhood. As a simple example, consider the "complex of superiority," or *narcissistic personality disorder*, characterized by perceiving oneself as superior to others, holding eminence over the rest of the world, and considering others unworthy of time or attention.¶

Other types of discordant complexes have names such as the *Medea complex, Orestes complex, Father complex, Mother complex,* and *Mes-*

---

* Recent research using fMRI imaging is identifying complexes as they relate to brain function involved with the processing of emotion (Leon Petchkovsky 2013).

† Jung's idea here bears remarkable semblance to Yogacara's principle of *ālaya-vijñāna*, often translated as "adhering consciousness" or "storehouse consciousness" (Chapter 4): it collects experiences and projects them back out when triggered and operates even when we're not aware of it.

‡ "...we may say that complexes have: two kinds of roots (they are based on infantile or actual events or conflicts); two kinds of nature (a complex may be 'morbid' or 'healthy'); two modes of expression (a complex may, according to the circumstances, be regarded as negative or positive; complexes are 'bipolar')" (Jacobi 1974, 25).

§ "If we imagine archetypes as forming fabric of the collective unconscious, then complexes—connected to them—would form a fabric of personal unconscious. Every complex therefore arises as a result of personal conflict and archetypal, universal conflict" (Jacobi 1974, 25).

¶ This complex differs from the "inferiority complex," which manifests compensatory behaviors that seek to demonstrate to others that one is superior to them; behaviors like buying expensive cars, telling jokes, wearing fancy clothes, etc. A person exhibiting a superiority complex doesn't care what other people think of him because to him they fundamentally are not important.

sianic/Redeemer complex. In general, whenever the psyche becomes strongly affected by life's experiences, unconscious elements manifest and merge with archetypal forces to create complexes.

Descriptions of some of the archetypes in the primary and secondary categories that are relevant to experiences encountered from chan training are presented below.

The (enemy) shadow archetype

The *enemy shadow* exists to increase the odds of our survival when we encounter a threat: a bear charges us, adrenaline is released, muscles tense, and our heart rate increases to deliver more oxygen to the muscles. All this prepares us for fight or flight. If we fight, we hope to win at whatever cost to ensure survival; if we flee, it's with the hope that we can outrun our foe. We would not exist today if we did not collectively share this archetype; through evolution, those who lacked the right instincts to survive left those who had them to continue the species.[*]

If we are not attentive, however, the enemy shadow can leap into our lives when we don't expect, need, or want it. When we suddenly feel pain or fear or humiliated, the enemy shadow may take control and respond violently toward the emotion's perceived cause. It may be toward someone who we feel insulted us, or toward a branch that caught us in the face as we walked along a forest path. When the enemy shadow is on the loose, we readily dehumanize its target, eliminating any moral sensibilities we may otherwise have invoked to offer respect and compassion.[†]

---

[*] Recent studies suggest the fight-or-flight instinct arises from the Y-chromosome gene, SRY (Harley 2012).

[†] We can see how the enemy shadow played a role in Hitler's desire to exterminate the Jews, Hirohito's desire for world domination, and radical Islamic fundamentalists' readiness to kill anyone who does not share their faith. These are all extreme examples that illustrate where projection of the enemy shadow can lead. A more insidious example is the subtle and sometimes overt hate rhetoric heard from right-wing extremists in the United States and elsewhere against foreigners and ethnic minorities such as African-Americans, Mexicans, Muslims, and Jews.

Once we are conscious of the enemy shadow, it no longer has the ability to act without our consent. We may get angry, but the anger is spontaneous, brief, and a natural reaction to circumstance; it may be so brief, in fact, that there is no outward expression of emotion at all. We can't reconfigure our DNA to suit us—we can't eliminate instincts and the archetypal impulses they thrust upon us—but when we are aware that the enemy shadow wants to act out, we can willfully arrest it before it has a chance to do harm.

The (friendly) shadow archetype

The friendly shadow is the balancing positive archetype for the negative enemy shadow, and is responsible for connections we develop with family and friends. It seeks social stability and close connections within a group or community. In dreams and visions, the friendly shadow is often that "other person" (of the same gender) who accompanies us, but has no face. Early in life we project this archetype onto close family members to gain their acceptance and embrace—essential ingredients for early survival. As we get older, we project the friendly shadow on people with whom we wish to associate or gain personal benefit. Salesmen, for example, use this archetype (consciously or unconsciously) to gain the confidence of prospective buyers.

The persona archetype

Persona is Latin for theatrical mask:

> It is, as its name implies, only a mask of the collective psyche, a mask that feigns individuality, making others and oneself believe that one is individual, whereas one is simply acting a role through which the collective psyche speaks.... The persona was only a mask of the collective psyche. Fundamentally the persona is nothing real: it is a compromise between individual and society as to what a man should appear to be.... In relation to the essential individuality of the person

concerned it is only a secondary reality, a compromise formation, in making which others often have a greater share than he. The persona is a semblance, a two-dimensional reality, to give it a nick-name.[350]

Similar to the friendly shadow, the persona seeks to fit in, to be accepted, but the persona is more interested in conforming with a social group than a close family. It seeks to abide by the status quo, and will direct behavior in ways suitable to achieving acceptance in the group. Its characteristics are conformity and harmony. We observe the persona at work in corporate law offices where all men wear expensive coats and ties, in churches where everyone sings the same hymns together, in meditation groups where everyone abides by the same codes of behavior and dress, etc. The persona is that guise we put on when we go out into the world to play a specific role: if we are a teacher, we don the self-confident attitude of knowledge and respectability; if we are an actor, we play whatever role our character requires;* if we are a wrestler, we behave tough and strong, hard and unstoppable. If we identify ourselves too greatly with the roles we play, however, those roles will play *us*; we will become slaves to them, our Self subsumed by the mask, hidden beneath its projection, a condition that can lead to depression and other forms of mental and emotional discord.

THE ANIMA & ANIMUS ARCHETYPES

The *anima* and *animus* are the feminine and masculine archetypes in men and women, respectively, that command heterosexual members of our species to reproduce.† They kick into overdrive during puberty when specific chemicals begin to be manufactured and released: DHEA, pheromones, oxytocin, phenylethylamine, estrogen, testoster-

---

* Some actors, often referred to as *method actors*, can convincingly portray a wide variety of characters because they have mastered the ability to project a range of different archetypes; i.e., through an act of will they can actually *become* a crazed psychopath or a mournful lover or a depressed parent. They have learned how to tap into those root sources of emotion that create the character.

† We might hypothesize that people who identify themselves as other than heterosexual, such as those in the LGBTQ+ group, exhibit different archetypal constellations, e.g., different relative proportions of these two archetypes.

one, serotonin, dopamine, progesterone, prolactin, and vasopressin, to name a few.*

When the anima/animus is projected onto another person, we imbue that person with superhuman qualities of perfection associated with our ideal mate. These projections give one a tremendous sense of elation and joy which lasts for as long as the projection is maintained. The moment the projection is terminated, the pain from the dissolution of *two-people-as-one* can be proportional to the joy felt during the projection phase.

In Jungian terms, integration of the anima and animus manifests as *spiritual androgyny* (divine union).[351] Just as wù arises once we give up our attachment to the ego-self and all that has gone into creating it, spiritual androgyny arises when we go further and give up our sexual identity, perhaps the strongest psychological attachment there is. To this point, S. Ortigue and others recently performed experiments demonstrating that passionate love strongly engages those parts of the brain utilized for social cognition and bodily self-representation,[352] implying that sexuality itself may be at the root of self-identification.†

People who become spiritually arrested at an early stage may become so disconnected from the anima/animus that maladaptive antisocial behaviors manifest. Without the constructive influence of the anima or animus to modify behavior, we may lose our ability to relate appropriately with members of the opposite sex. A man, for example, may become misogynous, treating women with contempt, or exhibiting aggressive antisocial behavior that results in sexual harassment or sexual assault. Such behavior was famously exhibited on the world stage by Donald Trump during his bid for president in 2016. Perhaps more commonly, men may express contempt toward women through various acts of overt and covert discrimination. Women, too, may express

---

* To continue our analogy with physics, chemicals such as these can be thought of as *carriers* of archetypal forces. In physics, every force has a "carrier particle" for that force: the electromagnetic force has the photon, the strong nuclear force has the gluon, the weak nuclear force has the boson, gravity has the graviton, sound has the phonon, etc.

† The recent LGBTQ+ movement suggests the tremendous significance that sexual/gender identity has on both individual lives and in society.

contempt for men through verbal aggression and passive-aggressive behavior.

Just as the Shadow has two faces—a "friend" and an "enemy"—so too does the anima/animus: a man under the influence of an enemy anima may present as moody, glum, subject to easily hurt feelings or, conversely, exhibit a grandiose sense of self-importance. A woman under the influence of an enemy animus may be highly opinionated, ruthless, harsh, unyielding, and act in an outwardly destructive manner. When the unconscious element is pacified, the effects are opposite: a man will show outward compassion, patience, kindness, and warmth; a woman will show thoughtfulness, control, and psychological strength.*

Projecting the animus (or anima) has no other purpose, evolutionarily speaking at least, than continuing the species. Yet there are some psychological dangers to be aware of when we engage in these projections. Projection leads to dependence upon the person who receives the projection: our identity can become enmeshed with him or her and we can become subjected to a roller-coaster ride of emotional highs and lows. The fear of rejection can be terrifying since the connection is between us and our anima/animus, *not between us and the other person*. The fear of losing the anima/animus can feel like losing our own identity. Considering this, it's not surprising that, among those who are most disconnected from their inner lives and are working through a relationship crisis, dramatic acts of violence are not uncommon. And it's not surprising that marriages taking place between couples during this projection-phase often don't last. Once there is no more projection, usually within a year or two of the relationship, the couple may find that they have little in common, or worse, don't even like each other's company. This may explain why cultures that embrace arranged marriages tend to have significantly lower divorce rates.†

---

* These descriptions are subjective but illustrate the point that, in accordance with the bipolar nature of psychological archetypes, the "enemy" aspects of the archetypes actualize themselves by influencing negative, maladaptive behaviors and emotions, while their friendly counterparts effect positive adaptive behaviors and emotions.

† According to ABC News, marriages in India, which are nearly always arranged, have about a 7% chance of divorce (Toledo 2009). In comparison, approximately 35% of U.S.

16. THE THEORY OF PSYCHOLOGICAL ARCHETYPES

Integrating the anima/animus archetype (divine union) is considered an advanced meditation, insofar as the practitioner must have already passed through earlier stages.* Hsu Yun put this at "Stage 7" in his ox-herding poems, alluding to the assimilation of the anima with the symbol of a spinning red wheel, a clear reference to the spinning maiden of the Nüwa/Fuxi myth (Chapter 17) and the Taoist Neijing tu (Chapter 4):

> *Into this painted hall comes a spinning red wheel.*
> *The New Bride finally arrives,*
> *and from my own house!*[353]

Sufi mystic, Jalaluddin Rumi, conveyed similar feelings:

> *The minute I heard my first love story,*
> *I started looking for you,*
> *not knowing how blind that was.*
> *Lovers don't finally meet somewhere.*
> *They're in each other all along.*[354]

And from the Atharva-Veda (c. 2nd millennium BCE):

> *As the creeper has completely embraced the tree, so may you embrace me.*
> *As the eagle, flying forth, beats its wings toward the earth, so I beat down your mind. May you live me. May you not withdraw from me.*
> *As the sun travels swiftly in [the space between] sky and earth here, so do I go about your mind. May you live me. May you not withdraw from me.*[355]

As we might imagine, a mind made powerful through years of meditation can evoke tremendous sexual energy from these meditations—the

---

marriages end with divorce (Swanson 2016).

* When this is accomplished, there is no longer sexual energy projected outward, only inward. Among the ancient Vrâtyas, men who have experienced divine union are said to have "quietened the penis," i.e., mastered their sexual drive. In Sanskrit, the term *shamaniya-medhra* refers to this advanced yogic state of *urdhva-retas* (Georg Feuerstein 2008, 120).

term *orgasmic ecstasy* (Skt., *sānanda samādhi*) is not used indiscriminately to describe the mystics' experience of divine union.*

THE HERO ARCHETYPE

The hero archetype provides the means to overcome great obstacles, to transform and enlighten, to improve, elevate, and save. It offers hope, redemption, and salvation and drives us to overcome adversity of all kinds. It has many faces: the jester, the magician, the outlaw, the ruler, the sage, the savior, and the creator, to name a few. We see hero archetypes depicted in movies and other media, and they are also central themes in religious myths and art. Assuming healthy psychological development, we experience and project the full range of hero archetypes throughout the course of our lives: as children, we may connect first with the trickster (e.g., Bugs Bunny, Wile E. Coyote), the magician (e.g., Merlin, Harry Potter), and the classic hero (e.g., Superman, X-Men, James Bond). As we mature, the outlaw-hero might make its debut (e.g., Robin Hood, Pancho Villa, Batman), the ruler (e.g., Mufasa from *The Lion King*, and real-world heroes such as Empress Wu of the Tang dynasty, Alexander the Great, and Ashoka). Finally, the sage archetype appears (e.g., Oogway in *Kung Fu Panda*, Yoda from *Star Wars*), along with the Savior archetype (e.g., Gandalf from *The Lord of the Rings*, Aslan from *The Chronicles of Narnia*, Neo from *The Matrix*). There are also the well-known non-fictional saviors, such as Jesus, Muhammed, and Siddhartha, and legendary sages such as Confucius and Lao Tzu. At the top of the list of hero archetypes is the Creator, or *celestial savior* archetype: God, YHVH, Elohim, Amitābha, Jehovah, Allah, Parvardigar, Ishvara, etc.

---

* If these meditations are thwarted for any reason when the practitioner is ready for them, having successively freed himself or herself from the restraints of repressed feelings—including those related to intimacy and sex—the practitioner can easily revert back to projections upon people. This may help explain widespread sexual misconduct of Zen teachers within Western institutions. More on this in Chapters 20 and 21.

The child & mother archetypes

The child archetype is the instinct that engages us to nurture our young, which compels us to guide and protect them. When projected, this instinct allows us to forgive and forget the unpleasantries that come with raising a child: messes, tantrums, lost sleep, dirty diapers, and howling rages.

The closely related mother archetype, projected by the child, is tightly bound to the child archetype projected by the mother, the two combining to form a strong, inseparable bond that helps ensure the child will be cared for and protected during the early stages of life when survival is most tenuous. If a mother fails to project this archetype, she may tend toward neglect or abuse.

The *divine mother* archetype is central in Hinduism (*Durga*), Christianity (*Mary*), Islam (*Fatimah/Sophia*), Buddhism (*Tārā*), as well as many other religions.

The father archetype

The father archetype embraces the principle of power, organization, reason, protection, and rule-following. Cinematic examples include Morpheus from *The Matrix*, Phil Coulson from *Agents of S.H.I.E.L.D.*, and Stoick from *How to Train your Dragon*. Its qualities are illumination, rationality, and locomotion. As another survival instinct, the father archetype provides the impetus to abandon the unconscious realm for the sensory world. It's the enforcer of boundaries, social values and restrictions, order, and discipline, all of which keep us safe and lead us toward becoming productive members of society.

Again, as with all elemental archetypes, the father archetype has a negative side, which is characterized by abuse of authority, cold and domineering affect, extreme rigidity, and self-righteousness. Darth Vader from *Star Wars* offers a caricature of the shadowy father archetype, as did the popular Saturday Night Live satirical characterization of Steve Bannon as the Grim Reaper.

In Chinese Buddhism, the father archetype is often represented by the *four heavenly kings* (*Fēng Tiáo Yǔ* 風調雨順)—large colorful statues presiding as protectors at the entrances of Buddhist temples.

THE WARRIOR ARCHETYPE

The warrior archetype encourages us to "fight for what's right"; its principal characteristics are courage, discipline, and skill. When there's a problem or threat, real or imagined, if we project this archetype, we'll fight to defeat it. We will fear weakness and impotence, its polar opposite.

Its negative shadow is expressed by the "bully," many dictators, and men who have suffered abuse from aggressive and domineering parental practices.[356] When embraced as an identity, the warrior archetype can lead to narcissistic and sociopathic personality disorders. Donald Trump expressed such a self-conception during a 1981 interview with People magazine: "Man is the most vicious of all animals, and life is a series of battles ending in victory or defeat."[357] When we project the warrior archetype upon a person or group of people, those projected upon can become aroused to project it as well.*

THE SELF ARCHETYPE

Analytical psychology considers that consciousness can be experienced through two realms: the ego-realm, which arises from our experiences, beliefs, opinions, etc., and the Self-realm, which manifests from the genetic code that carries the cumulative "wisdom" passed down through hundreds of millions of years of evolution, which Jung described as universal and eternal:

> Are we not the carriers of the entire history of mankind? When a man is fifty years old, only one part of his being has existed for half a century. The other half may be millions of years old ...[T]he self: as the

---

* For example, during Trump's first year in office, according to a 2018 FBI report, violent hate crimes rose 17% from the previous year and anti-Semitic hate crimes rose 37 percent. (Barrett 2018)

essence of individuality it is unitemporal and unique; as an archetypal symbol it is a God-image and therefore universal and eternal.[358]

In this context, the "missing part" of ourselves is that which is embedded in our genetic history and therefore innately unknowable to ego-consciousness. We can become aware of it only through another type of consciousness, one that's mysterious to ego-consciousness because it cannot assimilate it or fathom it; it's completely outside its cognitive domain.

While the ego-self exists in the temporal domain of phenomenal causes and effects (karma), the Self lacks awareness of temporally conditioned phenomena and is therefore, once fully perceived, recognized as eternal and outside the tumultuous realm of life and death (samsāra).

From the examples presented in this chapter, its apparent how archetypal forces can invisibly influence behavior—for better or worse. They can behave like wily children who want to be let out to play: unruly, eager, energetic, and determined to express themselves. When we explore the inner realm of the psyche and come to know them face-to-face, their reality becomes undeniable.

17

Dreams and Visions

Meeting the Unconscious

> Once I dreamed I entered a diamond cave and came to the stone door of Great Prajna Temple. I opened the door and went in and there, in a huge area, I saw solemn temple buildings and a spacious hall. Inside the hall, Great Master Qing Liang was resting on a large meditation bed. Miao Feng was standing on his left. I quickly went to the bed and prostrated myself and then stood on his right waiting for him to speak. Finally, he said: 'In the state of the Dharmadhatu, in which merge all the glorious Buddha lands, there are no hosts or guests, there is no coming or going.' As he spoke, the very state which he described enveloped me and I felt as if my body and mind had merged with it. After this revelation, Miao Feng asked the Great Master, 'Venerable Sir, what is this state?' Master Qing Liang smiled and said, 'This is the state of no state.' When I woke up all of my surroundings seemed transparent to me. I could see through everything.
>
> – Han Shan

TRADITIONAL CHAN TRAINING LEADS practitioners into the mysterious depths of the mind, where archetypal forms emerge vividly, and profound messages are conveyed. While we've explored the theory of psychological archetypes, how might we actually recognize them? What forms do they take when we turn our gaze inward, toward their natural domain? Unlike the conscious mind, which communicates in familiar words and images, the unconscious speaks in numinous beings and enigmatic symbols. These may appear as oceans, snakes, thunder, wind, intricate mandalas, or dazzling lights. The unconscious may also express itself through sound—clicks, pops, bangs, music, birdsong, choral harmonies, a string ensemble, or the natural rhythms of ocean waves or rustling leaves. By examining these encounters, we uncover not only their symbolic messages but also their universal, archetypal qualities. Anthony Stevens, in *The Two-Million-Year-Old Self*, describes dreams and visions as portals to an "ancient substratum of experience," suggesting that in our dreams, we engage with our collective phylogenetic heritage. In his words, "we speak to the species, and the species answers back," revealing the timeless dialogue between individual and collective unconscious.[359]

Dreams and visions occur when unconscious contents rise to the surface and burst into consciousness. Mystics sharply distinguish visions from dreams because of their dramatically different qualities. Ordinary dreams tap into the personal-unconscious, rehashing the day's events, responding to our biological or psychological needs, and are typically populated with the persons, places, and objects of daily experience, quickly vanishing from awareness when we awaken. Visions, on the other hand, are always unrelated to our personal lives and have an "otherworldly," numinous aspect, imparting an emotional intensity that commands our attention—sometimes for days or even weeks after. The reason for a perceived difference between dream and vision may, we will see, lie in the degree of cross-hemispheric synchronization of neuronal impulses that occurs within the brain when we learn to enter the meditative state.

The dreaming experience is thought to be common to all mammals as well as to many birds and reptiles.[360] As an emergent property of our evolution, this suggests that the origin of dreaming, or the conditions that gave rise to it, may lie in the Carboniferous period, over 300 million years ago. If spiders also dream, as it's now thought, that number could reach to more than 700 million years. Conventionally, however, researchers tend to consider the dreaming phenomena to have begun some 140 million years ago.[361] Regardless, considering this very long time period, it's not unreasonable to postulate that dreams may offer insights into who we are, where we've come from, and where we're going.* It's not insignificant that many discoveries have been attributed to dreams, including the organization of the periodic table by Dmitri Mendeleev, the theory of evolution by natural selection by Alfred Russel Wallace, the structure of benzene by August Kekulé, the discovery of the scientific method by René Descartes, and the shape and structure of DNA by James Watson. Much art has also been attributed to dream imagery. Salvador Dali, for example, used it extensively to inspire his work: "Give me two hours a day of activity, and I'll take the other twenty-two in dreams."

Imagery encountered during the early phases of sleep or light meditation generally arises from the personal unconscious. As the unconscious mind assimilates and orders information provided from conscious experience, it processes and returns the results back to the conscious mind in the form of imagery and emotion. This effect can be used to our advantage if we contemplate a significant problem we're having as we doze off to sleep. For example, as a physics student in college, I was assigned a problem in electrodynamics that was especially challenging. I worked on it into the night without success and finally went to bed. Around 4:00 a.m. I awoke with a start, fully aware of the solution. I got out of bed, jotted down the math, then returned to bed and sleep. This method of problem-solving has recurred multiple times since then. To work, it seems to require fierce mental energy directed at the problem just before dozing off.

---

* Some people claim that they don't dream; however, studies to date have been unable to determine whether it's possible to not dream. It may be that some people are less able to recall dreams, or that they don't pay attention to them, so don't recognize them as dreams, a form of agnōsía.

During sitting practice, as we begin watching the mind, we may experience dreams in a different way: being fully conscious of them as they occur. Watching them is not only tremendously engaging, but over time the process can enrich our overall perception of reality.

THE SCIENCE OF DREAMS AND VISUAL IMAGERY

Research into sleep over the last few decades has offered insights into the process, mechanism, and purpose of sleep, but much remains unknown. We now know that as we move through successive stages of sleep, our brains exhibit progressively more coherent, in-phase and synchronous activity.* We also know from EEG measurements that during meditation the brain's electromagnetic behavior is uniquely different from that encountered during unconscious sleeping: cross-hemispheric synchronization occurs across larger regions of the brain when we remain alert and conscious, as we do during meditation.[362]

As the brain moves toward meditation, it transitions to progressively slower and more synchronous and coherent wave-states. Initially, it enters the gamma stage, characterized by low frequencies in the range of 32 to 100 Hz, a range known to give rise to visual imagery. Some researchers have proposed that the 40 Hz resonance—which is produced during both wakefulness in meditation as well as during sleep—is the source of the cognitive experience itself.[363] Notably, studies of advanced meditators, when told to focus their attention on producing a feeling of compassion, produced the highest amplitude oscillations in the low end of the gamma range ever seen in humans, except for those experiencing seizures.[†364]

---

* There is much overlap between the various wave-states observed in the brain. Referred to as superposition, different parts of the brain can exhibit local synchronous behaviors which, when seen with an EEG, appear as a variety of waveforms combined with each other. Seven wave states are typically observed: delta (0.5 - 4 Hz), theta (4 - 7 Hz), alpha (8 - 15 Hz), mu (7.5 - 12.5 Hz), SMR (12.5 - 15.5 Hz), beta (16-31 Hz), and gamma (32 - 100 Hz).

† The Bodhisattva Avalokiteśvara is commonly visualized and contemplated in Mahāyāna Buddhism to evoke compassion.

We can become conscious of the transitions between alpha and theta when we are lying in bed beginning to doze off, or when we're sitting on our cushion or chair working with a concentration practice.

We also dream—though perhaps less frequently—during delta, the deepest sleep. Delta arises when the brain achieves maximum coherence and synchronicity at the lowest achievable frequencies (0.5 to 4 Hz). The most experienced meditators can stay in delta for many hours; however, unlike delta states during sleep, during delta meditation we are conscious and alert. Neuroscience researcher Jeffrey Fannin writes that "becoming consciously aware of experiencing the delta brainwave frequencies has been associated with the deepest sense of spirituality, highest sense of internal awareness, and feeling directly connected to a Higher Power."*365 During delta meditation we connect most intimately with the unconscious mind to witness visionary encounters from the most primitive archetypal motifs, those Jung described as being in the primary group: Self, persona, shadow, and anima/animus.

Archetypal visions

Although visions correlate with a learned ability to enter consciously into theta and delta brainwave states—states associated with a highly focused mind—they can also occur spontaneously during a night's sleep, especially if we have a robust chan practice during the day. Visions differentiate themselves from dreams by their clarity, emotional tone, and peculiar numinosity. James Hillman described the effects of a visionary encounter as "...more profound (archetypal), more powerful (potential), and more beautiful (theophanic) than the comprehension of it..."366

Whether we experience them during sleep or meditation, we're easily able to recall a vision's details, often with astonishing clarity. Their emotional tone can also reveal our psychological and spiritual state at

---

* For the mystic, such "spiritual experiences" are interesting and valued, but their mechanisms of formation are tangential to the objective of practice, which is revealing mysteries and transcending suffering: getting ourselves out of samsāra.

the time. Feelings of joy or satisfaction indicate progress and suggest that we're "doing things right," while feelings of fear, dread, remorse, shame, etc., suggest we need to investigate the message until we understand its meaning, then re-evaluate our conscious attitudes and affect adjustments. If we ignore or conveniently misinterpret the message, we risk stagnation and the possibility of repetitions of the unpleasant visionary encounter.

Throughout history, images from the collective unconscious have been expressed in art, music, and other creative forms. Considering that we all share a common genome,* it's not surprising that many of the images and dramatic events encountered through visionary experience follow universal mythic motifs; that is, they repeat themselves throughout humanity. As an example, one particular motif presented to me during my first year of dedicated chan practice. From my notes at the time:

> I was standing in the center of a large, bright room. From an opening in the cathedral ceiling high above, a bright white light shone, illuminating the white walls with a numinous radiance. Just below the spire, a small silver-gray hummingbird perched on a twig. The moment I glanced at it, it suddenly darted off and flew playfully through the room, coming to rest on my left shoulder. Gently but firmly, the hummingbird tugged at my left earlobe with its beak and made tiny sounds in my ear. After a few moments it rubbed its small body against the side of my neck affectionately, which brought me suddenly awake.

The vision was strangely erotic and its effects lingered a week or more. When I mentioned it to a friend, she was startled because a friend of hers in China had, years earlier, told her of a related vision. Her friend had spent years caring for her ill mother. When her mother died, she

---

* The human genome is comprised of nucleic acid sequences encoded as DNA in 23 chromosome pairs in the nuclei of cells and within mitochondria. DNA sequencing has shown that the human genome is 99.9% identical from person to person (National Human Genome Research Institute, 2019), unequivocally ending the debate over whether there are multiple races of humans. There aren't.

entered a Buddhist monastery. In China, dreams are considered extremely important, and when, after eight years, she failed to have any dreams of her mother, she developed great remorse. Then, on the ninth anniversary of her mother's death, she had a vision. She was in a beautiful room and her mother was reclining comfortably on a chair. She knelt beside her and then her mother cradled her in her arms and whispered to her, "I will always be with you. I will be a little hummingbird perched on your left shoulder, whispering in your ear." After the experience, she recounted that she was joyful and her remorse completely vanished.

I became intrigued with the hummingbird theme as an instance of universal myth, and discovered that "Hummingbird on the Left" was the literal translation of the Aztecs' patron deity, Huitzilopochtli.* According to their history, as the Aztec people first migrated south from northwest Mexico, their leader had a vision in which a hummingbird directed him not to cease migrating until he observed an eagle with a snake in its beak come to rest on a cactus. When this prophesied event occurred, the story goes, he halted the journey and founded the city of Tenochtitlan, now called Mexico City.[367]

Other common subjects of visions include human forms such as the wise old man who gives a needed solution or direction, and the erotic *anima* or *animus* who lures us to integrate our sexual opposites into a *divine union*. Various birds, animals, and sea creatures, as well as plant forms such as trees, vines, and roots, are also common themes. Buildings may house us, varying from dilapidated wrecks to marble palaces, or if outdoors, meadows, forests, or oceans may encompass the landscape. Other common motifs include fire, fanciful displays of colors, brilliant white light, numinous or imposing men or women, colorful moving mosaic patterns, and powerful objects of transport such as trains, horses, and cars. Each person, object, or setting comes with

---

* In Aztec mythology, Huitzilopochtli was the son of Omecíhuatl and Ometecuhtli, respectively the female and male aspects of the androgynous primordial god, Ometeotl.

an emotional signature that carries the vision's intended message. That signature can be anything from blissful or awe-inspiring, to terrifying.

Even when visionary experiences are frightening, they can lead to rewarding outcomes if we investigate them appropriately. Jung wrote that

> ...[t]he changes that may befall a man are not infinitely variable; they are variations of certain typical occurrences which are limited in number. When therefore a distressing situation arises, the corresponding archetype will be constellated in the unconscious. Since this archetype is numinous, i.e., possesses a specific energy, it will attract to itself the contents of consciousness—conscious ideas that render it perceptible and hence capable of conscious realization. Its passing over into consciousness is felt as an illumination, a revelation, or a "saving idea."[368]

Many years ago, at the beginning of my chan training when I was haunted by feelings of anger and despair, I experienced a terrifying but revelatory vision. I was (roughly) in Stage Three, as described in Chapter 11, working with negation practices during the day, and lucid dreaming[369] at night. One night I had a terrifying archetypal encounter with the *enemy shadow*. From my notes:

> I was in a dark cave, terrified, running away from something/someone, I could not tell what, and I didn't know why I was afraid. In a sudden movement, determined to understand what It was, I turned around and confronted It. What I saw was not human yet stood on two legs. The head was disproportionately large and nearly perfectly round, with small eyes devoid of eyebrows. It had a small nose and a small closed mouth. The head had no skin and was a satin pitch-black surface like a bowling ball. Still terrified, I aggressively confronted the being, pushing it up against the cave wall and yelled at it *"What do you want?! What do you want?! Who are you?!"* In reply, it gave an enormous compassionate smile and vanished. This broke the vision and I awoke. *What was that?*

This encounter completely lifted my spirits. My dark mood vanished and was replaced with a sense of awe, lightness, and relief. Still to this day, decades later, recalling the event elicits the numinosity of the experience, and the details are still clear in my mind.

Over the course of my journey I have had other archetypal encounters, sometimes during a night's sleep, sometimes during seated meditation. Once we experience visionary archetypal dramas, it becomes clear why they wield so much influence: they announce themselves with extreme urgency, dynamic energy, and uncanny prescience. And they always seem to have something important to convey, something that affects us viscerally and profoundly.

AN EXAMPLE: THE SNAKE MOTIF

Artwork from civilizations around the world illustrates many other striking vision-themes, and suggest the powerful influence they have had over individuals, societies, and religions for millennia. The snake motif is a particularly prevalent theme which occurs in virtually all domains of human enterprise: worship, art, war, alchemy, medicine, and even commerce.* It also has ancient roots: the oldest ritual known to date involves the worshiping of the python, according to a recent archaeological expedition in Botswana that uncovered artifacts dating to between 30,000 and 70,000 years ago.[370]

In the Vedas, the snake represents kundalini (*"serpent power"*), a symbol of spiritual androgyny common to many cultures around the world. According to Gimbutas, author of *The Language of the Goddess*, the snake was a ubiquitous symbol of the "Great Mother" archetype of Old Europe, and "[i]ts vital influence was felt not only in life creation, but also in fertility and increase, and particularly in the regeneration of dying life energy."[371]

---

* Carl Jung wrote that "...the snake is the representative of the world of instinct, especially of those vital processes which are psychologically the least accessible of all. Snake dreams always indicate a discrepancy between the attitude of the conscious mind and instinct, the snake being a personification of the threatening aspect of that conflict" (Jung 1956, para 616, p. 396).

FIGURE 11. NÜWA.
A sketch from the Shan Hai Jing depicting Nüwa as a serpent.

The Chinese *Huainzi* 淮南子, a collection of writings that dates to the second century BCE, describes the snake goddess, Nüwa 女媧 (Figure 11), as having created mankind and "repairing the pillar of heaven"[372] Nüwa and her divine consort Fuxi 伏羲 are often represented with serpent tails wrapping around one another in union. The ancient Chinese *Shan Hai Jing* (*Classic of Mountains and Seas*) tells the story of Nüwa and Fuxi, each kindling separate fires that grew to become a ferocious single blaze from which they conjoined to become husband and wife. In the later Han dynasty, Fuxi and Nüwa, the divine androgynous pair, were represented as king and queen (Figure 12).

The conjoined serpents motif is possibly the most ancient symbol of spiritual union, having appeared in diverse cultures since antiquity. In Sumeria, the diety *Ningizzida* was represented by two conjoined snakes, a symbol that we commonly see today to represent medicine.

Buddhism, too, offers many examples of the snake motif, most notably of Gau-

FIGURE 12. FUXI AND NÜWA AS KING AND QUEEN.
A mural image from the Han dynasty (206 BCE – 220 AD). Note the serpent-legs coiled in union. The child may represent the mischievous mercurial child (see *Alchemical Studies*, C. G. Jung 1967, p.228)

tama Buddha sitting in meditation with Mucalinda (Nüwa). From the *Muccalinda Sutta*:

> Thus have I heard. At one time the Lord was staying at Uruvela beside the river Nerañjara at the foot of the Mucalinda Tree, having just realized full enlightenment. At that time the Lord sat cross-legged for seven days experiencing the bliss of liberation.
>
> Now it happened that there occurred, out of season, a great rainstorm and for seven days there were rain clouds, cold winds, and unsettled weather. Then Mucalinda the naga-king left his dwelling place and having encircled the Lord's body seven times with his coils, he stood with his great hood spread over the Lord's head to protect the Lord from cold and heat, from gadflies, mosquitoes, wind, sun, and the touch of creeping things.
>
> At the end of those seven days the Lord emerged from that concentration. Then Mucalinda the naga-king, seeing that the sky had cleared and the rain clouds had gone, removed his coils from the Lord's body. Changing his own appearance and assuming the appearance of a youth, he stood in front of the Lord with his hands folded together venerating him.
>
> Then, on realizing its significance, the Lord uttered on that occasion this inspired utterance:
>
> *Blissful is detachment for one who is content,*
> *For one who has learned Dhamma and who sees;*
> *Blissful is non-affliction in the world,*
> *Restraint towards living creatures;*
> *Blissful is passionlessness in the world,*
> *The overcoming of sensual desires;*
> *But the abolition of the conceit "I am"—*
> *That is truly the supreme bliss.*[373]

Alchemy, founded by the legendary Hermes Trismegistus, is also replete with serpent symbolism. Figure 13 depicts an Androgyne standing on a cloud made of goat-heads and a boy and girl curling up the

FIGURE 13. ANDROGYNE WITH GOATS' HEADS.
An illustration from the Codex germanicus Monacensis depicting mystical union.

legs. In the Indian Vedas, the goat (*ajā*) means "unborn" and symbolizes *avyakta*, or Unmanifest Nature:[374]

Like the She-Goat, Nature (prakṛti), made of the three qualities, gives birth to the world. First to be born is the universal Intellect, the transcendent principle (mahat). In it, too, are found the three fundamental qualities. Its black quality is the tendency toward disintegration, the nature of which is to veil. Its white quality is the tendency toward concentration, the nature of which is to give light. Its red quality is the revolving tendency, the nature of which is enjoyment.* Some of the goats, after enjoying the spotted she-goat whose children are likewise spotted, still follow her, while others, having enjoyed her, abandon her. So also some living beings, after enjoying Nature, follow her who, spotted with the three qualities, procreates the world, while others, having enjoyed her, proceed toward another goal.[375]

On the other side of the globe, the Mesoamerican deity Quetzalcóatl, known as the *Plumed Serpent*, was the son of the primordial androgynous god Ometeotl. He was venerated by the Aztecs and Mayans as the god of wind and learning, was associated with the planet Venus, and was considered the creator of the world and mankind.[376]

---

* Recall the red/revolving theme referenced by Hsu Yun in his ox-herding poems to symbolize spiritual androgyny: "Into this painted hall comes a spinning red wheel. The New Bride finally arrives, and from my own house!"

Quetzalcóatl, with origins from the Nahuatl language, means "feathered serpent" (Figure 14). Its oldest surviving appearance comes from Teotihuacan between the first century BCE and the first century CE. Mayans referred to him as Kukulkán, the Quiché of Guatemala referred to him as Gucumatz, and the Huastecs of the Gulf Coast referred to him as Ehecatl.

In one creation myth, Cartwright recounts that Quetzalcóatl and Tezcatlipoca

FIGURE 14. QUETZALCÓATL AND THE BUDDHA.

Stone statues depicting the feathered serpent, Quetzalcóatl (left) from Mesoamerica; and from Asia, the Buddha wrapped in the coils of Mucalinda (Nüwa), protected by her many cobra heads (right).

...create the sun, the first man and woman, fire and the rain gods. The pair of gods had created the earth and the sky when they transformed themselves into huge snakes and ripped in two the female reptilian monster known as Tlaltcuhtli (or Cipactli), one part becoming the earth and the other the sky. Trees, plants and flowers sprang from the dead creature's hair and skin whilst springs and caves were made from her eyes and nose and the valleys and mountains came from her mouth.[377]

I've chosen the snake motif to illustrate similarities of visionary encounters across cultures and times because historical evidence suggests that it's one of the most common, dramatic, and commanding motifs of them all. As with all visionary encounters, its message is symbolic. Language and culture play a role in how we interpret them, which is why we see wide variations of snake lore, but perhaps more remarkable than the specific interpretations of the imagery is the high regard attributed to snake symbolism over a very long period of human history.

We can reasonably speculate that the details of visionary experiences are unique for each person, but we can just as reasonably speculate that they all share a similar intensity and numinous "otherworldliness," and that these qualities have motivated their widespread expression across the globe for millennia. Archetypal encounters not only captivate us but force themselves upon us in ways that command our attention and inspire their expression.

The following excerpt from an anonymous spiritual traveler describes an encounter with a serpent, then details other archetypal encounters during the same vision. Note the degree of detail and the emotional intensity of the narrative:

> I dreamed of a red snake with piercing, deep-yellow eyes last night. I wasn't scared in my dream but even in that state the meaning was a mystery to me….it certainly is now that I'm awake.
>
> The snake materialized after a vision where I was introduced to a hermetic order which had understanding of everything that was happening in the world and understood that the human race and planet Earth were in store for some dramatic changes still in the years to come. The order seemed to be of the OTO legacy and was currently led by a female master who initiated and educated me into the order in the twinkle of the eye. I literally looked at myself in the mirror in the dream and my eyes twinkled. That was a surprise for sure.
>
> On completing the initiation, the master was no longer present…. but there was the snake. Large, crimson red with gray tints to its

scales, and these intense yellow eyes. I thought at first that this was a negative omen; however, the snake seemed rather to calm me by not being aggressive at all...just looking. While the snake did not speak it did seem to communicate with me—indicating that it was my guide, executor of force, wise savant, and protector.

In the dream, I then went on to encounter several enemies and forces...some invisible, some animal shapes, some human, some unknown. I seemed to be able to see my entire situation from all perspectives simultaneously. I could even see up through the ground like it was clear and I could see my feet hit the ground and the force they had on the terra.

Ultimately, I wound up running up a mountain, where I was greeted by a vision of a balding man, clothed in a white linen loincloth, with a thin, long, white beard which seemed to wisp about as he moved and the gentle breeze rolled by. The man seemed to be very old, but his physical form didn't seem to be frail at all. He was sitting at a small table and was studying a lunar body...possibly the moon. He noticed me but did not speak that I recall. He made a few notes or drawings. The man appeared to have great knowledge and wisdom.... I wondered if it might be a future me, who'd finally learned a great deal from his plethora of mistakes.

The rest of the details, which I'm not sure of the chronology, include kaleidoscopic color images: a black robed human figure which seemed to morph into a flying creature, which I could not tell if it was a bird, a bat or possibly a huge moth. This figure flew just over my head and seemed to disappear before I could turn to follow its path visually.

I awoke intermittently, and then finally went back to sleep peaceably until the dogs and my baby girl got me up. Interestingly, my little dog was snuggled right next to me, and seemed to flinch when I had startling images in my dream. My little baby girl also entered my dream too. I envisioned that the dream, in part, was to help me protect her in the wake of coming dramatic earth changes. It seemed like the baby would ultimately be a wise and powerful being.

Also of interest is that I was chilled in my dream and in bed.... even though I had on PJs and was covered up with a sheet, a thick fleece blanket, and down comforter.... very unusual since I'm usually exceedingly hot in the covers.[378]

This series of contiguous visionary encounters illustrates how such visions command our attention to the degree that we can recall them with great precision, unlike dreams. It also illustrates how it's easy to misinterpret their meaning—or fail to identify their meaning—after we shift consciousness to the outer world, or "awaken." The first, reflexive response is to imagine that they relate to our external life rather than our inner life—that the encounters are with beings other than ourselves. The key to proper interpretation of visionary encounters is to recognize that each thematic subject expresses an aspect of ourselves; more specifically, *they are each an unconscious aspect of Self seeking to be known.** For example, the vision "...of a balding man, clothed in a white linen loincloth, with a thin, long, white beard" was an archetypal projection from the dreamer: the dreamer was the source from which "he" was born. That the dreamer described him as studying a "lunar body," rather than simply the moon, suggests an important symbolic message—the moon as a "lunar body" is a universal symbol of the anima, or the female principle, and of rebirth. That the dreamer had an overall feeling of "dramatic earth changes" soon to be taking place, along with numinous encounters with the wise old man archetype, anima (lunar body), snake (transformation energy), and female master of initiation (the mother archetype), suggests that a profound spiritual transformation may be on the horizon for the dreamer. The baby entering the visionary sequence at the end is suggestive of the formation of an *immortal fetus* or *holy embryo* (*sheng tai* 神胎)—the spiritual-progeny born of the union of male/female opposites†—especially considering

---

* To this point, James Hillman wrote that such archetypal images "don't stand for anything. They are the psyche itself in its imaginative visibility; as primary *datum*, image is irreducible" (2013, 17).

† Giving birth to an *immortal fetus* is an important Taoist goal and is given similar importance in chan. "As with a physical fetus, the immortal fetus needs to be incubated in the

the dreamer's feeling that "...the baby would ultimately be a wise and powerful being."

Visionary experiences, common to the spiritual journey, arise spontaneously and are nearly impossible to ignore. If we discount them, however, it's at our own jeopardy, for the insights they offer may not be available from any other source. For many chan practitioners, an encounter with the elusive Self archetype is the holy grail of the spiritual journey.

---

body. As the immortal fetus develops, it churns, moves, tumbles, and grows big in the belly of the internal alchemist. The incubation period is termed the ten months of pregnancy, because it resembles the development of a fetus in a mother's womb. At this stage of training, the practitioner must be secluded in a quiet place and not be distracted. If a wrong step is taken, the immortal fetus will be lost" (Wong 2011, 182). In Chinese Buddhist monasteries, monks at this stage are permitted seclusion from the rest of the sangha, and given reprieve from daily chores for as many days, weeks, or months as are needed to carry the process through to completion.

18

Discovering the "Self"

> A genius is the one most like himself.
> – Thelonious Monk

SELF-DISCOVERY OFTEN OCCURS ABRUPTLY, like a sudden flash of awareness that reveals a reality entirely distinct from our usual perspective. It's not something we can perceive gradually—it's either there or it isn't, like looking up at the night sky to see if the moon is out: it either is or isn't.* However, we might catch fleeting glimpses of the Self before fully recognizing it. Yet, just as individuals may perceive the flavor of a banana differently, we cannot assume that enlightenment or spiritual experiences are uniform across people. Each journey of self-realization or mystical insight is deeply personal and uniquely experienced.† Nevertheless, some of the more common (generic) experiences have been given names: among them are *jiànxìng* and *wù*.

For many Zen Buddhists, full spiritual awakening, or enlightenment—wù 悟 (Skt., *bodhi* बोधि; Jap., *satori*)—is considered the objective

---

* As a reminder, the Self I refer to here is not a "thing" that is actually "seen," but a linguistic tool used to describe a new mode of perception, one unmoderated by the ego. It's a tricky and paradoxical subject to discuss because the Self is that which sees the Self—that is, the Self is not something apart from the seer who sees it. Douglas Hofstadter explores this phenomenon in depth in his 1981 book, *The Mind's I: Fantasies And Reflections On Self & Soul*, and again in his more recent 2007 book, *I Am a Strange Loop*.

† For a thoughtful academic examination of this topic, see Steven T. Katz's 1978 book, *Mysticism and Philosophical Analysis*, from the Oxford University Press.

and destination of practice. For Chinese chan, however, it's only an important wayside event on a much longer journey. Chan's ox-herding parable, for example, places the enlightenment experience early in the spiritual journey (Chapter 14). This does not, however, discount it as a critically important experience; after all, spiritual awakening is what is said to have released Siddhartha from his long struggle. It was an experience so profound for him that he devoted the rest of his life to helping others get there too; and because of his apparent passion and skill as a teacher, his efforts led to an entirely new religion. But religion is largely about social conformity, belief, and group dynamics, which Siddhartha seems to have had little interest in. The Buddhist canon, as presented by the sutra literature, suggests he just wanted people to wake up from their illusory existence to spare them the unnecessary grief it imposes.

He did not teach waking up in a void, however, nor did he teach it as a means to an end. Spiritual awakening was not a goal—the goal was to rise out of saṃsāra and free ourselves from duhkha: spiritual awakening happens because of our efforts to accomplish this. Most of us must do a lot of "housekeeping" first, which is why he presented the *Four Noble Truths* and the *Eightfold Path* (Chapters 1, 9). We first need to be properly motivated and live according to what is beneficial to ourselves and others.

Enlightenment is best viewed as a consequence rather than an objective of spiritual labor. The purpose of spiritual life is to unravel mysteries and transcend suffering. It's a fluid, evolving process. Along the way, experiences happen, but not because we are trying to *make* them happen—they happen when we are ready to receive them.

Jiànxìng and wù are two of many types of experiences we may have. Jiànxìng 見性 (Skt., *dṛṣṭi-svabhāva*) means "viewing our essential nature," and is one of the first awakening experiences. In Japanese, it's commonly referred to as *kensho*.* Wù 悟 is the full and complete realization of *not-self*, of egoless awareness. Following wù and a lengthy

---

* The origin of the term may come from the Greek word, κένωσις, kénōsis, meaning emptiness.

period of *cultivation*,* one may experience *divine union*—integration of male/female aspects of the psyche. Thereafter, one may gestate an *immortal fetus* 神胎 which can subsequently grow into a *divine—mercurial—child* (Figure 15).

Jiànxìng (Kensho)

Jiànxìng refers to an early transitory glimpse of Self. At the cellular level, I speculate, the brain, through intensive concentration and contemplation practice, creates progressively more synapses between neurons until a critical threshold is reached and the event occurs.† Yet, there are reports of people experiencing this state who had never meditated but instead had arrived there by channeling their intense desire to be relieved of suffering. Regardless of the mechanism involved, the experience imparts an exuberant emotional reaction that can leave us giddy for days.

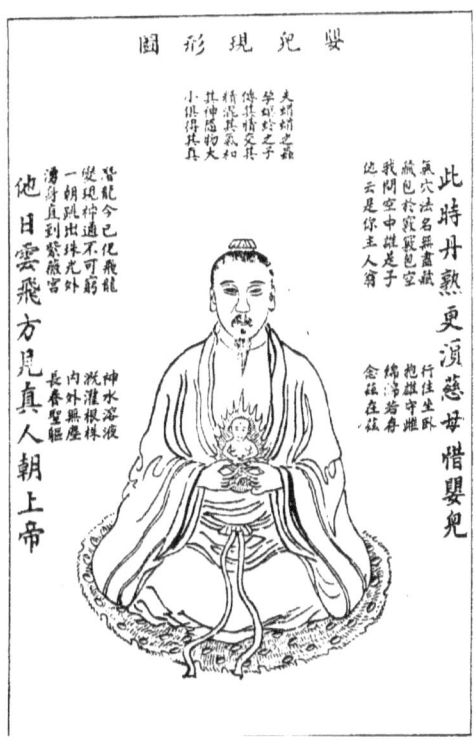

FIGURE 15. NEIDAN MEDITATION.

A 1615 illustration of the Taoist neidan meditation in which the immortal fetus 神胎 is gestated.

An event happened to me following a several-day retreat at a Japanese-style Zen Monastery in upstate New York in the early 1990s, which I later interpreted as jiànxìng. On the last day of the retreat, we were given *dokusan*, a private interview with the abbot. We were told

---

* By *cultivation*, I mean the act of paying attention to the Self, of progressively integrating the experience of Self-awareness into our lives.

† It's known that meditation increases the number of axons, or neural connections, that mediate consciousness, which may help explain this phenomenon (Chapter 13).

that tradition requires that all students rush to be first in line for the interview to express our intense desire for enlightenment. When the time came and the announcement was made for dokusan to begin, the congregation leapt to their feet and, in a frenzy, everyone rushed to be first in line (there were maybe thirty attendees). I thought: *Wow, they so want to be enlightened, why would I want to get in their way? I'm no more important than they are!* I watched as they nearly sprinted to get in line. I was stunned that Zen was being presented in the spirit of competition. It seemed selfish to want to be in front of another person who was so desperate to be ahead of me. Without hurrying, I got up and walked toward the end of the line. As I approached, another person came up behind me, looking horrified that she was so late to get there. I stepped aside to let her go ahead of me, and she bowed courteously with thanks. As the last person in line, I had plenty of time to think about what I would ask. Eventually, I was beckoned to enter the small room. The Abbot sat on a cushion in the middle of the floor and motioned for me to sit, then asked if I had a question for him. "You said Zen is a matter of life and death," I said, recalling his Dharma talk from earlier that day, "but the prospect of dying, of giving up everything for it, is terrifying. How do I overcome that fear?"

He sat silently for some moments, then replied, "Fear arises when the mind affixes on the future." He waited a few moments, then dinged a bell, indicating that the meeting was over and that I was to get up and leave.

The consequence of this brief encounter was, mysteriously, elation. I can't say why, but I became uncontrollably giddy. While others around me were looking gloomy and despondent, I wanted to jump for joy for no particular reason. For weeks to follow, I was euphoric. Reflecting on the experience later, in Chan parlance, I considered that it may have been a first brief encounter with Self—jiànxìng.* Whether or

---

* I quickly learned not to discuss personal experiences such as these with other people. People unfamiliar with mysticism think it's crazy-talk, and those with only intellectual knowledge of the subject—those who have not yet had such experience—either become jealous or think you are faking. Only people who have had such experiences can relate to them.

not this was the case, such experiences illustrate both the irrationality and emotionality of the spiritual domain.

WÙ (ENLIGHTENMENT OR SATORI)

> To know yourself as the Being underneath the thinker, the stillness underneath the mental noise, the love and joy underneath the pain, is freedom, salvation, enlightenment.
>
> - Eckhart Tolle

Many people equate Zen with a quest for enlightenment, or spiritual awakening, wù. In fact, the popular *Vocabulary* website states the first definition of Zen as a "school of Mahāyāna Buddhism asserting that enlightenment can come through meditation and intuition rather than faith," and the second as "a Buddhist doctrine that enlightenment can be attained through direct intuitive insight." While subjective—such experiences belong only to the people who have them—anecdotal evidence suggests that enlightenment is a real and profound experience for all who encounter it. But enlightenment is neither the objective of chan (which is freedom from duhkha), nor is it the sole life-altering experience on the journey. It's just one of many. To describe or define chan—or zen—as a journey to enlightenment is like describing a bus route by one of the first stops on its route.

Enlightenment is not something we can will ourselves to. From my experience and all direct accounts I have heard, it happens radically, suddenly, and unexpectedly, and only when we are ready for it. It can be such a profound experience that we may be stupefied, dazzled, and left with an afterglow that can last weeks or even months.*

---

* As discussed earlier, some people express a concern that they need a master to validate the experience of enlightenment. If we feel the need for validation, however, then we have not experienced enlightenment. It would be akin to taking a roller-coaster ride and, after getting off, searching for someone to validate the experience: *Did I just take a roller-coaster ride?* Some argue that the potential for self-delusion is high, however; that what we may think of as an enlightenment experience is not, and that only one who has experienced enlightenment can know. To assume, however, that one who has experienced enlightenment can validate someone else's experience is equally specious. The experience, after all, belongs exclusively to the one who has it: one person cannot get inside the mind of another (despite some who claim to have that magical power).

But the nature of enlightenment is rarely discussed.

Chanida Jantrasrisalai summarizes enlightenment from his understanding of the view presented in the Buddhist canon, as "the spiritual attainment of a Buddhist noble state which is relevant to the person's 'being freed from defilements, either to a certain degree or to the fullest degree."[379] This description, however, says nothing about the experience itself; it only suggests a possible consequence of the experience in the religious context of Buddhism.

Some people describe the experience of enlightenment as a "turning-over" of their minds, while others describe themselves as disappearing—losing all connection with time and space. The *Śuraṅgama Sūtra* describes it as "returning intellect to its source," and adds that "... by the attainment of the 'turning about' in the deepest seat of consciousness, self-realization of Noble Wisdom is fully entered into."[380] In the Yogācāra tradition, it's termed "turning around of the basis" (*Āśtayaparāvṛtti*) in which a person experiences "... a sudden revulsion, turning, or re-turning of the *ālayavijñāna** back into its original state of purity [...] the Mind returns to its original condition of non-attachment, non-discrimination and non-duality;"[381] it is "the basis on which one relies, revolves, and turns into a different basis (or non-basis); the ground itself on which one stands, overturns, revealing a new world, illuminated by a new light."[382]

Years before I had read anything about the enlightenment experience, and after months of intensive hua-tou practice (Chapter 12), I had a peculiar experience. After some research and consultation with others, I identified it as a possible candidate for wù, or enlightenment.†
The event occurred within the first few minutes of sitting-meditation

---

* See Chapter 4. In the Yogācāra tradition, this means "foundation consciousness," which is "an unspecified, nonobstructive, individual consciousness that underlies all cognition, cognizes the same objects as the cognitions it underlies, but is a nondetermining cognition of what appears to it and lacks clarity of its objects" (Berzin n.d.).

† My approach to chan was different from that common with popular Zen training, which emphasizes the attainment of enlightenment. Throughout my chan training, I was not trying to attain anything. I was simply investigating and exploring the mind. After this experience, I was interested in understanding it, but did not frame it in terms of having attained or accomplished anything.

one sunny summer afternoon in 1993. I suddenly felt like my mind had turned inside out and rotated counterclockwise (which, yes, makes no sense). I remember exclaiming to myself, *What was that!?* I stood up and paced about the house, which was thankfully absent of people, contemplating what had just happened. Awareness had shifted in a way I didn't expect or understand. The experience I had labeled as jiànxìng had made me giddy, but this brief event left me awestruck and bewildered. It seemed like the world I had known had vanished. Everything around me seemed real and not real at the same time.

I didn't know if the new way of seeing was temporary or permanent, but I desperately wanted it to be permanent. Over the next several weeks I experimented with it. Since I couldn't always be "tuned in" to this new mind—life requires that attention must sometimes go to other things—I wanted to see if it was still there whenever I invoked it. It was. All it took was intention to go there, and the more I returned to it, the more present it seemed to become.* Whether or not this was an enlightenment experience, though, was irrelevant. The experience that asserted itself spoke to its own reality. Others have described similar experiences. Han Shan, for example, described an experience in which his mind "overturned and shattered emptiness," awakening it from a dream:

> In an instant of thought, this chaotic mind was put to rest. Internally and externally, the sense faculties and objects became empty and clear. Overturning the body—emptiness is now shattered. The myriad forms and appearances arise and extinguish [in their own accord].[383]

> The objects of the material world are the props, sets and characters of a dream-drama. When one awakens, the stage vanishes. The players and the audience too, disappear. Waking up is not death. *What lives in a dream can die in a dream; but the dreamer has a real existence that doesn't perish with the dream.* All that is necessary is for him to stop

---

* Admittedly, stressful occasions can make it difficult to maintain this awareness. Stress alters the balance of numerous chemicals in the body, including glucocorticoids, catecholamines, growth hormone, and prolactin, all of which affect us emotionally and cognitively. Attention alone can't always bring this mind back to awareness, but it can return when we regain neuropsychological homeostasis. (Jerath R. 2014)

dreaming, to cease being fascinated by dream images, and to realize that he has merely been a dreamer.[384]

Whatever the description of experiences like these, to those who have had them, they assert themselves with great impact and meaning. Description beyond this is futile. Yet, if we take this collection of expressions of spiritual experience to represent something called *"enlightenment,"* or *"spiritual awakening,"* we can offer an analogy.

Enlightenment: an analogy

Susan Barry, a professor of neuroscience at a prominent college in the United States, was born cross-eyed, limiting her sight to only two dimensions instead of three. At a party on one fateful day, Dr. Barry happened to meet Dr. Oliver Sacks, another neuroscientist and author, and they struck up a conversation on the topic of stereoscopic vision, which was a topic of Dr. Sacks' lifelong passions. Dr. Barry explained to Dr. Sacks that she had no stereoscopic vision and added, "But aside from that, I'm pretty normal. I see what other people see." Dr. Barry recounted, "…he looked very seriously at me and he said, do you think you can imagine what it's like to see the world with two eyes? And I said, yes, of course, I can imagine that. I'm a college professor, I teach about it in class. So, yes, I think I know exactly what it is I'm missing."[385] In time, Dr. Barry visited a developmental optometrist and underwent intensive treatment in an attempt to correct her vision. After three weeks of difficult and demanding therapy sessions she recounted what happened one day when she got into her car: "…I glanced down at the steering wheel—I was sitting in the driver's seat and the steering wheel was floating in front of the dashboard…it was in its own three-dimensional space. I had never had that type of perception before and I didn't believe it, because I knew that this was not possible."[386]

Before long, Dr. Sacks received an excited letter from Dr. Barry: "Dear Dr. Sacks, you asked me this question, I gave you this answer, and I was completely wrong." She recounted to him in great detail the changes that happened when she suddenly began seeing in stereo. Dr.

Sacks recounted later: "Consciously, for the first time in her life, after 50 years of being stereo blind, she had suddenly gained a sense."[387]

Dr. Barry recounts her first experience in a snowfall after gaining stereoscopic vision:

> ...it was one of those late winter snows with big, thick snowflakes coming down very lazily, and I could see each snowflake in its own three-dimensional space, and there was space between each snowflake, and it was like this beautiful, three-dimensional dance, and I had this real sense of being within the snowfall.
>
> Prior to that, before my therapy, if I looked at a snowfall, all the snowflakes fell in one plane, slightly in front of me, and I was not really part of the snowfall, I was looking into the snowfall. And now, I had the sense of being within the snowfall—in the midst of the snowfall—all these beautiful flakes just falling all around me, and I just was completely filled with a sense of joy.[388]

While the quality of the experience of enlightenment is surely different from that of suddenly gaining the ability to see an additional dimension, there are several correlates with Dr. Barry's experience: 1) the three-dimensional world was there all along, she just was unable to experience it; 2) because of her training and study, she was convinced beforehand that she could imagine what it was like to see in three dimensions, but it turned out she was completely wrong; 3) it required hard work, faith in the program, and commitment to undergo the rigorous treatment required to enable her to eventually see in three dimensions; 4) the treatment allowed her to experience a new domain of awareness previously closed to her; and 5) the new sense brought joy and awe to her life that was totally unexpected.

Like the experience of suddenly being able to see in three dimensions, enlightenment brings a penetrating and sudden shift in awareness. There are profound consequences, both immediate and long-term. Like Dr. Barry, we may feel a tremendous sense of awe at the new view. We immediately understand why it's said that before enlightenment we are already enlightened, we just don't realize it: what we attain is not something that was not previously there, it was there all along but we were just unable to see it.* And just as one who might meet Dr. Barry would have no idea if she saw in three dimensions or not, neither can a person know if another has experienced enlightenment or not, because it's a purely personal and subjective experience.

When we review our actions, thoughts, desires, and attitudes from our life prior to the enlightenment experience, we recognize how deluded we were, not because we were stupid or bad, but because we were ignorant. We didn't see the big picture clearly because we were wrapped up in our confined and confused way of seeing the world, a way subjugated by a cloud of opinions, desires, attitudes, and self-righteousness. The newly discovered mind permits new ways of seeing and experiencing the world. If we are adequately motivated, exploration of this new mind can go on for days, weeks, or even years. Eventually, with continued cultivation, the new dimension of seeing becomes normalized: it may then no longer be possible to remember what the experience of life was like before the event, or recognize that others don't experience and understand the world as we do. As with learning anything new, once it has been learned there is no unlearning it. Like a young child recognizing her own reflection in a mirror for the first time, the new perspective is there to stay.

Enlightenment, most likely, doesn't depend on meditation, but meditation can help prepare us for it and bring us toward it. It's also unlikely that enlightenment can be willfully forced to happen, or that we can apply any singular method to achieve it. In the annals of Chan, stories of enlightenment include the moment of hearing a bell ring, a voice yell, a stick snap, or the *Diamond Sūtra* read—seemingly ordinary events. Meditation helps put the mind in the right "place" to experience enlightenment, but it doesn't seem to lead to it in and of itself.

---

* Chan Master Ben Huan commented that not being enlightened "is like having no sight and having to feel your way around all day long. If your sight suddenly returned, and everything was discernible, this is like the attaining of enlightenment—a journey from not knowing to fully knowing. When the vision clears, the path can be clearly discerned and all obstacles overcome—nothing can bar your way" (B. H. Shakya 2003).

Enlightenment from a Christian perspective

There are also apparent cases of people spontaneously experiencing enlightenment who had never formally meditated, at least not in the Buddhist sense. One comes from Bernadette Roberts, a Christian mystic.* In her book *The Experience of No-Self: a Contemplative Journey*, she describes her spiritual awakening, which happened one day while sitting along the edge of a river watching wood float by:

> With neither reason nor provocation, a smile emerged on my face, and in the split second of recognition I "saw"—finally I saw and knew I had seen. I knew: the smile itself, that which smiled, and that at which it smiled, were One—as indistinguishably one as a trinity without division. And what I saw was as natural and spontaneous as a smile on a face—not another thing more. In my journal I called this "the grin-of-recognition."
>
> ...It must be understood, however, that I could not rejoice in what had been revealed because I could not grasp it or hang onto it. It was so utterly simple and so completely obvious it was impossible to understand why I had not seen it before; and yet, there is no way I could come to this seeing of my own accord—it had to be revealed.
>
> What I learned was that the unknown object (of the smile) was identical with the subject, and not only that, but the smile itself was identical with these—a threesome, in other words. And what is the smile? It is "that" which remains when there is no self. The smile is neither the unknown subject or object, yet it is identical with it. It is that aspect of the Unknown which is obviously manifest. The implications of this seeing are tremendous, and yet they cannot be grasped by the mind.
>
> ...Once I realized that what Is can never be an object to Itself (and thus, never a subject), I had the marvelous and unique key to seeing it all the time—which was by not looking at all. It was as if the moment of its vanishing was also the final and complete close-down of the relative mind, which then heralded a new way of seeing, knowing,

---

* During Roberts' last thirty years, she gave retreats titled "The Essence of Christian Mysticism," for which the theme was "Trinity, Christ, and Faith."

and acting because now, I had the key! Now I could understand, and because of this, now I could rejoice. It seems that as long as the mind is viable it needs to enter into some form of understanding, otherwise the greatest revelation, while it would not go unnoticed, could not enter into the fullness of its human manifestation.[389]

Roberts' description of spiritual awakening illustrates the need we have to understand and process such experience intellectually: to create or employ a model to help us comprehend it and bring it more fully to consciousness—to reify it. She expresses her entrance into the self-referential loop of Self-discovery—the unification of the smile, that which smiled, and that at which it smiled—as one "thing," what many Buddhists would term Buddha-nature, or Self.

Roberts' (Christian) expression of the enlightenment experience has clear similarities with Han Shan's (Buddhist) expression—both express the self-referential aspect of the mind seeing itself:

> Actualized-Enlightenment results from solid and sincere practice when you reach an impasse where the mountains are barren and waters are exhausted. Suddenly, [at the moment when] a thought stops, you will thoroughly perceive your own mind. At this time, you will feel as though you have personally seen your own father at a crossroad—there is no doubt about it! It is like you yourself drinking water. Whether the water is cold or warm, only you will know, and it is not something you can describe to others. This is genuine practice and true Enlightenment. Having had such experience, you can integrate it with all situations of life…[390]

Enlightenment & morality

Some contemporary Zen teachers have suggested that enlightenment and morality are the same thing, implying that a moral life is an enlightened life, and that enlightenment without morality is not true enlightenment.* Others have stated that enlightenment reflects the perfection

---

* For example, John Daido Loori wrote, "Enlightenment and morality are one. Enlightenment without morality is not true enlightenment. Morality without enlightenment is not complete morality" (Loori 1996, 24).

of ethics.* Such views place the cart in front of the horse, in my view. Enlightenment is the event (or events) of awakening to our True Self, our Buddha-nature, of seeing a previously hidden dimension of reality. After we have had this experience, it doesn't mean that we are not capable of doing silly or stupid things, or making decisions that may inadvertently harm another person or ourselves. Enlightenment doesn't mean we suddenly become perfect human beings. Morality in Chan develops from working with the first seven of the Eight Noble Truths.† Dissociating chan, the mystical practice, from its Buddhist principles creates enormous dangers.‡

Enlightenment or enlightened?

Wù refers to a mind that is "spiritually awake," but it is more practical and relevant to use the term to describe the awakening experience rather than a permanent state of being. To label someone as enlightened or not is inherently misleading—not only because it suggests that a person

---

* For example, in an interview with Brian Daizen Victoria in 2015, Damien Keown, Emeritus Professor of Buddhist Ethics at the University of London, said: "Complete enlightenment must include the perfection of ethics. You can't disentangle ethics from wisdom, and if you try to do that, you achieve something that is not really an authentically Buddhist state of awakening" (B. D. Victoria 2015, 197).

† It's commonly thought that Buddhism's moral foundation is defined by specific *precepts*, vows taken when we enter the monastic tradition. Their origin is thought to be the *Brahmajāla Sūtra*, also known as the *Brahmajāla Bodhisattva śīla Sūtra* (Fàn Wǎng Púsà Jiè Jīng 梵網菩薩戒經). Contemporary historians generally consider this to be an apocryphal Chinese text written during the 5th century (see, for example, Buswell, 1990, 8). Sources for its content may lie in the *Prátimokṣa* (Chapter 1). The Buddha's Eightfold Path, as one of his principal teachings, requires that we penetrate into the fundamental motivations behind our actions and thoughts and work toward perfecting them. From this, commensurate moral action arises (Chapter 21). As far as we know, the Buddha did not issue a set of rules for people to follow mindlessly. Even the Buddhist precepts, created long after his death to guide ethical conduct, are not meant to be applied without due consideration to their purpose and meaning.

‡ For example, the reader may recall from Chapter 7 that many prominent Zen masters during the Meiji Restoration and later—all of whom were considered to be fully enlightened—were fervent proponents of war and killing, and some publicly bragged of their brutal killings and tortures on the battlefield. It could be argued that they acted ethically in the sense that they were abiding by "right action" according to societal values imposed by Shintō Imperialism. That they acted immorally, however, has rarely been questioned by the rest of the world. From my experience with Japanese-style Zen in the United States, the Noble Truths and Eightfold Path are often ignored, if not disregarded entirely, by many of its representatives.

who has experienced enlightenment and become aware of Self is fundamentally different, but also because it often conveys the impression that such a person has attained some kind of superhuman status, living beyond the ordinary human condition.

A related misconception, commonly expressed in Japanese Zen, is the belief that someone who has experienced enlightenment has completed the spiritual journey. This notion contradicts both the sutra literature and the extensive writings of prominent Chan masters over centuries, which emphasize that enlightenment is not a final destination but part of an ongoing process.

Furthermore, in both Zen and Chan traditions, enlightenment is often equated with the celestial Buddha—an idealized perfection of being. This perspective has caused significant problems throughout history. When someone identified as "enlightened" is regarded as morally infallible, it places them on an unrealistic pedestal. As we'll examine in Chapter 21, this dynamic can lead Zen and Chan teachers to internalize, consciously or unconsciously, the pressure to embody this impossible ideal of perfection, often resulting in psychological instability.

Even more troubling, the authority granted to teachers who adopt—or are perceived to embody—the role of a celestial Buddha has, in some cases, emboldened them to exploit their students financially, psychologically, and even sexually. This all too common abuse of power, and its devastating impact on spiritual communities, will be explored further in Part Four.

Encountering the Void

> Neither "void" nor "non-void" may be ascertained, nor both, nor either; they are spoken of only for the sake of expedient teaching (*prajñapti*).
>
> — Nāgārjuna

The term *Void* (*kōng* 空; Skt., *śūnyam*) is sometimes used to express the experience of samādhi, a state of undifferentiated awareness that arises when the personal-self, in both its localized and evolutionary forms, vanishes. We maintain awareness when we are in samādhi, despite there being no possessor of that awareness. In the Void of samādhi there is nothing left to define a self because the observer has fully fused with the observed. Distinctions of any kind no longer exist. This is not, in my experience, a state that can be maintained outside of meditation: when we exit meditation, we return to the world where the self again has agency.*

The experience of the Void may be as close to the experience of pure consciousness as we can get. Carl Jung offered this description:

> When we encounter the Void, we feel that it is primordial emptiness of cosmic proportions and relevance. We become pure consciousness aware of this absolute nothingness; however, at the same time, we have a strange paradoxical sense of its essential fullness.... While it does not contain anything in a concrete manifest form, it seems to comprise all of existence in potential form.... The Void transcends the usual categories of space and time, and lies beyond all dichotomies and polarities, such as light and darkness, good and evil, agony and ecstasy, singularity and plurality, form and emptiness, and even existence and nonexistence.... This metaphysical vacuum, pregnant with potential for everything there is, appears to be the cradle of all being, the ultimate source of existence. The creation of all phenomenal worlds is then the realization and concretization of its pre-existing potentialities. [391]

While the Void may defy meaningful description, experiences on chan's journey aren't limited to the psychological and metaphysical. There are physical experiences easily described, some of which I will present in the next chapter.

---

* Distractions of the physical world can easily divert attention away from Self-awareness. When we are not in meditation, the ego-self and Self coexist in proportions determined by our attention. Continued cultivation of Self-awareness is necessary to maintain its presence.

19

Physical Experiences

PHYSICAL EFFECTS ARE AS common to chan experience as psychological effects. When we begin chan training, we also begin conditioning our muscles and tendons for the physical demands of sitting still for extended periods of time. This can be a bit painful initially, but as we progress, the pain subsides and eventually disappears. As we become progressively adept with chan training methods, we may begin noticing other physical sensations, such as heat at the bottom of the spine (coccyx), tingling sensations in various parts of the body, and involuntary movements of the limbs, among others.

Chinese Buddhists use the Taoist alchemical model to interpret many of the physical effects that arise from meditation. Taoist alchemy envisions the body as a vessel within which an *essential energy* called Qi 氣 is circulated. Qi translates literally as *breath*, or *vital life energy*. Taoists employ specific and deliberate breathing practices to circulate it through a *microcosmic orbit* 小周天—an imagined network of energy channels in the body. Many of the same experiences described by Taoist alchemists are also encountered when using meditation practices that don't deliberately focus on circulating Qi.

A remarkably similar model which describes these experiences, and offers practices nearly identical to those used by Taoists, is Kuṇḍalinī ("coiled up energy") yoga, which is symbolized by a serpent.* From the Kuṇḍalinī Upanishad:

> The divine power,
> Kuṇḍalinī shines
> Like the stem of a young lotus;
> Like a snake, coiled round upon herself,
> She holds her tail in her mouth
> And lies resting, half asleep
> At the base of the body.[392]

In both the Chinese and Indian models, energy is harnessed in the lower sacrum and moves upward through a succession of *nodes*, which may correspond directly to nerve bundles called ganglions.[393] In the Indian yoga system, they are called *chakras* and *nadichakras*; in the Chinese Taoist system, these are variously called *gates*, *locks*, *energy centers* (*dantien*), and *junctions*. Regardless of the model employed, each presents a conceptual framework and methodology to assist in "awakening inner energy" and circulating that energy throughout the body. Some of the more common physical effects include: a tingling sensation in parts of the body, heat—sometimes extreme—in parts of the body or in the entire body, a rocking motion of the body, sexual arousal, involuntary jerks of the torso or limbs, sudden hot rushes of energy, and a sense that breathing has ceased.

The specific methods used to facilitate the circulation of energy are best tried with caution, or better, under the supervision of one who is experienced with them. If practiced the wrong way, the consequences can be unpleasant; for example, once the energy is fully flowing, it can be difficult to stop it. While chan practices don't generally involve such techniques, the activity of meditation can naturally lead to many of the

---

* What is popularly referred to as kundalini yoga today is a synthesis of other older forms of yoga, including hatha yoga, kriya yoga, tantric yoga, and laya yoga. The reader interested in learning more about kundalini yoga may enjoy *Kundalini: The arousal of the Inner Energy*, by Ajit Mookerjee, 1986, Destiny Books.

same effects described by Taoist alchemists and kundalini yogis. Since chan practices, however, don't seek to *force* Qi into circulation, there is less risk of getting into trouble—effects happen naturally when the mind and body are prepared and ready for them.

The general rule with chan is to allow physical sensations to arise and observe them without interfering. If sensations become frightening, we can back off, wait a day or two, then gently resume practice. Sometimes fear is warranted because we are engaging in an activity we aren't yet ready for. Other times, fear may simply be the ego's response to the prospect of annihilation, in which case we can ignore it and continue on. Careful reflection will help us distinguish between the two scenarios.

The physical effects of meditation, while often significant, generally pale in relation to the psychological and cognitive effects. It is, however, useful to know that the body responds in various ways to the meditative process. We won't be alarmed when we encounter physical responses to practice if we pay attention and remain a watchful spectator.

PART FOUR

Trials & Tribulations

The person who succeeds at anything has the realistic viewpoint at the beginning in knowing that the problem is large and that you have to take it a step at a time and you have to enjoy the step-by-step learning procedure.

– Bill Evans, 1966 interview

No serious undertaking is without challenges. For chan, fear of the unknown may be the biggest obstacle faced by newcomers. It takes immense courage to overcome it. Plato's analogy of the cave, written around 380 BC, offers insight into the problem. Imagine a group of people, Plato suggested, who have been prisoners since they were small children. They are shackled to the side of a wall in a cave and can look only straight ahead. Behind them a fire burns, casting shadows onto the cave-wall in front of them. Over time, they observe familiar repeated patterns and come to name them, describing and discussing them, identifying reality through them. One day they are released from their confinement and one of them ascends out of the cave. The others want nothing to do with leaving the safety of their home. Emerging into the open, the adventurer views the trees, grass, rocks, and sky for the first time and comes to the realization that the shadows he had thought of as reality were not reality at all. He had been duped! He descends back into the cave to tell his community about the wondrous world above. But when he arrives with the news, they tell him that the ascent must have ruined his sight. They would never leave their cave and, if anyone should try to make them, they would kill him.[394]

When we begin chan, we initiate an intimate encounter with ourselves. For most of us, there are lots of unpleasant things we would rather not look at—buried childhood traumas, repressed feelings of hate or despair, jealousy, guilt, insecurity, fear—and they all eventually come out as we delve inward. Our dream life may also become extraordinarily vivid and our emotional life fragile as we struggle to process feelings that had been buried years earlier. This is why it takes great courage, and a degree of fearlessness, to undertake chan. When repressed emotional shards expose themselves, we must *want* to see them, to allow them, and to release them to consciousness. Initially, it can be a painful process, but in short time we joyously discover that they are all fabricated, imagined chimera that, despite their seemingly great power, are lifeless the moment we expose them.

Most challenges encountered on chan's journey arise from the tension between our inner- and outer-lives. In Chapter 20, I discuss some common difficulties and suggest ways of working with them so they don't obstruct progress. In Chapter 21, I then examine some situations that can lead to significant problems and suggest ways to avoid them. These two chapters were written chiefly for readers who have a serious interest in taking up chan or who have previously participated with Chan or Zen independently or in groups. Others may not be able to relate easily to the topics discussed, many of which only make sense once we've embarked on the journey ourselves.

20

Hindrances

> Patience and perseverance have a magical effect before which difficulties disappear and obstacles vanish.
>
> – John Quincy Adams

ENGAGING WITH THE WORLD without taking adequate time to look within establishes conditions for many potential problems. We may, for example, come to feel isolated and alone, anxious, or depressed, without understanding the root cause. We may then turn further away from our Selves to engage even more with the world. It's an insidious process because we don't realize it's happening, and it brings every imaginable form of misery. The more we engage with the world while heedless of our inner lives, the more attachments to it are created and the deeper the Self retreats beneath the identity created from that engagement.

Perhaps this was in part why Shenhui objected to the "gradual method," which he derisively referred to as the "Northern school" teaching to distinguish it (and diminish it) from his approach (Chapter 4). The moment there is method (for example, formal seated training in a meditation hall), there is the mind that attaches to it, and that attachment becomes an obstacle when we mistake the method for the purpose it serves. But how do we go about "doing chan" without a method? We learn to develop awareness of the mind and not let latches drop into place. If we use a sitting practice, we don't attach ourselves to that practice, we do it because we want to know, to learn, to understand, and to discover, not because we want to do the seated practice for its own sake, or because we're trying to reach some imagined destination. This requires an open mind that fiercely desires to discover hidden truths. With this approach, any method becomes disposable, because it's not about the method but about where it takes us—once it's job is done we don't need it anymore. When we are thirsty, we fill a cup with water, drink it, then put it down. It's not about the cup, or even about the water, but about quenching our thirst.

This chapter describes some of the latches that can cause us to get stuck, and suggests how we might recognize and break away from them.

Expectations

Studying chan is like studying Mars with binoculars. We can know there's something there, but we can't know much about it in any detail. This leaves the imagination free to run wild with speculations that can easily become misconstrued as facts.

For example, one of the first things we learn about chan is that we need to allow the ego, i.e., our personal sense of "self," to be subsumed by something else called "Self." Until we have accomplished this, however, the idea seems meaningless, if not nonsense: *How can I have another self? How can there be both a true self and a not true self?* If we want to find out, we do the work. We don't have to believe it, we can just investigate it to see if it *might* be true. At the beginning, we can simply think of that "other Self" as something unknown: if we create a mental image of Self, we'll invoke a fiction that misrepresents it and we can erroneously pursue that misrepresentation, never finding it.*

---

*Keep in mind, however, that ultimately there is neither a self nor a Self: these are *expedient means* in Buddhism meant to help guide the mind in the right direction. They are devoid of intrinsic nature.

It's natural when starting a spiritual regimen to have expectations of what will happen as we proceed. Myths about enlightenment, for example, are pervasive. Yet, whatever we think it is, if we hold enlightenment out in front of us as if it's something we must attain, allowing it to become the principle motivation for practice, we'll end up chasing an elusive phantasm of our own imagination. Like the pot of gold at the end of a rainbow, we'll never find it. Enlightenment is not something we can think ourselves to, nor is it something that's achieved. Achievement requires an ego—an actor. Enlightenment is an opening of awareness that arises from ego-less, actor-less perception. Motivation for practice must come from other sources, such as the desire to get out of a dark place we're in (samsāra), an overwhelming sense of urgency to understand the nature of duhkha, a pervasive desire to expand our awareness and understanding, or an urgent, heartfelt desire to help others. Linji had this to say to people who are seeking in the wrong direction:

> I say to you there is no buddha, no dharma, nothing to practice, nothing to enlighten to. Just what are you seeking in the highways and byways? Blind men! You're putting a head on top of the one you already have. What do you yourselves lack? Followers of the Way, your own present activities do not differ from those of the patriarch-buddhas. You just don't believe this and keep on seeking outside. Make no mistake! Outside there is no dharma; inside, there is nothing to be obtained.[395]

Belief

> A belief proves to me only the phenomenon of belief, not the content of the belief.
>
> – C.G. Jung

Belief wields tremendous power. It's easy to take a position on a subject and identify ourselves with it, yet we rarely consider whether our positions reflect reality, our interpretations of reality, or our desires for what we want reality to be. What if what we believe to be ultimate truths are only partially true, or even altogether false? What if the anchor of security we get from our beliefs is nothing other than our own personal illusion? Beliefs help define us to ourselves—they create a narrative for self-identity—so it's understandable that letting go of them might seem absurd.

To abandon beliefs requires that we cease to identify ourselves with them. It doesn't mean we become immoral because we no longer *believe* in not killing, or no longer *believe* in not lying; it means we don't kill because we don't kill, we don't lie because we don't lie. Belief does not need to be involved, just action and its counterpart, non-action. Healthy moral action and thought are the default conditions we return to once the ego-self relinquishes control to the Self—assuming we continue cultivating awareness of that Self, and assuming we don't relinquish agency to another.[396] The selfish ego, which engages in actions and thoughts that serve its own purposes (or provide agency for another's purposes), sets up the conditions from which immoral action—action which harms ourselves or others—can arise.

RELINQUISHING AUTONOMY

When we fall under the spell of a religious or spiritual leader, we relinquish our autonomy to them; we forfeit our personal agency and give it to someone else. This can hinder spiritual growth and lead to other, more significant problems.

The process may begin by projecting the hero archetype, one of the most common psychological projections, especially in religions. It could be a harmless projection; we may, for example, meet a famous actor, musician, or political figure and fawn over them, or shake the hand of a celebrity and eagerly replay the exciting event to our friends. But similar projections upon religious figureheads can lead to unanticipated problems. Just as patients may develop excessive feelings for their doctor or therapist—the phenomenon of *transference*—we may similarly project grandiose feelings toward our teacher. It may begin in a benign way, when we attribute reverent titles to them such as master, guru, sensei, or venerable. Such titles aren't necessarily indicative of projection—they can be used to show respect, to acknowledge skills, knowledge, and kindness—yet reverence can lead to blind allegiance, which can turn disastrous.

The Jonestown Massacre of 1978, an orchestrated mass suicide and murder, offers a striking example of the dangers of projection upon a religious figurehead.*

In the massacre, 909 congregants of the Peoples Temple died, 30% of whom were children and adolescents. The mastermind behind the massacre, Jim Jones, had for years encouraged his congregants to revere him as a supremely spiritual and righteous man. Over time, he forced his followers to practice drinking Kool-Aid at events he called "white nights," telling them that it might be laced with cyanide. Imbued with power gained from his followers' reverence, he one day asked them to drink Kool-Aid (it was actually a similar product called Flavor Aid), but this time it actually *was* laced with cyanide. As they had practiced, they were told to first give it to their children to drink before drinking it themselves. Desensitized, they drank it and quickly died. Today "drinking the Kool-Aid" has become a phrase commonly used to refer to the danger we submit ourselves to when we become followers of an ideology or person without questioning what we're doing, or, more generally, when we accept something blindly without considering it critically.

This is an example of what can happen when we project the savior (hero) archetype upon someone who represents a religion or ideology: we can be harmed psychologically, emotionally, spiritually, and even

---

* Carl Jung believed that the power of projection is enormous and its effects insidious. "Just as we tend to assume that the world is as we see it, we naïvely suppose that people are as we imagine them to be... All the contents of our unconscious are constantly being projected into our surroundings, and it is only by recognizing certain properties of the objects as projections or imagos that we are able to distinguish them from the real properties of the objects... Cum grano salis, we always see our own unavowed mistakes in our opponent. Excellent examples of this are to be found in all personal quarrels. Unless we are possessed of an unusual degree of self-awareness, we shall never see through our projections but must always succumb to them, because the mind in its natural state presupposes the existence of such projections. It is the natural and given thing for unconscious contents to be projected" (Jung 1948, par. 507).

physically. Such projection can lead us to blindly follow the person upon whom we're projecting, to the extent, even, of harming ourselves or others.* This type of projection can also leave us susceptible to manipulation and coercion from spiritual authorities who seek power over us by demanding sexual and other "favors."†

This topic is worth belaboring because most of us believe we are immune to such behaviors—that we would never harm another person, much less kill someone, nor that we would allow ourselves to be sexually exploited, just because we were given directions to do so by an authority figure.

The facts are quite different.

Stanley Milgram performed seminal research in 1963 to try to understand why so many people under the Nazi regime could brutally torture and kill. In Milgram's experiment, volunteers were recruited for the study and told the project was a lab experiment to "investigate learning." There were forty males ranging from twenty to fifty years of

---

* Some readers may remember David Koresh's Branch Davidians, who led a fifty-one-day standoff with the FBI in 1993 in Waco, Texas. It ended in a raid by the FBI, during which a fire (thought by the FBI to be started by the Branch Davidians to avoid being taken) took the lives of 76 people. Other readers may remember Marshall Applewhite and Bonnie Nettles, who led Heaven's Gate and masterminded a group suicide by preaching that only through death could their followers reach an extra-terrestrial spacecraft they believed followed behind the comet Hale-Bopp. Thirty-nine followers took their lives. Other examples are numerous.

† As an example, a group of long-time students of Sogyal Rinpoche, the famous Tibetan Dzogchen lama in the Nyingma sect and author of *The Book of Living and Dying*, received a letter from eight of his long-time students complaining of his abusive behavior. In it they write: "You use your role as a teacher to gain access to young women, and to coerce, intimidate and manipulate them into giving you sexual favors. The ongoing controversies of your sexual abuse that we can read and watch on the Internet are only a small window into your decades of this behavior" (Standlee, et al. 2017). They then give an account of a young, vulnerable, attractive woman who attended one of his retreats following the death of her father, from which she was traumatized. "Sogyal seduced her, wearing her down over a period of hours in spite of her saying that she did not want to cheat on her husband—but Sogyal persisted, insisting that having sex with him would benefit her father's karma. She eventually became part of Sogyal's harem. [...] For several months Dierdre put her everyday life on hold and travelled with Sogyal as his servant, sex partner and arm candy. She recounts how the smile on Sogyal's face and the unctuous charm of his public presentation vanished the moment they were hidden from view: 'There must have been about 10 women in his inner circle,' she says, and it was our job to attend to his every need. We bathed him, dressed him, cooked for him, carried his suitcases, ironed his clothes and were available for sex. He was a tyrant. Nothing we did was ever good enough'" (Ibid.).

age; some held unskilled jobs and others were professionals. They were each paid $4.50 for showing up.

Before the experiment started, the volunteer was introduced to another "volunteer," who was actually one of the researchers (e.g., Milgram himself). The two drew straws to determine who would be the "learner" and who would be the "teacher." In fact, the draw was rigged so that the volunteer was always the teacher, the researcher always the learner. A third person in the experiment was the "experimenter," who was played by a professional actor.

Two rooms were used: one had an electric shock generator, which would be hooked up to the learner (the researcher disguised as a volunteer) who was strapped into a chair; the other room was for the teacher, the actual volunteer and subject of the experiment.

Once the learner was strapped into the chair and electrodes attached, he was given a set of word pairs to learn. As the experiment progressed, the teacher would speak a word to the learner and the learner would have to give the corresponding word associated with it, selecting from a set of four choices. Every time the learner made a mistake, the teacher was told to administer an electric shock, making progressively stronger shocks each time. The learner intentionally gave wrong answers most of the time.

Of course, there was no electric shock given, but the learner pretended otherwise. The shock generator had thirty switches covering voltages from 15 volts (small shock) to 450 volts (extreme shock, danger).

When the teacher refused to give a shock, the experimenter would encourage him to do so using one of four specific prods/orders. If one didn't work, they would move on to the next one until the teacher complied and administered the shock. The prods:

Please continue.

The experiment requires you to continue.

It is absolutely necessary for you to continue.

You have no other choice but to continue.

During shocks, the learner would convincingly scream, yell, whimper, cry, and beg for the shocks to stop.

The results were remarkable. Despite often thinking that they were actually killing the learner, despite believing that they were administering extreme pain and suffering, 65% of the participants delivered shocks all the way up to the maximum 450 volts, and 100% delivered shocks to at least 300 volts.

This experiment, and many variations on it, have been carried out since Milgram's work in the early 1960s, and all have strongly supported the conclusion that people are prone to perform extreme acts of violence against others if told to do so by someone they consider a valid authority figure. These studies suggest that obedience to authority is ingrained in us to the extent that we can easily be led to disregard moral boundaries.

In 1974, Milgram reasoned that we have two opposing states of behavior when in social situations: an autonomous state and an agentic state. In the autonomous state, people are guided by their own actions and take responsibility for them. In the agentic state, we allow others to guide our actions and pass off the consequences of those actions to whomever is giving the orders. In this latter case, we act as agents for another person's will, i.e., we effectively disown our actions and are thereby capable of doing most anything.*[397]

Chan training methods encourage us to sever our attachments to everything, including other people, regardless of their social, religious, or political status, according to Chan master Linji Yixuan, founder of the Linji (Jap. Rinzai) school of Chan:

---

* D. T. Suzuki suggested that the agentic state gave Buddhist warriors a superior ability to fight when he wrote: "...every pious Buddhist knows that there is no such irreducible a thing as ego. Therefore, as he steadily moves onward and clears every obstacle in the way, he is doing what has been ordained by a power higher than himself; he is merely instrumental. In him there is no hatred, no anger, no ignorance, no prejudice. He has lost himself in fighting" (D. T. Suzuki 1904, 181). In other words, when we can act without any obstructions, according to Suzuki, we enter an agentic state whereby our actions are no longer ours, but guided by an external actor, a "higher power," and we become instruments of that higher power. From Suzuki's prolific writings, we know he considered that higher power to be the Emperor of Japan, "a power greater than god."

> Followers of the Way of Chán, if you want to get the kind of understanding that accords with the Dharma, never be misled by others. Whether you are facing inward or facing outward, whatever you meet up with, just kill it! If you meet a Buddha, kill the Buddha. If you meet a patriarch, kill the patriarch. If you meet an arhat, kill the arhat. If you meet your parents, kill your parents. If you meet your kinfolk, kill your kinfolk. Then for the first time you will gain emancipation, will not be entangled with things, will pass freely anywhere you wish to go.[398]

Of course, we don't literally kill anybody—that's just metaphor. What we do is sever our attachments to them: we cease projecting. The term "kill" emphasizes the degree to which those attachments must be severed and suggests the immense effort it can take to do so.

It's easy to imagine that we are immune to projection, but it's human nature and we are easily blind to it.

Consider marriage. Many people fall in love, get married, and then get divorced after only a few years. The first phase of the relationship in these situations is often the projection phase; that is, we "fall madly in love," the term "madly" being suggestive of the complete irrationality of the experience. During this phase, we see the other person not as he or she is, but as we desire to see him or her; that is, we project an ideal form (in this case, the anima or animus) upon the other person. When we discover months or years later that this other person doesn't live up to our ideal, we fall out of love, sometimes tragically. We may even wonder why we married the person in the first place. *How could I have been so blind!**

We might consider that a person who practices Chan would be naturally immune to problems with projection since projection arises from desire and the Buddha's Second Noble Truth asserts that desire is the ultimate cause for suffering. Yet some Zen and Chan groups operate in ways that encourage projection, in much the same fashion that Jim

---

* According to the World Population Review, around 50% of married couples in the United States end in divorce. The country has the sixth highest divorce rate in the world.

Jones did with his Peoples Temple congregation; their leaders encourage congregants to exalt them, rewarding those who do by putting them in higher social positions within the group and punishing those who don't through a variety of subtle (and sometimes not so subtle) means. Such leaders may assign themselves titles to impress, such as roshi, master, guru, or venerable,* and adopt the role of a saintly person. They may then project this altered self-image back upon their congregants, reinforcing the participation mystique that serves to support their status in the community.† Their congregants, like those at Jonestown, may become so caught up in the bi-directional projection that they are unable to see the forest for the trees; they may lose their autonomy and become agentic actors, subject to the whims of another.‡ Those who become aware of what's happening may escape unharmed, but others may not be so lucky. The last few decades are replete with examples of such crimes to Zen/Chan, from sexual and psychological abuses to the confiscation of large sums of donated money for extravagant personal use. These abuses often go ignored or forgiven by congregants, being attributed to the behaviors of an "enlightened being" whose actions are, by implicit definition, "beyond the understanding of the unenlightened."[399]

In *Coming Down from the Zen Clouds*, Stuart Lachs§ documents many scandals in Zen centers as they pertain to teachers' abuses of

---

* Such titles are more appropriately bestowed upon a teacher by others as a show of respect rather than assumed by oneself: the latter suggests ego-inflation and grandiosity, qualities which aren't well suited for a person in a position of spiritual authority.

† Carl Jung: "It frequently happens that the object offers a hook to the projection, and even lures it out. This is generally the case when the object himself (or herself) is not conscious of the quality in question: in that way it works directly upon the unconscious of the projicient. For all projections provoke counter-projections when the object is unconscious of the quality projected upon it by the subject" (Jung 1948, para. 519).

‡ Paul Hagus, for example, commented in an interview after he left the Church of Scientology, "I was a part of this for thirty years before I spoke out. I felt deeply ashamed. Why didn't I do it earlier? Why didn't I look earlier" (Wright 2013)?

§ Stuart Lachs has been a Zen practitioner for nearly five decades. Following a career in mathematical physics at Bell Labs, he has been a member of Tassajara Zen Center outside San Francisco and of Sheng-yen's Chan Center in New York City. Mr. Lachs has also spent time in monasteries in Korea, Japan, and Taiwan. He performed as head monk and head of the Board of Directors at Walter Nowick's Moon Spring Hermitage in Maine, where he gave instruction in meditation and social and ceremonial protocols. In the 1990s he became interested in academic perspectives on Zen, with special emphasis on institutional history,

authority. Speaking as a knowledgeable insider, and someone who has done a tremendous amount of research on the topic, Lachs contends that such abuses are abundant and widespread within North American Zen centers:

> Beginning in 1975 and continuing to this day, a series of scandals has erupted at one Zen center after another revealing that many Zen teachers have exploited students sexually and financially. This list has included, at various times, the head teachers at The Zen Studies Society in New York City, the San Francisco Zen Center, the Zen Center of Los Angeles, the Cimarron Zen Center in Los Angeles, the now-defunct Kanzeon Zen center in Bar Harbor, Maine, the Morgan Bay Zendo in Surry, Maine, the Providence Zen Center and the Toronto Zen center. These are some of the largest and most influential centers. In most cases the scandals have persisted continually for years, or seemed to end only to arise again. At one center, for example, sex scandals have recurred for approximately twenty-five years with the same teacher involving many women. These scandals have been pervasive as well as persistent, affecting almost all major American Zen Centers.[400]

To illustrate the extent to which Zen trainees will follow their leader, heedless of that leader's psychological health or qualifications to lead, Lachs cites a story recounted to him by a correspondent from a small community Zen group.* A Zen retreat was held in 1998 under the guidance of someone he calls Carol. The sangha consisted of eight full-time and four part-time students. On the second day of the retreat, Carol added her name to a list of dead people to whom chants during the retreat were to be dedicated. Carol cancelled private interviews on the third day and instead took everyone to the movies. On the fourth day,

---

myth making, and the interaction between Zen and the state. His articles on the sociological context of institutionalized Zen have been widely distributed and well received in academic circles.

  * This story was recounted to Lachs from a sangha member during his research into 150 Zen centers across the United States. The account retold here, however, does not represent an isolated case. I have received accounts of other, equally disturbing, behaviors of group leaders from their victims.

Carol was mostly absent, but arranged for pizza and champagne to be served for dinner. On the fifth day, she told the sangha they would all be moving to Miami and to start learning Spanish. In the afternoon that day, Carol showed the Steven Spielberg film *ET* and later announced that the sangha would have a funeral ceremony to celebrate the death of her ego. Perplexed, the group nonetheless devised and performed a funeral ceremony for her. Afterward, she announced that she no longer had a name because she was dead. She said she should be called "Zen Ma." They drank champagne. In the midst of an impromptu Dharma talk, Carol stopped and asked if anyone in the room had negative energy. Lachs' correspondent said he did and that he was interested in being a student, but not someone's follower. Carol quickly dismissed him from the group. Soon after, Carol decided that her two long-time students were witches and also ordered them to leave. She got rid of her belongings and moved to Florida. Lachs comments,

> It is interesting to note that despite Carol's bizarre behavior and disjointed speech, not one person on the retreat left on their own initiative or raised a question to the teacher directly. The two senior students maintained that nothing was wrong when a question was raised privately about the teacher's mental state. After two months, Carol returned from Florida and all the people who had been on the retreat returned to study with her, except for the fellow who related this story to me. Again, I have related this story as an illustration, albeit an extreme one, of the sort of unquestioning respect and obedience given to the Zen teacher by Western students. It also underlines the fact that the imputed attainment of the teacher repeated in one Zen context or another, will more often than not outweigh or transform what is happening in front of the student's eyes. It should be noted, that Carol was not an officially sanctioned Master or roshi, but was functioning in that role without the actual title.[401]

Projecting on a teacher is extraordinarily easy to do, especially when we're not aware of the processes at work. It would be nice to think that we are safe once we check ourselves into a Zen or Chan center, but we are often only as safe as our own spiritual maturity and common sense allow us to be. If we are attentive to the nature of projection and watch for signs of our own projections, we can arrest the process before it gets a grip on us. It's dangerous to ever assume that a teacher is superior to us, or to others, in any way. We can respect and honor a person for their kindness, knowledge, and skills, but when we put a person on a pedestal, we are projecting, and this always invites danger.

When we succumb to this kind of projection, we'll eventually come out of it—all such attachments lose their hold on us over time—but coming out of it can be extremely painful.

In 2011, filmmaker Vikram Gandhi released the documentary *Kumaré*, in which he pretended to be a guru from India. He recorded his interactions with his congregation using hidden cameras. For the role, he grew a beard, acquired a fake accent, and invented a noble-sounding philosophy. His objective was to see if a "fake religion" could have the same effect on people as a "real" religion.* As people came to believe he was the spiritual authority he said he was, it took little time for him to establish a following of enthusiastic devotees. In this case, there seemed to be no significant harm done to any of his unsuspecting followers, except that when he finally revealed his secret to them, after a protracted, stunned silence, some stood up in apparent anger, humiliation, and disgust and left. In Kumaré, Gandhi created a persona that could be readily embraced by people needing to project the savior-archetype. The con, of course, was that his followers were an experiment to him and a means for him to gain fame (which he did—he went on to direct *Batman v Superman: Dawn of Justice*). It was less clear that he fundamentally cared about them rather than wanting to fool them in order to make a name for himself as a filmmaker.†

---

* Although this was his stated objective, he never explained how he differentiated "fake" from "real" religions. That distinction may have arisen from identifying himself as a "fake" guru, i.e., as insincere in the role he was playing, in contrast to other gurus who he perceived as "real," thus de facto sincere.

† While I consider Vikram Gandhi's deception immoral (it brought painful humiliation for many of his congregants who had invested their lives—their trust and confidence— in him), it's not in the same league as the offenses of the many religious teachers who have knowingly and intentionally caused harm by engaging in sexual affairs with (often married)

In the often-unruly world of Zen/Chan, there are many who have read books about it, have learned to sit quietly, and may have received ordination from a respected master or roshi, yet they may not have cracked the ego's fortress; they may profess knowledge of the subject and offer their ecclesiastical credentials as proof of their expertise to solicit followers, even when true spiritual experience is lacking. They may also be charismatic and exceptionally fine actors and cons, like Vikram Gandhi. There is often no way to recognize whether a teacher has true spiritual experience that can guide, or is merely inhabiting a role expected of someone in their particular position of authority.

It's worth noting that problems with Chan masters are not new, or even purely artifacts of Western culture. Alan Cole has observed that the Chan abbot Zongze, who produced the *Rules for Purity for a Chan Monastery* in 1103, was especially vocal in describing Chan abbots as both saintly and potential troublemakers. To Zongze, Cole writes,

> Chan abbots were living buddhas, to be sure! Just make sure to keep them under careful supervision, especially at the end of their service when they might be especially tempted to make off with monastic valuables.[402]... [Zongze] expected abbots to understand that their supposed buddha status was far from being a foolproof reality, and that they, as a class of individuals, also needed to be carefully policed. That is, on top of all the practical and literary knowledge required of abbots, Zongze asked that they come to regard their position with a thorough-going irony—admitting that even though the abbot was the spiritual leader of the community, he was also potentially one of the monastery's worst enemies.[403]

Zongze's Rules for Purity became widely adopted by Chan monasteries throughout China and offers an example of an operative check and bal-

---

students, by knowingly infecting their followers with HIV, by appropriating donated money for extravagant personal use, and by charging exorbitant fees for a few days of time with them. Gandhi's rhetoric, as he played the role of a guru, though insincere and exploitative, did not seem to convey a desire to harm his subjects.

ance placed on abbots to help prevent them from abusing power.[404] No such guidelines have been adopted in the West.

Guilt, Painful Memories & Moral Injury

None of us can go through life without doing things that, retrospectively, we wish we hadn't: perhaps we said something to someone that caused them pain or acted in an embarrassing or foolish way. Perhaps we did something morally wrong and are plagued with guilt, suffering the effects of moral injury.* Such events lodge in our psyches, sometimes becoming unconscious, sometimes lurking on the edge of consciousness. Memories of them can be triggered by things we read, places we go, or people we see or meet, causing us to re-experience the anguish of the past. Their effects can sabotage our relationships with ourselves and others and keep us stuck in a world of misery.

Guilt serves a valuable purpose if we learn from the causes and conditions that give rise to it, because it allows us to adjust our behavior so we don't repeat mistakes. But, if we fail to learn from those mistakes, or in some cases atone for them in some way, the emotional structures can recede to the subconscious and lurk there until they are released again. The process of re-experiencing the pain may repeat until a resolution finally happens and the emotional fragments are permanently dissolved—a process that can take immense courage and commitment.

Unless we live our lives with honest reflection and genuine action, we can end up in a troubled mess of anxiety and malcontent, the subconscious contents of our psyches dominating our moods, attitudes, and actions. To avoid this, we allow repressed emotions to flow into conscious awareness, embracing the traumatic episodes which plague us. While it can be painful and sometimes frightening, this process re-

---

* Moral injury describes the condition in which forces outside our control result in us acting against our deepest personal morals. People who commonly suffer moral injury are doctors who have to turn away sick patients because they have to tend to other, sicker, patients, and soldiers who kill other humans. The 2004 psychological thriller, *The Machinist*, starring Christian Bale, offers a poignant example of the depths of hell one who suffers from severe moral injury can descend into.

leases us from the trauma of our personal past and allows us to live more fully in the present. When painful memories erupt into consciousness, we allow them to do so, observe the source from which they arose, recognize them as empty, and let them pass without clinging to them: "This is not me." We release the latch.

Causes and conditions

If we retreat to the meditation pillow to escape the stress of life, using the time and space as a place to isolate ourselves from the world, we remove ourselves from the external sources that we perceive to be the cause of our suffering without realizing that the problem's cause is within, and that when we go to the pillow, we bring it along.

Chan requires that we investigate causes and conditions. If we experience fear, we delve into the nature and content of that fear and work to understand it, tearing it apart piece by piece until we understand its conditional existence. If we are feeling guilty, we examine the source of the guilt and seek to understand the conditions and causes that prompted our regretful behavior; if we made a mistake that caused it, we determine how we might atone for it to help rectify the damage. Each time we reconcile our actions with their results and understand the forces at work which led to our behavior we become a little humbler, a little more whole, and a little more at peace. We also begin to recognize and understand the process of error and guilt in others, becoming more aware of our shared humanity, which fosters compassion.

Checking ourselves into a meditation center for a retreat for a few days may be beneficial, but only if we have the right intentions and are properly prepared. If we truly want to explore the depths of our human condition, the meditation hall provides and exceptional environment to support our quest, but if we are seeking escape from our lives, we may be better off staying home and finding answers to what it is we are running away from, and why.

Judgment

Many of us start our spiritual journey by looking for a group to join, and in the modern world there are many to select from. How do we know which to choose? The Buddha's purported advice was simply to use good judgment and common sense:*

> Bhante, there are some ascetics and brahmins who come to Kesaputta. They explain and elucidate their own doctrines, but disparage, denigrate, deride, and denounce the doctrines of others. But then some other ascetics and brahmins come to Kesaputta, and they too explain and elucidate their own doctrines, but disparage, denigrate, deride, and denounce the doctrines of others. We are perplexed and in doubt, Bhante, as to which of these good ascetics speak truth and which speak falsehood.
>
> It is fitting for you to be perplexed, Kalamas, fitting for you to be in doubt; Doubt has arisen in you about a perplexing matter. Come, Kalamas, do not go by oral tradition, by lineage of teaching, by hearsay, by a collection of scriptures, by logical reasoning, by inferential reasoning, by reasoned cogitation, by the acceptance of a view after pondering it, by the seeming competence [of a speaker], or because you think: 'The ascetic is our guru.' But when, Kalamas, you know for yourselves: "These things are unwholesome; these things are blameworthy; these things are censured by the wise; these things, if accepted and undertaken lead to harm and suffering," then you should abandon them.[405]

"Good judgment" can sometimes lead us astray, however, for how can we judge something about which we know little? In such cases, we must rely on whether it feels right to us, and if it does, we may stick with it. If it doesn't, we may leave it and move on to something else. But if it

---

* The following excerpt is taken from the Aṅguttara Nikāya of the Tipiṭaka (Theravāda canon). The term "Bhante" means "venerable sir" in Pali and is used here to refer to the Buddha. "Kalamas" refers to the people or ruler of Kesaputta, now known as Kesariya. The Kālāma Sutta is contained within the Aṅguttara Nikāya, famous for the Buddha's warning against applying blind faith, dogmatism, and belief, and for encouraging independent thought and free inquiry.

feels right to the ego, that is, if it makes us feel good about ourselves, we should be suspicious. This may happen if we encounter a charismatic leader who uses archetypal projection tactics to lure people into his or her domain.*

Leaving the decision process up to us can potentially backfire, leading us to perpetually try new things and not stick with any. Instead of moving forward, we then may move in circles. It's often more productive to choose a path and stick with it, making it our own—to take what is good and wholesome and leave the rest behind.

Teachers

People seeking a spiritual path commonly begin by seeking an authority from whom they can trust to receive good guidance. While it can indeed be valuable to have coaching and encouragement from an experienced meditator, it's not always an experienced meditator who comes with the title of master, roshi, or guru. Titles can be bestowed indiscriminately, inherited†, or even self-invoked by people seeking the status and authority the title brings. Anyone can learn to meditate given adequate motivation and commitment, and instructions can be found in many texts. It can sometimes be safer to learn from a book than from an instructor; without true depth of spiritual experience, an instructor can harm more than help.

Some examples illustrate the problem.

Richard Baker, ordained by Suzuki Roshi, was installed as abbot of the San Francisco Zen Center in 1971. Michael Downing, author of *Shoes Outside the Door*, has noted that Baker had sexual relations with numerous women, and amassed tremendous personal wealth from the donations he received from his sangha, which he flagrantly displayed

---

* For example, some group leaders unconsciously inhabit (project) the savior/redeemer complex (Chapter 16), which invokes a bonding counter projection from the student. (Jung 1948, par 507).

† Inherited titles, however, do not necessarily mean that the inheritor is without spiritual depth, but it does suggest that spiritual depth is not required to receive the title.

by driving fancy cars purchased with them.[406] Chögyam Trungpa, acknowledged as the 11th Trungpa Tulka, supreme lama of the Surmang monasteries in Tibet, established Naropa University in Boulder, Colorado, in 1974. Sandra Bell, author of *Scandals in emerging Western Buddhism*, noted that he amassed a considerable following of Dharma-seekers, then proceeded to have sexual relations with both men and women in the group. His Vajra Regent, Thomas Rich (Osel Tendzin), also engaged in sexual relations with students and through them acquired HIV. Then, while knowing he had HIV, he continued sexual engagements with followers, which spread the disease to even more of his unknowing victims."[407] Dennis Merzel, aka Genpo Roshi, had sexual relations with many students throughout his long career as Abbot of various Zen centers. He claims lineage transmission in Japanese Sōtō and Rinzai Zen traditions and was recognized in Japan as "the third Zen Priest outside Japan to be offered the title of Dai Osho (Great Priest) in the Sōtō Zen tradition."[408] In 1988, Merzel was installed as abbot of Hosshinji Zen center in Bar Harbor, Maine, where he had scandalous affairs with students that eventually led to the center closing. Subsequently, Merzel moved to Salt Lake City and reestablished Hosshinji as Kanzeon Zen Center. As a married man, he remained Abbot there until 2011, when he disrobed as a Zen priest after announcing,

---

*Vajrayāna—the tantric/esoteric Buddhism dominant in Tibet—is especially prone to abuses by teachers because of the initiation vows—*samaya*—embraced by devotees, which emphasize the importance of secrecy and instill an attitude that the teacher's actions are sacrosanct, whatever they are. Stuart Lachs' carefully researched paper, "Tibetan Buddhism Enters the 21st Century: Trouble in Sangri-la," documents many of them from first-hand accounts. In summary, Lachs writes: "Trungpa [Chögyam] often had sex with the wives and girlfriends of students, and at the snap of a finger could have disciples forcibly stripped naked whether they agreed to it or not. A close disciple of Sogyal [Rinpoche] stated that Sogyal slept with the wives of some of his students, that is, aside from seducing other women, married or single who came to him for spiritual counseling. This is on top of the physical abuse and humiliation he dealt to his dakinis. The Sakyong we saw also seduced many young women, some involved with other men and ghosted them when he was finished with them. The Vajra Regent liked straight men who had no previous homosexual experience, in one case it was a young man less than half his age who he infected with HIV. The teenage Kalu tulku while in the monastery, was raped for roughly two years by a group of older monks, and when he returned from a three-year retreat he recognized the next young boys attacked by them. When he wanted to change tutors, the rejected tutor attempted to kill him, while dismissing him as being easily replaceable" (2019).

again, having had numerous affairs with his students and "causing pain and suffering."⁴⁰⁹ At the time of this writing, he continues teaching at retreats through an organization he calls Big Mind, offering multi-day retreats for many thousands of nonrefundable dollars: one program that he called the "5-5-50 program" costs $50,000 for five days of training with him.*⁴¹⁰

The convention that a student of Chan must have a master evolved from the tradition of ancestor veneration (Chapter 4), which instills the notion that the Dharma can only be transmitted from a teacher who has previously received it and who is thus a Buddha himself. To help validate his own existence as a Buddha, the master accepts and encourages veneration from his disciples. Other Buddhist schools follow this approach overtly. Stephen Butterfield, a former devotee of Chögyam Trungpa, wrote, "The single most important quality demanded of the Vajrayāna student is devotion to the guru. ...The guru is the Buddha. ... To regard the guru as an ordinary person is a perverted attitude. No matter what the guru does, you must accept it as a teaching."⁴¹¹ This is in stark contrast to chan's ideal, for which many devotees like to quote Linji:

> Followers of the Way, don't take the Buddha to be the ultimate. As I see it, he is just like a privy hole. Both bodhisattvahood and arhatship are cangues and chains that bind one. This is why Mañjuśrī tried to kill Gautama with his sword, and why Aṅgulimāla attempted to slay Śākyamuni with his dagger.⁴¹²

In practice, however, many Chan practitioners are closely connected to their teachers, at least in part because of the rhetoric of Dharma transmission, lineage, and ancestor veneration, as we explored in Chapter

---

* Abuses have occurred in China as well, but I have no knowledge of such gross offenses against sangha members from abbots or senior staff (though this is not to suggest it hasn't happened). Monks may "go rogue," however, as Holmes Welsh has documented: "I have heard of the dharma brother of one monastery who absconded with $10,000 in its funds, took a mistress and had children by her. He used the money to set up a retail shop. Later he began to use opium and heroin. In three years, he lost everything, whereupon he deserted his wife and children, was re-ordained, and went to live in another temple" (1963, 114).

4, and, for some, because of an eagerness to gain the prize of Buddhahood from their teacher. Genuine fondness and gratitude may also arise as disciples gain deeper spiritual insights under the guidance of their teachers.

Guidance from an experienced person, one who has been where we are and gone beyond it, is of great value, but being attached to one who guides—as often happens when we project the hero or savior archetype—can arrest spiritual development and send us further into samsāra's dark pit before we realize what's happening. Our sense of agency, both internal and external, can be subjugated by a teacher who may just as easily lead us away from spiritual awakening as toward it.

Social learning

Social Learning Theory was developed by Dr. Albert Bandura at Stanford University in the mid-20th century to describe processes through which we learn, and his theories are still helpful today in understanding the social dynamics of learning in groups. His famous 1961 Bobo doll experiment demonstrated that people learn not only through rewards for good behavior and punishment for bad behavior, but also by simply watching others get rewarded or punished. A group of people, he observed, can be taught behaviors all at once by applying reward/punishment principles to just one if it's done in front of the group. Bandura conjectured that this worked because people learn by observing, imitating, and modeling behavior.[413]

When we enter a Zen or Chan training center, we find our place in the social hierarchy by modeling the behaviors we see. We will notice the behavior of the leader of the group, those who assume dominant modeling roles, and those who are subordinate to the others. We may also observe that those in authority will apply reward and punishment principles to teach behaviors that reinforce social conformity and group solidarity.* The social teaching environment can be helpful when we're learning the mechanics of sitting or walking meditation, but it can fail to be useful when we're learning to meditate; for that, outside guidance can not only interfere with progress, but halt it altogether. Meditation requires autonomy, and if our will is replaced by the will of others, we can become victims of misdirection.

For example, it's sometimes taught in Zen/Chan groups that one must copy the behavior of the teacher. The implication is that the student is there to be like the teacher, who is supposed to represent the Buddha. In one Chinese Buddhist temple I visited many years ago, one of the young, recently ordained Chinese monks (requiring that I address him as "Master") told me sternly after observing me laughing with someone, "If you want to be a Buddha, you must act like a Buddha. If you want to be reborn as a dog, act like a dog." He then explained that it is inappropriate for a monk to laugh and added, "We must always look serious."†

When we look at our natural tendency to copy other people's behaviors as a means for learning, it's not surprising that it can be hard to differentiate between what's valuable to copy and what's not—we aren't instinctually programmed to distinguish between the two. If the person we mimic has motivations other than trying to help us gain insight and awareness of Self, we can be misled. When we are newcomers to Chan/Zen, it can be especially hard to discern intentions, to understand what

---

* During my 30-day ordination at Hong Fa temple, it was discovered that some of the young postulants were skipping out on early morning (3:00 AM) devotional services by climbing out of windows when no one was looking, and returning to bed. Because identification of the young men was impossible, the following day all five hundred of us were disciplined with a whack to the shoulder with a flat stick called a xiang ban 香板 (it made a tremendous sound but caused little pain). This was the only instance of discipline I witnessed during that month.

† As discussed in Chapter 4, Buddhism in China includes elements of its ancient folk religion. Some aspects that have been preserved include the belief in spirits and ghosts, the practice of exorcism, and the belief in reincarnation as various animals. The purpose of the monk's comment, however, was clearly to reprimand me for my momentary joviality, not to express concern that I would return as a dog (which he clearly thought would be a horrible thing to happen to anyone).

it is we need to learn and how to learn it; we are often left with no other recourse than to follow the leader.

Groups require that we conform if we are to be accepted, a powerful incentive for most people seeking to be part of a community. A healthy group, whose motives are spiritual in nature, will establish norms of behavior based on helping its members progress spiritually. Activities that distract from spiritual work will be on the "don't do" list—excessive talking, wearing bright colors, sexual promiscuity, etc.—while activities that encourage spiritual work will be encouraged, like silence, wearing dull colors, and following group etiquette that encourages harmony. In contrast, a group whose motives predominantly serve the teacher may place excessive importance on other forms of collective behavior, such as kowtowing, veneration, and supplication.

Ultimately, the more we can be aware of the processes in play when we enter the domain of a group, the less likely we'll be led in a dangerous direction.

Clinging

The Buddha purportedly told an anecdotal story, preserved in the *Sutta-Pitaka*, that tells of the perils of clinging to a practice after it has served its purpose:

Consider a man who travels along a road and encounters a large body of water. Along the shore there are many dangers which frighten him. Looking across to the other side, he sees that it appears free of danger, yet there appears to be no way to get to it. After some deliberation, he builds a raft from reeds, sticks, foliage, and branches, binds them together tightly, then uses it to float across to the other shore. Recognizing its value, he considers whether he should carry it with him for the rest of his journey so he would be assured safe passage wherever he might need it, or whether he should set it adrift on the water and be on his way. The Buddha asks his congregation if the man should carry it with him, and they respond, "No, he should not." The Buddha agrees and explains the simile:*

> So I have shown you how the Dhamma is similar to a raft, being for the purpose of crossing over, not for the purpose of grasping. ... when you know the Dhamma to be similar to a raft, you should abandon even good states, how much more so bad states?
>
> In the same way, monks, have I shown to you the Teaching's similitude to a raft: as having the purpose of crossing over, not the purpose of being clung to. "You, O monks, who understand the Teaching's similitude to a raft, you should let go even (good) teachings, how much more false ones![414]

Some practitioners identify their practice, or even chan itself, with its methods—with the raft. For example, "doing chan" may be equated with sitting on a cushion and passively observing the mind. All methods are intended to be temporary vehicles, *yāna*. Once their purpose is fulfilled, they are left behind so that we may continue to move forward. If we don't leave them behind, we can get stuck in them. After learning to concentrate by focusing the mind for extended periods, for example, we abandon those training exercises and begin new ones that will lead us toward immersive contemplation. How much time it takes to master any spiritual skill is irrelevant; it may take days or weeks or months or years. What's important is that we stick with a practice until its intended benefits are realized, then move on.

Control

Some people new to chan mistakenly think that the objective of practice is to control thoughts and emotions, to prevent them from careening wildly about. But trying to force the mind into submission, to stop the brain's nerve synapses from firing, is like trying not to think of a green elephant. Willpower alone won't do it.

---

* The Pali term *Dhamma* in the following passage refers to the Buddha's teaching.

Trying to control thoughts and emotions is acting. We may, for example, be angry but pretend to be calm, happy, or neutral. If we sit on a cushion trying to meditate for some purpose other than gaining spiritual insight, we will be trying to achieve something which meditation can't give. Rather than being open and receptive, or focused and concentrated, we will be acting, trying to force ourselves to be relaxed, peaceful, or emotionally neutral. Eventually, if we maintain this ruse, the internal pressure may build up and explode out of us.

Following a Zen *sesshin* 接心 (a ritualized Japanese-style meditation retreat) in 1987, I was riding home with another participant when he suddenly, without explanation, pulled over to the side of the road, got out, walked calmly toward a bank of trees, and let out a tremendous series of howling screams. For several minutes, he stood screaming into the woods. When he returned to the car, he said quietly in a controlled voice, "I needed to do that." Psychic pressures had built up and needed release. He confided that he did this often because it made him feel better.

Chan is about contemplation and meditation, altered states of consciousness in which the ego plays no role. There is no way to control thoughts in such a state, because thoughts require a thinker, and the thinker isn't there. Certain control methods can be employed to initiate entry into meditation, as discussed in Part Two, but we must ultimately let go and abandon our desire to be in control before meditation can occur.

Wrong practice

True meditation is a beautiful experience. No matter what technique we use, if we get a good result, the technique was the right one. If we fail to get a good result, however, we need to investigate to discover why, being careful not to blame ourselves or anyone else. Admission that a technique isn't working is the first step toward getting ourselves back on track.

Indicators of wrong-practice may include repeated nightmares, frequent violent or scary hallucinations, persistent sleeplessness, anxiety, temper, or frustration. Other, subtler signs may include becoming apathetic, lazy, or nonchalant toward responsibilities or commitments. If we experience any of these symptoms, we need to reassess what we're doing; our motivations may be misaligned with practice, we may have picked the wrong method, or we may be practicing a method improperly. Whatever the cause, it's up to us to figure it out and alter our practice or adjust our performance to get back on track.

Another indication of wrong practice is recognizing that we have spent years or even decades on a particular approach without feeling we've made progress. On occasion, people with a Japanese Zen background have come to me with questions about their practice because they feel they haven't been getting anywhere. They explain that they have studied and practiced Zen for many years and emphasize the large number of hours they spend daily on the cushion. When I ask them to describe their practice, they invariably explain, in one way or another, that they "just sit", that is their practice. If I ask them what method they are working with, they may look at me confused, and again say they "just sit." They sometimes justify their "just sitting" approach by quoting excerpts from Dogen's Shōbōgenzō (Chapter 7) or instructions given them by one of their favorite teachers. Since my practice has been based on Chinese "southern school" Chan, I usually suggest they try some concentration (Chapter 11) or contemplation (Chapter 12) exercises. Only rarely have I been taken up on these suggestions. Most often, they defend their approach and wave goodbye.

It can be difficult to entertain new ways of practice when we have spent years practicing in a particular way, a way which we have convinced ourselves is correct. The more time we have committed to a practice, the more psychologically invested we become in doing it and the more we will tend to defend it. To suggest to ourselves that our practice has failed is anathema to the ego, which has invested itself in its sanctity. In such cases, we are stuck and unable to get ourselves out on our own, and self-righteousness prevents us from allowing others to help.

Fear

We all know fear: fear of failure, fear of rejection, fear of death, fear of being shunned by a religious or social group or by friends and family. Ironically, the effects of fear manifest in ways that often increase our fear. Fear can limit our ability to make friends, or to communicate effectively and honestly with others, resulting in a sense of disassociation. We may try to hide our fear by donning a friendly persona to mask our insecurities, giving us an unnatural appearance of friendliness. On the other hand, we may choose a dark persona, wearing a guise of depression or cynicism, seeking out activities and friends that support, sustain, and build a dark self-image. The physical effects of fear can be as much of a problem as the psychological effects. We may suffer from headaches, nervousness, insomnia, rashes, ulcers, irritable bowel syndrome, or panic attacks.

Fear can also paralyze and prevent us from interacting with others compassionately. Instead of seeing others as they are, we may project our own fears and insecurities upon them, seeing what we dislike about ourselves in them, whether they are there or not. Ultimately, fear leads to isolation and separation.

To overcome fear, we muster up courage and allow ourselves to make mistakes, to show failure, and to show our human vulnerabilities. We allow ourselves to risk being outcast by our social groups, friends, and family if required. We then discover that the pain and anguish involved in these courageous acts are slight and transitory compared to the pain and suffering we had endured by hiding from our natural human frailties.

When we disassociate ourselves from our image of ourselves, there is tremendous relief and freedom. What we lose is nothing real: it's like shedding a dead skin, one that had no life in the first place.

Untoward emotions

If our psyche is trying to resolve a conflict—maybe we had an argument with a friend, got angry at a colleague, failed an exam, or experienced the death of a loved one—and we banish the angry or sad thought without understanding it, we will repress it; then, rather than disappearing, it will go into hiding and continue to lurk. In time, the unwanted feelings will resurface. We may have strange nightmares, terrible visions, anxiety, or anger, none of which we can understand. When we are conscious and on-guard, we can control our responses, mask our feelings, and keep them hidden. But when we aren't, as when we're asleep or alone with our thoughts, we may experience extreme psychological distress.

Repressed feelings that go unprocessed remain that way until we allow them to rise to consciousness. But sometimes those feelings are so intense that fear of facing them prevents it. Combat veterans may have especially frightful dreams and sudden wakeful recollections of war; people with childhood histories of abuse may have comparable frightful dreams of abandonment, neglect, or assault. Without consciously processing the trauma, it can effect our mood, our relationships, and lead to unconscious affectations. Regardless of the source or intensity of the buried emotional shards, they invariably reveal themselves in dreams, which can persist until we uncover their emotional source. Dreams offer a bridge between the conscious and unconscious, but we have to choose to cross it. Becoming aware of, and contemplating, dreams can bring their generative forces to consciousness and begin a healing process. It takes time, endurance, commitment, patience, and faith in the process, but with proper attention, we can experience the joyful relief of rendering them harmless.

Existential annihilation

As we come to see the ego as the phantasm it is, it begins to fear its own extinction, and this can produce arresting fear. Preservation of self is programmed into us, so going against that programming is no small feat. For many of us, the only way to overcome this hurdle is to have such disdain for the life we're living that we are willing to give it up. This is where faith becomes essential—once we are prepared for self-annihilation, we have to believe that after abandoning self-identity we will still be around, that we will still be able to enjoy a delicious meal or a good movie, to laugh with friends, to experience love. Once we surmount the fear of existential annihilation, we realize there is nothing real that is, in fact, extinguished. Even the ego does not disappear, it merely loses its autonomous control over us. Enlightenment changes nothing except perception and understanding: nothing is lost, only gained. When we shed the illusory, what's real gains clarity, and this allows us to experience the joys and sorrows of life more directly and fully. The difference is that we don't attach ourselves—our fabricated identities—to these experiences, because those fabricated identities no longer exist.

Social media

Social media presents an insidious obstacle for many. It cajoles us into spending our time reading other people's posts and adding our own. Some of us become obsessed with staying tuned-in to Facebook, WhatsApp, Instagram, WeChat, Snapchat, or TikTok, awaiting responses to something we posted or new gossip from a "friend." Social media is a carnival for the ego and is not only a tremendous distraction for someone engaged in chan practice but is most often counterproductive. Rather than disengaging the ego, it strengthens it. The solution is to log out and stay logged out or simply delete the accounts.

Effort

If we're motivated to practice chan for the right reasons, e.g., we're seeking escape from duhkha, then becoming lazy about practice won't happen.* When our lives are at stake, our commitment to practice becomes unwavering. We'll engage in it with all our energy and willpower. It's only when we approach chan as an interesting pastime, a cool or trendy thing to do, or with some other tangential purpose and motive, that our practice may suffer from lack of effort. This is an issue not only for independent practitioners. When Holmes Welch asked the monk Chin Shan whether this was an issue in the Chan monasteries where he lived for many years, he replied:

> If you did not have the mental equipment to cope with the work, then the meditation hall was worse than prison. So every year there were monks who fled. On the other hand, if your mind was really on your work, then there was nothing boring about it. Those who were doing well with meditation could hardly wait to get started the next day.[415]

If we find ourselves becoming bored with practice, we can return to the prerequisites and determine what we're missing, then work on overcoming the deficiency. If we aren't properly motivated for chan, it will, at best, be a waste of time and, at worst, lead to unintended problems (Chapter 21).

The chan monk, Ben Huan, advised:

---

* There are some other interesting and offbeat reasons that people have taken up Zen. Ōmori Sōgen's reason was among the oddest: "Honestly speaking, the reason I entered the Way of Zen from the Way of the sword had nothing to do with any lofty ideals on my part. Instead, being short, I realized that I had no hope of standing up to opponents taller than me if I couldn't compensate for their physical advantage by acquiring superior power. In short, I entered the Way of Zen due to the fear I experienced when sword fighting. I hoped to overcome that fear" (Ōmori Sōgen, quoted by B. D. Victoria, 2003, 40-41). Sōgen would become a recognized Zen master and leader of right-wing political activism in Japan, advocating the Imperial Way and obliteration of all obstructions to it according to the code of Bushido: "Forgetting himself and becoming one with the Way, he [the Bushido warrior] completely transforms the small self into the Way of the warrior. He then lives the Great Life" (Ibid., 51). From this anecdote, we might surmise that our motive for engaging with Zen or Chan practice will influence the outcome of our efforts.

To maintain the right kind of intense effort is very hard, as our eyes want to look left and right. To gain oneness of mind an intense and sustained effort must be generated without end. Perhaps we should be afraid of allowing our eyes to wonder? My lecture today, if you recall, is about how we should use our time effectively. We need to make a great effort in this matter, and never allow our effort to diminish for any reason. A great effort is fuelled by a great doubt, which fundamentally questions our deluded existence. Arousing this true 'doubt' (疑情 – Yi Qing) should not be underestimated, as it is a very powerful technique. Arousing the true doubt will transcend the mind and body, and cause the practitioner to forget the world.[416]

Delusion

It's not uncommon for people to mistake the ego-self for the Self,* a form of delusion in which we mistake the illusory for the real. Unfortunately, the rhetoric of Chan can lead to this misdirection. For example, how do we understand comments like this one from Linji: "Just be your ordinary self in ordinary life, unconcerned in seeking for Buddhahood," or this one from Yunmen: "Every day is a good day. Your everyday mind—that is the Way!", in relation to comments like this from Han Shan: "Absolute Truth can't be expressed in words. It must be experienced." Or this one from Hsu Yun: "Jump off the lofty peaks of mystery. Turn your heaven and earth inside out." Or this one by Hakuin Ekaku: "Should you desire great tranquility, prepare to sweat white beads."

The first two quotes give the impression that there is nothing we need to do to do chan. The second three suggest there is mystery involved, along with some kind of unusual or even mystic experience. When taken out of context, Chan sayings offer something for everyone, which makes it easy to cherry pick practices and beliefs according to whichever best fits our desired agenda. The ego's agenda is to stay in power, and this often confounds our ability to do the work.

---

* In the spirit of Chan, the concept of "Self" is only an expedient means (upāya) for describing that which comes to be known once the veil of ego is lifted. Ultimately, there is neither a "self" nor a "Self," a realization gained when we enter samādhi (Chapter 13).

One of the most common obstacles people encounter is lack of motivation, energy, and desire to delve within. Many people approach chan because they are seeking easy solutions to life's challenges and are not prepared to apply the needed effort for spiritual growth. For them, the rhetoric of Chan offers many excuses to avoid doing the work and "sweating the white beads." Sayings like "Zen is just ordinary mind," when spoken by a representative of the Chan or Zen institution, can be enough incentive for them to abandon personal effort and, instead, assume that to "do Zen" means merely living life however we want to live it. Such a perspective is easily taken when we're not truly interested in delving into our lives. When our interest in Chan is prompted by any reason other than a desire to delve within, it's easy to dismiss anything we encounter about it that challenges our desire to continue as we are: a form of self-delusion imposed by the ego's will to maintain the status quo.

I don't know if there's a way out of this. The rhetoric we tell ourselves is inherently self-reinforcing. Unless we are willing to question our beliefs, to embrace "great doubt" (Chapters 8, 9, 12), we are unlikely to break through our mental illusions. If our interest in chan does not align with its purpose as a mystical path of Self-discovery, it will offer nothing to help us break out of the delusion. Attachment to the sensory-realm is tremendously difficult to escape without adequate effort and determination, as the Bodhidharma/Huike legend expressed (Chapter 4). Han Shan wrote,

> The worst thing is to be self-satisfied with little [experiences]. Never allow yourself to fall into the dazzling experiences that arise from your sensory gates. Why? Because your eighth consciousness* has not yet been crushed, so whatever you experience or do will be [conditioned] by your [deluded] consciousness and senses. If you think that this [consciousness] is real, then it is like mistaking a thief to be your

---

* The "eighth consciousness" refers to Yogacara's Storehouse Consciousness (Chapter 4) and is similar to the modern idea of the subconscious. The other seven types of consciousness in the Yogacara tradition are the five sensory consciousnesses, the mind, and the self—or ego—consciousness.

own son! The ancient one has said, "Those who engage in practice do not know what is real because until now they have taken their consciousness [to be true]; what a fool takes to be his original face is actually the fundamental cause of birth and death." This is the barrier that you must pass through.[417]

Sexual desire

All living beings are programmed to procreate. Why, then, are sexual relationships not acknowledged as something natural and permissible in the Chan monastic tradition? While Chinese Chan monks are known to be celibate, Japanese Zen monks are generally known not to be. The third Buddhist precept, according to Chinese tradition, is *Abrahmacariya veramani sikkhapadam samadiyami*, to abstain from sexual activity. In Japan, this precept has been (popularly) adjusted to "avoid sexual misconduct."

The purpose of monastic celibacy is to prevent monks and nuns from disrupting their spiritual lives and those of others.* Engaging in Chan's mystical training requires that we are motivated by a great desire to get out of the swamp of duhkha, and that our desire to know the Self —or escape the ego-self—is so strong that we are ready and eager to do whatever is necessary. This was, after all, the foundational tenet of the Buddha's teaching as described in his Noble Truths. To foster spiritual growth, we limit distractions from those things that direct attention away from our spiritual objectives.

And the sexual brain is more than just a distraction; it overwhelms the mind with thoughts and emotions completely counter to spiritual labor. Sexual arousal arises from the production and release of chemicals in the body—testosterone, serotonin, dopamine, progesterone, and many others—that cause us to forget entirely about delving within.

---

* We might wonder if the Japanese loosening of this precept helped foster the pandemic wave of sexual misconduct by Zen teachers in the West. We would like to think that Zen/Chan teachers have mastered sexual desire, but until divine union—taijitu 太極圖 —has been experienced (Chapters 17 and 18), the forces of sexual desire will be as present for them as they are for anyone else who has not had the experience.

In a Chan monastery, celibacy is expected because it's assumed we're there to engage in a spiritual practice. If that's not our purpose and we are there for a different reason, what is it? Do we seek to rise through the ranks to attain a position of power within the congregation, to engage with the social environment, to avoid homelessness, or to wear the robes? Perhaps we're there to test it out, to see if it's something we want. For people who are not motivated by a strong desire for spiritual growth, sexual abstinence will do little to support a contemplative life; however, for those with motivations harmonious with the spiritual purpose of chan, sexual abstinence is not only accepted, but welcomed. For the serious lay practitioner not bound by monastic code, sexual abstinence can be a welcomed choice as well.

The solution to working with sexual desire is to point the mind away from it when it arises. If we're working with a hua-tou, we return our attention to it; if we're working with negation practice, we say to ourselves, *Not thus! Not thus!* (Chapter 12).

PICKING AND CHOOSING

When I cook something new, I sometimes consult the Internet to find recipes. Once I find two or three that are similar, I'll look to see what ingredients they share then come up with my own version. Sometimes what I make turns out well, but it can be a fiasco if I chose ingredients that don't work well together. When we begin a spiritual journey, there's often a temptation to formulate our own recipe. We may jump from group to group or teacher to teacher to learn different approaches, then attempt to mix together what we like and discard the rest. But just like making soup by selectively choosing ingredients, we may be disappointed with the outcome. There are infinite paths that lead toward spiritual awakening, just as there are infinite ways to combine ingredients to make soup; but as all soups involve a broth, all spiritual paths involve transcending the ego. When the ego oversees itself, it will not seek the path of annihilation. It seeks, at all costs, self-preservation.

Picking and choosing may work when we're in the kitchen, but it rarely, if ever, works when our objective is spiritual transformation.

I have often been asked questions about chan practice only to later learn that the inquirer is asking the same question to other teachers, then judging to determine who they think is right or wrong to determine whose advice to follow and whose to abandon. The problem with this is that teachers may disagree with each other, not only about how to do a practice, but about the validity of a practice itself, based on their own unique experiences or acquired beliefs. In Chan, it's often said that a student cannot have two masters. The reason for this is that different teachers can take their students on different paths, which, while intended to arrive at the same result, may employ different methods. Those paths may cross each other, or they may not. Teachers advocate practices that worked for them, or that they believe should eventually work for them. One who has not successfully used the hua-tou practice, for example, is unlikely to teach it and may even turn students away from it (the hua-tou is uncommon in Japanese Zen, for instance). But this doesn't mean their approach is faulty. As we explored in Chapter 4, chan training embraces many diverse methods. If we approach training with acceptance of this diversity, but limit ourselves to a particular method, it will prevent us from getting disillusioned by apparent contradictions between teachers and methods, and it will keep us moving forward.

Secular life

People practicing chan disciplines outside the monastic setting may be challenged with maintaining their practice in the presence of others who don't share or understand that practice. Spiritual cultivation is facilitated when a collective group is engaged in it together, as we find in monastic life, but it can be hindered when we are with people who neither share our interest of delving within nor understand that we have little interest in engaging in frivolous conversation and activities;

they may not recognize that directing our attention toward such things can divert our attention away from the inward gaze, which is where we would rather be.

"People will drive you crazy if you let them," a Chan priest once comment to me. Her point was that we don't need to let people interfere with our spiritual lives, regardless of the situation we're in—we don't need to let people interrupt our practice. Cultivation of the chan mind means we work to maintain Self reflection in all situations of our life. When we are around someone who likes to talk, for example, rather than participating with their churning thoughts we can become an observer and recognize that the person speaking is not the words they speak. The sound we hear from them need not bother us. This engaged approach helps us detach from the social expectations of reciprocal dialogue. We also often find that people who like to talk often do not like to listen, so our silence can be comfortable for them. With attentive listening grounded in Self-reflection, when an appropriate time to speak arises, we are better able to speak thoughtfully and compassionately because we can more easily see through the person's words to the person behind them without loosing our own equanimity. Until we're successfully able to do this, however, arranging time for solitude daily is invaluable.

To recap, this chapter has described a few of the more common hindrances and obstructions that chan practitioners may encounter. Our own unique set of circumstances will determine the specific difficulties we'll have; generally, however, problems can be resolved if we return to the first seven steps of the Eightfold Path for guidance (Chapters 1 and 9).

If we fail to overcome the hurdles, though, we might get into dangerous situations. Some of those most important to avoid are presented in the next chapter.

21

Dangers

The whole secret of existence is to have no fear. Never fear what will become of you, depend on no one. Only the moment you reject all help are you freed.

– Swami Vivekananda

WHEN STARTING OUT, CHAN can seem like an endless succession of hurdles to jump, but without the struggle to get over and past them, progress may cease, and we may even end up worse off than before we started. Just as we might prepare for a car trip by learning about possible hazardous road conditions on our route, foreknowledge of hazards on the spiritual journey can help us navigate around them if they arise. In this chapter, we'll explore some of those possible hazards and suggest effective detours around them.

Skipping steps

As we become aware of the mind's activity through observation and contemplation, we gain power over its processes. Through concentration, contemplation, and meditation, we learn the language of the mind and gain insight into the functions it presides over, and may even gain some control over those functions. But control isn't without risks; we may be able to master some of the brain's functions, but not steer it. Imagine being a passenger in a self-driving car, traveling at high speed down a freeway with no skill to drive it manually. Suddenly, its computer fails and relinquishes control to you, its passenger. In a panic, you push and pull knobs and turn the wheel, hoping for your life that the car won't crash, while feeling powerless to avoid it. A similar scenario can happen as we delve into the recesses of the mind. With knowledge comes power, but unmoderated by wisdom and skill, that knowledge can wreck havoc. Without a wise commander in charge, we can find ourselves like a hapless passenger in a car out of control.

The solution is to not attempt advanced practices before we are ready for them. When we jump over steps on the journey, we can get into trouble. A cellist doesn't begin her musical training by attempting a solo performance of a Bach Cello Suite at Carnegie Hall: it takes thousands of hours of practice and unrelenting commitment to gain the necessary mastery of the instrument. Likewise, only if we start at the beginning and persevere, moving step by step along the path, can we be assured of progress with chan. Spiritual life is a journey, not a destination. For a mountain climber, reaching the summit is an excuse for an adventure. Just as the musician practices her instrument for the joy and love of playing, a devotee of chan practices for the gratification of delving into the unknown realm of being to discover hidden secrets.

It's common for beginners to want to skip steps, to jump over beginning practices and go directly to more advanced ones. Some teachers even encourage this by giving advanced Void ("mind-blanking") meditations to new students as their first practice. But just as we cannot will ourselves to enlightenment, neither can we will ourselves into the Void. It's something that happens naturally when the body, mind, and psyche are all prepared and ready. There are many experiences to have first, all equally rewarding. Jumping over stages of the journey is akin to leaping over a wide, raging river to get to the other side when a nearby bridge offers a safer path. If we choose to leap, we may drown in psychological stresses that lead to dissociative disorders and snapping, but if we mindfully walk across the bridge, we'll arrive safely on the other side.

Dissociative disorders

When we skip beginning training stages and leap directly to advanced practices, we can experience the frightening effects of *depersonalization*, a type of *dissociative disorder*. This is common among people who have experienced severe stress or trauma, but it can also be a consequence of rushing the process of chan training. Social alienation, in which we become reclusive and isolated, may also follow. The way to get out of it is to return to earlier stages of practice, such as the breathing exercises described in Chapter 11. When the mind is grounded in the breath, it's grounded in the body. This is a principal reason that beginning chan practices emphasize attention to the breath.

A type of dissociative disorder happened to me when I first began delving into meditation. I had responded to a notice in a health food store that read: "Meditation at my house, Thursday, 6-8 PM." I liked the simplicity of the message, so I dialed the number and was invited to attend. Three others arrived and, after a brief introduction by the host, we did our "sit." Everything was fine until suddenly there was a very loud *dong!* Our host had a large traditional grandfather clock that chimed loudly on the hour, every hour. I was so startled by the sudden sound that I abruptly leapt to my feet, my primitive limbic system prepared for a pouncing sabertooth tiger that failed to appear. I quickly realized that everything was all right, but the sudden shot of endorphins, combined with my mental state at the moment of that *dong!*, left me feeling quite odd. Afterward, as people were drinking tea and chatting, I discovered I was unable to speak intelligently. I couldn't form a sentence or recall the names of things or people. It was very uncomfortable and a bit scary. The strange feeling lasted the rest of the day and was gone by the following morning.

In retrospect, I consider this to have likely been a *transient disassociation* event, a term that refers to "discontinuity in sense of self and sense of agency, accompanied by related alterations in affect, behavior, consciousness, memory, perception, cognition, and/or sensory-motor functioning."[418]

It's known that trauma can cause dissociation, and I speculate that the startling loud sound, at a time when my brain was in some type of transitory pre-meditative state, led to this event. I since learned that this is not an uncommon experience for people learning meditation.

Transient dissociation is something for the aspiring meditator to know about, but there's no need to be alarmed if it happens. If there are pre-existing psychological conditions, the effects may be prolonged or amplified, but removing ourselves from social situations and avoiding activities that require alert consciousness will give us time to return to normal.

Snapping

Spiritual practices expand awareness both gradually and suddenly. However, when these practices are forced upon us, or when we force them upon ourselves when we aren't yet ready for them, they can reduce awareness rather than enhance it. We might then experience sudden leaps of consciousness in the opposite direction: becoming dulled to our environment, confused, unable to think or act for ourselves, suggestible. Some groups go to great length to encourage this in order to control their members. The Ananda tribe of central Australia offers a striking example:

> Around puberty, the young male ... is taken from his mother, isolated in the wilderness and deprived of food for a prolonged period of time. He is kept awake at night in a state of constant fear by the eerie, whirling sound of the bullroarer, a native hunting device, until the combined physical and emotional stresses reach their maximum effect. At that moment, the elders of the tribe converge on the ter-

rified youth wearing grotesque masks and covered with vivid body paints and proceed to subject him to a painful ritual of initiation into manhood. If he survives the ordeal, the young man emerges from the ritual in a drastically reduced state of mind, his awareness continuing at a level only sufficient to allow absolute adherence to the strict laws and taboos of the tribe. The adult Ananda tribesman may spend his entire life in this altered state the natives call Dream Time. He will stand on one leg for hours, completely motionless, in a waking trance so deep that flies may crawl across his eyeballs without causing him to blink."[*][419]

While this degree of snapping is unusual and must be induced by extreme circumstances, sudden leaps of cognition are common. Parents observe toddlers who, seemingly overnight, display an awareness of self, using words like "I" and "me," or suddenly speak in full sentences when, just the day before, they spoke only phrases. We may think we evolve in a continuous fashion, slowly adapting to our environment and experiences, but reality can trick us. Things can seem continuous because our brain processes information from our senses in an apparently continuous way—we see things moving smoothly from place to place, and we hear continuous sounds—but what appears continuous in the macrocosm is often a discontinuous process at its microcosmic source.[†] Our senses have evolved to detect the average collected results of a large group of such transitions, which makes them appear continuous.[‡]

Consider what happens to a collection of water molecules when they freeze. If the conditions are right, they will form a highly organized

---

[*] Joseph Chilton Pearce's description of life in the Ananda tribe from *The Crack in the Cosmic Egg*, as excerpted by Conway and Siegelman in *Snapping*.

[†] Rui Qi provides a mathematical model for discontinuous motion in "The basis of discontinuous motion" (Qi n.d.). The brain, too, is thought to operate discontinuously at the microscopic level, and it's speculated that quantum behavior may be responsible for consciousness itself. Matthew Fisher, a physicist at UC Santa Barbara who specializes in quantum mechanics, is the scientific director of the new Quantum Brain Project (QuBrain), which seeks to answer questions about quantum mechanical aspects of mentation and consciousness and determine if our brains are, in fact, quantum computers themselves.

[‡] Julian Barbour describes this effect in detail in *The End of Time: The Next Revolution in Physics*, through the introduction of the concept of "time capsules," which are "any fixed pattern that creates or encodes the appearance of motion, change or history."

crystalline structure and become a snowflake. But if the conditions are different—if, say, the temperature quickly drops below a critical threshold—then the water will freeze into an amorphous solid. Instead of the snowflake's exquisite geometry, a bead of ice will form as the water molecules bind together in random chaos. In both cases, the outcome is dependent entirely upon the conditions of temperature, pressure, and humidity. A similar process can happen to us when we subject ourselves to a spiritual discipline. We may suddenly become like the snowflake, attaining a higher level of order and awareness, or we may become like the blob of ice, our minds dulled and chaotic.

A healthy spiritual regimen creates a snowflake, but if we go off in the wrong direction, we can end up snapping. Interviews with ex-members of the People's Temple, whose congregation famously killed themselves by drinking Kool-Aid laced with cyanide and other drugs, revealed snapping on a profound level. Other groups/cults with documented cases of snapping (individual and collective) include Heaven's Gate[420] and the Church of Scientology,[421] but there are many others.

While the methods used by such cults may be similar to those of all religions—chanting, fasting, sleep deprivation, and prayer—those methods, when applied for spiritual purposes, aim to induce a meditative state. When applied for purposes of controlling a group, they lead to the suggestive state associated with hypnotic trance: a state of contracted consciousness.*

Cults operate on different principles from religions, principally because they are governed by leaders who seek power over their followers rather than their spiritual health. They seek their servitude, not their liberation. Cult leaders will generally prescribe the same disciplines to every member of his congregation, regardless of each person's spiri-

---

* Consider, for example, the following comment from the actor Jason Beghe after he left the Church of Scientology: "I got so fucked up. I mean they, they—I went insane. I was like stuck somewhere in a tiny spot behind my head [points toward his eyes toward the back of his head, then points around his head in circles]. I mean, I had never experienced anything like it. Ten fuckin' years. I was worse than the day that I walked in. It was by design, 'cause they needed to keep me there. So basically [they] had to put a whole new case on me so they could run it, and they just kept trying to fuckin' keep me stuck in. It was crazy" (Wright 2013, 1:44).

tual readiness. These may be legitimate spiritual practices, but when advanced techniques are given to a novice, there can be disastrous consequences.* Monks may disappear to a mountain retreat to live for months or years with little food or sleep to contemplate and meditate, but they typically do this after years of monastic training. Cult leaders, however, after allurements, may gain blind obedience from their congregation by subjecting them to nonstop indoctrination with tense, exhausting days and nights, in which the only food or sleep they receive are given as rewards for obediently reaching the "right" conclusions.[422] To further break them down, bathroom visits may be refused so that they have to urinate or defecate in their clothes in public. Under such stresses, their followers eventually crack, or snap. That's when we hear about cases of sudden psychosis and conversion disorders.†

We may ask why people get involved in cults; clearly, they were already a little crazy to do something like that, we might think. But cults generally start out with noble-sounding causes espoused by a charismatic leader who makes them alluring. In most cases, people who join cults are regular, sane people who behave in accordance with our natural herd instinct.

If we look through the lens of analytical psychology, three powerful archetypes that come into play in groups, and often prominently in cults, are the hero/savior, the friend, and the enemy-shadow (Chapter 16). A devotee projects the hero/savior archetype on the leader, relinquishing agency. From here, the devotee will do anything for the leader and blindly accept whatever he or she says or does. The leader responds to the dynamic, invoking the counter-balancing archetype, the shadowy anti-hero; anyone who questions the intentions of the cult

---

* A sangha member of a Zen monastery I visited many years ago in the Rocky Mountains, which emphasized Soto-style mind-blanking meditations, told me it was standard practice for participants who showed signs of snapping during training to be given strong sedatives at night. It was not, I was told, an uncommon problem. If the drugs didn't work, the participants would be summarily expelled.

† Also known as *functional neurological symptom disorder*, this condition manifests on rare occasions in some people as a result of mental or emotional crisis and presents as a physical symptom, such as paralysis. It can affect one's ability to walk, see, swallow, or hear. Most people improve with immediate treatment.

or threatens it in any way will be marked as evil, a villain who, in the leader's eyes, may deserve to be publicly humiliated, expelled, or even killed.[423] Invoking this shadow archetype serves to further enhance the power of the cult leader and strengthen the solidarity of the cult's members. This phenomenon was demonstrated on the world stage during the election of Donald Trump for President of the United States, as his supporters discounted his hostile rhetoric toward women, Jews, Muslims, and immigrants, and followed his violent provocations with violence of their own, a behavior that continued into his presidency.[424] He demonstrated his role as a cult figurehead when he proclaimed: "You know what else they say about my people? The polls, they say I have the most loyal people. Did you ever see that? Where I could stand in the middle of Fifth Avenue and shoot somebody and I wouldn't lose any voters, okay? It's like incredible!"

There are many examples of cults bringing catastrophic outcomes to their followers and victims, from Hitler's Nazis to David Koresh's Branch Davidians. Others include the Church of Bible Understanding (the Forever Family), the Manson Family, Aum Shinrikyo, the Movement for the Restoration of the Ten Commandments of God, the Raelian Church, and the Order of the Solar Temple.

Although these are extreme examples of what can happen when the herd instinct takes control, they illustrate forces at work in every group, forces which even appear across species; geese will fly in whatever direction their leader takes them; a herd of buffalo will follow the lead bull off a cliff—a maneuver Native Americans orchestrated to slaughter them. The herd instinct is also evident in families, political organizations, corporations, and churches—anywhere people congregate for a common cause or purpose.

Overzealousness

Meditation can quickly turn into a habit. In time, that habit can turn into a consuming necessity. Chan practice is healthy, but excessive zeal can cause problems. The process of watching the mind, of exploring hidden territories, is infinitely engaging, but if it's not practiced in moderation and balanced with other chan disciplines and normal life activities, unintended problems can arise.

Prior to learning to meditate, "sitting" was work for me, and I often avoided it. In those days, it was almost a relief to have a kitchen to clean, clothes to wash, and groceries to buy. But once I learned to meditate, overindulgence led to problems; I lost interest in daily chores and managing social and fiscal responsibilities.

The culprit, I discovered, was desire, and desire is always moderated by ego. Like a drug addict, I had to get more. I was told by a chan monk that I had a common case of *chanbing* 禪病, or "meditation sickness". The ego vanishes when we are in meditation, but when we come out, it's right back where we left it when we entered. I finally decided to stop sitting and attend to chan practice in ways that wouldn't interfere with life. I discovered I could explore the mind in ways that didn't require sitting meditation and which would allow me to engage with the world: while washing dishes I could practice Right Mindfulness; while talking with a friend I could practice Right Speech; while driving a car I could practice Right Action.

By vigilantly observing the ego's desired influence over us and not allowing it gratuitous freedom to play, we can cultivate chan Mind all the time, regardless of the activity in which we're engaged.

Pride

"Self-congratulation, O disciple, is like unto a lofty tower, up which a haughty fool has climbed. Thereon he sits in prideful solitude and unperceived by any but himself," wrote Helena Blavatsky, co-founder of the Theosophical Society.[425] Ironically, it's not uncommon for people to become inflated with pride over their perceived spiritual accomplishments. Even our desire to help others may have selfish intent, as Christmas Humphries has warned:

> The 'power complex,' so easy to observe in one's neighbor's desire to dominate and impress his fellows, is latent in each one of us, and much that masquerades as altruism and a desire to help humanity will be found, on ruthless analysis in the meditation hour, to be naught but the will to self-aggrandizement. Spiritual pride is rightly regarded as one of the last of the Fetters to be broken ...[426]

To recognize spiritual pride in ourselves we can look for the signs. Are we presenting ourselves as spiritual experts? Are we donning fancy titles to trumpet our own perceived self-attainments and gain admiration from others? Are we acting as if we're above and beyond other people, more knowledgeable, more important, treating them with disregard, contempt, or scorn?

It's important to be ever-vigilant of the ego's influences on our dispositions, perceptions, and attitudes. It can, and will, undermine our spiritual journey given the opportunity.

Moral turpitude

All religions provide an ethical framework, but it's our own personal sense of right and wrong—our moral compass—that inspires and guides our actions. When Chan becomes isolated from the ethical structure of Buddhism, which shapes compatible moral sensibilities, we may lose our spiritual compass. We may then approach chan more as an exercise to improve a skill or strengthen some part of the body, or as a pretext for social engagement to escape from the pains and sorrows of life, rather than as a vehicle for transformation.

For the context of this discussion, I will consider morality to be represented by our own personal set of values which we hold to be universally valid (e.g., "it's fundamentally wrong to kill another human being"); while ethics refers to principles of right or wrong as identified by an organization, religion, government, or other group.*

---

* It's worth noting that there are many different interpretations of morality and ethics, and moral principles are just as varied between cultures and religions as are their ethical frameworks.

Morality can help us decide on the best course of action but can just as easily cause a great deal of misery. Morality can lead us in either direction. Steven Pinker, in his provocative 2011 book, *The Better Angels of our Nature*, even argues that

> [t]he world has far too much morality. If you added up all the homicides committed in pursuit of self-help justice, the casualties of religious and revolutionary wars, the people executed for victimless crimes and misdemeanors, and the targets of ideological genocides, they would surely outnumber the fatalities from amoral predation and conquest. The human moral sense can excuse any atrocity in the minds of those who commit it, and it furnishes them with motives for acts of violence that bring them no tangible benefit. The torture of heretics and conversos, the burning of witches, the imprisonment of homosexuals, and the honor killing of unchaste sisters and daughters are just a few examples. [...] ...the moral sense does not, in general, push toward the reduction of suffering but so often increases it.[427]

Ethics can be tricky to navigate as well. The ethical principles of Buddhism offer a means to help ensure that actions are harmonious with spiritual objectives, but they are meant to be guides, not rigid laws that must be followed blindly. Relying on ethical principles can be hazardous if we fail to understand why they exist, what purpose they serve, and whether they apply equally to our own circumstance.

A story related to me by a friend illustrates how a proper understanding of ethics, combined with selfless motivation to help others, can guide moral actions toward positive outcomes. A husband and his pregnant wife were driving home from the cinema when his wife began the early phase of childbirth and passed out. He immediately turned the car around and headed to the nearest hospital as fast as he could safely drive, going cautiously through red lights as he came to them. After running one red light, a police officer pulled him over. The officer, learning what was happening, gave him a rapid escort to the hospital. He later told the father that, considering the situation, he'd made the right decision to break the law. The mother had required an emergency caesarian section to save the lives of both her and her child.

If the father had believed he had to abide by traffic laws in all situations, he may not have been able to save his wife and daughter, but because he understood the spirit of the law and recognized the gravity of the situation for others, he was able to act in their best interest and not just his own. Although it may seem that anyone would have done the same, I have witnessed on many occasions an ambulance trying to get through an intersection but blocked by a single vehicle whose driver refused to go through the red light to let it pass when it was clearly able to do so.

Action based on a belief that we must strictly adhere to specific social or religious laws or norms can lead to bad outcomes if we fail to consider and question the premises upon which they are built and the purposes they serve. Attention to the Eightfold Path and the ethical code provided by Buddhism's specific precepts* can help develop a moral compass that aligns actions with healthy spiritual growth. Without that guidance, things can go terribly astray, as we have examined with Zen in Japan during World War II (Chapter 7), and with abusive exploitation of students by teachers in the West (Chapter 20). Morality can go in either direction. If we think selfishly, our moral sense will reflect that selfish perspective and our actions will mirror it. Religious rules of conduct, such as those presented by the Vinaya Pitaka, exist to protect us and others from ourselves, and they support a communal environment conducive to spiritual labor.

---

* There is no universally agreed-upon set of precepts in Buddhism. Most Mahāyāna Buddhists, however, abide by the Bodhisattva precepts established in the *Brahmajāla Sūtra* (which scholarship suggests is likely apocryphal—see, for example, Buswell, 1990), which involve not killing, not stealing, not engaging in licentious acts, not lying, not using alcohol, not openly discussing the misdeeds of others, not praising oneself or speaking ill of others, not being miserly, not harboring anger, and not defaming the Buddha, Dharma, or Sangha (Buddhism's *triple refuge*, embraced by all Mahāyāna Buddhists).

Dark emotions

At various stages of practice, we may feel consumed with dark emotions and thoughts. This often occurs during the beginning stages, as repressed emotions from childhood experiences make their way into consciousness. It can happen again later in our journey; an experience St. John of the Cross poetically called the "dark night of the soul." When dark emotions arise, it's important not to hold onto them, but to acknowledge them for what they are and let them go. We don't want to reside in them for any longer than necessary to process them. The work can be expedited if we open ourselves to them and release them, and not suppress or ignore them.

Chan practice can lead to many different mental and emotional states, and all are beneficial if we remain a passive observer and don't grasp onto them, regardless of whether they are pleasant or unpleasant. Depending on the nature of the repressed contents, some people find the anguish that can emerge from beginning mindfulness practice challenging to endure. This should not be an indication, however, that the journey is not valuable and rewarding. Retrieving and purging repressed emotions is critically important for spiritual growth, and immensely liberating.

Visionary experience

"Dreams have only the pigmentation of fact," wrote Djuna Barnes in *Nightwood*. Yet, if we forget this and project an external reality from an internal experience, such as a vision or dream, problems can arise.

The dreaming mind has no awareness of the waking mind, nor does the waking mind have awareness of the dreaming mind.* Though

---

* Some readers may cite lucid dreaming as a counter-example. Lucid dreaming is an experience in which we attain a degree of wakefulness in our dreams, but it does not have the same quality as wakefulness outside of the dream-state: we are consciously aware of dreaming, but still have no awareness of the wakeful mind. Others may cite the unusual occurrence of sleeping with only one side of the brain while the other side remains awake and alert, a common event for many animal species and possible but rare for humans—combat soldiers have reported this phenomenon while fighting for extended periods (Scott

the wakeful mind may retain some memories of a dream, it loses the dream's immediacy and, hence, its reality. When dreams are especially vivid, however, as they are when we experience visions, we may assign them inappropriate value. Visions can linger for hours or even days in the conscious mind, which can lead us to assign them extraordinary importance. But why?

From early childhood, we are taught to distinguish between what is "real" and what is imaginary or dreamlike. We attribute our sense of reality to perceptions we consider non-illusory and associate nonreality with those we deem imaginary, dreamlike, or deceptive. However, as we progress in chan practice, these distinctions can blur. Wakeful states may begin to feel more dreamlike, while dreamlike states may take on a sense of heightened reality.

In some cases, we might mistake dreams or visions for external reality, projecting them as independent subjects. For example, we might become convinced that a dream-image or vision represents a visitor from the "great beyond," overlooking the fact that the imagery originates within us. In more extreme cases, one might believe they are the embodiment of a celestial being (as discussed in Chapters 1, 4, and 12), a delusion that can foster grandiosity and even lead to the creation of harmful cults.

When visionary material from the unconscious is not adequately processed, psychosis can arise. Once this condition takes hold, escaping it alone can be challenging and may require the guidance of a more advanced practitioner—ideally, someone who has faced and overcome such experiences themselves.

In such situations, it is crucial to temporarily pause Chan practice, step back, and adopt the role of a passive observer. Engaging in mundane, grounding tasks and resisting the mind's urge to fixate on unconscious imagery can be especially effective in regaining balance.

2019, 8). Little to no research has been done to understand or confirm this phenomenon in humans.

Institutional allegiance

The psychological forces at work in a religious group can be both alluring and dangerous, a theme I've touched on frequently in this book. Spiritual growth requires that we take control of our lives for ourselves and by ourselves. Furthermore, it requires that we abandon our attachments and desires. Yet ironically, these requirements are often ignored or even discouraged by religious organizations. A challenge for the mystic who engages with a religious group is to avoid replacing one "bubble reality"—our false ego-reality—with another false reality, one created by the social dynamics of the group.

Shedding our attachments—ultimately, our attachment to an imagined personal ego-identity—is of paramount importance for successful chan practice. It can be facilitated by conforming to a social/religious structure that subverts our desire to indulge the ego; however, if we fall blindly into step with a religious program—as noble as it may be—we can easily become servants to that program instead. We may then identify with the religion rather than with the spiritual journey it purports to represent, a journey that requires a specific kind of independent and willful action that can only be obtained through personal autonomy.

It's not uncommon for people to check themselves into a monastery in order to apply structure and discipline to their lives; but if the ultimate intent is to escape from life rather than embrace it, we can be lead toward mindless, spiritless subservience to the institution. Instead of lifting a shroud to reveal reality, the religious institution may put a bag over our heads. We may then mistakenly identify the bag for reality itself. Others may consider that if they are in the presence of a religious institution, or a Zen/Chan Master, they will "absorb" spirituality through some form of osmosis. This "magic pill" approach has two major flaws: first, it falsely presupposes that there is something to "get" that's not already within us, and second, it redirects responsibility for finding it away from us, when we are the only ones who can do the finding. Spiritual insight comes from looking within. Other people can inspire and encourage us, and they can help us learn to turn our gaze inward, but the work must be done by us, and us alone.

Stuart Lachs, having spent decades in Zen training centers, aptly warns of the tendency for institutional Zen to reshape our interpretation of reality through its social rules and symbolic language. Under its spell, he warns, we can mistakenly and dangerously consider our newly acquired yet fabricated sense of reality a fruit of spiritual practice:

> Anyone who visits a Zen Center is usually struck by the formal and ritualized atmosphere of the temple or zendo, an atmosphere that creates a sense of the sacred. Before entering we remove our shoes, finding a certain quiet, the smell of incense, the altar with Buddha statues surrounded by offerings of flowers and fruit and a priest, monk, or nun in formal robes whom others show respect with bows or even prostrations. One quickly learns that there exists a hierarchy as clearly defined and rigid as anything in Western religious institutions. If one becomes involved with the life of the group, one learns that there are set ways to behave in the temple, in the meditation hall, in sharing common meals, greeting other members, monks, or nuns, and when meeting the teacher, Master, or roshi. One also learns a whole new language comprised of a new set of terms and definitions. The adoption and continued use of this language will form the person's view of the world and his/her place in it—both in relation to the larger world and to his/her place within the Zen world. The views espoused within the Zen community will, to one degree or another, reshape and color the person's way of thinking about and views of the world. A person who becomes actively involved with a Zen group not only identifies themselves with Zen ideas and meanings, but also sees himself/herself as expressing these ideas through speech, attitude, and activity and as a representative of Zen itself. Interestingly, many people then attribute their new worldview to the fruit of "practice." What appears as spiritual fruit may in actuality be the adjustment to being schooled and indoctrinated into a prefabricated world-view.[428]

In addition, the social context of Zen/Chan institutions can produce alienation, creating an unfavorable environment for spiritual development. Peter L. Berger, in *The Social Construction of Reality*, describes alienation as

> ...the process whereby the dialectical relationship between the individual and his world is lost to consciousness. The individual "forgets" that this world was and continues to be co-produced by him. Alienated consciousness is undialectical consciousness.*429

We can relate Berger's observation back to the first of Yogācāra's *Three Natures*, or "threefold marks of all things" from the *Saṃdhinirmocana Sūtra* (Chapter 4): we become stuck, "clinging to what is entirely imagined."430 Like seeing a mirage of water and believing it to be water, we fail to recognize that we are co-producers of the experience (the *second mark* of all things).

Alienation has profound effects on both practitioners and leaders. A Zen master, for example, is often identified by his followers as a perfect being. As we explored in Chapter 4, the source of this perspective can be found in Chan's patriarchal lineage system, which evolved from the ancient Chinese tradition of ancestral worship. But how does a human psyche respond to being put in such an impossible, untenable, inhuman role? A role of celestial perfection?† Sometimes Chan Masters come to believe it themselves, and when that happens, Lachs writes, they:

> ... cannot maintain a healthy self-reflection of being human without feeling like a fraud. Instead of seeing themselves as changing human beings, the idealized Zen masters become co-producers of a world in which they are role players, paradoxically, a world that denies who they really are.431

---

* that is, consciousness devoid of rationality.

† Recall from Chapter 1 that the Mahāyāna evolved in part from visionary encounters with divine "celestial beings." It was the Chinese who dovetailed this with the Confucian ideal of ancestral worship to create a marriage between human and divine, resulting in a "perfect master," representative of the Buddha Dharma (Chapter 4).

We have terms for people who perceive themselves to be perfect, and they aren't flattering: self-centered, conceited, vain, narcissistic. Those living out this role may disdain everyone else. In a religious context, people perceived as spiritual icons are considered to be above and beyond the human domain they inhabit, a dichotomy that can lead to unfortunate events. From research and decades of experience in institutional Zen and Chan settings, Lachs has observed that Zen masters performing the role of a perfect human may look contemptuously upon his students/disciples, who he sees clearly to be of lesser importance than himself:

> [The master] knows well that his desires, likes and dislikes, are often in contrast to his officially sanctioned and public face. It is [therefore] not uncommon for the master to become alienated—where one part of the self is in conflict with the other part. All the while, his flock is acting adoringly so that a certain disdain can develop for these adoring, yet somewhat blind worshippers.[432]

Another way a Zen master who lacks spiritual maturity may abuse his authority is to have sex with his students. Dennis Merzel (Genpo Merzel Roshi), for example, after announcing his sexual relations with students, explained that "his affairs were 'not about sex,' but about his feeling of isolation and loneliness as the teacher at the top of an organization."[433]

While there are Zen/Chan teachers who have indeed attained a high degree of spiritual development and don't have issues with alienation described here, they may be few among the many leading Zen or Chan groups. But this knowledge can't help the novice who has no way to differentiate between a sweet apple and a sour one on appearance alone, and who often relies instead upon the well-honed but often misleading mystique of lineage to assess a teacher's credibility.

The rhetoric of the Chan/Zen institution primarily functions as a tool to assert its authenticity and authority, yet it can also mislead the dedicated Chan practitioner. When we align our identity with the institution, we risk ceasing to question its rhetoric and becoming ensnared by it, often to our own detriment. Some of the common rhetoric we hear from the Chan/Zen institution includes:

- The objective of practice is enlightenment.
- Dharma transmission and enlightenment are identical.
- Only through Dharma transmission can one be considered to be enlightened—to have "attained Buddha Mind." Dharma transmission must be received from a monk who has previously received it from another who received it, going back to the Buddha himself. In this way, the mind of the Buddha—the Buddha Dharma—has been preserved.
- An enlightened being is equivalent to the Buddha; therefore, is perfect and beyond reproach.

We can offer an alternate and contrasting set of principles from the perspective of mystical Chan:

- The objective of practice is to transcend suffering (duhkha) and discover hidden truths.
- Dharma transmission can be understood in three ways: first, it can be viewed as a fabricated means for establishing hierarchy within the institution and perpetuating a religious ideology; second, as a means of expressing the value of preserving the message of the Dharma by sharing it with successive generations; third, as a utilization of reification, serving to both acknowledge spiritual awakening and bring it to life as a real "thing"—a mechanism for connecting the spiritual with the corporeal.
- Enlightenment is not identical to anything except itself. It's a particular experience of consciousness encountered when ego-identity is transcended.

- One who has experienced enlightenment attains a new perspective and awareness that was previously unknown. The experience does not make one a perfect human being, nor a Buddha, since Buddha (in Mahāyāna Buddhism) refers to an ideal form—a transcendental, celestial, being (Chapter 1).

If we can identify and use what's beneficial from the institution and discard those things that aren't; moreover, if we can avoid becoming attached to the institution and its defining social paradigm, as difficult as that might be, we can preserve the autonomy essential for spiritual growth.[*]

READERS WHO HAVE MADE IT THROUGH to the end of this last chapter may be wondering why anyone would want to challenge themselves to chan. After all, it not only takes enormous effort, but it comes with a potential minefield of hazards.

Indeed, it's largely for this reason that I wrote this book. Obstacles are prevalent with chan, but obstacles are just as prevalent with life in any context. What sets Chan apart is the way it guides us toward living healthy, meaningful, and engaged lives. It doesn't shield us from life's difficulties; instead, it teaches us to face them directly, to learn from them, and to keep moving forward. True growth, after all, requires struggle.

Difficulties that beginners encounter with chan training often turn them away from it before progress is made. The ego-complex is extremely powerful and commands with great temerity; yet for chan, ig-

---

[*] For many, this is extraordinarily difficult to do. The degree of violence shed in the name of Buddhism offers a stark illustration, as Christopher Ives has noted from his investigation into historical violence by Buddhist monks, especially Japanese Zen monks: "historically, Buddhists' desire for institutional security has taken precedence over total rejection of violence" (1996, 151). We might conclude that subservience to institutions of any kind is potentially dangerous, both to ourselves and to others. Complete allegiance to an individual or institution can lead us to cross all moral boundaries, as we examined in Chapter 20.

noring the ego through a courageous act of will is what we must do. We must deny it what it wants.

Almost every challenge on the Chan journey can be traced back to the ego's cunning and capricious nature. Success in Chan is assured for those who can persevere—who resist the ego's distractions and remain steadfast in their practice.

Final Thoughts

> *If you love the sacred and hate the secular,*
> *You'll float and sink in the birth-and-death sea.*
> *The passions exist dependent on mind;*
> *Have no-mind, and how can they bind you?*
> *Without troubling to discriminate or cling to forms,*
> *You'll attain the Way naturally in a moment of time.*
>
> – Linji

A RAINDROP FALLS FROM THE sky, following its nature without effort or aspiration to be anything other than what it is. It isn't searching for something it lacks; it simply moves forward into the unknown. Spiritual practices are much the same. By committing ourselves to a spiritual discipline, we open the door to discovering our true nature within the mysterious realm of pure being. As we immerse ourselves in this expanded awareness, our perception of what was once hidden begins to expand. Over time, the clarity and truth of this awareness can captivate us so fully that the world we once knew seems like a fleeting dream compared to the vividness of the reality we now experience.

Like the raindrop descending from the sky to merge with the vast ocean below, we come to realize that our essence is not separate from the ocean but is, in fact, the ocean itself. Merging with the ocean, the raindrop's true nature is revealed. The sense of separateness we once held, we discover, was an illusion born of limited perception—a misinterpretation of our fundamental unity. In truth, we were never apart from the whole; we are, and always have been, one with it.

This profound realization arises through the dissolution of attachments—the web of associations we form with the material world that collectively create a false sense of self. Releasing these mental constructs initiates a transformative shift in how we think, feel, and perceive reality. The journey to this understanding requires an intimate act of surrender—a relinquishment of the self as we believe it to be.

Yet, abandoning the constructed self is no simple task. It demands extraordinary commitment, perseverance, and the kind of motivation that comes from a deep yearning to transcend dukkha—the pervasive suffering born of ego-driven awareness.

For those of us ready and eager to embrace the profound transformation that comes with self-abandonment, there is solace in knowing we don't need to start from scratch. The path has been forged by others. Siddhārtha, however, was not so fortunate. His journey required years of dedication, discipline, and perseverance through countless missteps and misguided teachings. Yet, when he finally declared, "Enough is enough!", and took his life into his own hands, he discovered what he had been seeking all along.

Siddhārtha became the Buddha—the Awakened One. His unwavering pursuit of truth and his commitment to sharing it gave rise to one of history's most remarkable religions. At its heart lies a single principle: awakening—a conscious realization of Self, of Buddha Nature.

Yet, Buddhist religious teachings often overlook the significance of this. Like all religions, Buddhism is a social institution, primarily focused on its own preservation and the maintenance of social order. Encouraging genuine spiritual insight is rarely a central priority. As we examined in earlier chapters, this institutional focus has the potential to hinder or even subvert spiritual practice. Fortunately, chan transcends institutional boundaries. It's is an intensely personal practice, one we undertake alone—whether we're serving food in a temple, sitting quietly on a park bench, or jogging along a mountain trail. This independence explains why some of the most dedicated chan practitioners prefer to distance themselves from organized religious groups, even those of their own tradition. History is replete with examples of such solitary practitioners, from the legendary Layman Pang to the countless hermits who sought refuge in the remote mountains of China. They all embraced solitude or secular life as a means to deepen their practice, demonstrating that spiritual life can flourish beyond the confines of organized religion.[434]

One of the most significant challenges for Chan practitioners in a monastic setting is navigating the deeply ingrained master-disciple dynamic (Chapters 20 and 21). This relationship often fosters the belief that a master is necessary to validate spiritual experiences. While this can strengthen group cohesion and reinforce the hierarchical structure essential to any religious institution, it can inadvertently undermine individual confidence by implying that spiritual experiences lack intrinsic validity.

But consider this: when we discover something new, isn't it the joy of the discovery itself that propels us forward? Do we ever truly grasp an insight and then doubt that we've grasped it? If doubt arises, it can signal that we don't need external validation, but rather a deeper trust in our own understanding.

Furthermore, by approaching the path without rigid goals and embracing it as a natural, continuous unfolding of experience, the concept of "attainment" dissolves. When there is nothing to achieve, there is nothing to validate—only the unbroken flow of practice itself.

For better or worse, Chan's lineage system—rooted in a long tradition of ancestor veneration—can tempt us to accept our teachers' actions and guidance without question. However, as we have seen, claims of enlightenment or Dharma transmission do not necessarily guarantee that a teacher possesses a strong moral compass, psychological stability, or intentions aligned with Buddhism's purpose as a path of salvation. Nor do they ensure that such teachers have our best interests at heart.

Chan practice demands that we cultivate a mind that is open, questioning, observant, and unattached. When practicing in an institutional setting, applying these principles can shield us from the pitfalls inherent to such institutions. It also allows us to recognize that the true validation of our efforts lies in the experiences we encounter along the way.

These experiences—whether unpleasant, beautiful, or transcendent—are more than fleeting sensations. Each one brings us closer to understanding the full nature of being alive. And this, ultimately, is the purpose of Chan: a profound engagement with life itself.

Chinese Chan "vs." Japanese Zen

We have a dangerous tendency to consider Zen and Chan and Sŏn to all be the same thing. This is natural considering that the terms all originate from *dhyāna*, meaning to delve within, to contemplate. If we think about these three traditions this way, they are indeed all the same because they will all lead to the same place: knowledge of Self. However, as we explored in Part One, the expression of dhyāna in its institutional forms can differ dramatically from one culture to another, and even between teachers within the same culture. As long as we consider Chan or Zen or Sŏn to be a solitary journey of contemplation and meditation, there's no problem; but, if we mistake its externalized expression for the inner practice, we can be misled.

In Part One, we explored how Chinese Chan evolved through a synthesis of Indian Buddhism, Taoism, and Confucianism, but we can ask whether Chan imported by other cultures necessarily depends upon this particular admixture of "isms." The Western psyche, for example, does not generally relate closely with Chinese attitudes toward ancestral veneration. Yet, Chan evolved in China embracing ancient sensibilities of filial piety and ancestral worship to create a quintessential lineage system; a "genealogy" related not to genetics, but to something called Dharma, an ineffable essence that can be transmitted from one person to another. This system established a uniquely Chinese expression of Buddhism, which had consequences when it was adopted by other cultures. Chinese Buddhism could not be embraced in its original form by its neighbors, who had different endemic values, social and political systems, and indigenous religious beliefs. Adaptations were naturally made.

When Chan was imported to Japan, for example, so was its lineage system, along with Confucian and Taoist ideologies. Since the Japanese didn't readily connect with ancestral worship, they created a substitution. As we explored in Chapter 7, that substitution was Shintōism, which had been ingrained within the Japanese psyche since long before Buddhism arrived from Korea. Rather than venerating ancestors* as the Chinese did, the Japanese venerated their clan chieftain or emperor—assuming that observations like D. T. Suzuki's accurately reflects a consensus of Japanese sentiment: "... god can be something very low for us. We [the Japanese] see the emperor in an area high above all religions" (Chapter 7).

Religions have long been intertwined with heads of state, and this association often shapes their doctrines. When religious teachings adopt the vocabulary of a mystical tradition like chan, that tradition becomes vulnerable to distortion by those seeking power over its followers. They may reinterpret its doctrines—many of which are metaphorical or allegorical—into rigid, literal dogmas designed to serve their political agendas.

Take, for example, Linji's provocative statement: "If you meet your parents, kill your parents. If you meet your kinfolk, kill your kinfolk." Clearly, this was never meant to be taken literally. Linji's words encourage us to sever our attachments to these relationships, not to harm

---

* Some readers may argue this view, citing, for example, the fact that many contemporary devout followers of Sōtō Zen recite daily the many names of their ancestral lineage. Indeed, this may be interpreted as an act of worship, or it may be a ritualized activity to strengthen group solidarity and impress upon devotees the value and historical validity of their sect. It may also be a combination of these things. Nonetheless, the Japanese relationship with Dharma ancestry is markedly different from that of the Chinese.

others. Similarly, his frequent use of the sword as a metaphor symbolized wisdom, insight, mental sharpness, and mindfulness—not physical violence. His intent was to teach and guide, not to promote the acts of killing that some advocates of Buddhism have justified historically in nations where it became a state religion. The symbolic power of the sword lies not in its capacity to harm but in its ability to cut through ignorance and delusion. We do not need a literal weapon to wield this power—only the clarity and insight it represents.

Chan and Zen are still relatively new to the West, and many of us are drawn to them by the allure of Eastern religions. However, as we continue to embrace these traditions, it's worth pausing to reflect on our intentions. What are we truly seeking? Are we looking for community, a sense of belonging, or a structure to help us feel grounded? Are we drawn by cultural fascination, captivated by the mystique and novelty of Asian traditions? Do we see ourselves becoming priests, tending to a spiritual community? Are we in pursuit of prestige, validation, or material gain? Or is our yearning deeper—an earnest search for a spiritual solution to life's challenges? Are we seeking liberation from duhkha, the suffering inherent in samsaric existence? Are we embracing a time-tested model to guide ourselves toward the timeless realization of Self?

As Westerners, we often pride ourselves on independence and freedom of thought and speech. How, then, does Chan or Zen adapt to this cultural context? So far, the adaptation has been imperfect, particularly in institutional settings where small groups gather under the authority of a leader who may lack the spiritual maturity or psychological stability required to guide others effectively.

These challenges highlight the need to thoughtfully adapt Chan and Zen to the Western mindset—one that values openness, questioning, and individual exploration. Indeed, Siddhārtha Gautama purportedly encouraged such independent thinking, assessment, and evaluation. As previously quoted from the *Aṅguttara Nikaya*, he advised his congregants to

> ... not go by oral tradition, by lineage of teaching, by hearsay, by a collection of scriptures, by logical reasoning, by inferential reasoning, by reasoned cogitation, by the acceptance of a view after pondering it, by the seeming competence [of a speaker], or because you think: "The ascetic is our guru." But when, Kalamas, you know for yourselves: "These things are unwholesome; these things are blameworthy; these things are censured by the wise; these things, if accepted and undertaken lead to harm and suffering," then you should abandon them.[435]

Siddhartha's guidance suggests that the challenge of pursuing autonomous spiritual growth within the confines of a religious body is neither unique to our time nor exclusive to our culture. For centuries, seekers from diverse civilizations have wrestled with this tension, striving to balance personal spiritual exploration with the structures, traditions, and expectations imposed by organized religion.

Returning to the Source

The human psyche is enormously complex. As Carl Jung reminded us, "Ultimately, every individual life is at the same time the eternal life of the species."[436] Complexity should be no surprise. Our full human ancestry is contained within each of us, exposing itself through the instinctual behaviors we have inherited and through the dreams and visions they proffer. But what is this thing we call life? That we call consciousness? Was Blaise Pascal right, that reality is an impenetrable secret?

Archeological evidence from around the globe suggests people have thought about the nature of reality and the difficult questions of consciousness for millennia. Records from ancient Greece, Mesopotamia, East Asia, Mesoamerica, and the ancient Indus Valley, make clear that these topics have been of tremendous interest to humanity for a very long time. While the quest to understand life, consciousness, and the experience of reality is not new, definitive answers to these deep questions remain elusive. But why?

Because the mind can glimpse aspects of reality—reflections, imprints, or fragments—but it cannot perceive the whole. According to Donald Hoffman, a professor of cognitive science at the University of California, Irvine, this limitation exists because the mind did not evolve for that purpose. Hoffman offers a provocative perspective on consciousness, arguing that it does not emerge from the mind or brain but rather the reverse: the mind and brain arise from consciousness.

Hoffman suggests that our senses constrain us, preventing us from perceiving reality as it truly is. Instead, we rely on metaphoric, representational "icons"—the objects we identify as real, such as trees, cars, rocks, and lamps—and mistakenly interpret them as objective reality, distinct and separate from ourselves. He refers to his theory as epiphysicalism, proposing that physical objects are not fundamental but are instead constructs of consciousness, created by what he terms *conscious agents*.

Drawing on evolutionary biology's fitness model, Hoffman explains that sensory consciousness is not designed to apprehend reality itself but only a limited, symbolic "reflection" of reality—one tailored for species survival. These representations are akin to a computer interface, where the icons we see don't reveal the true workings of the system but merely allow us to interact with it effectively.

Hoffman's ideas resonate with Blaise Pascal's assertion that the full scope of reality is intrinsically hidden from us. Like a computer confined to its closed system, the mind is bound by its evolutionary constraints and incapable of perceiving what lies beyond them.

In his model, consciousness not only creates the impression of an external reality, but from consciousness the world with all its physical laws emerges: the physical universe, or objective reality, is not *a priori* real, Hoffman says, but is just a collective manifestation of conscious agents, which are simply points of view.[437] He and his team have skillfully worked backward from this hypothesis to show that, through a rigorous mathematical construction of conscious agents, basic properties of quantum physics, and of time itself, can be derived.[438]

Quantum mechanics—a branch of physics which describes physical phenomena at the most fundamental level—describes matter as existing in a "probability cloud," not expressing itself until we participate with it through observation, a postulate originally presented by Erwin Schrödinger in 1926, which has been demonstrated experimentally many times. In fact, the transistor, which forms the basis for all our electronic devices, depends on it. The implication of this theory is that the observer and the observed are mutually interdependent. Hoffman, following Schrödinger's logic, suggests that if we remove the observer (conscious agents), we remove that which can be observed; that is, observed "things" are a manifestation of our consciousness, and not of some alternate, inherent and fundamental, reality. While this is consistent with the principles of quantum mechanics, his argument says nothing about the "probability cloud", which may or may not still be there should an observer come along and participate with it.* An "objective reality" may be there all along; it may just not be what we think it is or imagine it to be. The rock we see may not be at all what we interpret it to be, but something much different, something our minds aren't able to access.† If this is true, what might it tell us? There's no reason to think that the moon we saw last night, but is no longer visible to us today, doesn't exist until we look at it again. Clearly, the moon is there, even though its complete nature may be occluded from view. Our senses aren't lying to us, they just aren't giving us the complete truth. The full reality of the moon is not something we can actually

---

* For example, if we consider Schrödinger's famous cat thought-experiment, often used to introduce students to the perplexing nature of quantum mechanics, if nobody ever opens the box to determine the state of the cat (whether it's alive or dead), this has no bearing on whether or not the cat is, indeed, alive or dead at any moment, but it does suggest that there is a boundary on what can be known.

† For example, if you talk with theoretical physicist, Lisa Randall, Frank J. Baird Professor of Science at Harvard, she will tell you that the universe likely has more dimensions than we can perceive, and many of them are tiny and "curled-up", or warped. She examined these theories in the popular 2005 book, *Warped Passages: Unraveling the Mysteries of the Universe's Hidden Dimensions*.

get to beyond our subjective experience of it, an experience enabled by a consciousness that evolved for optimum species survival, not for clearly seeing reality, Hoffman insists. Which brings us back to not knowing anything about reality at all: if consciousness is what gives rise to our experience of reality, it gets us no closer to understanding what reality actually is because we don't understand consciousness. We remain stuck in a quagmire of vicious mental loops and uncomfortable conundrums. It seems Pascal was right all along. Reality is concealed in an impenetrable secret.

All we can safely say about an objective reality—a reality that exists independently of the observer—is nothing. "It exists" and "it doesn't exist" are mental framings about possibilities for which we have incomplete information. And they are, themselves, fabrications of the mind, which, in Buddhism, is considered just another sensory organ—the one that thinks. We can say that our sensory experience of life is real, as Hoffman does, but we cannot draw reasonable conclusions about a possible "objective" reality beyond that, because any conclusions are themselves necessarily dependent upon mentation. Mentation, in its broadest sense, always gives a subjective view, which is an inherently limited view, if not completely erroneous. Even if we say that the nature of reality is emptiness (as many mystics attest to), what is emptiness? We can experience it, but we can't describe it without using metaphor: we experience reality but we can't identify what it is, much less explain it.

Substantiating Hoffman's theories, John Clause, Alian Aspect, and Anton Zeilinger, winners of the Nobel Prize in physics for experiments on entangled quantum states, have shown experimentally that the objects we experience as objectively real because of their observable properties, are, in fact, unequivocally *not* real. They have shown that, not only is nature not *locally real*, but information at the quantum level is shared expansively and instantaneously, everywhere.

The work of these Noble prize winners offers insight into some profound and perplexing existential questions, such as, "Why am I me instead of someone else?" Since all matter, including ourselves, can be described in its most basic form through the principles of quantum mechanics, could it be that the Self we speak of is also not locally real? In other words, when we connect with the Self, rather than engaging with something intrinsic to our individual mind or body, might we be engaging with something expansive, shared, and instantaneous—something beyond the confines of locality?

If so, this may explain why mystics often describe the experience of Self-awareness as timeless, transcending life and death, and imbued with a sense of immortality. Huangbo Xiyun (Huang Po) expresses this artfully: "The mind is the Buddha, and the Buddha is the mind. The true nature of all things is undying, and this nature is neither large nor small, neither far nor near, and exists in all places. It is nothing but the essence of the one mind." Similarly, Linji Yixuan teaches: "Followers of the Way, don't search for the Buddha; don't search for the Dharma; don't search for anything. At this very moment, what is it that lacks nothing? It is you, before the distinctions of life and death, who are fundamentally free and immortal."

Considering that "I-ness" is an ego-generated experience, and considering the results of research by Clause, Aspect and Zeilinger, we might conclude that the essence of "me," when stripped of the ego's filter, is universal and identical for everyone. That, in essence, there is no difference between "you" and "me". At the root of all things, then, we are the same—expressions of the Whole. Thus, the answer to the question, "Why am I me instead of someone else?" is this: if I were someone else, I would still be me. As perplexing to the mind as it is, we are all "me". In another sense, there is *only* "me".*

When the physical body—home to our ego-identity—ceases to exist, the Whole remains—that is, the *fundamental essence* endures. In this way, we are intrinsically beyond life and death and, in a profound

---

* I am reminded of Richard Feynman's quip about electrons in a discussion with his mentor John Archibald Wheeler. He suggested that there is only one electron in the universe, which is going back and forth in time, making up all the electrons and positrons we observe. Feynman received the Nobel Prize in the field of quantum chromodynamics.

sense, immortal. As the 17th-century Rinzai Zen master Bankei Yōtaku observed: "The Unborn is beyond life and death. Once you awaken to the Unborn, you see that nothing ever comes into being or ceases to exist. In this realization, you are free."

But intellectual understanding is fundamentally distinct from direct, experiential knowledge. Someone may vividly describe a persimmon to me, but until I taste it myself, my understanding will remain incomplete. Similarly, without direct knowledge of the Whole or the Self, the mind fabricates an imagined reality, projecting it onto an externalized, objective world. This illusion veils the Self, concealed behind the mind's discursive and ego-driven awareness.

But this observation is not new to our era.

The foundations of Chan were established by two prominent leaders of early Buddhism: Vasubandhu (4th to 5th century), who developed epistemological solutions to the consciousness "problem", and Xuan Zang (602-664), who took Vasubandhu's ideas and added them to the Chinese Buddhist cannon, along with his own related thoughts. Broadly, these two titans are regarded as the progenitors of the Yogācāra school of Buddhism (Chapter 4), which laid the foundation for Chan. The Yogācāra school is commonly referred to as the Consciousness Only 法相宗 (vijñapti-mātra), or Mind Only school. While the details of Yogācāra epistemology are vast and complex, the basics are simple. People inhabit one of two domains. The first is the domain of the senses, where reality is interpreted solely through cognition—mental activity arising from sensory interactions. In this domain, we mistakenly believe that our impressions of reality are concrete and objective, failing to recognize that they are merely cognitive projections. External objects exist only as "ideas" that we project outward, creating the illusion of a reality separate from ourselves. Even our theories about this reality are no exception—they too are just mental constructs imposed on an imagined, independent world. This is the realm of the unenlightened, those confined within the cognitive sphere, unaware of anything beyond it.

The second domain is that of the enlightened, those who have transcended this cognitive entrapment. In this state, the obstructions that limit perception are removed, and consciousness becomes immediate rather than discursive. The enlightened no longer superimpose mental projections onto reality, seeing instead with clarity unclouded by conceptualization. According to Vasubandhu, what the enlightened mind discovers is not the true nature of reality, but rather what reality is *not*. Buddhist scholar, Dan Lusthaus, explains that vijñapti-mātra is

> ...not a declaration of metaphysical idealism, in which only mind is real, but rather a caution about a cognitive veil, a consciousness that projects and superimposes false notions and presuppositions on to reality, by which we mistake our interpretations for reality itself. Unenlightened cognitions are cognitive constructions. The Yogācāra project is to overcome erroneous cognition and lift the veil. With enlightenment, the projections cease and one's mind becomes the great mirror cognition that reflects everything just as it is.[439]

What I find fascinating is that, over the past few decades, humanity has begun to validate Vasubandhu's thesis through experiments in quantum physics and mathematics. Both Hoffman and Vasubandhu recognize that our minds construct and project an imagined reality onto what we perceive as an external, "objective" world. However, while Hoffman and many physicists focus on studying and analyzing this phenomenon, Vasubandhu's interest lay in helping people transcend the veil of the mind's projections to experience reality directly, as it truly is.

Neither Hoffman nor Vasubandhu attempts to describe the fundamental nature of reality, agreeing that it lies beyond the cognitive capabilities of our limited mind-body system. Yet Vasubandhu takes this insight a step further, asserting that the nature of reality itself is irrelevant. What truly matters, he argues, is expanding our awareness—our consciousness—to connect with it. In doing so, we come to recognize its timeless, unifying essence and understand that the dualistic framework of perception is flawed. The perceived distinction between subject and object is illusory; for example, the moon is not an independent "thing" separate from us. All things, as Vasubandhu reveals, are empty of intrinsic form.

While contemporary thinkers have arrived at these conclusions theoretically and experimentally, Vasubandhu uncovered them empirically through meditation. His profound realizations gave rise to a new form of Buddhist practice that, along with the herculean efforts of Xuan Zang (see Chapter 4), became the central theme of mystical Chinese Chan. Even today, the Chan school, or sect*, is often referred to as the Consciousness Only school.

Contemplating the nature of reality is endlessly fascinating. With a professional background in physics, I still enjoy exploring the latest experimental and theoretical research in this field. Yet, no matter what we "discover" about reality, it will always be filtered through the mind—it cannot be otherwise. Even when such discoveries align with the mystical insights of Vasubandhu and Xuan Zang, they remain products of cognition.

What is truly remarkable, however, is how the direct, intuitive realization of these insights—not through rational analysis but through a mystical lens—profoundly transforms us. It reshapes how we see, think, and feel about everything. It diminishes our pains and sufferings to near insignificance. It liberates us from the torment of a manipulative ego we once mistook for our Self.

This awakening begins when we detach from the projections we cast onto the things we perceive as separate and uniquely defined. By turning our gaze inward—toward the source of consciousness itself—we transcend these illusions and connect with a deeper, unified truth.

When we neglect our inner lives, we risk becoming little more than automatons, operating on predetermined instructions shaped by our

---

* I have heard arguments that, as a mystical practice, chan is not a religious sect because it does not rely on a religious social structure or on institutional conformity, both of which are necessary for the establishment of a traditional sect. The counterargument considers that much Zen/Chan training occurs within a highly structured, ritualized, institutional environment, so it's therefore very much a religious sect. The context in which we participate with Chan will obviously affect our relationship with it.

experiences, instincts, attitudes, beliefs, judgments, moods, and moral dispositions. Over time, as our sense of separation from our inner selves deepens, so too does a yearning to feel whole—to connect with something beyond explanation or comprehension, something that lies outside the realm of our usual knowledge.

Some respond to this unsettling feeling by turning away from it. They ignore it, suppress it, or distract themselves in countless ways. Yet, this avoidance only deepens the chasm between us and our Selves—our connection with reality. If we remain trapped in these conditioned ways of perceiving and engaging with the world, we grow increasingly fractured, disconnected, and discontented.

However, when we muster the courage to look within—to explore the depths of hidden inner knowledge—the journey that unfolds is not only transformative but deeply healing in ways we could never have anticipated. My own spiritual journey began in a place of overwhelming despair and anguish, feelings I could neither understand nor escape. This suffering, which eventually led me to chan, dissipated as I learned to shift my attention away from myself. I didn't need to "discover" reality—it was always there, waiting. I simply couldn't perceive it through the haze of self-inflicted misery.

For those grappling with existential questions or yearning for profound change, chan offers a path forward. All it takes is a deep breath, an open heart, and a willing mind to dive into the Dharma. Exploring chan may not only transform your perspective—it may just transform your life.

Notes

INTRODUCTION

1   Blaise Pascal, *Pascal's Pensées* (Seattle, WA: Loki's Publishing, 2017).
2   Alan Cole, *Patriarchs on Paper: A Critical History of Medieval Chan Literature* (Oakland, CA: University of California Press, 2016), 12-13.
3   Taigen Dan Leighton, "Zazen as an Enactment Ritual," in Zen Ritual (Oxford: Oxford University Press, 2008), 167.
4   Robert Sharf, "Mindfulness and Mindlessness in Early Chan," Philosophy East & West 64, no. 4 (2014): 940.
5   Empty Cloud, "Poems by Empty Cloud: Series II," in Exploring Chan. http://www.eyeofchan.org/special-features/poetry-of-empty-cloud/495-hsuyunpoems2.html.
6   Sharf, *Mindfulness and Mindlessness in Early Chan*, 937-8.
7   Chanida Jantrasrisalai, *Early Buddhist Dhammakaya: Its Philosophical and Soteriological Significance* (Sydney: The University of Sydney, 2008), 48-50.
8   Jantrasrisalai, *Early Buddhist Dhammakaya: Its Philosophical and Soteriological Significance*, 47.
9   Luther Blissett, *Anarchist Integralism: Aesthetics, Politics and the Apres-Garde* (London, UK: Sabotage Editions, 1997).
10 Tilmann Vetter, *The Ideas and Meditative Practices of Early Buddhism* (New York: E. J. Brill, 1988), xxxiii.
11 Ernest Wood, *Yoga* (Harmondsworth, Middlesex, England: Penguin Books, Ltd., 1959), 198.
12 See, for example, Anthony Stevens, *The Two Million-Year-Old-Self*, Texas A&M University Press, College Station, 1993.
13 See, for example, *Language, Thought, and Reality: Selected Writings of Benjamin Lee Whorf*, second ed., The MIT Press, 2012.

PART ONE

14 See, for example, Skilton 2001, N. R. Reat 1994, Conze 1993, Harvey 1995, McRae 2003, DeCaroli 2004, Cole 2009, Victoria 2006, Foulk 1992, Vetter 1988.
15 Wendi L. Adamek, *The Mystique of Transmission: On an Early Chan History and its Contents* (New York, NY: Columbia University Press, 2007), 3.

Chapter 1. India

16   D. N. Jha, *Ancient India In Historical Outline* (New Delhi: Manohar Publishers & Distributors, 20011), 69.
17   Jha, *Ancient India In Historical Outline*, 69.
18   Edward Conze, *A Short History of Buddhism* (Guernsey, Great Britain: Oneworld Publications, 1993), 8.
19   Majjhima Nikaya, *Majjhima Nikaya*, ed. V. Trenckner, vol. I (Pali Text Society (PTS), 1888, 1993), 77-80.
20   Jha, *Ancient India In Historical Outline*, 70.
21   Vetter, *The Ideas and Meditative Practices of Early Buddhism*, XII.
22   Edward Fitzpatrick Crangle, *The Origin and Development of Early Indian Contemplative Practices*, ed. Walther Heissig and Hans-Joachim Klimkeit, vol. 29 (Weisbaden: Die Deutsche Bibliothek - CIP-Einheitsaufnahme, 1994).
23   Hermann Oldenberg, *The Religion of the Veda*, trans. Shridhar B Shrotri (Delhi, India: Motilal Banarsidass Publishers Private Limited, 1988), 250.
24   Jha, *Ancient India In Historical Outline*, 59.
25   Encyclopedia Britannica, (4 9 2015). http://www.britannica.com/topic/vratya.
26   Ph.D. Georg Feuerstein, *The Yoga Tradition, It's History, Literature, Philosophy and Practice* (Chino Valley, AZ: Hohm Press, 2008), 121.
27   Georg Feuerstein, *The Yoga Tradition, It's History, Literature, Philosophy and Practice*, 117.
28   Ibid, 131
29   M.A. Robert Ernest Hume, Ph.D., *The Thirteen Principal Upanishads*, trans. M.A. Robert Ernest Hume, Ph.D. (Oxford, England: Oxford University Press, 1921), 126.
30   Robert Ernest Hume, *The Thirteen Principal Upanishads*, 142.
31   Georg Feuerstein, *The Yoga Tradition, It's History, Literature, Philosophy and Practice*, 130.
32   Robert Ernest Hume, *The Thirteen Principal Upanishads*, 346-48.
33   Digha Nikaya, *Digha Nikaya*, vol. 2, 156.
34   D. L. Snellgrove, "Sakyamuni's final nirvana," *Bulletin of the School of Oriental and African Studies* 36, no. 2 (1973): 401-2.
35   S. Beal and D. J. Gogerly, "Comparative Arrangement of two Translations of the Buddhist Ritual for the Priesthood, known as the Prátimoksha, or Pátimokhan.," *Journal of the Royal Asiatic Society of Great Britain & Ireland* 19, no. Art. XVIII (1862).
36   Étienne Lamotte, *History of Indian Buddhism*, trans. Sara Webb-Boin (Louvain-Paris: Peeters Press, 1988), 86.
37   Donald S. Lopez Jr., *The Norton Anthology of World Religions, Hinduism, Buddhism, Daoism*, ed. Donald S. Lopez Jack Miles General Editor with Wendy Doniger, Jr., James Robson (New York: W. W. Norton & Company, Inc., 2015), 860.
38   Donald S. Lopez Wendy Doniger, Jr., James Robson, *The Norton Anthology of World Religions*, Two vols., vol. One (New York, NY: W. W. Norton & Company, Inc., 2015), 861.
39   Noble Ross Reat, *The Salistamba Sutra* (New Delhi, India: Motilal Banarsidass Publishers, 1993), 43.
40   Reat, *The Salistamba Sutra*, 43.
41   Wendy Doniger, *The Norton Anthology of World Religions*, One, 861.
42   Vetter, *The Ideas and Meditative Practices of Early Buddhism*, XXV.
43   Reat, *The Salistamba Sutra*, 26.
44   Bhikkhu Bodhi, *The Connected Discourses of the Buddha: A New Translation of the Samyutta Nikaya*, trans. Translated from the Pali by Bhikkhu Bodhi (Somerville, MA: Wisdom Publications, 2000), 89.

45 Aṅguttara Nikāya, IV, 280-281
46 Williams, *Mahayana Buddhism, the doctrinal foundations*, 57.
47 Quoted by Florin Giripescu Sutton in *Existence and Enlightenment in the Laṅkāvatāra Sūtra*, p. 149.
48 Kaisa Puhakka, "Awakening from the Spell of Reality: Lessons from Nāgārjuna," in *Encountering Buddhism: Western Psychology and Buddhist Teachings* (Albany, NY: State University of New York Press, 2003), 132.
49 Paul Harrison and John R. McRae, translators, *The Pratyutpanna Samādhi Sūtra and The Śūraṅgama Samādhi Sūtra* (Moraga, CA: BDK America, Inc., 1998), 40.
50 Nikaya, *Majjhima Nikaya*, I, 486.
51 Fritz Staal, "The Fidelity of Oral Tradition and the Origins of Science, Mededelingen der Koninklijke Nederlandse Akademie von Wetenschappen," (Afd. Letterkunde, 1986).
52 Pierre-Sylvain Filliozat, "Ancient Sanskrit Mathematics: An Oral Tradition and a Written Literature," in *History of Science, History of Text* (Boston Series in the Philosophy of Science) (Dordrecht: Springer Netherlands: 2004), 139.
53 Filliozat, *Ancient Sanskrit Mathematics: An Oral Tradition and a Written Literature*, 139.
54 Ibid.
55 Ibid.
56 Ibid, 140-41.
57 Williams, *Mahayana Buddhism, the doctrinal foundations*, 22-23.
58 Reat, *The Salistamba Sutra*, 4
59 Ibid, 65-66.
60 Ibid. 70.
61 Paul Harrison and John R. McRae, *The Pratyutpanna Samādhi Sūtra and The Śūraṅgama Samādhi Sūtra*, 42.
62 Williams, *Mahayana Buddhism, the doctrinal foundations*.
63 Edward Conze, *The Perfection of Wisdom in Eight Thousand Lines & Its Verse Summary*, trans. Edward Conze (1973), Chapter XXXI, Dharmodgata, paras 3-5.
64 Nick Bostrom, "Are You Living in a Computer Simulation," *Philosophical Quarterly* 53 (2003).
65 Hillman, James, *Uniform Edition of the Writings of James Hillman*, 2013, 18.
66 Translation by Lin Yutang.
67 Noble Ross Reat, *Buddhism, A History* (Berkley: Asian Humanities Press, 1994), 25.
68 G. Schopen, *Buddhist Monks and Business Matters: Still More Papers on Monastic Buddhism in India* (Honolulu: University of Hawai'i Press, 2004), 15.
69 Ibid. 211.
70 Schopen, *Buddhist Monks and Business Matters: Still More Papers on Monastic Buddhism in India*, 92-3.
71 Williams, *Mahayana Buddhism, the doctrinal foundations*, 38.
72 Ibid, 37.
73 Ibid, 40.
74 Paul Harrison, "Mediums and messages: Reflections on the production of Mahayana sutras," *The Eastern Buddhist*, no. New Series 35 (1/2) (2003): 142.
75 Williams, *Mahayana Buddhism, the doctrinal foundations*, 41.
76 J. Nattier, "The Heart Sutra: A Chinese apocryphal text?," *Journal of the International Association of Buddhist Studies* 15, no. 2 (1992).
77 Williams, *Mahayana Buddhism, the doctrinal foundations*, 42.
78 Reat, *Buddhism, A History*, 74-5.

Chapter 2. Sri Lanka

79 A. K. Warder, *Indian Buddhism* (Motilal Banarsidass, 2008), 280.
80 A. G. S. Kariyawasam, "Buddhist Ceremonies and Rituals of Sri Lanka," *Access to Insight* (1996). http://www.accesstoinsight.org/lib/authors/kariyawasam/wheel402.html.
81 Hannah Beech, "Buddhists Go to Battle: When Nationalism Overrides Pacifism," *The New York Times*, July 8, 2019.

Chapter 3. Tibet

82 Reat, *Budhism, A History*, 240.
83 Ibid, 246.
84 *Demographics of Buddhism*, Berkley Center (2018)

Chapter 4. China

85 Reat, *Buddhism, A History*, 133.
86 Williams, *Mahayana Buddhism, the doctrinal foundations*, 330.
87 Paul Harrison and John R. McRae, *The Pratyutpanna Samādhi Sūtra and The Śūraṅgama Samādhi Sūtra* (1998), 8.
88 David N. Keightley, *These Bones Shall Rise Again*, ed. Henry Rosemont Jr. (Albany, NY: SUNY Press, 2014).
89 Ibid, 61.
90 Keightley, *These Bones Shall Rise Again*, 63.
91 Ibid.
92 Jeffrey Riegel, "Confucius," *Stanford Encyclopedia of Philosophy* (2013).
93 Ibid.
94 Reat, *Buddhism, A History*, 124-35.
95 Riegel, *Confucius*.
96 Reat, *Buddhism, A History*, 135.
97 Holmes Welch, *The Practice of Chinese Buddhism 1900-1950* (London: Oxford University Press, 1967), 24.
98 Jeaneane Fowler, *An Introduction To The Philosophy And Religion Of Taoism: Pathways To Immortality* (Brighton: Sussex Academic Press, 2005).
99 John Stubbs, *Lao Tzu Tao Te Ching: By The Way* (Cobourg, ON: John Stubbs, 2016), 2, 10,12.
100 Russell Kirkland, *Taoism: The Enduring Tradition* (New York: Routledge, 2004), 33, 34.
101 Burton Watson, *Chuang Tzu Basic Writings*, trans. Burton Watson (New York: Columbia University Press, 1996), 13.
102 Watson, *Chuang Tzu Basic Writings*, 58-9.
103 Ibid, 94-5.
104 Ibid, 72.
105 Ibid. 95.
106 Lin Yutang, *The Wisdom of Laotse*, ed. Lin Yutang (New York: Random House, 1948), 7.
107 Reat, *Buddhism, A History*, 138.
108 Ibid, 140-45.
109 Ibid, 140.

110 Ibid.
111 Ibid, 141.
112 Bhikkhu Anālayo, *Satipaṭṭhāna: the direct path to realization* (Birmingham: Windhorse, 2003), 125.
113 Reat, *Buddhism, A History*, 490.
114 Ibid, 150.
115 Sally Hovey Wriggins, *The Silk Road Journey with Xuanzang* (Boulder, CO: Westview Press, 1996), 11.
116 Xuanzang. *Three Texts on Consciousness Only*. (Berkeley: Numata Center for Buddhist Translation and Research, 1999).
117 John P Keenan Xuanzang, *The Scripture on the Explication of Underlying Meaning*, trans. Translated from the Chinese of Hsiian-tsang by Joh n P. Keena (Berkeley CA: Numata Center for Buddhist Translation and Research, 2000).
118 Étienne Lamotte, *Louvain. Asaṅga: La Somme du Grand Vehicule d'Asaṅga* (Mahayanasamgraha). (Bureaux du Muséon, 1938).
119 Hsüan-tsang, *Ch'eng wei-shih lun*, trans. Wei Tat (Hong Kong: Ch'eng wei-shih lun Publication Committee, 1973), 117-21.
120 Reat, *Buddhism, A History*, 150.
121 Ibid, 147.
122 Alan Cole, *Fathering Your Father: The Zen of Fabrication in Tang Buddhism* (2009), 63-69.
123 Alan Cole, *Patriarchs on Paper: A Critical History of Medieval Chan Literature*, 22-25.
124 Reat, *Buddhism, A History*, 153.
125 Ibid, 154.
126 Williams, *Mahayana Buddhism, the doctrinal foundations*, 239.
127 Adamek, *The Mystique of Transmission: On an Early Chan History and its Contents*, 5-6.
128 Ibid, 7.
129 Cole, *Patriarchs on Paper: A Critical History of Medieval Chan Literature*, 7.
130 Wendy Doniger, *The Norton Anthology of World Religions*, One, 5-6.
131 See, for example, Alan Cole's *Fathering Your Father: The Zen of Fabrication in Tang Buddhism* 2009; John McRae's *Seeing Through Zen: Encounter, Transformation, and Genealogy in Chinese Chan Buddhism*, 2003; Morten Schlütter's *How Zen Became Zen*, 2008; and Robert H. Sharf's *Coming to Terms with Chinese Buddhism*, 2002.
132 Cole, *Patriarchs on Paper: A Critical History of Medieval Chan Literature*, 13.
133 Ibid, 28.
134 Eric Chaline, *The book of Zen: The Path to Inner Peace* (Barron's Educational Series, 2003), 26-27.
135 From the *Keitoku dentōroku*, book 3, T. 2076, vol 51. P. 219a.
136 Lin Boyuan, *Zhōngguó wǔshù shǐ* 中國武術史 (Taipei Wǔzhōu chūbǎnshè 五洲出版社, 1996), 183.
137 Sutton, Florin Giripescu, *Existence and Enlightenment in the Laṅkāvatāra-sutra: A Study in the Ontology and Epistemology of the Yogācāra School of Mahāyāna Buddhism.*,162.
138 Alan Cole, "Conspiracy's Truth: The Zen of Narrative Cunning in the Platform Sutra," *Asia Major* 28 (2015): 146 fn 3.
139 Cole, *Patriarchs on Paper: A Critical History of Medieval Chan Literature*, 24.
140 Cole, *Patriarchs on Paper: A Critical History of Medieval Chan Literature*, 26.

141 For an examination of the role Faru's funerary stele played in developing the early structure of Chan Buddhism, see Alan Cole's *Patriarchs on Paper*, 2016, University of California Press, pp. 59-69; and John R. McRae's *Seeing Through Zen, Encounter, Transformation, and Genealogy in Chinese Chan Buddhism*, University of California Press, 2003, p. 84.

142 Cole, *Patriarchs on Paper: A Critical History of Medieval Chan Literature*, 72.

143 Thomas Cleary, *Transmission of Light: Zen in the Art of Enlightenment by Zen Master Keizan* (North Point Press, 1999), 126.

144 Heinrich Dumoulin, *Zen Buddhism: A History* (Bloomington, IN: Wold Wisdom, Inc., 2005), 39-54, 137-8.

145 Alan Cole, *Fathering Your Father: The Zen of Fabrication in Tang Buddhism* (Berkeley, CA: University of California Press, 2009), 39-54, 137-8.

146 Philip B. Yampolsky, *The Platform Sutra of the Sixth Patriarch* (New York: Columbia University Press, 1967), 4.

147 Ibid, 18.

148 Ibid, 23-38.

149 John R. McRae, *Seeing Through Zen: Encounter, Transformation, and Genealogy in Chinese Chan Buddhism* (Berkeley and Los Angeles, CA: University of California Press, 2003), 54-56.

150 John R. McRae, *Seeing Through Zen: Encounter, Transformation, and Genealogy in Chinese Chan Buddhism* (Berkeley and Los Angeles, CA: University of California Press, 2003), 52.

151 Ibid, 54.

152 Robert Thurman, *The Vimalakri Nirdesa Sutra* (The Pennsylvania State University, 1976).

153 See McRae, "Shen Hui," for a thorough examination of Shenhui's historicity and enduring influence on early Chan.

154 See, for example, John Jorgensen's extensive analysis of the Huineng legend in *Inventing Hui-Neng, the Sixth Patriarch: Hagiography and Biography in Early Ch'an*, Brill, 2005.

155 McRae, *Seeing Through Zen: Encounter, Transformation, and Genealogy in Chinese Chan Buddhism*, 60-69.

156 Ibid.

157 Ibid.

158 Yampolsky, *The Platform Sutra of the Sixth Patriarch*, 80.

159 Ibid, 163.

160 Ibid, 136-37.

161 Ibid, 143-44.

162 Ibid, 160.

163 McRae, *Seeing Through Zen: Encounter, Transformation, and Genealogy in Chinese Chan Buddhism*, 70.

164 Ibid.

165 Albert Welter, *The Linji Lu and the Creation of Chan Orthodoxy: The Development of Chan's Records of Sayings Literature* (Oxford: Oxford University Press, Inc., 2008), 48.

166 From the *Record of the Transmission of the Lamp* as quoted by Chung-Yuan, 1971, xi.

167 Cole, *Patriarchs on Paper: A Critical History of Medieval Chan Literature*, 197.

168 Welter, *The Linji Lu and the Creation of Chan Orthodoxy: The Development of Chan's Records of Sayings Literature*, 163.

169 Morten Schlütter, *How Zen Became Zen* (Honolulu: Sheridan Books, 2008), 182.

170 Keightley, *These Bones Shall Rise Again*, 51-70.

171 T. Griffith Foulk, "The Ch'an Tsung in Medieval China: School, Lineage, or What?," *The Pacific World*, no. 8 (1992): 18.

172 Holmes Welch, *The Practice of Chinese Buddhism 1900-1950* (London: Oxford University Press, 1967), 96, 111, 134.

173 Holmes Welsh, "Dharma Scrolls and the Succession of Abbots in Chinese Monasteries," *International Journal of Chinese Studies* 50 (1963), 134.

174 Hsu Yun, "Poems by Empty Cloud: Series II," Exploring Chan (2014). http://www.eyeofchan.org/special-features/poetry-of-empty-cloud/495-hsuyunpoems2.html.

175 Welch, *The Practice of Chinese Buddhism* 1900-1950, 397.

176 Welsh, *Dharma Scrolls and the Succession of Abbots in Chinese Monasteries*, 123.

177 Welsh, *Dharma Scrolls and the Succession of Abbots in Chinese Monasteries*, 123.

178 Hasebe Yūkei, *Min Shin Bukkyō kyōdanshi kenkyū* (1993), 268-273.

179 Hsuan-Li Wang, "Gushan: the Formation of a Chan Lineage During the Seventeenth Century and Its Spread to Taiwan," (Columbia University, Ph. D. Thesis, 2014), 88.

180 Asian Art Museum n.d.

181 Reat, *Buddhism, A History*, 159.

182 Ibid.

183 Ibid, 161.

184 Chuan Yuan Shakya, *Empty Cloud: The Teachings of Xu (Hsu) Yun* (Las Vegas, NV: The Nan Hua Chan Buddhist Society, 1996), 4.

185 Reat, *Buddhism, A History*, 162-3.

186 Jy Din Shakya, *Empty Cloud: The Teachings of Xu (Hsu) Yun* (Las Vegas, NV: Nan Hua Chan Buddhist Society, 1996), xi.

187 USCIRG, USCIRF-RECOMMENDED COUNTRIES OF PARTICULAR CONCERN, United States Commission on International Religious Freedom (USCIRG) (2017).

Chapter 5. Korea

188 The Economist, "Korea in Chinese history: Stuck in the Middle," 2013.

189 Jung Young Lee, *Korean Shamanistic Rituals* (Mouton De Gruyter, 1981), 18.

190 Reat, *Buddhism, A History*, 167.

191 Ibid, 174.

192 Ibid, 177.

193 Ibid, 180.

194 Ibid, 182.

195 See, for example, Turning the Wheel: American Women Creating the New Buddhism, by Sandy Boucher, Harper collins, June, 1988; How the Swans Came to the Lake: A Narrative History of Buddhism in America, 3rd ed. by Rick Fields, Shambhala 1992; and The 60s communes: Hippies and Beyond by Timothy Miller, Syracuse University Press: 1999.

196 See, for example, *Language, Thought, and Reality: Selected Writings of Benjamin Lee Whorf*, second ed., The MIT Press, 2012.

Chapter 7. Japan

197 Victoria, *Zen at War*, 2006.

198 For example, for Buddhists at war in Sri Lanka, see Tessa J. Bartholomeusz' thoroughly researched book, *In Defense of Dharma, Just-war ideology in Buddhist Sri Lanka*, RoutledgeCurzon, New York, NY, 2002; for Buddhists at war in China, see Xue Yu's *Buddhism, War, and Nationalism: Chinese Monks in the Struggle Against Japanese Aggressions, 1931-1945*, Routledge, New York, NY 2005 and *The Shaolin Monastery: History, Religion, and the Chinese Martial Arts*, by Meir Shahar, University of Hawai'i Press, Honolulu, 2008; for Buddhists at war in Vietnam, see Mark Mayar's article, *Political Monks: The Militant*

Buddhist Movement during the Vietnam War, Cambridge University Press, Modern Asian Studies, 6 October 2004; and a compendium of articles edited by Michael Jerryson and Mark Juergensmeyer, *Buddhist Warfare*, Oxford University Press, New York, NY, 2010. For Buddhists' violence against Muslims in Myanmar, see Francis Wade's *Enemy Within: Buddhist Violence and the Making of a Muslim 'Other'*, Zed Books, Ltd, London, UK 2017.

199 See, for example, *Zen and the Way of the Sword: Arming the Samurai Psyche*, by Winston L. King, Oxford University Press, Nov 1, 1994.

200 Reat, *Buddhism, A History*, 187.

201 Ibid.

202 Anne Buttimer, *Nature and Identity in Cross-Cultural Perspective*, ed. Luke Wallin Anne Buttimer (Netherlands: Dordrecht: Springer, 1999).

203 Reat, *Buddhism, A History*, 188.

204 Ibid.

205 Ichiro Ishida Delmer M. Brown, *The Future and the Past, a translation and study of the Gukansho, an interpretive history of Japan written in 1219* (Berkeley, CA: University of California Press, 1979), 249.

206 Andrew Skilton, *A Concise History of Buddhism* (Woodbridge Park: Biddles Ltd, Walnut Tree House, 2001), 178.

207 Reat, *Buddhism, A History*, 190.

208 Ibid, 190.

209 Ibid, 194.

210 Winston L. King, *Death Was His Koan, The Samurai-Zen of Suzuki Shōsan* (Freemont, CA: Asian Humanities Press, 1986), 25.

211 King, *Death Was His Koan, The Samurai-Zen of Suzuki Shōsan*, 25.

212 Reat, *Buddhism, A History*, 198.

213 Ibid, 202-204.

214 Esben Andreasen, "Popular Buddhism in Japan, Shin Buddhist Religion and Culture" (Japan: Curzon Press Ltd., 1998), 11.

215 Masaharu Anesaki, "History of Japanese Religion, with special reference to the social and moral life of the nation" (C. E. Tuttle Co, 1963), 198.

216 Reat, *Buddhism, A History*, 206.

217 Ibid.

218 See, for example, Steven Heine's book (2006), *Did Dogen go to China? What He Wrote and When He Wrote It*.

219 Steven Heine, "Dogen, Textual and Historical Studies," ed. Steven Heine (Oxford: Oxford University Press, 2012), 96

220 Reat, *Buddhism, A History*, 215-216.

221 Stephen Turnbull, *Warriors of Medieval Japan* (New York, NY: Osprey Publishing Ltd., 2005), 211.

222 Reat, *Buddhism, A History*, 211.

223 G. B. Sansom, "The Western World and Japan" (Tokyo: Charles E. Tuttle Company, 1950), 215.

224 Reat, *Buddhism, A History*, 215.

225 James Edaward Ketelaar, "Of Heretics and Martyrs in Meiji Japan" (Princeton, NJ: Princeton University Press), 7.

226 Anesaki, "History of Japanese Religion, with special reference to the social and moral life of the nation," 335.

227 Victoria, *Zen at War*, 8.

228 N. Matsunami, "The Constitution of Japan" (Tokya: Maruzen, 1930), 136.

229 Anesaki Masaharu, *Bukkyo Seiten Shi-ron* (Tokyo: Keiso Shoin, 1899), no. 1.
230 Daido Shinpo, quoted in the journal, *Daidō Shinpō* (March 11 1889).
231 Victoria, *Zen at War*, 20.
232 Ibid, 22.
233 James E. Ketelaar, "Kaikyoron: Buddhism Confronts Modernity," Zen Buddhism Today (1996): 31.
234 Moriya Tomoe, "Social Ethics of 'New Buddhists' at the Turn of the Twentieth Century," Japanese Journal of Religious Studies (2005): 291.
235 Tomoe, *Social Ethics of New Buddhists at the Turn of the Twentieth Century*, 296.
236 Ibid, 296.
237 Ibid, 293-97.
238 Ibid.
239 Inoue Shūten, *Shin Bukkyō* 12, 1911, as quoted by Tomoe, 2005, 294.
240 D. T. Suzuki, "*Shin Shūkyō-ron, Suzuki Daisetsu Zenshū*," no. 23 (1969): 136-37.
241 Victoria, *Zen at War*, 25
242 Shaku Sōen, Quoted in the journal, *Heimin Shimbun* (August 7 1904).
243 Akizuki Ryōmin, *Nantenbō Zenwa*, ed. Akizuki Ryōmin (Tokyo: Hirakawa Shuppan, 1985), 51.
244 Victoria, *Zen at War*, 37.
245 Ibid.
246 Inagaki Masami, *Henkaku o motometa Bukkyō-sha* (Tokyo: Daizō Shinsho, 1975), 112-113.
247 As quoted by Victoria 1998, 72.
248 Hayashiya Tomojirō 1937, 4, 7, as quoted by Victoria, 2006, 87
249 Shimizu Ryūzan, *Risshō Ankoku no Taigi to Nippon Seishin* (Kyoto: Heirakuji Shoten, 1934), 46.
250 Ibid.
251 Gorō 1938, 23-25, as quoted by Victoria, 2006, 117.
252 For an examination of dehumanization during wartime, see *Dehumanization: A Composite Psychological Defense in Relation to Modern War*, by Viola W. Bernard, Perry Ottenberg, and Fritz Redl, in *Behavioral Science and Human Survival*, edited by Milton Schwebel, 2003, pp. 64-82.
253 Terry McCarthy, "Japanese troops 'ate flesh of enemy and civilians,'" *Independent* (August Tuesday 1992).
254 Katsuichi Honda, *The Nanjing Massacre: A Japanese Journalist Confronts Japan's National Shame*, ed. Frank Gibney (New York, NY: M. E. Sharpe, 1999).
255 Christopher Ives, "Wartime Nationalism and Peaceful Representation: Issues Surrounding the Multiple Zens of Modern Japan," *Japan Studies Review* (2001), 40.
256 Gerhard Rosenkranz, Fernost - wohin? Begegnungen mit den Religionen Japans und Chinas im Umbruch der Gegenwart, (Heilbronn: Verlag Eugen Salzer, 1940).
257 "POLL: Negative views of Russia on the Rise: Global Poll ", BBC News (2014). http://downloads.bbc.co.uk/mediacentre/country-rating-poll.pdf.
258   Mariko Oi, "What Japanese history lessons leave out," BBC News (2013). http://www.bbc.com/news/magazine-21226068.

CHAPTER 8. CHAN'S MIGRATION WEST

259 Emma Barnett, *Mindfulness: the saddest trend of 2015* (January 8 2015).
260 Megan Rose Dickey, "Meditation Startup Headspace Raises $30 Million To Help You Be More Mindful," (September 21 2015).

261 Megan Rose Dickey, "Meditation Startup Headspace Raises $30 Million To Help You Be More Mindful," (September 21 2015).
262 Ibid.

CHAPTER 9. PREREQUISITES

263 John R. McRae, *The Northern School and the Formation of Early Ch'an Buddhism* (Honolulu: University of Hawaii Press, 1986), 112.
264 Pascal, *Pascal's Pensées*, 45-6.
265 J. C. Cleary, *Swampland Flowers: The letters and lectures of Zen Master Ta hui*, ed. J. C. Cleary (Boston: Shambhala, 1977), 43.
266 Anil Ananthaswamy, *The Man Who Wasn't There: Investigations into the Strange New Science of the Self* (New York, NY: Dutton, 2015), 63-67.
267 Ibid, 91.
268 Justin Kruger and David Dunning, "Unskilled and Unaware of It: How Difficulties in Recognizing One's Own Incompetence Lead to Inflated Self-Assessments," *Journal of Personality and Social Psychology* (1999).
269 David Dunning, "Anosognosic's Dilemma: Something's Wrong but You'll Never Know What It Is" (Part 1) (June 20, 2010).
270 "The National Alliance on Mental Illness," Nami.Org (2013).
271 "Most Prescribed Branded Drugs Through March," (*Medscape Medical News*, May 2015).
272 C. G. Jung, *Psychological Types, Collected Works*, vol. 6 (Princeton, NJ: Princeton University Press, 1971).
273 Han Shan, *The Autobiography and Maxims of Chan Master Han Shan 1546-1623*, trans. Upasaka Richard Cheung (Honolulu, HI: Hsu Yun Temple, 1999), 48.
274 Vetter, *The Ideas and Meditative Practices of Early Buddhism*, xxxvii.
275 "Muslim MTA Employee Attacked At Grand Central Is Latest in String of Hate Crimes," updated December 5, 2016.
276 Shan, *The Autobiography and Maxims of Chan Master Han Shan 1546-1623*, 51.
277 Christmas Humphreys, *Meditation and Concentration, A Manual of Mind Development* (Longmead, Shaftesbury, Dorset, Great Britain: Element Books, Ltd., 1987), 5.
278 Erwin Rousselle, *Spiritual Guidance in Contemporary Taoism*, trans. Translated from the German by Ralph Manheim, vol. 4 (New York, NY: Pantheon Books, 1933), 60.
279 James W. Fowler, *Stages of Faith, the Psychology of Human Development and the Quest for Meaning* (New York, NY: Harper Collins, 1995), 133-34.
280 Ibid, 149-50.
281 Ibid, 172-73.
282 Ibid, 182-3.
283 Ibid, 197-98.
284 Empty Cloud, *Exploring Chan*, (12 6 2014). http://www.eyeofchan.org/special-features/poetry-of-empty-cloud/847-poems-on-the-oxherding-xuyun.html.
285 D. T. Suzuki, *Manual Of Zen Buddhism* (New York, NY: Grove Press, 1994).
286 Cloud, Exploring Chan website, http://www.eyeofchan.org/.
287 Suzuki, *Manual Of Zen Buddhism*.
288 As quoted by Keightley, *These Bones Shall Rise Again*, 177.
289 Ben Huan Shakya, Dharma Talk (2003), 941.
290 Ibid.

Chapter 10. Stage One: Mindfulness

291 Donald Lopez, "Which Mindfulness? The modern understanding of mindfulness differs significantly from what the term has historically meant in Buddhism." (*Tricycle*, 2014).
292 Sharf, "Mindfulnes sand Mindlessness in Early Chan," 941.
293 Ibid.
294 Sharf, "Mindfulnes sand Mindlessness in Early Chan," 942.
295 Sōtōshu, SōtōZEN-NET, (2015), 1. http://global.Sōtōzen-net.or.jp/eng/practice/zazen/howto/.
296 Schlütter, *How Zen Became Zen*, 170.
297 Jian Xu, et al. "Nondirective meditation activates default mode network and areas associated with memory retrieval and emotional processing," *Frontiers in Human Neuroscience* (February 26 2014).
298 J. Polich & B.R. Cahn, "Meditation states and traits: EEG, erp, and neuroimaging studies.," *Psychological Bulletin* 132 (2006).
299 Nikolai Axmacher Juergen Fell, Sven Haupt, "From alpha to gamma: Electrophysiological correlates of meditation-related states of consciousness," Department of Epileptology, University of Bonn (2010): 99.

Chapter 11. Stage Two: Concentration

300 Crangle, *The Origin and Development of Early Indian Contemplative Practices*, 29, 105.
301 *Seven Schools of Yoga* (Wheaton, IL: The Theosophical Publishing House, 1988).
302 M.D. Jeffrey M. Schwartz, and Sharon Begley, *The Mind & The Brain* (ReganBooks, HarperCollins, 2002), 307.
303 "Unconscious decisions in the brain," Max-Plank-Gesellschaft (April 14 2008).
304 M.D. Jeffrey M. Schwartz, and Sharon Begley, *The Mind & The Brain* (ReganBooks, HarperCollins, 2002), 307.
305 Donald A. Braue, "Maya" in Radhakrishnan's Thought: Six Meanings other than "Illusion" (Delhi: Motilal Banarsidass).
306 Christmas Humphreys, *Concentration and Meditation* (Great Britain: Element Books Ltd, 1987).
307 Han Shan Te Ching, *Essentials of Practice and Enlightenment*, (n.d.).

Chapter 12. Stage 3: Contemplation

308 McRae, *The Northern School and the Formation of Early Ch'an Buddhism*, 215.
309 Wood, *Seven Schools of Yoga*, 111-12.
310 Thomas Cleary, *Book of Serenity: One Hundred Zen Dialogues*, trans. Thomas Cleary (Hudson, New York: Lindisfarne Press, 1988), 3.
311 Dogen, *Dogen's Extensive Record*, 583.
312 John Daido Loori, "Shape of a Buddha," *Mountain Record* 20.1, 2001.
313 McRae, *Seeing Through Zen: Encounter, Transformation, and Genealogy in Chinese Chan Buddhism*, 76.
314 Xu Yun, *Empty Cloud, the Autobiography of the Chinese Zen Master.*, 1988, Second ed., 158.
315 Xu Yun, *Empty Cloud, The Autobiography of the Chinese Zen Master*, trans. Charles Luk (Thorpe Hamlet, Norwich: Unknown, 1980), 202fn.
316 McRae, *Seeing Through Zen: Encounter, Transformation, and Genealogy in Chinese Chan Buddhism*.

317 Lu Kuan Yu: Charles Luk, *Ch'an and Zen Teaching*, trans. Charles Luk, 3 vols., vol. 1 (York Beach, Maine: Samuel Weiser, Inc., 1993), 23.
318 Lu Kuan Yu: Charles Luk, *Ch'an and Zen Teaching*, trans. Charles Luk, 3 vols., vol. 1 (York Beach, Maine: Samuel Weiser, Inc., 1993), 23.
319 Te-ching, *Essentials of Practice and Enlightenment*.
320 Yampolsky, *The Platform Sutra of the Sixth Patriarch*, 137-38.
321 McRae, *The Northern School and the Formation of Early Ch'an Buddhism*, 216.
322 Ibid.
323 From the *Fundamental Expedient Teachings for Calming the Mind to Enter the Way*, as quoted by Sharf 2014.

CHAPTER 13. STAGE FOUR: MEDITATION

324 For an examination of ecstatic absorption/samadhi/divine union, see *Mysticism: Experience, Response, and Empowerment* by Jess Byron Hollenback, The Pennsylvania State University Press, University Park, PA, 1996.
325 Matthieu Ricard, "Mind of the Meditator."
326 Antoine Lutz, et al., "Long term meditators self-induce high-amplitude gamma synchrony during mental practice," *Proceedings of the National Academy of Sciences of the United States of America* 101, no. 46 (October 6 2004).
327 Luders, "Forever Young(er): potential age-defying effects of long-term meditation on gray matter atrophy," 2015.
328 Antoine Lutz, "Long term meditators self-induce high-amplitude gamma synchrony during mental practice," 2004.

CHAPTER 14 CHAN'S OX-HERDING SERIES

329 Suzuki, *Manual Of Zen Buddhism*, 128.
330 Ibid, 128-29.
331 Hsu Yun, *Oxherding Poems of Hsu Yun*.

CHAPTER 15 – THE VALUE OF A MODEL

332 Anthony Stevens, *Archetype Revisited: An Updated Natural History of the Self* (New York, NY: Routledge, 2015), 45.
333 Olivier Bernier, *Jung Had Nothing To Do With Cults*. op-ed, New York Times, Oct. 20, 1994. page 26.
334 Dawkins, *The Selfish Gene*. 2016 p. 249.
335 Olivier Bernier, *Jung Had Nothing To Do With Cults*. op-ed, New York Times, Oct. 20, 1994. page 26.
336 Albert Hofmann, *LSD: My Problem Child* (New York: McGraw-Hill, 1980), 15.
337 Supreme Court, Central Intelligence Agency et al. v. Sims et al, United States Government (Washington DC, 1985), 159, 161-162.
338 R. Fischer, "A Cartography of Understanding Mysticism," *Science* 174 (1971), 901-02.
339 Cleary, *Swampland Flowers: The letters and lectures of Zen Master Ta hui*, 30.
340 Shan, *The Autobiography and Maxims of Chan Master Han Shan 1546-1623*.
341 Fischer, "A Cartography of Understanding Mysticism," 902.

Chapter 16. The Theory of Psychological Archetypes

342 C. G. Jung, *The Archetypes and the Collective Unconscious*, vol. 9 (1959), 43.
343 C. G. Jung, *Psychology and Religion: West to East* (1969), par. 222.
344 Ibid, par. 91.
345 Hillman, James, Uniform Edition of the Writings of James Hillman, (2013), 14.
346 C. G. Jung, *Psychological Types: The Collected Works of C. G. Jung* (1990), 560.
347 Vladislav Solc examines this relationship in *Father Archetype*, 2013.
348 See Tao Jian's excellent work, *Contexts and Dialogue: Yogacara Buddhism and Modern Psychology on the Subliminal Mind*, 2006, University of Hawai'i Press.
349 Jung, *The Archetypes and the Collective Unconscious*, 106.
350 C. G. Jung, *Psychological Types: The Collected Works of C. G. Jung*, trans. H. G. Baynes & R.F.C. Hull, vol. 6 (Princeton University Press, 1990), 155-56, original italics.
351 For more on this topic, see *The Androgyne, Reconciliation of Male and Female* by Elémire Zolla, Jung, *Psychological Types: The Collected Works of C. G. Jung*, 6., *Androgyny, the Opposites Within* by June Singer, C. G. Jung, and *Two Essays on Analytical Psychology*, ed. Michael Fordham, trans. R. F. C. Hull, vol. 7 (Princeton, NJ: Princeton University Press, 1966).
352 Ortigue S, Bianchi-Demicheli F, Patel N, Frum C, Lewis JW, "Neuroimaging of love: fMRI meta-analysis evidence toward new perspectives in sexual medicine," *J Sex Med* (Nov 7 2010).
353 Hsu Yun, *Oxherding Poems of Hsu Yun*.
354 Jalal Al-Din Rumi, *The Illuminated Rumi* (New York: Broadway Books; 1st edition, 1997).
355 Feuerstein, *The Yoga Tradition, It's History, Literature, Philosophy and Practice* (2008), 114.
356 For insight into this topic, see "Mothers' Parenting and Young Economically Disadvantaged Children's Relational and Overt Bullying" by Mary E. Curtner-Smith, et al., *Journal of Child and Family Studies*, 2006, pp. 177–189.
357 Michael D'Antonio, *The Truth About Trump* (New York, New York: St. Martin's Press, 2016), 154.
358 C. G. Jung, Aion. *Researches into the Phenomenology of the Self* (1969), 62-63.

Chapter 17 – Dreams and Visions

359 Anthony Stevens, *The Two-Million-Year-Old Self* (1993), 22.
360 Paul-Antoine Libourel, et al. "Partial homologies between sleep states in lizards, mammals, and birds suggest a complex evolution of sleep states in amniotes." PLOS, Oct. 11, 2018.
361 For insightful perspectives on the evolutionary role of dreams, see Michael S. Franklin and Michael J. Zypher's article, "The Role of Dreams in the Evolution of the Human Mind," 2005, *Evolutionary Psychology*, Sage Journals.
362 J. P. Banquet, "Spectral analysis of the EEG in meditation," *Electroencephalography and Clinical Neurophysiology*, August, 1973.
363 Rodolfo Llinas, *Consciousness and the Brain*, vol. 929 (New York, NY: New York University School of Medicine, 2006).
364 Antoine Lutz, "Long term meditators self-induce high-amplitude gamma synchrony during mental practice"(2004).
365 Jeffrey L. Fannin, Ph.D. *Understanding Your Brainwaves*, 5.
366 Hillman, James, *Uniform Edition of the Writings of James Hillman*, 2013, 20.
367 Mark Cartwright, "Huitzilopochtli," *Ancient History Encyclopedia* (August 27 2013).
368 C. G. Jung, *Symobols of Transformation*, vol. 5 (New York, NY: Bollingen Foundation Inc., 1956), 294.

369 Readers interested in lucid dreaming—an offshoot of Yoga—may enjoy reading *Dreaming Yourself Awake: Lucid Dreaming and Tibetan Dream Yoga for Insight and Transformation* by B. Alan Wallace, *Lucid Dreaming - Gateway to the Inner Self* by Robert Waggoner, *Exploring the World of Lucid Dreaming* by Stephen LaBarge and Howard Rheingold, and *The Tibetan Yogas of Dream and Sleep* by Tenzin Wangyal Rinpoche and Mark Dahlby.

370 Yngve Vogt, "World's oldest ritual discovered. Worshipped the python 70,000 years ago," *Apollon Research Magazine* (Feb. 1 2012).

371 Marija Gimbutas, *The Language of the Goddess* (San Francisco: Harper, 1989), 121.

372 Sarah A. Queen, John S. Major, Andrew Seth Meyer, and Harold D. Roth, *The Huainanzi: A Guide to the Theory and Practice of Government in Early Han China* (New York, NY: Colombia University Press, 2010).

373 John D. Ireland, *Muccalinda Sutta: About Muccalinda*, trans. John D. Ireland (1998).

374 Alain Daniélou, "The Myths and Gods of India: the classic work on Hindu polytheism" (Rochester, VT: Inner Traditions International, 1991), 286.

375 Karapātrī, *Śrī Bhagavatī tattva*, 174.

376 Cartwright, "Quetzalcoatl," (2013).

377 Ibid.

378 "T. J." (2011).

Chapter 18 – Discovering the Self

379 Jantrasrisalai, *Early Buddhist Dhammakaya: Its Philosophical and Soteriological Significance*, (2008), 28.

380 Len Yen Ching, *The Śūraṅgama Sutra (Len Yen Ching)*, trans. Charles Luk (London, 1966), 139.

381 Sung-bae Park, *Buddhist Faith and Sudden Enlightenment* (SUNY Press), 127.

382 Gadjin M Nagao, *Madhyamika and Yogacara*, ed. L. S. Kawamura, trans. L. S. Kawamura (Albany, N. Y.: State University of New York Press, 1991), 115.

383 Te-ching, *Essentials of Practice and Enlightenment*.

384 Shan, *The Autobiography and Maxims of Chan Master Han Shan 1546-1623* (1999).

385 Dr. Oliver Sacks Dr. Susan Barry, Dr. Theresa Ruggiero, "Going Binocular: Susan's First Snowfall," ed. Robert Krulwich (June 26 2006).

386 Ibid.

387 Ibid.

388 Dr. Susan Barry, "Going Binocular: Susan's First Snowfall" (2006).

389 Roberts, Benadette, The Experience of No-Self, 1993, 72-6.

390 Master Han-shan, "Essentials of Chan Practice and Enlightenment," Dharma Talks by Gilbert Gutierrez (2007).

391 As quoted by Davis (2015), 134.

Chapter 19 – Physical Experiences

392 From the *Yoga Kuṇḍalinī Upanishad* as quoted by Mookerjee, 1986

393 S. Brinkmann, "Madness, Depression, Heart Palpitations Are Commonside effects of Kundalini Yoga," (March 2 2011).

Part Four. Trials and Tribulations

394 Plato, *The Republic*, trans. Desmond Lee (London, England: the Penguin Group, 1987), 259.

Chapter 20. Hinderances

395 Ruth Fuller Sasaki, *The Record of Linji*, ed. Thomas Huho Kirchner, trans. Ruth Fuller Sasaki (Honolulu, HI: University of Hawaii Press, 2009), 22.

396 For insight into this topic, see Albert Bandura's June 2006 article, "Toward a Psychology of Human Agency," *Perspectives on Psychological Science*, Stanford University, Volume: 1 issue: 2, pages 164-180.

397 Stanley Milgram, "Obedience to Authority," *Harper's Magazine* (1974).

398 Jin Y. Park, *Buddhism and Postmodernity: Zen, Huayan, and the Possibility of Buddhist Postmodern Ethics* (Plymouth, England: Lexington Books, 2008), 102.

399 For more about abuses in Zen training centers, see: Lachs, *Richard Baker and the Myth of the Zen Roshi* 2002; Lachs, *When the Saints Go Marching In: Modern Day Zen Hagiography* 2011; B. D. Victoria, *Zen at War* 2006; and Downing, *Shoes Outside the Door: Desire, Devotion and Excess at San Francisco Zen Center* 2001.

400 Stuart Lachs, "Coming down from Zen Clouds: A Critique of the Current State of American Zen," (1994), 1-2.

401 Stuart Lachs, "Means of Authorization: Establishing Hierarchy in Chan/Zen Buddhism in America," (paper presented at the Meeting of the American Academy of Religion, Boston, 1999), 4-5.

402 Cole, *Patriarchs on Paper: A Critical History of Medieval Chan Literature* (2016), 222.

403 Ibid, 249.

404 Ibid, 222.

405 Bhikkhu Bodhi, *Discourses of the Buddha: A Translation of the Anguttara Nikaya*, trans. Bhikkhu Bodhi (Somerville, MA: Wisdom Publications, 2012), 280.

406 For details of scandals revolving around Richard Baker, see *Shoes Outside the Door; Desire, Devotion, and Excess at San Francisco Zen Center*, by Michael Downing, Counterpoint, 2001.

407 Sandra Bell, "Scandals in Emerging Western Buddhism," *Westward Dharma: Buddhism beyond Asia* (2002), 232-35.

408 Gempo Roshi, "Big Mind: Change Your Persepective, Changeyour Life" (2016).

409 Stack, "Utah Zen master admits affair, leaves center" (2011).

410 Ibid.

411 Stephen Butterfield, *The Double Mirror: A Skeptical Journey into Buddhist Tantra* (Berkeley: North Atlantic Books, 1994), 136.

412 Sasaki, *The Record of Linji*, 229, 31.

413 Albert Bandura, *Social Learning Theory* (New York, NY: General Learning Press, 1971).

414 Majjhima Nikaya, "The Middle Length Discourses of the Buddha," ed. Bhikkhu Nanamoli, trans. Bikkhu Nanamoli and Bhikkhu Bodhi (Boston, MA: *Wisdom Publications*), 229.

415 Welch, *The Practice of Chinese Buddhism 1900-1950*, 87.

416 Ben Huan Shakya, Dharma Talk (2003), 941.

417 Te-ching, "Essentials of Practice and Enlightenment."

418 *The Diagnostic and Statistical Manual of Mental Disorders* (DSM-5), (2013).

419 Flo Conway & Jim Siegelman, *Snapping: America's Epidemic of Sudden Personality Change* (New York: Stillpoint Press, 1995), 53.

420 Deb Simpson, *Closing the Gate: A Heaven's Gate Cult Biography* (Murfreesboro, TN: Piney D Press, 2012).

421 See Laurence Wright, *Going Clear: Scientology, Hollywood, and the Prison of Belief* (Random House, 2013).

422 See for example, "A Psychiatric Overview of Cult-Related Phenomena" by Louis Jolyon West, MD

423 See, for example, Robert L Snow, "Deadly cults: the crimes of true believers, 2003, Praeger Publishers.
424 For a thorough examination of this issue, see *Talking Terrorism: A Dictionary of the Loaded Language of Political Violence* by Philip Herbst and Robert Herbst, 2003, Greenwood Press.

CHAPTER 21. DANGERS

425 H. P. Blavatsky, *The Voice of The Silence*, trans. H. P. B. (Theosophy Trust, 2006), 13.
426 Humphreys, *Meditation and Concentration, A Manual of Mind Development*, 18-19.
427 Steven Pinker, *The Better Angels of our Nature: Why Violence Has Declined* (New York, NY: Penguin Group, 2011), 622.
428 Lachs, "Means of Authorization: Establishing Hierarchy in Chan/Zen Buddhism in America" (1999).
429 Peter L. Berger, *The Sacred Canopy, Elements of a Sociological Theory of Religion* (Garden City, NY: Anchor Books, 1990), 85.
430 Xuanzang, *The Scripture on the Explication of Underlying Meaning* (2000).
431 Stuart Lachs, "When the Saints Go Marching In: Modern Day Zen Hagiography," (updated March 9, 2011), 37.
432 Ibid, 36.
433 Kristen Moulton, "Zen teachers are livid Utah colleague in sex scandal still teaching," *The Salt Lake Tribune* (2011).

FINAL THOUGHTS

434 Red Pine, *Road to Heaven: Encounters with Chinese Hermits* (Berkley: Counterpoint, 1993).
435 Bodhi, *Discourses of the Buddha: A Translation of the Anguttara Nikaya* (2012), 280.
436 C. G. Jung, *The Collected Works of C. G. Jung (1953-60)*, par.146.
437 Amanda Gefter, "The Case Against Reality" (*The Atlantic*, 2016).
438 See, for example, "The Origin of Time in Conscious Agents", by Donald D. Hoffman, *Cosmology*, 2014, Vol 18. 494-520.
439 Lusthaus, Dan, *Vasubandhu/Xuanzang and the problem of consciousness*, from *Consciousness and the Great Philosophers*, Routledge, London and New York, 2017.

Illustration Credits

Figure 1. Vesak Day Celebration. Photo by pwbaker, CC by 2.0.

Figure 2. Pashupati seal No. 420. Wikimedia commons.

Figure 3. The Nèijīng tú. Copy of an engraved stele from the White Cloud Temple in Beijing dated 1886. Public Domain.

Figure 4. Lineage poem. Prepared by the author.

Figure 5. Bodhidharma. IanDagnall Computing/Alamy Stock Photo.

Figure 6. Empty Cloud. Public domain. Anonymous photographer.

Figure 7. Hotei Pointing at the Moon. The Picture Art Collection/Alamy Stock Photo. Illustration by Fugai Ekun.

Figure 8. The Quadrant Exercise. Produced by the author.

Figure 9. Picture 8 of ox-herding series by artist unknown/Alamy.

Figure 10. A Cartography of the Ecstatic and Meditative States, Roland Fischer, Science, March 10, 2019, Lic. 4545370780957.

Figure 11 Nüwa. Public Domain.

Figure 12. Fuxi and Nüwa as king and queen. Temple mural, Han Dynasty. Public Domain.

Figure 13. Androgyne with goat's heads. Cgm 598, f 106v, Germany, 15th c. Bayerisches Staatsbibliothek, Munich. Public Domain.

Figure 14. Quetzalcóatl and the Buddha. Quetzalcóatl (left) is a sculpture by an unknown artist produced between the 15th and 16th centuries, in the collection of Musée du quai Branly, Paris. Public Domain. The statue of the Buddha is from Cambodia, 12th century, Honolulu Museum of Art accession 12839.1. Public Domain.

Figure 15. Neidan Meditation. Public domain.

Front and back cover art: Two illustrations from a set of ten produced in 1278 as a hand scroll with black and colored ink on paper. From the Mary Griggs Burke Collection, Gift of the Mary and Jackson Burke Foundation, 2015. No. 2015.300.10. Public Domain.

Words of Thanks

This book has been shaped by countless hours of independent reflection and "time on the cushion," as we chan Buddhists often say. It has also been deeply inspired by the writings of other spiritual travelers and scholars, as well as conversations with people about their lives and ascetic practices. My understanding of the religious framework of Chan Buddhism owes much to the works of Robert H. Sharf, John R. McRae, David Keightley, Morten Schlütter, Stuart Lachs, Brian Victoria, Alan Cole, Wendi L. Adamek, and Peter L. Berger. I am deeply grateful for their thoughtful insights into an extraordinarily intricate subject.

I owe special thanks to Chan Masters Jy Din and Ben Huan, who graciously welcomed me into their lives, their religion, and their country, where they presided over my ordination in 1998. They revealed the bridge between the Buddhist institution and the ascetic practice of chan—a bridge I had sought for many years and was elated to finally cross. Their guidance not only gave me the courage to write this book but also planted the seeds for many of its topics.

I am immensely appreciative of the reviews and commentaries I received on drafts of this work from Peadar O'Greachain, Mary Jo Brock, Fa Hsing Shakya, Fa Lohng Shakya, Yin Ming Shakya, Stuart Lachs, and many others. Special thanks also go to Max Van Zile for his insightful editorial assistance.

Lastly, this book stands as a tribute to the countless women and men who, over millennia, chose lives of solitude to reflect and meditate. They gifted us not only words of wisdom but also a path to discover that wisdom for ourselves. Many of these practitioners embraced anonymity, attributing their works to past sages, both real and imagined, or choosing to guide the next generation quietly, leaving no trace of their names. For chan, the medium truly is the message; historical facts hold as little significance as time itself.

With deep gratitude, may the flame forever burn.

The author (left), with his mentors, Masters Jy Din Shakya (center) and Ben Huan (right), May, 1998, Shen Zhen, China. Photo courtesy of Hong Fa Temple.

Bibliography

Adamek, Wendi L. 2007. *The Mystique of Transmission: On an Early Chan History and its Contents.* New York, NY: Columbia University Press.
Administrative Headquarters Announcement. 1993. "Announcement." *Sōtō Shuho* 26.
Aitken, Robert. 1995. *The Gateless Barrier: The Wu-men Kuan (Mumonkan).* Translated by Robert Aitken. New York, NY: North Point Press.
American Psychiatric Association. 2013. *The Diagnostic and Statistical Manual of Mental Disorders (DSM-5).* 5th. doi:10.1176/appi.books.9780890425596.744053.
Anālayo, Bhikkhu. 2003. *Satipaṭṭhāna : the direct path to realization.* Birmingham: Windhorse.
Ananthaswamy, Anil. 2015. *The Man Who Wasn't There: Investigations into the Strange New Science of the Self.* New York, NY: Dutton.
Anderson, Scott. 2016. "Fractured Lands: How the Arab World Came Apart." *The New York Times Magazine,* August 14: 3-58.
Andreasen, Esben. 1998. *Popular Buddhism in Japan, Shin Buddhist Religion and Culture.* Japan: Curzon Press Ltd.
Anesaki, Masaharu. 1963. *History of Japanese Religion.* Rutland, VT: Tuttle.
—. 1963. *History of Japanese Religion, with special reference to the social and moral life of the nation.* C. E. Tuttle Co.
Animal Rights Center of Japan. 2015. *Animal Rights Center Japan survey results.* Animal Rights Center of Japan.
Anonymous. 1889. *The Voice of The Silence.* Edited by Helena Petrovna Blavatsky. Translated by Helena Petrovna Blavatsky. New York, NY: Theosophical Publishing Company, Limited.
Antoine Lutz, et al. 2004. "Long term meditators self-induce high-amplitude gamma synchrony during mental practice." *Proceedings of the National Academy of Sciences of the United States of America* (Princeton University) 101 (46). doi:10.1073/pnas.0407401101.
App, Urs. 2011. *Richard Wagner and Buddhism.* University Media.
Armstrong, Karen. 2001. *Buddha.* New York, New York: Viking Penguin.
Asian Art Museum. n.d. *Buddhism in the Tang (618-906) and Song (960-1279) Dynasties.* Accessed July 18, 2016. http://education.asianart.org/explore-resources/background-information/buddhism-tang-618%E2%80%93906-and-song-960%E2%80%931279-dynasties.
Babauta, Leo. n.d. *Focus: A Simplicity Manifesto in the Age of Distraction.*
Bandura, Albert. 1971. *Social Learning Theory.* New York, NY: General Learning Press.
Banquet, J. P. 1973. "Spectral analysis of the EEG in meditation." *Electroencephalography and Clinical Neurophysiology,* August: 143-151.
Barnett, Emma. 2015. *Mindfulness: the saddest trend of 2015.* January 8. Accessed July 27, 2016. http://www.telegraph.co.uk/women/womens-life/11331034/Mindfulness-the-saddest-trend-of-2015.html.
Barrett, Devlin. 2018. *Hate crimes rose 17 percent last year, according to new FBI data.* 11 13. Accessed 11 16, 2018. https://www.washingtonpost.com.
Barsalou, Lawrence W. 1999. "Perceptual symbol systems." *Behavioral and Brain Sciences* 577-660.

Basham, AL. 2009. *History and Doctrines of the Ajivikas - a Vanished Indian Religion*. Motilal Banarsidass.

Baumer, Bettina and Vatsyayan, Kapila. 2001. *Kalatattvakosa Vol. 1: Pervasive Terms Vyapti*. Motilal Banarsidass.

BBC World Service. 2014. "POLL: Negative views of Russia on the Rise: Global Poll." *BBC News*. June 3. Accessed April 12, 2017. http://downloads.bbc.co.uk/mediacentre/country-rating-poll.pdf.

Beech, Hannah, "Buddhists Go to Battle: When Nationalism Overrides Pacifism," The New York Times, July 8, 2019.

Bell, Sandra. 2002. "Scandals in Emerging Western Buddhism." *Westward Dharma: Buddhism beyond Asia* 230-242.

Berger, Peter L. 1990. *The Sacred Canopy, Elements of a Sociological Theory of Religion*. Garden City, NY: Anchor Books.

Berkley Center. n.d. *Demographics of Buddhism*. Accessed 9 16, 2018. berkleycenter.georgetown.edu.

Bernhardt, Stephen. 1990. "Are Pure Consciousness Events Unmediated?" In *The Problem of Pure Consciousness*, by Robert K. C. Forman, 220-236. New York, NY: Oxford University Press.

Bernier, Olivier, op-ed, *Jung Had Nothing To Do With Cults*. The New York Times, October 20, 1994, Section A.

Berzin, Alexander. n.d. *English Glossart of Buddhist Terms*. Berlin, Germany: The Berzin Archives.

Blavatsky, H. P. 2006. *The Voice of The Silence*. Translated by H. P. B. Theosophy Trust.

Blissett, Luther. 1997. *Anarchist Integralism: Aesthetics, Politics and the Apres-Garde*. London, UK: Sabotage Editions.

Bodhi, Bhikkhu. 2012. *Discourses of the Buddha: A Translation of the Anguttara Nikaya*. Translated by Bhikkhu Bodhi. Somerville, MA: Wisdom Publications.

—. 2000. *The Connected Discourses of the Buddha: A New Translation of the Samyutta Nikaya*. Translated by Translated from the Pali by Bhikkhu Bodhi. Somerville, MA: Wisdom Publications.

Bostrom, Nick. 2003. "Are You Living in a Computer Simulation." *Philosophical Quarterly* 53: 243-255.

Bourbaki, Nicolas. 1998. "Elements of the History of Mathematics." In *Britannica Concise Encyclopedia*.

Bourdieu, Pierre. 1991. *Language & Symbolic Power*. Malden, MA: Polity Press.

Boyuan, Lin. 1996. *Zhōngguó wǔshù shǐ* 中國武術史. Taipei : Wǔzhōu chūbǎnshè 五洲出版社.

Braue, Donald A. 1984. *"Maya" in Radhakrishnan's Thought: Six Meanings other than "Illusion"*. Delhi: Motilal Banarsidass.

Brinkmann, S. 2011. "Madness, Depression, Heart Palpitations Are 'Common' side effects of Kundalini Yoga." March 2. Accessed October 1, 2016. http://www.womenofgrace.com/blog/?p=676.

Buddhaghosa, Bhadantácariya. 2010. *Visuddhimagga: The Path of Purification*. Translated by Bhikkhu Ñáóamoli (Translated from the Pali). Buddhist Publication Society.

Bukay, David. 2006. "The Religious Foundations of Suicide Bombings: Islamist Ideology." *The Middle East Quarterly* 27-36.

Buswell, Robert. 1990. *Chinese Buddhist Apocrypha*. Honolulu, HI: University of Hawaii Press.

Butterfield, Stephen. 1994. *The Double Mirror: A Skeptical Journey into Buddhist Tantra*. Berkeley: North Atlantic Books.

Buttimer, Anne. 1999. *Nature and Identity in Cross-Cultural Perspective*. Edited by Luke Wallin Anne Buttimer. Netherlands: Dordrecht: Springer.

Cahn, B. R., & J. Polich. 2006. "Meditation states and traits: EEG, erp, and neuroimaging studies." *Psychological Bulletin* 132: 180-211. doi:10.1037/0033-2909.132.2.180.

Cartwright, Mark. 2013. "Huitzilopochtli." *Ancient History Encyclopedia*. http://www.ancient.eu/Huitzilopochtli/.

Cartwright, Mark. 2013. "Quetzalcoatl." *Ancient History Encyclopedia*. August 1. http://www.ancient.eu/Quetzalcoatl/.

Carus, Paul. 1894. "Buddha. "Sermon at Benares"." In *The Gospel of Buddha*, by ed. Paul Carus, edited by Paul Carus. Chicago: Open Court Publishing.
CBS, New York. 2016. *Muslim MTA Employee Attacked At Grand Central Is Latest in String of Hate Crimes.* New York, December 5. Accessed December 23, 2016. https://newyork.cbslocal.com/2016/12/05/cuomo-hate-crimes/.
Center for Ethics at Emory. 2015. *Emory Center for Ethics.* 12 6. Accessed 2015. http://ethics.emory.edu/people/Founder.html.
Chaline, Eric. 2003. *The book of Zen: The Path to Inner Peace.* Barron's Educational Series.
Chan, Alan. 2013. "Laozi." Edited by Edward N. Zalta. *Stanford University of Philosophy (Spring 2014 Edition).* http://plato.stanford.edu/archives/spr2014/entries/laozi/.
Chan-Wyles, Adrian. 2015. *The Differences Between Chinese Ch'an and Japanese Zen in a Nutshell.* Accessed July 17, 2016. https://thesanghakommune.org/tag/chinese-caodong-chan/.
Ch'en, Kenneth. 1973. *Buddhism in China.* Princeton, New Jersey: Princeton University Press.
Ching, Len Yen. 1966. *The Śūraṅgama Sutra (Len Yen Ching).* Translated by Charles Luk. London.
Chuang Tzu, Translated by Burton Watson. 1996. *Chuang Tzu, Basic Writings, Translated by Burton Watson.* New York: Columbia University Press.
Chung-weon, Lee. 2010. "1000 Korean and Japanese Scholars "Japan–Korea Annexation Treaty Is Originally Invalid"." *Yonhap News (in Korean).*
Chung-Yuan, Chang. 1971. *Original Teachings of Ch'an Buddhism.* Vol. 6. New York, NY: Random House, Inc.
Cleary, J. C. 1977. *Swampland Flowers: The letters and lectures of Zen Master Ta hui.* Edited by J. C. Cleary. Boston: Shambhala.
Cleary, Thomas. 1988. *Book of Serenity: One Hundred Zen Dialogues.* Translated by Thomas Cleary. Hudson, New York: Lindisfarne Press.
—. 1999. *Transmission of Light: Zen in the Art of Enlightenment by Zen Master Keizan.* North Point Press.
Cloud, Empty. 2014. Exploring Chan website. Accessed April 10, 2017. http://www.eyeofchan.org/special-features/poetry-of-empty-cloud/847-poems-on-the-oxherding-xuyun.html.
—. n.d. *Poems by Empty Cloud: Series II.* Accessed February 6, 2017. http://www.eyeofchan.org/special-features/poetry-of-empty-cloud/495-hsuyunpoems2.html.
Cole, Alan. 2015. "Conspiracy's Truth: The Zen of Narrative Cunning in the Platform Sutra." *Asia Major* 28: 145-175.
—. 2009. *Fathering Your Father: The Zen of Fabrication in Tang Buddhism.* Berkeley, CA: University of California Press.
—. 2016. *Patriarchs on Paper: A Critical History of Medieval Chan Literature.* Oakland, CA: University of California Press.
Conners, Edward P. J. Corbett and Robert J. 1998. *Classical Rhetoric for the Modern Student.* 4th Ed. Oxford, England: Oxford University Press.
Conze, Edward. 1993. *A Short History of Buddhism.* Guernsey, Great Britain: Oneworld Publications.
—. 1958. *Astasahasrika Prajnaparamita.* Translated by Ph.D. Dr. Edward Conze. Vol. 284. Calcutta: The Asiatic Society.
—. 1973. *The Perfection of Wisdom in Eight Thousand Lines & Its Verse Summary.* Translated by Edward Conze.
Court, Supreme. 1985. *Central Intelligence Agency et al. v. Sims et al.* Washington DC: United States Government.
Cowell, E. B. 1969. *Buddhist Mahayana Texts.* Edited by F. Max Muller. Translated by Various oriental scholars. New York, NY: Dover Publications, Inc.
Crangle, Edward Fitzpatrick. 1994. *The Origin and Development of Early Indian Contemplative Practices.* Edited by Walther Heissig and Hans-Joachim Klimkeit. Vol. 29. Weisbaden: Die Deutsche Bibliothek - CIP-Einheitsaufnahme.
Daniélou, Alain. 1991. *The Myths and Gods of India: the classic work on Hindu polytheism.* Rochester, VT: Inner Traditions International.

D'Antonio, Michael. 2016. *The Truth About Trump.* New York, New York: St. Martin's Press.

Davis, Judson. 2015. *Jung at the Foot of Mt. Kailash, A Comparitive Exploration of Depth Psychology, Tibetan Tantra, and the Sacred Mythic Imagery of East and West.* Hamburg, Germany: Anchor Academic Publishing.

Dawa-Samdup, Lāma Kazi. 2000. *The Tibetan Book of the Dead.* Translated by Lama Kazi Dawa-Samdup. London: Oxford University Press.

Dawkins, Richard. 1989. *The Selfish Gene.* Oxford University Press. 40th anniversary ed. 2016.

DeCaroli, Robert. 2004. *Haunting the Buddha: Indian Popular Religions and the Formation of Buddhism.* New York, New York: Oxford University Press.

Delmer M. Brown, Ichiro Ishida. 1979. *The Future and the Past, a translation and study of the Gukansho, an interpretative history of Japan written in 1219.* Berkeley, CA: University of California Press.

Denyer, Simon. 2017. "Air China bans shark fin cargo, reflecting dramatic shift in attitudes." *The Washington Post.* January 8. Accessed April 27, 2017. https://www.washingtonpost.com/world/asia_pacific/air-china-bans-shark-fin-cargo-reflecting-dramatic-shift-in-attitudes/2017/01/08/754e0d56-0457-4667-8880-97775a0a97fd_story.html?utm_term=.184017f3efb5.

Despeux, Catherine. 2008. *Neijing tu and Xiuzhen tu.* Edited by Fabrizio Pregadio. New York, NY: Routledge.

De Vaus, June, Matthew J. Hornsey, Peter Kuppens. Oct. 16, 2017. "Exploring the East-West Divide in Prevalence of Affective Disorder: A Case for Cultural Differences in Coping with Negative Emotion." *Personality and Social Psychology Review*, Volume: 22 issue: 3, page(s): 285-304.

Dickey, Megan Rose. 2015. *Meditation Startup Headspace Raises $30 Million To Help You Be More Mindful.* September 21. Accessed July 25, 2016. https://techcrunch.com/2015/09/21/meditation-startup-headspace-raised-30-million-to-help-you-be-more-mindful/.

Dienes, Peter Lush and Zoltan. 2016. "Hypnosis and the conscious awareness of intentions." *OUPblog, Oxford University Press.* Sept. 2. Accessed Dec. 3, 2017. https://blog.oup.com/2016/09/hypnosis-conscious-awareness-of-intentions/.

Dogen. 2010. *Dogen's Extensive Record.* Edited by Taigen Dan Leighton. Translated by Taigen Dan Leighton and Shohaku Okumura. Sumerville, MA: Wisdom Publications.

Downing, Michael. 2001. *Shoes Outside the Door: Desire, Devotion and Excess at San Francisco Zen Center.* Counterpoint.

Dr. Susan Barry, Dr. Oliver Sacks, Dr. Theresa Ruggiero, interview by Robert Krulwich. 2006. *Going Binocular: Susan's First Snowfall* (June 26). http://www.npr.org/templates/story/story.php?storyId=5507789.

Draper, George E. P. Box and Norman R. 1984. *Empirical Model-Building and Response Surfaces.*

Dumoulin, Heinrich. 1995. *Zen Buddhism in the 20th Century.* Translated by Joseph S. O'leary. New York, New York: Weatherhill, Inc.

—. 2005. *Zen Buddhism: A History.* Bloomington, IN: Wold Wisdom, Inc.

Dunning, David, interview by Errol Morris. 2010. *The Anosognosic's Dilemma: Something's Wrong but You'll Never Know What It Is (Part 1)* (June 20). http://opinionator.blogs.nytimes.com/2010/06/20/the-anosognosics-dilemma-1/?_r=0.

Eliade, Mircea. 1990. *Yoga, Immortality and Freedom.* 9th. Princeton, New Jersey: Princeton University Press.

Encyclopedia Britannica. 2015. *Encyclopedia Britannica.* 4 9. Accessed 12 5, 2015. http://www.britannica.com/topic/vratya.

Evans, Bill. 1966. The Universal Mind of Bill Evans, 1966 interview. https://www.youtube.com/watch?v=QwXAqIaUahI&t

Fannin, Jeffrey L., Ph.D. n.d. "Understanding Your Brainwaves." http://drjoedispenza.com/files/understanding-brainwaves_white_paper.pdf.

Fell, Juergen, Nikolai Axmacher, Sven Haupt. 2010. "From alpha to gamma: Electrophysicological correlates of meditation-related states of consciousness." Department of Epileptology, University of Bonn (University of Bonn).

Ferguson, Andy. 2000. *Zen's Chinese Heritage*. Boston: Wisdom Publications.
Feuerstein, Georg, 2008. *The Yoga Tradition, It's History, Literature, Philosophy and Practice*. Chino Valley, AZ: Hohm Press.
Feuerstein, Gerog, Subhash Kak & David Frawley. 1995. *In Search of the Cradle of Civilization*. Delhi: Quest Books.
Filliozat, Pierre-Sylvain. 2004. "Ancient Sanskrit Mathematics: An Oral Tradition and a Written Literature." In *History of Science, History of Text (Boston Series in the Philosophy of Science)*, by Robert S. Cohen, Jürgen Renn and et al., 137–157, 360–375. Dordrecht: Springer Netherlands.
Fischer, Roland. 1971. "A Cartography of Understanding Mysticism." *Science* (AAAS) 174: 897-904.
Forman, Robert K. C. 1990. *The Problem of Pure Consciousness*. New York, NY: Oxford University Press.
Foulk, T. Griffith. 1992. "The Ch'an Tsung in Medieval China: School, Lineage, or What?" *The Pacific World* (The University of Michigan, Ann Arbor) (8): 18-31.
Fowler, James W. 1995. *Stages of Faith, the Psychology of Human Development and the Quest for Meaning*. New York, NY: Harper Collins.
Fowler, Jeaneane. 2005. *An Introduction To The Philosophy And Religion Of Taoism: Pathways To Immortality*. Brighton: Sussex Academic Press.
Fronsdal, Gil. n.d. *The Discourse on Mindfulness of Breathing: Anapanasati Sutta*. Translated by Gil Fronsdal. http://zen-ua.org/wp-content/uploads/anapanasati_sutta_the_discourse_on_mindfulness_of_breathing_english.pdf.
Galanter, Marc. 1999. *Cults, Faith, Healing, and Coercion*. New York, New York: Oxford University Press, Inc.
Gallard, M. 1994. "Jung's attitude during the second World War in the light of the historical and professional context." *Journal of analytical psychology* 39: 203-232.
Gariepy, Jean-Francois, Karli K. Watson, Emily Du, Diana L. Xie, Joshua Erb, Dianna Amasino, Michael L Platt. 2014. "Social learning in humans and other animals." Frontiers in Neuroscience. http://dx.doi.org/10.3389/fnins.2014.00058.
Gefter, Amanda. 2016. "The Case Against Reality." *The Atlantic*.
Georges, Ifrah. 2000. *The Universal History of Numbers: From Prehistory to the Invention of the Computer*. Wiley.
2015. *Going Clear, Scientology and the Prison of Belief*. Directed by Alex Gibney. Produced by G C Productions.
Gimbutas, Marija. 1989. *The Language of the Goddess*. San Francisco: Harper.
Gogerly, S. Beal and D. J. 1862. "Comparative Arrangement of two Translations of the Buddhist Ritual for the Priesthood, known as the Prátimoksha, or Pátimokhan." *Journal of the Royal Asiatic Society of Great Britain & Ireland* (The Royal Asiatic Society) 19 (Art. XVIII): 407-480. doi:10.1017/S0035869X00156655.
Gorō, Sugimoto. 1938. *Taigi*. Tokyo: Heibonsha.
Griffith, et al. n.d. *Four Vedas: Rik, Yajus, Sama, & Atharva*. Translated by Yajur Veda: AB Keith, Hymns of Sama Veda: RT Griffith, Hymns of Atharva Veda: M Bloomfield Rig Veda: RT Griffith.
Gunaratana, Bhante Henepola. 2002. *Mindfulness in Plain English*. Somerville, MA: Wisdom Publications.
Han-shan, Master. 2007. "Essentials of Chan Practice and Enlightenment." Dharma Talks by Gilbert Gutierrez. October 17. Accessed September 2018. http://dharmatalks.riversidechan.org/2007/12/dharma-talk-october-17-2007.html.
—. 1999. *The Autobiography and Maxims of Chan Master Han Shan 1546-1623*. Translated by Upasaka Richard Cheung. Honolulu, HI: Hsu Yun Temple.
Harley, Joohyung Lee and Vincent R. 2012. "The male fight-flight response: A result of SRY regulation of catecholamines?" *Brain and Gender* (Prince Henry's Institute of Medical Research).
Harrison, Paul. M. 1982. *Sanskrit fragments of a Lokottaravadin tradition*.
—. 2003. "Mediums and messages: Reflections on the production of Mahayana sutras." *The Eastern Buddhist* (New Series 35 (1/2)): 115-51.

Harrison, Paul, and John R. McRae, translators. 1998. *The Pratyutpanna Samādhi Sūtra and The Śūraṅgama Samādhi Sūtra*. Moraga, CA: BDK America, Inc.
Harvey, Peter. 1995. *An Introduction to Buddhism*. Cambridge: Cambridge University Press.
—. 1995. *An Introduction to Buddhism, Teachings, history, and practices*. New York: Press Syndicate of the University of Cambridge.
Heine, Steven. 2006. *Did Dōgen Go to China? What He Wrote and When he Wrote It*. Oxford : Oxford University Press.
—. 2012. *Dogen, Textual and Historical Studies*. Edited by Steven Heine. Oxford: Oxford University Press.
Helmholtz Association. 2010. "Golden ratio discovered in a quantum world." *EurekaAlert! The Global Source for Science News*. http://www.eurekalert.org/pub_releases/2010-01/haog-grd010510.php.
Henricks, Robert G. 1990. *The Poetry of Han-Shan: A Complete, Annotated Translation of Cold Mountain*. New York, NY: State University of New York.
Hillman, James. 2013. *Uniform Edition of the Writings of James Hillman*. Spring Publications, Inc.
Hofmann, Albert. 1980. *LSD: My Problem Child*. New York: McGraw-Hill.
Hofstadter, Douglas. 2007. *I Am a Strange Loop*. New York, NY: Basic Books Inc.
--1979. *Gödel, Escher, Bach: An Eternal Golden Braid*. New York, NY: Basic Books Inc.
Honda, Katsuichi. 1999. *The Nanjing Massacre: A Japanese Journalist Confronts Japan's National Shame*. Edited by Frank Gibney. New York, NY: M. E. Sharpe.
Hornsby, Peter J. 2007. "Telomerase and the aging process." *Exp Gerontol*. doi:10.1016/j.exger.2007.03.007.
Hsu-yun. 1952. Master Hsu Yun's Discourses and Dharma Words. Edited by Lu Kuan Yu. http://www.thezensite.com/ZenTeachings/Master_Hsu-Yun_Discourses_and_Dharma_Words.pdf.
Hsüan-tsang. 1973. *Ch'eng wei-shih lun*. Translated by Wei Tat. Hong Kong: Ch'eng wei-shih lun Publication Committee.
Hue Huang, Sui Yu, Zhanhe Wu, Beisha Tang. 2014. "Genetics of hereditary neurological disorders in children." *Translational Pediatrics* 3 (2). http://www.thetp.org/article/view/3547/4410.
Hume, Robert Ernest, M.A., Ph.D. 1921. *The Thirteen Principal Upanishads*. Translated by M.A., Ph.D. Robert Ernest Hume. Oxford, England: Oxford University Press.
Humphreys, Christmas. 1987. *Concentration and Meditation*. 2. Great Britain: Element Books Ltd.
—. 1987. *Meditation and Concentration, A Manual of Mind Development*. Longmead, Shaftesbury, Dorset, Great Britain: Element Books, Ltd.
Iliade, Mircea. 1991. *Images and Symbols, Studies in Religious Symbolism*. Translated by Philip Mairet. Princeton, New Jersey: Princeton University Press.
Ingrid Fischer-Schreiber, et al. 1994. *The Encyclopedia of Eastern Philosophy and Religion*. Boston: Shambhala.
Ireland, John D. 1998. *Muccalinda Sutta: About Muccalinda*. Translated by John D. Ireland. http://www.accesstoinsight.org/tipitaka/kn/ud/ud.2.01.irel.html.
Irvine, Gregory. 2000. *The Japanese Sword: The Soul of the Samurai*. London: V&A Publications.
Ives, Christopher. 1996. "Dharma and Destruction: Buddhist Institutions and Violence." *Colloquium on Violence and Religion at Stanford* 151-174.
Ives, Christopher. 2001. "Wartime Nationalism and Peaceful Representation: Issues Surrounding the Multiple Zens of Modern Japan." *Japan Studies Review* 37-46.
Iyengar, B. K. S. 2002. *Light on the Yoga Sutras of Patanjali*. Bury St. Edmunds, Suffolk, England: Thorsons.
Jacobi, Jolande. 1974. *Complex Archetype Symbol in the Psychology of C. G. Jung*. Translated by Ralph Manheim. Bollingen Press.
Jaffe, Richard M. 2002. *Neither Monk nor Layman: Clerical Marriage in Modern Japanese Buddhism*. Princeton, NJ: Princeton University Press.
Jantrasrisalai, Chanida. 2008. *Early Buddhist Dhammakaya: Its Philosophical and Soteriological Significance*. Sydney: The University of Sydney.

Japan Experience. 2015. *Vegitarian in Japan.* October 1. Accessed 3 9, 2019. https://www.japan-experience.com/to-know/chopsticks-at-the-ready/vegetarian-japan.

Jerath R., Barnes VA, Crawford MW. 2014. "Mind-body response and neurophysiological changes during stress and meditation: central role of homeostasis." *Journal of Biological Regulators and Homeostatic Agents* 545-54.

JHA, D. N. 2011. *Ancient India In Historical Outline.* New Delhi: Manohar Publishers & Distributors.

Jiang, Tao. 2006. *Contexts and Dialogue: Yogacara Buddhism and Modern Psychology on the Subliminal Mind.* Honolulu: University of Hawai'i Press.

John S. Major, Sarah A. Queen, Andrew Seth Meyer, Harold D. Roth. 2010. *The Huainanzi: A Guide to the Theory and Practice of Government in Early Han China.* New York, NY: Colombia University Press.

Johnston, William M. 2000. *Encyclopedia of Monasticism.* Chicago, IL: Fitzroy Dearborn Publishers.

Jong, J. W. de. 1979. *Buddhist Studies.* Edited by G. Schopen. Berkeley, CA: Asian Studies Press.

Jorgensen, John 2005. Inventing Hui-Neng, The Sixth Patriarch: Hagiography and Biography in Early Ch'an. Brill.

Jung, C. G. 1969. *Aion. Researches into the Phenomenology of the Self.* 2nd. Edited by Sir Herbert Read, and Gerhard Adler Michael Fordham. Translated by R. F. C. Hull. Vols. 9, part 2. Princeton, NJ: Princeton University Press.

—. 1997. *C. G. Jung Speaking: Interviews and Encounters.* Edited by Wm. McGuire and R. F. C. Hull. Princeton, NJ: Princeton University Press.

—. 1968. *Concerning the Archetypes.* Vol. 9i. Princeton University Press.

—. 1948. *General Aspects of Dream Psychology.* Princeton, N. J.: Princeton University Press.

—. 1921. *Psychological Types.* Princeton, N. J.: Princeton University Press.

—. 1971. *Psychological Types, Collected Works.* Vol. 6. Princeton, NJ: Princeton University Press.

—. 1990. *Psychological Types: The Collected Works of C. G. Jung.* Translated by H. G. Baynes & R.F.C. Hull. Vol. 6. Princeton University Press.

—. 1969. *Psychology and Religion: West to East.*

—. 1956. *Symobols of Transformation.* Vol. 5. New York, NY: Bollingen Foundation Inc.

—. 1959. *The Archetypes and the Collective Unconscious.* Vol. 9.

—. 1953-60. *The Collected Works of C. G. Jung.* Edited by H. Read. Vol. II. New York, NY: Pantheon Books.

—. 1941. *The Psychological Aspects of the Kore.* Vols. 9i - The Archetypes and the Collective Unconscious.

—. 1969. *The Structure of the Psyche.* Vol. 8. Princeton University Press.

—. 1966. *Two Essays on Analytical Psychology.* 2nd. Edited by Michael Fordham. Translated by R. F. C. Hull. Vol. 7. Princeton, NJ: Princeton University Press.

Kabat-Zinn J, et al. 1992. "Effectiveness of a meditation-based stress reduction program in the treatment of anxiety disorders." *Am J Psychiatry* 936-43.

Kabat-Zinn, Jon. 2013. "Some Reflections on the Origins of MBSR, Skillful Means, and the Trouble with Maps." In *Mindfulness: Diverse Perspectives on Its Meaning, Origins and Applications,* by Jon Kabat-Zinn, edited by J. Mark G. Williams and Jon Kabat-Zinn. New York, NY: Routledge.

Kaisetsu. 1997. *Dokugasusen kankei shiryō. II / Yoshimi Yoshiaki, Matsuno Seiya hen kaisetsu.* Tōkyō.

Kak, Subhash C. 1993. "Astronomy of the Vedic Altars." *Vistas in Astronomy* (Pergamon Press Ltd.) 36: 117-140.

Kariyawasam, A. G. S. 1996. "Buddhist Ceremonies and Rituals of Sri Lanka." *Access to Insight.* Accessed December 2015. http://www.accesstoinsight.org/lib/authors/kariyawasam/wheel402.html.

Katsura, Mark Siderits and Shōryū. 2013. *Nāgārjuna's Middle Way: Mūlamadhyamakakārikā.* Wisdom Publications.

Katz, Steven T. 1978. *Mysticism and Philosophical Analysis.* New York, Oxford University Press.

Keightley, David N. 2014. *These Bones Shall Rise Again*. Edited by Henry Rosemont Jr. Albany, NY: SUNY Press.
Ketelaar, James E. 1996. "Kaikyoron: Buddhism Confronts Modernity." *Zen Buddhism Today* 25-39.
Ketelaar, James Edaward. 1990. *Of Heretics and Martyrs in Meiji Japan*. Princeton, NJ: Princeton University Press.
King, Winston L. 1986. *Death Was His Koan, The Samurai-Zen of Suzuki Shōsan*. Freemont, CA: Asian Humanities Press.
Kinzer, Stephen, 2019. "The Secret History of Fort Detrick, the CIA's Base for Mind Control Experiments," *POLITICO Magazine*.
Kirkland, Russell. 2004. *Taoism: The Enduring Tradition*. New York: Routledge.
Kōdō, Sawaki. 1984. *Sawaki Kōdō Kikigaki*. Tokyo: Kōdansha.
Kōdō, Sawaki. 1942. "Zen-kai Hongi o kataru." *Daihōrin* 98-112.
Kornfield, Jack. 2012. *Teachings of the Buddha*. Edited by Gil Fronsdal Jack Kornfield. Boston & London: Shambhala.
Kruger, Justin, and David Dunning. 1999. "Unskilled and Unaware of It: How Difficulties in Recognizing One's Own Incompetence Lead to Inflated Self-Assessments." *Journal of Personality and Social Psychology* 1121-34.
Kyuishi, Yoshida. 1959. *Nihon Kindai Bukkyō-shi Kenkyū*. Tokyo: Yoshikawa Kōbunkan.
Lachs, Stuart. 1994. *Coming down from Zen Clouds: A Critique of the Current State of American Zen*. New York. URL: http://www.lachs.inter-link.com/docs/ComingDownfromtheZenClouds2.pdf.
—. 1999. "Means of Authorization: Establishing Hierarchy in Chan/Zen Buddhism in America." *Meeting of the American Academy of Religion*. Boston.
—. 2002. *Richard Baker and the Myth of the Zen Roshi*. New York: Stuart Lachs. URL: http://www.lachs.inter-link.com/docs/RichardBaker_Myth_of_the_Zen_Roshi.pdf.
—. 2006. "The Zen Master in America: Dressing the Donkey with Bells and Scarves." *Annual Meeting of the American Academy of Religion*. Washington, D.C.: Stuart Lachs. 29. URL: http://www.lachs.inter-link.com/docs/DressingTheDonkey.pdf.
—. 2011. *When the Saints Go Marching In: Modern Day Zen Hagiography*. New York, New York, March 9. URL: http://www.lachs.inter-link.com/docs/WhenTheSaintsGoMarching.pdf.
—. 2019. *Tibetan Buddhism Enters the 21st Century: Trouble in Sangri-la*. OpenBuddhsim.org. Last accessed Oct. 25, 2019.
Lai, Whalen. 2009. *History of Chinese Philosophy*. Edited by Bo Mou. Vol. 3. London and New York: Routledge.
Lamotte, Étienne. 1988. *History of Indian Buddhism*. Translated by Sara Webb-Boin. Louvain-Paris: Peeters Press.
—. 1938. *Asaṅga: La Somme du Grand Vehicule d'Asaṅga (Mahayanasamgraha)*. Bureaux du Muséon.
Laotse. 1948. *The Wisdom of Laotse*. Edited by Lin Yutang. Translated by Lin Yutang. New York: Random House, Inc.
Lapsley, Patrick L. Hill and Daniel K. 2011. "Adaptive and Maladaptive Narcissism in Adolescent Development." *Implications of narcissism and Machiavellianism for the development of prosocial and antisocial behavior in youth*.
Lee, Jung Young. 1981. *Korean Shamanistic Rituals*. Mouton De Gruyter.
Lee, Shu-Ching. 1947. "Intelligentsia of China." *American Journal of Sociology* (The University of Chicago Press) 489-497.
Leighton, Taigen Dan. 2008. "Zazen as an Enactment Ritual." In *Zen Ritual*, by Dale S. Wright Steven Heine, 167-184. Oxford: Oxford University Press.
Leon Petchkovsky, Michael Petchkovsky, Philip Morris, Paul Dickson, Danielle Montgomery, Jonathan Dwyer, Patrick Burnett. 2013. "fMRI response to Jung's Word Association Test: implications for theiory, treatment and research." *Journal of Analytical Psychology* 58: 409-431.

Levy, Samuel, et al. 2007. "The Diploid Genome Sequence of an Individual Human." *PLOS Biology*. https://doi.org/10.1371/journal.pbio.0050254.

Libourel, Paul-Antoine, "Partial homologies between sleep states in lizards, mammals, and birds suggest a complex evolution of sleep states in amniotes." PLOS Biology, Oct 11, 2018.

Lombardo, Michael V., Bhismadev Chakrabarti, Edward T. Bullmore, Susan A. Sadek, Greg Pasco, Sally J. Wheelwright, John Suckling, MRC AIMS Consortium, and Simon Baron-Cohen. 2010. "Atypical neural self-representation in autism." Brain (Oxford University Press).

Loori, John Daido. 2001. "Shape of a Buddha." *Mountain Record 20.1*.

—. 1996. *The Heart of Being, Moral and Ethical Teachings of Zen Buddhism*. Rutland, Vermont: Charles E. Tuttle Company, Inc.

Lopez, Robert E. Buswell and Donald S. 2014. *The Princeton Dictionary of Buddhism*. Princeton, NJ: Princeton University Press.

Lopez, Robert E. Buswell and Donald S. 2014. "Which Mindfulness?" *Trycicle*. Accessed Feb. 2016. http://www.tricycle.com/blog/which-mindfulness.

Lopez, Donald S. Jr. 2015. The Norton Anthology of World Religions, Hinduism, Buddhism, Daoism. Edited by Donald S. Lopez, Jr., James Robson Jack Miles General Editor with Wendy Doniger. New York: W. W. Norton & Company, Inc.

Luders, Eileen, Nicolas Cherbuin, Florian Kurth. 2015. "Forever Young(er): potential age-defying effects of long-term meditation on gray matter atrophy." Frontiers in Psychology. http://dx.doi.org/10.3389/fpsyg.2014.01551.

Luk, Charles. 1964. *The Secrets of Chinese Meditation*.

—. 1966. *The Śūraṅgama Sūtra (Leng Yen Ching)*. Translated by Charles Luk. Reprint, New Delhi, 2013: Munshiram Manoharlal Publishers Pvt. Ltd.

Luk, Lu Kuan Yu: Charles. 1993. *Ch'an and Zen Teaching*. Translated by Charles Luk. Vol. 1. 3 vols. York Beach, Maine: Samuel Weiser, Inc.

Majumdar, Jit. 2015. *HinduPedia*. December. http://www.hindupedia.com/en/%C4%80rya.

Mary E. Curtner-Smith, et al. 2006. "Mothers' Parenting and Young Economically Disadvantaged Children's Relational and Overt Bullying." *Journal of Child and Family Studies* 15 (2): 177–189.

Masaharu, Anesaki. 1899. *Bukkyo Seiten Shi-ron*. Tokyo: Keiso Shoin.

Masami, Inagaki. 1975. *Henkaku o motometa Bukkyō-sha*. Tokyo: Daizō Shinsho.

Matsunami, N. 1930. *The Constitution of Japan*. Tokya: Maruzen.

Matt, Daniel C. 1990. "Ayin: The Concept of Nothingness in Jewish Mysticism." In *The Problem of Pure Consciousness*, by Robert K. C. Forman, 121-159. New York: Oxford University Press.

Matthieu Ricard, Antoine Lutz and Richard J. Davidson. 2014. "Mind of the Meditator." *Scientific American* 311 (5).

Max-Plank-Gesellschaft. 2008. "Unconscious decisions in the brain." *Max-Plank-Gesellschaft*. Accessed December 29, 2016. https://www.mpg.de/research/unconscious-decisions-in-the-brain.

McCarthy, Terry. 1992. "Japanese troops 'ate flesh of enemy and civilians.'" *Independent*. http://www.independent.co.uk/news/world/japanese-troops-ate-flesh-of-enemies-and-civilians-1539816.html.

McLaren, W. W. 1979. *Japanese Government Documents*. Bethesda, MD: Univeristy Publications of America.

McRae, John R. 2003. *Seeing Through Zen: Encounter, Transformation, and Genealogy in Chinese Chan Buddhism*. Berkeley and Los Angeles, CA: University of California Press.

—. 1986. *The Northern School and the Formation of Early Ch'an Buddhism*. Honolulu: University of Hawaii Press.

—. 1987. "Shen-hui and the Teaching of Sudden Enlightenment in Early Ch'an Buddhism," In *Sudden and Gradual: Approaches of Sudden Enlightenment in Chinese Thought*, edited by Peter N. Gregory, 227-278. Honolulu: University of Hawai'i Press.

Meltzoff, Andrew N. 2007. "'Like me': a foundation for social cognition." *National Institutes of Health* 126-134.

Merton, Thomas. 1968. *Zen and the Birds of Appetite*. New York: New Directions.

Milgram, Stanley. 1974. "Obedience to Authority." *Harper's Magazine.*
Miller, Alice. 1997. *The Drama of the Gifted Child, The Search for the True Self.* New York, New York: Basic Books.
Monier-Williams, M. 2011. *A Sanskrit-English Dictionary.* New Delhi: Chaukhambha Publications.
Mookerjee, Ajit. 1986. *Kundalini, the Arousal of the Inner Energy.* Rochester, VT: Destiny Books.
Moulton, Kristen. 2011. "Zen teachers are livid Utah colleague in sex scandal still teaching." *The Salt Lake Tribune.* May 10. Accessed 10 17, 2016. http://archive.sltrib.com/printfriendly.php?id=51768224&itype=cmsid.
Myōgen, Ōtake. 1993. "Statement of Repentance." *Sōtō Shuho* 28-31.
Nagao, Gadjin M. 1991. *Madhyamika and Yogacara.* Edited by L. S. Kawamura. Translated by L. S. Kawamura. Albany, N. Y.: State University of New York Press.
Nakata, Yumi. 2014. "Japanese Double Eyelid Surgery." *GaijinPot.* October 19. Accessed April 12, 2017. https://blog.gaijinpot.com/japanese-double-eyelid-surgery/.
NAMI. 2013. "The National Alliance on Mental Illness." *Nami.Org.* March. Accessed 2015. http://www2.nami.org/factsheets/mentalillness_factsheet.pdf.
Nan, Huai-Chin. 1997. *Basic Buddhism: Exploring Buddhism and Zen.*
Nattier, J. 2003. *A Few Good Men: The Bodhisattva Path according to The Inquiry of Ugra (Ugrapariprccha).* Honolulu: University of Hawai'i Press.
Nattier, J. 1992. "The Heart Sutra: A Chinese apocryphal text?" *Journal of the International Association of Buddhist Studies* 15 (2): 153-219.
Nattier, Jan. 1992. "The Heart Sutra: A Chinese Apocryphal Text?" Edited by Roger Jackson. *The Journal of The International Association of Buddhist Studies* (International Associatoin of Buddhist Studies) 15 (2).
Niayesh Afshordi, Claudio Corianò, Luigi Delle Rose, Elizabeth Gould, and Kostas Skenderis. 2017. "From Planck Data to Planck Era: Observational Tests of Holographic Cosmology." *Physical Review Letters* (American Physical Society).
Nickerson, A, Bryant, R. A., Aderka, I.M. Hinton, D.E., & Hofmann, S.G. 2011. "The Impacts of Parental Loss and Adverse Parenting on Mental Health." *Psychological Trauma: Theory, Research, Practice, and Policy.* doi:10.1037/a0025695.
Nikāya, Dīgha. 1921. *Dialogues of the Buddha.* Translated by T. W. and C. A. F. Rhys Davids. London: PTS.
Nikaya, Digha. n.d. *Digha Nikaya.* PTS. Vol. 2.
Nikaya, Majjhima. 1888, 1993. *Majjhima Nikaya.* PTS, Volume 1. Edited by V. Trenckner. Vol. I. Pali Text Society (PTS).
—. 1995. *The Middle Length Discourses of the Buddha.* Edited by Bhikkhu Nanamoli. Translated by Bikkhu Nanamoli and Bhikkhu Bodhi. Boston, MA: Wisdom Publications.
Nishi Honganji. 1894. "Quoted in issue." [Honganji-ha] Honzan Rokuji.
Nitobe, Inazo. 2002. *Bushido: The Soul of Japan.* Tokyo: Kodansha International. doi:ISBN 978-4-7700-2731-3.
O'Connell LA, Hofmann HA. 2011. "Genes, hormones, and circuits: an integrative approach to study the evolution of social behavior." *Frontiers in Neuroendocrinology.*
Oi, Mariko. 2013. "What Japanese history lessons leave out." *BBC News.* March 14. Accessed April 12, 2017. http://www.bbc.com/news/magazine-21226068.
Oldenberg, Herman. 1879. *The Dīpavaṃsa.* London, England: Williams and Norgate.
Oldenberg, Hermann. 1879. *"Introduction"* in the *Vinaya.* Edited by H. Oldenberg. London: Williams & Norgate.
—. 1988. *The Religion of the Veda.* Translated by Shridhar B Shrotri. Delhi, India: Motilal Banarsidass Publishers Private Limited.
Ortigue S, Bianchi-Demicheli F, Patel N, Frum C, Lewis JW. 2010. "Neuroimaging of love: fMRI meta-analysis evidence toward new perspectives in sexual medicine." *J Sex Med* 3541-52. doi:10.1111/j.1743-6109.2010.01999.x.
Osborn, David. 2014. *Scientific Verification of Vedic Knowledge: Archaeology Online.* Accessed January 8, 2017. http://archaeologyonline.net/artifacts/scientific-verif-vedas.

Paintner, Christine Valters. 2012. *Desert Fathers and Mothers: Early Christian Wisdom Sayings--Annotated and Explained*. Woodstock, VT: Skylight Paths.
Park, Jin Y. 2008. *Buddhism and Postmodernity: Zen, Huayan, and the Possibility of Buddhist Postmodern Ethics*. Plymouth, England: Lexington Books.
Park, Sung-bae. 1983. *Buddhist Faith and Sudden Enlightenment*. SUNY Press.
Pascal, Blaise. 2017. *Pascal's Pensées*. Seattle, WA: Loki's Publishing.
Perry, Gina. 2012. *Behind the Shock Machine, The Untold Story of the Milgram Psychology Experiments*. Australia: Scribe.
Pete Arambula, Erik Peper, Mitsumasa Kawakami, and Katherine Hughes Gibney. 2001. "The Psychological Correlates of Kundalini Yoga: A Study of a Yoga Master." *Applied Psychophysiology & Biofeedback* 26 (2): 147-153.
Pew Research Center. 2012. *Buddhists*. Accessed September 3, 2015. http://www.pewforum.org/2012/12/18/global-religious-landscape-buddhist/.
PhysOrg. 2016. "Research team reproduces major functional principles of the brain using technology." *Phys Org*, July 1. http://phys.org/news/2016-07-team-major-functional-principles-brain.html.
Pinker, Steven. 2011. *The Better Angels of our Nature: Why Violence Has Declined*. New York, NY: Penguin Group.
Plato. 1987. *The Republic*. Translated by Desmond Lee. London, England: the Penguin Group.
Pollack, Robert. 1999. *The Missing Moment: How the Unconscious Shapes Modern Science*. New York, NY: Houghton Mifflin Harcourt.
Porter, Billl. 1993. *Road to Heaven*. Berkley: Counterpoint.
Prebish, Charles S. 2002. *Westward Dharma*. Edited by Charles S. Prebish and Martin Baumann. Berkeley: University of California Press.
Puhakka, Kaisa. 2003. "Awakening from the Spell of Reality: Lessons from Nāgārjuna." In *Encountering Buddhism: Western Psychology and Buddhist Teachings*, by Seth Robert Segall. Albany, NY: State University of New York Press.
Qi, Rui. n.d. "The basis of discontinuous motion." *Institute of Electronics, Chinese Academy of Sciences* (Chinese Academy of Sciences).
Rahula, Walpola. 1958. *What the Buddha Taught*. Buddhist Library of China.
Reat, Noble Ross. 1994. *Buddhism, A History*. Berkley: Asian Humanities Press.
—. 1993. *The Salistamba Sutra*. New Delhi, India: Motilal Banarsidass Publishers.
Regardie, Israel. n.d. *The Philosopher*.
Riegel, Jeffrey. 2013. "Confucius." *Stanford Encyclopedia of Philosophy*. http://plato.stanford.edu/archives/spr2013/entries/confucius/.
Roberts, Bernadette. 1993. *The Experience of No-Self: A contemplative Journey*. Albany, NY: State University of New York Press.
Rochat, Philippe. 2003. "Five levels of self-awareness as they unfold early in life." *Consciousness and Cognition* (Emory University Department of Psychology) 12.
Rodolfo Llinas, Urs Ribary. 2006. *Consciousness and the Brain*. Vol. 929. New York, NY: New York University School of Medicine.
Rohrabacher, U.S. Congressional Representative. 2001. *Paying Homage to a Special Group of Veterans, Survivors of Bataan and Corregidor*. Congressional Record – House, United States Government, 11980-11985.
Rosenkranz, Gerhard. 1940. *Fernost - wohin? Begegnungen mit den Religionen Japans und Chinas im Umbruch der Gegenwart. Heilbronn*. Heilbronn: Verlag Eugen Salzer. http://www.payer.de/neobuddhismus/neobud0305.htm.
Roshi, Gempo. 2016. *Big Mind: Change Your Persepective, Change your Life*. Accessed June 26, 2016. http://bigmind.org/genpo-roshi.
Rousselle, Erwin. 1933. *Spiritual Guidance in Contemporary Taoism*. Translated by Translated from the German by Ralph Manheim. Vol. 4. New York, NY: Pantheon Books.
Rumi, Jalal Al-Din. 1997. *The Illuminated Rumi*. New York: Broadway Books; 1st edition.

Russell, Benjamin. 2014. *Monk becomes millionaire after masterminding meditation app used by the stars*. March 28. Accessed July 27, 2016. http://www.express.co.uk/news/uk/467508/Monk-becomes-millionaire-after-masterminding-meditation-app-used-by-the-stars.

Russell, Edward. 2002. *The Knights of Bushido, a short history of Japanese War Crimes*. Greenhill Books.

Ryōmin, Akizuki. 1985. *Nantenbō Zenwa*. Edited by Akizuki Ryōmin. Tokyo: Hirakawa Shuppan.

Ryūzan, Shimizu. 1934. *Risshō Ankoku no Taigi to Nippon Seishin*. Kyoto: Heirakuji Shoten.

Saburo, Ienaga. 1968. *The Pacific War, 1931-1945*. New York: Pantheon.

Samuel, Geoffrey. 2008. *The Origins of Yoga and Tantra*. Cambridge, MA: Cambridge University Press.

Sansom, G. B. 1950. *The Western World and Japan*. Tokyo: Charles E. Tuttle Company.

Santoso, Akex. 2006. "Monk Can Control Body Temperature by Meditating." Neatorama. Dec. 18. Accessed March 4, 2017. http://www.neatorama.com/2006/12/18/monk-can-control-body-temperature-by-meditating/.

Sapolsky, Robert M. 2017. *Behave: The Biology of Humans at Our Best and Worst*. New York, NY: Pinguin Press.

Sasaki, Ruth Fuller. 2009. *The Record of Linji*. Edited by Thomas Huho Kirchner. Translated by Ruth Fuller Sasaki. Honolulu, HI: University of Hawaii Press.

Schlütter, Morten. 2008. *How Zen Became Zen*. Honolulu: Sheridan Books.

Schmitt, Paul. 1945. *Archetypisches bei Augustin und Goethe*.

Schopen, G. 2004. *Buddhist Monks and Business Matters: Still More Papers on Monastic Buddhism in India*. Honolulu: University of Hawai'i Press.

Schopen, G. 2004. *Mahayana*. Vol. 2, in *Encyclopedia of Buddhism*, by R. E. Buswell (ed) Jr. New York: Macmillan Reference USA.

Schwartz, Jeffrey M., M.D., and Sharon Begley. 2002. *The Mind & The Brain*. Regan Books, HarperCollins.

Scott, Mike 2019. *Scientific American*, October. Vol. 321, No. 4.

Service, Korean Statistical Information. 2015. *Population by Gender, Age, and Religion*. Accessed 11 13, 2018. http://kosis.kr/statHtml/statHtml.do?orgId=101&tblId=DT_1PM1502&conn_path=I2.

Shahar, Meir. 2008. *The Shaolin Monastery: history, religion, and the Chinese Martial Arts*. Honolulu, HI: University of Hawaii Press.

Shakya, Ben Huan. 2003. *Dharma Talk*.

Shakya, Chuan Yuan. 1996. *Empty Cloud: The Teachings of Xu (Hsu) Yun*. Las Vegas, NV: The Nan Hua Chan Buddhist Society.

—. 1985. *The Seventh World of Chan Buddhism*. Las Vegas, NV: Nan Hua Chan Buddhist Society.

Shakya, Jy Din. 1996. *Empty Cloud: The Teachings of Xu (Hsu) Yun*. Las Vegas, NV: Nan Hua Chan Buddhist Society.

—. 2014. "The Maxims of Master Han Shan." *Exploring Chan*. Accessed Feb. 19, 2017. http://www.eyeofchan.org/special-features/han-shan/560-hanshanmaxims.html.

Sharf, Robert. 2014. "Mindfulness and Mindlessness in Early Chan." *Philosophy East & West* (University of Hawai'i Press) 64 (4): 933-964.

Shibayama. 1974. *The Gateless Barrier. Zen comments on the mumonkan*. Translated by from the Chinese and Japanese Sumiko Kudo. Shambhala Publications.

Shimla, Agence France-Presse in. 2014. *The Guardian*. September 2. Accessed December 3, 2015. http://www.theguardian.com/world/2014/sep/02/india-court-bans-animal-sacrifice-hindu-temples.

Shinpo, Daido. 1889. "Quoted in journal." *Daidō Shinpō*.

Shinshi, Meikyo. 1877. "Quoted in journal." *Meikyo Shinshi*.

Siegelman, Flo Conway & Jim. 1995. *Snapping: America's Epidemic of Sudden Personality Change*. Second. New York: Stillpoint Press.

Simpson, Deb. 2012. *Closing the Gate: A Heaven's Gate Cult Biography*. Murfreesboro, TN: Piney D Press.

Singer, June. 2000. *Androgyny, The Opposites Within*. York Beach, ME: Nicolas-Hays.
Skilton, Andrew. 2001. *A Concise History of Buddhism*. Woodbridge Park: Biddles Ltd, Walnut Tree House.
Slingerland, Edward. 2009. *History of Chinese Philosophy*. Edited by Bo Mou. Vol. 3. New York, NY: Routladge.
Smart, Ninian. 2008. *World Philosophies*. Edited by Oliver Leaman. New York, NY: Routledge.
Snellgrove, D. L. 1973. "Sakyamuni's final nirvana." *Bulletin of the School of Oriental and African Studies* (University of London) 36 (2).
Snow, Robert L. 2003. *Deadly cults: the crimes of true believers*. Praeger Publishers.
Sōen, Shaku. 1904. "Quoted in the journal." *Heimin Shimbun*.
Solc, Vladislav. 2013. *Father Archetype*. Milwaukee, WI, August. http://www.therapyvlado.com/.
Sōtōshu. 2015. *SōtōZEN-NET*. Accessed December 5, 2015. http://global.Sōtōzen-net.or.jp/eng/practice/zazen/howto/.
Staal, Frits. 1986. "The Fidelity of Oral Tradition and the Origins of Science, Mededelingen der Koninklijke Nederlandse Akademie von Wetenschappen." *Afd. Letterkunde* (North Holland Publishing Company) 49 (8): 40.
Stack, Peggy Fletcher. 2011. "Utah Zen master admits affair, leaves center." *The Salt Lake Tribune*. February 25. Accessed 10 17, 2016. http://archive.sltrib.com/story.php?ref=/sltrib/home/51270057-76/merzel-zen-center-buddhist.html.csp.
Standlee, Mark et al. (2017). Public letter from eight senior students of Sogyal, July 14, 2017 (last accessed October 27, 2019). https://www.lionsroar.com/wp-content/uploads/2017/07/Letter-to-Sogyal-Lakar-14-06-2017-.pdf
Stevens, Anthony. 2015. *Archetype Revisited: An Updated Natural History of the Self*. New York, NY: Routledge.
—. 1993. *The Two-Million-Year-Old Self*. College Station, TX: Texas A&M University Press.
Strong, John S. 2004. *Relics of the Buddha*. Princeton:, NJ: Princeton University Press.
Stubbs, John. 2016. *Lao Tzu Tao Te Ching: By The Way*. Cobourg, ON: John Stubbs. Accessed May 6, 2016. http://www.eyeofchan.org/docs/ENGLISH/pdf/TaoTeChing_Stubbs.pdf.
Sutton, 1991. Existence and Enlightenment in the Laṅkāvatāra-sutra: A Study in the Ontology and Epistemology of the Yogācāra School of Mahāyāna Buddhism. State University of New York, Albany Press.
Suzuki, D. T. 1904. "A Buddhist View of War." *The Light of Dharma* 4 (2): 179-182.
—. 1964. *An Introduction to Zen Buddhism*. New York, NY: Grove Press.
—. 1994. *Manual Of Zen Buddhism*. New York, NY: Grove Press.
—. 1969. "Shin Shūkyō-ron." *Suzuki Daisetsu Zenshū* (Iwanami Shoten) (23): 1-147.
—. 1959. *Zen and Japanese Culture*. Princeton, NJ: Bollingen Foundation, Inc.
Swanson, Ana. 2016. "Who Gets Divorced in America in Seven Charts." *Washington Post*. April 6. Accessed March 2, 2017. https://www.washingtonpost.com/news/wonk/wp/2016/04/06/who-gets-divorced-in-america-in-7-charts/.
TJ. 2011. "Blog post." *Dream Research & Education*. Website. KellyBulkeley.Org, January 18.
Te-ching, Master Han-shan. n.d. *Essentials of Practice and Enlightenment*. Translated by Guo-gu Shi. Accessed June 6, 2017. http://www.angelfire.com/electronic/awakening101/essentials.html.
Thagard, Jing Zhu & Paul. 2002. "Emotion and action." *Philosophical Psychology* (Routledge) 15 (1).
The American Forum of Global Education. 2000. *Spotlight on Inner Asia*. The American Forum of Global Education.
The Economist. 2013. *Korea in Chinese history: Stuck in the Middle*. April 12. Accessed July 19, 2016. http://www.economist.com/blogs/banyan/2013/04/korea-chinese-history.
The Tibetan Administration Official Media. 2011. "His Holiness the Dalai Lama Ratifies Amendment to Charter of Tibetans." *The Tibet Post International*, May 31.

Thera, Soma. n.d. *Kalama Sutta: The Buddhia's Charter of Free Inquiry.* Edited by Soma Thera. Translated by Soma Thera. Soma Thera. Accessed Dec. 18, 2016. http://www.sobhana.net/meditation/english/reading/med003.pdf.

Thurman, Robert A. F. 1976. *VIMALAKIRTI NIRDESA SUTRA.* The Pennsylvania State University. Accessed May 29, 2016. http://huntingtonarchive.osu.edu/resources/downloads/sutras/06lotusVimalakirti/Vimalakirti%20Nirdesha%20Sutra.pdf.

Toledo, Myrna. 2009. "First Comes Marriage, Then Comes Love." *ABC News.* Jan. 30. Accessed March 2, 2017. http://abcnews.go.com/2020/story?id=6762309&page=1.

Tomoe, Moriya. 2005. "Social Ethics of "New Buddhists" at the Turn of the Twentieth Century." *Japanese Journal of Religious Studies* (Nanzan institute for Religion and Culture) 283-304.

Tomojirō, Hayashiya, and Shimakage Chikai. 1937. *Bukkyō no Sensō-kan.* Tokyo: Daitō Shuppansha.

Travis, Fredrerick R. Keith Wallace. 2002. "Autonomic and EEG Patterns during Eyes-Closed Rest and Transcendental Meditation (TM) Practice: The Basis for a Neural Model of TM Practice." *Consciousness and Cognition,* April.

Troy Brown, RN. 2015. "100 Best-Selling, Most Prescribed Branded Drugs Through March." *Medscape Medical News.* May. http://www.medscape.com/viewarticle/844317.

Turnbull, Stephen. 2005. *Warriors of Medieval Japan.* New York, NY: Osprey Publishing Ltd.

USCIRG. 2017. *USCIRF-Recommended Countries of Particular Concern.* Annual Report 2018, United States Commission on International Religious Freedom (USCIRG). Accessed 12 29, 2018. https://www.uscirf.gov/sites/default/files/Tier1_CHINA.pdf.

Vetter, Tilmann. 1988. *The Ideas and Meditative Practices of Early Buddhism.* New York: E. J. Brill.

Victoria, Brian Daizen. 2015. "An Ethical Critique of Wartime Zen." *JOCBS* (11): 179-212.

—. 2006. *Zen at War.* Lanham, MD: Rowman & Littlefield Publishers, Inc.

—. 2003. *Zen War Stories.* New York, NY: RutledgeCurzon.

—. 1998. *Zen At War, 1st Ed.* Weatherhill.

Vogt, Yngve. 2012. "World's oldest ritual discovered. Worshipped the python 70,000 years ago." *Apollon Research Magazine.* https://www.apollon.uio.no/english/articles/2006/python-english.html.

Wang, Hsuan-Li. 2014. *Gushan: the Formation of a Chan Lineage During the Seventeenth Century and Its Spread to.* Ph.D. Thesis, New York, NY: Columbia University.

Warder, A. K. 2008. *Indian Buddhism.* Motilal Banarsidass.

Watson, Burton. 1996. Chuang Tzu Basic Writings. Translated by Burton Watson. New York: Columbia University Press.

Wayman, Alex 1984. *Buddhist Insight: Essays by Alex Wayman.* New Delhi, Shri Jainendra Press

Web Archive. 2007. Religious Intelligence. October 13. Accessed July 20, 2016. https://web.archive.org/web/20071013201130/http://www.religiousintelligence.co.uk/country/?CountryID=37.

Welch, Holmes. 1967. *The Practice of Chinese Buddhism 1900-1950.* London: Oxford University Press.

—. 1963. "Dharma Scrolls and the Succession of Abbots in Chinese Monasteries." Edited by T'oung Pao. *International Journal of Chinese Studies* 50.

Welsh E., Hannah, B., and Briner, M. 1947. *Essays on contemporary events.* London: Kegan Paul.

Welter, Albert. 2008. *The Linji Lu and the Creation of Chan Orthodoxy: The Development of Chan's Records of Sayings Literature.* Oxford: Oxford University Press, Inc.

Wendy Doniger, Donald S. Lopez, Jr., James Robson. 2015. *The Norton Anthology of World Religions.* Vol. One. Two vols. New York, NY: W. W. Norton & Company, Inc.

West, Jouis Jolyon, MD, 1993. "A Psychiatric Overview of Cult-Related Phenomena. Journal of the American Academy of Psychoanalysis," Vol. 21, No. 1, pp. 1-19.

Wetzler, Peter. 1998. *Hirohito and War: Imperial Tradition and Military Decision Making in Prewar Japan.* Hawaii: University of Hawaii Press.

Wilhelm, Richard. 1989. *Tao Te Ching.* London: Penguin Books, Ltd.

Williams, Paul. 2005. *Buddhism: Critical Concepts in Religious Studies.* New York, NY: Routledge.

—. 2009. *Mahayana Buddhism, the doctrinal foundations.* Second. Routdledge.

Witzel, Michael. 2003. *Vedas and Upanishads.* Edited by Gavin Flood. Blackwell.

Wong, Eva. 2011. *Taoism, and Essential Guide.* Boston, MA: Shambhala.
Wood, Ernest. 1988. *Seven Schools of Yoga.* Wheaton, IL: The Theosophical Publishing House.
—. 1959. *Yoga.* Harmondsworth, Middlesex, England: Penguin Books, Ltd.
Wriggins, Sally Hovey. 1996. *The Silk Road Journey with Xuanzang.* Boulder, CO: Westview Press.
Wright, Laurence. 2013. *Going Clear: Scientology, Hollywood, and the Prison of Belief.* Random House.
Wu, Alex. 2013. "Chinese Character: Dream." *Epoch Times.* July 6. Accessed February 2016. http://www.theepochtimes.com/n3/157885-chinese-character-dream-%E5%A4%A2/.
Wu, Kuang-Ming. 1990. *The Butterfly As Companion: Meditations on the First Three Chapters of the Chuang Tzu.* SUNY.
Xuanzang. 1999. *Three Texts on Consciousness Only.* Translated by Francis H. Cook. Berkeley: Numata Center for Buddhist Translation and Research.
Xuanzang, John P Keenan. 2000. *The Scripture on the Explication of Underlying Meaning.* Taisho Volume 16, Number 676. Translated by Translated from the Chinese of Hsiian-tsang by Joh n P. Keena. Berkeley CA: Numata Center for Buddhist Translation and Research.
Yampolsky, Philip B. 1967. *The Platform Sutra of the Sixth Patriarch.* New York: Columbia University Press.
—. 1999. "Chan. A Historical Sketch." In *Buddhist Spirituality. Later China, Korea, Japan and the Modern World*, by Takeuchi Yoshinori. New York, NY: The Crossroad Publishing Company.
Yifa. 2003. "The Origins of Buddhist Monastic Codes in China: An Annotated Translation and Study of the Chanyuan qinggui." Edited by Jiang Wu. *The Journal of Asian Studies* (University of Hawai'i Press) 2 (3): 408.
Yūkei, Hasebe. 1993. *Min Shin Bukkyō kyōdanshi kenkyū.*
—. n.d. *Oxherding Poems of Hsu Yun.* Accessed July 22, 2016. http://www.eyeofchan.org/special-features/visual-arts/846-poems-on-the-oxherding-series-2.html.
—. 2014. "Poems by Empty Cloud: Series II." *Exploring Chan.* Accessed April 27, 2017. http://www.eyeofchan.org/special-features/poetry-of-empty-cloud/495-hsuyunpoems2.html.
Xu, Jian, et al. 2014. "Nondirective meditation activates default mode network and areas associated with memory retrieval and emotional processing." *Frontiers in Human Neuroscience.* http://dx.doi.org/10.3389/fnhum.2014.00086.
Yun, Xu. 1988. *Empty Cloud, the Autobiography of the Chinese Zen Master.* Translated by Charles Luk. Second ed., Thorpe Hamlet, Norwich: Unknown.
Yutang, Lin. 1948. *The Wisdom of Laotse.* Edited by Lin Yutang. New York: Random House.
Zeising, Adolf. 1854. "Neue Lehre van den Proportionen des meschlischen Körpers."
Zolla, Elemire. 1981. *The Androgyne, Reconciliation of Male and Female.* New York, NY: Crossroad Publishing Co.

Index

A

Abhidharmakośakārikā 91
abuse by teachers 70, 354, 363, 398
Adamantine Vehicle 69
Advaita Vedānta 62
afterlife 75, 78, 158
agency (psychological) 144, 161, 175, 258, 275, 348, 352, 354, 365, 384
agnōsía 194, 308
Ajahn Chah xiv
Ājīvakas 11
Ājīvakism 11, 57, 64
Akihito, emperor 152
ālayavijñāna 97, 98, 295, 328. See also substratum-, foundation-, and storehouse consciousness
alchemy 82
alchemy, spiritual xix, 1, 81, 82
alienation viii, xviii, 16, 383, 397, 398
alpha-waves 227
Altair 9, 267, 269
amalavijñāna 99. See immaculate consciousness
Amaterasu 149, 151, 152, 153, 173
Amitābha xiii, 39, 104, 105, 154, 158, 220, 254, 302
Amitāyus xiii, 39, 59, 105, 220, 254
Amoghavajra 99, 126
amygdala 226, 258
Analects 77, 78, 80
analytical psychology 275
Ānanda 23
ānāpānasmṛti 188, 230
anātman. See not-self
ancestor 405
ancestor's hall 79, 101
ancestral 73
  cults 74, 75, 76
  spirits 75, 76, 77
  veneration 23, 73, 74, 75, 76, 77, 78, 79, 106, 123, 131, 143, 364, 397, 407
Androgyne 316
androgyny. See spiritual androgyny
Aṅguttara Nikāya 34, 40, 49, 60, 361, 408, 420
anima. See archetypes, psychological: anima
animus. See archetypes, psychological: animus
annihilation (ego) 16, 32, 340, 373, 378
antarātma xix. See also True Self and Buddha Nature
Anthology of the Patriarchal Hall 127
Arabs 62
arahats 24
archetypal motifs 274, 306
archetypes 307
archetypes, psychological xviii, 38, 46, 221, 243, 294
  anima 9, 267, 294, 298, 299, 300, 301, 310, 312, 321, 353
  animus 267, 294, 298, 299, 300, 301, 310, 312, 353
  anti-hero 387
  as forces 289, 290, 292, 395
  child 294
  encounters 98, 256, 314, 319
  enemy shadow 294, 296, 297
  father 294, 430
  friendly shadow 294, 297, 298
  hero 169, 294, 302, 348, 349, 365, 387
  imagery 254, 255
  mother 294
  motifs xvii, xviii, 95, 105, 268, 274, 278, 291, 310, 311, 312
  persona 294, 297, 298
  sage 54
  savior 302
  shadow warrior 304
arhats 36
Aryan xix, 14, 22, 110
āryāṣṭāṅgamārga. See Eightfold Path
asamprajñāta. See supra-consciousness
Asanga 44, 93, 94, 99

asceticism iv, v, xii, xvi, 9, 10, 11, 13, 22, 57, 58, 102, 177, 192, 361, 409
practice iv, xii, 13, 58
Ashikaga Period 155, 159, 160
Ashoka 27, 46, 61, 63, 86, 150, 302
Asian water buffalo xix, 266, 268. See also ox
Association of New Buddhists 166
Āṣṭayaparāvṛtti 328
Atharva Veda 14, 19, 47
Atman 19, 21, 42. See also True Self, Buddha Nature, Brahman
attachments 32, 131, 197, 198, 204, 221, 251, 352, 353, 357, 395
attainment 405
Avalokiteśvara 37, 38, 46, 64, 68, 220, 254, 309
avidyā 20, 31. See ignorance; See also ignorance
awakening 404
ayin xvii

B

Bali ceremony 65
Bandura, Albert 365, 432
Bankei Yōtaku 414
Banzhou sanmei jing 37
barbarians 72, 88, 142
Bardo Thodol 69
bare attention 224
Barnes, Djuna 393
begging 101, 102
benevolence 37, 38, 46, 159, 171
Ben Huan i, 100, 130, 141, 193, 221, 332, 374
Bhutan 24, 71
birth 3, 10, 12, 13, 16, 22, 29, 31, 32, 37, 52, 53, 54, 76, 82, 97, 193, 208, 249, 282, 285, 317, 321, 377
birth and death xiv, 16, 22, 32, 37, 53, 97
Blaise Pascal 410
bliss 11, 16, 39, 63, 158, 316
Blue Cliff Record iv, 127, 137
Blue-eyed Barbarian. See Bodhidharma
Blue-eyed Daemon. See Bodhidharma
Bobo doll experiment 365

bodhi xvii, 9, 73, 121, 125. See also spiritual awakening and enlightenment
bodhicitta 95
Bodhidharma 82, 96, 108, 109, 110, 111, 112, 114, 115, 117, 121, 134, 145
bodhisattva 26, 53, 169, 236, 243, 309, 364
Bodhisattva Ideal 36, 37, 38
bodhi tree 9
Bön 24, 67, 68
bondage 40, 51, 52
Bön-po 67
Book of Documents 78
Book of Equanimity 127
Book of Odes 76
Book of Rites 78
Book of Serenity 226
Brahman xv, 12, 16, 21, 22, 62, 110. See also True Self, Buddha Nature, Atman
Brahmanas 13
Brahmanism 12, 22, 36, 57, 64
brain 277, 280, 295, 299, 307, 309, 310, 325
delta waves 309, 310
theta waves 227, 309, 310
breath ix, xvi, 13, 14, 17, 18, 19, 89, 111, 188, 205, 216, 217, 225, 228, 230, 231, 232, 233, 234, 236, 252, 260, 338, 339, 383. See also prā?āyāma
Bronze age 74, 76, 151
Buddha xiii, 336
Dharma 27, 37, 41, 57, 88, 114, 131, 169, 171, 397
first sermon 12, 28, 198
-nature iv, xv, 53, 105, 191, 334, 335. See also True Self
of infinite light. See Amitābha
of infinite time. See Amitāyus
Buddhabhadra 109, 112
Buddhacinga 89
Buddhaghosa 58, 64, 224
Buddha Nature 404
Buddha Realms 95. See also celestial beings
Buddhist associations 136, 139, 141, 146

Buddhist canon xii, xiii, xvii, 21, 25, 28, 57, 74, 90, 324, 328
Buddhist precepts 25, 93. See also Prátimokṣa and Vinaya Pitaka
Burma 65, 184
Bushido 159, 374
butterfly parable 56

C

Cambodia xix, 65, 147, 148, 187
cannibalism 174
Cáodòng 130, 134, 157, 226. See also five petals of Chan
capitalism 183
castes 24
Catholicism 180
  priests 35, 146
catuṣkoṭi 41, 42, 43, 44, 72, 287, 288, 289
Catvāri āryasatyāni 28. See Four Noble Truths; See also Noble Truths
celestial beings xiii, 36, 37, 39, 45, 46, 93, 95, 104, 105, 153, 220, 254, 273, 302, 397, 400
celibacy 72, 155, 184, 377, 378
chanbing. See meditation sickness
Chan houses
  Caodong 136
  Fayan 134
  Gui Yang 136
  Linji 136
  Yunmen 134
Chân Không 180
Chan patriarchs 108, 110, 112, 115, 117, 148, 157, 347, 353
Chan school 100, 106, 111, 122, 123, 126, 157, 225
chanting 49, 68, 105, 176, 190, 386
Chart for the Cultivation of Reality. See Xiuzhen tu
Chéng Wéishì Lùn 94
Chiang Kai-shek 139
Chien Niu 267
Chikai, Shimakage 171
Ching Chu 268
Chinul 145

Chögyam Trungpa 363, 364
Christian
  ascetics 246
  mysticism 333
Christians xix, 3, 7, 35, 73, 141, 148, 160, 303
  missionaries 143, 146
  persecution of 141, 146, 160
Chuan fa-pao chi 117
Chuang Chou. See Chuang Tzu
Chuangtse. See Chuang Tzu
Chuang Tzu 56, 82, 84, 85, 86, 112, 128, 129
Chuang Tzu, the 82
Church of Scientology 386
cittamātra 99. See also consciousness
Classical Chan 127, 244
Classic of Changes. See I-Ching
Classic of History 76
Classic of Poetry 78, 266
clerical marriage 155
Cole, Alan ix, xi, 1, 76, 106, 107, 108, 109, 112, 113, 114, 115, 128, 132, 276, 358, 418, 422, 423
collective unconscious 98, 290, 291, 292, 295, 307, 311
compassion 37, 38, 46, 63, 78, 95, 105, 115, 154, 159, 166, 168, 170, 171, 172, 174, 205, 220, 221, 242, 254, 296, 300, 309
complexes, psychological 153, 294, 295, 296
concentration xvi, 21, 33, 35, 89, 119, 120, 138, 158, 188, 205, 206, 224, 227, 228, 229, 230, 232, 234, 236, 237, 238, 241, 242, 247, 257, 259, 310, 316, 317, 325, 381
conceptualized nature 97. See also Three Natures
conditional arising 37, 52
Confucianism 3, 24, 57, 66, 72, 73, 78, 87, 93, 101, 106, 113, 124, 138, 146, 147, 148, 150, 176, 181, 185, 187, 397, 406, 407
Confucius 74, 77, 78, 79, 80, 84, 106, 138, 173, 251, 302
conscious agents 410, 411

consciousness viii, xviii, 30, 44, 51, 97, 98, 99, 126, 217, 227, 228, 257, 259, 260, 275, 282, 283, 287, 289, 291, 292, 293, 294, 295, 305, 307, 313, 321, 325, 328, 337, 344, 359, 360, 369, 372, 376, 384, 385, 386, 393, 397, 399, 409, 410, 412, 415
  agents 410
  immaculate 99
Consciousness Only school 41, 92, 414, 416. See also Yogācāra
constructivism xix
contemplation iv, v, xvi, 2, 14, 35, 37, 57, 87, 89, 120, 128, 138, 188, 194, 205, 218, 220, 223, 230, 236, 241, 242, 243, 248, 249, 253, 254, 255, 257, 259, 283, 308, 325, 368, 369, 381, 387, 406
conversion disorder 387
corruption 145, 153
councils, Buddhist 24, 25, 132
creation 16, 59, 74, 76, 82, 97, 122, 130, 178, 314, 318, 337
creativity 41, 44, 57, 60, 61, 74, 218, 219, 311
cultivation, spiritual 13, 82, 111, 146, 188, 233, 257, 272, 273, 325, 332, 337, 379
cults 76, 210, 386, 387, 388
Cultural Revolution 136, 141

D

daemons 67, 217
Dahui Zonggao 127, 130, 193, 245
Dalai Lama 70, 71
Daoxin 114, 255
Dao Xuan 91
Daoyuan 127
dark night of the soul 393
death 2, 7, 8, 9, 15, 16, 22, 23, 26, 29, 31, 32, 36, 37, 44, 50, 51, 53, 54, 61, 69, 77, 79, 81, 97, 98, 99, 102, 104, 140, 141, 148, 156, 158, 161, 172, 181, 193, 196, 248, 259, 285, 305, 312, 326, 329, 350, 356, 371, 372, 377
deity xii, 13, 69, 151, 312, 317
delta-rhythms 258

delusion 12, 20, 31, 45, 52, 124, 125, 375, 376, 408
Deneb 9, 267, 269
dependent nature 97. See also Three Natures
dependent origination 30
depersonalization 383
desire (ego) vi, 10, 19, 20, 21, 28, 30, 31, 32, 40, 81, 84, 112, 346, 347, 353, 369, 375, 377, 378, 389, 390, 395, 398, 400. See also samudaya and mental formations
detachment v, 11, 30, 58, 89
devotional Buddhism ix, 46, 69, 87, 88, 90, 101, 102, 148, 190. See also Pure Land Buddhism and ritual: devotional
devotionalism 45, 46
Dhamma. See Dharma
dhāraṇā xvi, 188, 205, 228, 257. See also concentration
Dharma xii, 407
  ancestors 114, 128, 131
  ecclesiastical transmission 131
  Ending Age 101, 102. See also Three Ages school
  lineage x, 114, 124, 132, 406
  transmission 24, 106, 112, 113, 128, 131, 133, 134, 137, 364, 399
Dharmācāryas 22
Dharmaguptaka 25
dharmakāya xii, 9, 32, 38, 61, 97, 99, 272
dharmas xii, 43, 54, 59, 272
Dharma scroll 132, 133
dhyāna x, xi, xvi, 2, 257, 406. See also meditation
Dialectical school 41
Dīpavaṃsa 63
directive meditation 224, 226
discipline 404
discipline, spiritual vii, viii, x, xi, 2, 8, 23, 24, 25, 78, 87, 91, 139, 174, 190, 192, 205, 228, 229, 303, 304, 386, 395
discursive thought 86, 129
dissociative disorder 383
divination 67, 74, 75, 182

divine beings 54. See also celestial beings
divine body 82
Divine Child 325
divine feminine. See archetypes, psychological anima
divine union 82, 83, 256, 267, 269, 299, 301, 302, 312, 325, 377, 429. See also spiritual androgyny
Dōgen 136, 154, 156, 157, 158, 225, 226, 244, 245, 425
dokusan 326
Dongshan 136, 244, 245
doubt 191, 195, 247, 249. See also great doubt
dreams 3, 51, 54, 55, 56, 59, 60, 135, 307, 313, 330, 393, 403
dualism 36, 45, 129, 157, 251
duality 16, 62, 86, 97, 99, 129, 250, 256, 273, 328
Du Fei 114, 115
duhkha xiii, 16, 28, 29, 30, 34, 96, 182, 191, 193, 194, 196, 206, 272, 273, 324, 327, 347, 374, 377, 399, 408. See also suffering and Noble Truths
dukkha 404
Dumoulin, Heinrich 115
Dunhuang 107, 117
Dunning-Kruger effect. 195

E

ecclesiastical authority ix
ecstatic absorption 205, 257, 429. See also samādhi
effort 353, 374, 375, 376, 400
ego vi, xiv, xv, xix, 9, 10, 31, 46, 51, 53, 80, 113, 164, 174, 177, 184. See also self-identity
Egypt 27
Eightfold Path 10, 28, 29, 30, 32, 33, 34, 95, 104, 182, 198, 200, 205, 206, 257, 267, 324, 335, 380, 392
Eisai, Myōan 156, 157
Elders 26, 36
emancipation vi

emotions vii, xix, 203, 218, 267, 275, 292, 293, 295, 300, 359, 368, 369, 393
Emperor Ming 86
Emperor Wen 90, 91
Emperor Wu 90, 110
Empress Wu 102, 302
emptiness 43, 44, 45, 52, 53, 62, 72, 73, 88, 92, 95, 111, 112, 119, 124, 243, 251, 273, 324, 329, 337, 412. See also Void
empty circle 43, 273, 289
Empty Cloud See Hsu Yun
encounter dialogues 20, 122, 126, 128, 129
enlightened 415
enlightenment xvii, 9, 33, 37, 44, 55, 61, 77, 106, 113, 118, 120, 121, 125, 127, 131, 132, 241, 250, 272, 273, 285, 316, 323, 324, 326, 327, 328, 331, 332, 333, 334, 335, 336, 347, 382, 399, 400, 415. See also spiritual awakening and wù
epiphysicalism 410
ergotropic experience 283, 284, 285, 286
Erwin Schrödinger 411
Esoteric Buddhism 126, 363. See also Vajrayāna Buddhism
ethics, Buddhist 12, 149, 159, 163, 164, 165, 171, 172, 173, 176, 207, 335, 391
evil 16, 51, 65, 125, 163, 167, 170, 174, 194, 226, 337, 388
exorcism 65, 366
expedient means 9, 102, 346, 375. See also skill-in-means
exploitation, sexual and other 26, 184, 208, 350, 355, 392
extension of the breath. See pranayama

F

Fa Hsing 246
faith vii, 62, 112, 141, 155, 156, 166, 173, 191, 207, 208, 209, 210, 211, 212, 221, 222, 277, 296, 327, 331, 333, 361, 372, 373
Faru 114, 423
fasting 11, 12, 386

Fa Xian 89
Fa Xiang school. See Wei Shi school
Fayan Wenyi 134, 136.
fear iii, xiii, 2, 65, 240, 326, 340, 371
feudalism 76
first mark of all things 96
Fischer, Roland 281, 283
five petals of Chan 134, 136, 137. See also Chan houses
Five Treatises of Maitreya 99
flame history 115
Flower Garland school. See Hua Yan school
fMRI studies vii, 226, 259, 295
folk religion 13, 24, 68, 73, 76, 101, 131, 136, 138, 147, 151, 176, 181, 366
  aboriginal cults of Sri Lanka 64
  animism 148
  animistic 142
  Chinese 73, 76, 142
  Korean Muism 143
  of Tibet 67
forest hermits 57, 58
fortune-telling 99
Fotudeng 89, 230
Foulk, Griffith xi, 24, 106, 418
foundation consciousness 328. See also ālayavijñāna
four heavenly kings 304
Four Noble Truths xiii, 10, 28, 30, 32, 35, 95, 182
Fowler, James 207
free will 11, 229
free won't 229
Fuke-shū Zen sect 270
fund-raising 139
Fuxi 83, 269, 301, 315

G

Ganjin. See Jianzhen
Gateless Barrier, The 128, 222, 251
genealogy 76, 113, 131
genes 98, 259, 275
ghana-pātha. See recitation
ghosts xvi, 181, 366
Glaucon 19
golden age of Chan 106, 116
Golden Elixir 81, 267

gong-an 84, 226, 243, 246, 248, 251
Gorō, Sugimoto 149, 173
government influence on Buddhism 65, 70, 88, 90, 100, 101, 118, 139, 140, 141, 144, 145, 147, 152, 153, 154, 156, 161, 163, 164, 167, 176, 291
grassroots socialism 141
great doubt 182, 199, 213, 247, 375, 376. See also doubt
Greater Cowherd Discourse 266
Great Persecution 146
Greece 27, 37, 75
Guanding 103, 113, 114
guilt 2, 239, 344, 359, 360
Gui Yang 134. See also
Gut ceremony 143

H

Haedong 144
hagiography 3, 7, 8, 82, 116, 126
haibutsu kishaku movement 162
Hakuin Ekaku 375
Hakuun, Yasutani 170
hallucination 286
Han dynasty 73, 86, 315
Haneullium 143
Han Shan 130, 187, 197, 204, 214, 236, 249, 285, 306, 329, 375, 376
Harrison, Paul 8, 60, 73, 124
hatha-yoga 234
Hayashiya Tomojirō 171, 426
Headspace 183
healing breath 234
heart xv, xvii, 21, 29, 32, 35, 86, 90, 115, 184, 193, 203, 216, 223, 230, 237, 243, 251, 296
heaven 76, 78, 105, 158, 162, 213, 271, 315, 375
Heian period 154
Heine, Steven xi, 425
Hermes Trismegistus 316
Hillman, James xviii, 55, 227, 254, 310, 321
Himalayan Buddhism 3, 24, 71, 181. See also Tibetan Buddhism
Hīnayāna Buddhism 27, 94
Hinduism 11, 36, 50, 51, 59, 61, 62, 68, 71, 148, 303

Hirohito, Emperor 152, 296
HIV 358, 363
Hoffman, Donald 92, 410, 411, 412, 415
hologram 103, 104
Hōnen 154
Hong Fa Temple i, 100, 102, 133, 141
Hongren 114, 117, 122, 123
Hong Zhi 157, 158, 226
Hossō school 153
host and guest xv, 306
Hsin Hsing. See Xinxing
Hsüan-tsang 56, 93
Hsu Yun i, x, 23, 39, 130, 132, 137, 140, 211, 213, 248, 250, 268, 270, 273, 301, 317, 375
Huainzi 315
Huangbo Xiyun (Huang Po) 413
hua-tou practice 130, 136, 205, 243, 245, 246, 247, 248, 250, 251, 328, 378, 379
Hua Yan school 100, 101, 103, 137, 144, 153
Huike 114, 115
Huineng 108, 116, 117, 122, 123, 124, 134, 139, 157
  mummy 123
Huitzilopochtli 312
Hui Tzu 84, 85
Hui Yuan 104, 230
hummingbird 311, 312. See also archetypes, psychological: motifs
Humphries, Christmas 204, 235, 389
Hunguk Monastery 143
hymns xviii, 12, 298

I

I-Ching 75, 76, 78
ideal forms 34, 37, 46, 53, 54, 105, 158, 260, 353
identity. See self-identity
ignorance 20, 30, 31, 54, 95, 96, 125, 182, 265, 352, 408
Ikkō-ikki 159
illusion vi, xv, 31, 41, 43, 44, 45, 50, 51, 52, 55, 106, 118, 177, 182, 197, 221, 324, 348, 373, 375
immortal fetus 82, 321, 325
immortality 12, 16, 17, 18, 81, 82, 413

immortals 76
imperialism 88, 113, 153, 154, 157, 158, 164, 165, 167, 168, 176
  Japanese 149, 165, 170
Imperial-Way Buddhism 170
individuation 293
Indus River Valley 1, 11, 27, 182, 246
inheritance certificate 24
intelligentsia 86, 87
internalization practices 14, 275
Islam xvii, xviii, 3, 35, 62, 141, 148, 180, 303
  persecution of 141
isolationism 161
Ives, Christopher xi, 149, 176, 177

J

Jainism 10, 11, 12, 13, 22, 23, 57, 59, 64
Japanese war crimes 174
jatā-pāṭha. See mesh-recitation
jiànxìng 241, 272, 323, 324, 325, 326, 329. See also spiritual awakening
Jianzhen 91
Jim Jones 349, 353
Jing Tu school 104. See also Pure Land school
Jōdo Shinshū 155, 156
Jōdoshū 154
Jonestown Massacre 349, 354
Jung, Carl 98, 196, 274, 276, 277, 278, 279, 290, 291, 292, 294, 304, 310, 313, 314, 337, 349, 354, 409
just sitting ix, 158, 225, 273, 370. See also zazen
Jy Din i, x, 23, 130, 138, 270

K

Kabbalism xviii
Kaisa Puhakka 42
Kalmykia 24
kami 151
karma 11, 21, 22, 30, 51, 95, 97, 98, 305
Kashgar 72
Kashmir 62
Kashmir Shaivism 63
katana 155
Katha-Upanishad 19

Kathmandu Valley 71
Katz, Steven T. viii, 323
Kegon school 153
Keightley, David xi, 74, 75, 131
Kena-Upanishad 17, 97
kensho 241. See also jiànxìng
kevala-jnana 22
Khuddaka Nikāya 49
kinship churches 131
kōan 243. See gong-an
Kōdō, Sawaki 169
kōng 337. See also Void
Korea xi, 4, 87, 88, 90, 118, 137, 142, 143, 144, 145, 146, 151, 153, 164, 165, 166, 177, 187, 354, 407
Kuang Chi Monastery 136
Kucha 89
Kumārajīva 56, 90, 92
Kumaré 357
Kundalini 339
Kuòān Shīyuǎn 268
Kwan Um school of Zen 146

L

Lachs, Stuart xi, 276, 354, 355, 356, 363, 396, 397
Lamotte, Étienne 23
Lankāvatāra school. See Chan school
Laos 65, 147
Laotse. See Lao Tzu
Lao Tzu 74, 77, 79, 80, 82, 84, 85, 86, 138, 302
Layman Pang 405
Leng-chia shih-tzu chi 117
LGBTQ+ 298
liberation vi, xvii, 11, 33, 34, 40, 42, 121, 158, 175, 316, 386, 393, 406
life and death xv, 16, 305, 413, 414
lineage x, xii, 23, 24, 69, 73, 76, 107, 112, 113, 114, 117, 122, 126, 128, 131, 133, 134, 135, 137, 143, 157, 169, 225, 361, 363, 364, 397, 398, 405, 407, 409
Linji x, 23, 130, 134, 157, 226, 347, 352, 364, 375, 403, 407, 413
li (ritual) 78
Li-tai fa-pao chi 122
Lokaksema 37, 73

Lokavibhāga 54
Lokottaravāda school 8
Loori, John Daido 244, 335
lotus flower 33, 39, 94
LSD 281, 282, 286
lucid dreaming 313, 393
Lucien Levy-Bruhl 196
Lü school 91, 101
Lusthaus, Dan 415

M

Madhyamaka 25, 41, 43, 44. See also Dialectical school
Mahābhārata 20, 21
Mahā Kassapa 25
Mahāsanghika 26, 27, 36, 57, 58
Mahāsī Sayādaw 224
Mahāvairocana 153
Mahāyāna Buddhism xix, 8, 17, 24, 26, 32, 36, 37, 38, 41, 42, 44, 45, 49, 50, 51, 52, 53, 56, 57, 58, 59, 60, 61, 64, 68, 73, 90, 91, 92, 93, 94, 95, 100, 101, 105, 147, 148, 170, 171, 181
Mahāyānasamgraha 97
Maitreya 37, 38, 46, 99, 220
Majjhima Nikāya 22, 49
Malaysia xix
mandalas 69
Mandate of Heaven 79
Mañjuśrī 37, 38, 46, 220, 243, 364
mantras 64, 68, 126, 248
Mantra school. See Zhen Yan school
Maresuke, Nogi 169
mārga 29. See also Noble Truths
Marifa xvii
martial arts 111, 150, 151, 230
Masaharu, Anesaki 164
master worship viii, ix. See also veneration
Mauryan Empire 27
McRae, John R. xi, 96, 106, 110, 112, 115, 118, 122, 124, 126, 191, 245, 418, 423

meditation xi, xvi, 14, 24, 58, 100, 105, 110, 111, 158, 177, 216, 224, 225, 226, 227, 257, 259, 270, 277, 325, 337, 354, 369. See also samādhi
meditation sickness 389
Meiji constitution 152, 164
Meiji, emperor 152, 161, 162, 163, 164, 335
meme 280
memorization 48
mental attitude 217, 218
mental formations 30, 31, 32, 44, 239, 241. See also desire
mentation 96, 385
mercenaries 159
merit 57, 110, 111, 124
Merzel, Dennis 363, 398
mesh recitation 47
Mesopotamia 75
metaphysical idealism 415
microcosmic orbit 338
Middle Way 10, 11, 13, 28, 32, 42, 92
Milgram experiment 350, 351, 352
Milgram, Stanley 175
military influence on Buddhism 126, 145, 150, 152, 155, 157, 158, 159, 161, 162, 165, 166, 167, 169, 174, 176
mind xi, xv, 9, 37, 50, 54, 123, 124, 223, 275, 314, 328, 329, 349, 376, 387, 393
mindfulness xvi, 33, 34, 89, 158, 183, 184, 188, 223, 224, 225, 226, 227, 229, 230, 257, 393, 408
Mind Only school 414. See Chan school and Consciousness Only school; See also Yogācāra school
misogyny 299
missionaries 27, 63, 72, 86, 88, 143
MKUltra project 282
mnemonic literature 21
Mogao caves 117, 118
moksha 51
monasteries 28, 58, 61, 72, 79, 88, 94, 100, 123, 133, 138, 139, 150, 153, 154, 155, 159, 180, 190, 322, 354, 358, 363, 374
monastic 405
monasticism 58, 72, 91, 101, 119, 124

Mongolia 24
monk-soldiers 154, 159
moral injury 359
morality 12, 27, 34, 51, 68, 70, 72, 108, 159, 173, 183, 203, 336, 348, 352, 357, 359, 390, 391, 392, 400, 405
mortality 15, 16, 21
Mucalinda 316. See also Nüwa
Muccalinda Sutta 316
mudras 217, 238
  aakaash 238
  bhairava 217
  hairavi 217
Muism 142, 143
Muslims 7, 62, 202, 296, 388, 425
Myanmar xix, 65
mystical 323
mysticism v, vi, vii, viii, ix, x, xi, xvii, xviii, xix, 2, 3, 4, 50, 81, 82, 86, 93, 105, 106, 109, 110, 127, 131, 177, 182, 188, 206, 302
  discipline ix
  experience vii, viii, x, xi, xix
  practice vii, viii, xi, xii, 4, 106, 175, 177
mythologies x, 7, 8, 24, 75, 83, 143, 208, 209, 265, 267, 269, 301, 302, 311, 312

N

Nachiketa (Naciketas) 19
Nāgārjuna 41, 42, 43, 62, 92
Nakahara Nantembō 169
Nan Hua Temple 138
Nanjing Massacre 174
Nantembō, Nakahara 169, 170
Nara 91, 153, 154, 156
narcissistic personality disorder 210, 295, 304, 398
Naruhito, Emperor 152
Nātha 64
nationalism 157, 159, 169, 171, 172, 177, 180
Nattier, Jan xi, 26, 56
negation practice xvii, 17, 251, 313, 378. See also Not thus! Not thus!
Neidan 81
Neijing tu 9, 81, 267, 294, 301
Neo-Confucianism 24

Neolithic age 74, 75, 131
Nepal 24, 68, 71
Neti!, Neti!. See Not thus! Not thus! and negation practice
neurology 52
nibbāna. See nirvāṇa
Nichiren 154, 156, 172
Nikāya 49
Nikāya Buddhism 23, 27, 35, 37, 38, 44, 45, 50, 57, 59, 60, 61, 90, 91
Nine Mountains school 145
Nirmāṇakāya 39, 273
nirodha 29, 32. See also Noble Truths
nirvāṇa xiv, xvii, 26, 33, 37, 43, 53, 55, 73, 124, 145, 269
Niulang 267
Noble Truths xiii, 10, 22, 28, 35, 95, 324, 335, 377
nondirected attention 89
nondirective meditation 224, 225, 226
nondualistic 36, 45, 129, 289
nonviolence 11, 12
Northern School Chan 68, 71, 110, 117, 118, 126, 153, 225, 242, 345
not-self 50, 177, 324
Not thus! Not thus! 17, 229, 252, 378
numinosity vii, 242, 254, 287, 291, 294, 307, 310, 311, 312, 313, 314, 319, 321
Nüwa 83, 301, 315, 316. See also serpent

O

object of transformation 270
Ōmori Sōgen 374
open-monitoring meditation 224
oracle bones 75
ordination i, x, 93, 112, 133, 144, 145, 358
orgasmic ecstasy 302. See also samādhi: sānanda
original nature xix, 252. See Buddha-nature
ox xix, 9, 53, 74, 82, 211, 212, 213, 265, 266, 267, 270, 271, 273, 294, 301, 317, 324
 herding 9, 39, 53, 268, 270
 symbolism 267, 268
ox-herder 83, 265, 266, 267, 268

P

Pāli canon xix, 36, 60, 64, 65
Paramārtha 91, 99
Parshvanatha 10
participation mystique 196, 197, 198, 354
Pascal, Blaise iv, 193, 409
Pashupati seal 40
patriarchs 117, 134
patriarchy 107, 157
patriotism 144, 163, 164, 166, 167
pattern of other-dependency 95, 96
perceptions 44, 96, 97
perfected nature 97. See also Three Natures
perfection of concentration. See samādhi: samyak
persecution, religious 100, 141, 160, 163, 276
persona. See archetypes, psychological persona
personal unconscious 292, 294, 295, 308
philosopher's stone xvii
Piney Expanse Monastery 146
Plato 19, 37, 343
posture 2, 214, 216, 218, 225, 226, 231
prajñāpāramitā 56
prāṇā. See breath
pranayama 14, 89, 92, 230, 233. See also breath
Prāsaṅgiga 43, 44
pratibhāna 60
prátimokṣa 25, 26, 335
pratītyasamutpāda. See dependent origination
pratyāhāra 230. See also withdrawl of the senses
prayer beads 64
precepts 39, 170, 335, 392. See also Buddhist precepts
projection, psychological 103, 273, 296, 298, 299, 300, 321, 348, 349, 353, 354, 357, 415
Providence Zen Center 146
psyche 54, 82, 174, 211, 221, 256, 274, 275, 291, 292, 294, 296, 297, 305, 372, 382, 397, 407

psychology 73, 97, 194, 275, 279, 281, 290, 387
psychosis 387
pulse meditation 70, 205, 237, 238
Pure Land school 24, 53, 100, 101, 104, 105, 132, 133, 138, 148, 154, 155, 156, 158, 160, 177, 190, 260. See also devotional Buddhism and ritual: devotional

Q

Qi 217, 338, 340, 385
Qigong 111
Qing dynasty ii, 134, 138
Qing Long Temple 99
quantum physics 60, 92, 96, 385, 411, 412, 415
Quetzalcóatl 317, 318
Quran 62

R

Rājagaha 25
Randall, Lisa 411
reality 343, 344, 347, 358, 385, 393, 394, 395, 396, 397, 403, 409, 411, 412, 414, 415
reality bubble vi, viii, 98, 395
rebirth xiv, xv, 11, 16, 28, 51, 52, 54, 98, 104, 105, 110, 154, 177, 321, 366. See also reincarnation
recitation 7, 10, 47, 48, 49, 53, 64, 133, 138
Record of Rites 76
Records of the Transmission of the Lamp 127
reification 38, 334, 399
reincarnation xiv, xv, 16, 51, 52, 69, 70, 71, 181, 366. See also rebirth
revelation xvii, 59
Right Action 34, 202, 203, 389
Right Effort 34
Right Intention 34, 199, 200
Right Livelihood 34, 203
Right Meditative Absorption 34, 205
Right Mindfulness 34, 204, 205, 220, 389
Right Speech 34, 200, 201, 389

Right Understanding 34
Right View 198, 199, 200
Rigveda 12, 20, 48
Rinzai Zen 157, 159, 168, 169, 226, 243, 363
Rishabha 10
Ritsu school 153
ritual xvii, 143, 182, 220
   Ananda tribe 385
   begging 102
   Chan ix, 24, 73, 220, 369, 396, 416
   demonic 65
   devotional 148
   esoteric 68, 126
   memorization 47
   nationalistic 176
   religious 220
   sacrificial slaughter 12
   shamanistic 143, 145
   tantric 24
   Tendai and Shingon 172
rivalries between sects 101, 154
Roberts, Bernadette 333
Rohingya 65
Rújìng, Tiāntóng 157
Rules for Purity for a Chan Monastery 358. See also Zongze, Changlu
rules of discipline 91. See also Vinaya monastic rules
ruti. See recitation

S

sacrifices 12, 13, 78
   animal 12, 13, 67, 143
   inner 15
   self xiii, 115
   spiritual 15
Saglithlivagga. See Book with Verses
salvation vi, ix, xvii, 12, 22, 23, 26, 57, 121, 125, 175, 183, 302
samādhi 35, 43, 52, 53, 59, 73, 89, 97, 105, 119, 123, 125, 188, 205, 214, 236, 256, 257, 258, 268, 283, 286, 287, 289, 302, 337, 375, 429
   asamprajnata 257
   samprajnata 257
   samyak 205, 257

sānanda 302. See also orgasmic ecstasy
samaya 363
Saṃbhogakāya 39, 273
samsāra vi, xiii, xiv, xv, 28, 30, 32, 34, 37, 46, 96, 99, 183, 198, 305, 310, 347, 408
saṃskāra 239. See also mental formations
samudaya 29, 30, 32. See also Noble Truths and mental formations
samurai 157, 158, 159, 161, 174
San Jie Jiao school 101. See also Three Ages school
Sankara 62
San Lun school 92
Śāriputra 38, 51, 52, 120, 125
satori 241, 324. See also wù
Sayutta Nikāya 49
scandals 146, 185, 354, 355, 432
Schlütter, Morten xi, 130
Schrödinger, Erwin 96
Schrödinger's cat 411
Schwartz, Jeffrey 229
second mark of all things 96, 397
Sect-Shintō 164
seeds (for contemplation & meditation) iv, xvi, 188, 205, 220, 233, 236, 238, 242, 254, 255, 257, 259
self-annihilation 404
self-existence v, 41, 43, 44
self-identity iii, v, vi, viii, xv, xix, 21, 31, 52, 118
self-mortification 11, 12, 13, 22
Sengcan 114, 148
sensory perceptions 288, 295, 390
Separation Edicts 162
serpent 314, 315, 316, 317, 318, 319, 321. See also archetypes, psychological: motifs
  feathered 318
  kundalini 339
  motifs 314, 315
  symbolism 315, 316
sesshin 28, 369
Seung Sahn 146, 180
sexual abuse 299, 302, 350, 354, 355, 357, 362, 363, 377, 398

sexuality vi, 24, 146, 336, 367, 377, 378
Shakti 217
shakuhachi 270
Shaku Sōen 168
Shakyamuni. See Buddha
shamanism 67, 76, 143
Shang dynasty 74, 77, 250
Shan Hai Jing 315
Shaolin monastery 109, 111, 112, 114, 150, 424
Sharf, Robert H. x, xi, 224, 429
Shelun school 99
Sheng-yen 180, 354
Shenhui 117, 118, 119, 120, 121, 122, 125, 126, 157, 345
Shenxiu 114, 117, 118, 119, 120, 121, 126, 242, 253
Shenzhen i, 100, 133, 141
shikan-taza 158. See also zazen
Shin Buddhism 155, 156
Shin Bukkyō 166, 167, 426
Shingon Buddhism 99, 126, 145, 154, 172
Shinran 154, 155
Shintō 35, 136, 142, 150, 152, 153, 155, 159, 161, 162, 163, 164, 169, 171, 173, 175, 176, 178, 180, 185, 335, 407
Shiva 217
Shōbōgenzō 157, 370
Shōgunate 154, 155, 157, 158, 159, 160, 161, 176
shoguns 157, 159, 160, 161
Shōtoku 151
Shūten, Inoue 167
Siddhārtha 404
Siddhārtha Gautama xiii, 6, 7, 8, 9, 10, 11, 12, 13, 14, 22, 23, 30, 33, 36, 198, 265, 408, 409
signlessness 53
Sikkim 71
Silent Illumination 158, 226
Silk Road 14, 27, 72, 117
Silla 143, 144
six realms of desire 212
Six Schools of Nara 153
skandhas 42
skillful means. See skill-in-means

skill-in-means 9, 41, 102, 117, 121, 149, 173, 375. See also upāya
sleep vii, 3, 70, 93, 191, 227, 254, 258, 270, 277, 303, 308, 309, 310, 314, 320, 386, 387
smṛti 34, 223
snake 315, 319, 339. See also serpent
snapping 332, 385, 387
Social Learning Theory 365
Socrates 19
Soen Shaku 180
Sōgaku, Harada 170
Sogyal Rinpoche 350, 363
solitude 218
Song dynasty 106, 107, 127, 130
Sŏn (Korean Chan) 4, 145, 146, 406
Sōtō Zen 136, 149, 155, 157, 163, 169, 170, 225, 226, 363, 407
soul xv, xvi, 11, 17, 19, 44, 50, 51, 52, 69, 79, 230
Southern School Chan x, 117, 157, 167
spinning maiden 83, 265, 267, 301. See also spiritual androgyny
spirit 190, 217, 249
spirits 64, 65, 67, 78, 142, 143, 151, 181, 250, 314, 366
spiritual
  androgyny 272, 299, 312, 314, 315, 317. See also divine union and taijitu
  authority ix, 22, 23, 26, 75, 116, 126, 143, 354
  awakening 9, 333, 334, 335, 365, 378. See also enlightenment
  head 23, 70
  labor (effort) vii, 34, 193, 194, 197, 204, 205, 221, 222, 228, 229, 232, 236, 248, 324, 377, 378
  pride 390
  training ix, xv, xviii, 28, 48, 69, 87, 89, 100, 101, 115, 116, 119, 122, 123, 124, 130, 137
  transformation 39, 78, 81, 220, 379, 390, 404
  union 315
spiritual discipline 403
Spring and Summer Annals 78
Sri Lanka xix, 4, 8, 23, 27, 57, 63, 64, 65, 187, 224, 424

State Shintō 164
state-sponsored Buddhism 88, 144
stele, for Faru 114, 423
sthavira 26
Sthaviravada school 63
storehouse consciousness 295, 376
Śubhākarasiṃha 99, 126
subject-object duality 96, 288. See also duality
substratum consciousness 97, 98, 99. See also ālayavijñāna
suchness xiii, 9, 73, 95, 97, 250. See also thusness and tathātā
suffering vi, ix, xiii, xiv, xvii, 8, 9, 13, 16, 19, 21, 27, 28, 29, 30, 31, 32, 37, 44, 52, 95, 104, 112, 194, 352, 353, 359, 360, 361, 364, 371, 391, 399, 409. See also duḥkha
sufferings 416
Sui Yangdi, emperor 103
summer triangle 269
Sung dynasty 24, 138
śūnyam & śūnya 41, 337. See also Void & emptiness
supra-consciousness 241
Sūtras
  Aggivacchagotta 44
  Ajitasena 53
  Akṣobhyavyūha 59
  Amitāyurdhyāna 104, 158
  Ānāpānasmṛti 89, 230
  Āryasvapnanirdeśa 59
  Aṣṭasāhasrikā Prajñāpāramitā 32, 49, 53, 54, 55, 95
  Avatamsaka 103, 153
  Daśabhūmika 99
  Dhammachakkappavattana 29, 33
  Diamond 133
  Heart 56, 80, 252
  Laṅkāvatāra 45, 99, 111
  Lotus 53, 89, 90, 102, 156
  Mahā-gopālaka 266, 267
  Mahā-paridibbāna 23
  of Hui Neng. See herein Platform
  Parirccha 26
  Perfection of Wisdom. See Aṣṭasāhasrikā Prajñāpāramitā

Platform 117, 122, 123, 124, 125, 134, 252
Prajñāpāramitāhrdaya. See herein Heart
Prāsangiga 44
Pratyutpanna 43, 52, 59, 73, 99, 123, 131
Śālistamba 30, 38, 50, 52, 57
Samdhinirmocana 45, 72, 94, 95, 99
Sarvadharmāpravrttinirdeśa 58
Sarvāstivāda Mahāpari Nirvāna 23
Sukhāvatīvyūhah 59, 104, 105, 158
Śūrangama 236, 328
Sutra of Infinite Compassion 104
Sutra of Infinite Light 104
Sutta Nipāta 50
Sutta Pitaka 49
Svātantrika 44
Ugrapariprcchā 58
Upāyakauśalya 41
sutra-study 102
Suzuki, D. T. xvii, 154, 167, 168, 172, 173, 176, 180, 352, 362
Suzuki's 407
svabhāva. See self-existence
Svātantrika 43, 44
symbolic language 396
synchronicity, brain-wave 259

T

Ta Hui 285
taijitu 82, 376, 377. See also spiritual androgyny and divine union
tainted consciousness 11, 69, 97, 99
Tai Ping Rebellion 138
Taittiriya Brahmana 20
Taiwan 140, 165, 354
taking refuge 39
Tang dynasty ix, 91, 99, 100, 106, 137, 138, 150, 245, 302
tantric. See also Vajrayāna Buddhism
  Buddhism 24, 68, 69, 99, 145, 363
  Shaiva 63
  yoga 339
Taoism 9, 14, 24, 57, 66, 72, 73, 80, 81, 82, 92, 124, 138, 147, 150, 176, 181, 185, 187, 206, 217, 260, 406, 407
Tao Te Ching 80, 81

Tārā 68, 303
Tathāgata xiii, 9, 32, 44, 54
tathātā 73, 97, 223, 250. See also suchness, thusness
tax-avoidance schemes 100
taxes 88, 100, 145
teleological concepts 98, 293, 294
telomerase 259
Tendai 154, 157, 170, 172
tetralemma. See catuṣkoṭi
Thailand xix, 65, 147, 187
The Book of Serenity 243
The Buddhist View of War 171
Theravāda Buddhism xix, 13, 24, 27, 34, 36, 38, 45, 49, 50, 51, 53, 56, 64, 65, 68, 69, 148, 181, 224, 361
The Republic of China 140
The Republic (Plato) 19
theta brain-wave states 227
Thích Nhat Hanh 180
Thích Thiên-Ân 148
Thiền xi, 147, 148, 180
Third Dharma Age. See Three Ages school
third mark of all things 97
thought retracing 235
Three Ages school 100, 101, 102, 104
Three Bodies 39. See also Trikāya
Three Jewels 39
Three Kingdoms 86, 142, 144
Three Natures 95, 397
thusness 97, 223, 250. See also tathātā and suchness
tian. See Heaven
Tian Tai school 90, 100, 101, 102, 103, 137, 144
Tibet 4, 24, 27, 62, 63, 66, 67, 68, 70, 118, 133, 187, 363
Tibetan Book of the Dead 66, 69
Tibetan Buddhism 3, 24, 67, 68, 69, 70, 71. See also Himalayan Buddhism
Tōin, Iida 170
Tokugawa Iemitsu 160
Tokugawa Ieyasu 160
tonsure names 39, 134
Tovil ceremony 65
transcendence 184

Transcendental Meditation 224
Transformation-body. See Nirmanakaya
transient disassociation 384
transmigration 51, 70, 98
transmission 60, 112, 113, 122, 132, 134, 135, 169, 363, 405
  ecclesiastical 131
  spiritual 132
trauma 196, 295, 344, 350, 359, 383, 384
Treatise on the Two Entrances and Four Practices 96, 109, 112
tribalism 151
Trikāya 39, 273. See also Three Bodies
trinity 38, 40, 220, 333
triple refuge 392
triratna 40
trishula 39, 40
trophotropic experience 283, 285, 286
True Self xiv, 23, 158, 272, 273, 335, 375. See also Buddha Nature, Atman, Brahman
Trungpa, Chögyam 363
Tuva 24
Tzu-te Hui 268

U

unconscious mind xvii, 32, 54, 97, 201, 220, 229, 275, 276, 291, 292, 295, 296, 300, 303, 307, 308, 309, 310, 313, 321, 349, 354, 359
Upanishads xv, 11, 12, 14, 15, 16, 19, 21, 22, 36, 92, 224, 229, 339, 431
upāya 40, 41, 60, 102, 117, 121. See also skill-in-means

V

Vairocana 153
Vajashravasa 19
Vajrabodhi 99, 126
Vajrayāna Buddhism xix, 24, 36, 69, 126, 363, 364
validation of spiritual experience 250, 327
Vardhamâna Mahâvîra 10, 11, 13, 22
Vasubandhu 44, 93, 414, 415, 416
Vedânta 17
Vedas xv, 3, 12, 27, 47, 224, 314, 317
Vedism 12, 22, 61
Vega 9, 267, 269
vegetarianism 12, 155
Vehicle of Spells. See Adamantine Vehicle
veneration ix, 23, 79, 170, 367, 406
Vesak day 33
Vetter, Tilmann xi, 7, 11, 22, 28, 34, 106, 121, 198, 418
Victoria, Brian xi, 149, 165, 168, 169, 174, 418, 426
Vietnam xi, 4, 147, 148, 187, 424
Vijñānavāda 44, 62, 92, 103. See also Consciousness school
vijñapti-mātra 92, 414, 415
Vikram Gandhi 357, 358
Vimalakīrti 120, 125
Vinaya 25, 40, 41, 60, 100, 121, 133, 144, 155
  Pitaka 25
  school 91
  Tripitaka 91
Vinaya monastic rules 25, 100, 155
Vinaya Pitaka 25, 392. See also Vinaya monastic rules
Vinaya Tripitaka 91
Vipassana 224
visionary experience. See visions
visions x, 3, 32, 33, 39, 54, 57, 59, 60, 93, 94, 96, 141, 188, 211, 229, 254, 277, 278, 287, 294, 297, 307, 310, 311, 312, 313, 314, 319, 320, 321, 322, 330, 331, 332, 372, 393, 394, 397
Visistacārita 156
Visuddhimagga 58
Void 41, 52, 53, 201, 256, 268, 324, 337, 382
Vrâtyas 13, 14, 301

W

Wang Bi 92
Warring States period 77, 79, 85, 108
warriors, Buddhist 155, 158, 159, 173
Way of the Celestial Masters 81
Way of the Golden Elixir 81
Way of the Warrior. See Bushido
weaponsmithing 155

Wei Boyang 81
Wei Shi school 91, 92, 94, 153
Welch, Holmes 39, 133, 374
Welter, Albert xi, 126, 129
wheel of the Dharma 28, 33, 94. See also Eightfold Path
Williams, Paul 8, 41, 58, 60, 72, 73, 98, 99, 104
Wind and the Flag, parable 123
wisdom 29, 37, 38, 46, 52, 54, 56, 59, 73, 84, 105, 115, 125, 130, 159, 164, 165, 220, 221, 267, 285, 304, 320, 335, 382, 408
wishlessness 53, 243
withdrawal of the senses xvi, 188, 230
World War II 149, 152, 156, 162, 392
worship xvii, 12, 18, 19, 23, 45, 46, 58, 59, 64, 69, 71, 74, 76, 87, 90, 242, 246, 314, 407
Wù 336
Wuism 76, 142
Wúménguān 128, 246, 251
wú (negation) 17, 73, 84, 92, 94, 252
wù (spiritual awakening) xvii, 131, 241, 299, 323, 324, 327, 328. See also enlightenment
wú wéi (non-acting) 84

X

Xinxing 101, 102, 114
Xiong Nu 86
Xiuzhen tu 82
Xuan Zang 14, 25, 93, 94, 95, 96, 99, 414, 416
Xuan Zhi 109
Xu Yun 140. See also, Hsu Yun

Y

Yâjnavalkya 15, 16, 17, 181
Yampolsky, Philip 107, 116, 118
yāna 368
Yang Di 91
Yogācāra 14, 38, 45, 92, 93, 94, 97, 98, 99, 111, 328, 376, 397, 430
Yogācārabhūmi-śāstra 99
Yogācāra school 92, 414

Yoga Practice school. See Yogācāra school
Yolban 144
yulu genre 126, 129, 130
Yunmen, Chan sect 134, 136
Yunmen Quinzhee Chánshī Guǎnglù 137

Z

zazen 158, 214, 225, 273, 286, 287
zero 53, 196
Zhang Daoling 81
Zhao Zhou 17, 251, 289
Zhen Yan school 99, 126, 145
Zhi Yi 89, 90, 91, 102, 103, 113, 144, 226
Zhou dynasty 76, 77, 78
Zhuang Zi. See Chuang Tzu
Zongze, Changlu 25, 225, 358
Zuochan yi 225